#2

TRIGUN YASUHIRO NIGHTOW

DEEP SPACE PLANET FUTURE GUN ACTION!!

内藤泰弘
YASUHIRO NIGHTOW

TRANSLATION
JUSTIN BURNS

LETTERING
STUDIO CUTIE

DARK HORSE MANGA

DMP
Digital Manga Publishing

PUBLISHER
MIKE RICHARDSON
AND **HIKARU SASAHARA**

EDITORS
TIM ERVIN-GORE
AND **FRED LUI**

COLLECTION DESIGNER
DAVID NESTELLE

English-language version produced
by DARK HORSE COMICS and
DIGITAL MANGA PUBLISHING.

TRIGUN vol. 2

Published by
Dark Horse Manga
A division of Dark Horse Comics, Inc.
10956 S.E. Main Street
Milwaukie, OR 97222

www.darkhorse.com

Digital Manga Publishing
1123 Dominguez Street, unit K
Carson, CA 90746

www.emanga.com

To find a comics shop in your area, call the Comic
Shop Locator Service toll-free at 1-888-266-4226

First edition: January 2004
ISBN: 1-59307-053-5

10 9 8 7 6 5 4 3 2
Printed in Canada

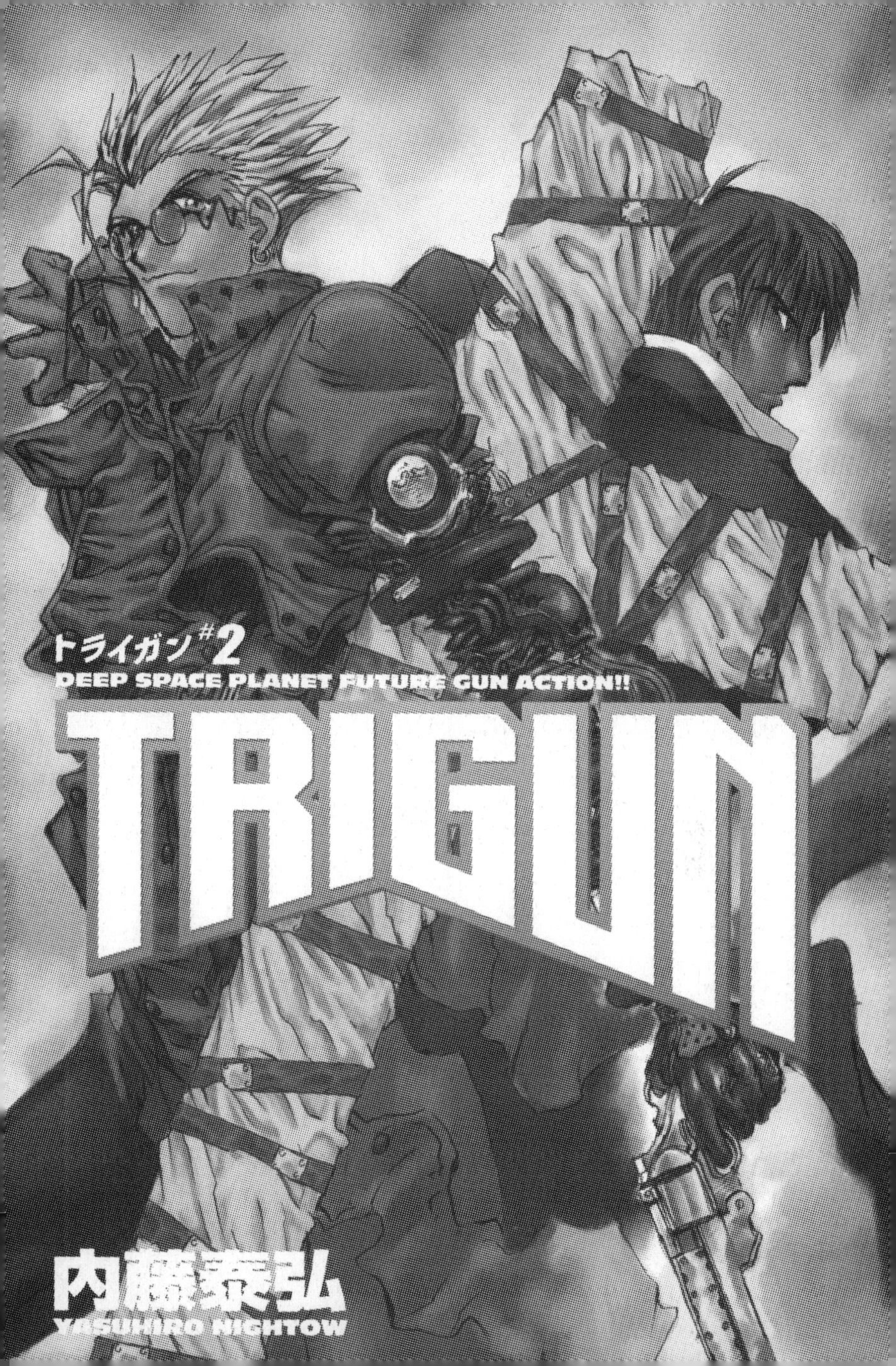
トライガン#2
DEEP SPACE PLANET FUTURE GUN ACTION!!
TRIGUN
内藤泰弘
YASUHIRO NIGHTOW

TRIGUN YASUHIRO NIGHTOW
DEEP SPACE PLANET FUTURE GUN ACTION!!
CONTENTS #2

#1

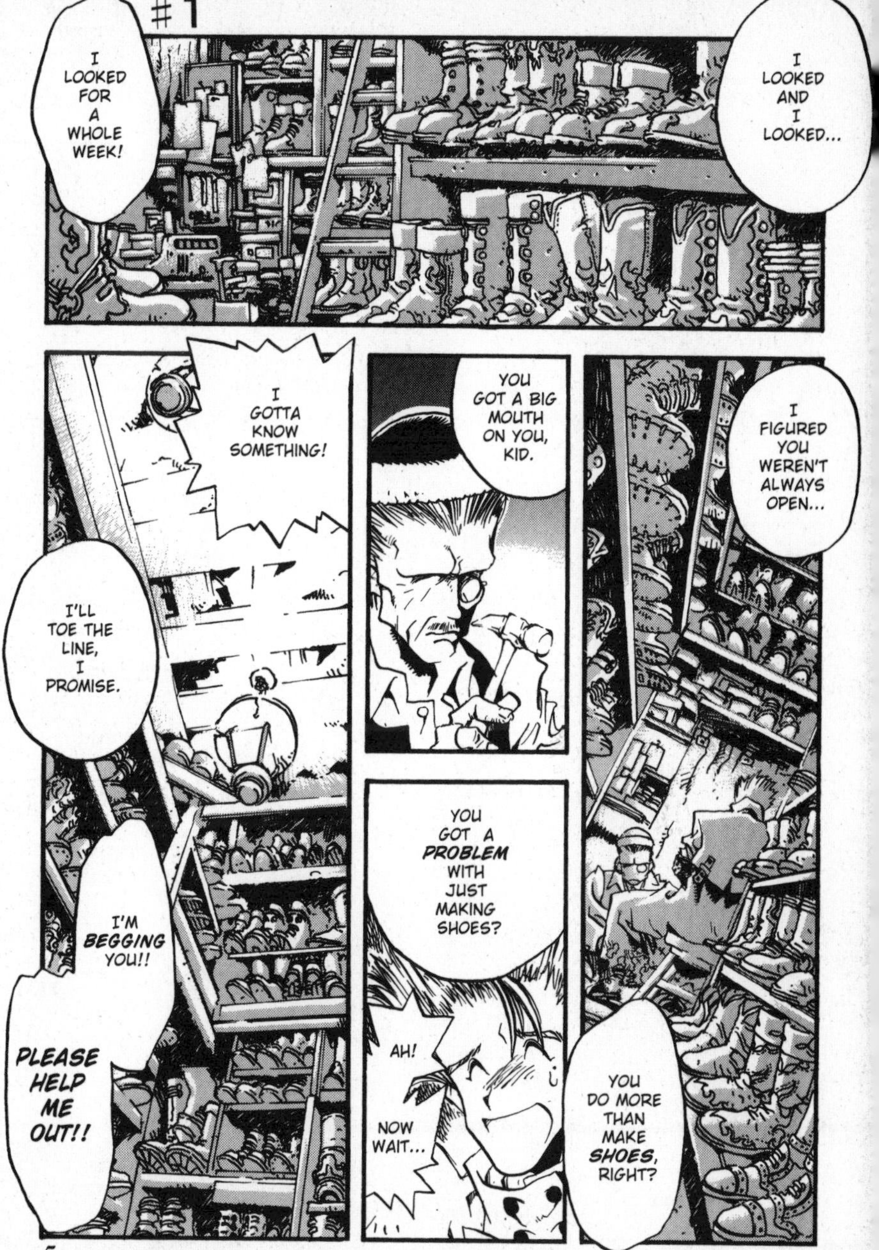

I LOOKED AND I LOOKED...
I LOOKED FOR A WHOLE WEEK!
I FIGURED YOU WEREN'T ALWAYS OPEN...
YOU DO MORE THAN MAKE SHOES, RIGHT?
YOU GOT A BIG MOUTH ON YOU, KID.
YOU GOT A PROBLEM WITH JUST MAKING SHOES?
AH!
NOW WAIT...
I GOTTA KNOW SOMETHING!
I'LL TOE THE LINE, I PROMISE.
I'M BEGGING YOU!!
PLEASE HELP ME OUT!!

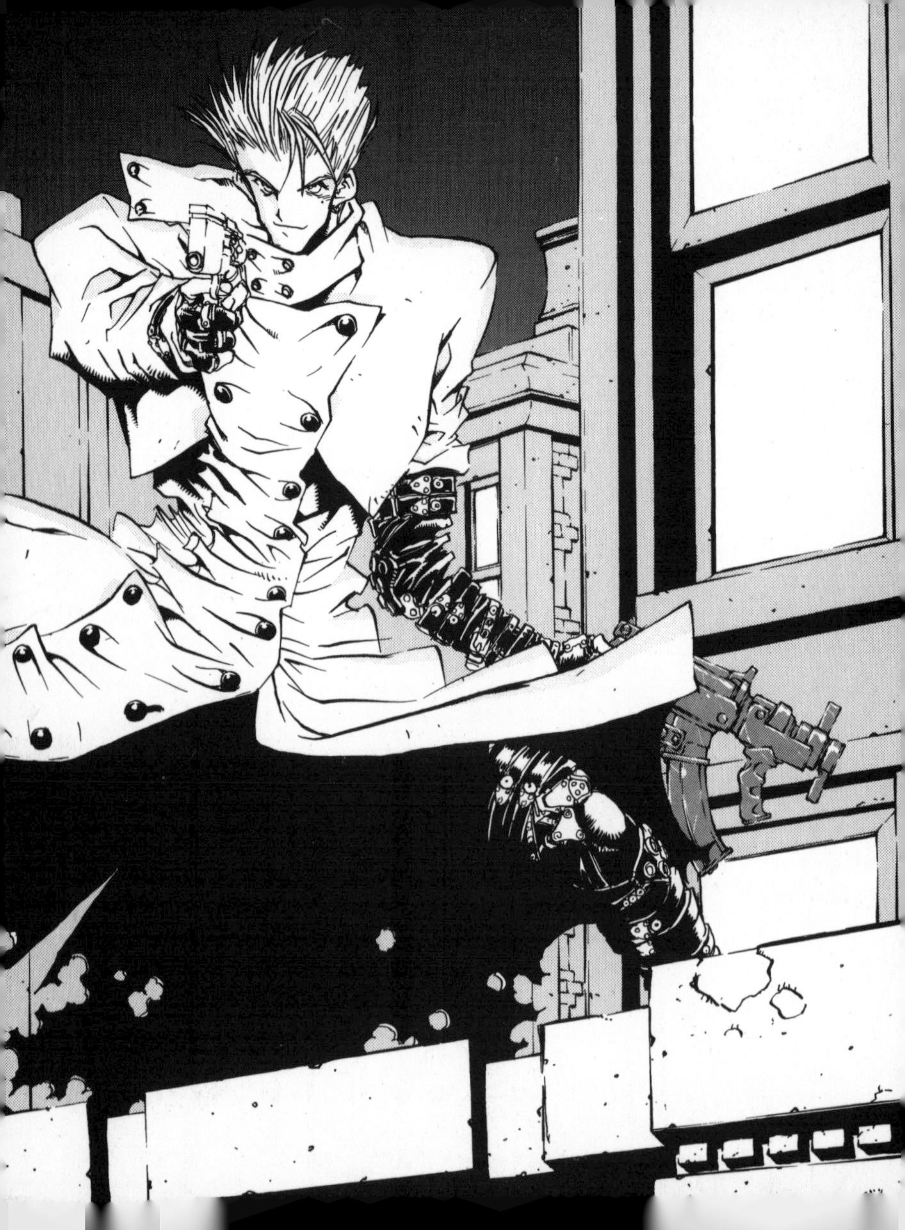

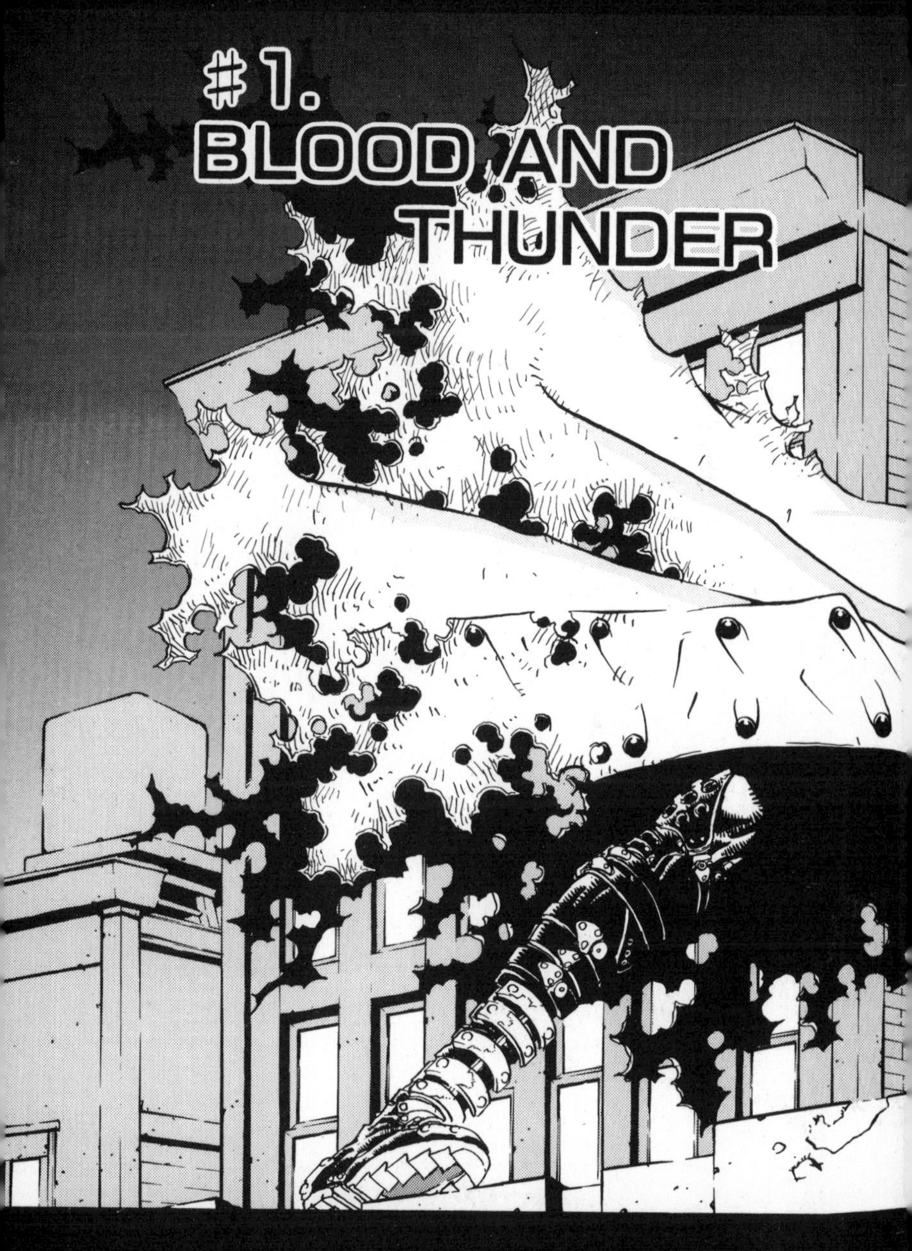

#1.
BLOOD AND
THUNDER

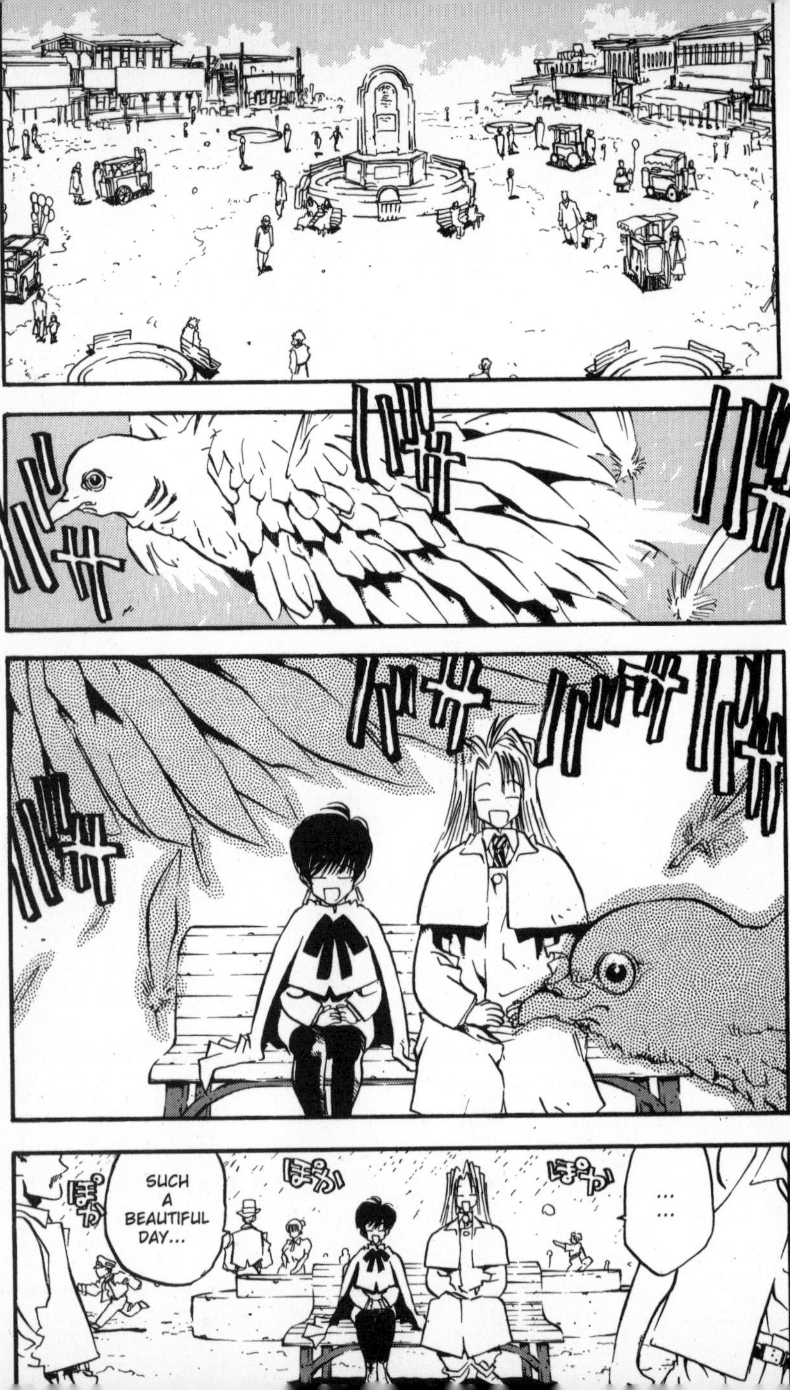
……
SUCH A BEAUTIFUL DAY…

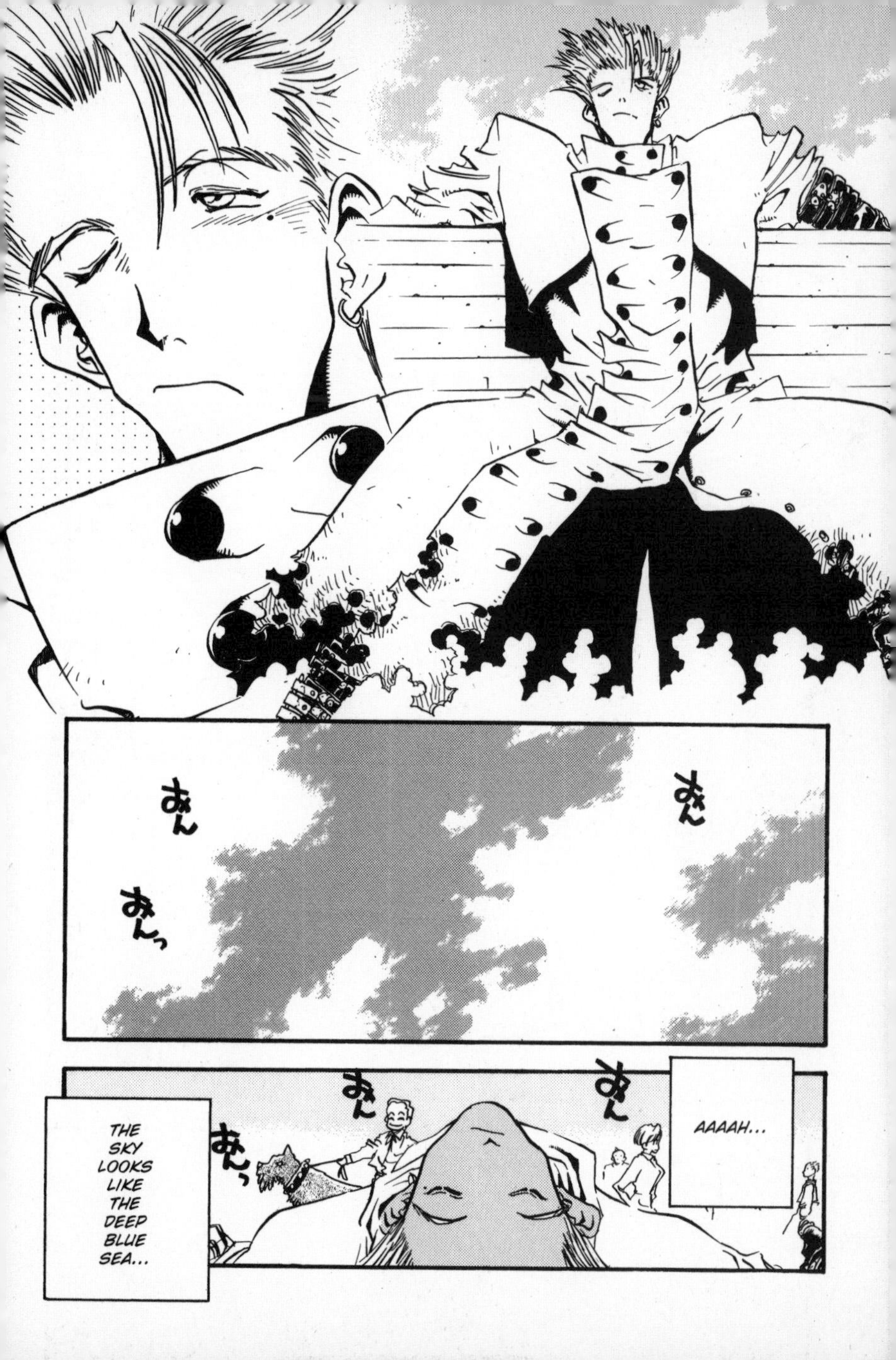
おん
おん
おんっ
AAAAH...
おん
おん
おんっ
THE SKY LOOKS LIKE THE DEEP BLUE SEA...

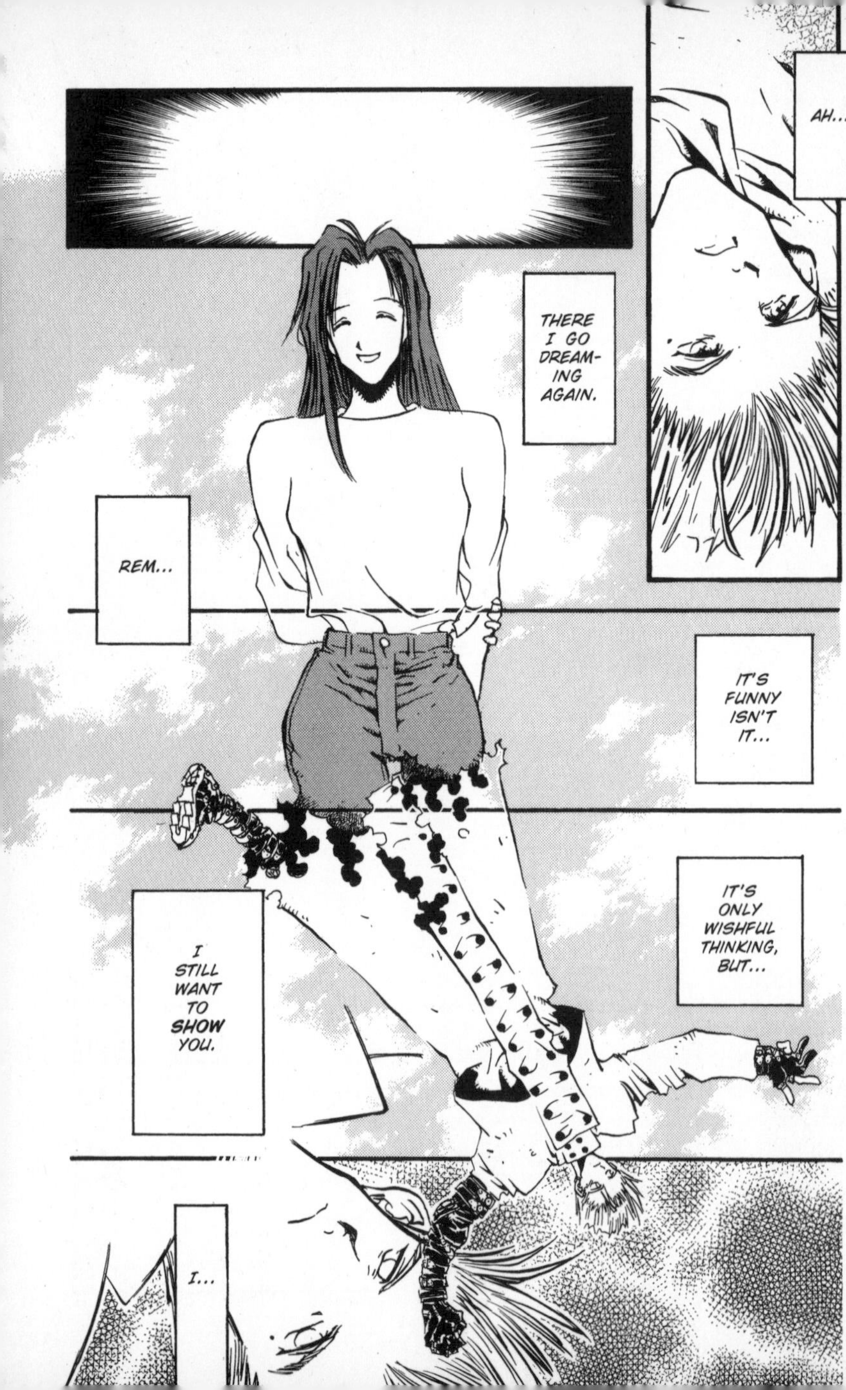
AH...
THERE I GO DREAMING AGAIN.
REM...
IT'S FUNNY ISN'T IT...
IT'S ONLY WISHFUL THINKING, BUT...
I STILL WANT TO SHOW YOU.
I...

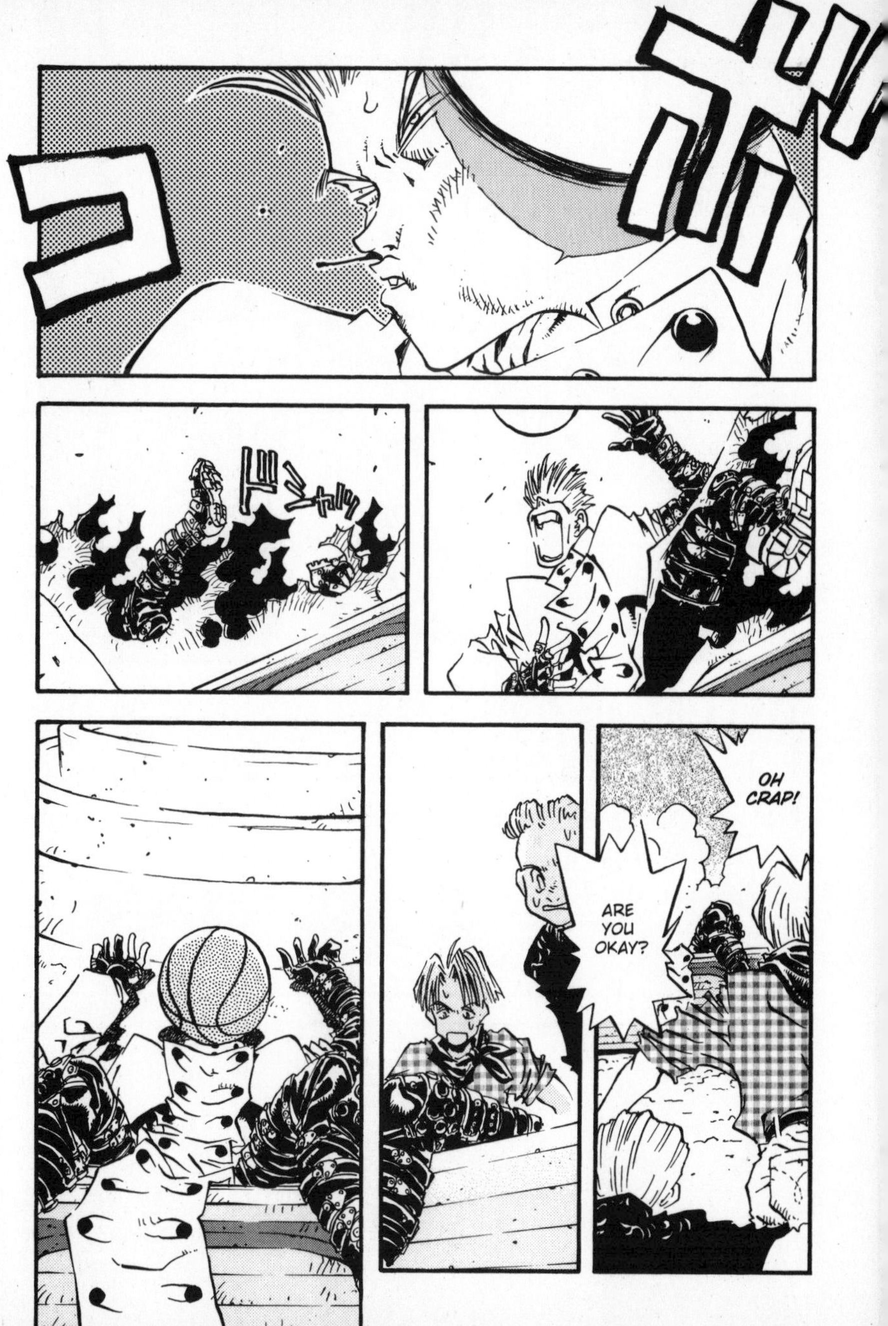
OH CRAP!
ARE YOU OKAY?

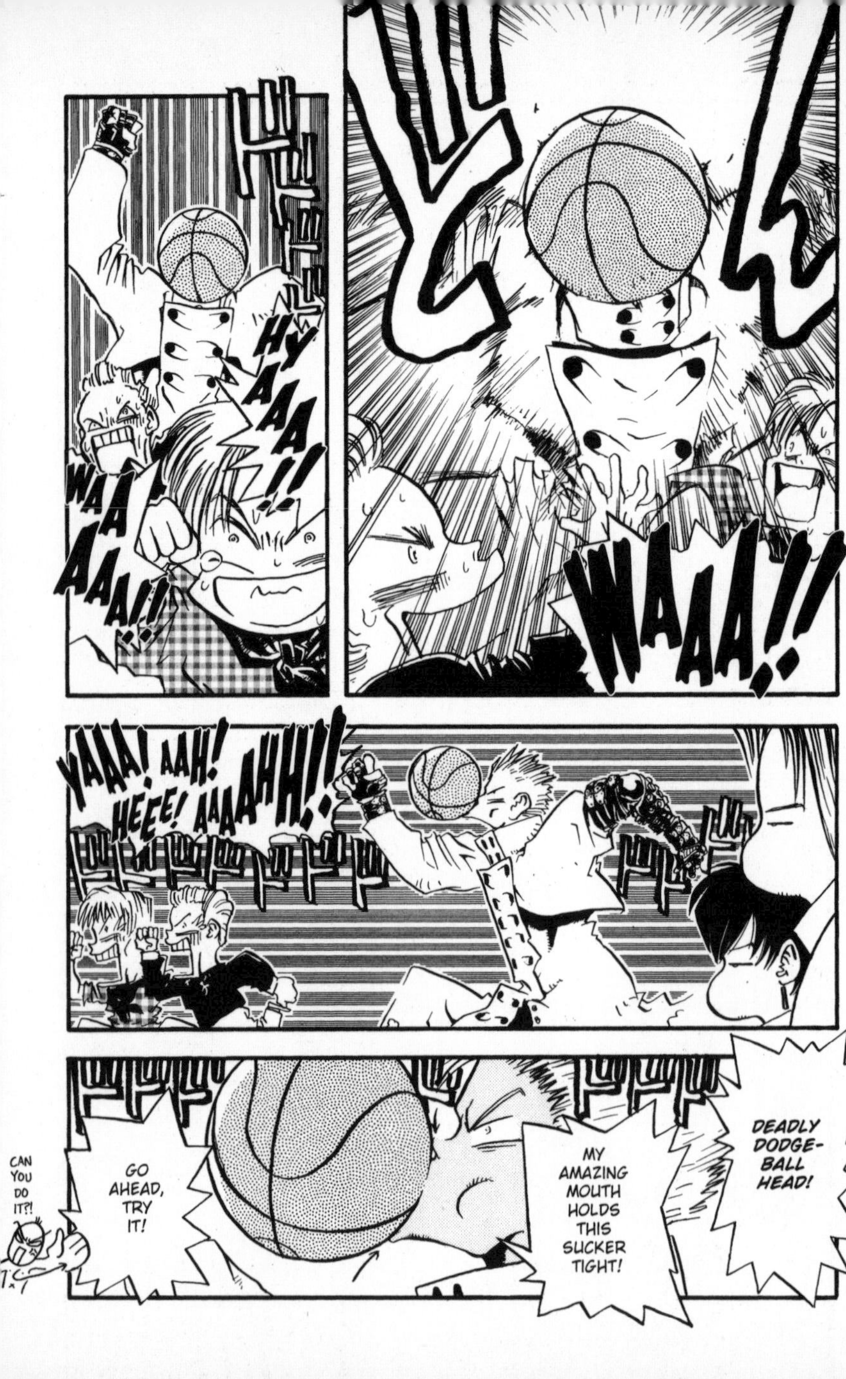
WAAA!!
HYAAAA!!
WAAAAAA!!
YAAA! AAH! HEEE! AAAAHH!!
DEADLY DODGE-BALL HEAD!
MY AMAZING MOUTH HOLDS THIS SUCKER TIGHT!
GO AHEAD, TRY IT!
CAN YOU DO IT?!

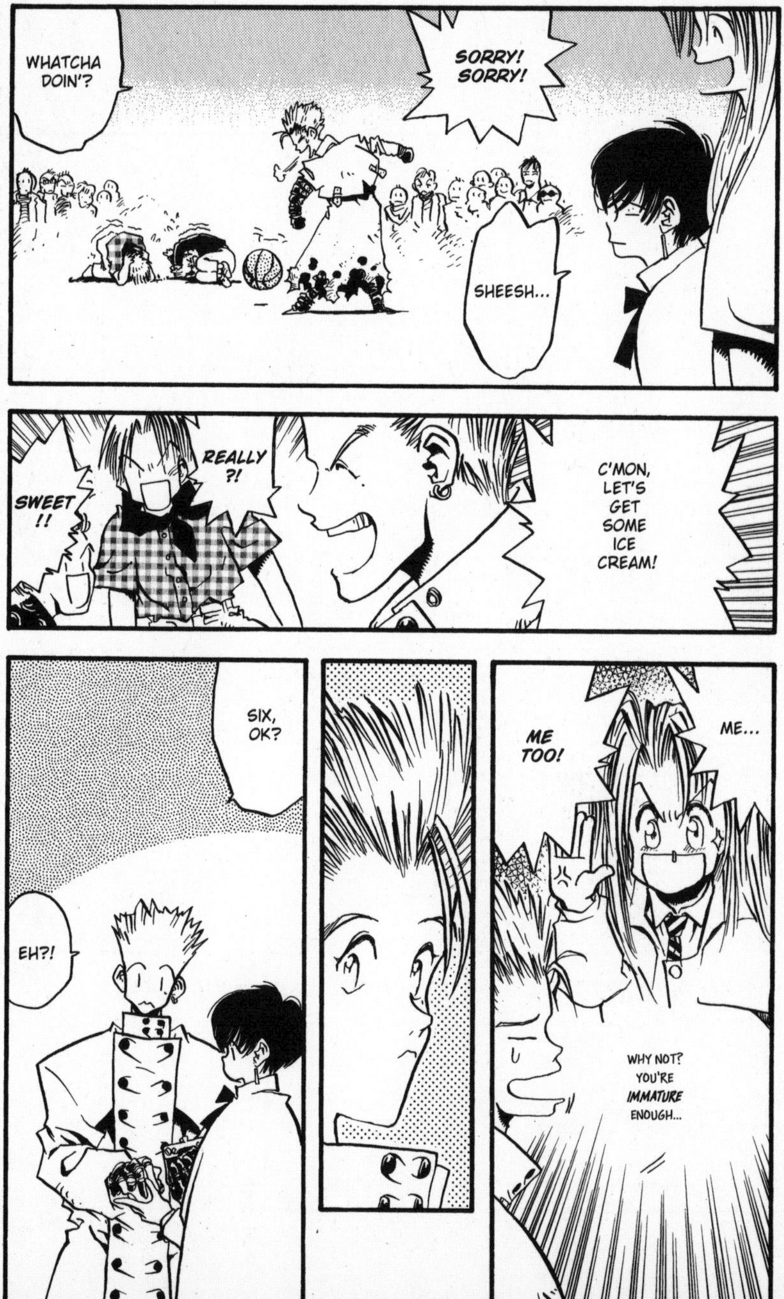
SORRY! SORRY!
WHATCHA DOIN'?
SHEESH...
C'MON, LET'S GET SOME ICE CREAM!
REALLY ?!
SWEET !!
ME...
ME TOO!
WHY NOT? YOU'RE IMMATURE ENOUGH...
SIX, OK?
EH?!

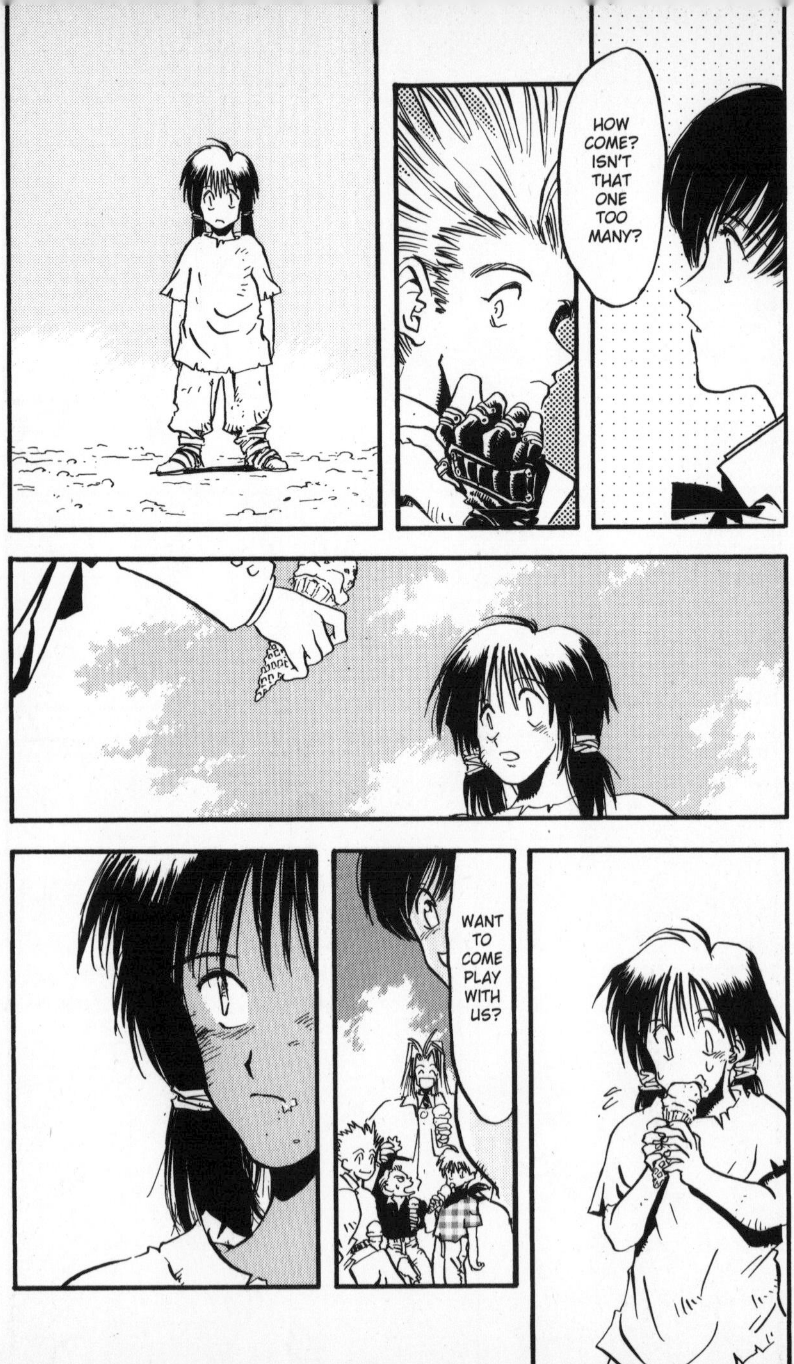
HOW COME? ISN'T THAT ONE TOO MANY?
WANT TO COME PLAY WITH US?

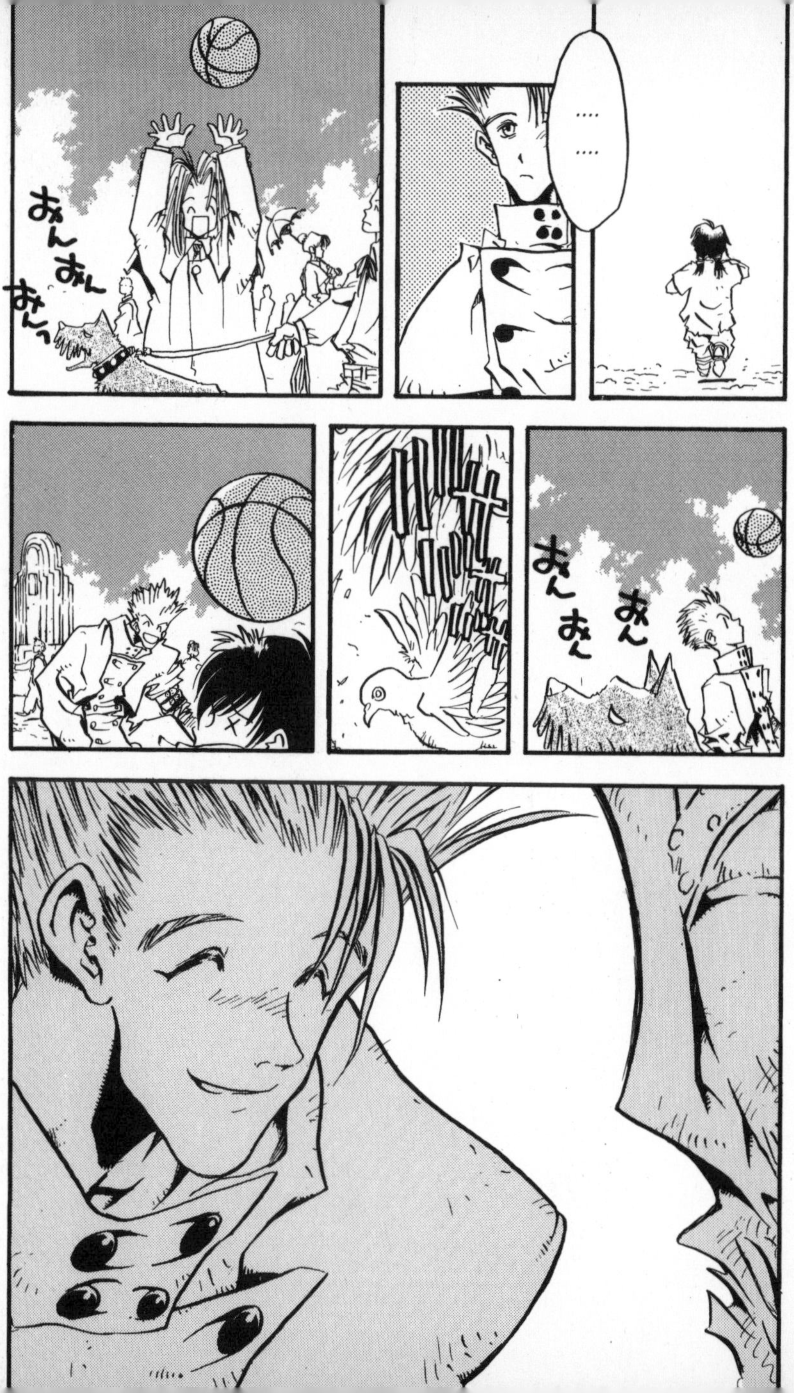
…… ……
おんおん
おんっ
おん
おん

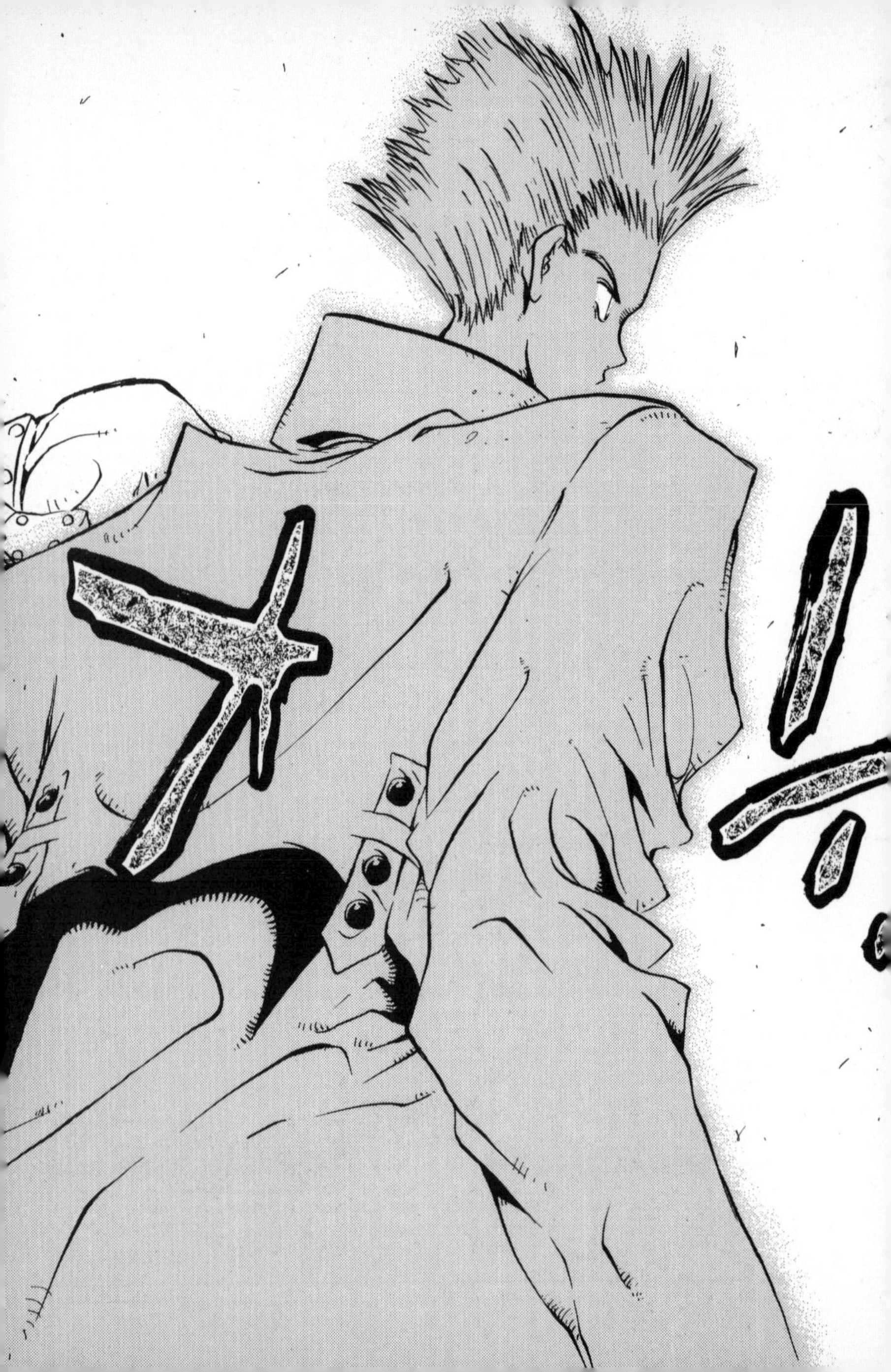

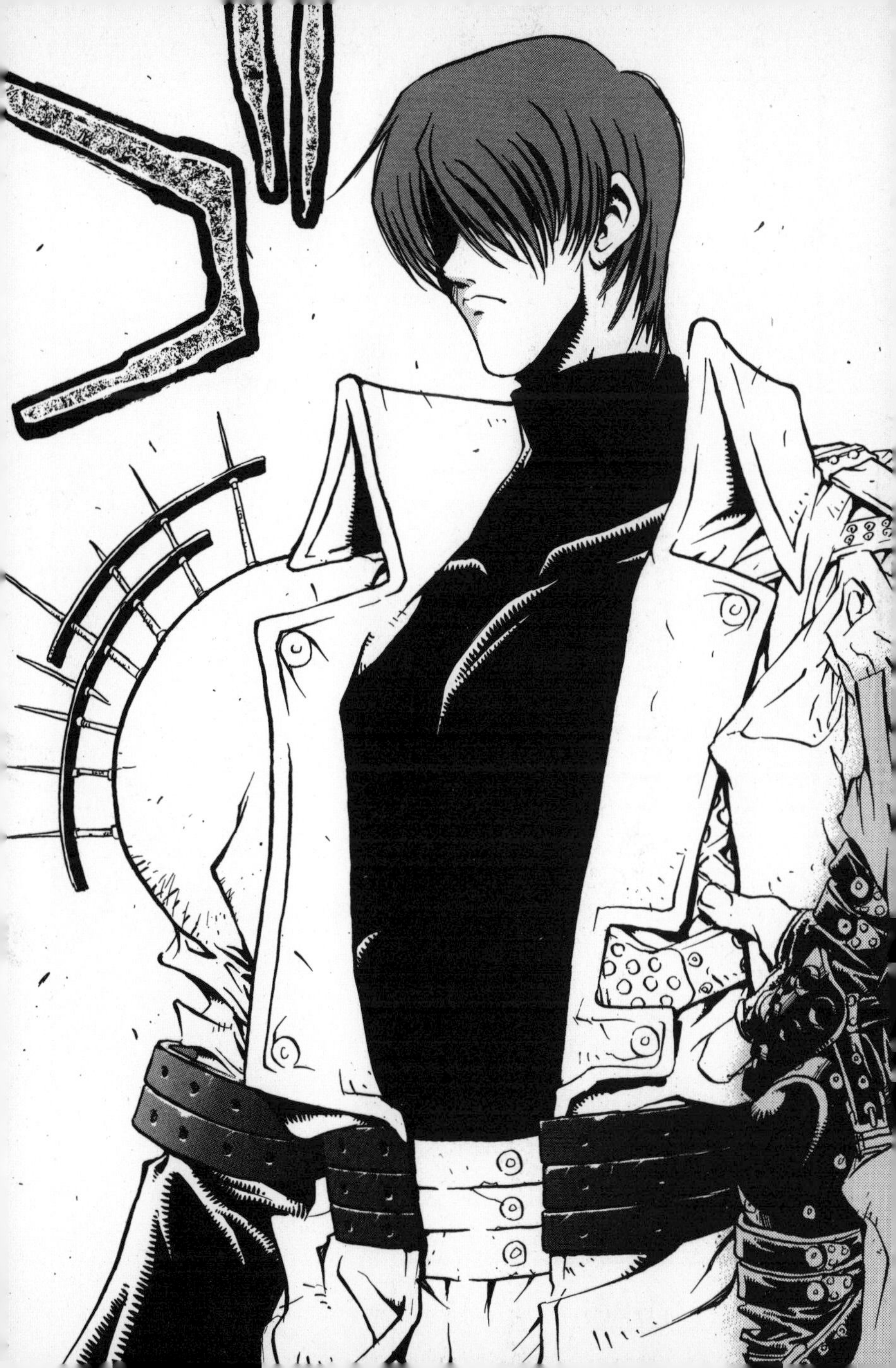

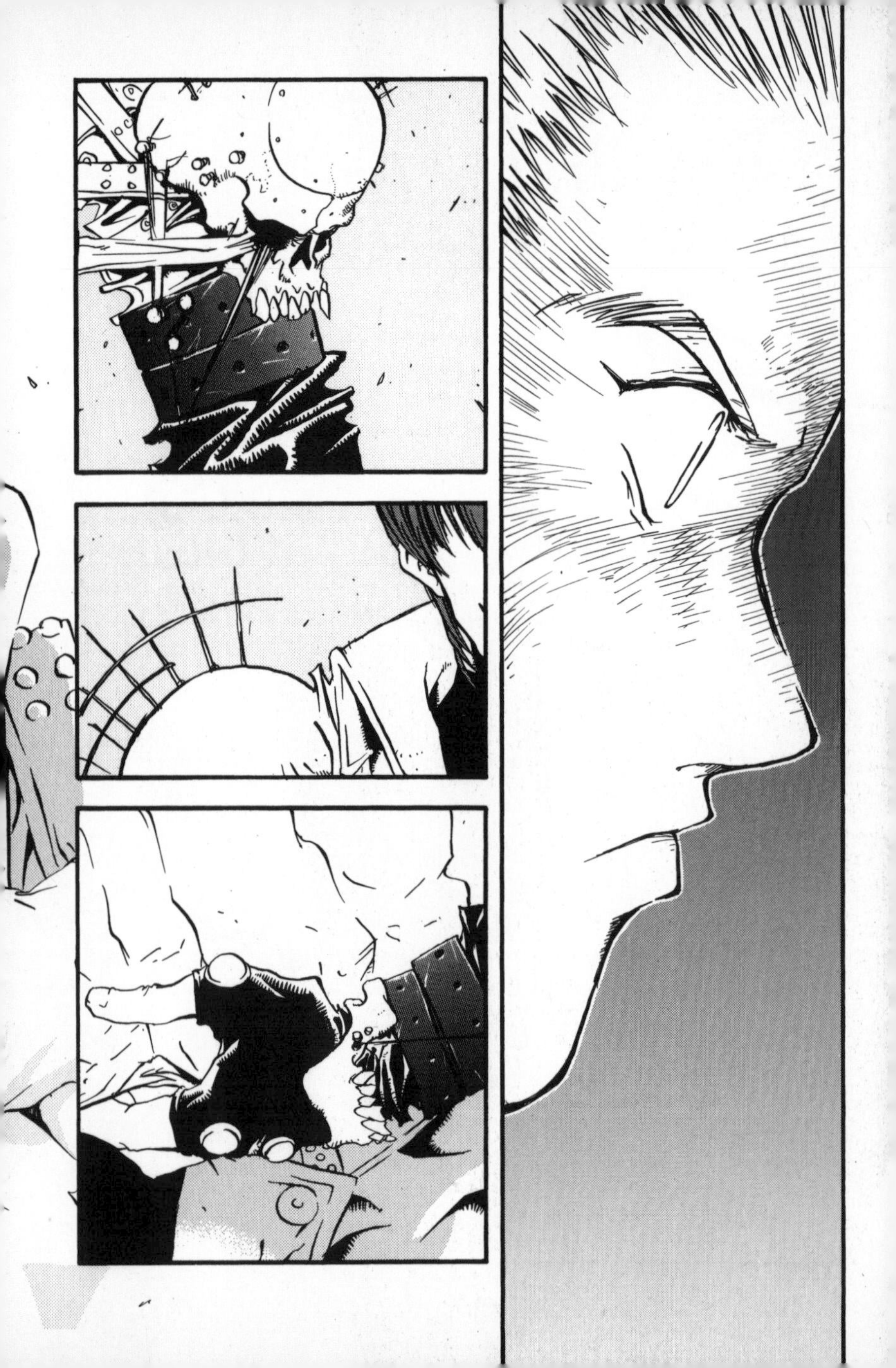

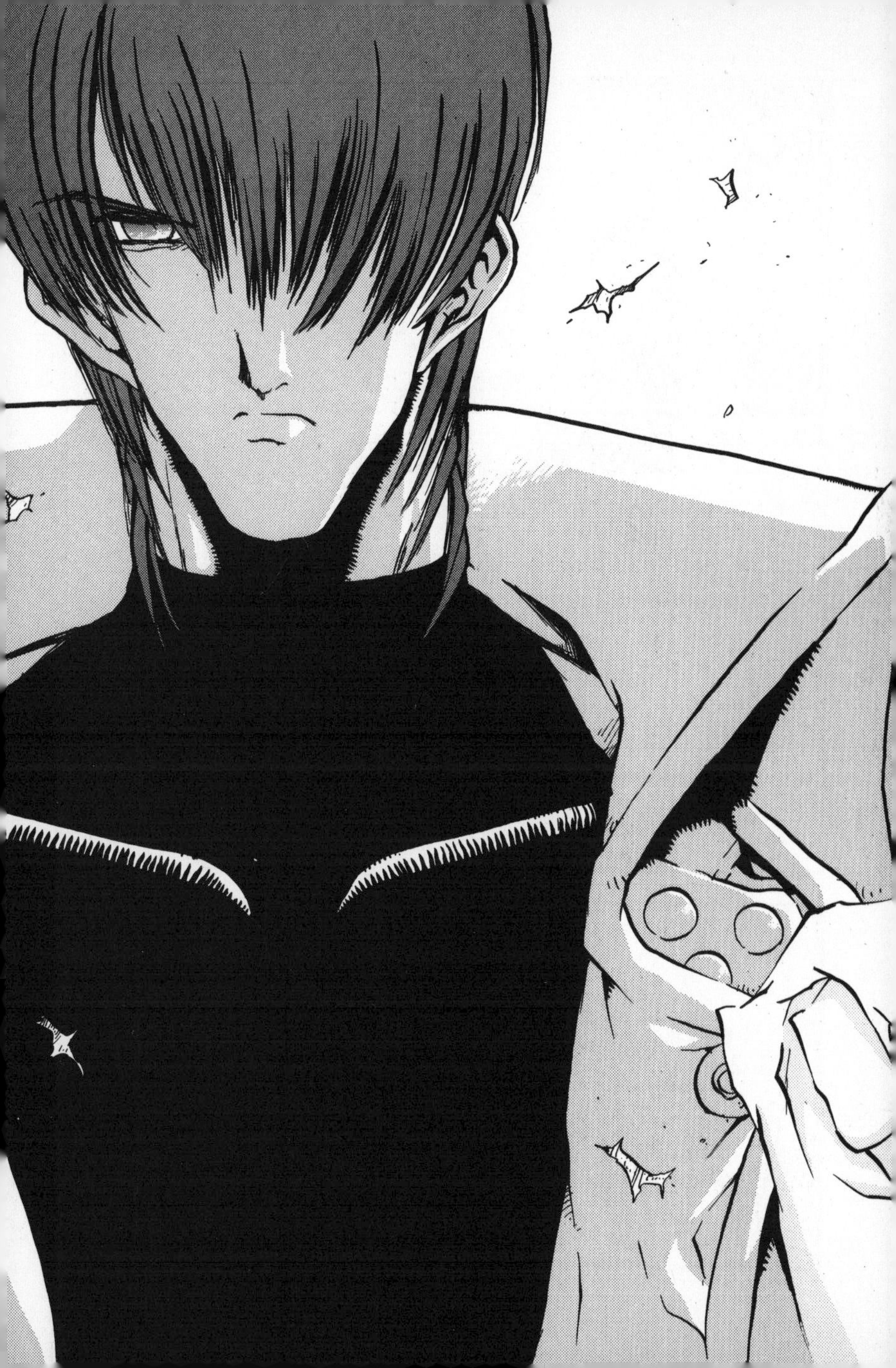

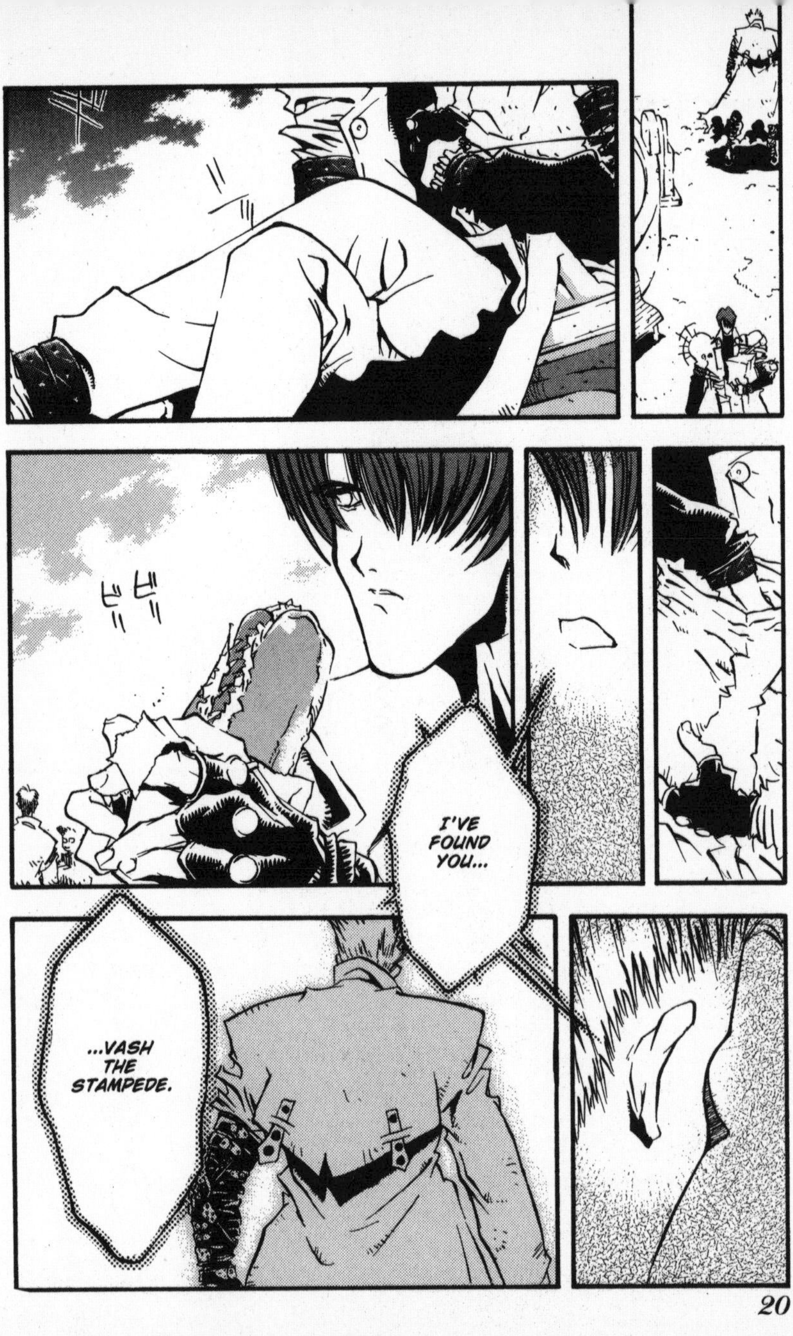
ビビ
I'VE FOUND YOU...
...VASH THE STAMPEDE.

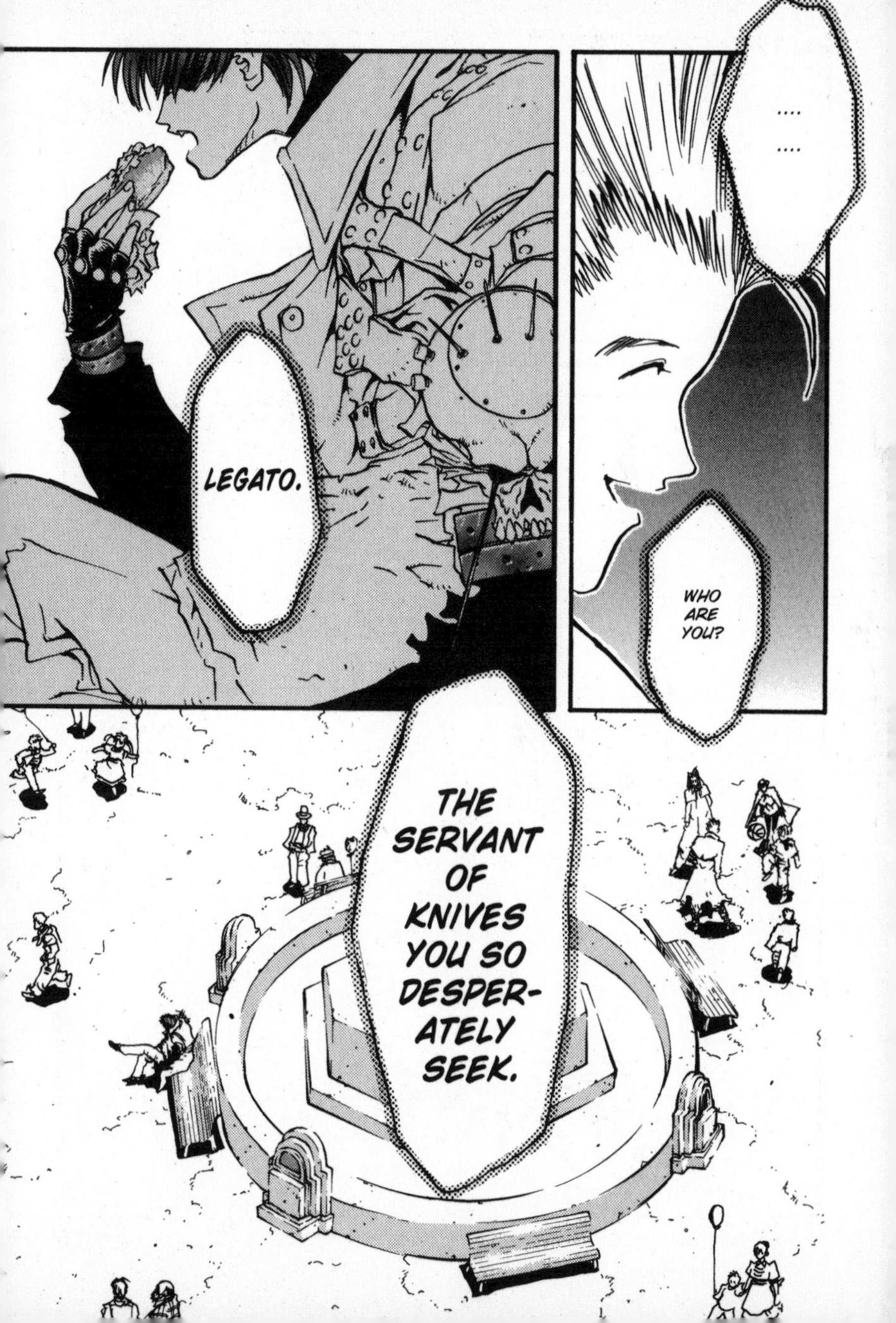
....
....
WHO ARE YOU?
LEGATO.
THE SERVANT OF KNIVES YOU SO DESPERATELY SEEK.

WHA--?

JUST
NOW,
VASH
LOOKED
SO
SERIOUSLY
SAD...

WHAT
WAS
THAT...?

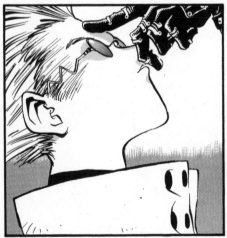

CHK

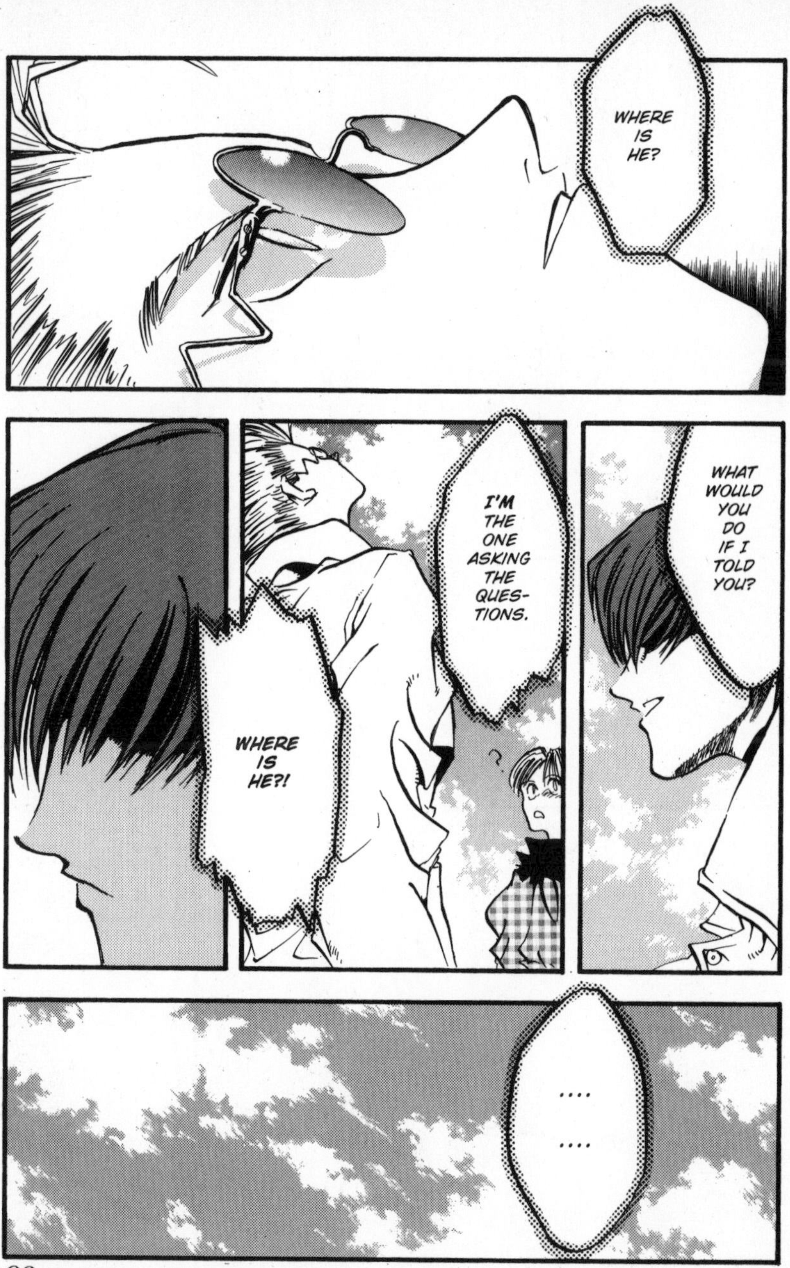
WHERE IS HE?
WHAT WOULD YOU DO IF I TOLD YOU?
I'M THE ONE ASKING THE QUES-TIONS.
WHERE IS HE?!
....
....

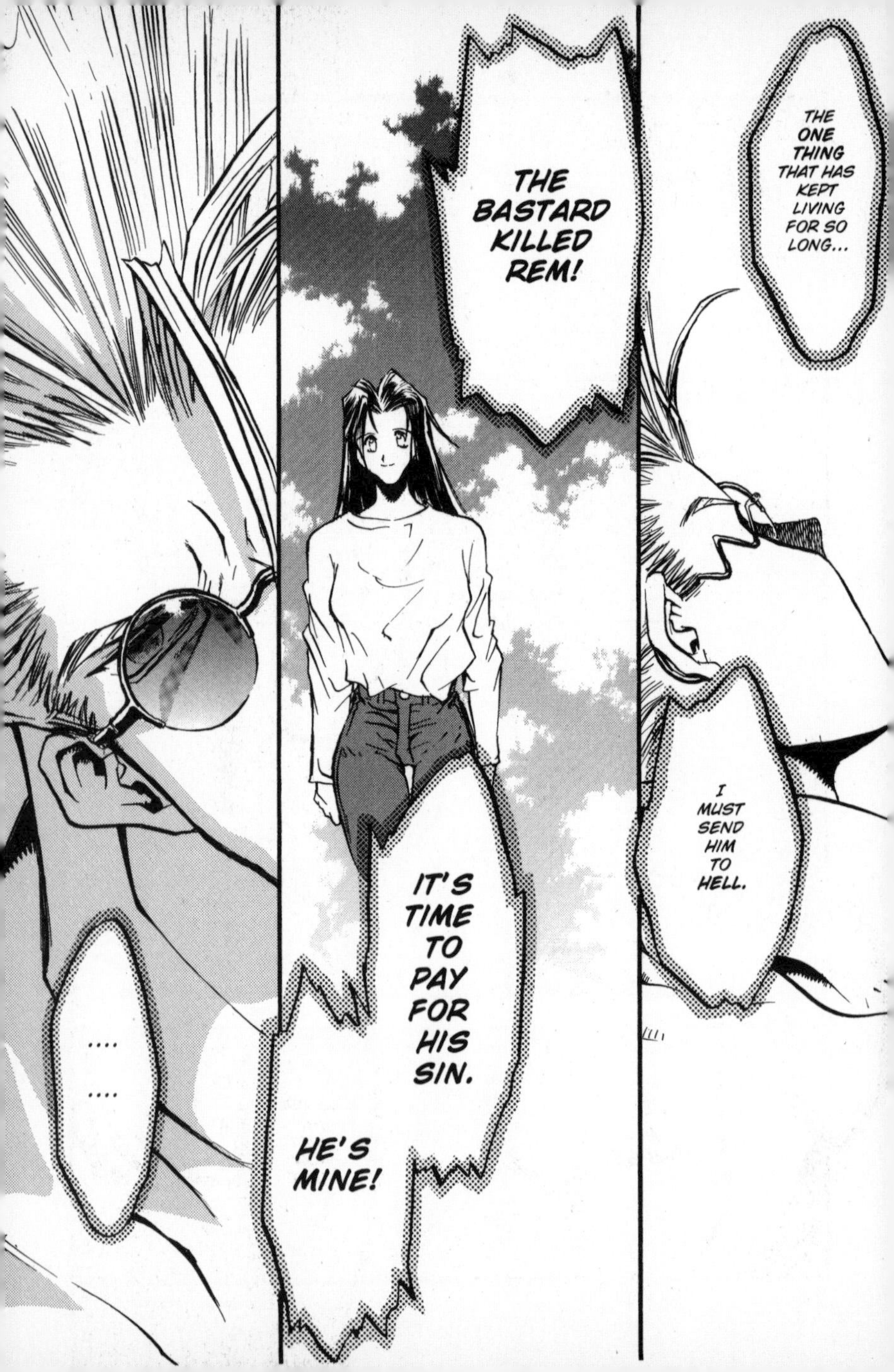
THE ONE THING THAT HAS KEPT LIVING FOR SO LONG...
I MUST SEND HIM TO HELL.
THE BASTARD KILLED REM!
IT'S TIME TO PAY FOR HIS SIN.
HE'S MINE!
....
....

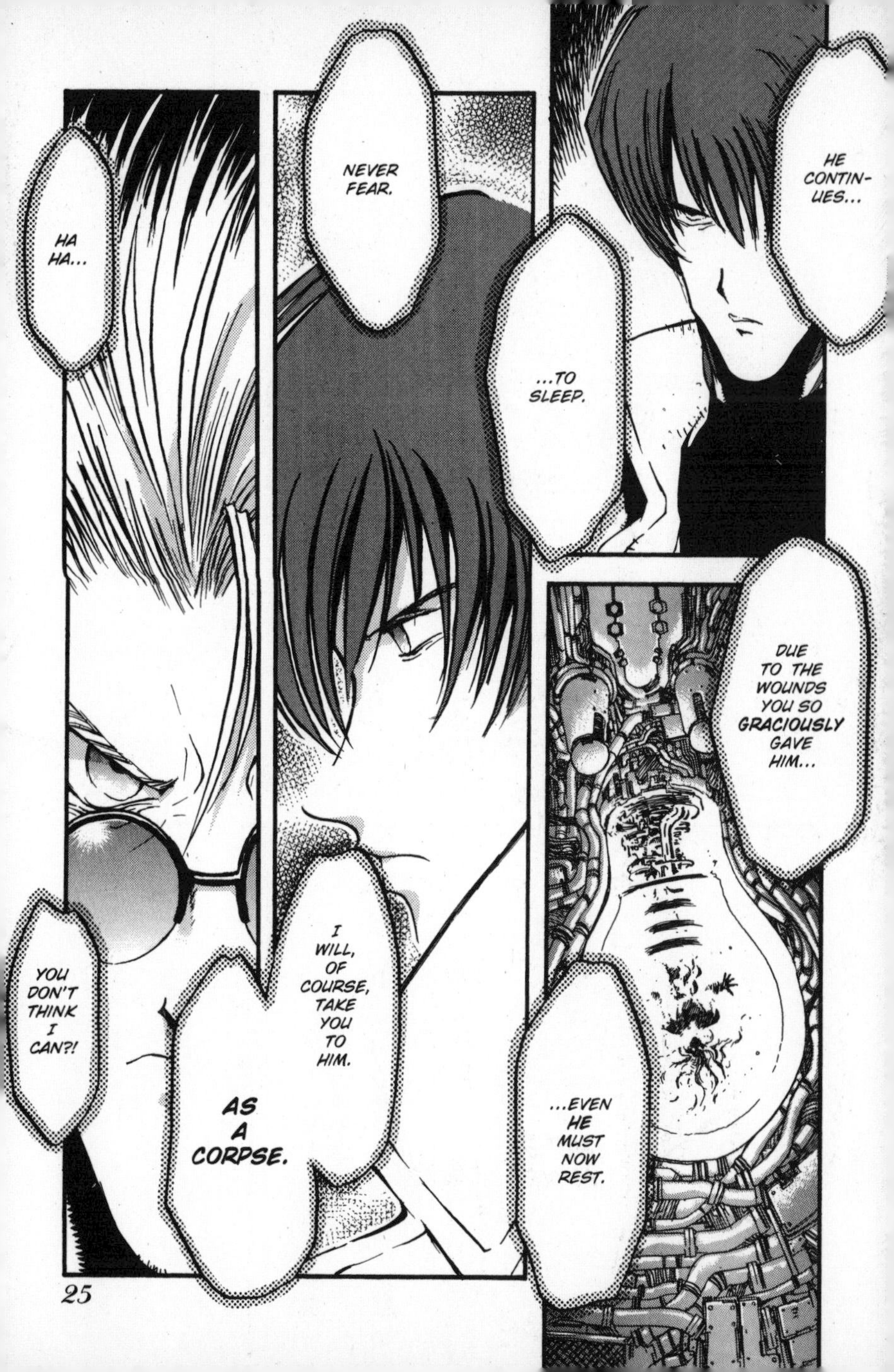
HE CONTIN-UES...
...TO SLEEP.
DUE TO THE WOUNDS YOU SO **GRACIOUSLY** GAVE HIM...
...EVEN HE MUST NOW REST.
NEVER FEAR.
I WILL, OF COURSE, TAKE YOU TO HIM.
AS A CORPSE.
HA HA...
YOU DON'T THINK I CAN?!

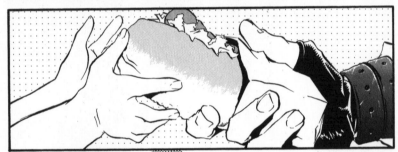

I STILL HAVEN'T GIVEN YOU...

...YOUR GIFT, HAVE I?

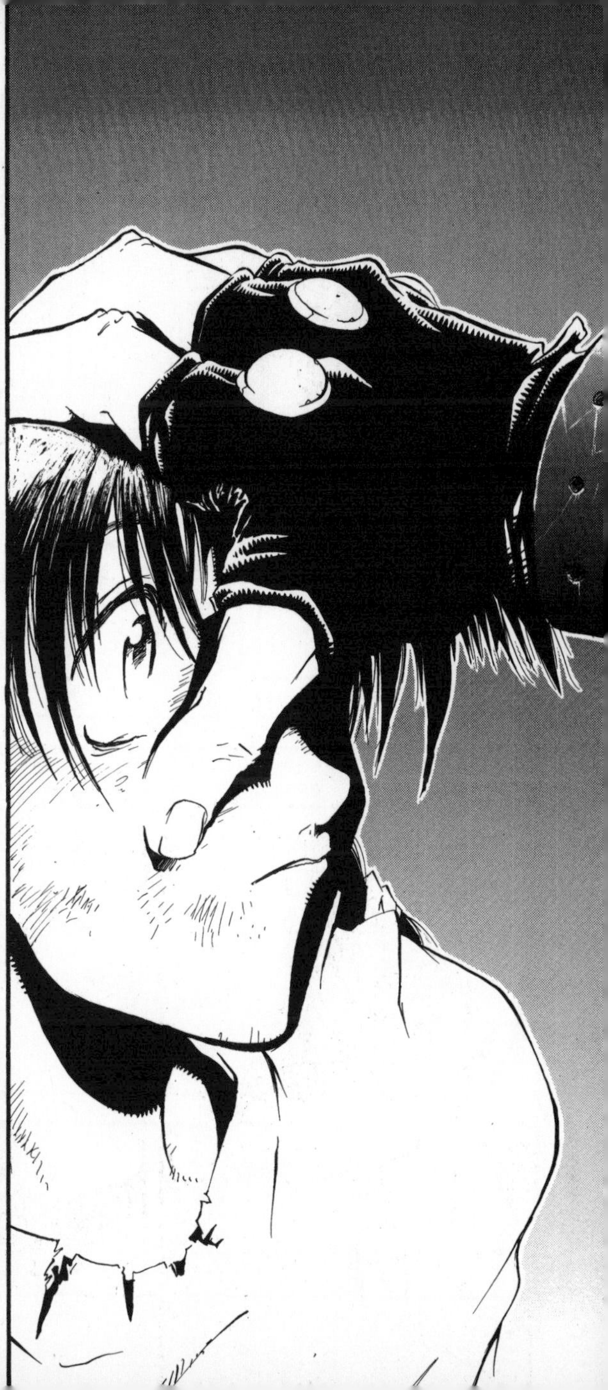
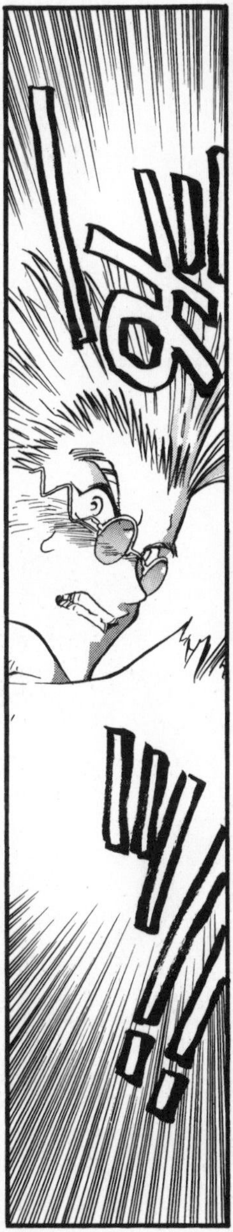

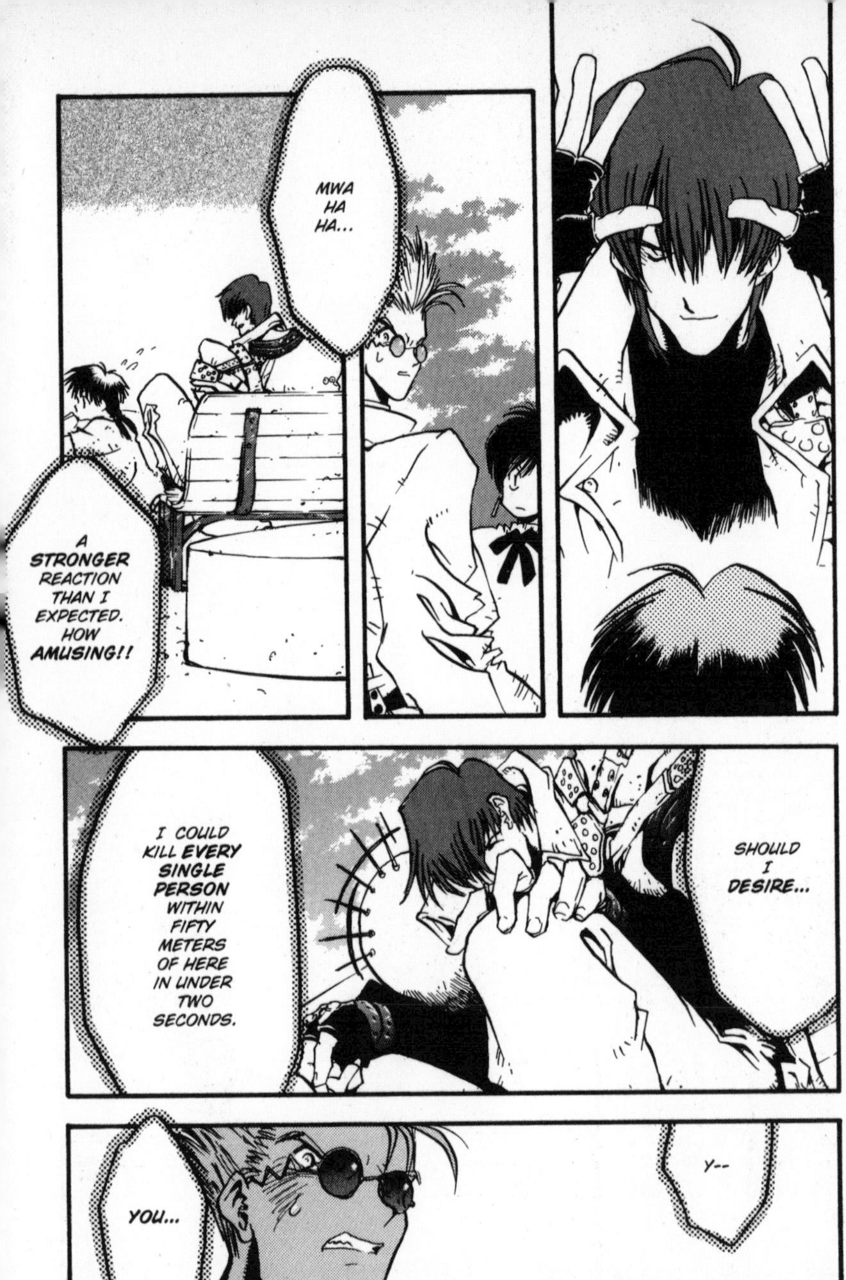
MWA HA HA...
A STRONGER REACTION THAN I EXPECTED. HOW AMUSING!!
SHOULD I DESIRE...
I COULD KILL EVERY SINGLE PERSON WITHIN FIFTY METERS OF HERE IN UNDER TWO SECONDS.
Y--
YOU...

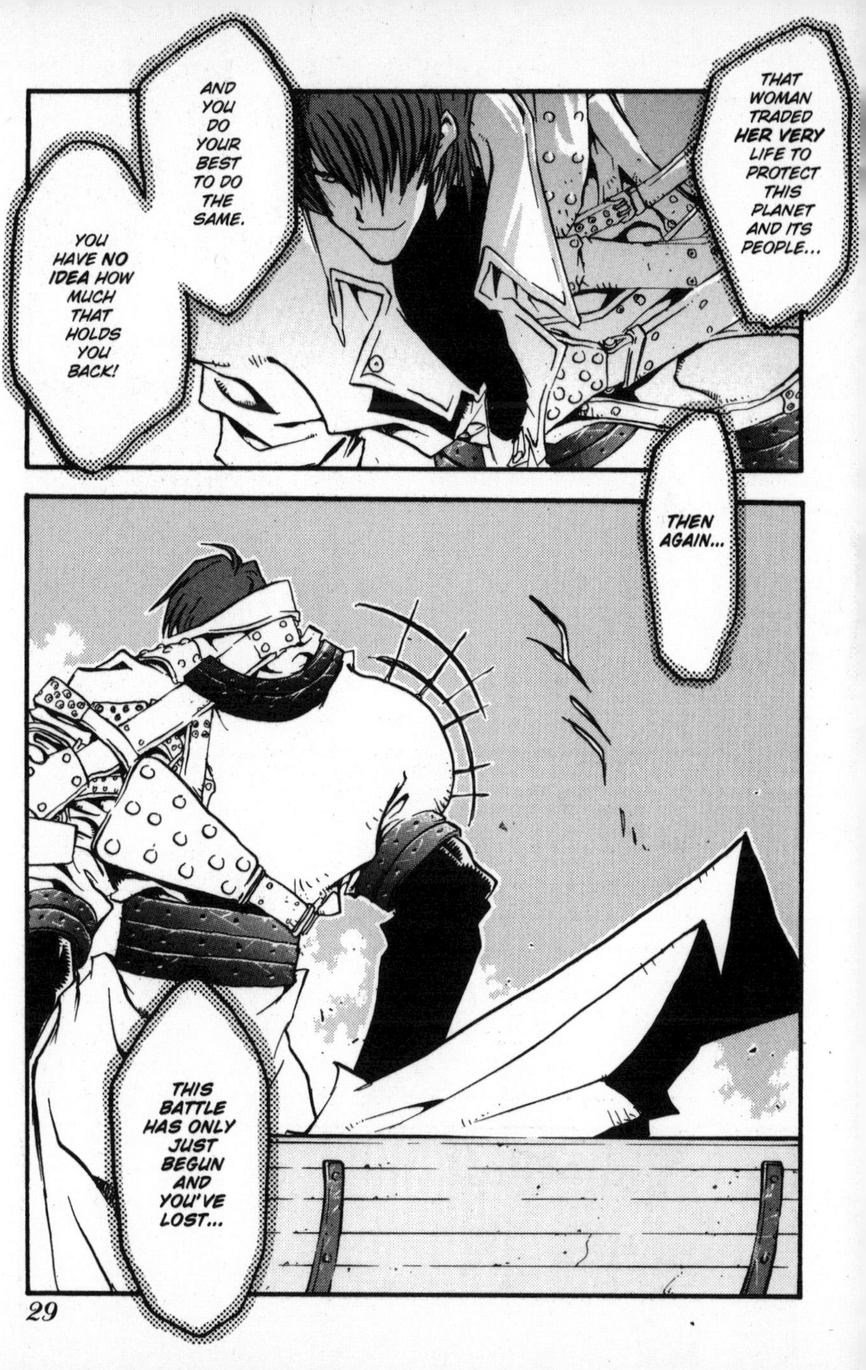
THAT WOMAN TRADED HER VERY LIFE TO PROTECT THIS PLANET AND ITS PEOPLE...
AND YOU DO YOUR BEST TO DO THE SAME.
YOU HAVE NO IDEA HOW MUCH THAT HOLDS YOU BACK!
THEN AGAIN...
THIS BATTLE HAS ONLY JUST BEGUN AND YOU'VE LOST...

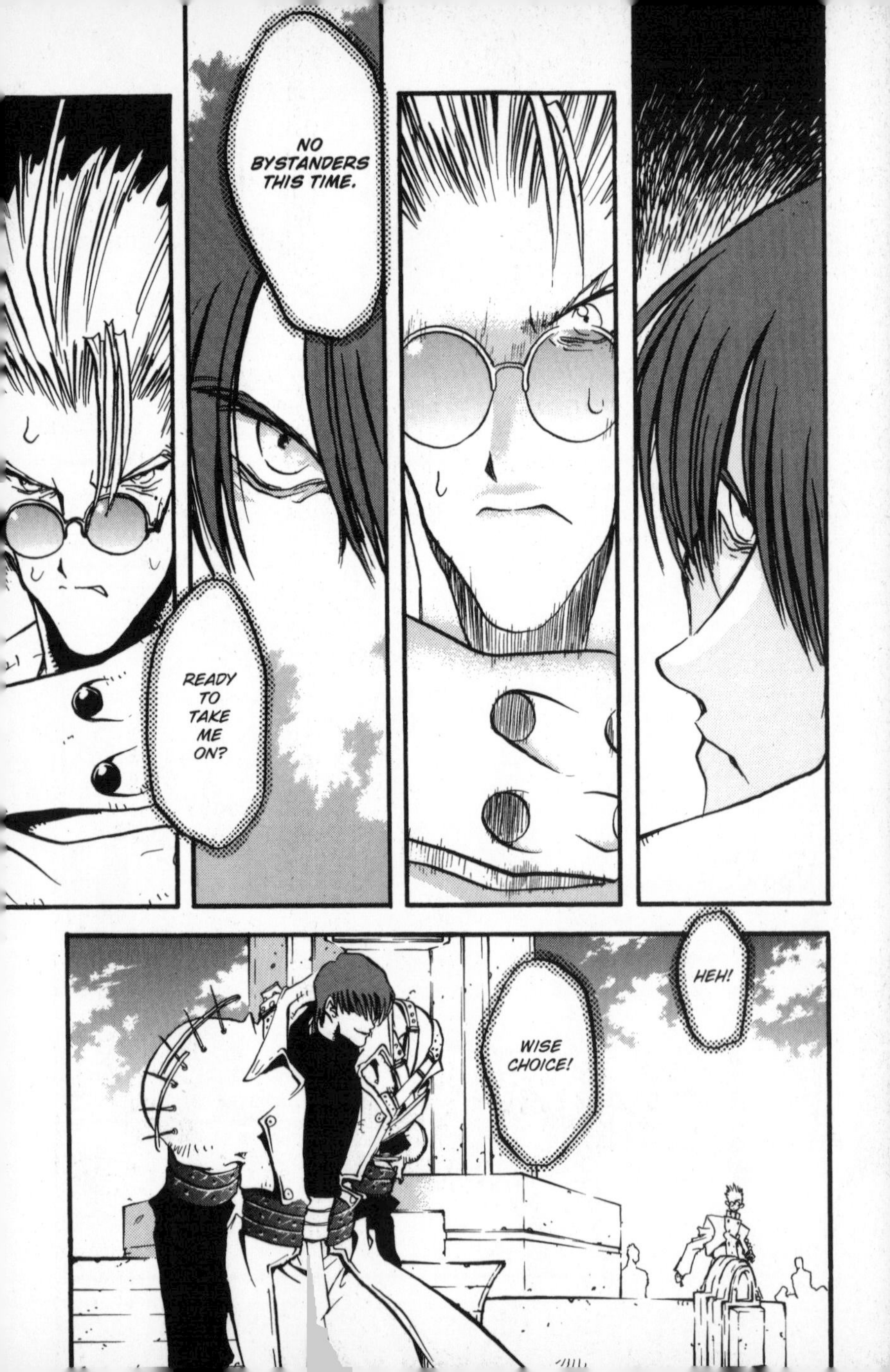
NO BYSTANDERS THIS TIME.
READY TO TAKE ME ON?
HEH!
WISE CHOICE!

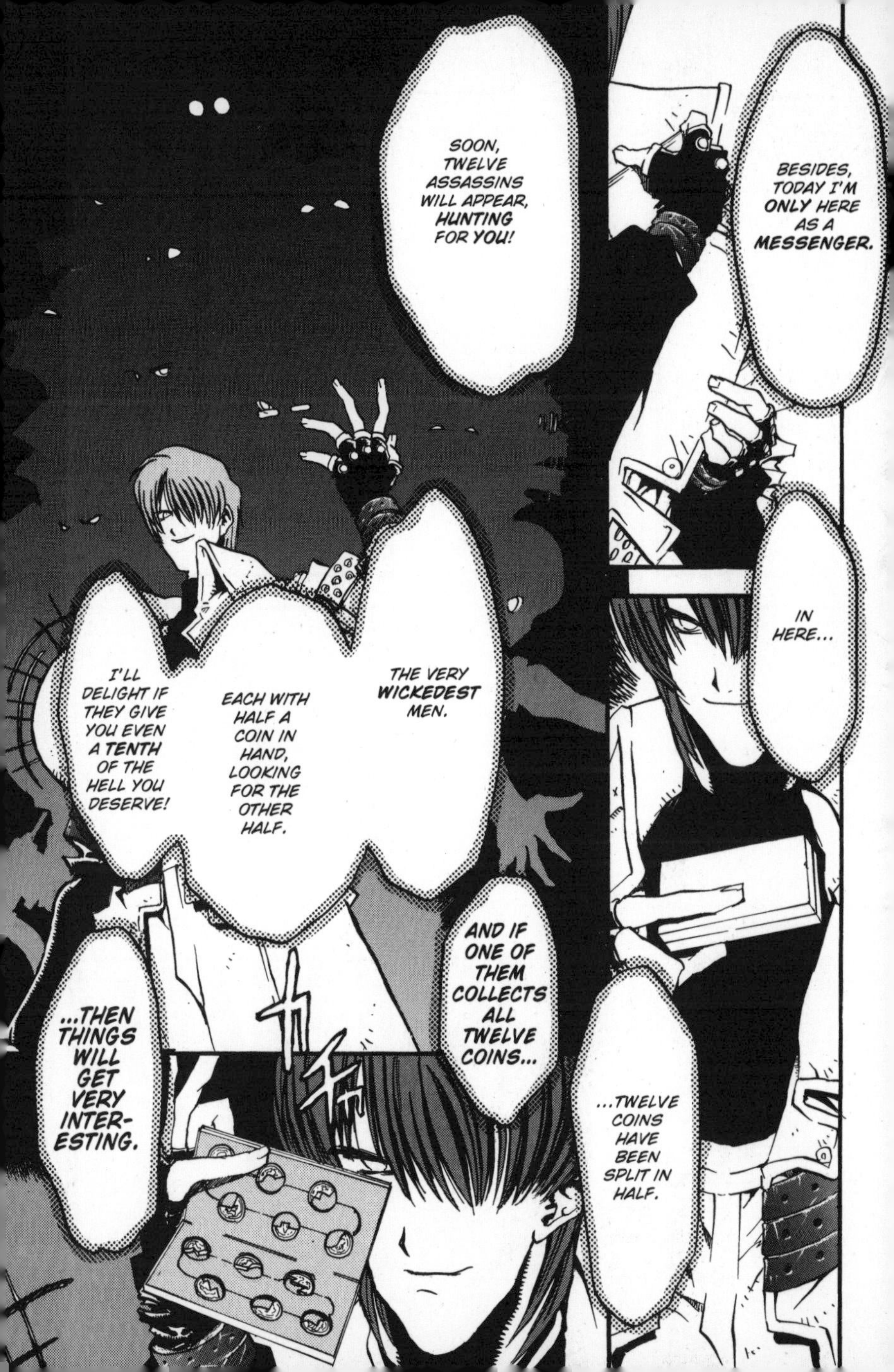
BESIDES, TODAY I'M ONLY HERE AS A MESSENGER.
IN HERE...
...TWELVE COINS HAVE BEEN SPLIT IN HALF.
SOON, TWELVE ASSASSINS WILL APPEAR, HUNTING FOR YOU!
THE VERY WICKEDEST MEN.
EACH WITH HALF A COIN IN HAND, LOOKING FOR THE OTHER HALF.
I'LL DELIGHT IF THEY GIVE YOU EVEN A TENTH OF THE HELL YOU DESERVE!
AND IF ONE OF THEM COLLECTS ALL TWELVE COINS...
...THEN THINGS WILL GET VERY INTER-ESTING.

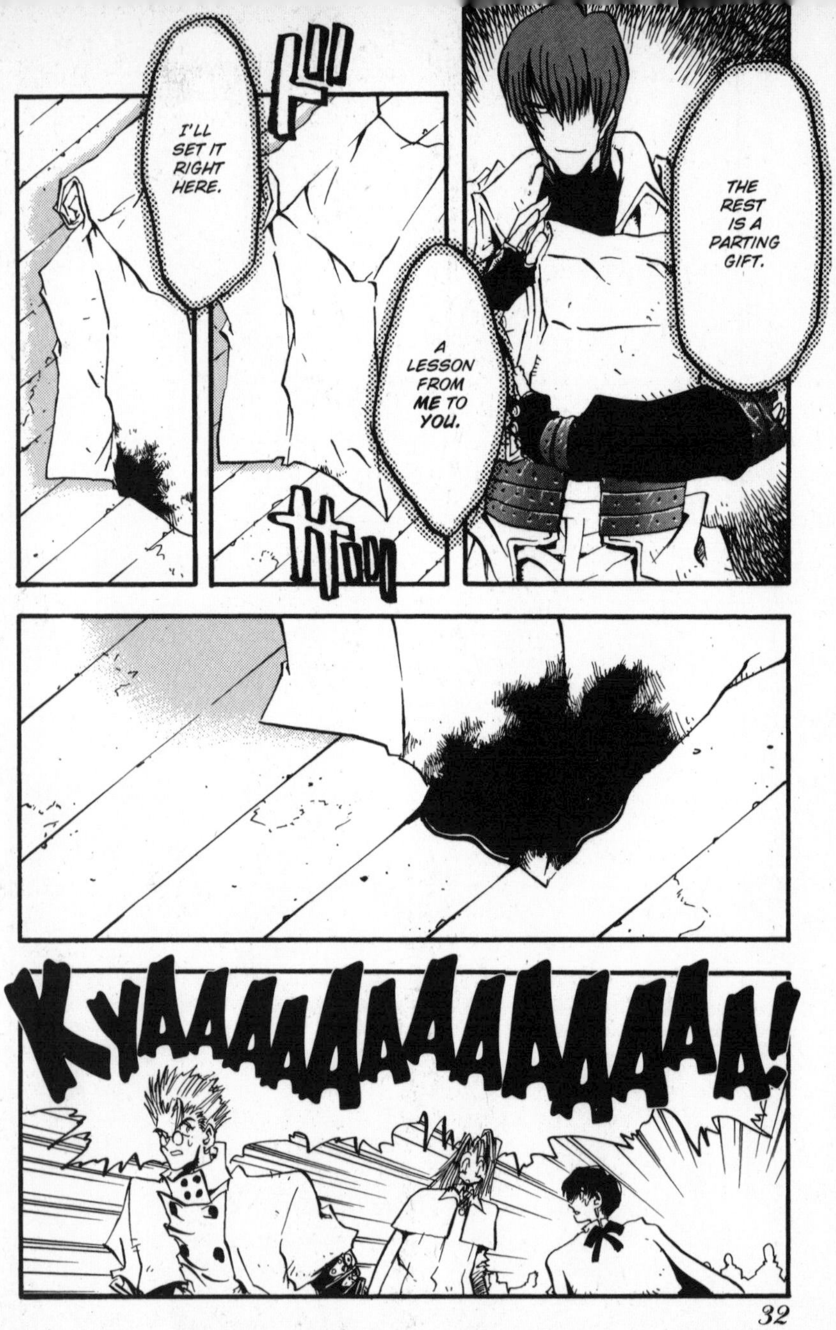
THE REST IS A PARTING GIFT.
A LESSON FROM ME TO YOU.
I'LL SET IT RIGHT HERE.
KYAAAAAAAAAAAA!

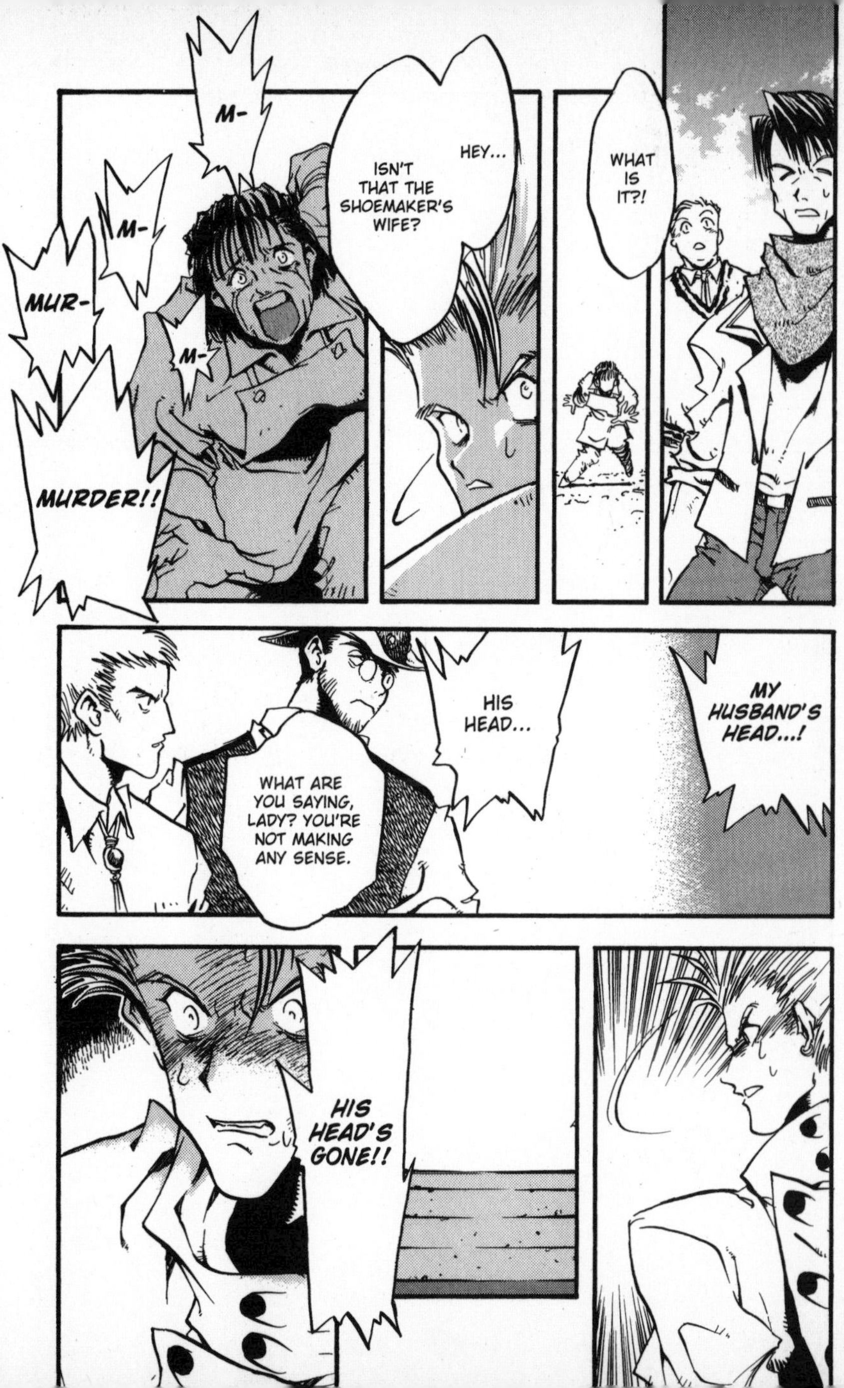
WHAT IS IT?!
HEY...
ISN'T THAT THE SHOEMAKER'S WIFE?
M-
M-
MUR-
M-
MURDER!!
MY HUSBAND'S HEAD...!
HIS HEAD...
WHAT ARE YOU SAYING, LADY? YOU'RE NOT MAKING ANY SENSE.
HIS HEAD'S GONE!!

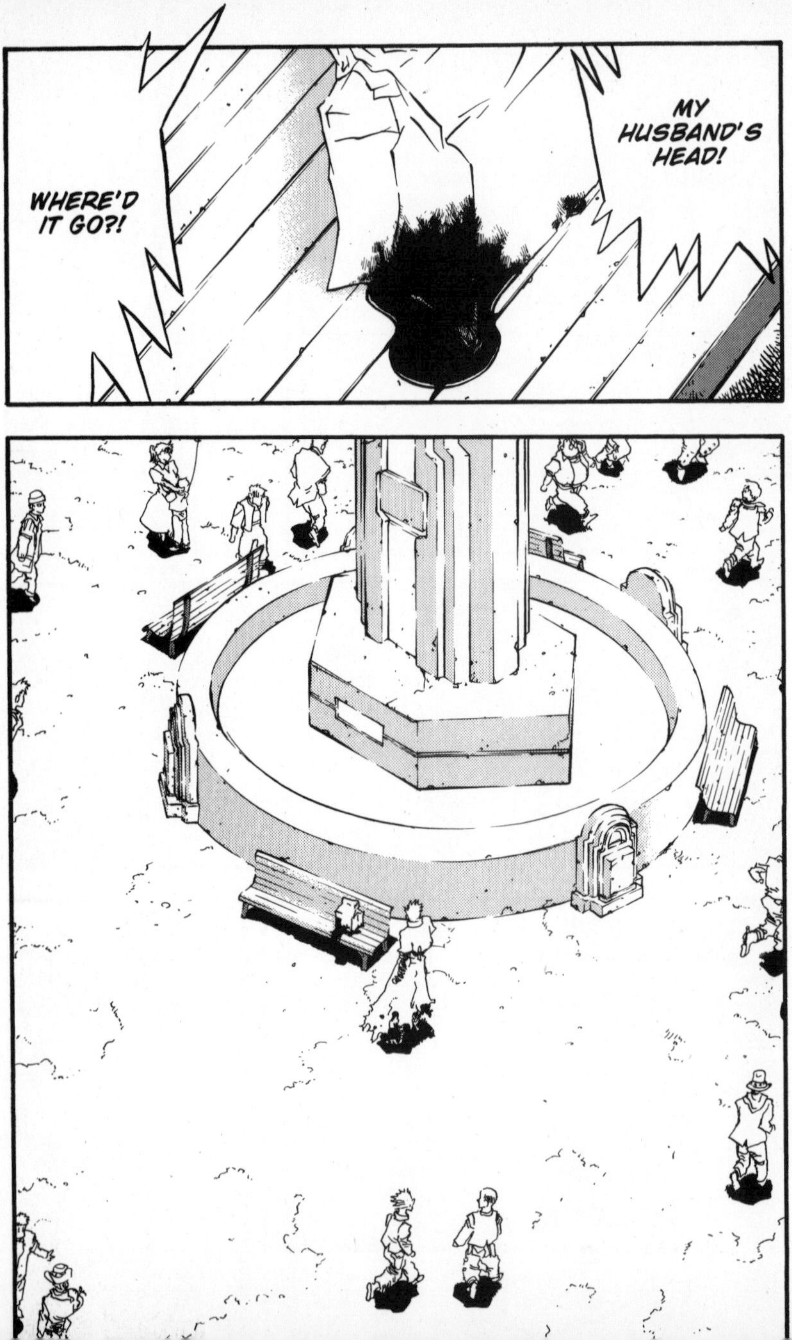
MY HUSBAND'S HEAD!
WHERE'D IT GO?!

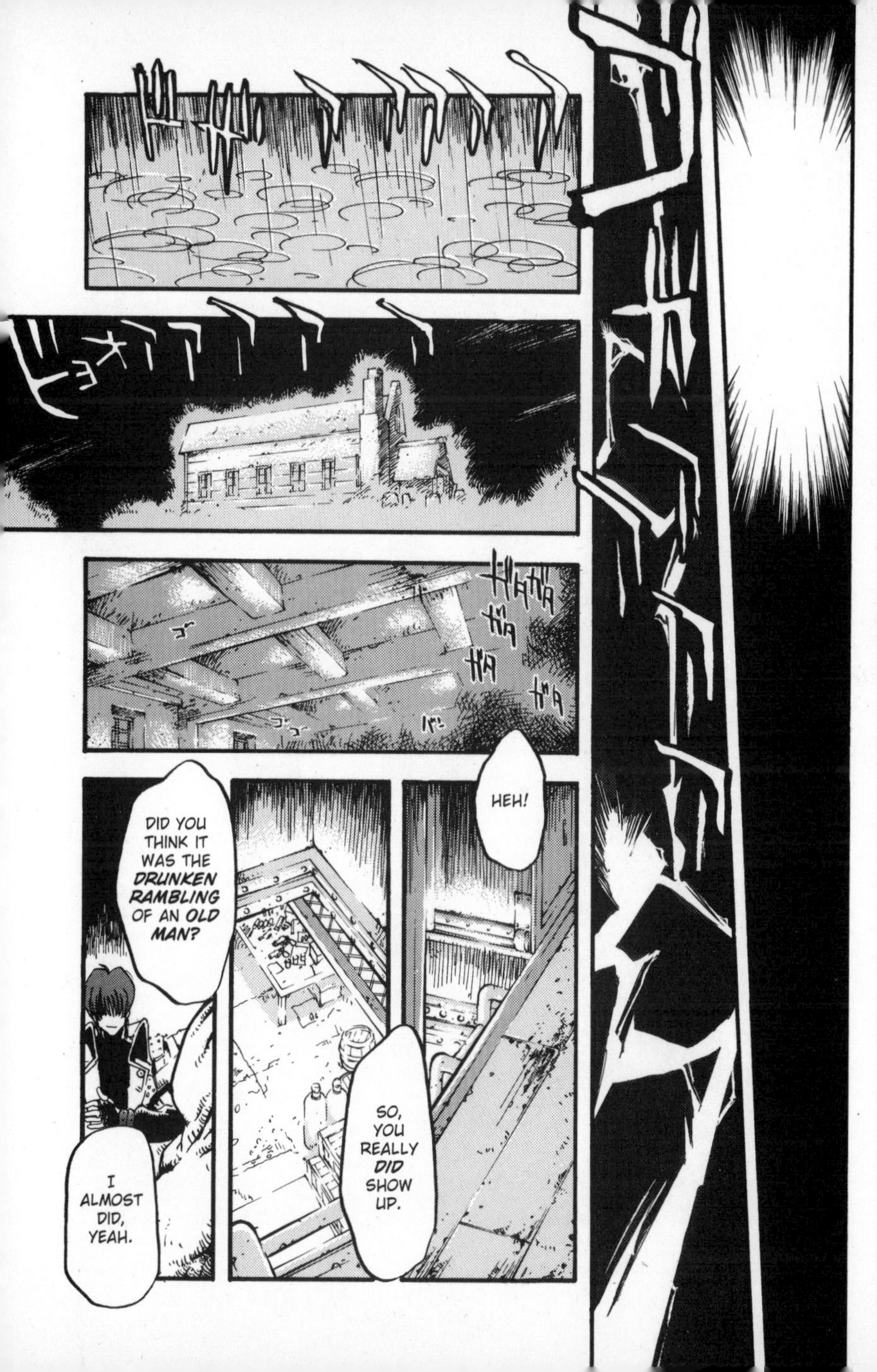
HEH!
SO, YOU REALLY DID SHOW UP.
DID YOU THINK IT WAS THE DRUNKEN RAMBLING OF AN OLD MAN?
I ALMOST DID, YEAH.

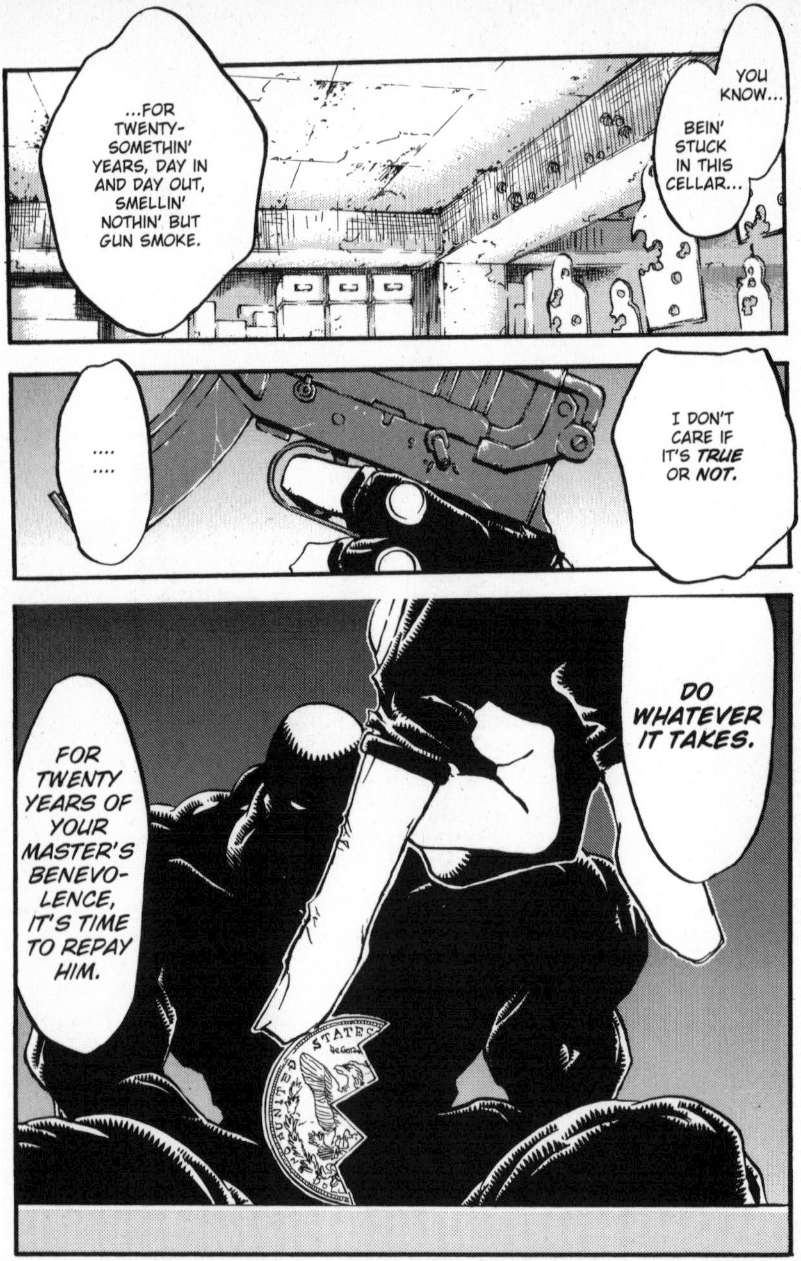
YOU KNOW... BEIN' STUCK IN THIS CELLAR...
...FOR TWENTY-SOMETHIN' YEARS, DAY IN AND DAY OUT, SMELLIN' NOTHIN' BUT GUN SMOKE.
I DON'T CARE IF IT'S *TRUE* OR *NOT*.
....
DO WHATEVER IT TAKES.
FOR TWENTY YEARS OF YOUR MASTER'S BENEVOLENCE, IT'S TIME TO REPAY HIM.

#1. BLOOD AND THUNDER/END

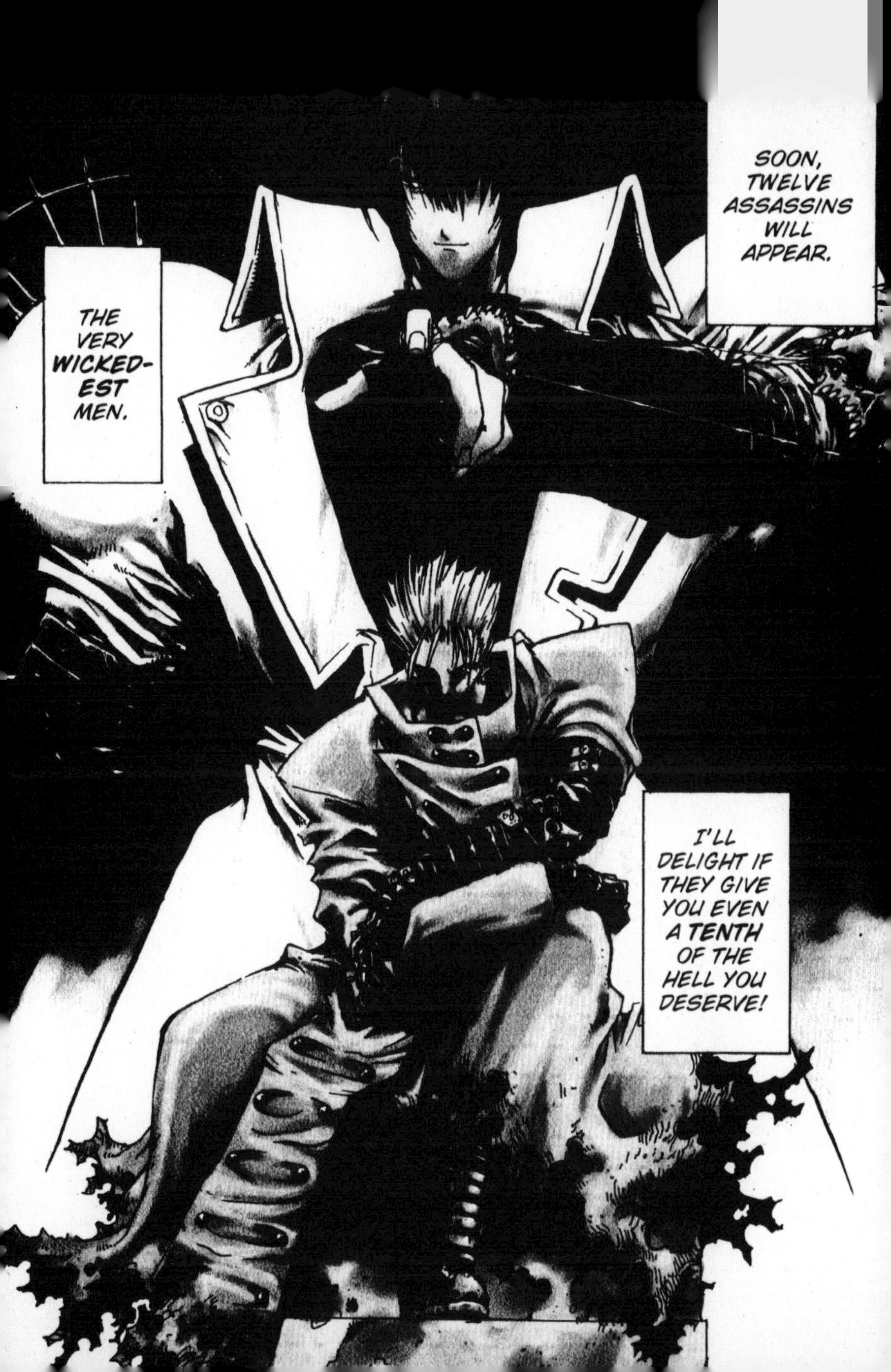
SOON, TWELVE ASSASSINS WILL APPEAR.
THE VERY WICKED-EST MEN.
I'LL DELIGHT IF THEY GIVE YOU EVEN A TENTH OF THE HELL YOU DESERVE!

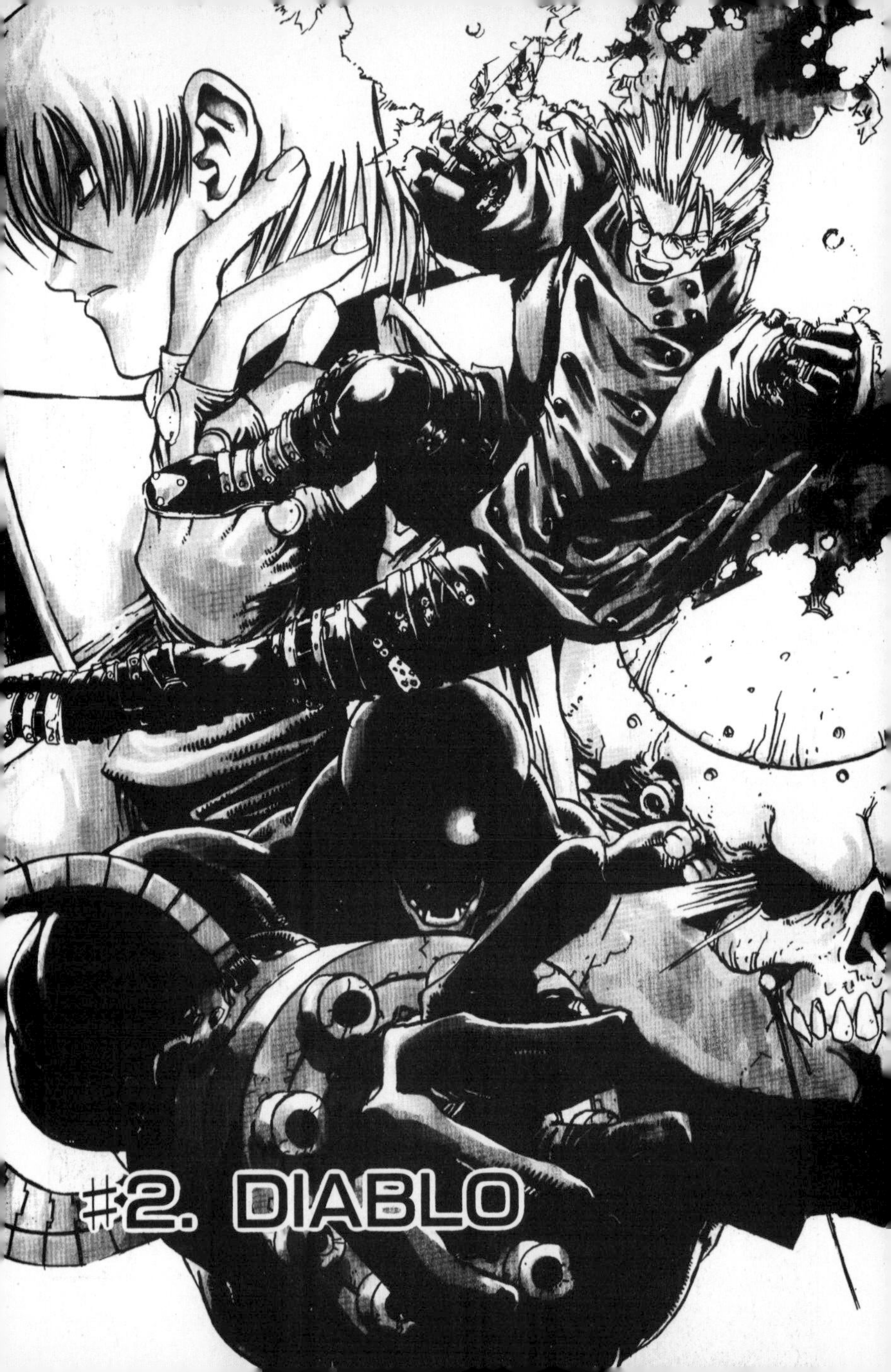
#2. DIABLO

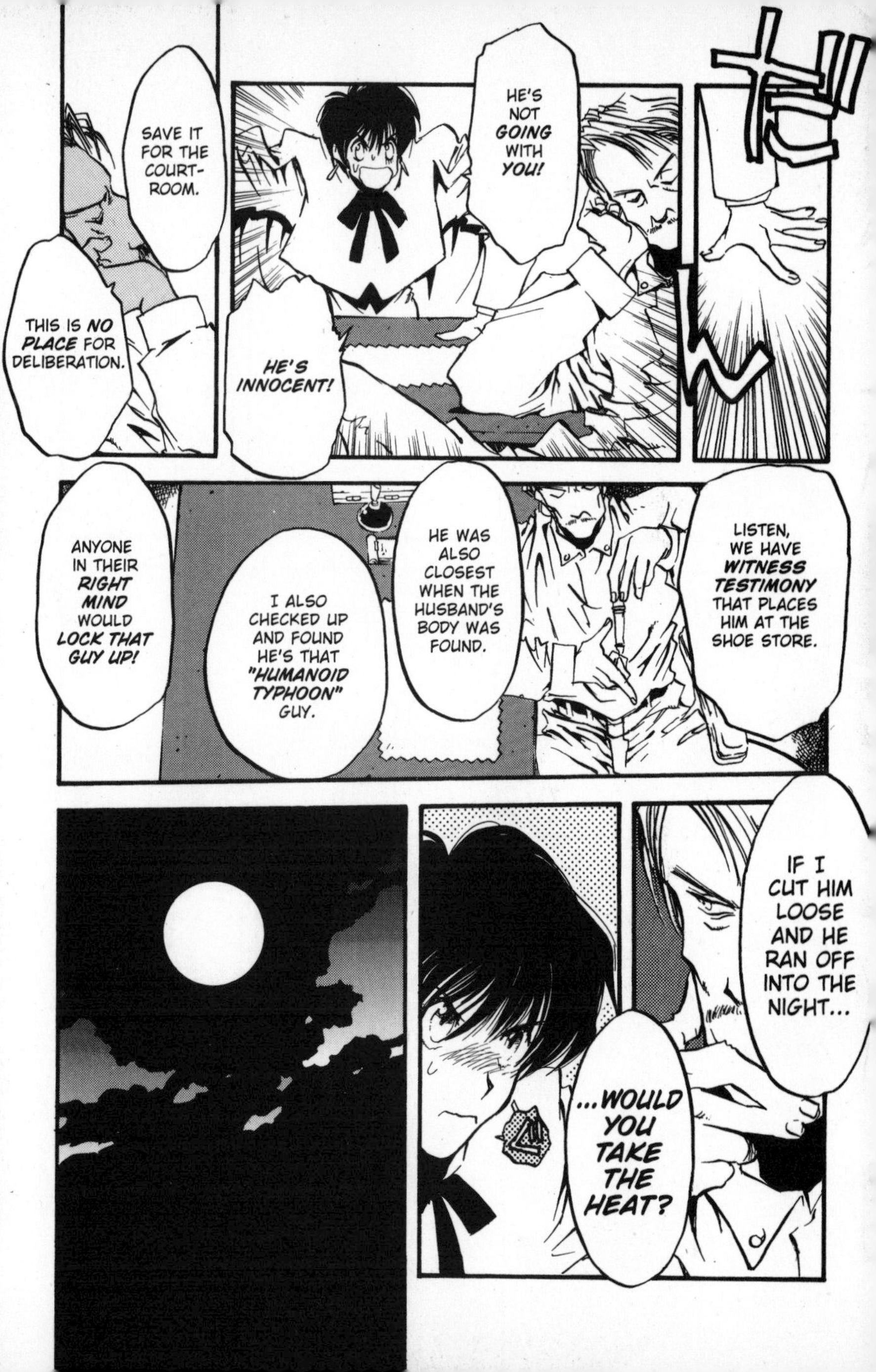
だん
HE'S NOT GOING WITH YOU!
HE'S INNOCENT!
SAVE IT FOR THE COURTROOM.
THIS IS NO PLACE FOR DELIBERATION.
LISTEN, WE HAVE WITNESS TESTIMONY THAT PLACES HIM AT THE SHOE STORE.
HE WAS ALSO CLOSEST WHEN THE HUSBAND'S BODY WAS FOUND.
I ALSO CHECKED UP AND FOUND HE'S THAT "HUMANOID TYPHOON" GUY.
ANYONE IN THEIR RIGHT MIND WOULD LOCK THAT GUY UP!
IF I CUT HIM LOOSE AND HE RAN OFF INTO THE NIGHT...
...WOULD YOU TAKE THE HEAT?

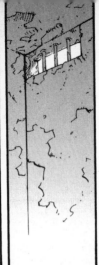

I'VE FINALLY PICKED UP YOUR SCENT...

DON'T WRITE ME OFF.

I'LL TRACK YOU *DOWN*. I *WON'T* LET YOU GET AWAY.

KNIVES...

COUNT ON IT!!

40

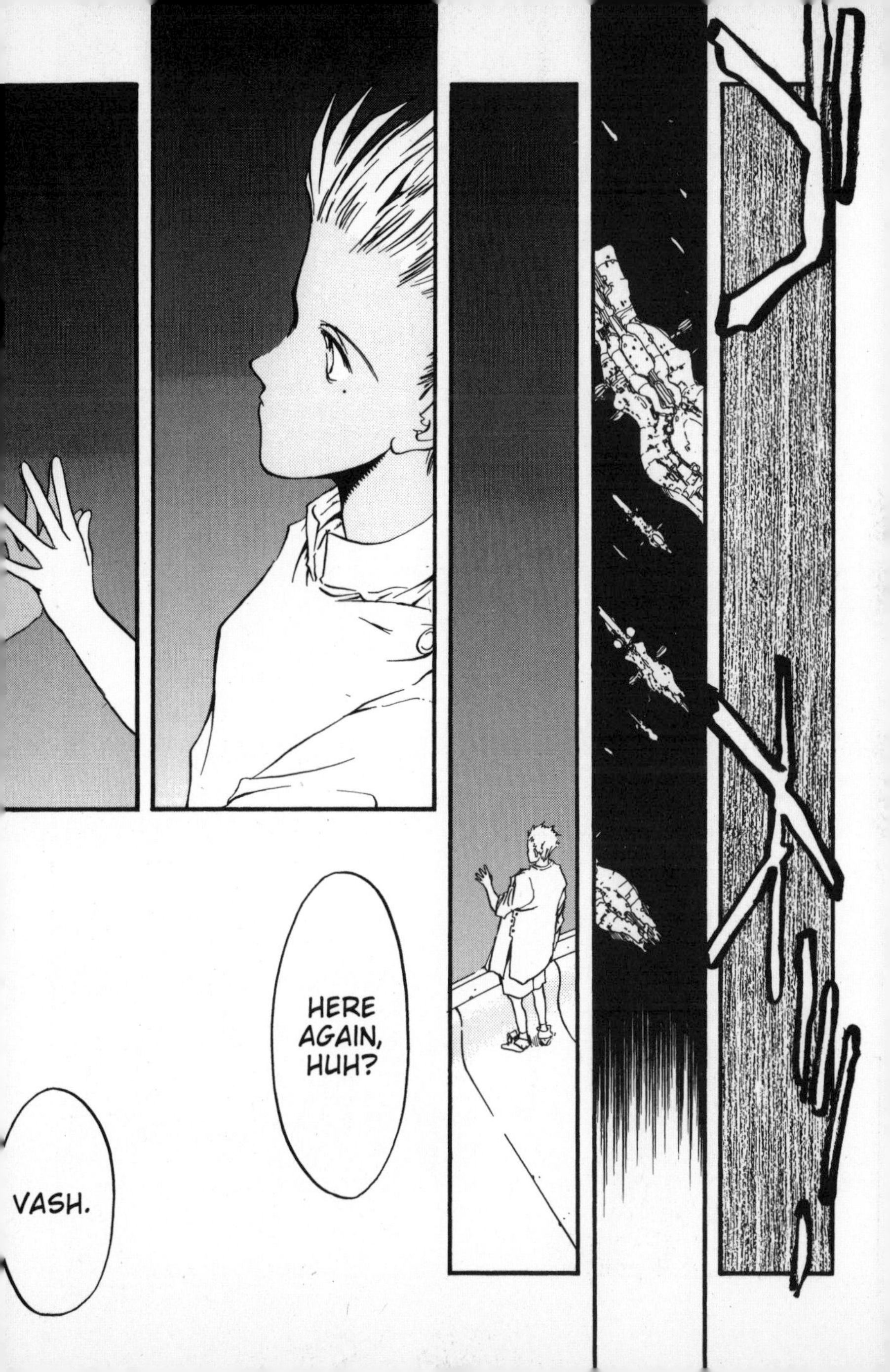
HERE AGAIN, HUH?
VASH.

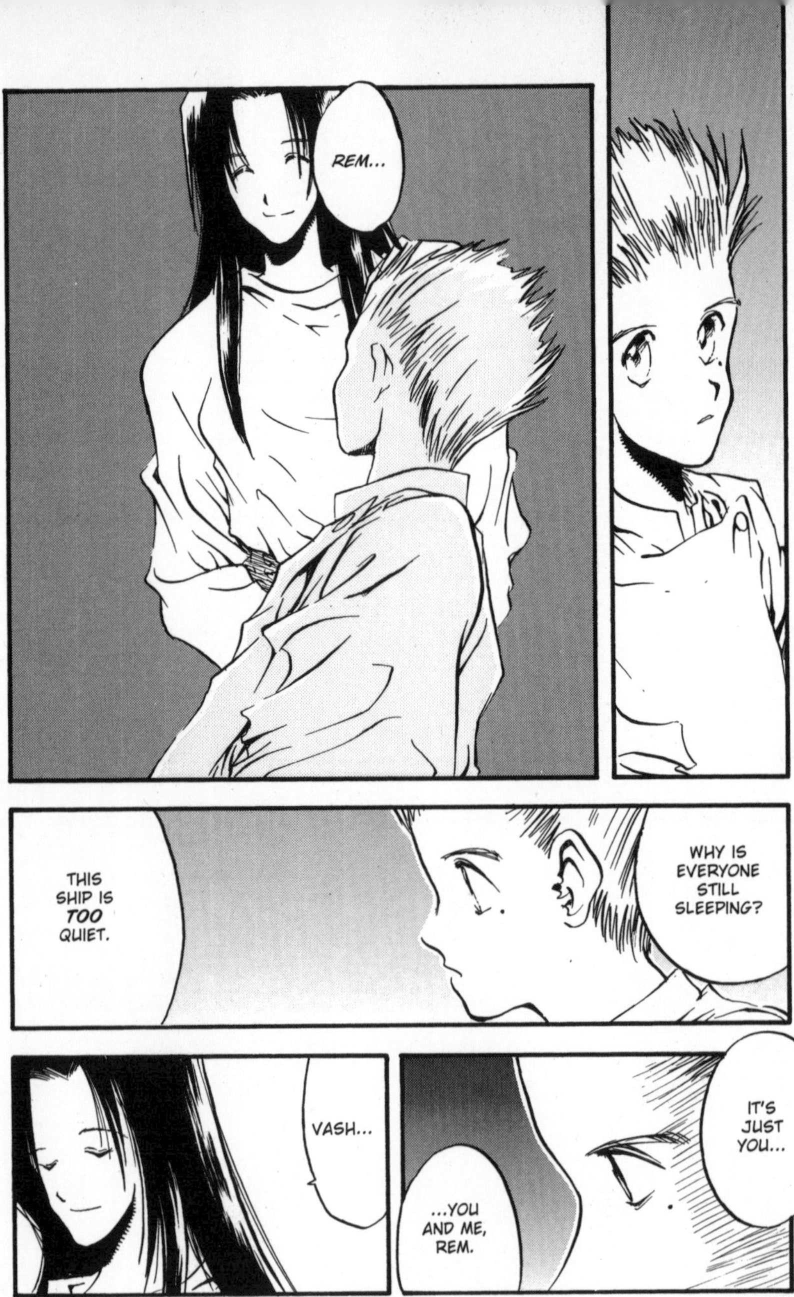
REM...
WHY IS EVERYONE STILL SLEEPING?
THIS SHIP IS *TOO* QUIET.
IT'S JUST YOU...
...YOU AND ME, REM.
VASH...

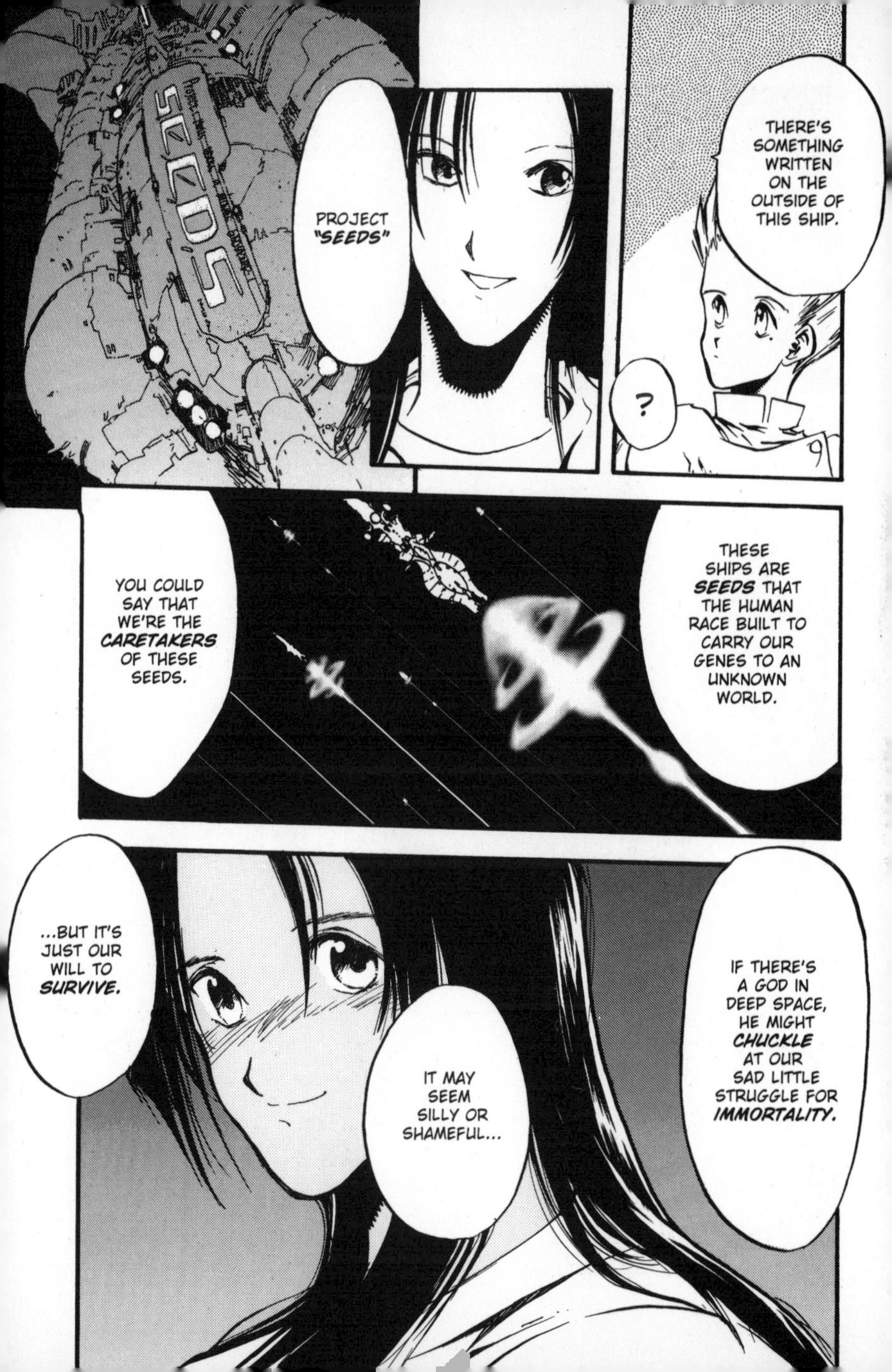
THERE'S SOMETHING WRITTEN ON THE OUTSIDE OF THIS SHIP.
?
PROJECT "SEEDS"
SEEDS
THESE SHIPS ARE SEEDS THAT THE HUMAN RACE BUILT TO CARRY OUR GENES TO AN UNKNOWN WORLD.
YOU COULD SAY THAT WE'RE THE CARETAKERS OF THESE SEEDS.
IF THERE'S A GOD IN DEEP SPACE, HE MIGHT CHUCKLE AT OUR SAD LITTLE STRUGGLE FOR IMMORTALITY.
IT MAY SEEM SILLY OR SHAMEFUL...
...BUT IT'S JUST OUR WILL TO SURVIVE.

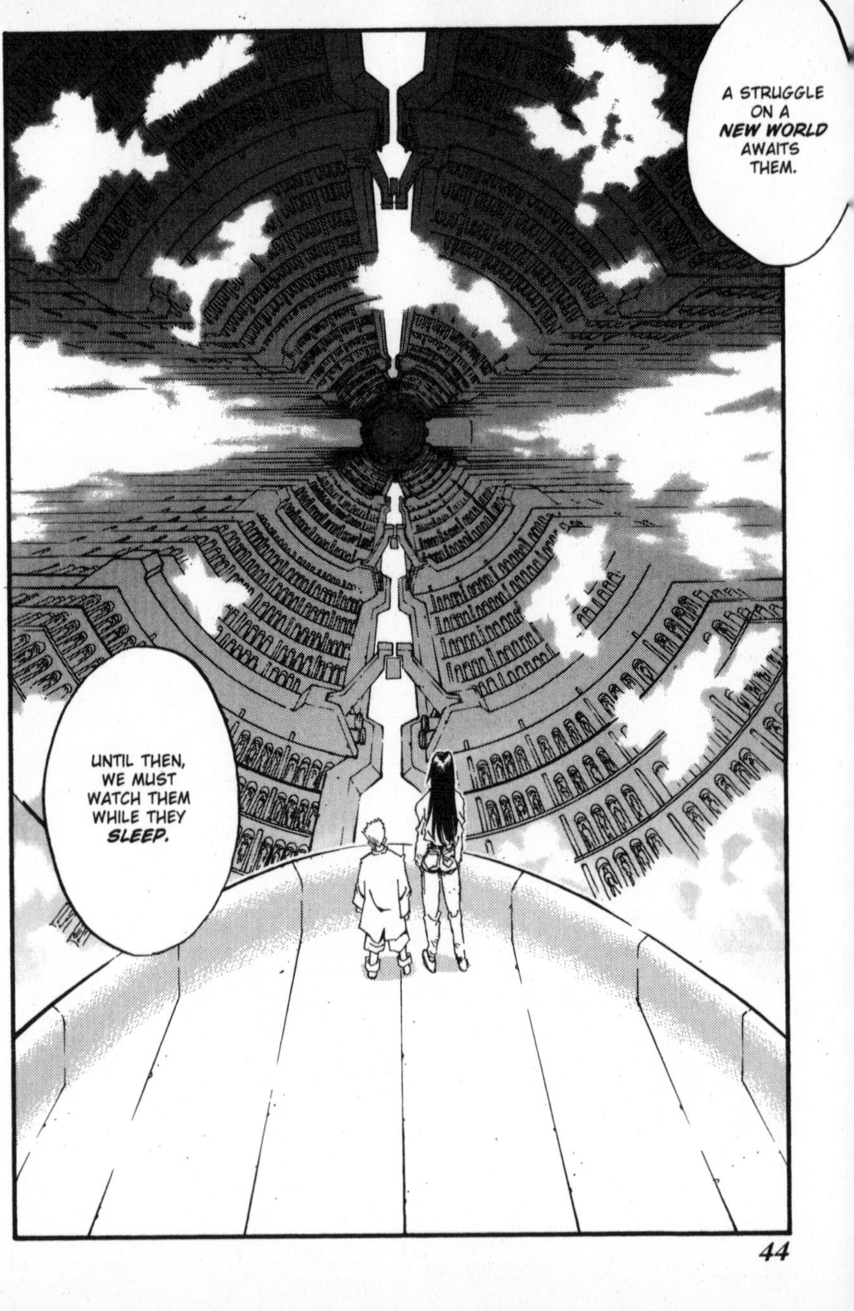
A STRUGGLE ON A NEW WORLD AWAITS THEM.
UNTIL THEN, WE MUST WATCH THEM WHILE THEY SLEEP.

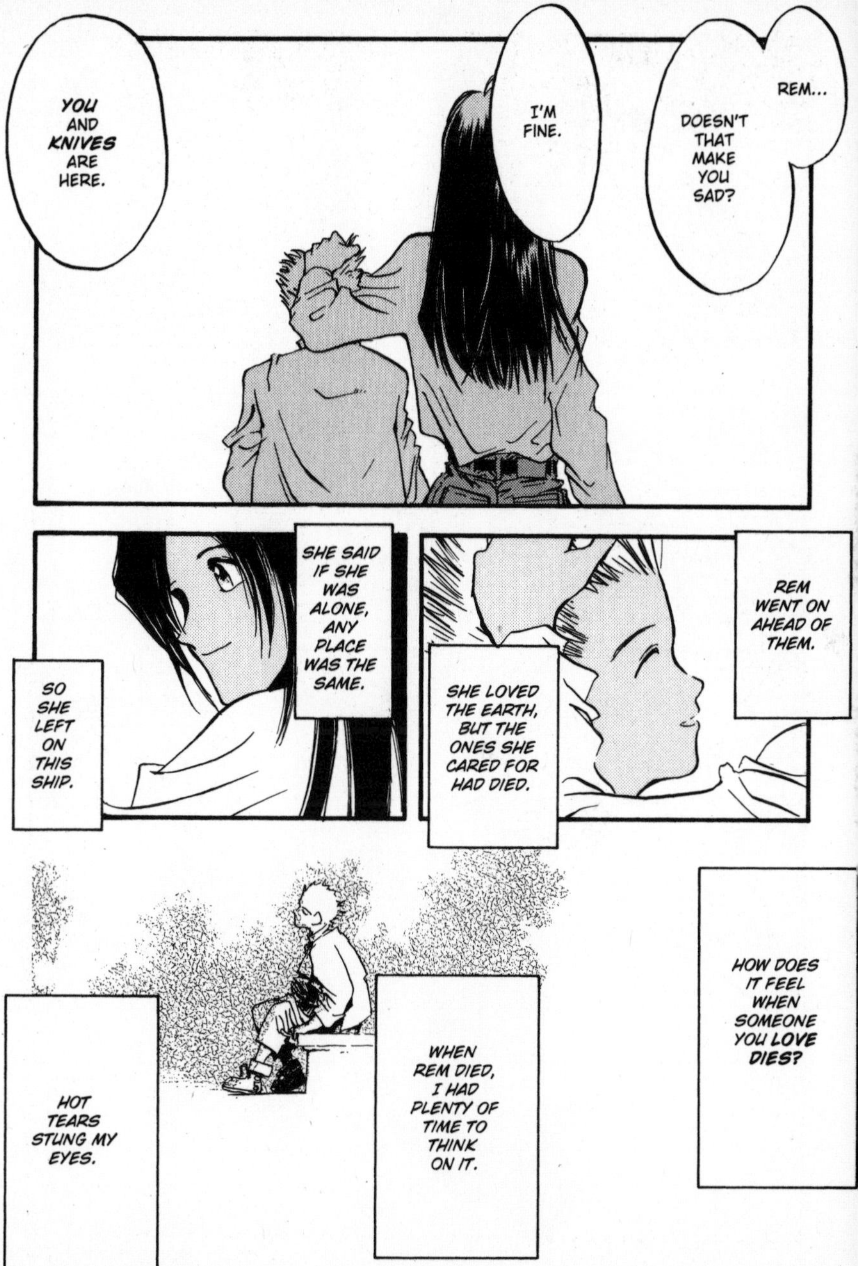
REM... DOESN'T THAT MAKE YOU SAD?
I'M FINE.
YOU AND KNIVES ARE HERE.
REM WENT ON AHEAD OF THEM.
SHE LOVED THE EARTH, BUT THE ONES SHE CARED FOR HAD DIED.
SHE SAID IF SHE WAS ALONE, ANY PLACE WAS THE SAME.
SO SHE LEFT ON THIS SHIP.
HOW DOES IT FEEL WHEN SOMEONE YOU LOVE DIES?
WHEN REM DIED, I HAD PLENTY OF TIME TO THINK ON IT.
HOT TEARS STUNG MY EYES.

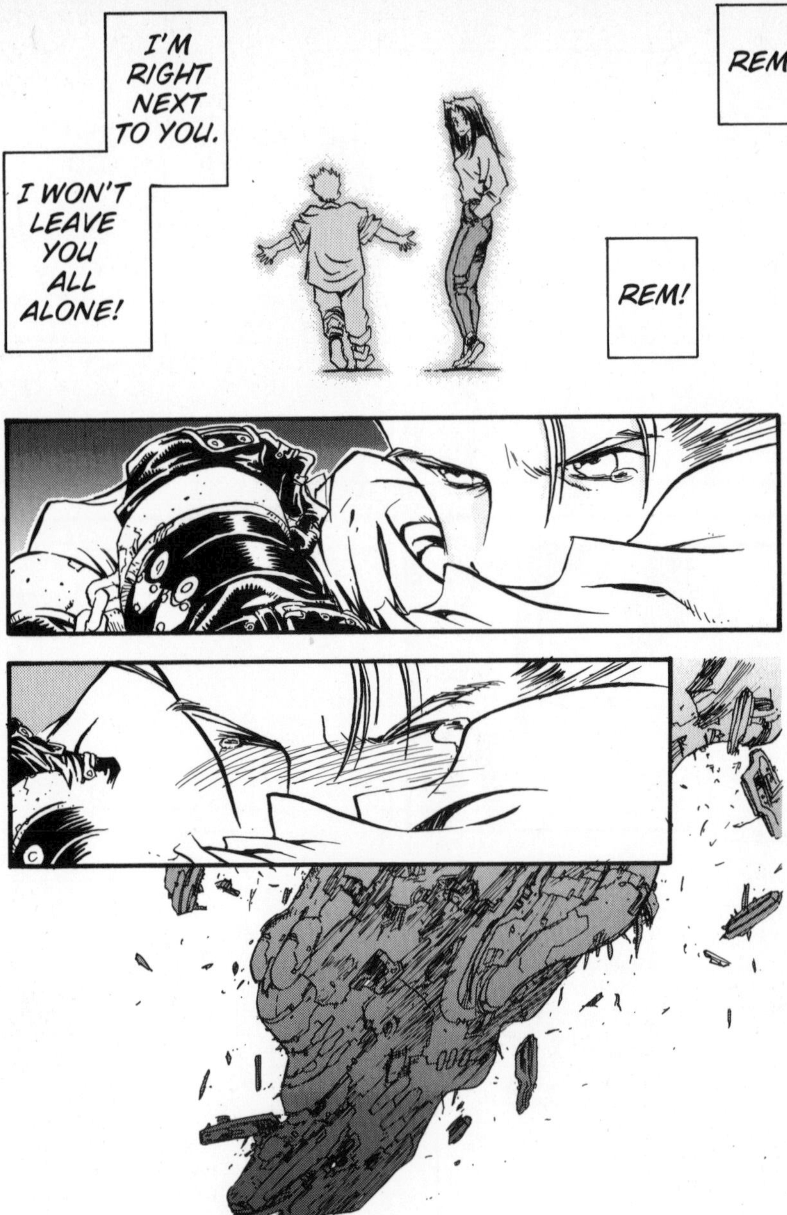
REM!
REM!
I'M RIGHT NEXT TO YOU.
I WON'T LEAVE YOU ALL ALONE!

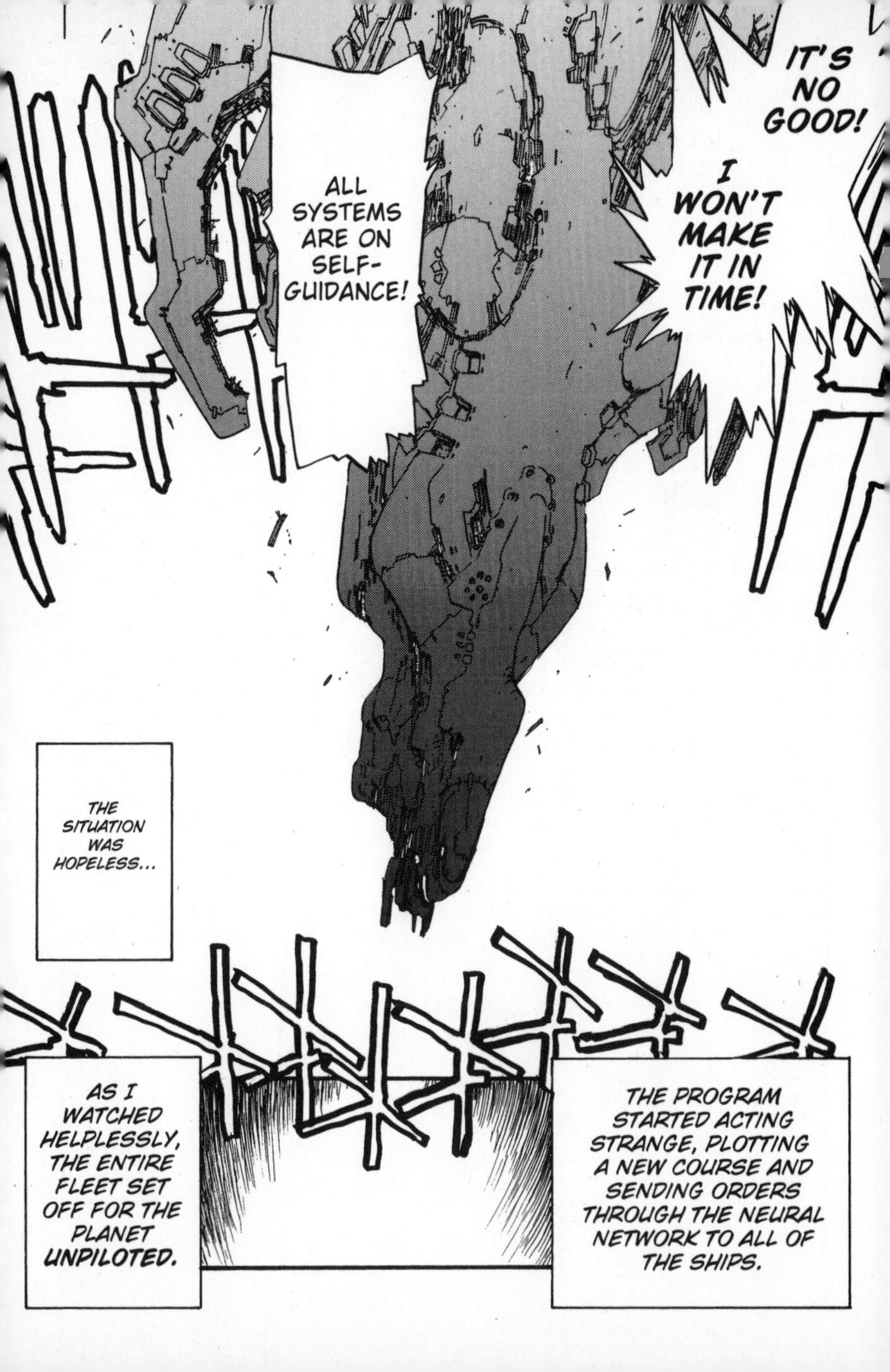
IT'S NO GOOD!
I WON'T MAKE IT IN TIME!
ALL SYSTEMS ARE ON SELF-GUIDANCE!
THE SITUATION WAS HOPELESS...
THE PROGRAM STARTED ACTING STRANGE, PLOTTING A NEW COURSE AND SENDING ORDERS THROUGH THE NEURAL NETWORK TO ALL OF THE SHIPS.
AS I WATCHED HELPLESSLY, THE ENTIRE FLEET SET OFF FOR THE PLANET **UNPILOTED.**

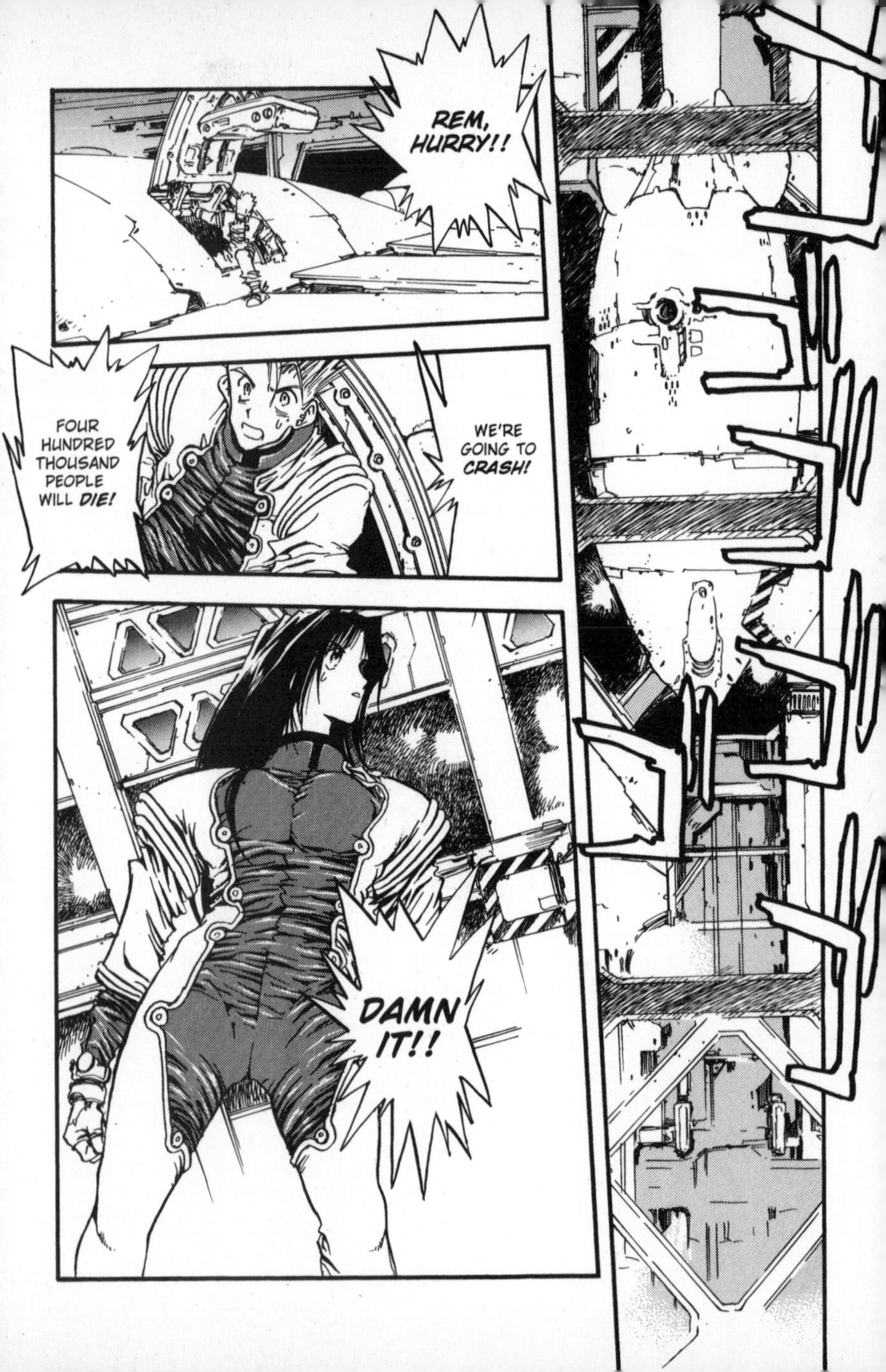
REM, HURRY!!
WE'RE GOING TO CRASH!
FOUR HUNDRED THOUSAND PEOPLE WILL DIE!
DAMN IT!!

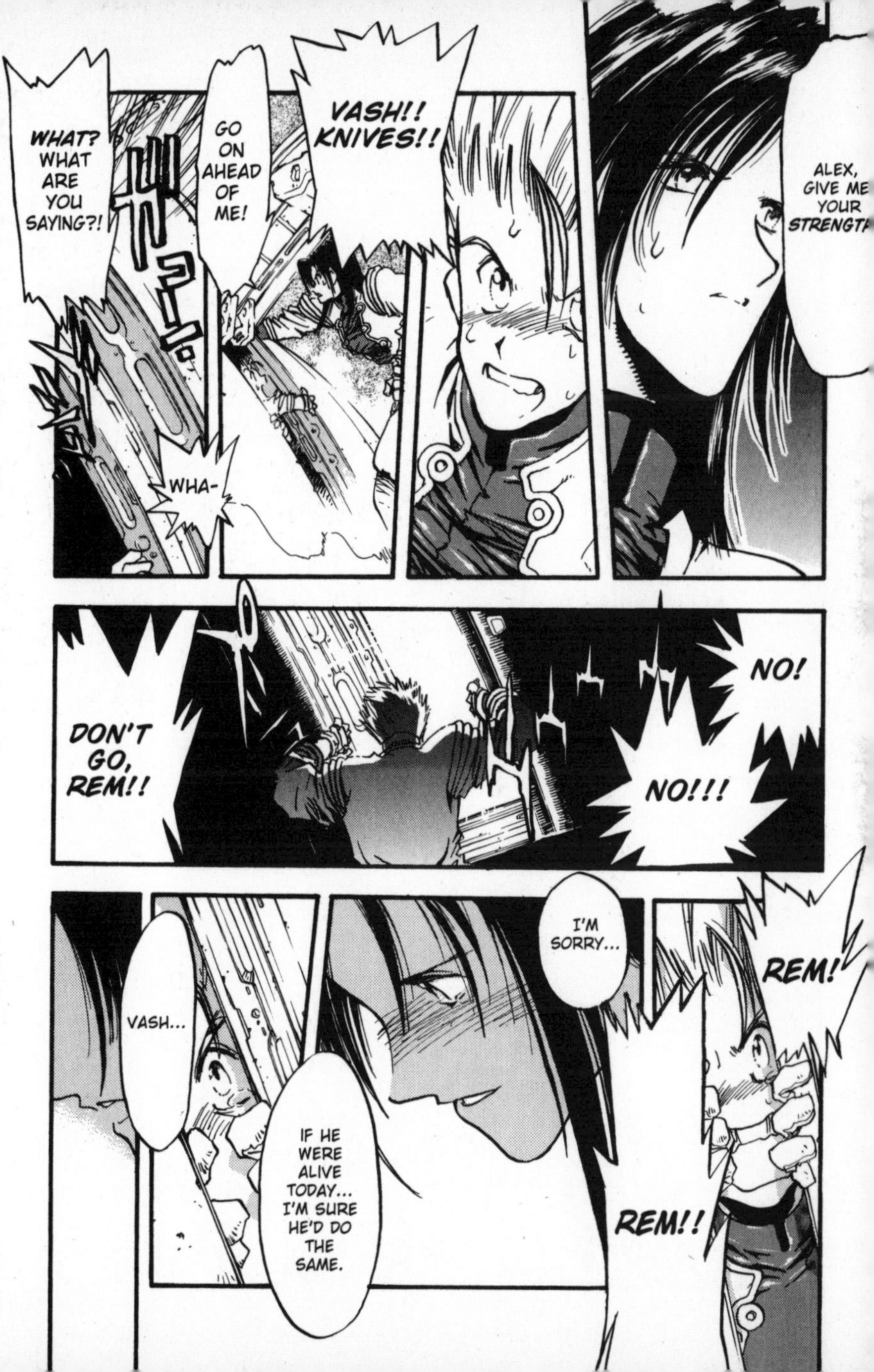
ALEX, GIVE ME YOUR STRENGT
VASH!! KNIVES!!
GO ON AHEAD OF ME!
WHAT? WHAT ARE YOU SAYING?!
WHA-
NO!
NO!!!
DON'T GO, REM!!
REM!
REM!!
I'M SORRY...
IF HE WERE ALIVE TODAY... I'M SURE HE'D DO THE SAME.
VASH...

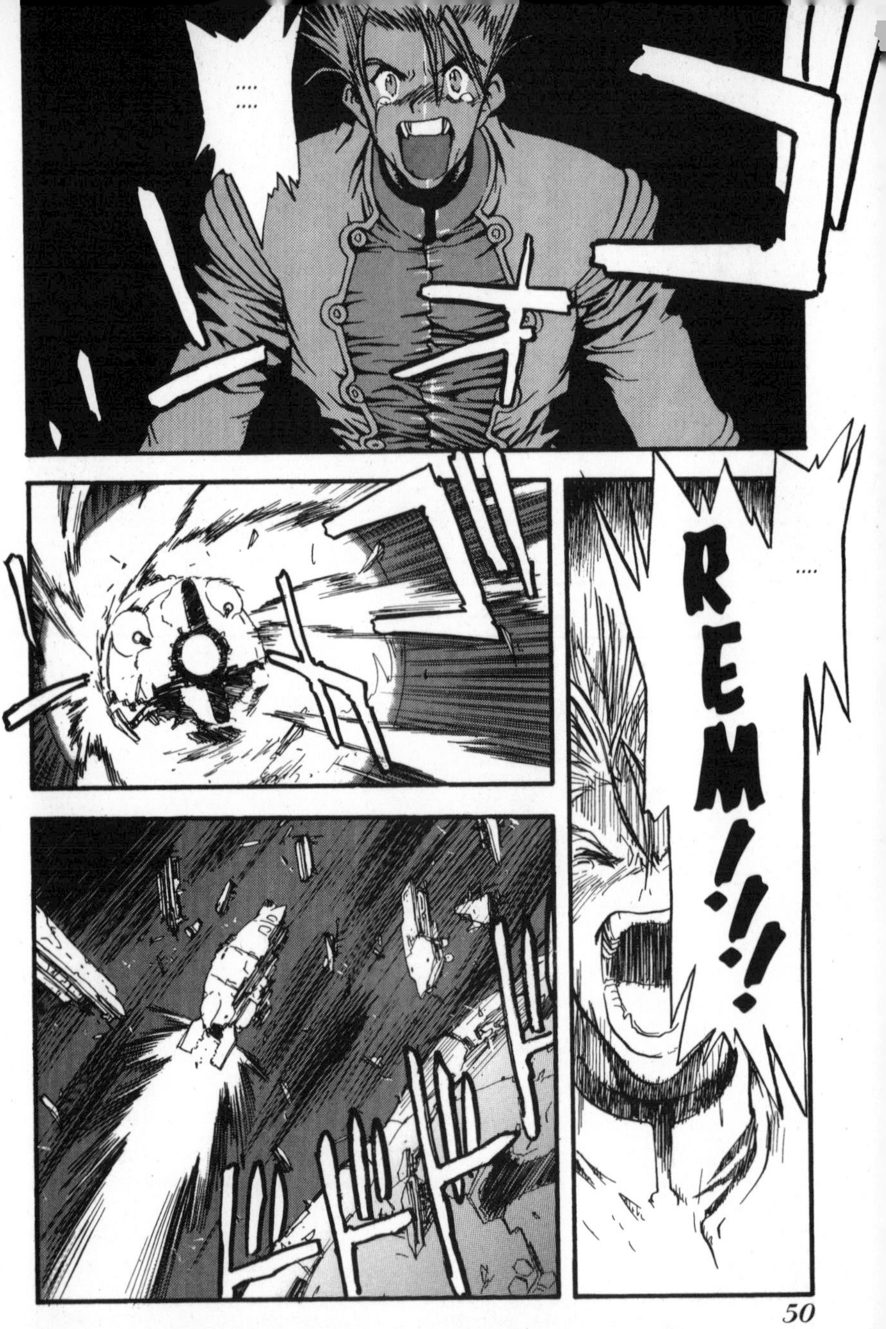

....
....
....
REM!!!!

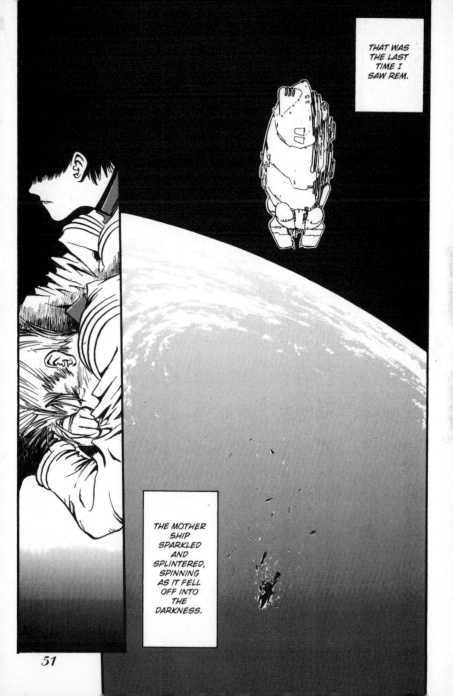

THAT WAS
THE LAST
TIME I
SAW REM.

THE MOTHER
SHIP
SPARKLED
AND
SPLINTERED,
SPINNING
AS IT FELL
OFF INTO
THE
DARKNESS.

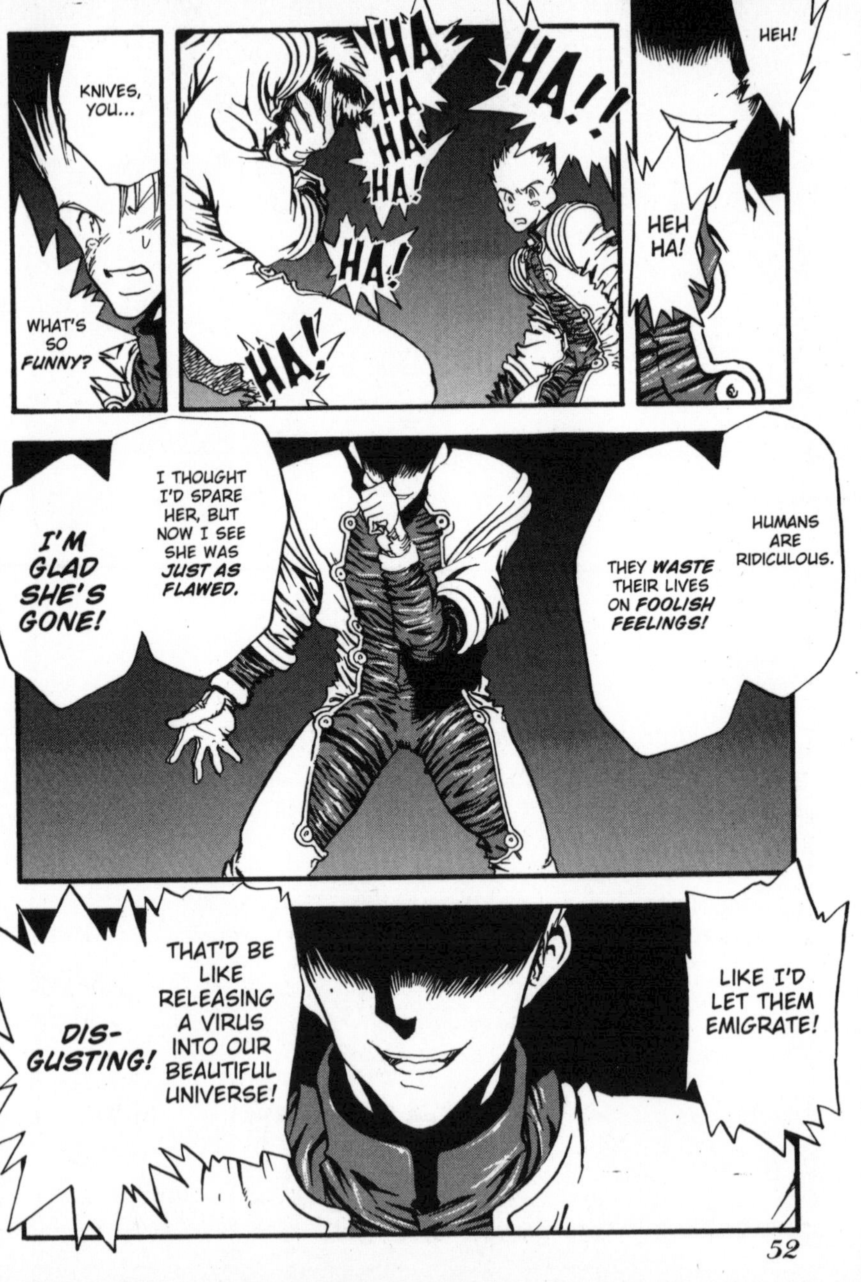
HEH!
HEH HA!
HA!!
HA HA HA HA HA!
HA!
HA!
KNIVES, YOU...
WHAT'S SO *FUNNY?*
HUMANS ARE RIDICULOUS.
THEY ***WASTE*** THEIR LIVES ON ***FOOLISH FEELINGS!***
I THOUGHT I'D SPARE HER, BUT NOW I SEE SHE WAS ***JUST AS FLAWED.***
I'M GLAD SHE'S GONE!
LIKE I'D LET THEM EMIGRATE!
THAT'D BE LIKE RELEASING A VIRUS INTO OUR BEAUTIFUL UNIVERSE!
DIS-GUSTING!

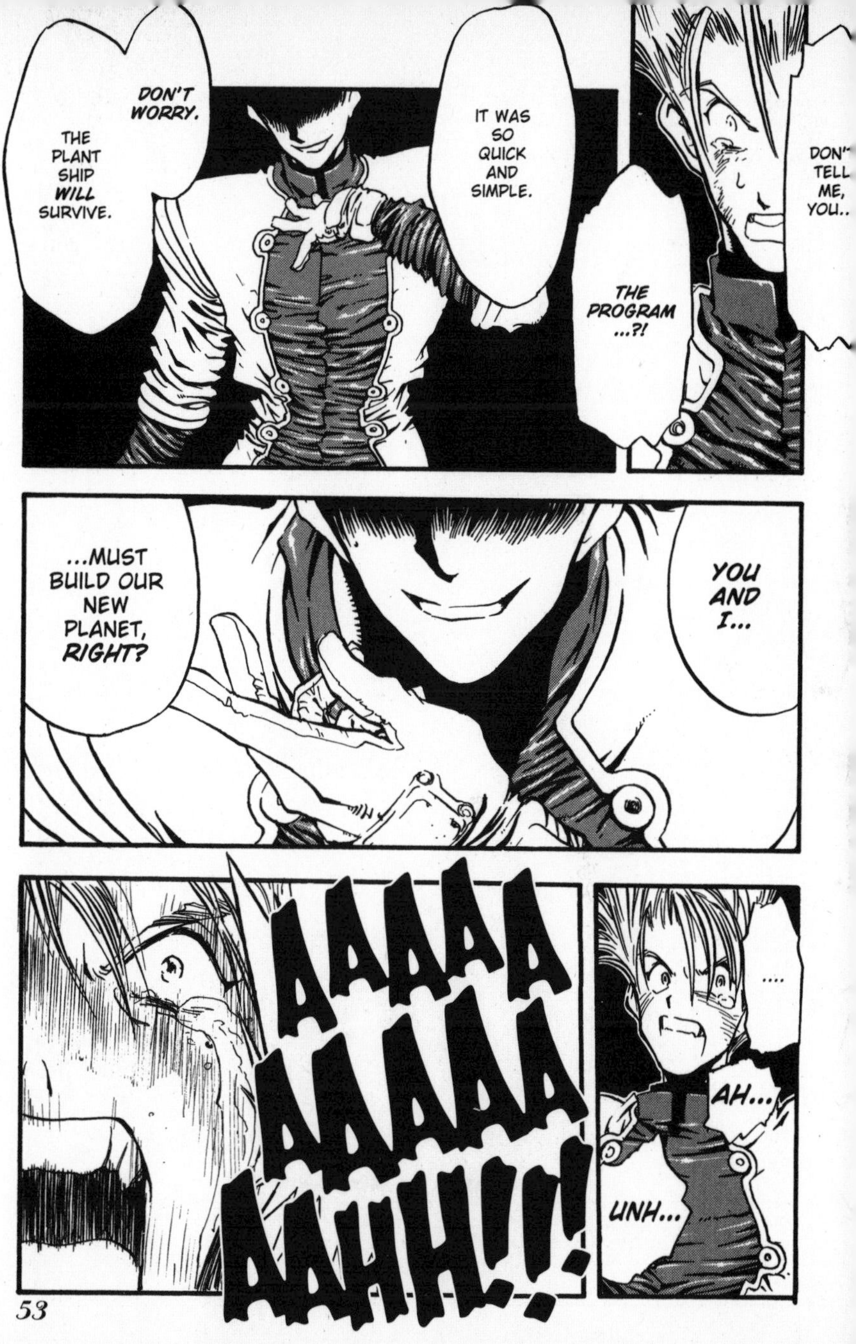
DON'T TELL ME, YOU..
THE PROGRAM ...?!
IT WAS SO QUICK AND SIMPLE.
DON'T WORRY.
THE PLANT SHIP *WILL* SURVIVE.
YOU AND I...
...MUST BUILD OUR NEW PLANET, *RIGHT?*
....
AH...
UNH...
AAAAAAAAAAAAAAHH!!!

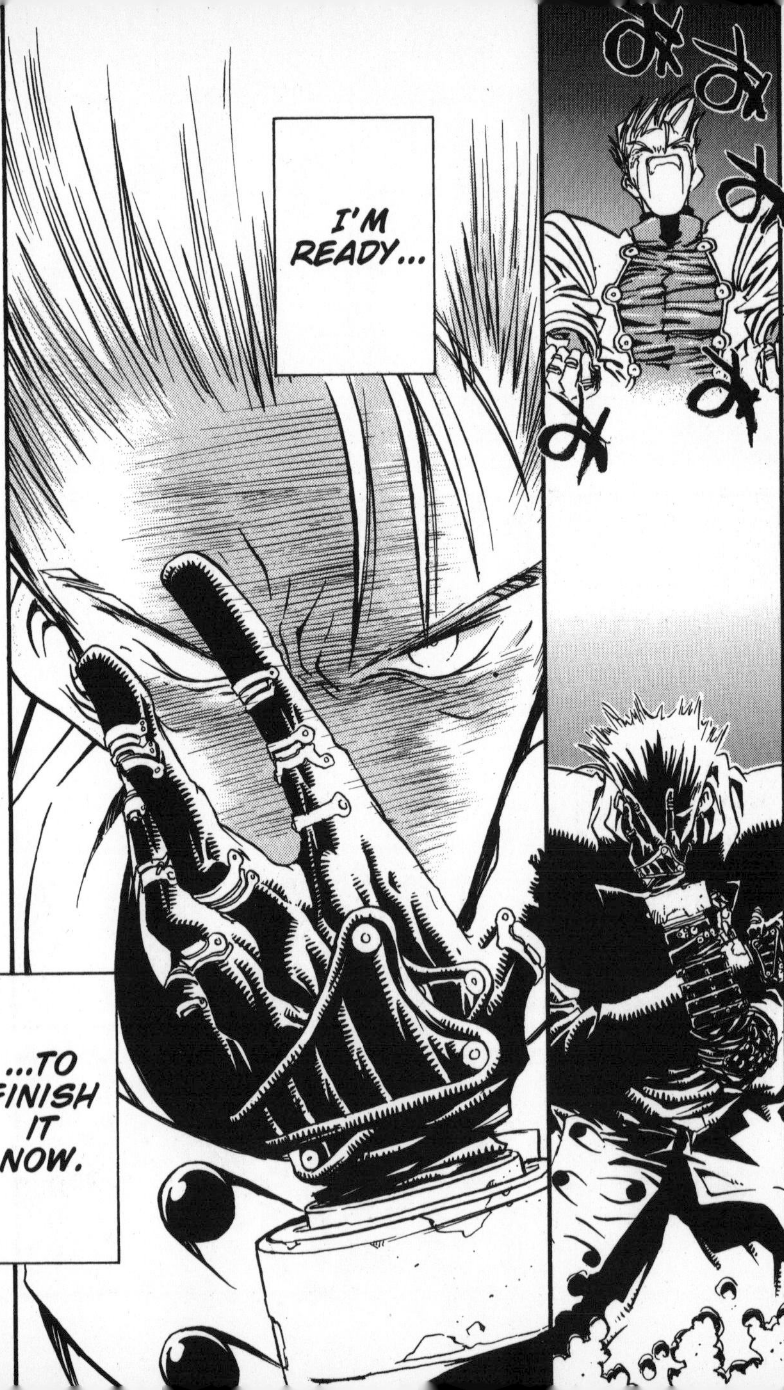
I'M READY...
...TO FINISH IT NOW.

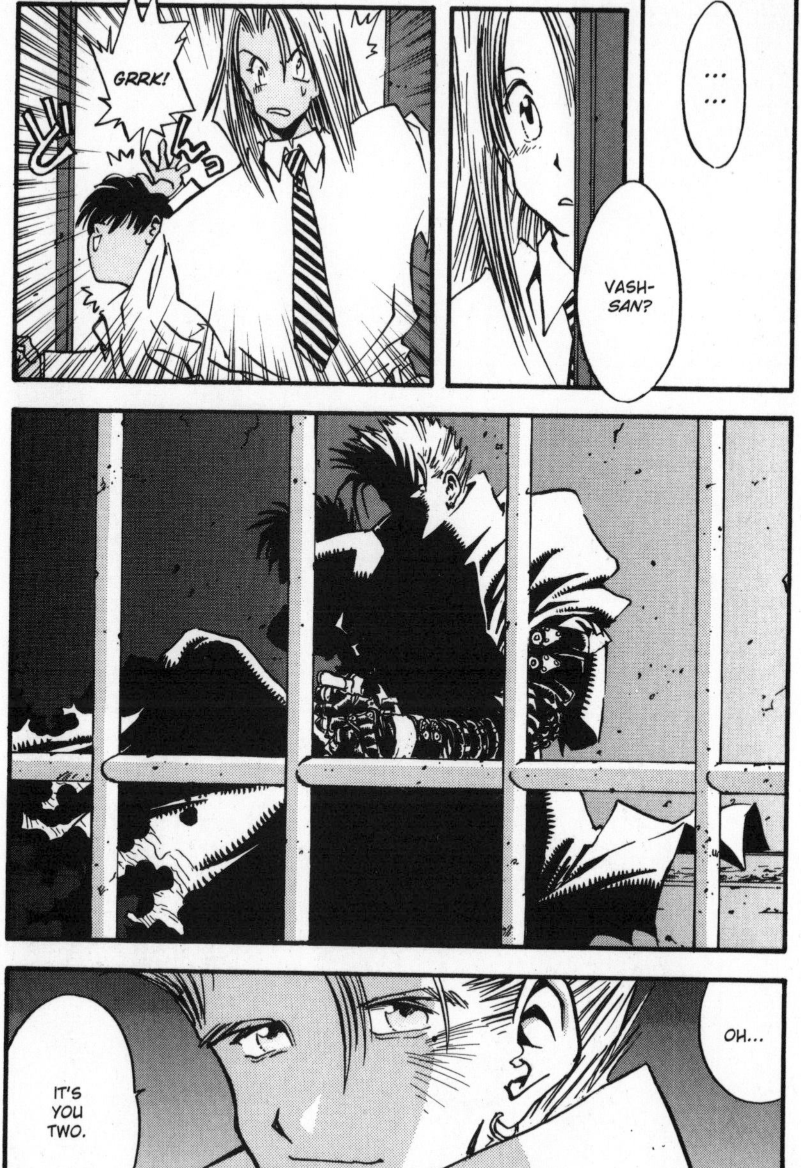
... ...
VASH-SAN?
GRRK!
OH...
IT'S YOU TWO.

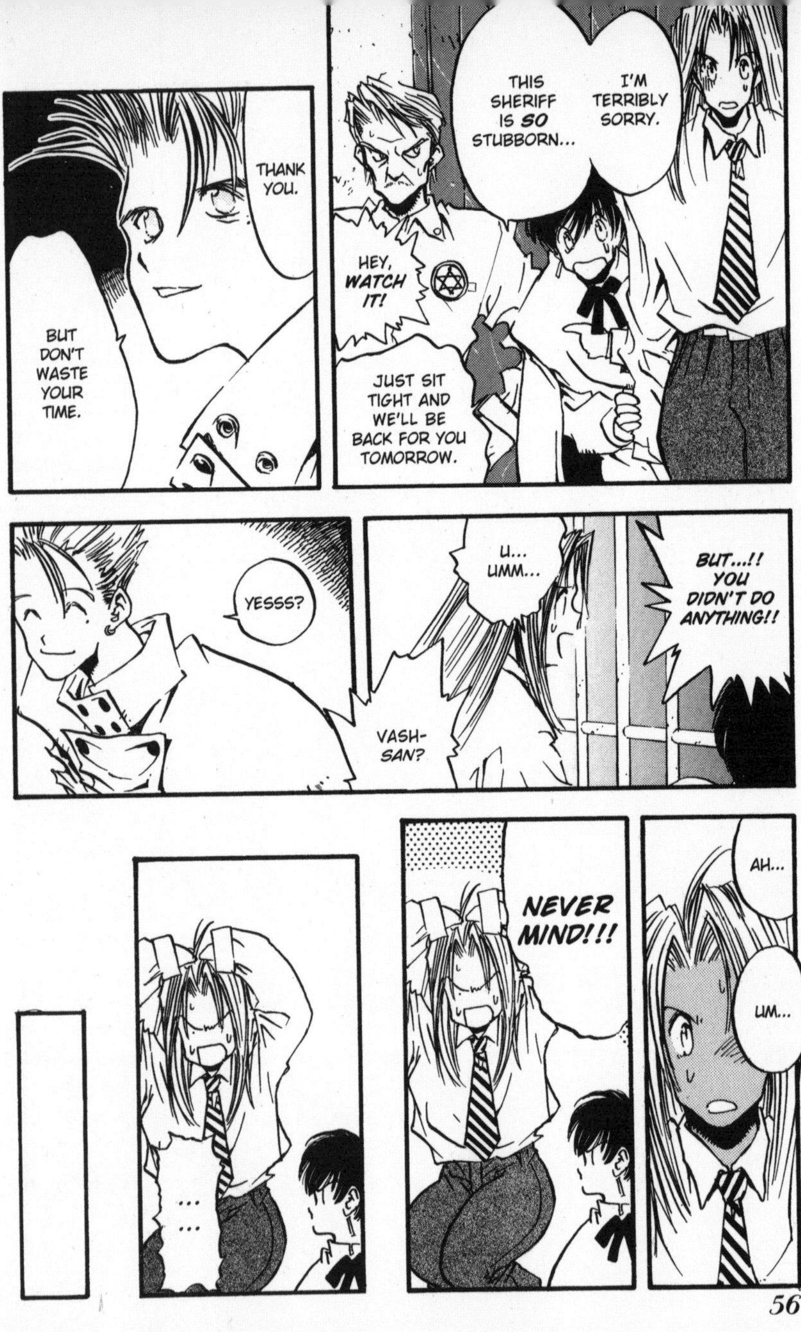
I'M TERRIBLY SORRY.
THIS SHERIFF IS SO STUBBORN...
HEY, WATCH IT!
JUST SIT TIGHT AND WE'LL BE BACK FOR YOU TOMORROW.
THANK YOU.
BUT DON'T WASTE YOUR TIME.
BUT...!! YOU DIDN'T DO ANYTHING!!
U... UMM...
VASH-SAN?
YESSS?
AH...
UM...
NEVER MIND!!!
...
...

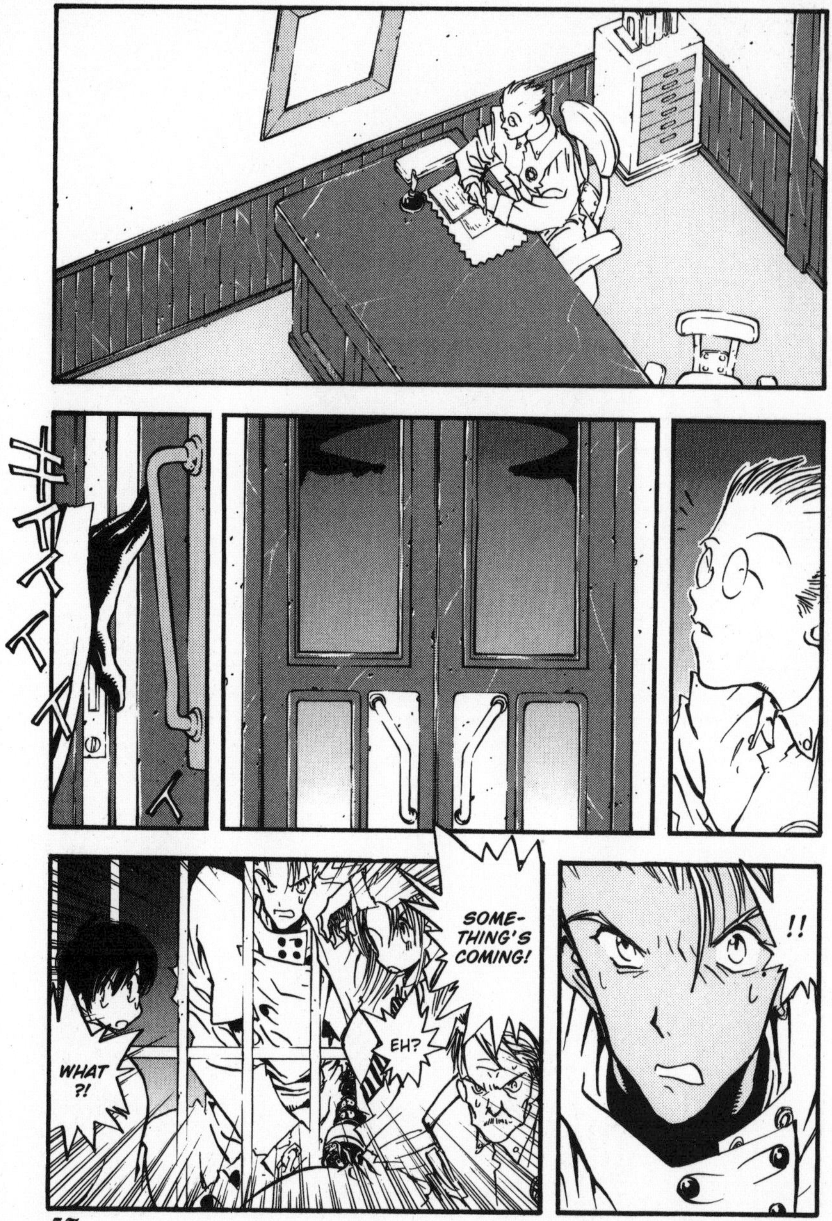
ギイイイイイ
!!
SOME-THING'S COMING!
EH?
WHAT ?!

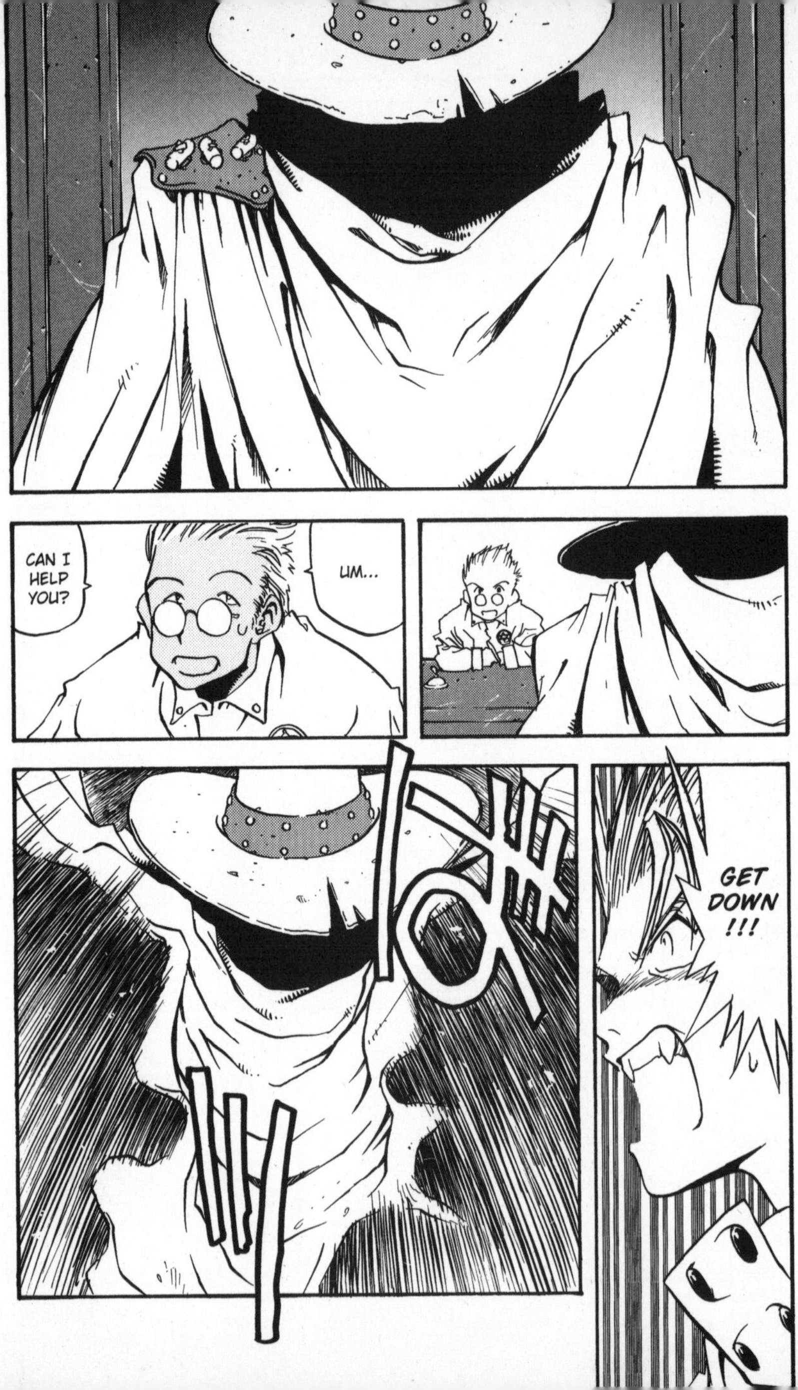
UM...
CAN I HELP YOU?
GET DOWN!!!

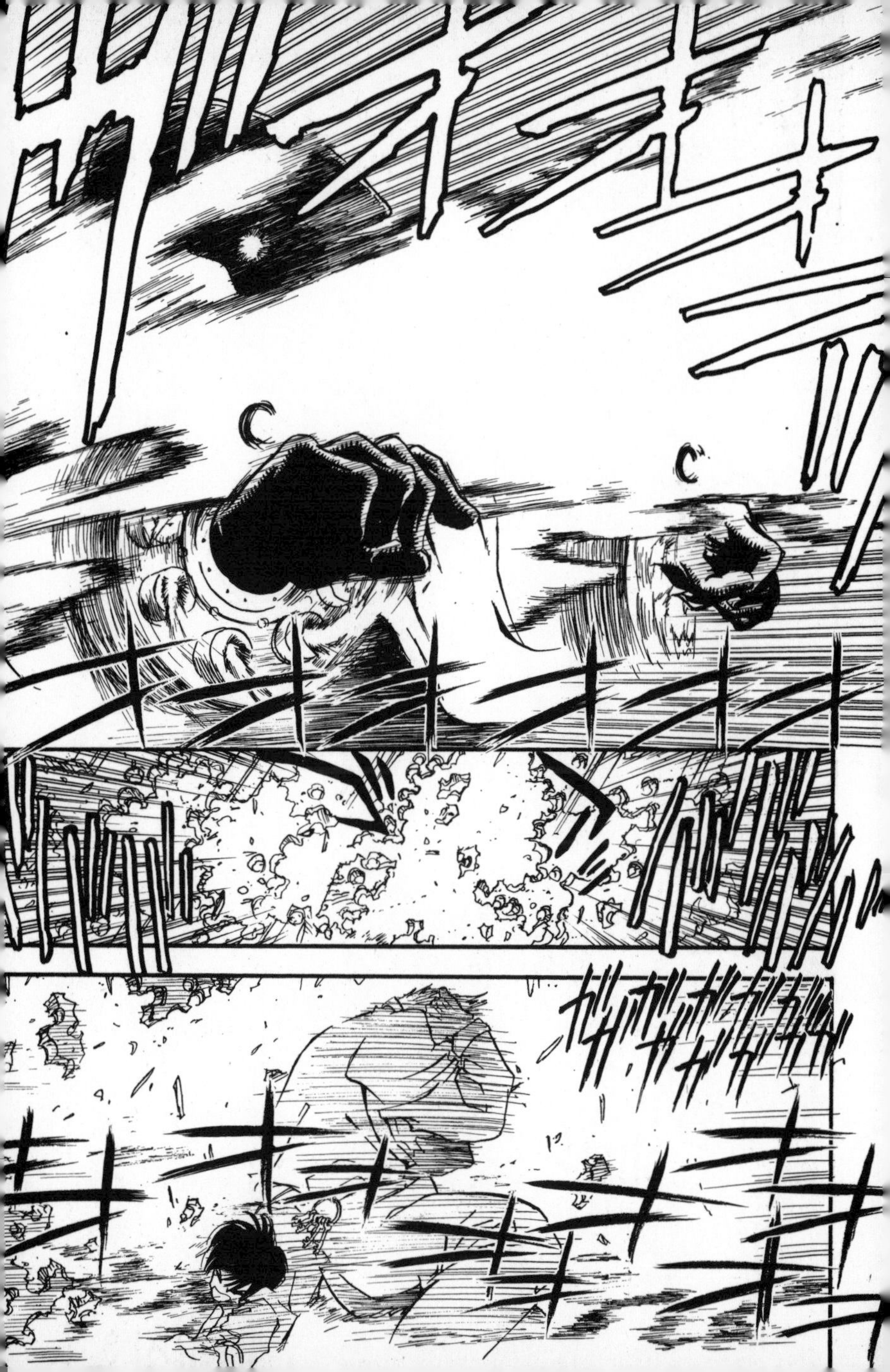

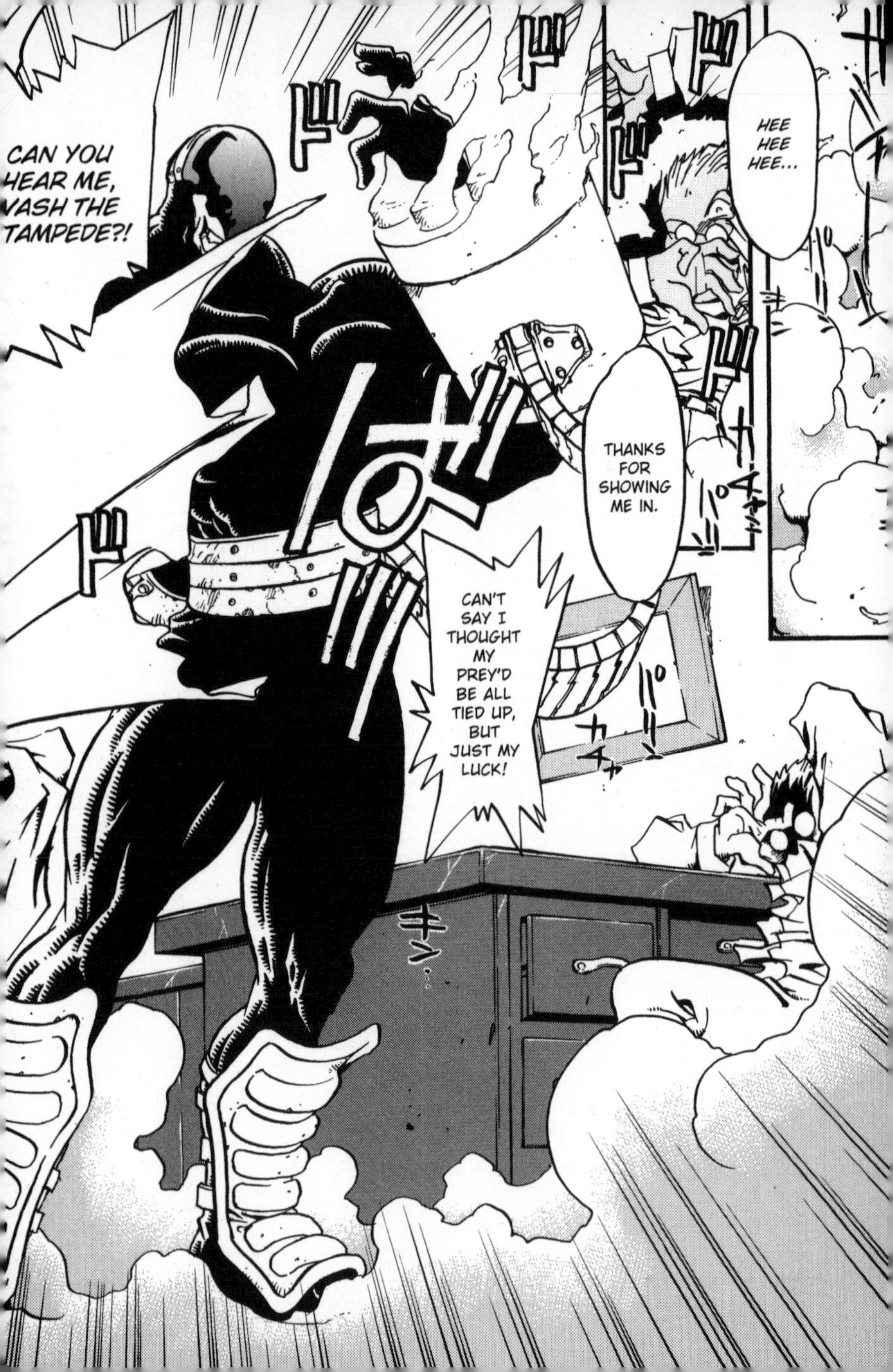
HEE HEE HEE...
THANKS FOR SHOWING ME IN.
CAN'T SAY I THOUGHT MY PREY'D BE ALL TIED UP, BUT JUST MY LUCK!
CAN YOU HEAR ME, VASH THE TAMPEDE?!

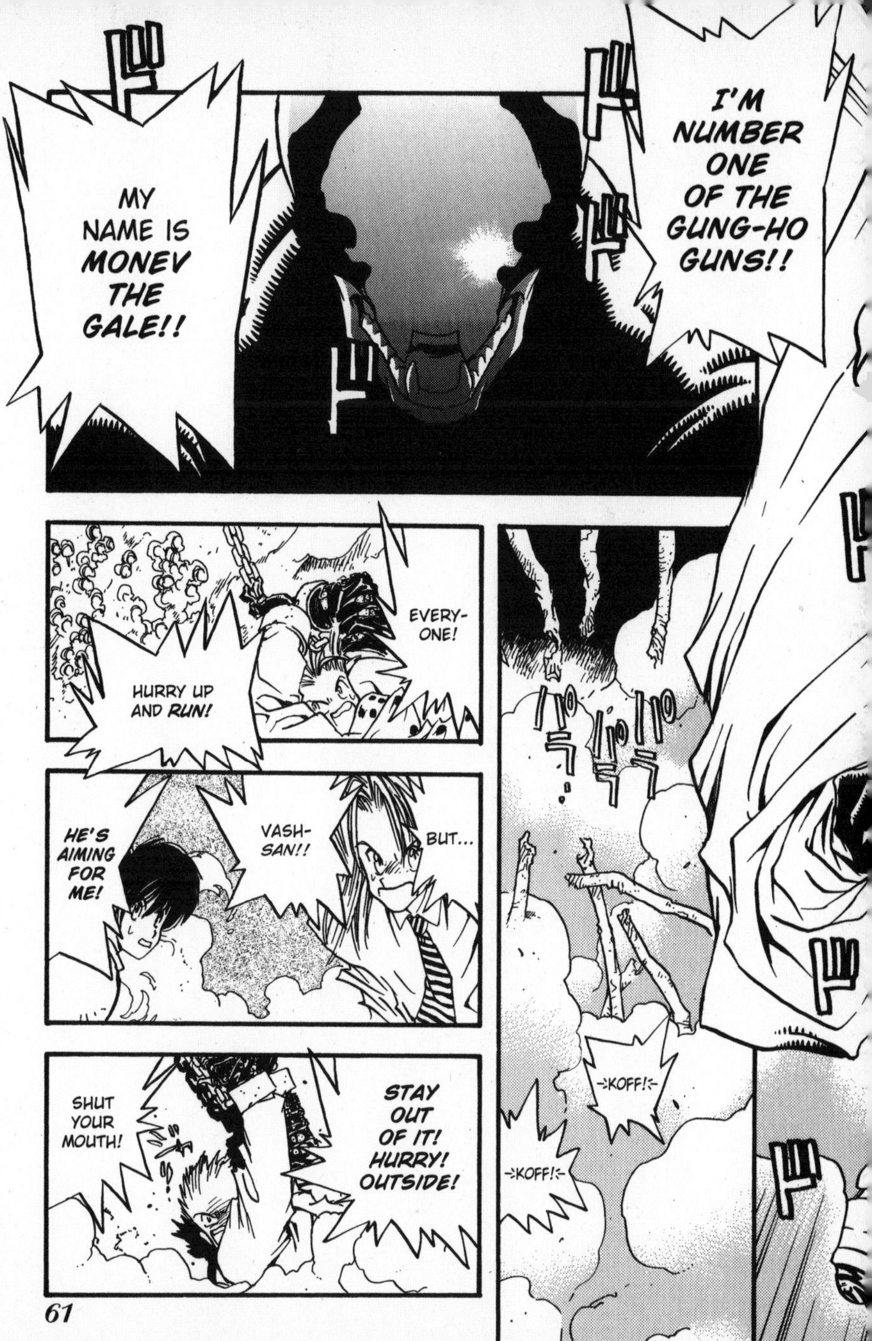
I'M NUMBER ONE OF THE GUNG-HO GUNS!!
MY NAME IS MONEV THE GALE!!
-KOFF!-
-KOFF!-
EVERY-ONE!
HURRY UP AND RUN!
BUT...
VASH-SAN!!
HE'S AIMING FOR ME!
STAY OUT OF IT! HURRY! OUTSIDE!
SHUT YOUR MOUTH!

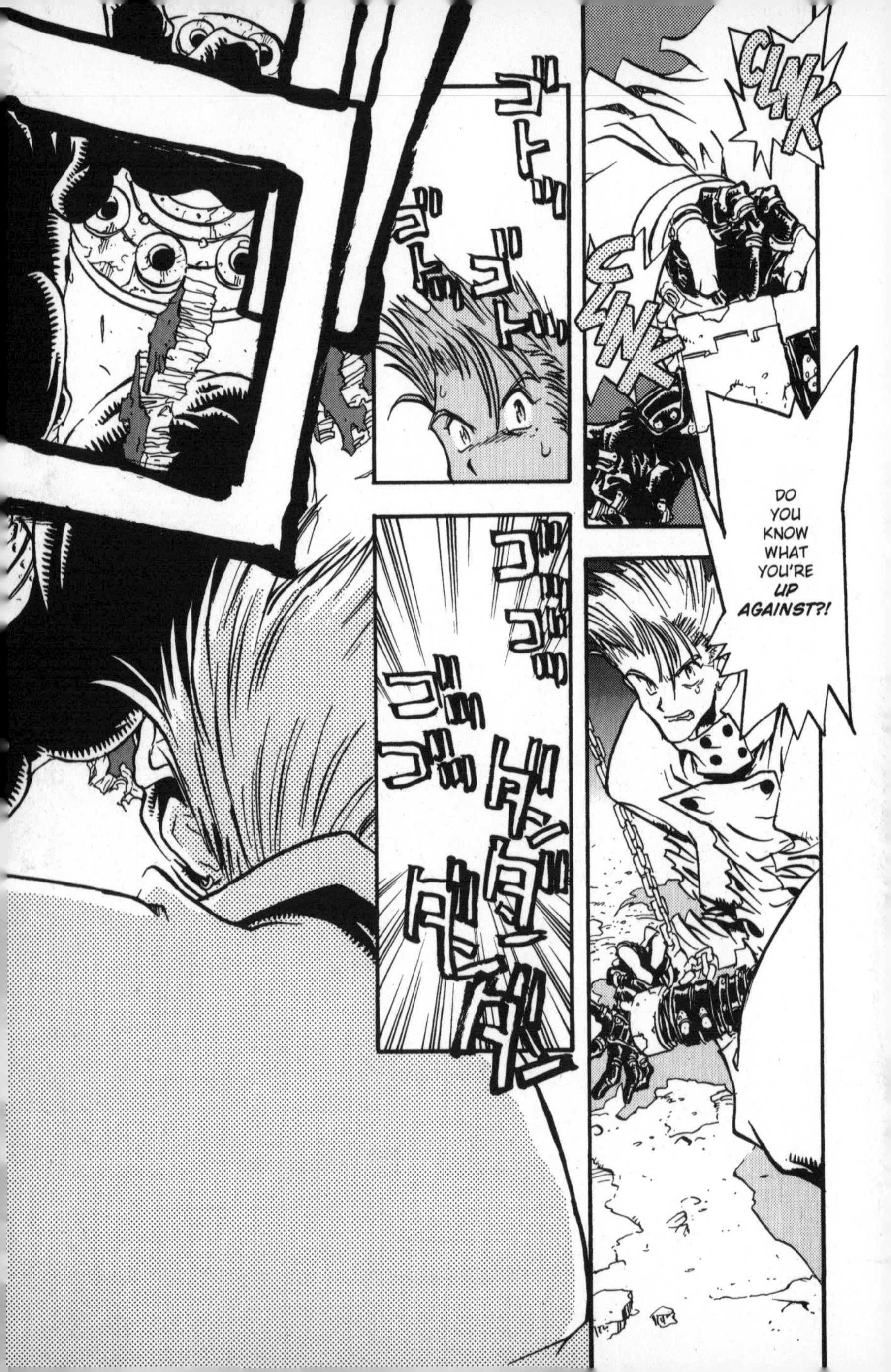
CLUNK
CLUNK
DO YOU KNOW WHAT YOU'RE *UP AGAINST?!*

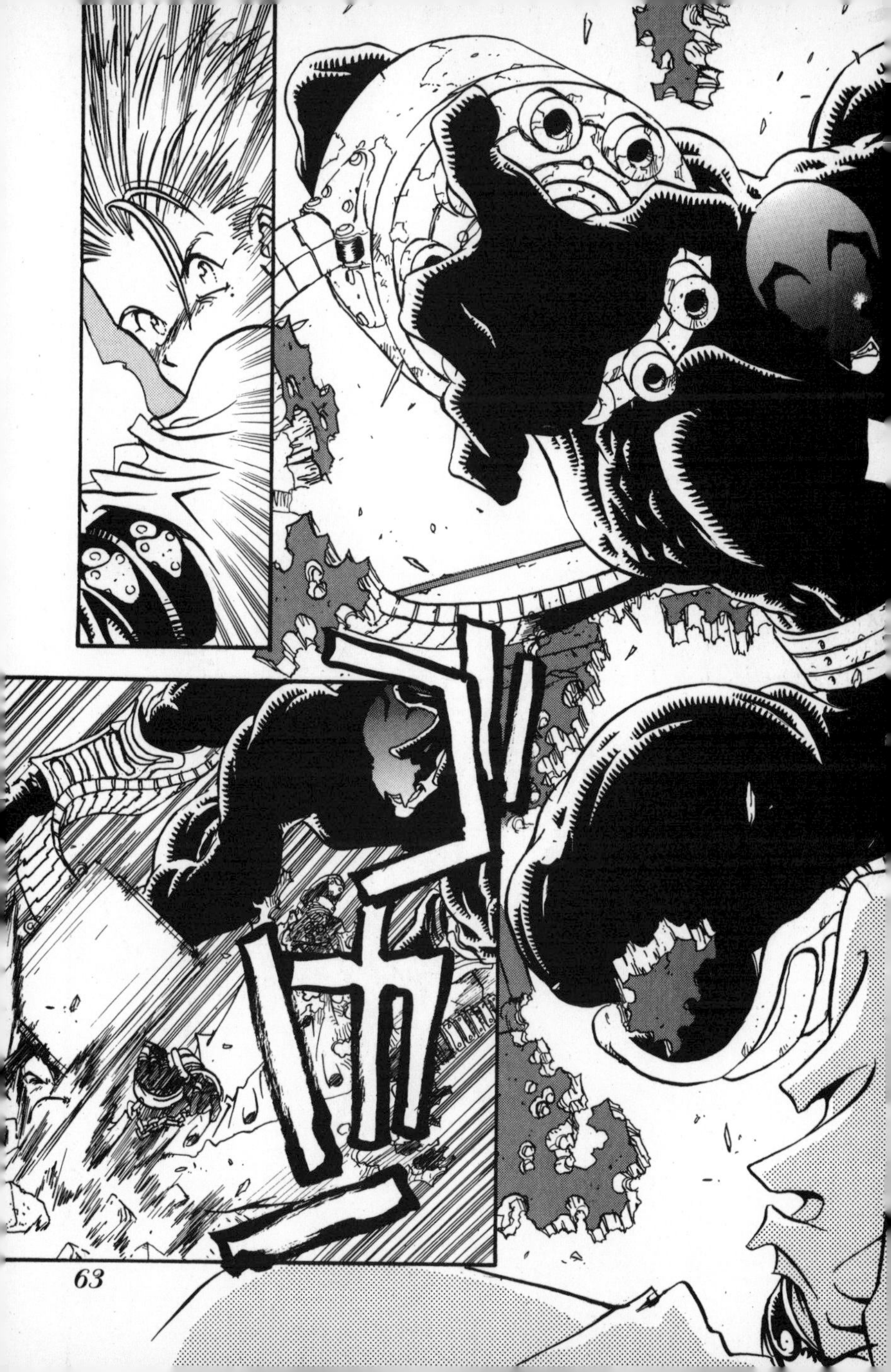

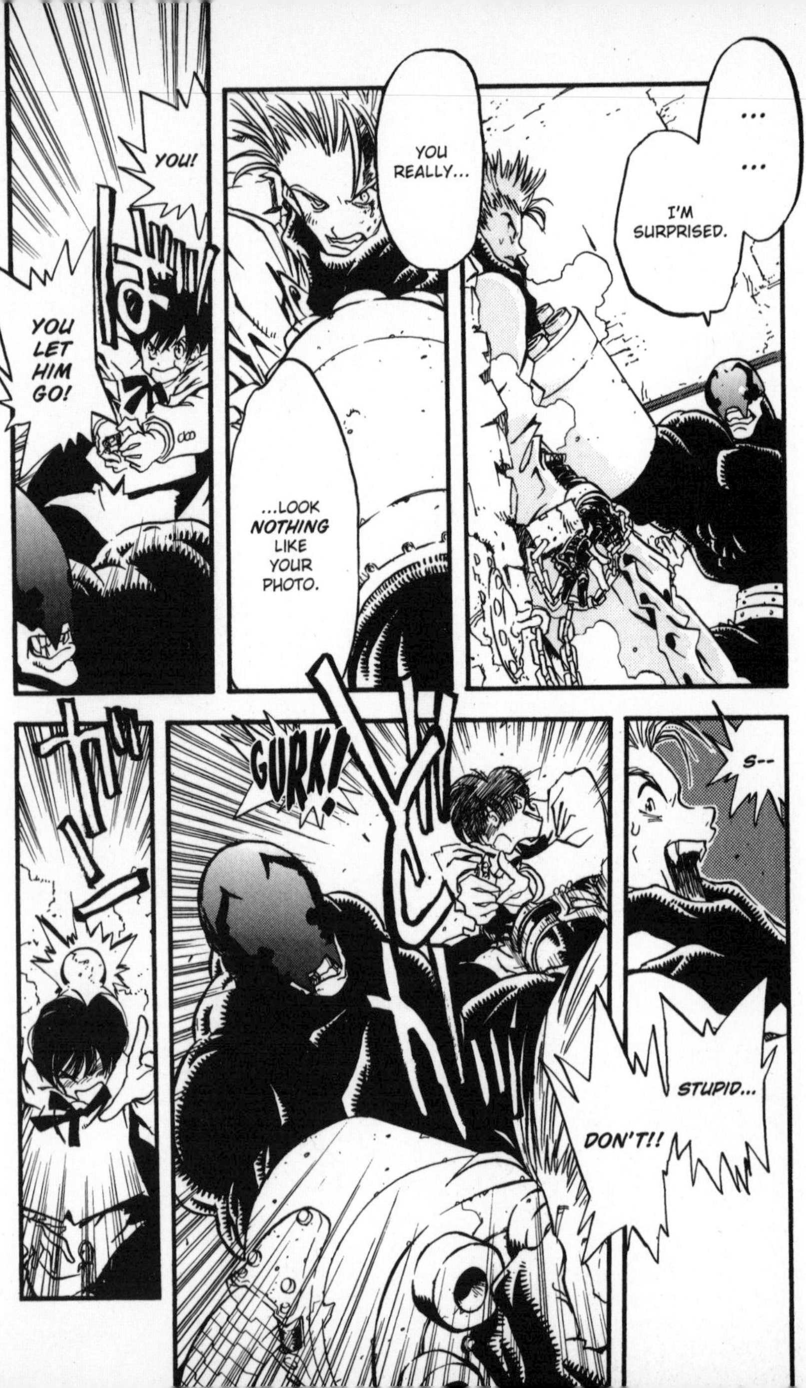
...
...
I'M SURPRISED.
YOU REALLY...
...LOOK NOTHING LIKE YOUR PHOTO.
YOU!
YOU LET HIM GO!
S--
GURK!
STUPID...
DON'T!!

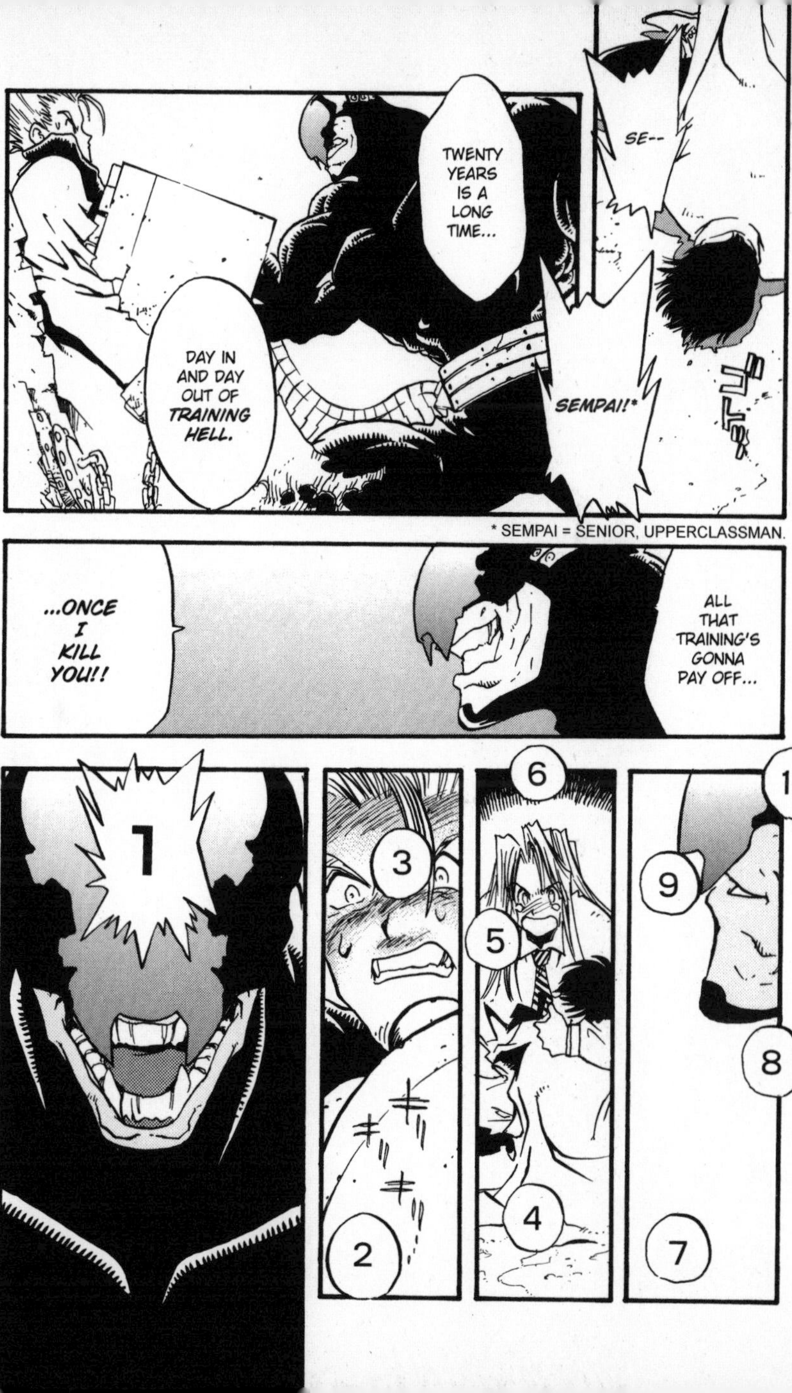
SE--
SEMPAI!*
TWENTY YEARS IS A LONG TIME...
DAY IN AND DAY OUT OF TRAINING HELL.
ALL THAT TRAINING'S GONNA PAY OFF...
...ONCE I KILL YOU!!
1
2
3
4
5
6
7
8
9
10

* SEMPAI = SENIOR, UPPERCLASSMAN.

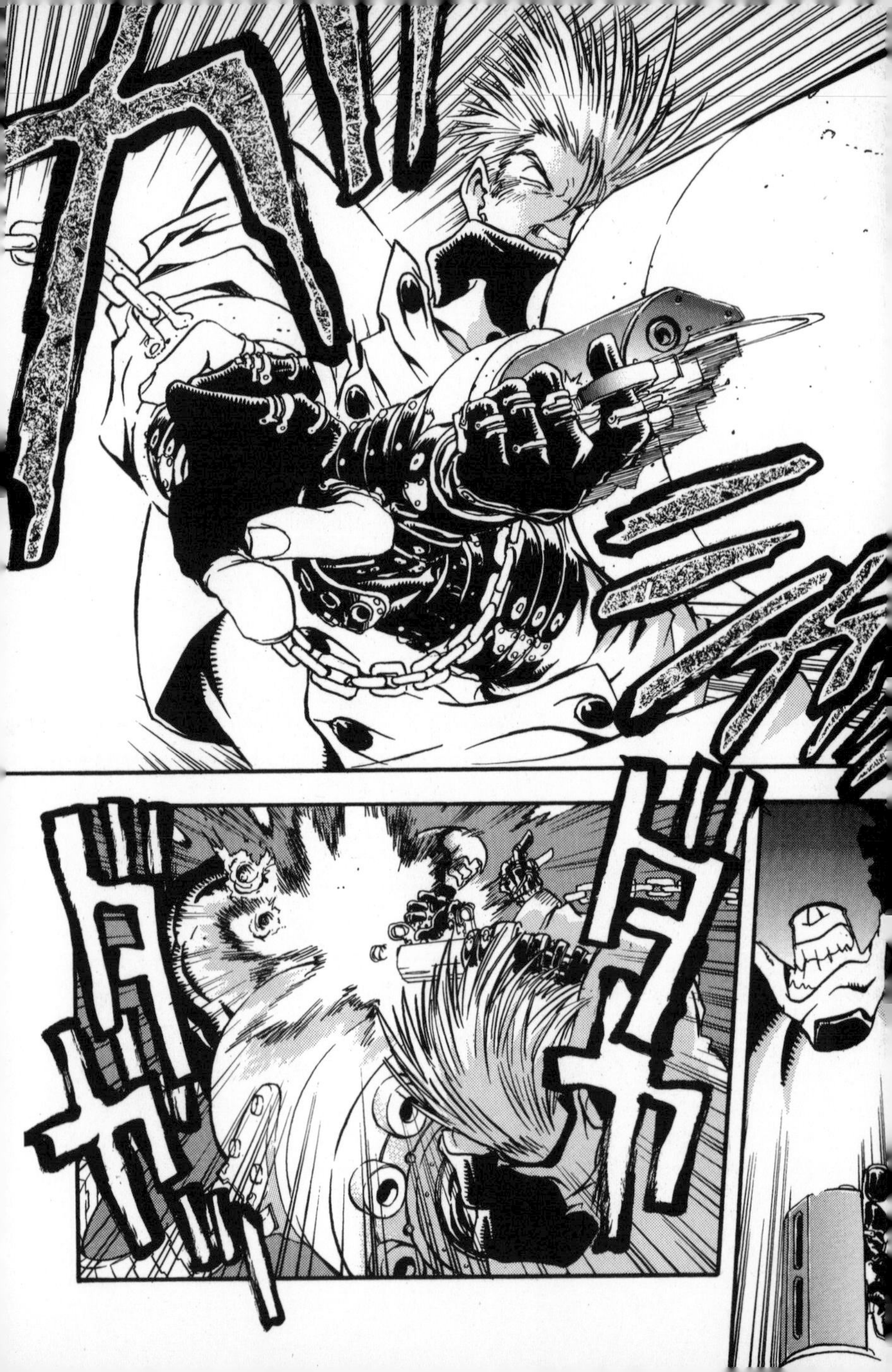

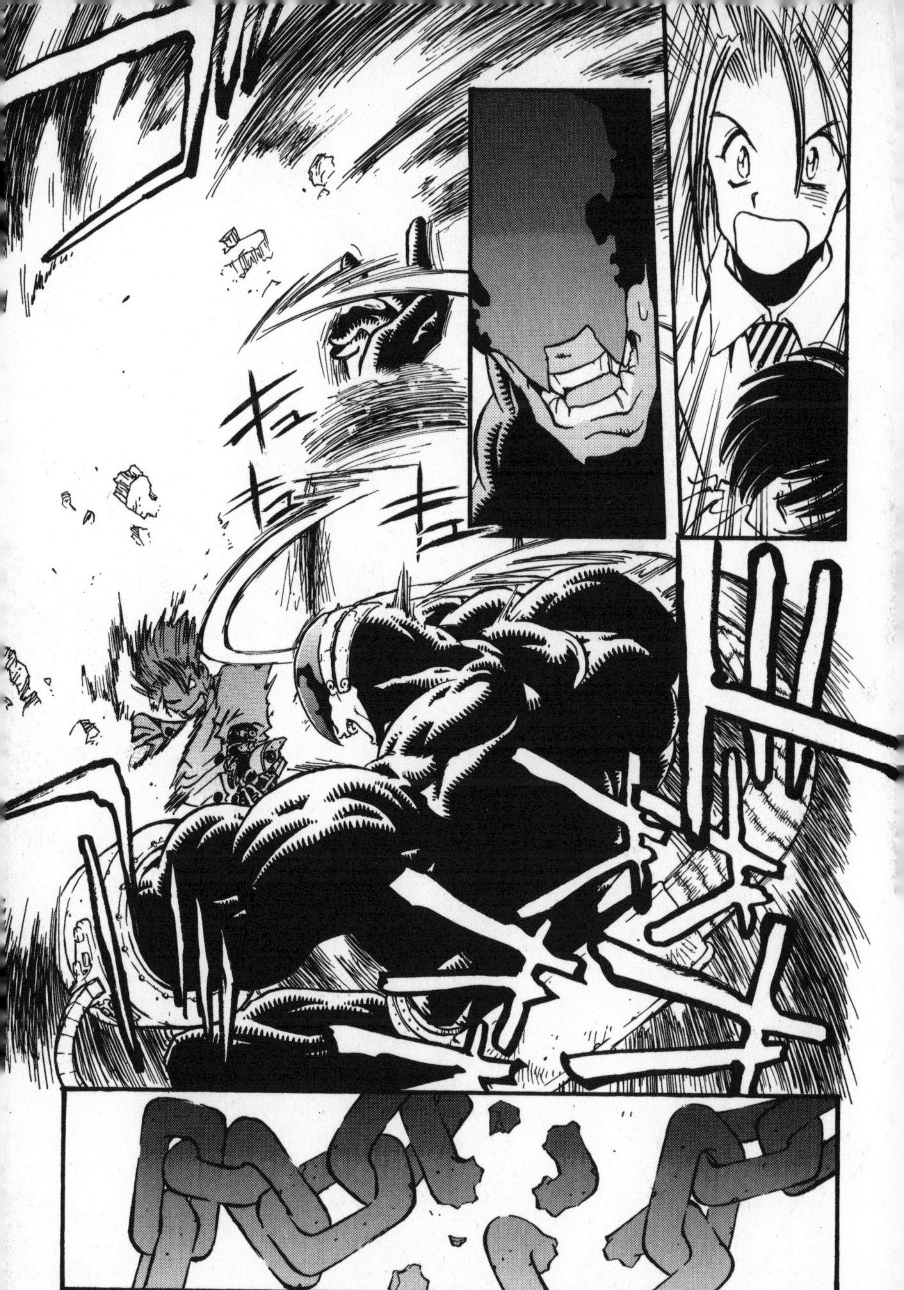
キュ
キュ
キュ

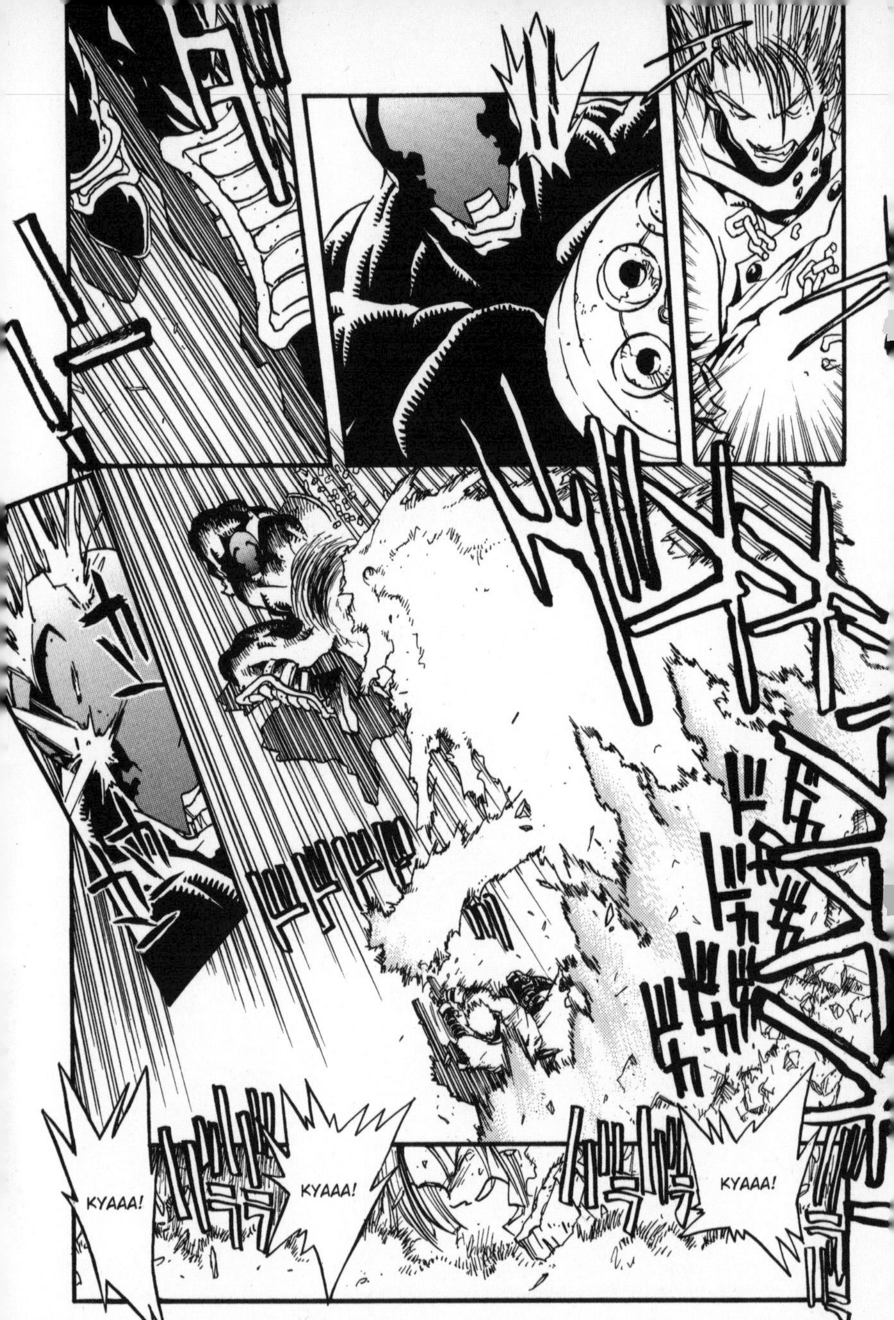
KYAAA!
KYAAA!
KYAAA!

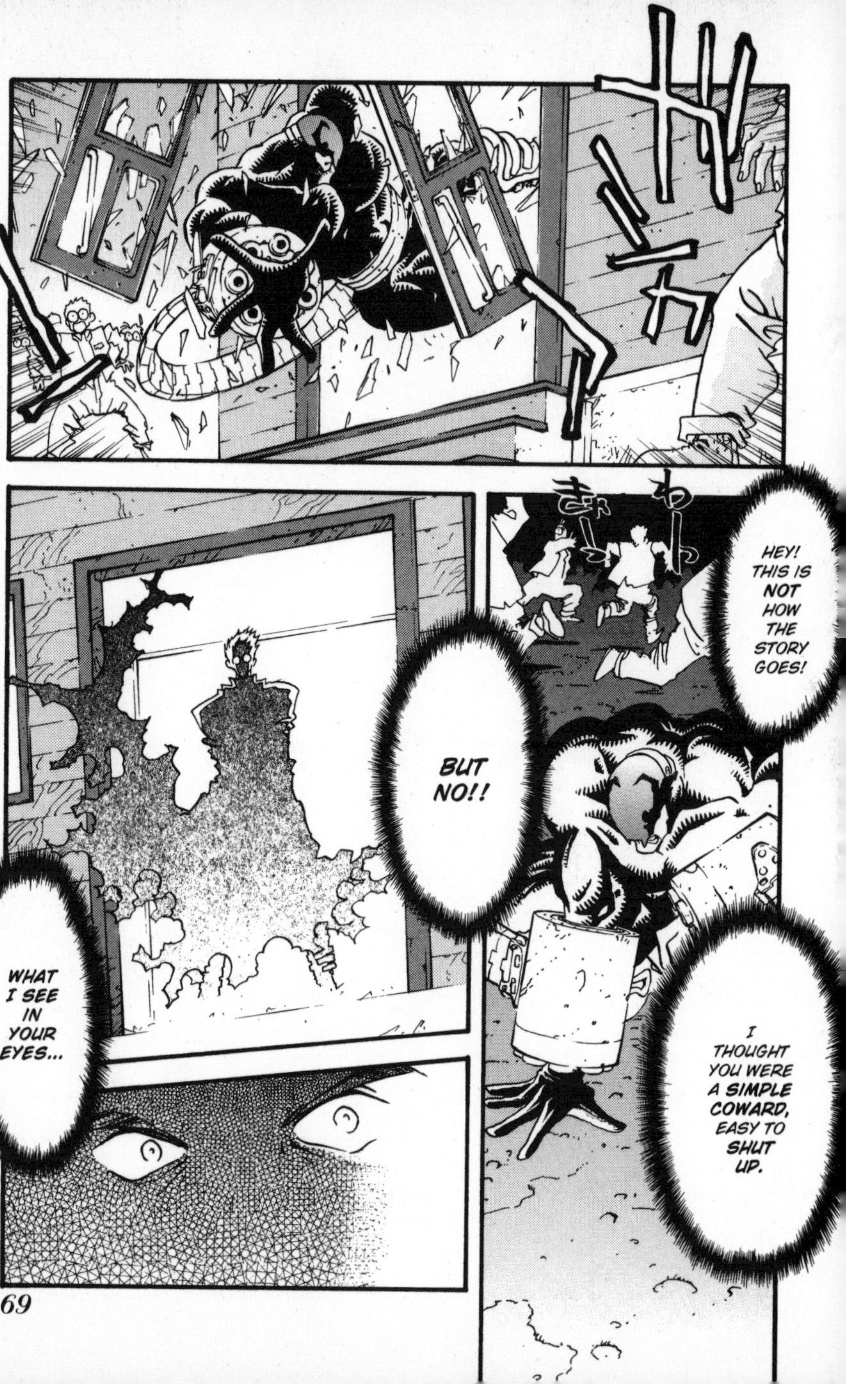

わー
きゃー
HEY! THIS IS **NOT** HOW THE STORY GOES!
BUT NO!!
I THOUGHT YOU WERE A **SIMPLE COWARD**, EASY TO **SHUT UP**.
WHAT I SEE IN YOUR EYES...

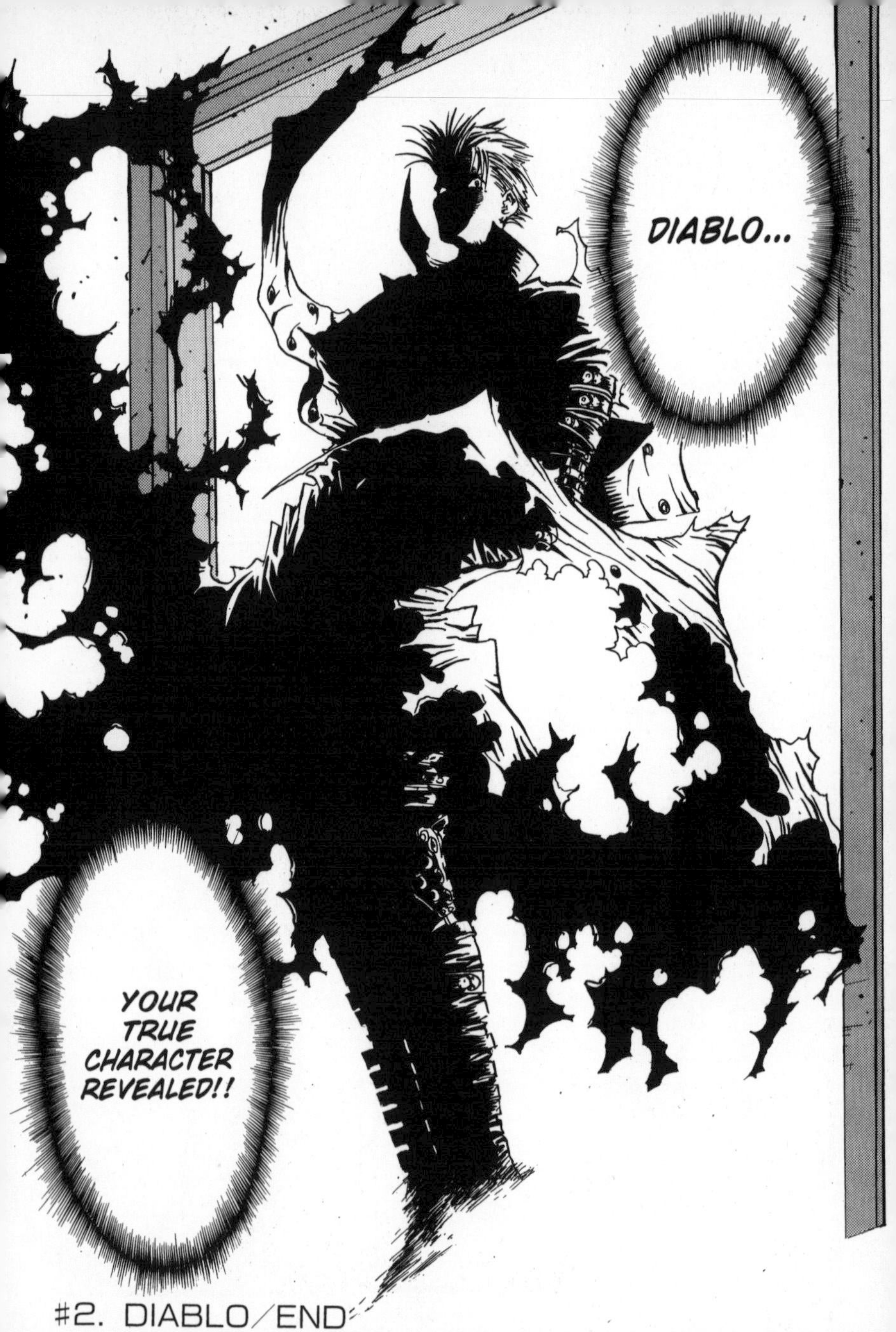
DIABLO...
YOUR TRUE CHARACTER REVEALED!!

#2. DIABLO/END

#3

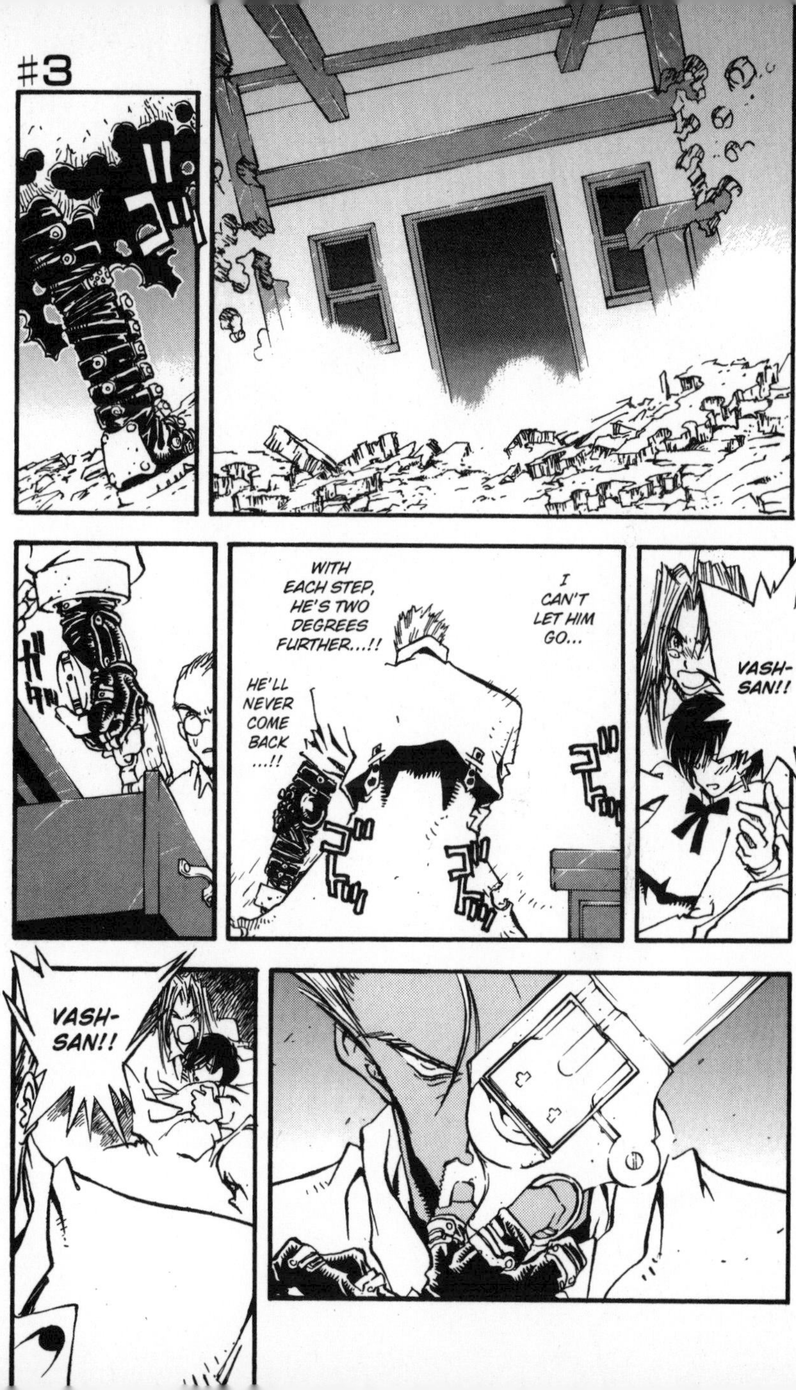
VASH-SAN!!
I CAN'T LET HIM GO...
WITH EACH STEP, HE'S TWO DEGREES FURTHER...!!
HE'LL NEVER COME BACK ...!!
VASH-SAN!!

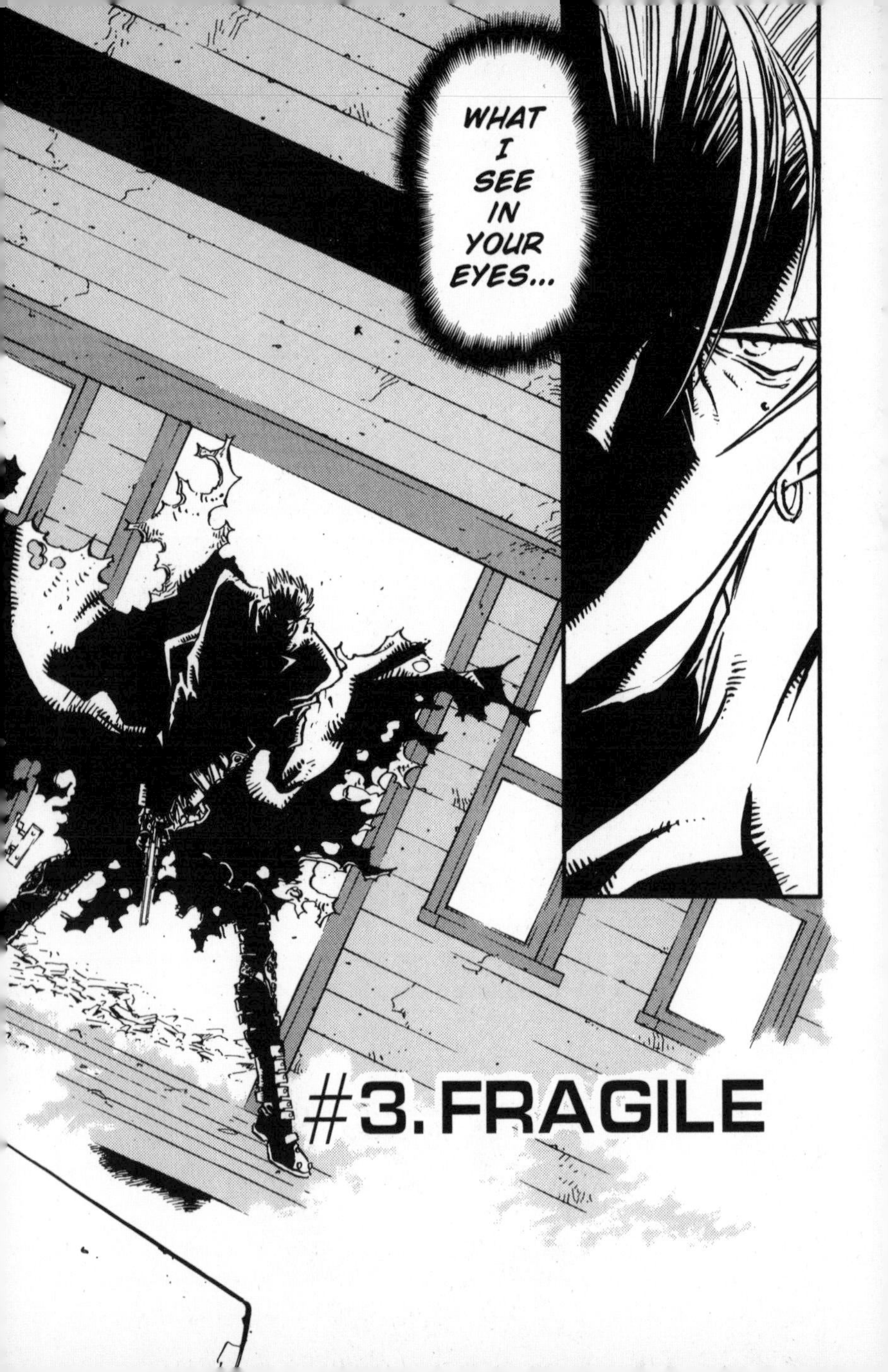
WHAT I SEE IN YOUR EYES...
#3. FRAGILE

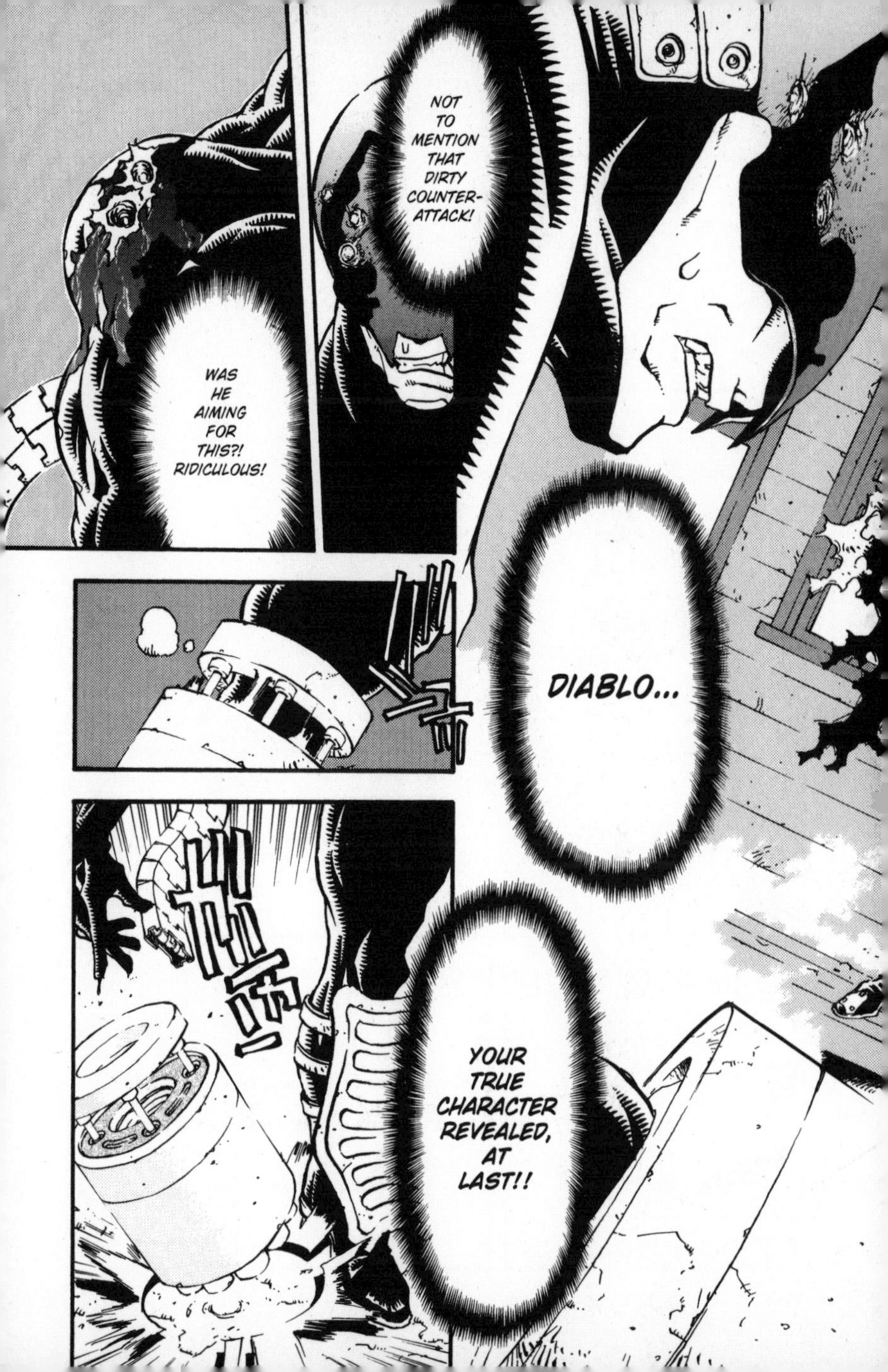
NOT TO MENTION THAT DIRTY COUNTER-ATTACK!
WAS HE AIMING FOR THIS?! RIDICULOUS!
DIABLO...
YOUR TRUE CHARACTER REVEALED, AT LAST!!

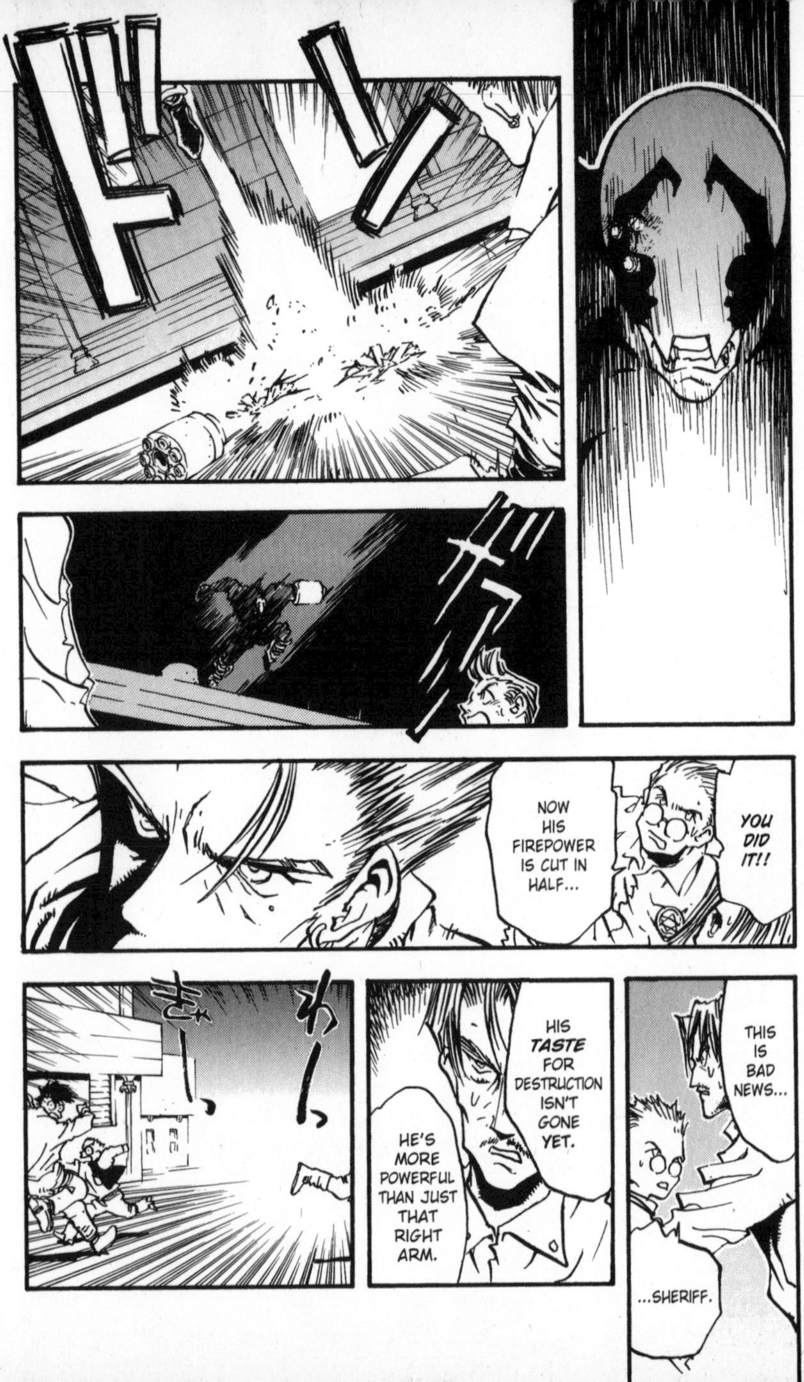
YOU DID IT!!
NOW HIS FIREPOWER IS CUT IN HALF...
THIS IS BAD NEWS...
...SHERIFF.
HIS TASTE FOR DESTRUCTION ISN'T GONE YET.
HE'S MORE POWERFUL THAN JUST THAT RIGHT ARM.
わーっ
きゃーっ

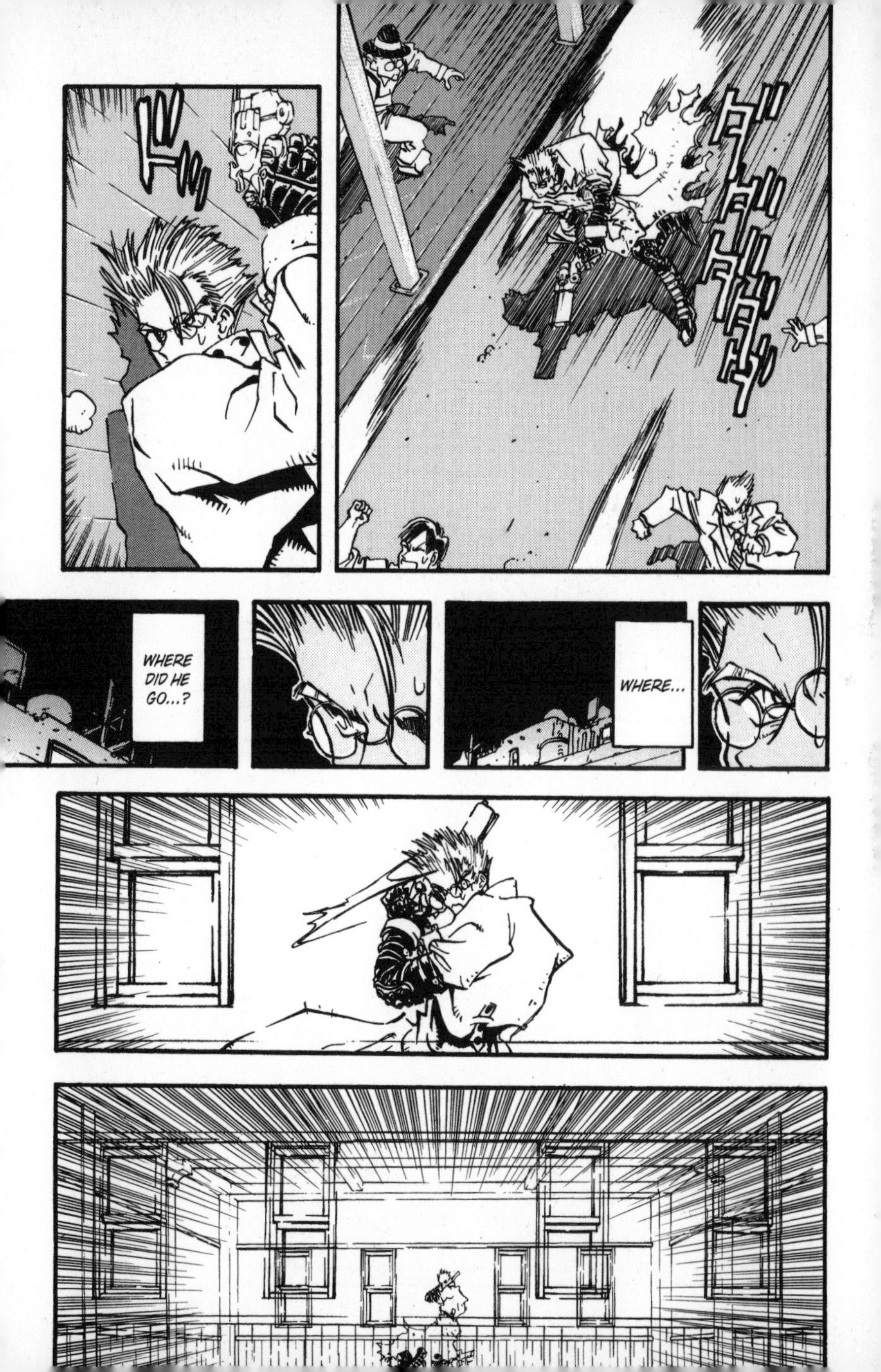
WHERE...
WHERE DID HE GO...?

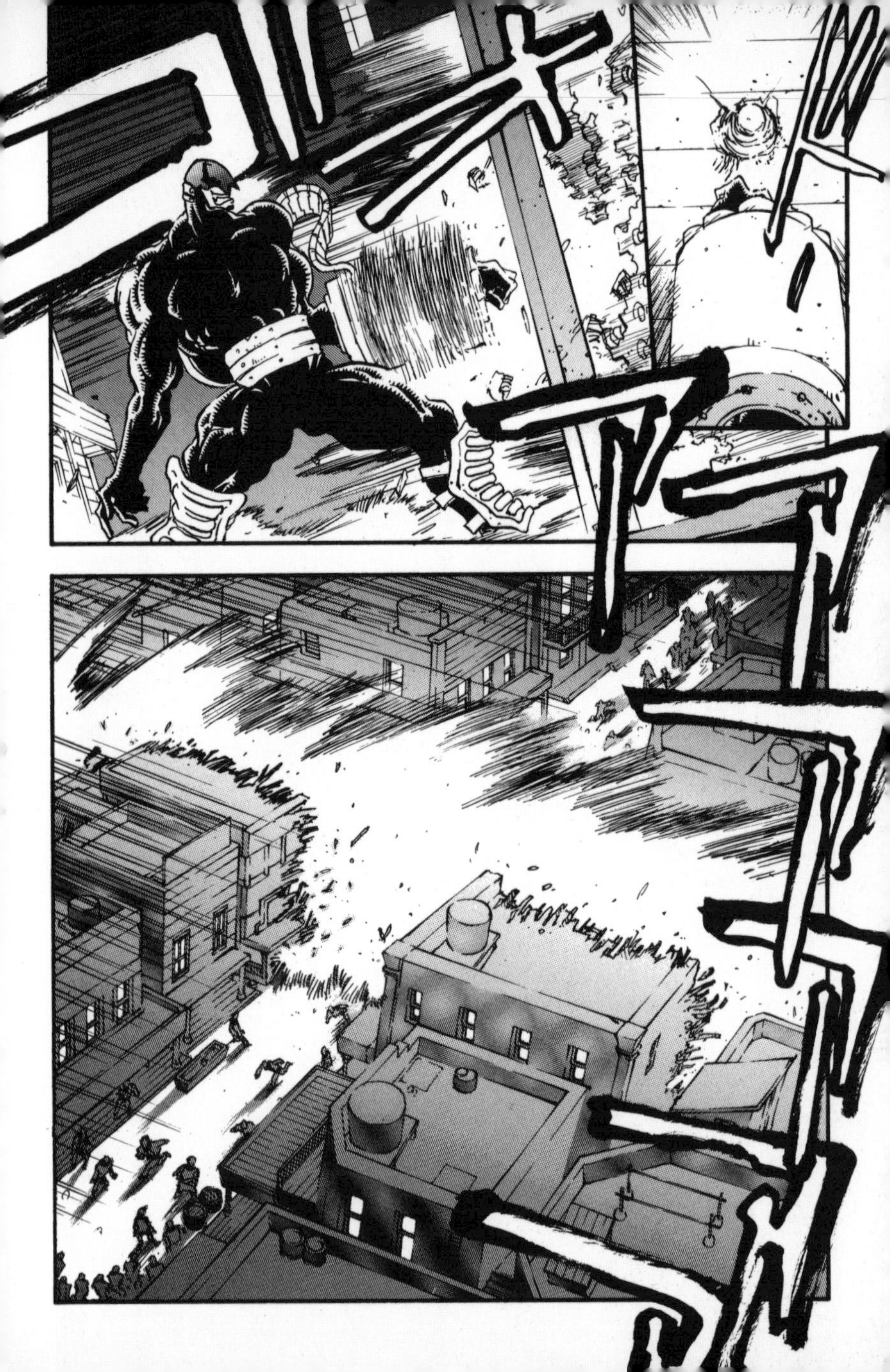

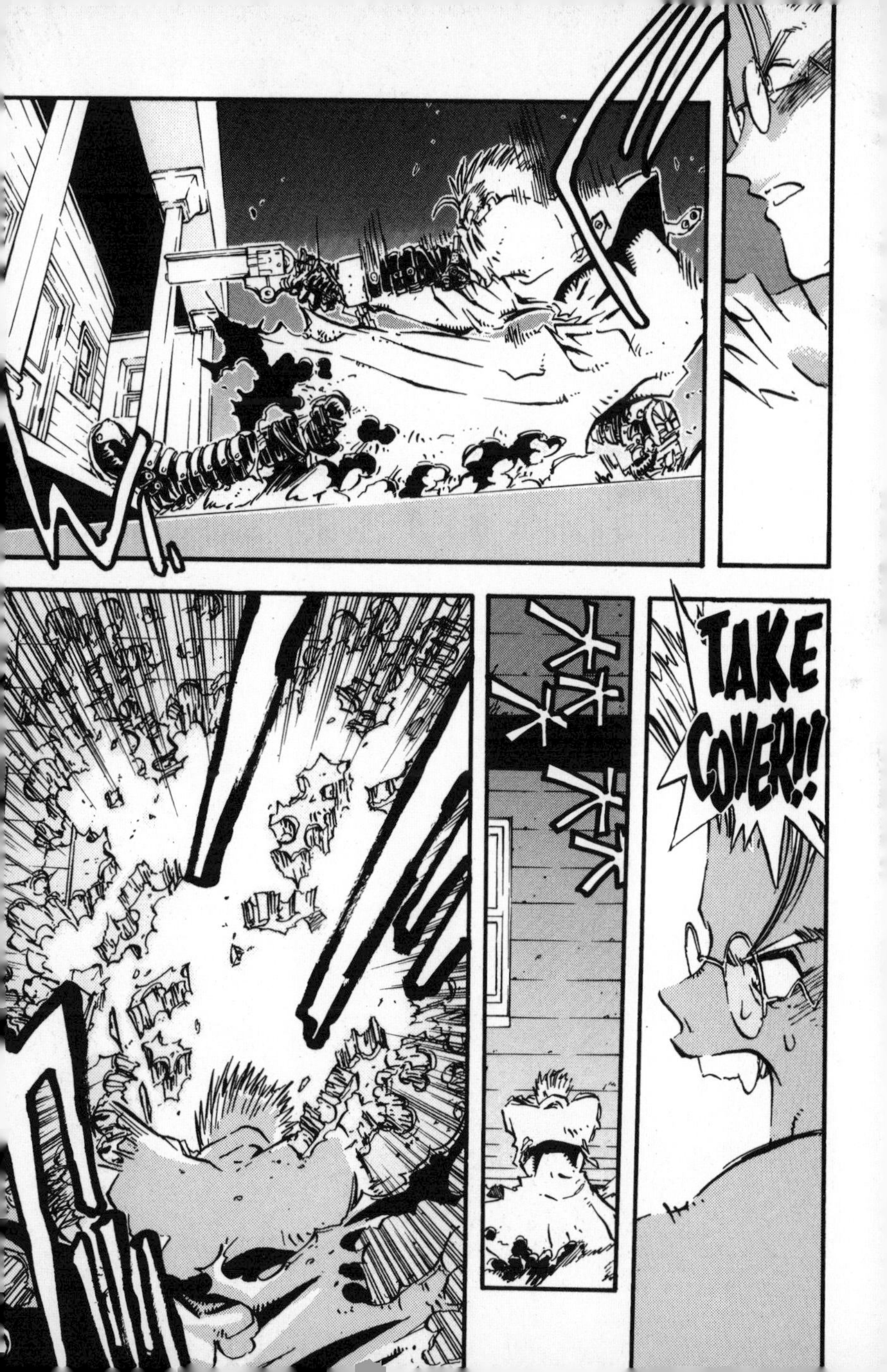
TAKE COVER!!

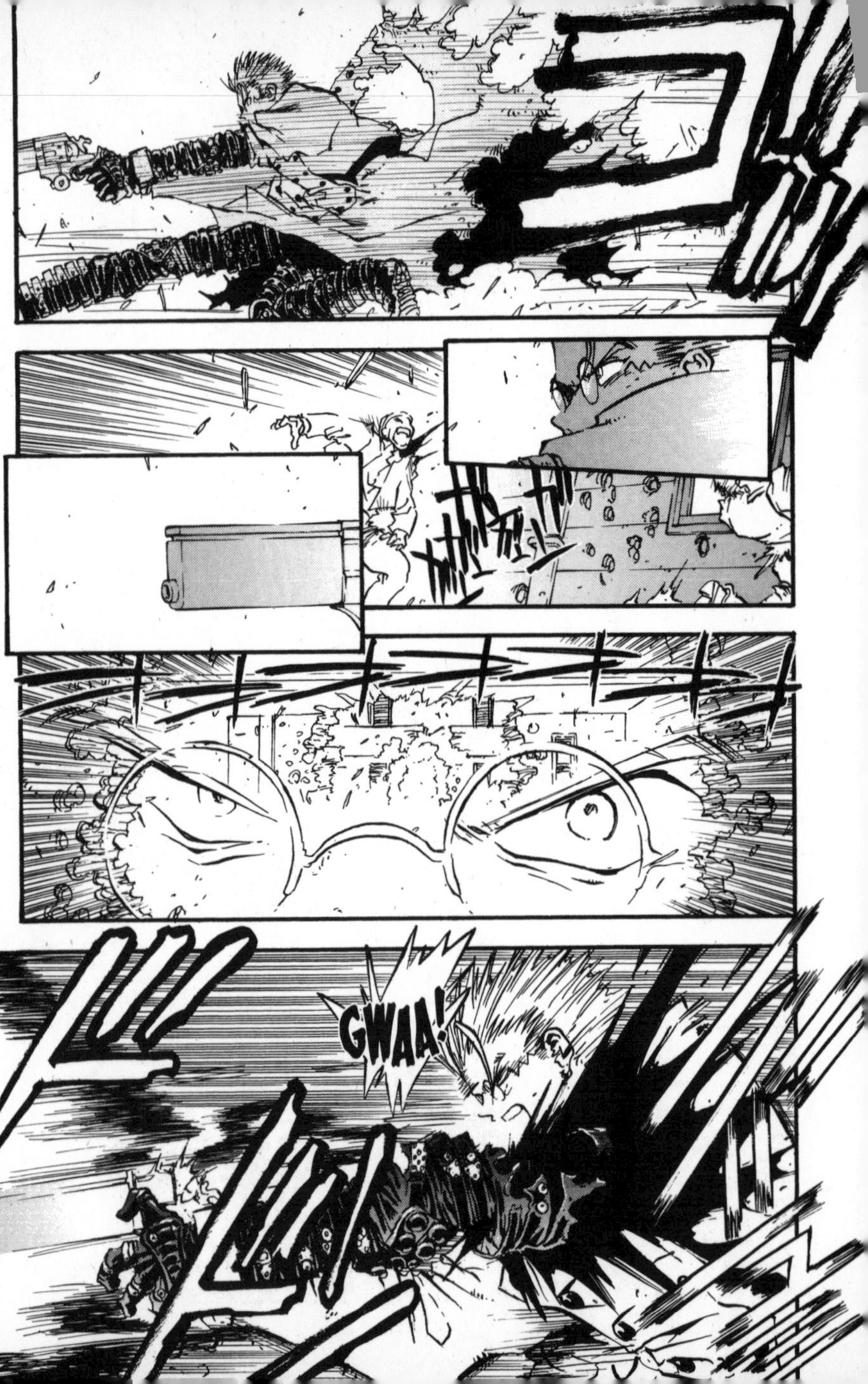
GWAA!

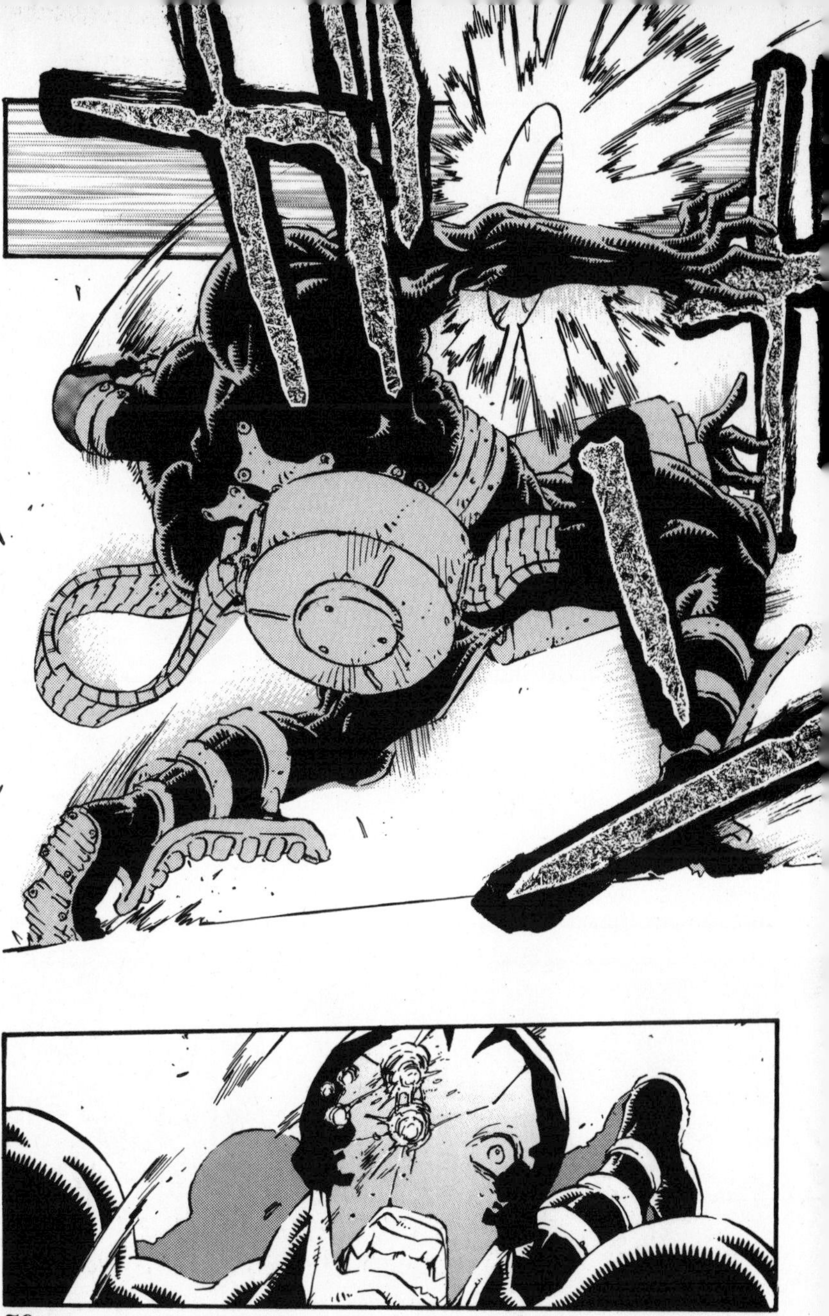

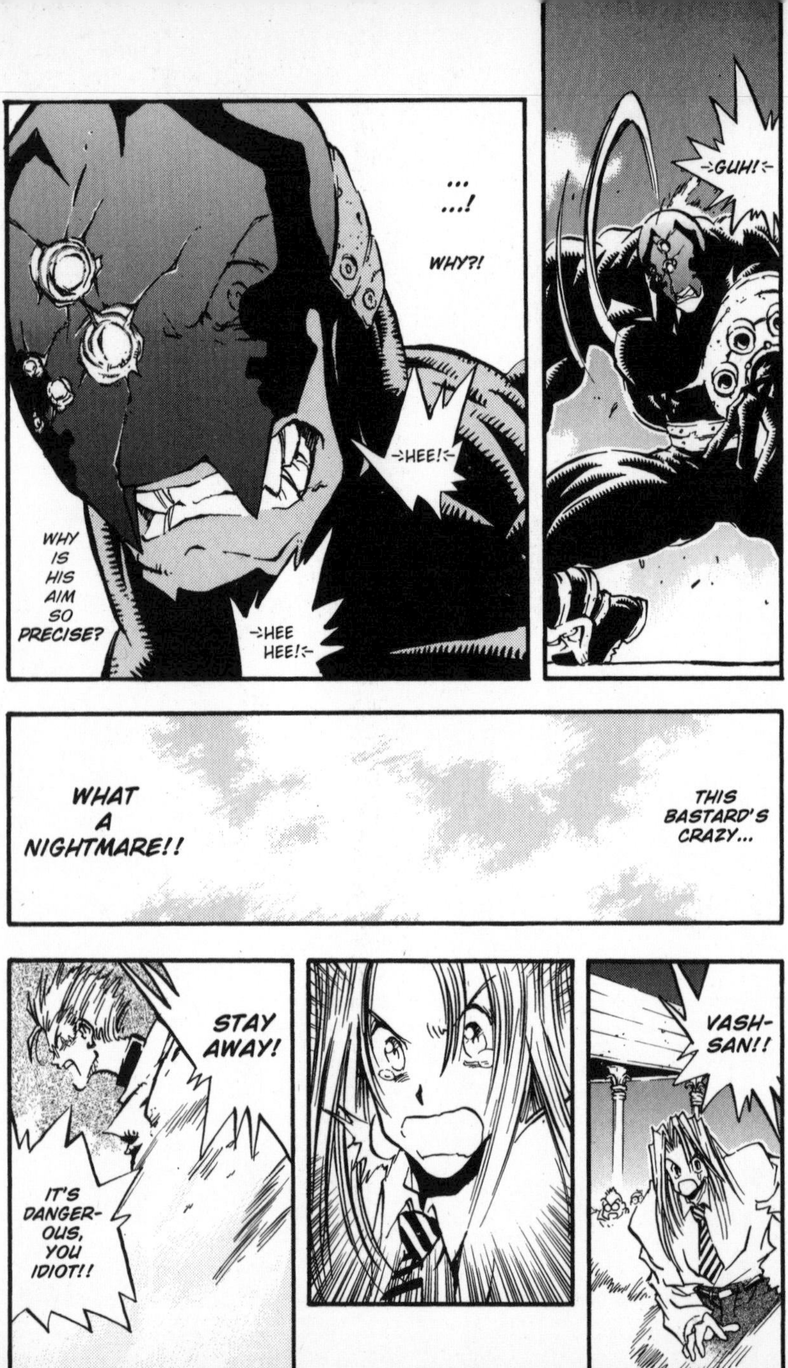
-GUH!-
...
...!
WHY?!
-HEE!-
-HEE HEE!-
WHY IS HIS AIM SO PRECISE?
THIS BASTARD'S CRAZY...
WHAT A NIGHTMARE!!
VASH-SAN!!
STAY AWAY!
IT'S DANGER-OUS, YOU IDIOT!!

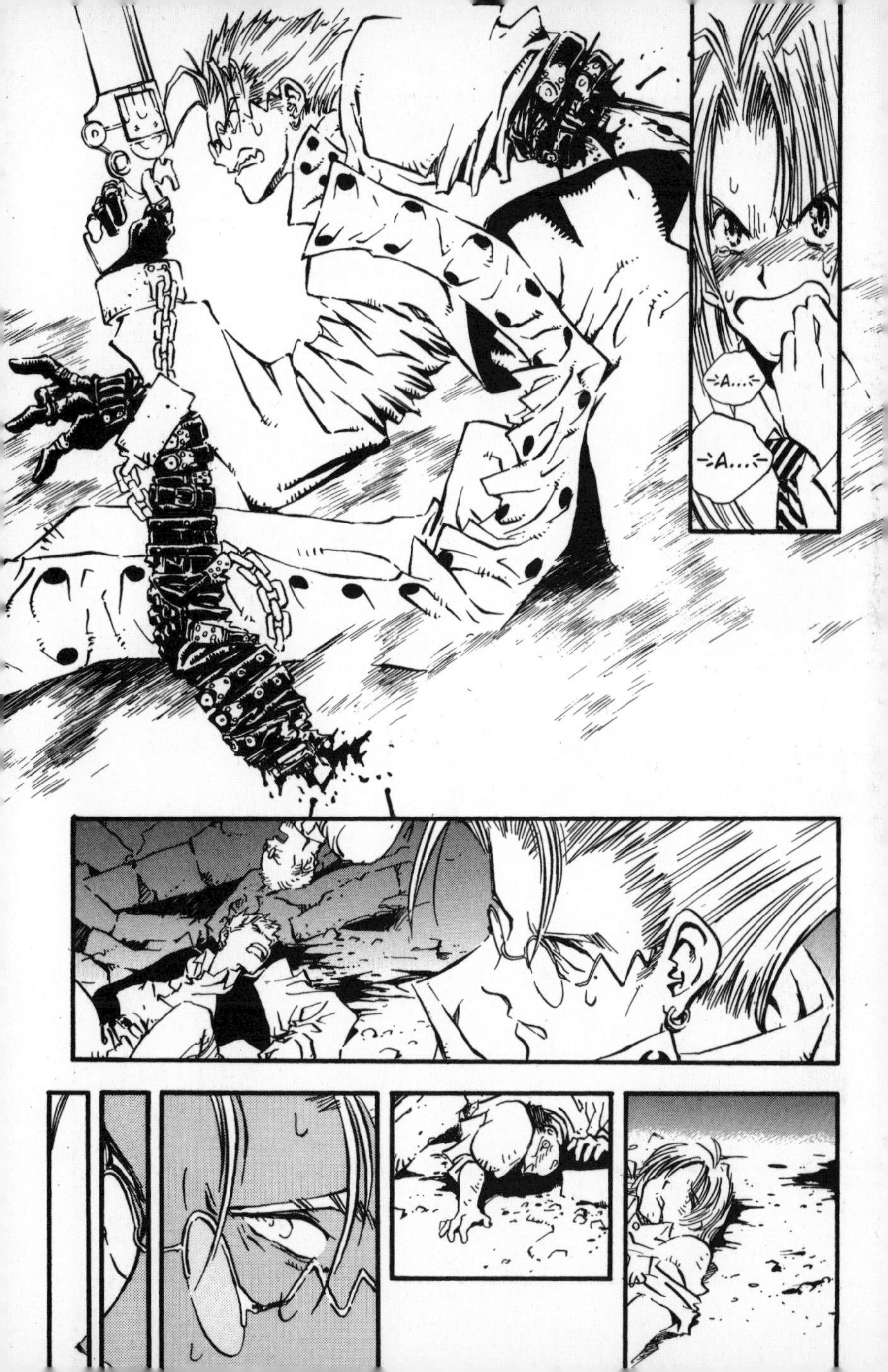
A...
A...

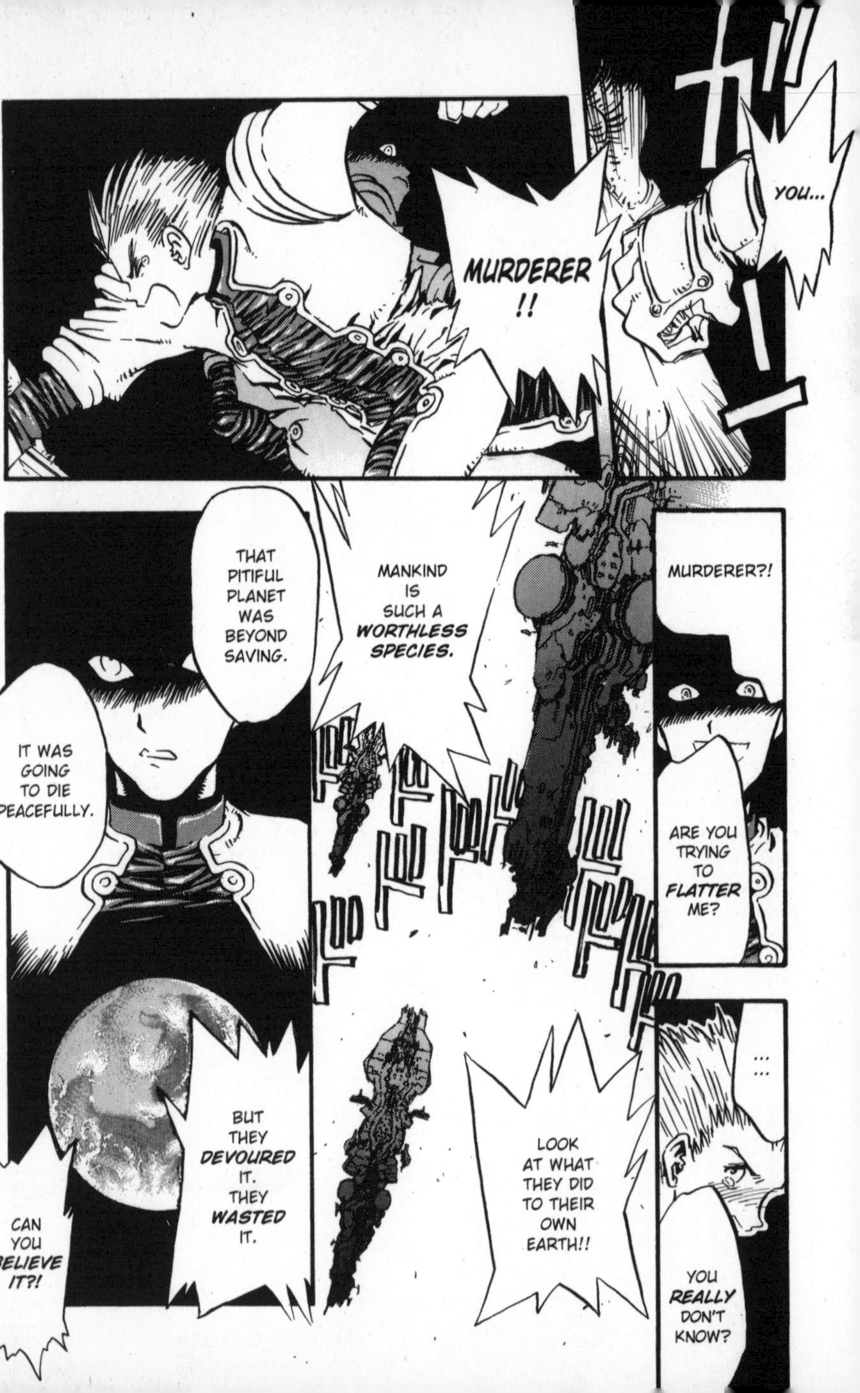
YOU...
MURDERER !!
MURDERER?!
ARE YOU TRYING TO FLATTER ME?
... ...
YOU REALLY DON'T KNOW?
MANKIND IS SUCH A WORTHLESS SPECIES.
LOOK AT WHAT THEY DID TO THEIR OWN EARTH!!
THAT PITIFUL PLANET WAS BEYOND SAVING.
IT WAS GOING TO DIE PEACEFULLY.
BUT THEY DEVOURED IT. THEY WASTED IT.
CAN YOU BELIEVE IT?!

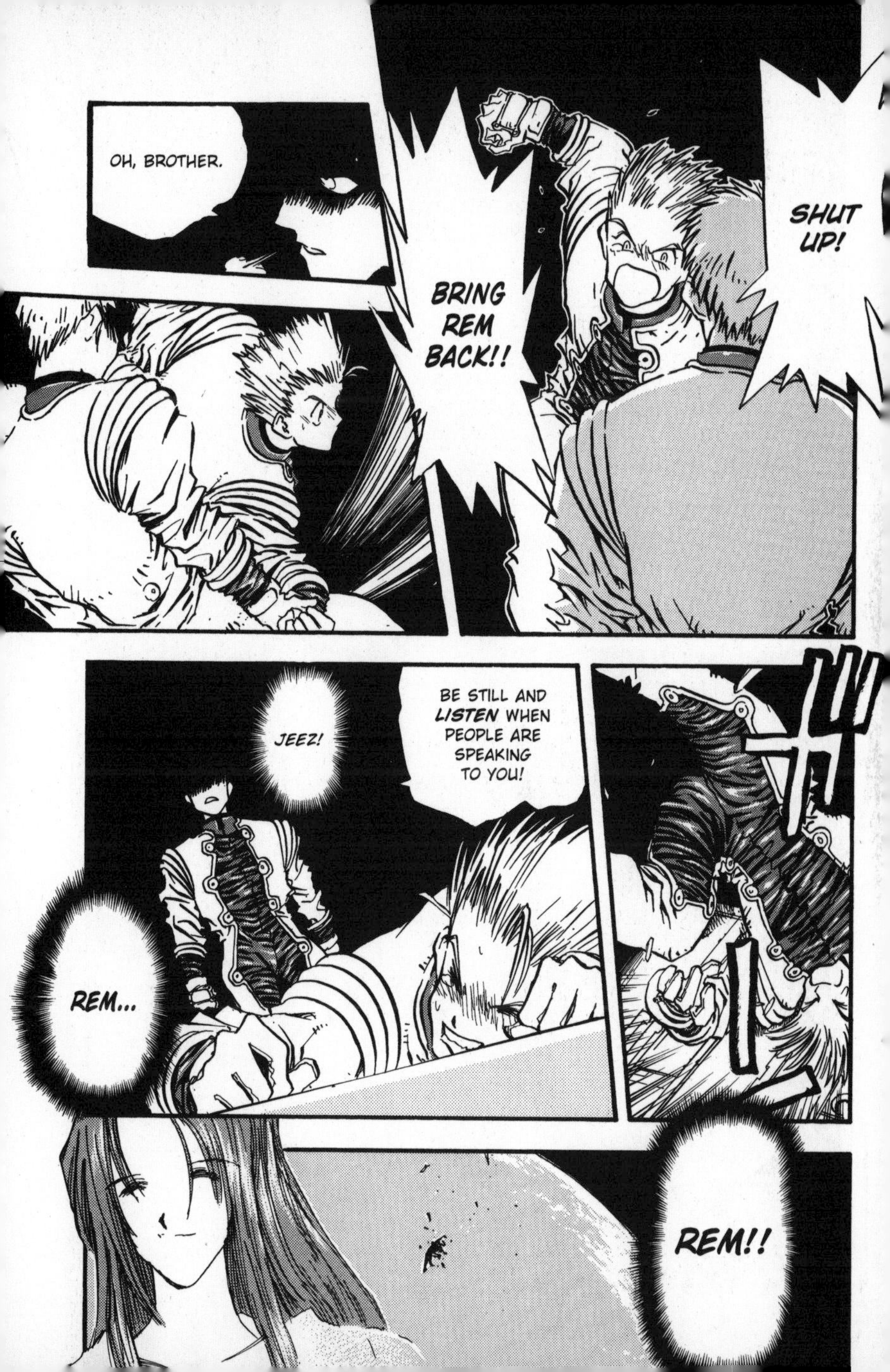
SHUT UP!
BRING REM BACK!!
OH, BROTHER.
BE STILL AND LISTEN WHEN PEOPLE ARE SPEAKING TO YOU!
JEEZ!
REM...
REM!!

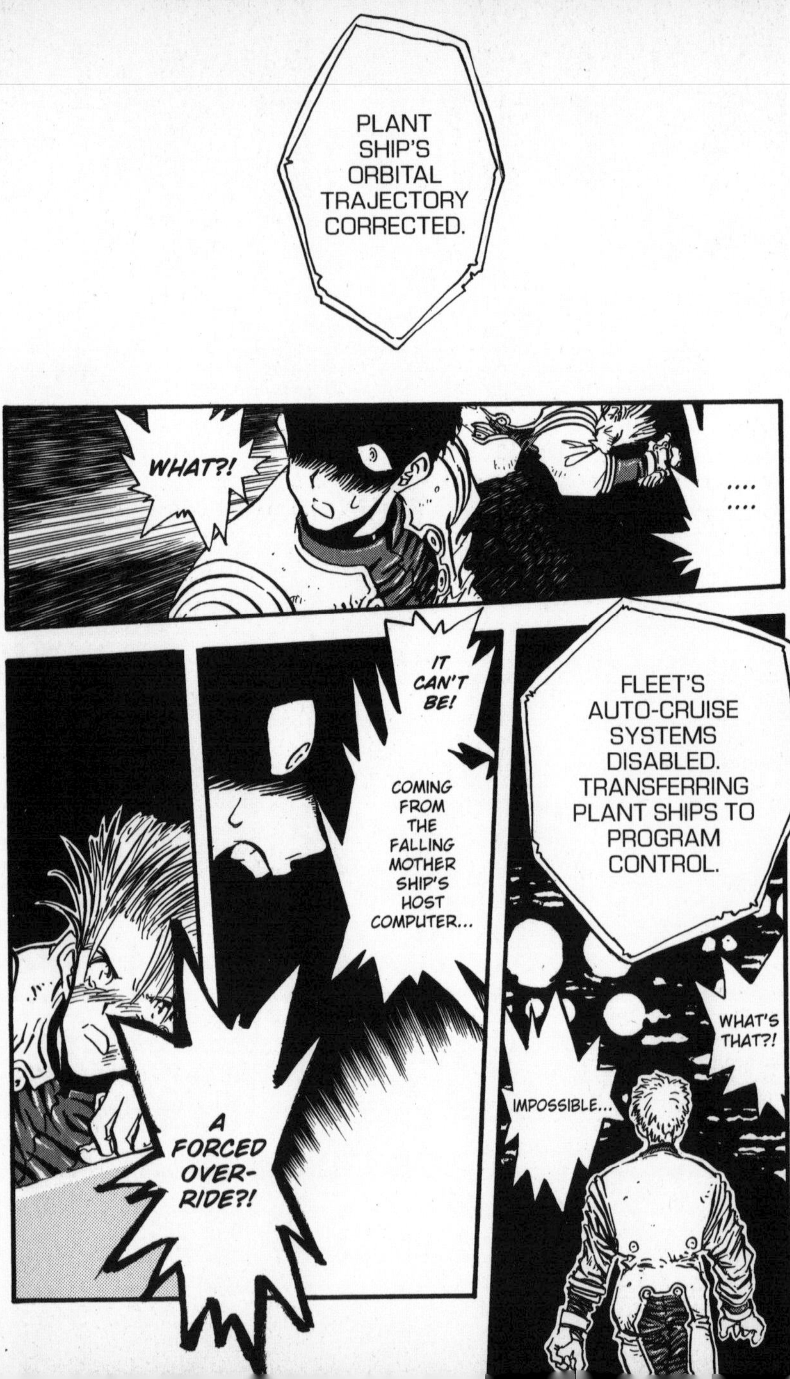
PLANT SHIP'S ORBITAL TRAJECTORY CORRECTED.
....
WHAT?!
FLEET'S AUTO-CRUISE SYSTEMS DISABLED. TRANSFERRING PLANT SHIPS TO PROGRAM CONTROL.
WHAT'S THAT?!
IMPOSSIBLE...
IT CAN'T BE!
COMING FROM THE FALLING MOTHER SHIP'S HOST COMPUTER...
A FORCED OVER-RIDE?!

REVERSE THRUSTERS...

SHE GOT ME.

DAMN.

SUCH SLIM ODDS THAT SHE COULD EVEN SAVE THEM...

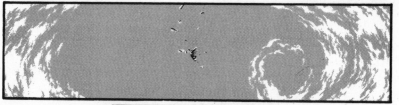

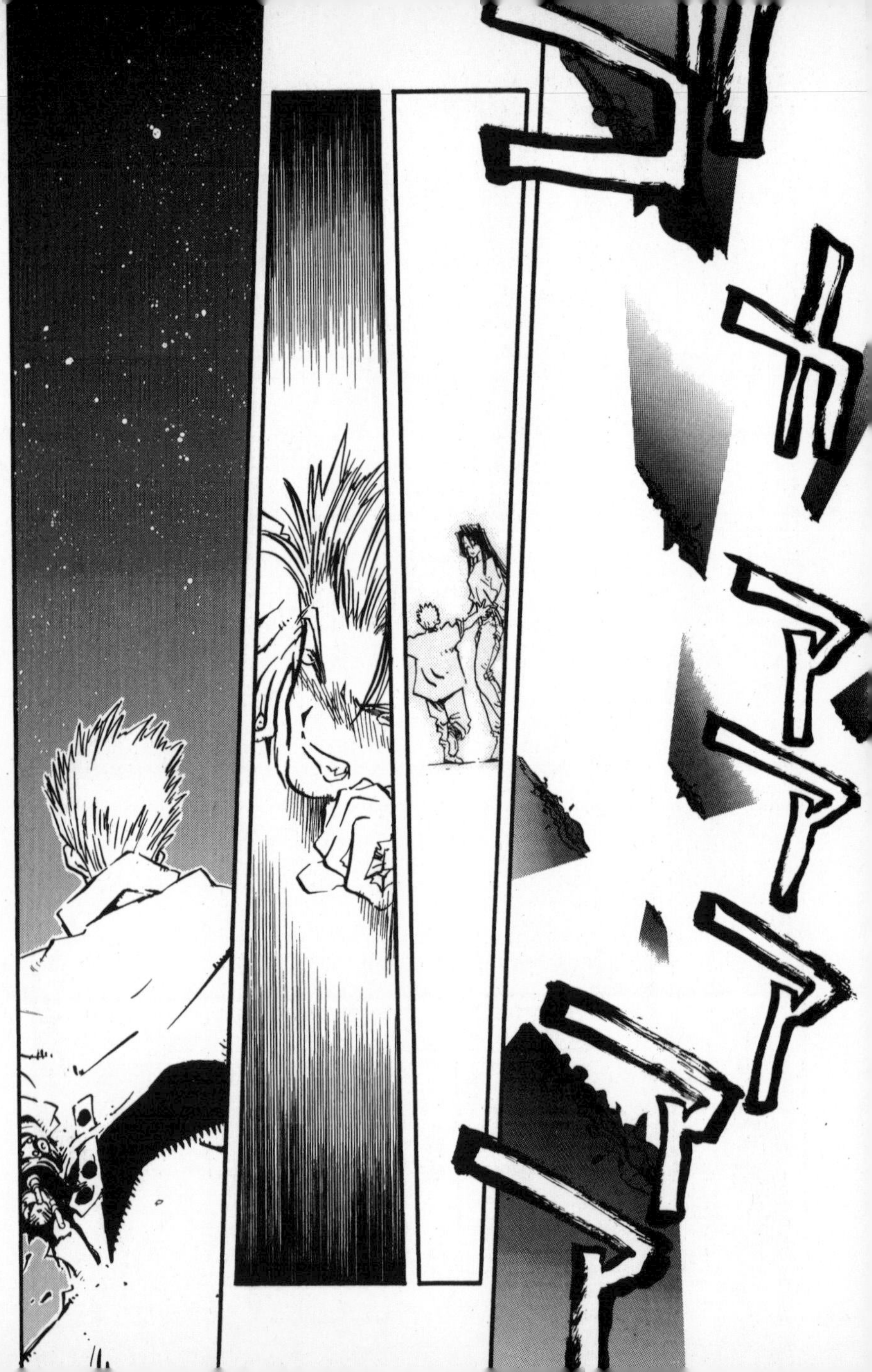
ゴオアアアア

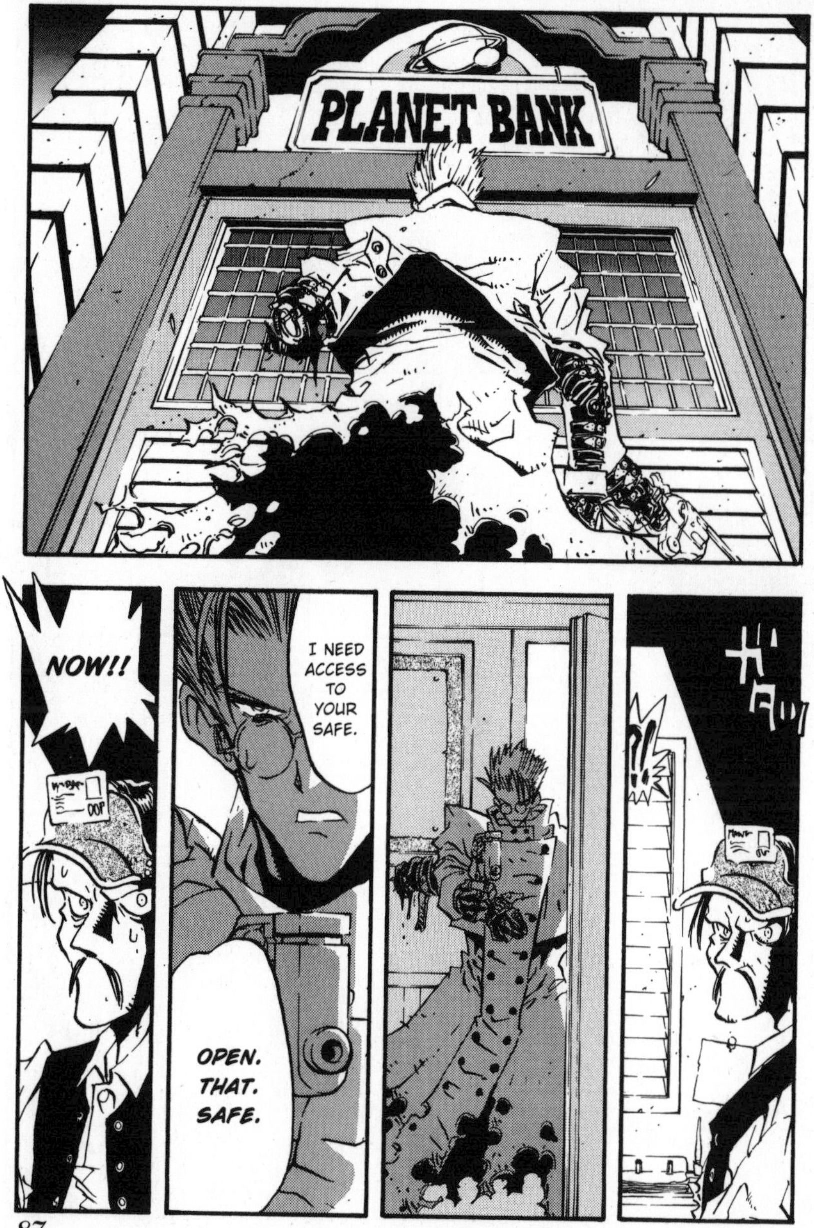
PLANET BANK
?!
I NEED ACCESS TO YOUR SAFE.
OPEN. THAT. SAFE.
NOW!!

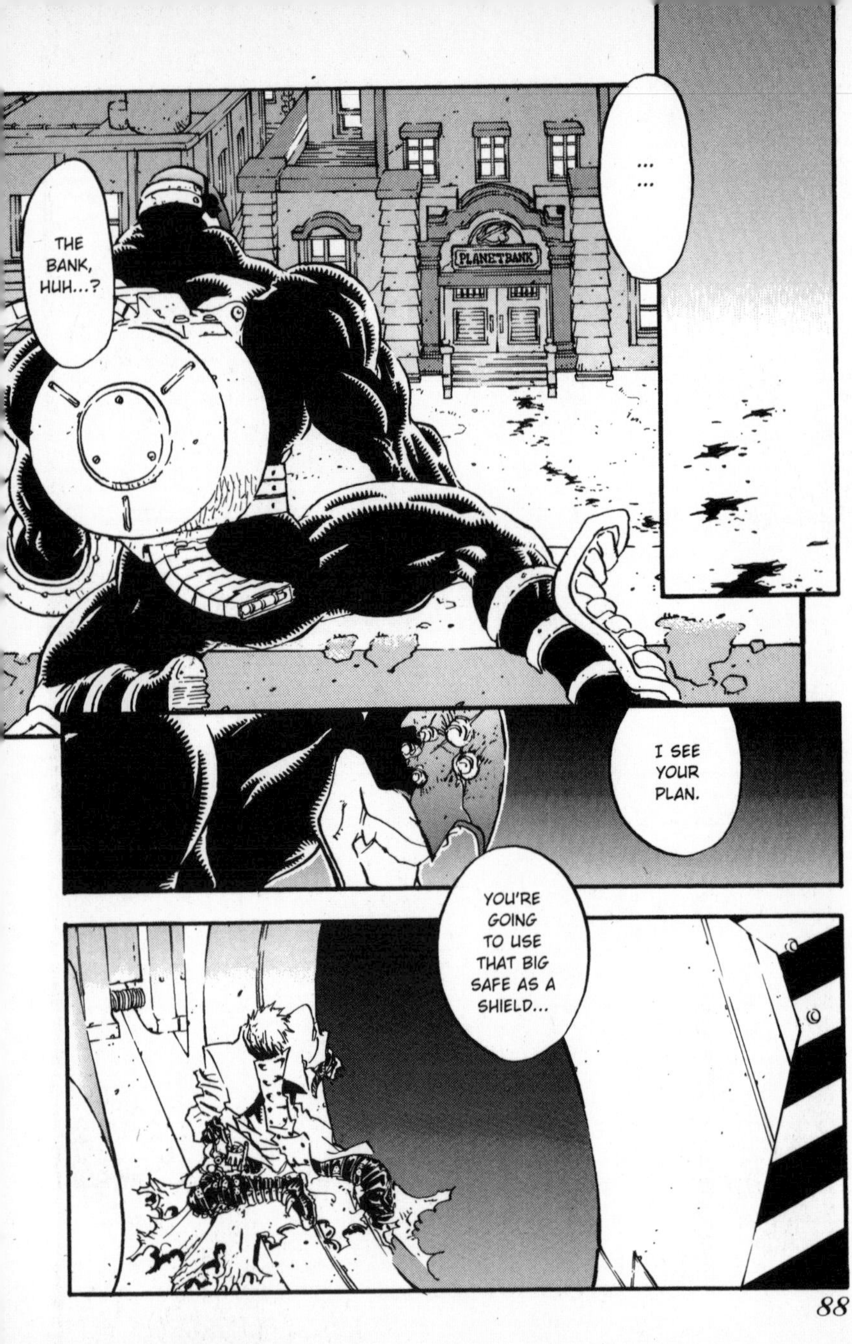
...
...
THE BANK, HUH...?
PLANETBANK
I SEE YOUR PLAN.
YOU'RE GOING TO USE THAT BIG SAFE AS A SHIELD...

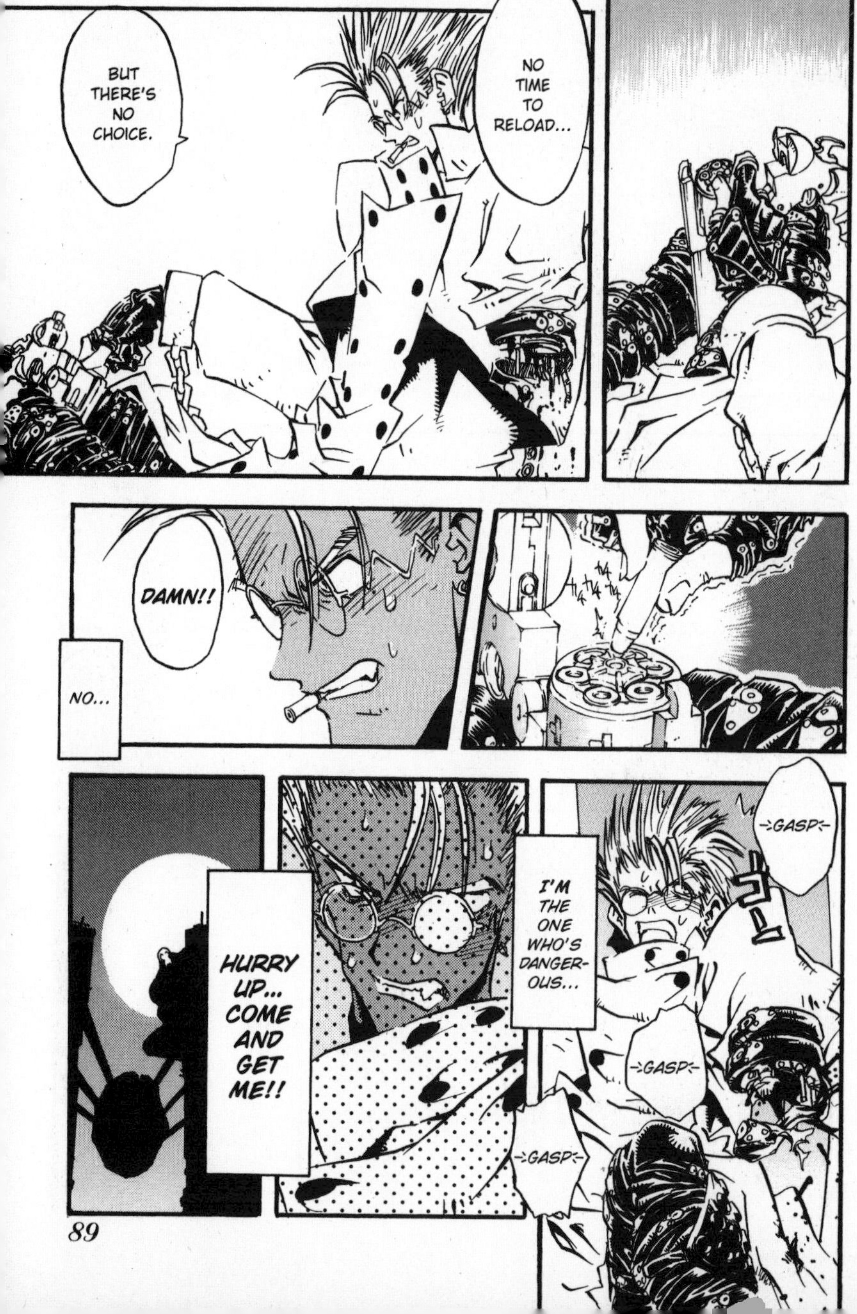
NO TIME TO RELOAD...
BUT THERE'S NO CHOICE.
DAMN!!
NO...
-GASP-
I'M THE ONE WHO'S DANGER-OUS...
-GASP-
-GASP-
HURRY UP... COME AND GET ME!!

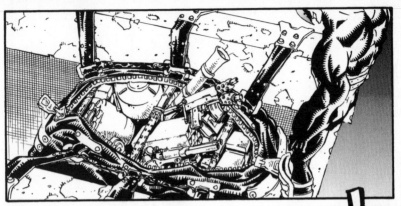

I'M GONNA **SMASH YOU** INTO TINY PIECES...

...VASH THE STAMP-EDE!!

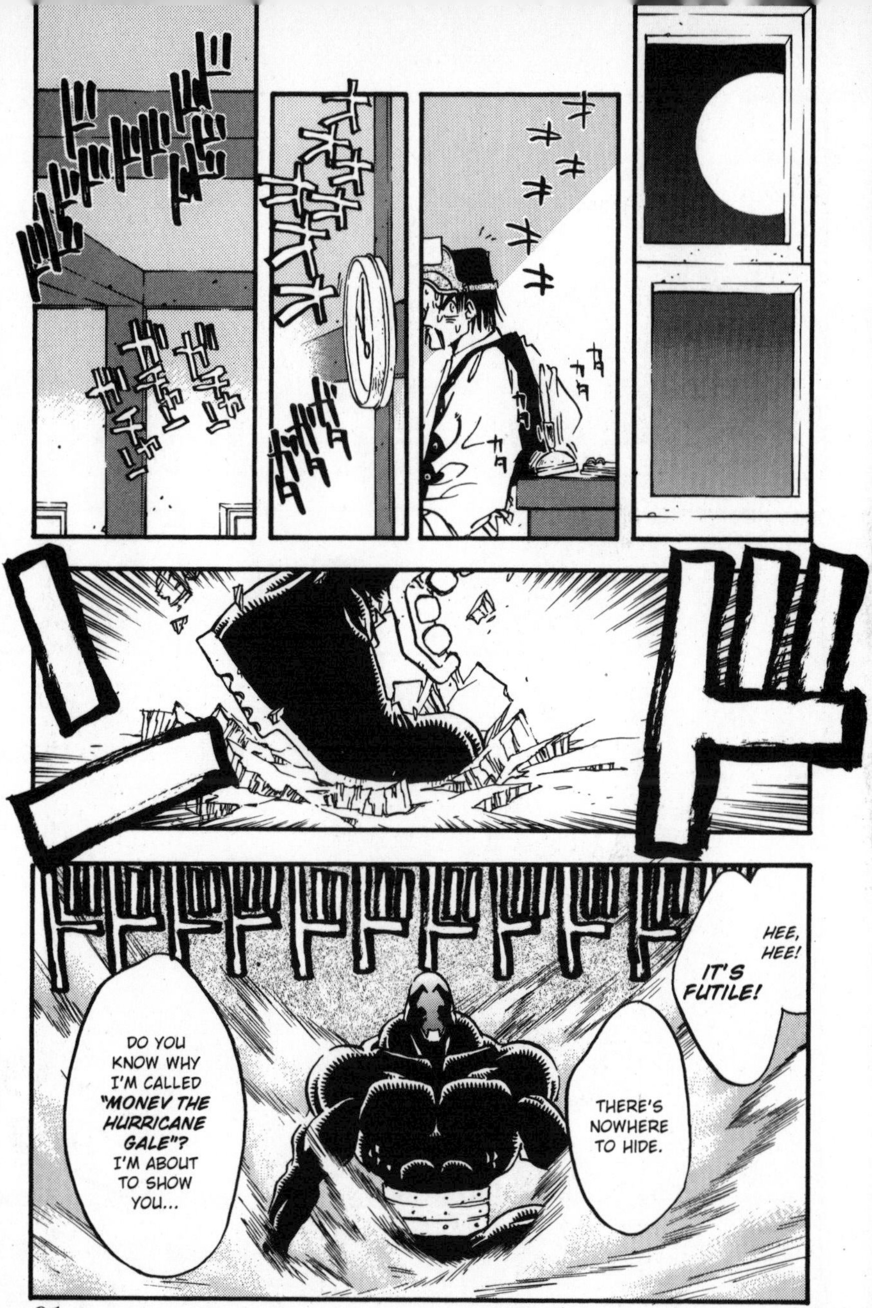
HEE, HEE! IT'S FUTILE!
THERE'S NOWHERE TO HIDE.
DO YOU KNOW WHY I'M CALLED "MONEV THE HURRICANE GALE"? I'M ABOUT TO SHOW YOU...

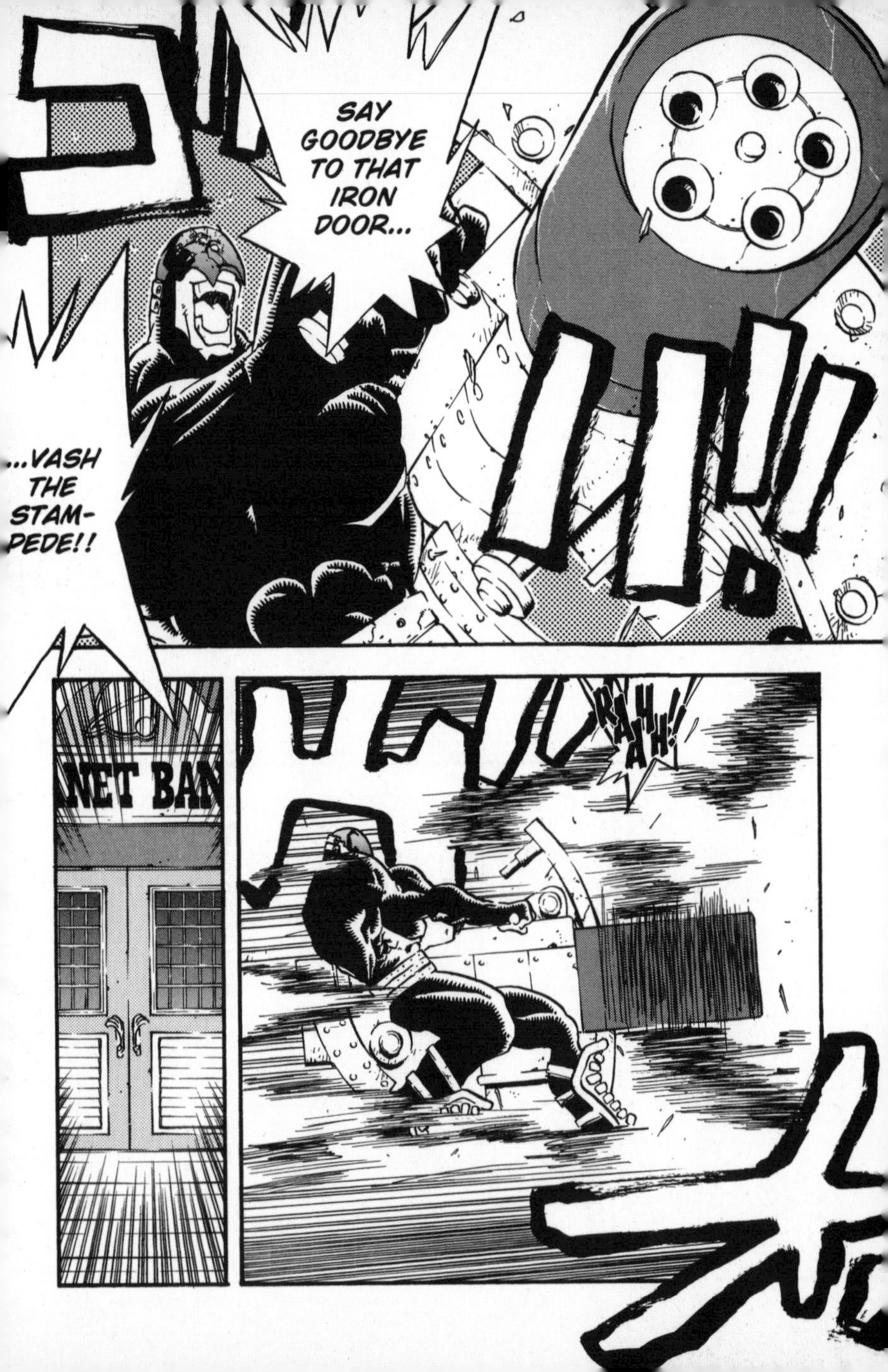
SAY GOODBYE TO THAT IRON DOOR...
...VASH THE STAMPEDE!!
NET BAN

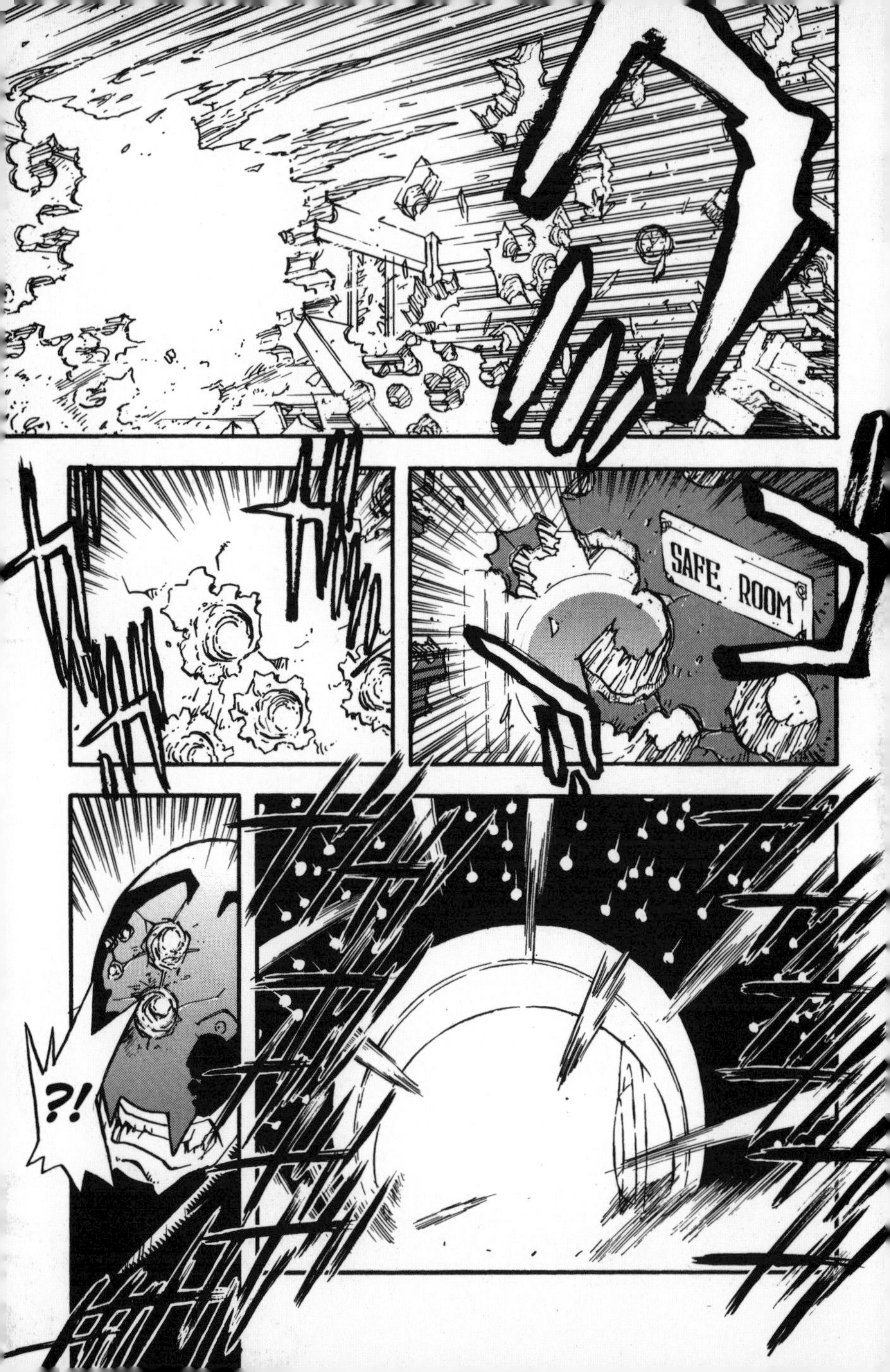
SAFE ROOM
?!

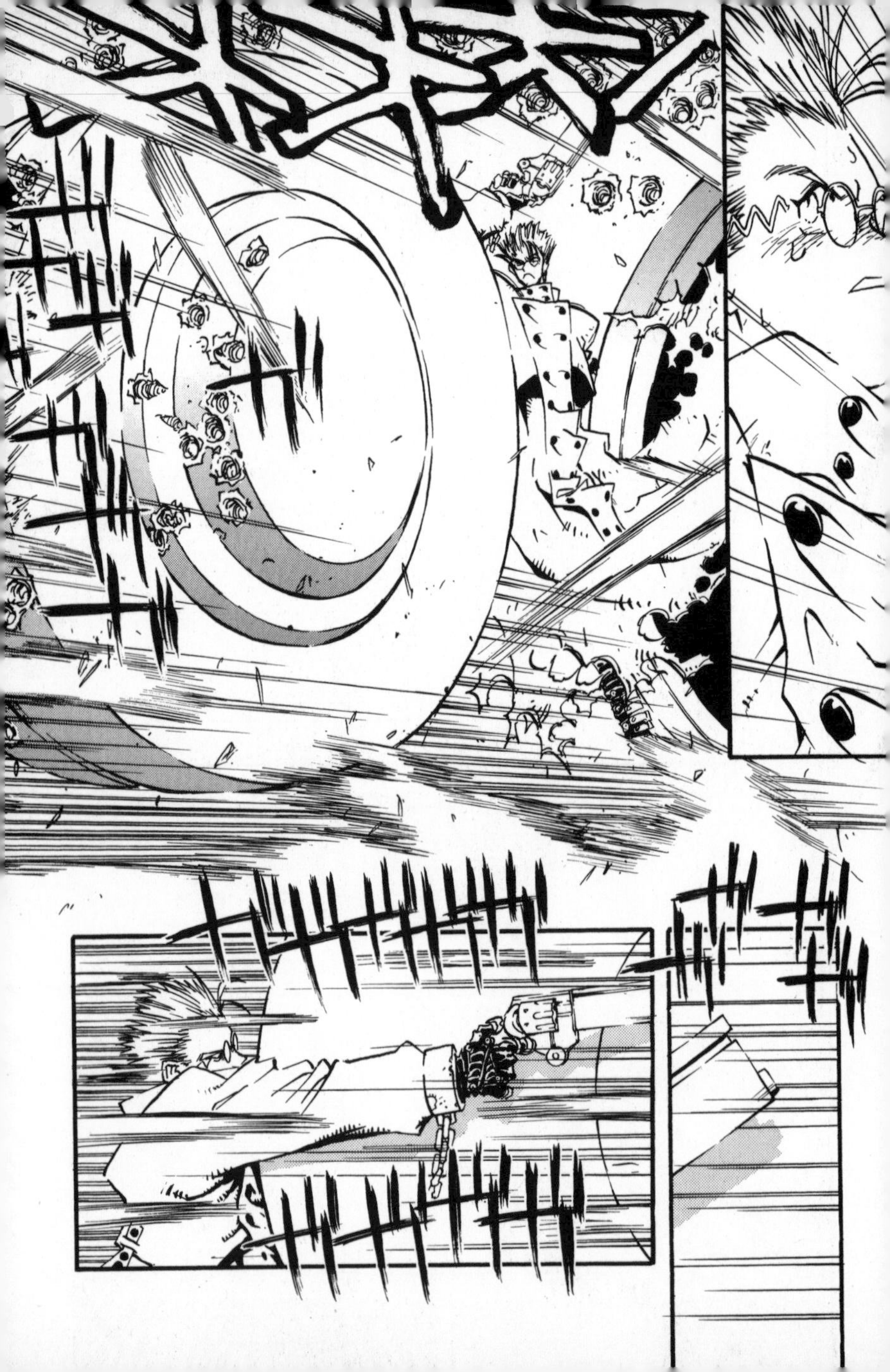

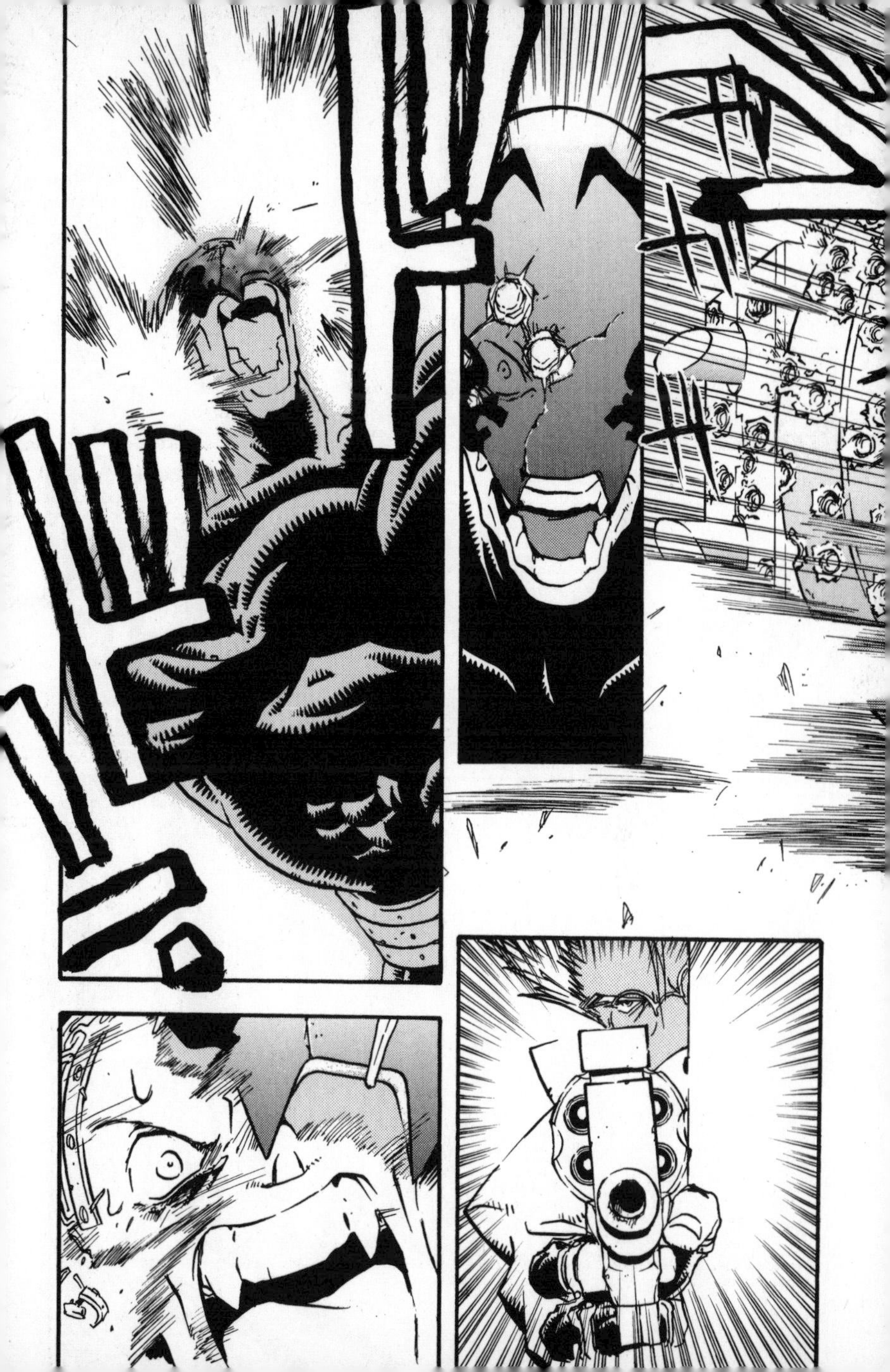

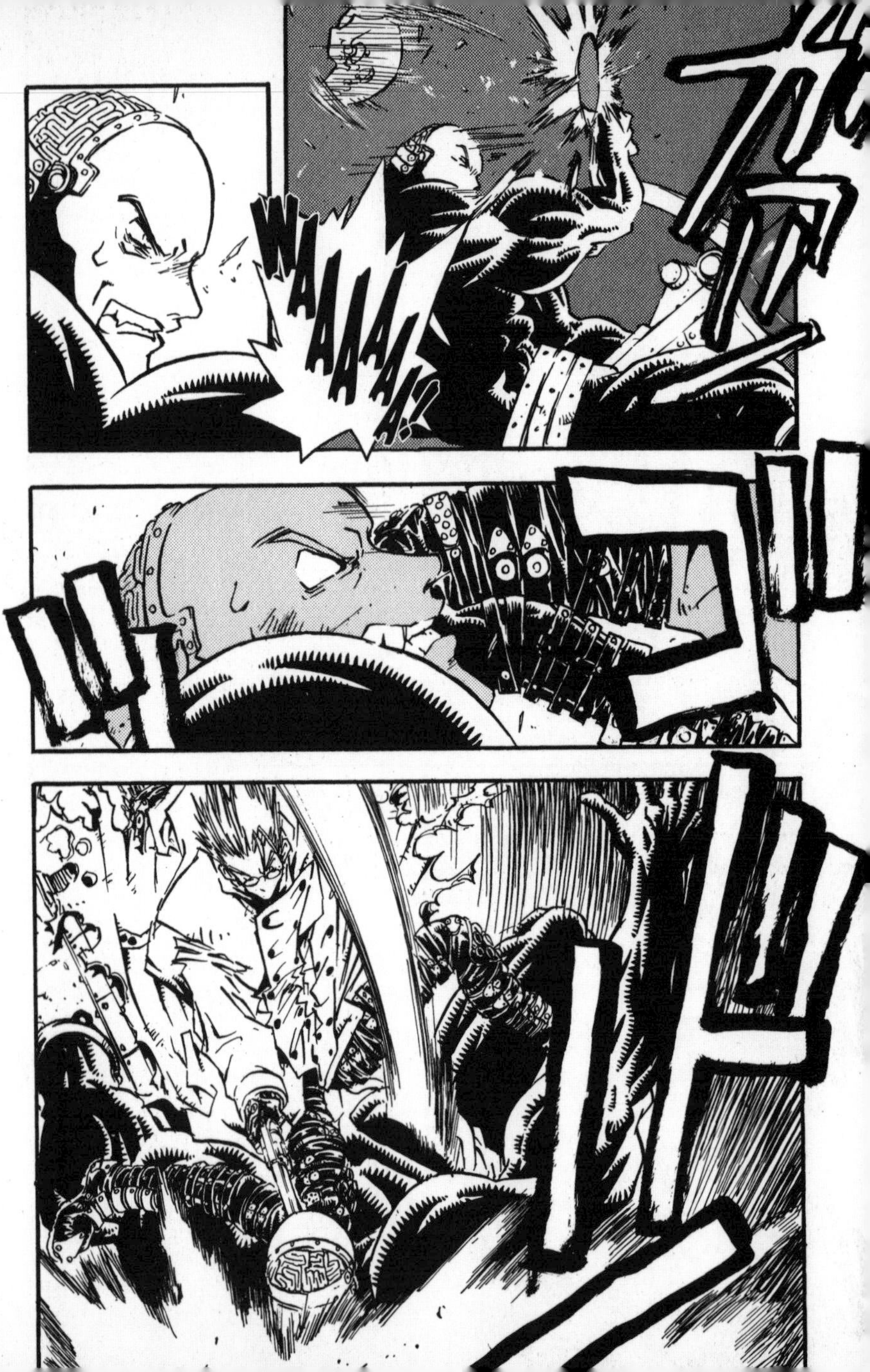
WAAAAAA!

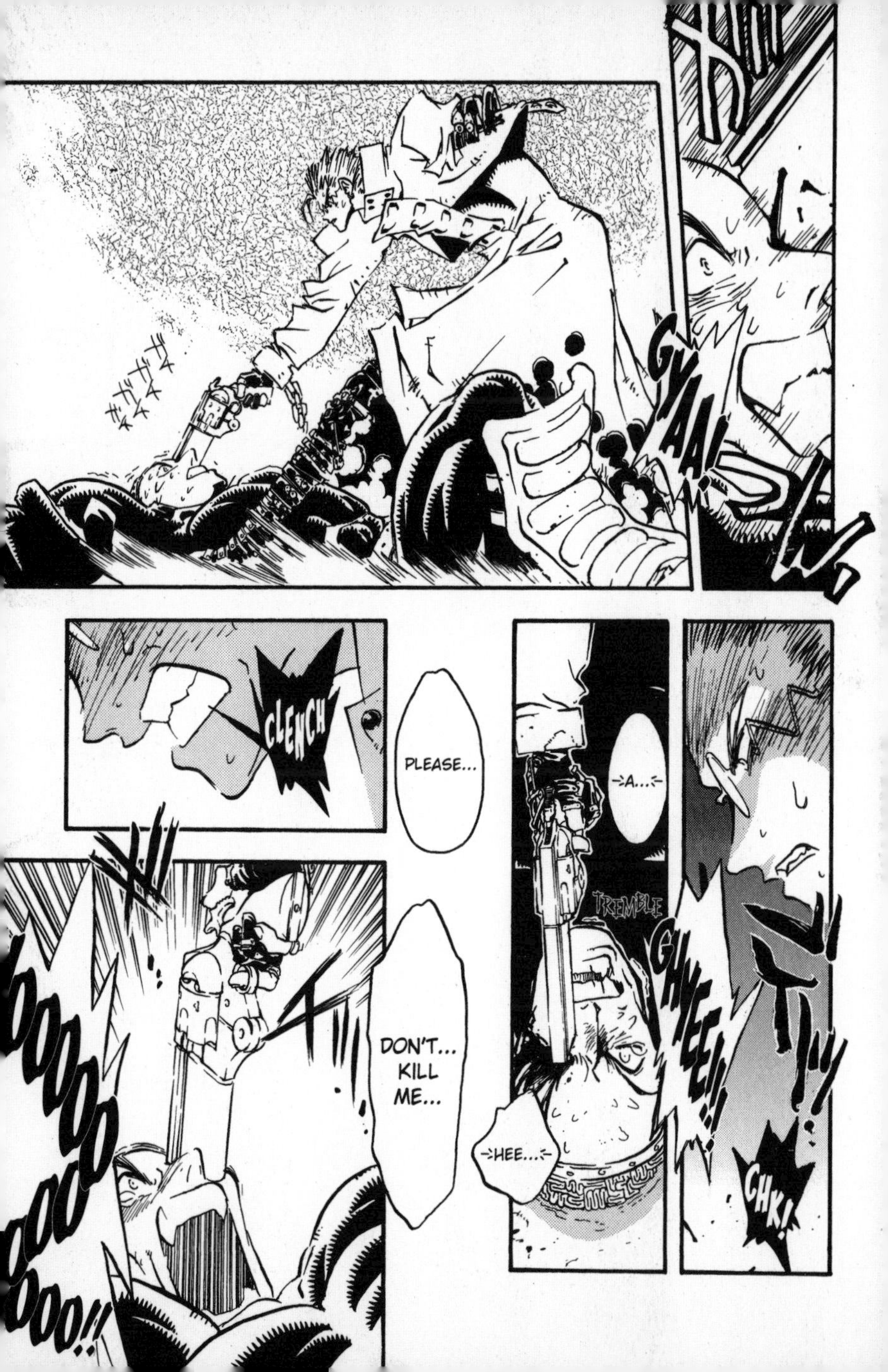
GYAA!
CHK!
—A...—
TREMBLE
GHWEE!!!
—HEE...—
CLENCH
PLEASE...
DON'T... KILL ME...

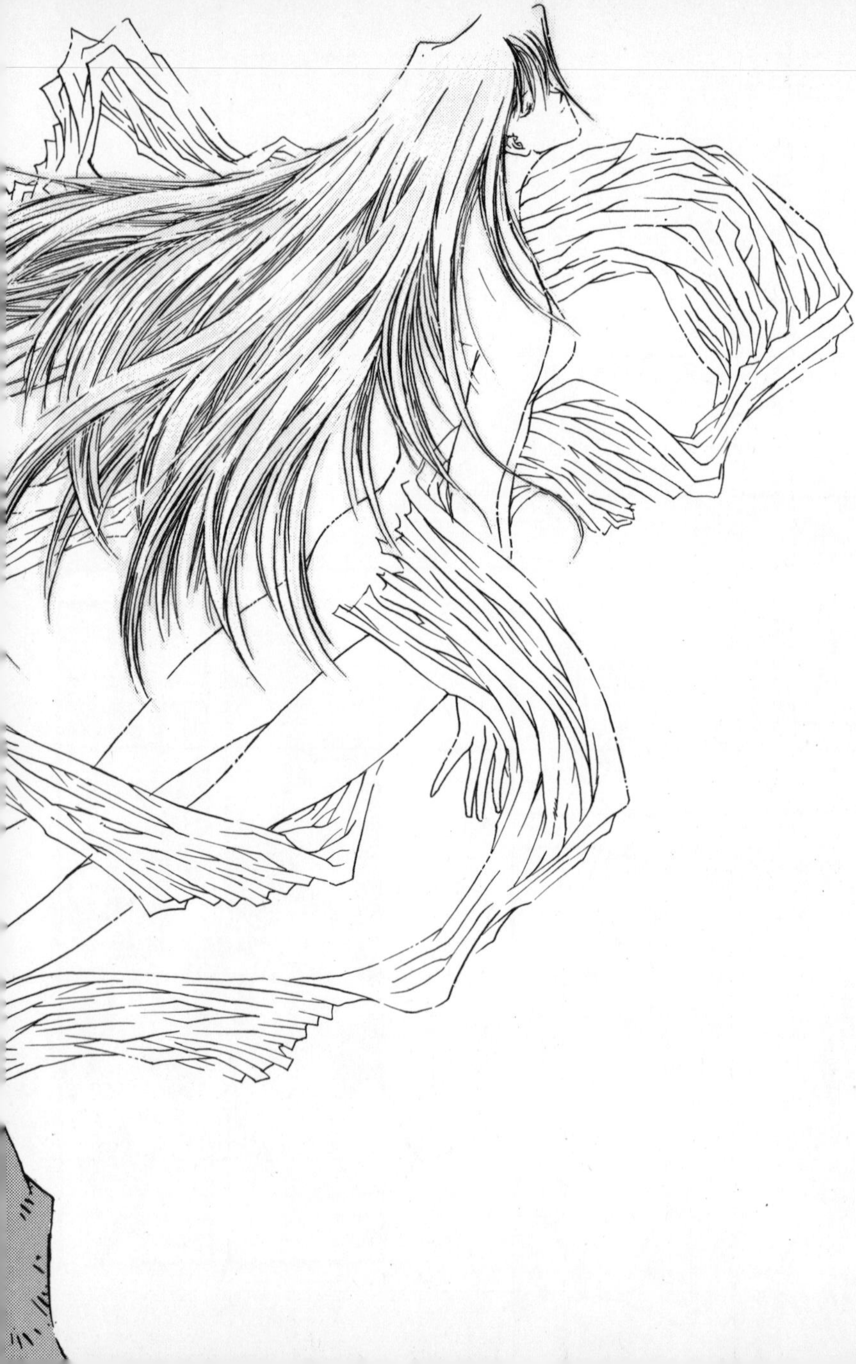

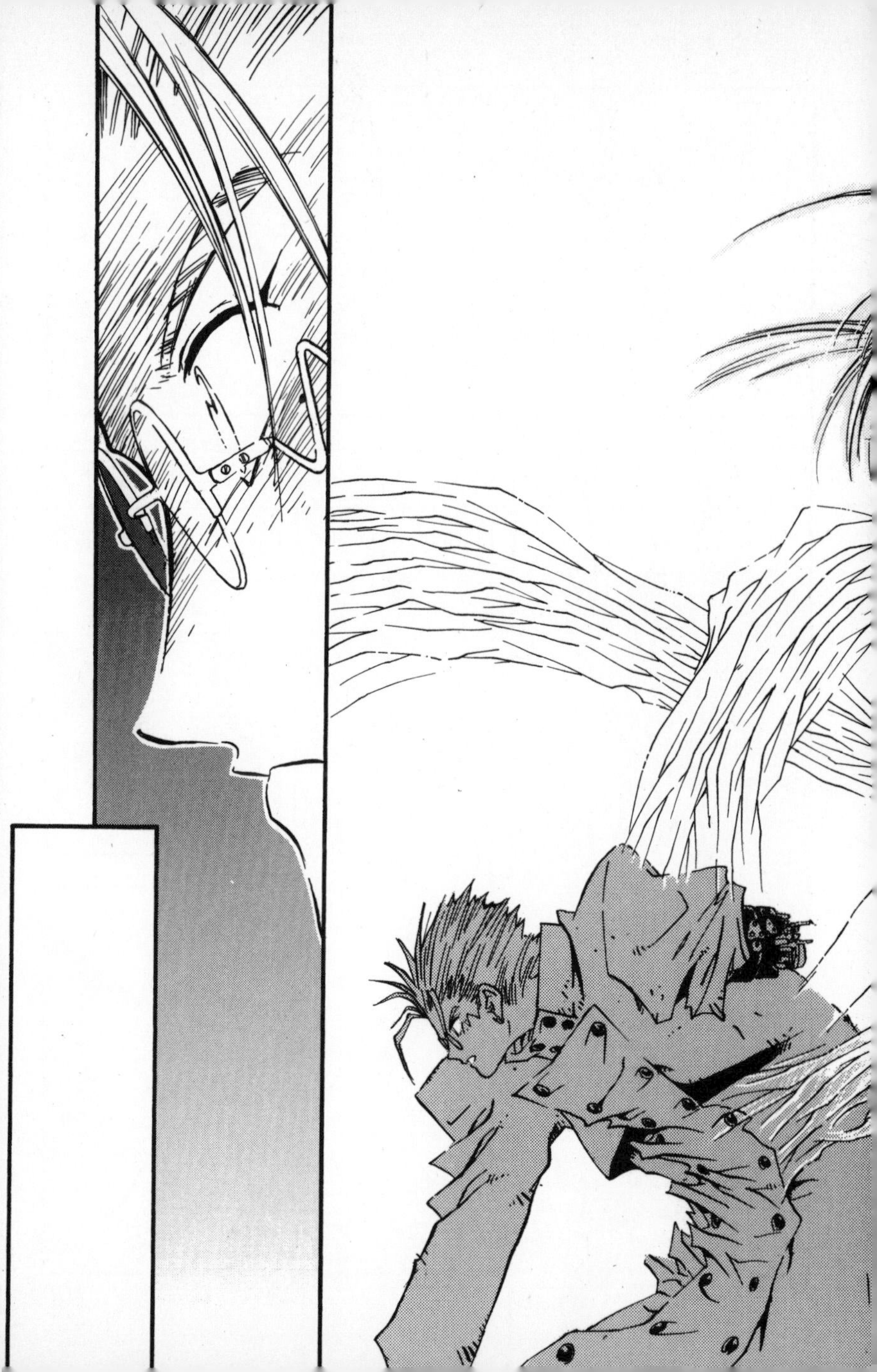

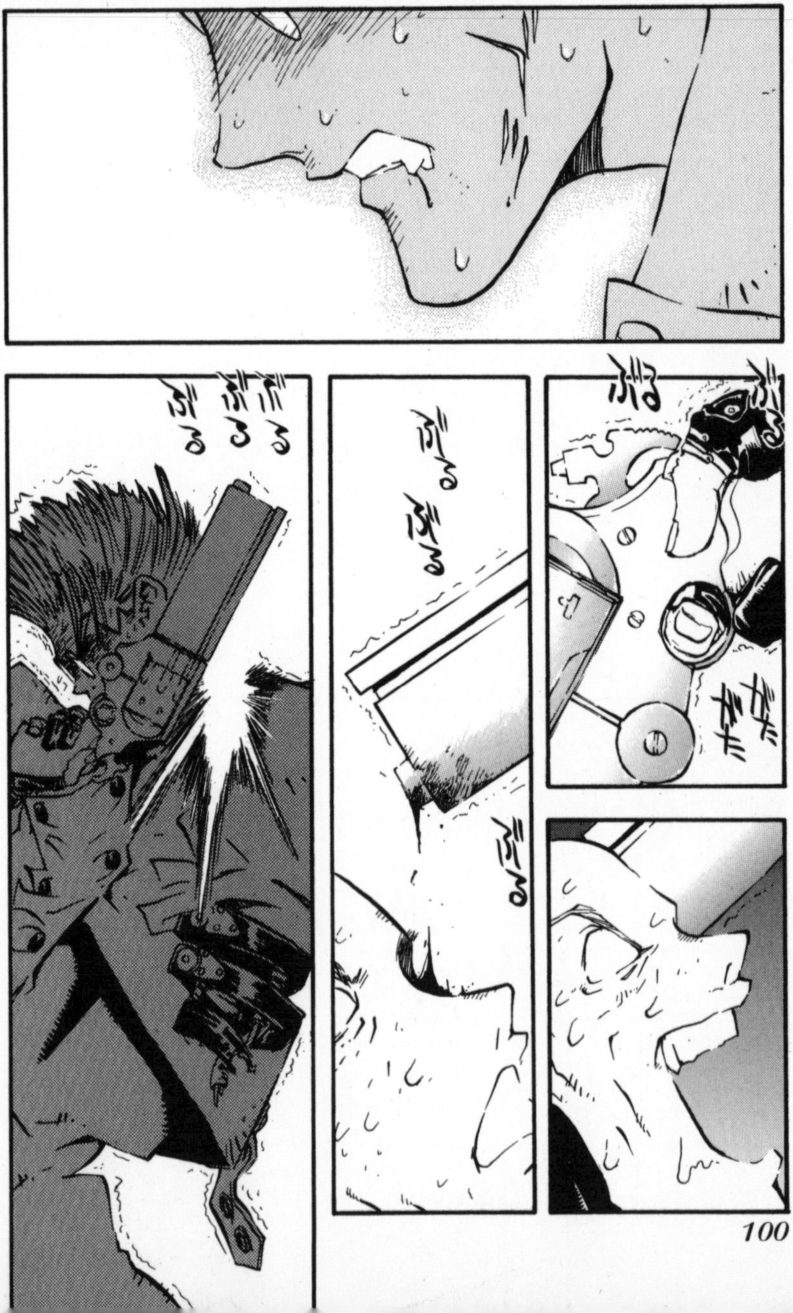
ぶる
ぶる
ぶる
ぶる
ぶるる
ぶるる
ぶるる

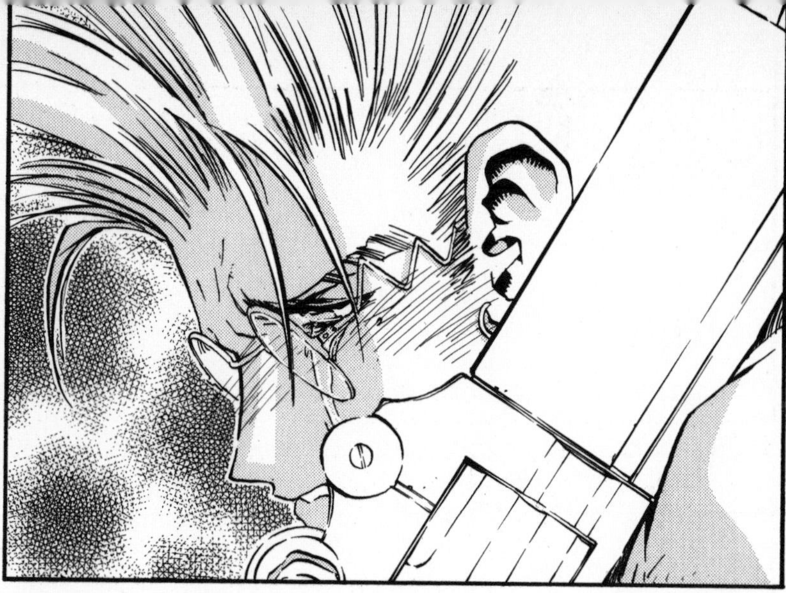

IF I SHOOT HIM NOW...

...THEN SHE'LL DIE.

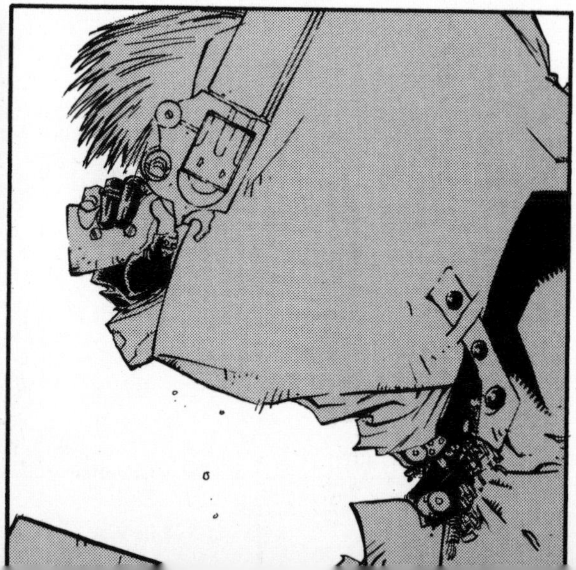

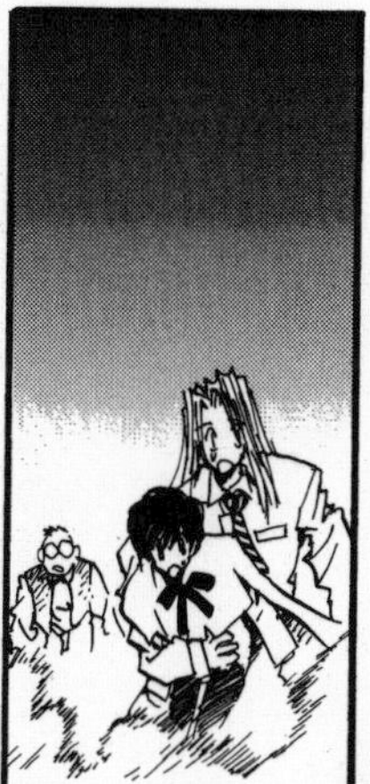

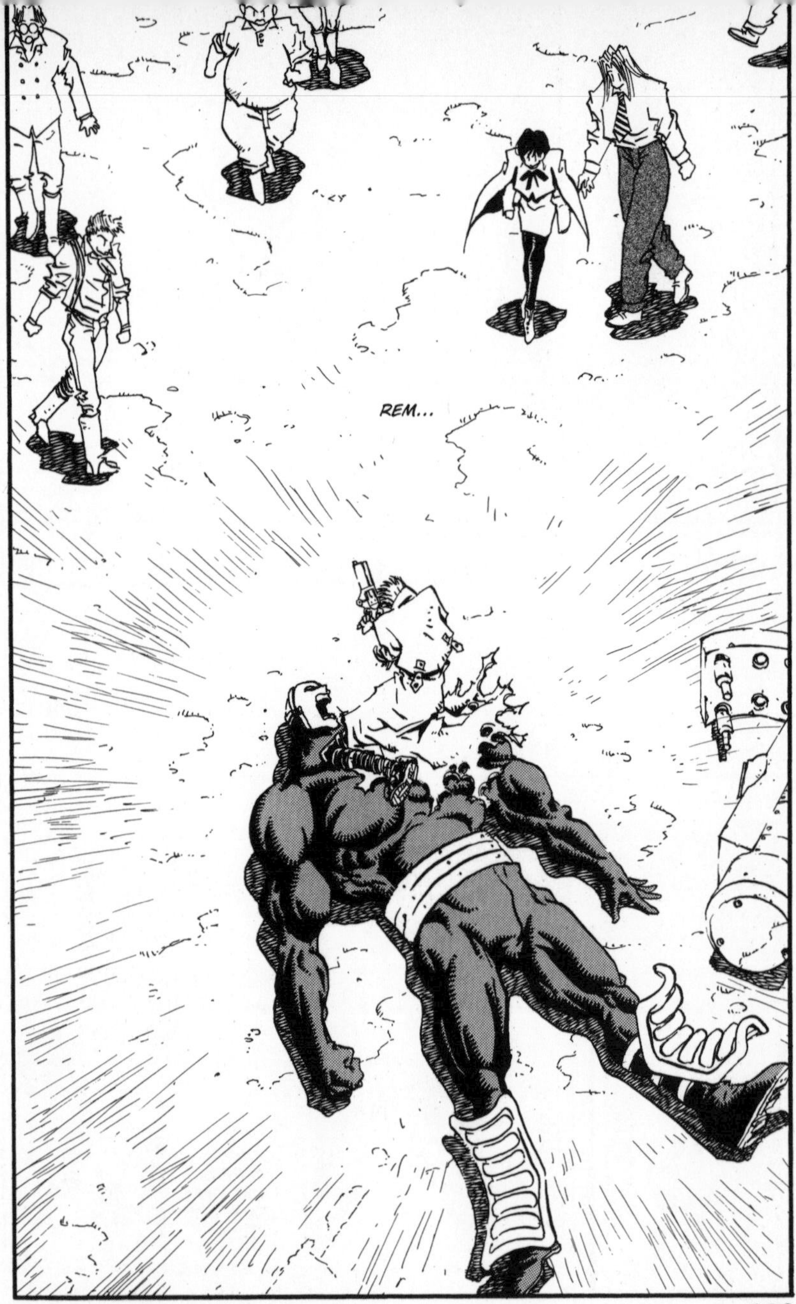
REM...

#3. FRAGILE / END

#4

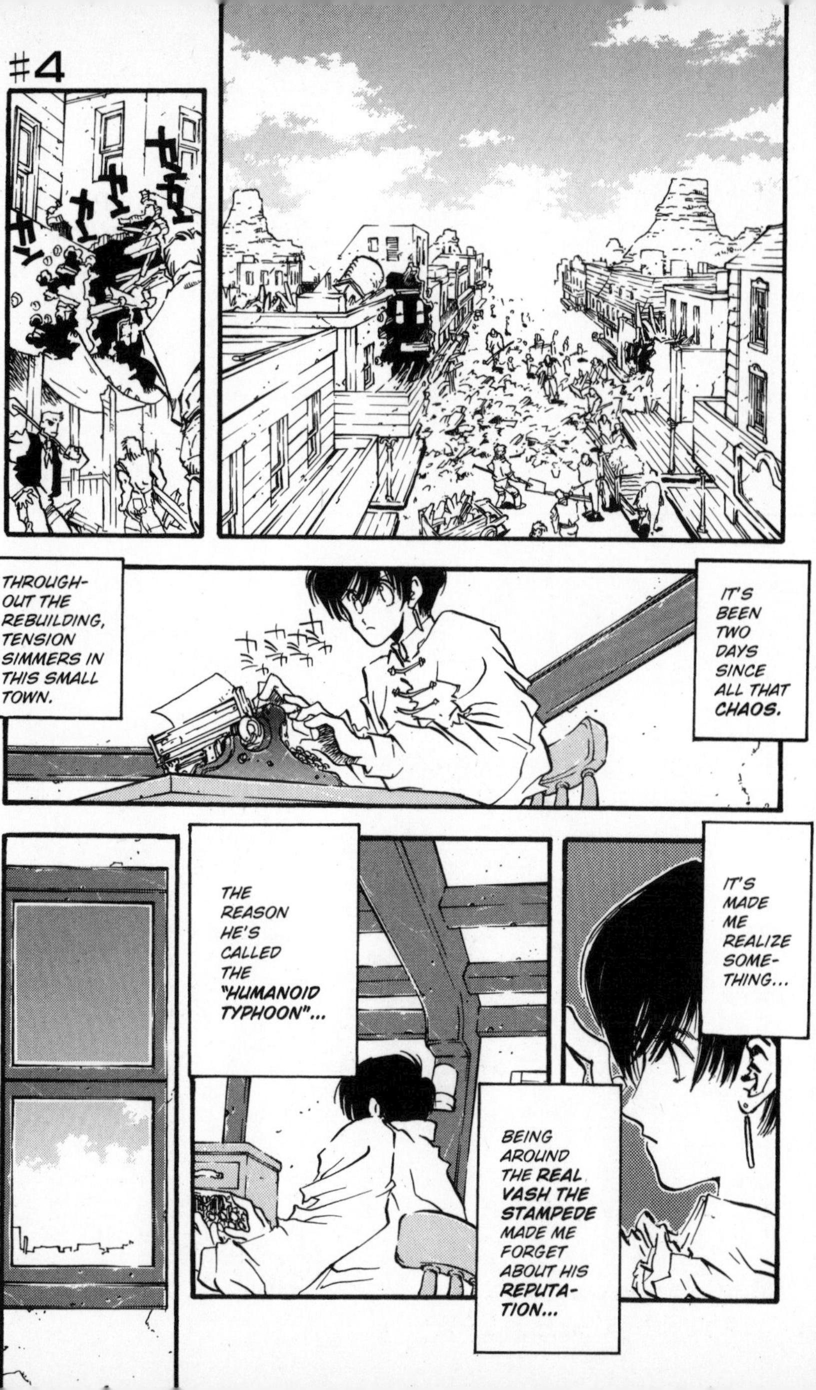

IT'S BEEN TWO DAYS SINCE ALL THAT **CHAOS.**
THROUGHOUT THE REBUILDING, TENSION SIMMERS IN THIS SMALL TOWN.
IT'S MADE ME REALIZE SOMETHING...
BEING AROUND THE **REAL VASH THE STAMPEDE** MADE ME FORGET ABOUT HIS **REPUTATION...**
THE REASON HE'S CALLED THE **"HUMANOID TYPHOON"...**

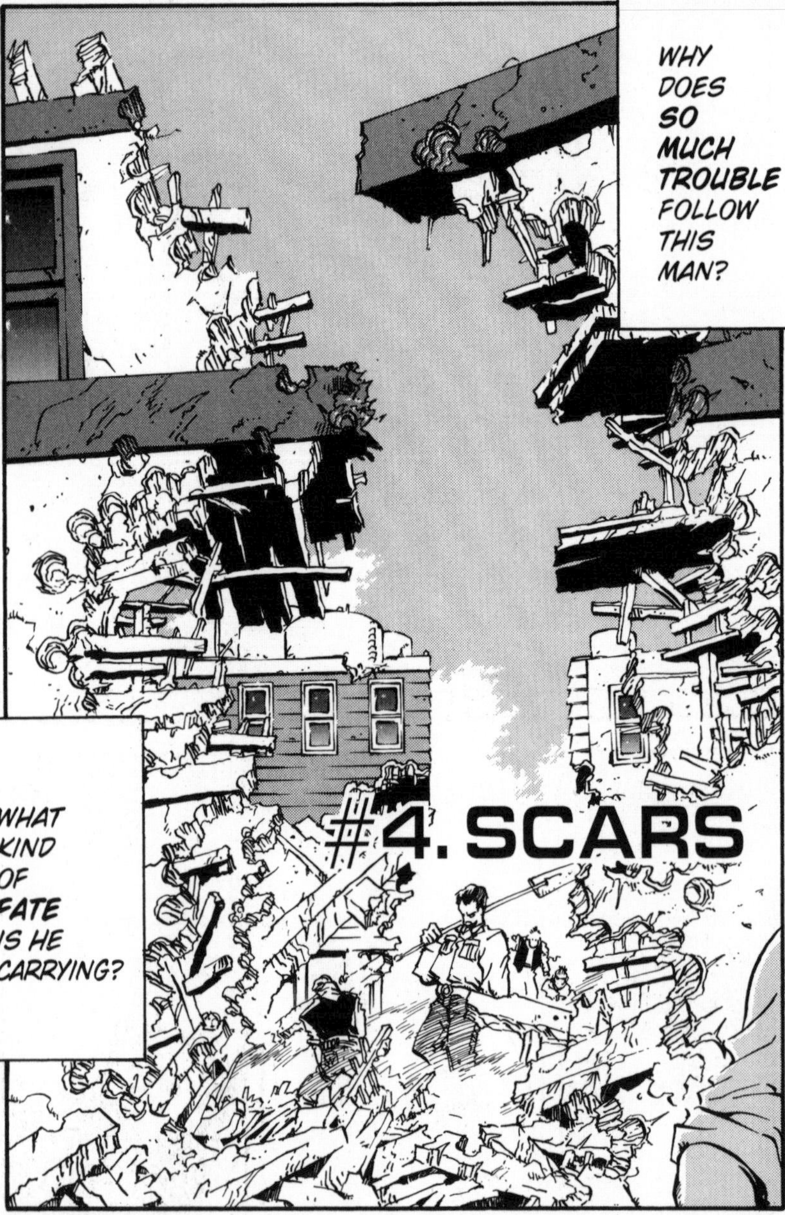
WHY DOES SO MUCH TROUBLE FOLLOW THIS MAN?
#4. SCARS
WHAT KIND OF FATE IS HE CARRYING?

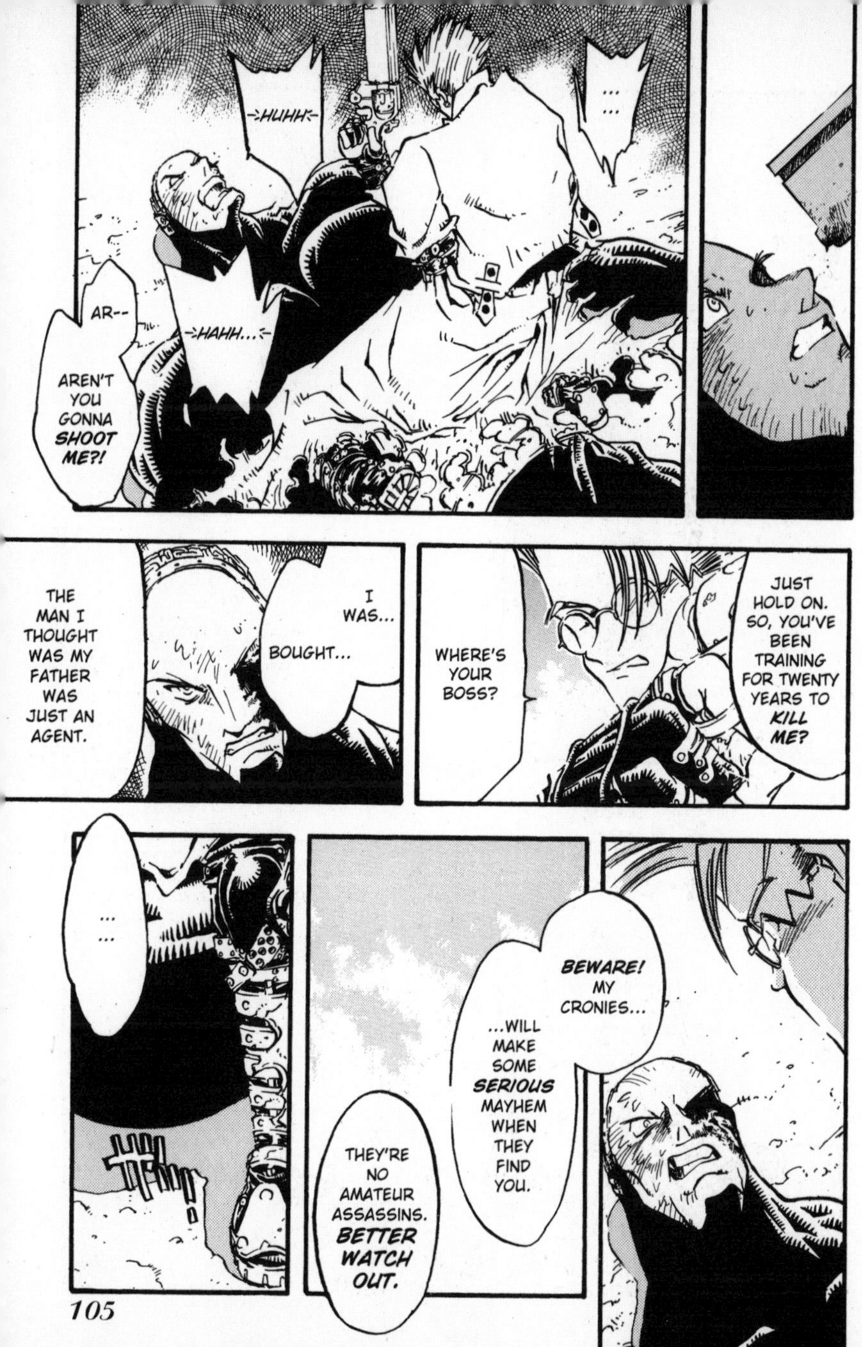
... ...
HUHH
AR--
HAHH...
AREN'T YOU GONNA SHOOT ME?!
JUST HOLD ON. SO, YOU'VE BEEN TRAINING FOR TWENTY YEARS TO KILL ME?
WHERE'S YOUR BOSS?
I WAS... BOUGHT...
THE MAN I THOUGHT WAS MY FATHER WAS JUST AN AGENT.
BEWARE! MY CRONIES...
...WILL MAKE SOME SERIOUS MAYHEM WHEN THEY FIND YOU.
THEY'RE NO AMATEUR ASSASSINS. BETTER WATCH OUT.
... ...

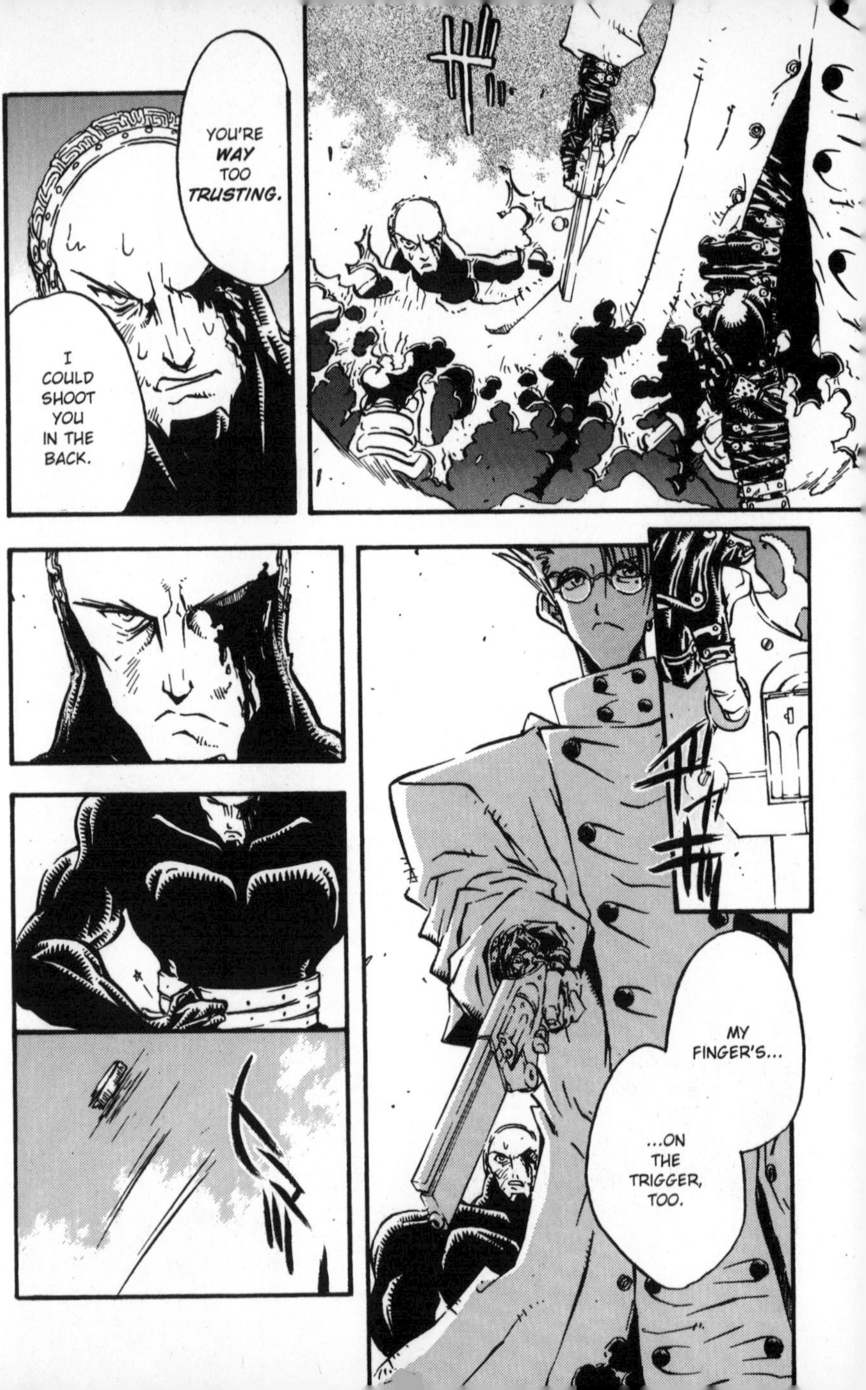
YOU'RE **WAY** TOO **TRUSTING.**
I COULD SHOOT YOU IN THE BACK.
MY FINGER'S...
...ON THE TRIGGER, TOO.

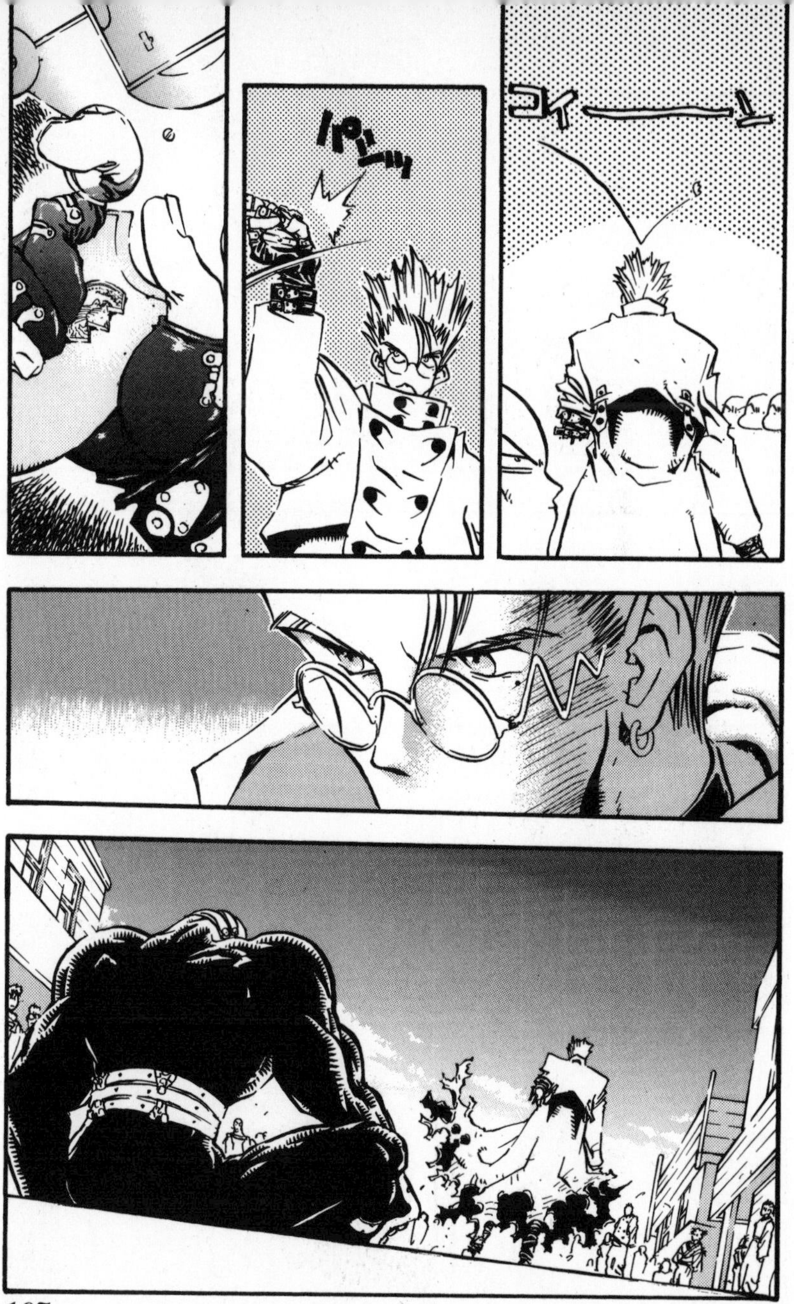

コイーーーン
パシーン

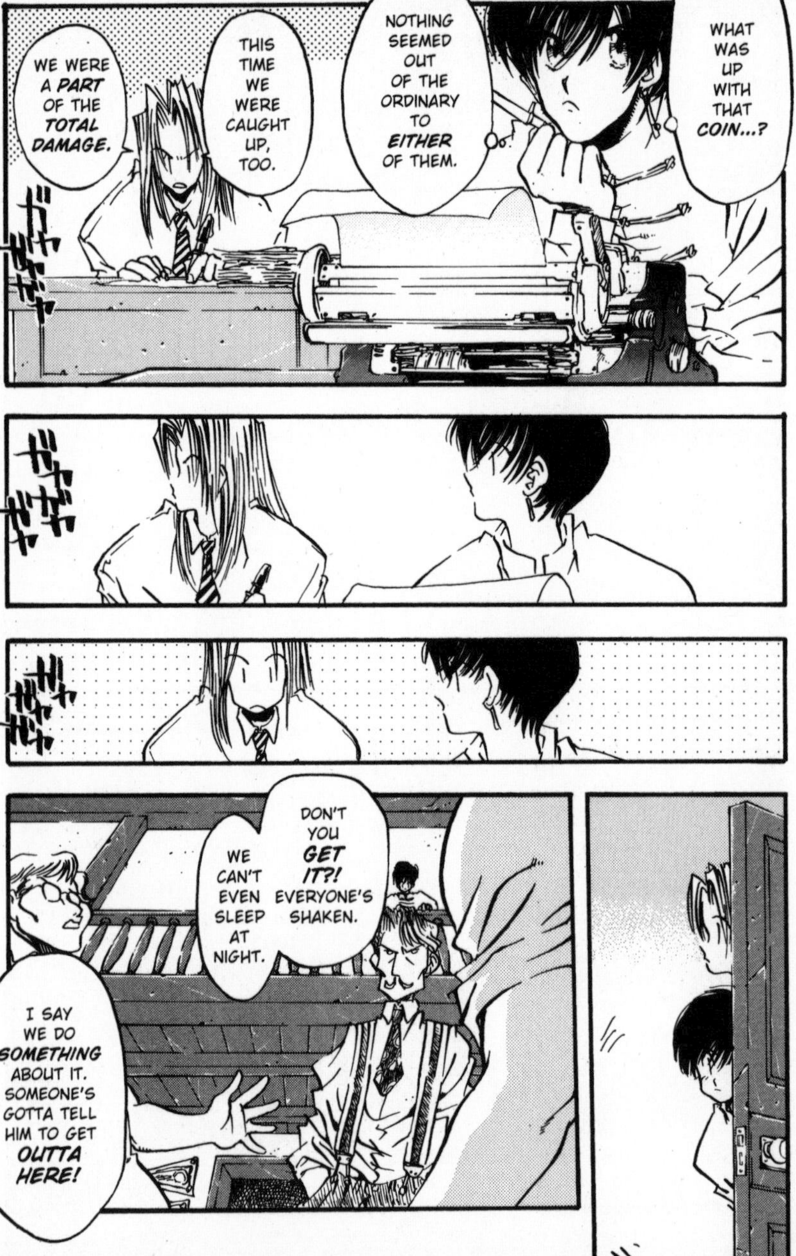
WHAT WAS UP WITH THAT COIN...?
NOTHING SEEMED OUT OF THE ORDINARY TO EITHER OF THEM.
THIS TIME WE WERE CAUGHT UP, TOO.
WE WERE A PART OF THE TOTAL DAMAGE.
DON'T YOU GET IT?! EVERYONE'S SHAKEN.
WE CAN'T EVEN SLEEP AT NIGHT.
I SAY WE DO SOMETHING ABOUT IT. SOMEONE'S GOTTA TELL HIM TO GET OUTTA HERE!

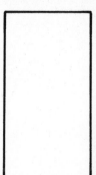

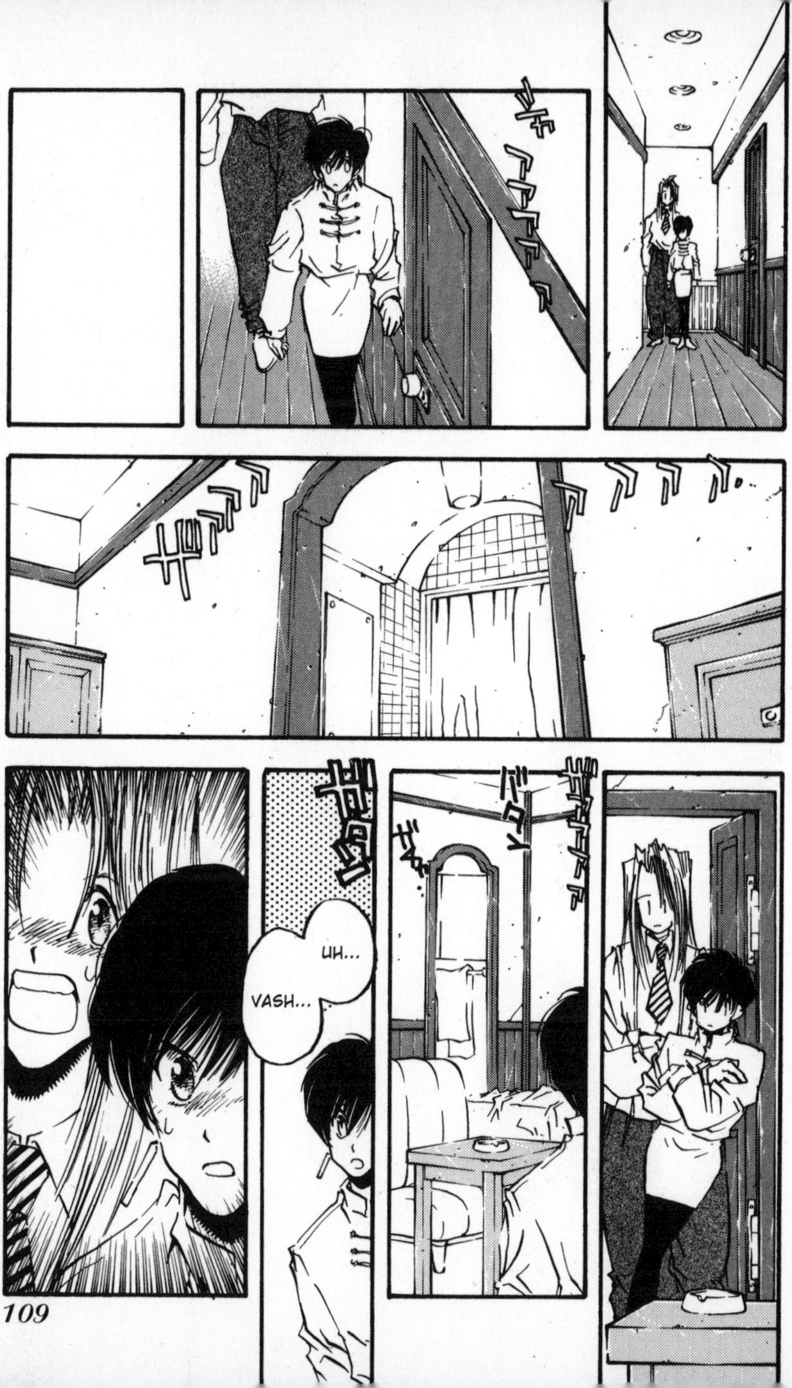
UH... VASH...

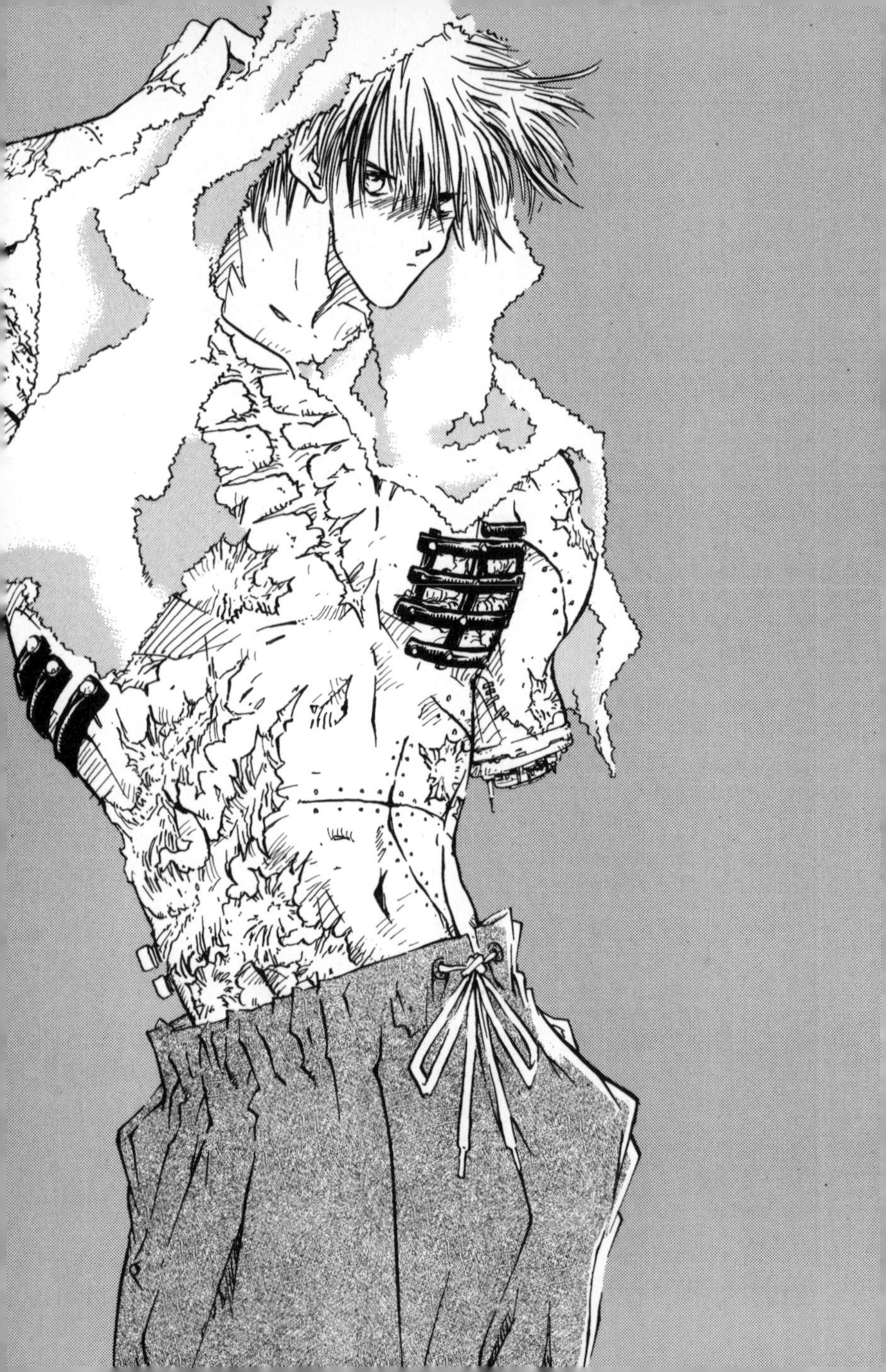

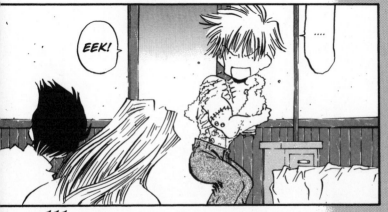

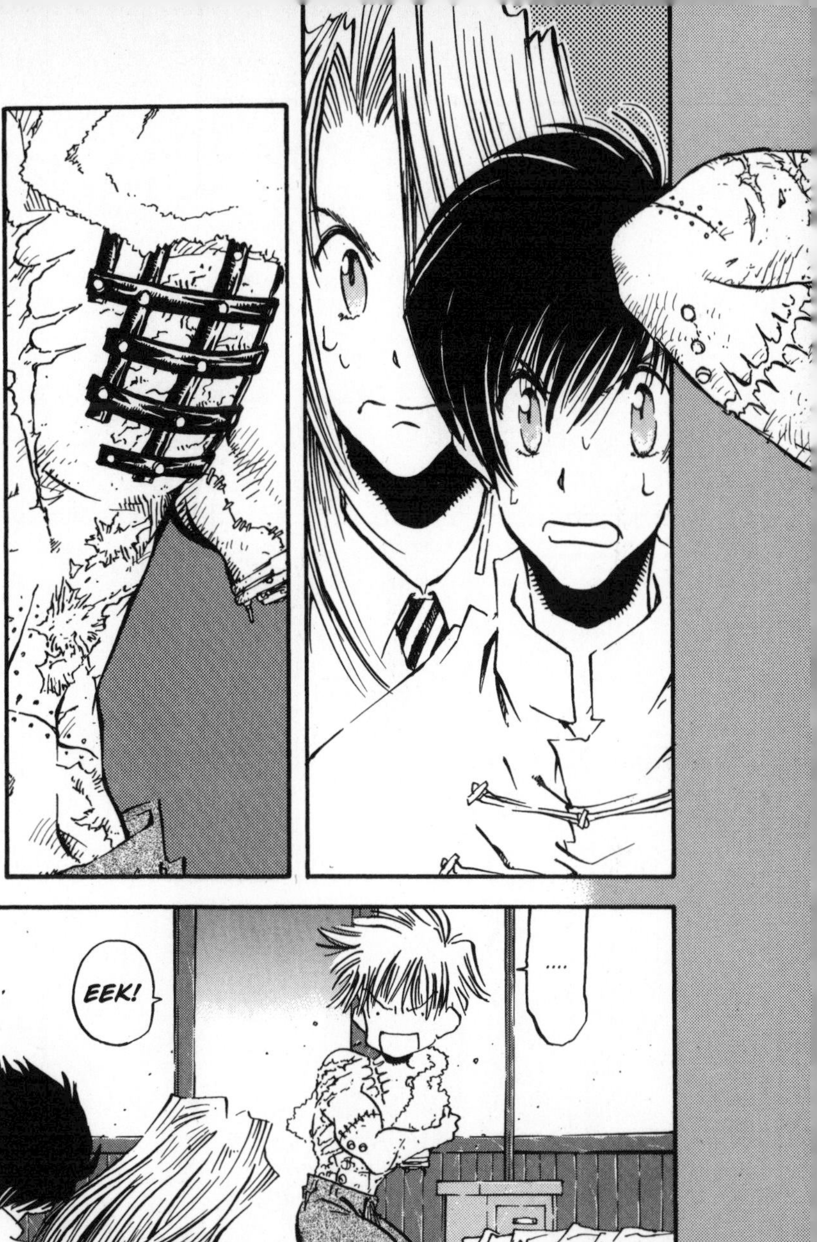
....
EEK!

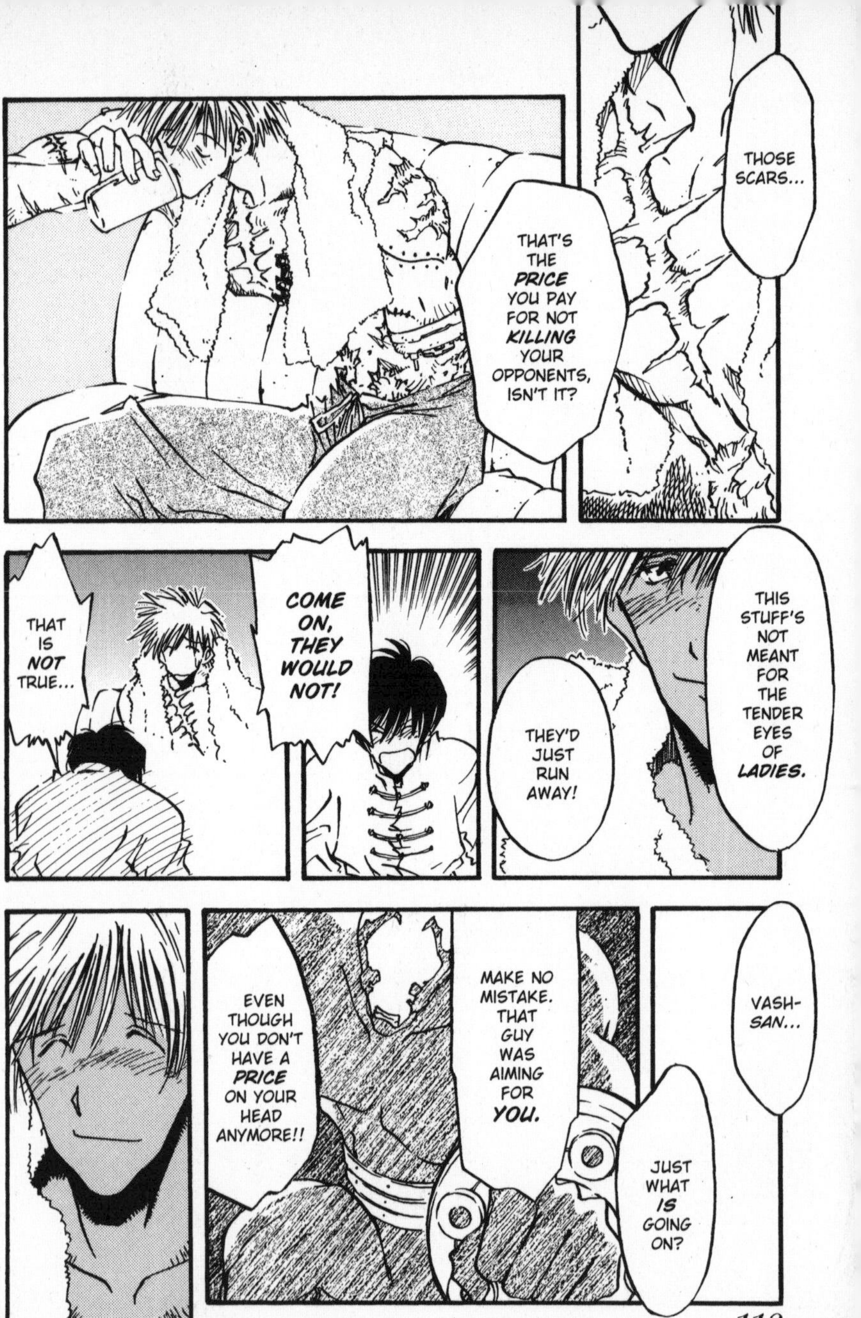
THOSE SCARS...
THAT'S THE PRICE YOU PAY FOR NOT KILLING YOUR OPPONENTS, ISN'T IT?
THIS STUFF'S NOT MEANT FOR THE TENDER EYES OF LADIES.
THEY'D JUST RUN AWAY!
COME ON, THEY WOULD NOT!
THAT IS NOT TRUE...
VASH-SAN...
JUST WHAT IS GOING ON?
MAKE NO MISTAKE. THAT GUY WAS AIMING FOR YOU.
EVEN THOUGH YOU DON'T HAVE A PRICE ON YOUR HEAD ANYMORE!!

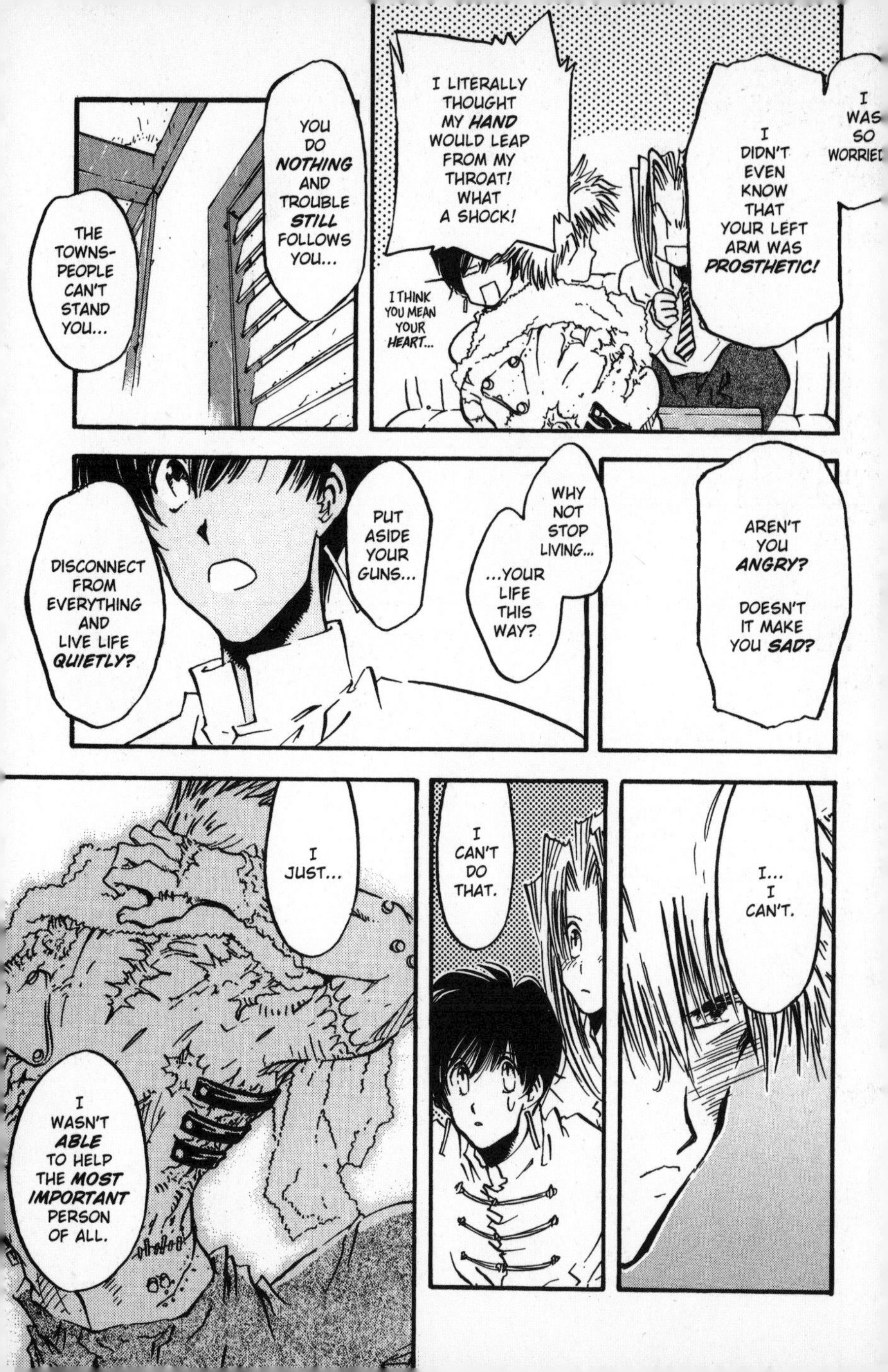

I WAS SO WORRIED
I DIDN'T EVEN KNOW THAT YOUR LEFT ARM WAS ***PROSTHETIC!***
I LITERALLY THOUGHT ***MY HAND*** WOULD LEAP FROM MY THROAT! WHAT A SHOCK!
I THINK YOU MEAN YOUR ***HEART...***
YOU DO ***NOTHING*** AND TROUBLE ***STILL*** FOLLOWS YOU...
THE TOWNSPEOPLE CAN'T STAND YOU...
AREN'T YOU ***ANGRY?*** DOESN'T IT MAKE YOU ***SAD?***
WHY NOT STOP LIVING...
...YOUR LIFE THIS WAY?
PUT ASIDE YOUR GUNS...
DISCONNECT FROM EVERYTHING AND LIVE LIFE ***QUIETLY?***
I... I CAN'T.
I CAN'T DO THAT.
I JUST...
I WASN'T ***ABLE*** TO HELP THE ***MOST IMPORTANT*** PERSON OF ALL.

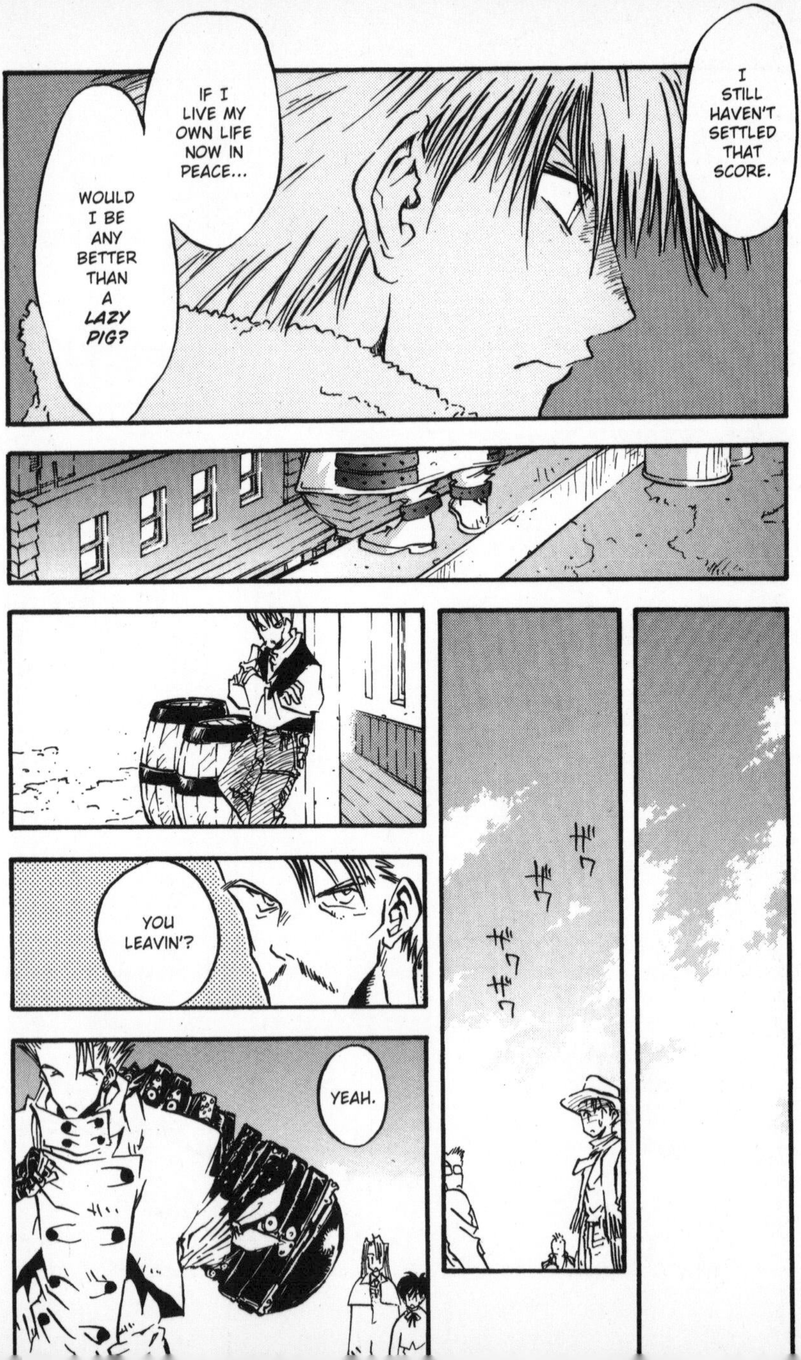
I STILL HAVEN'T SETTLED THAT SCORE.
IF I LIVE MY OWN LIFE NOW IN PEACE...
WOULD I BE ANY BETTER THAN A *LAZY PIG?*
ギワ
ギワ
ギワギワ
YOU LEAVIN'?
YEAH.

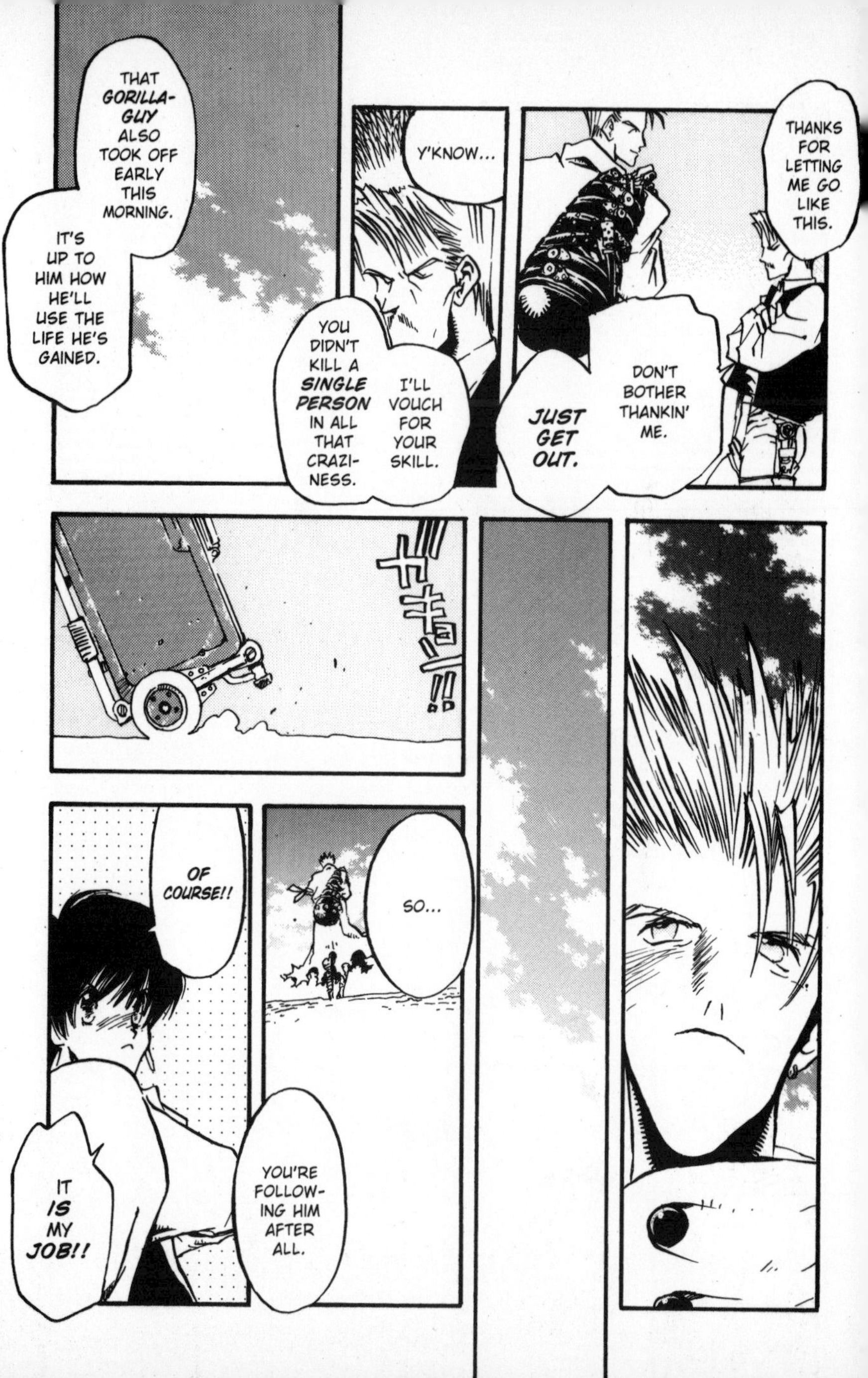
THANKS FOR LETTING ME GO LIKE THIS.
DON'T BOTHER THANKIN' ME.
JUST GET OUT.
Y'KNOW...
YOU DIDN'T KILL A SINGLE PERSON IN ALL THAT CRAZINESS.
I'LL VOUCH FOR YOUR SKILL.
THAT GORILLA-GUY ALSO TOOK OFF EARLY THIS MORNING.
IT'S UP TO HIM HOW HE'LL USE THE LIFE HE'S GAINED.
SO...
YOU'RE FOLLOWING HIM AFTER ALL.
OF COURSE!!
IT IS MY JOB!!

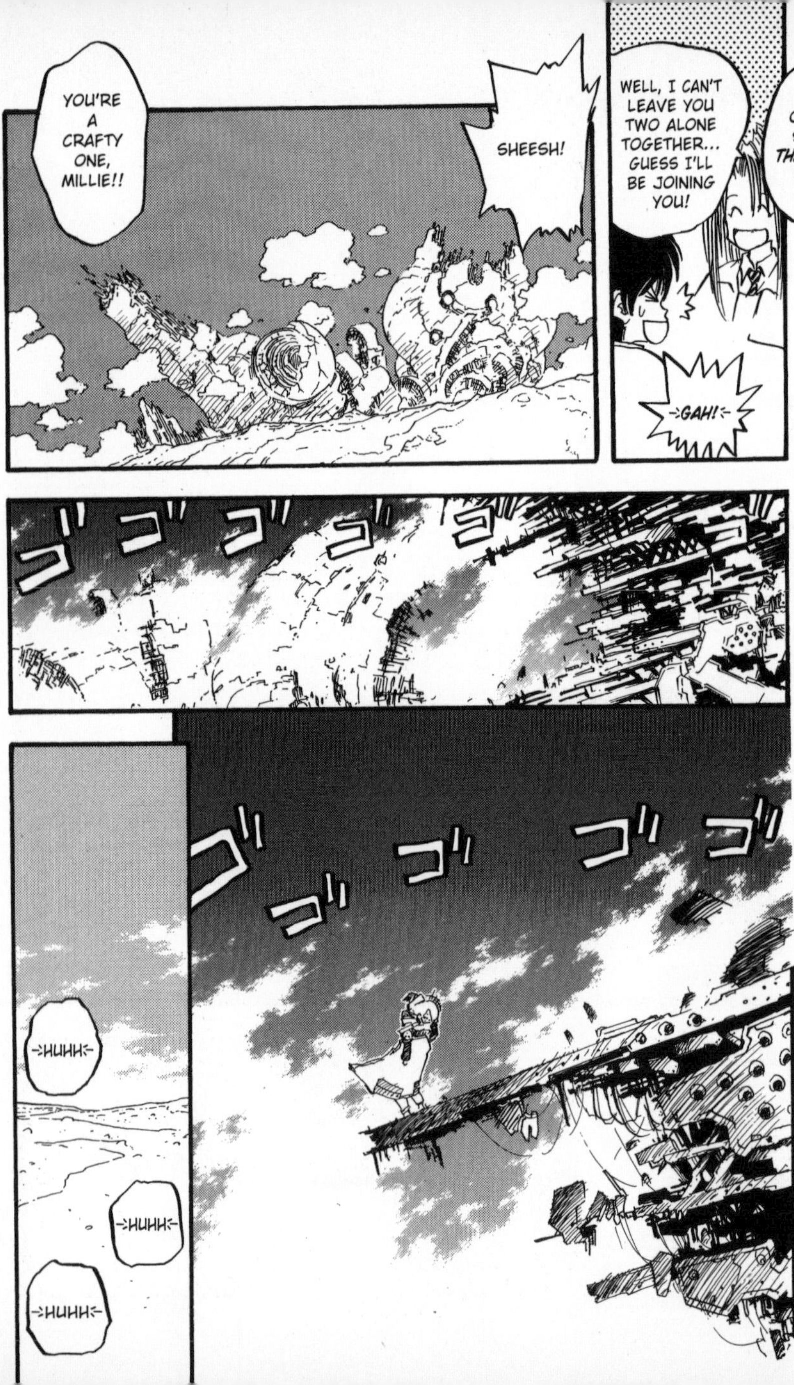
WELL, I CAN'T LEAVE YOU TWO ALONE TOGETHER... GUESS I'LL BE JOINING YOU!
OH, SO *THAT'S* IT!
GAH!
SHEESH!
YOU'RE A CRAFTY ONE, MILLIE!!
ゴゴゴゴゴ
ゴゴゴゴゴ
HUHH
HUHH
HUHH

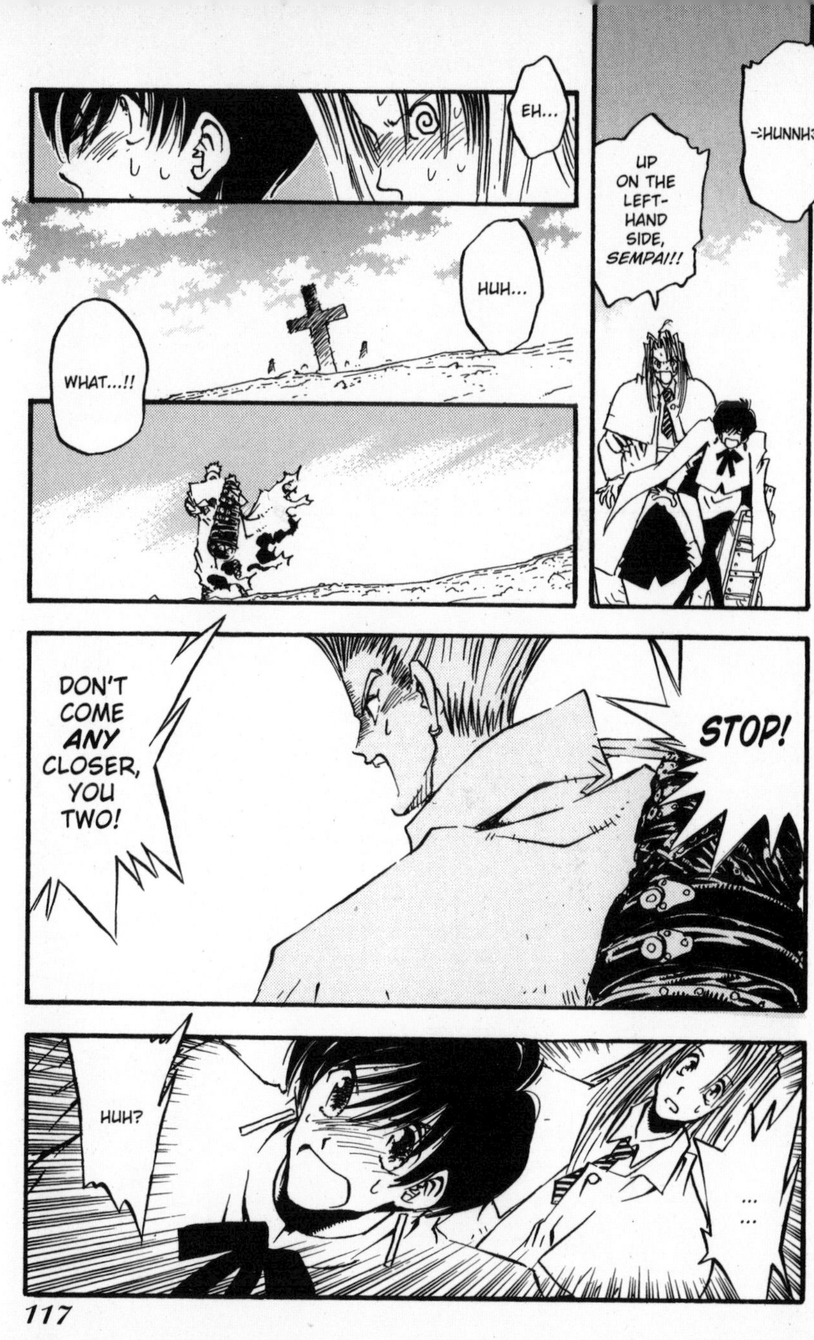

-HUNNH-
UP ON THE LEFT-HAND SIDE, SEMPAI!!
EH...
HUH...
WHAT...!!
STOP!
DON'T COME **ANY** CLOSER, YOU TWO!
... ...
HUH?

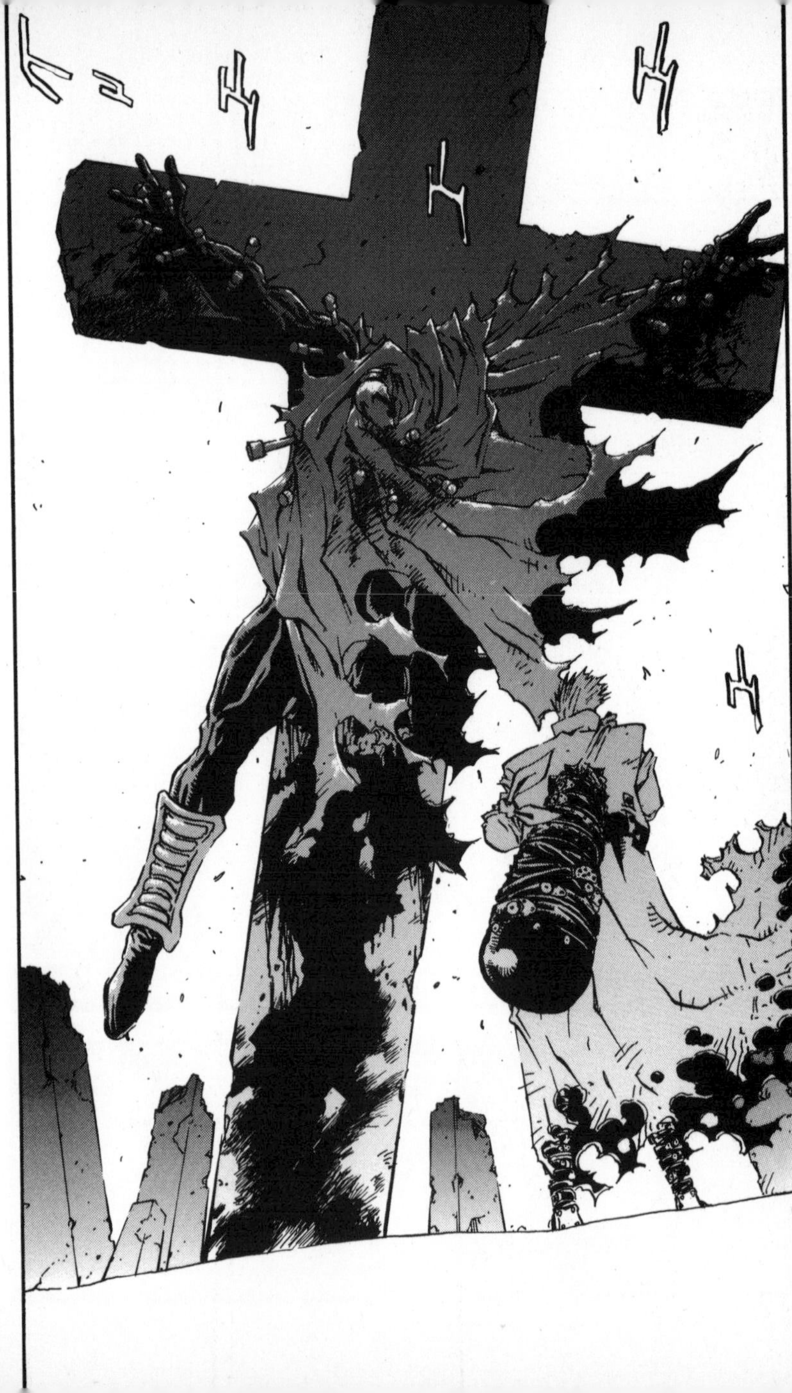
ヒュ

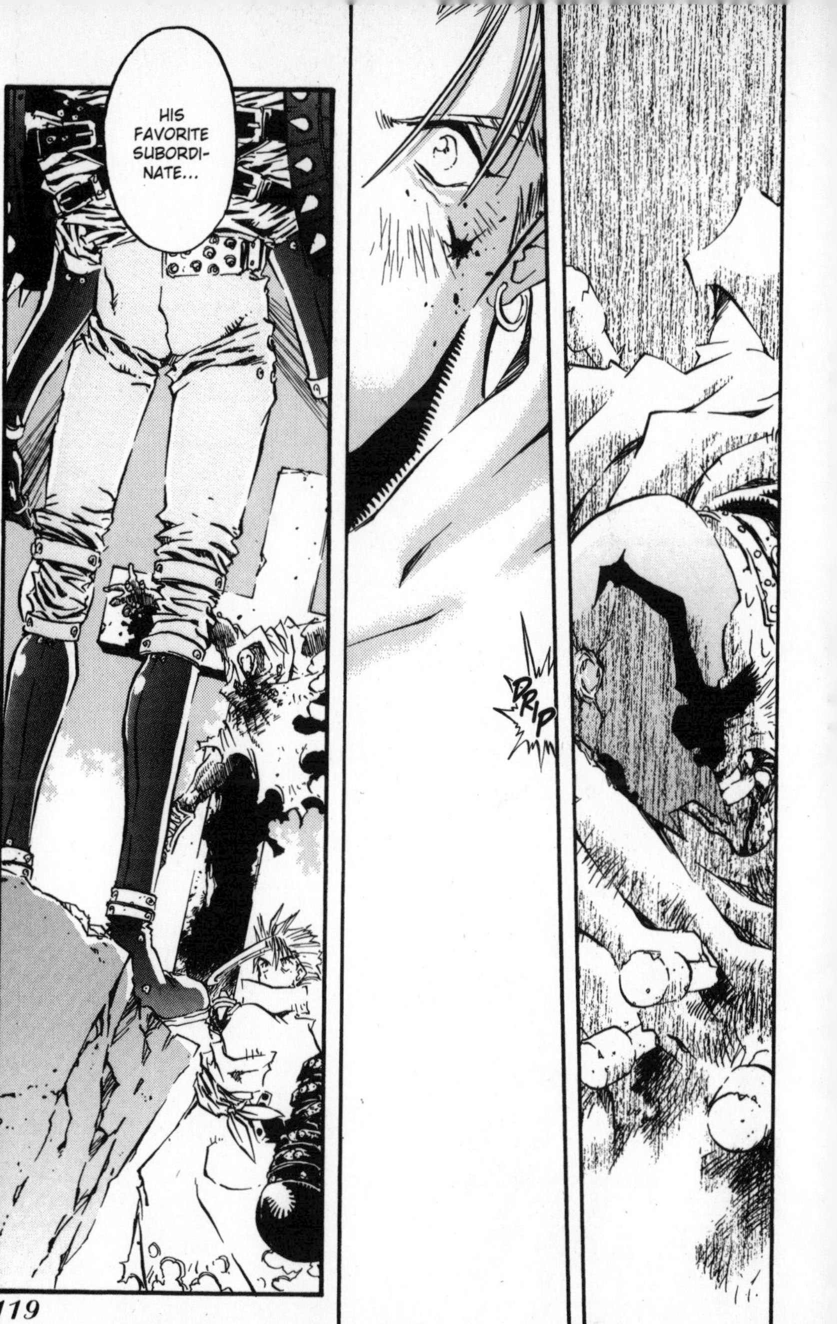
DRIP
HIS FAVORITE SUBORDINATE...

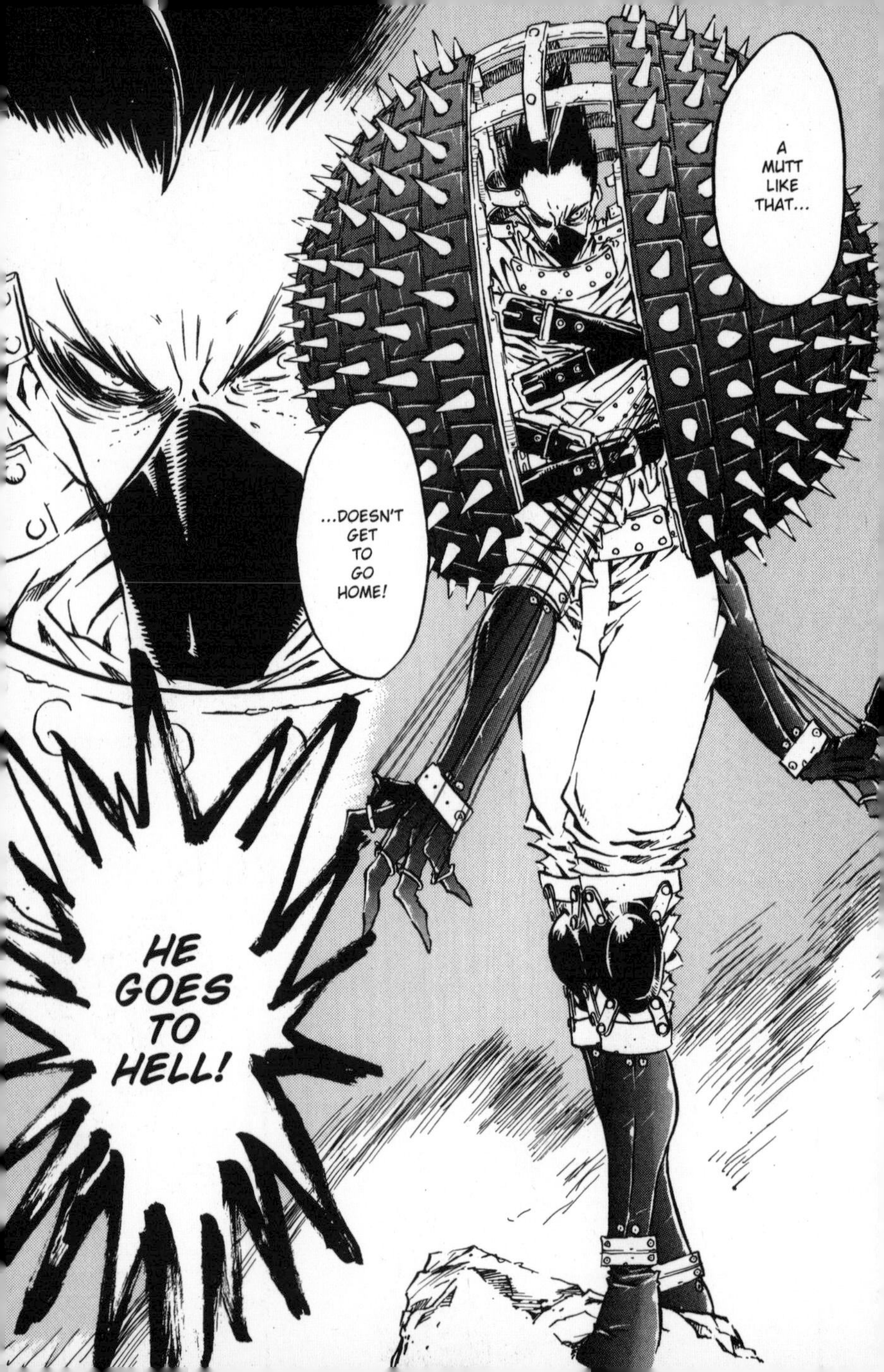
A MUTT LIKE THAT...
...DOESN'T GET TO GO HOME!
HE GOES TO HELL!

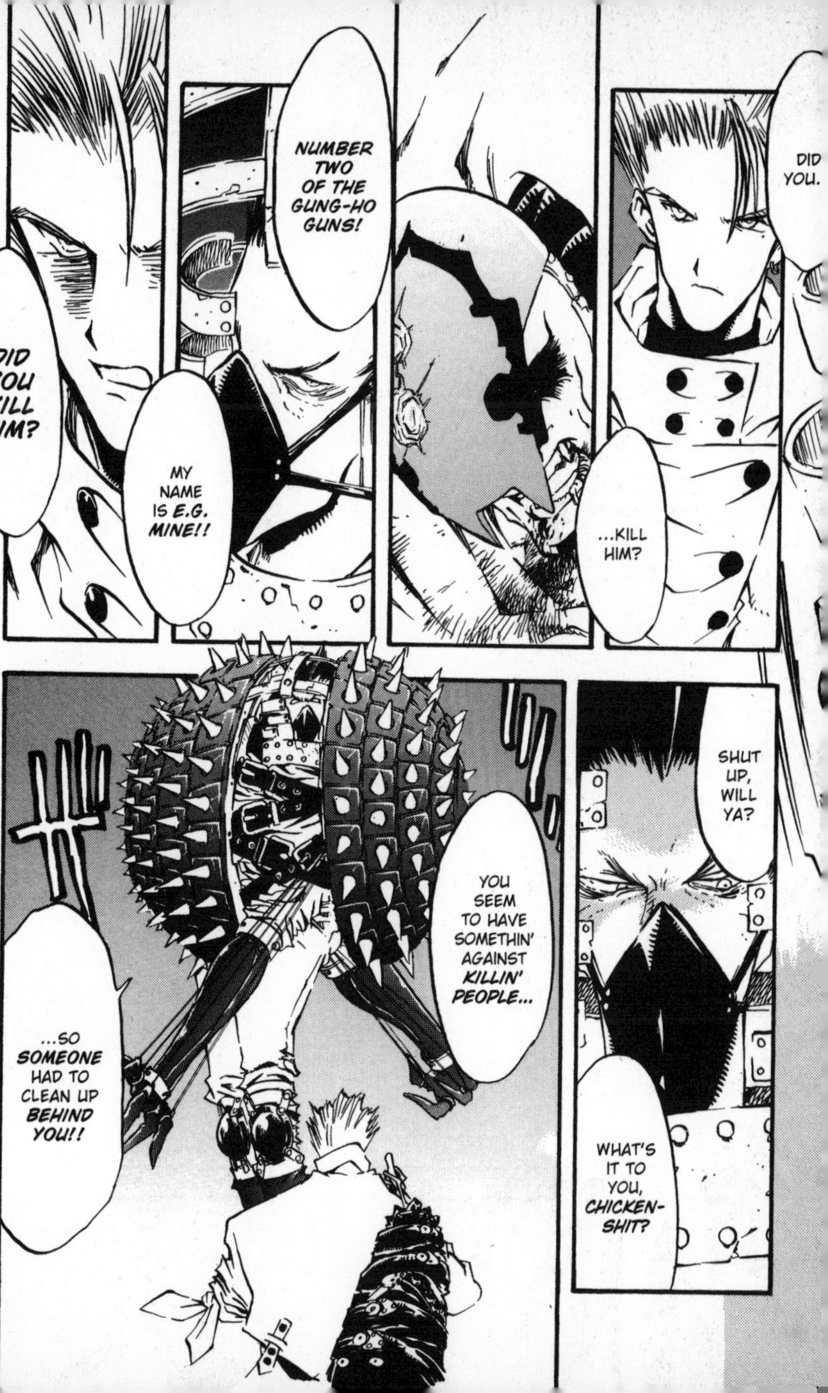
DID YOU.
...KILL HIM?
NUMBER TWO OF THE GUNG-HO GUNS!
MY NAME IS E.G. MINE!!
DID YOU KILL HIM?
SHUT UP, WILL YA?
WHAT'S IT TO YOU, CHICKEN-SHIT?
YOU SEEM TO HAVE SOMETHIN' AGAINST KILLIN' PEOPLE...
...SO SOMEONE HAD TO CLEAN UP BEHIND YOU!!

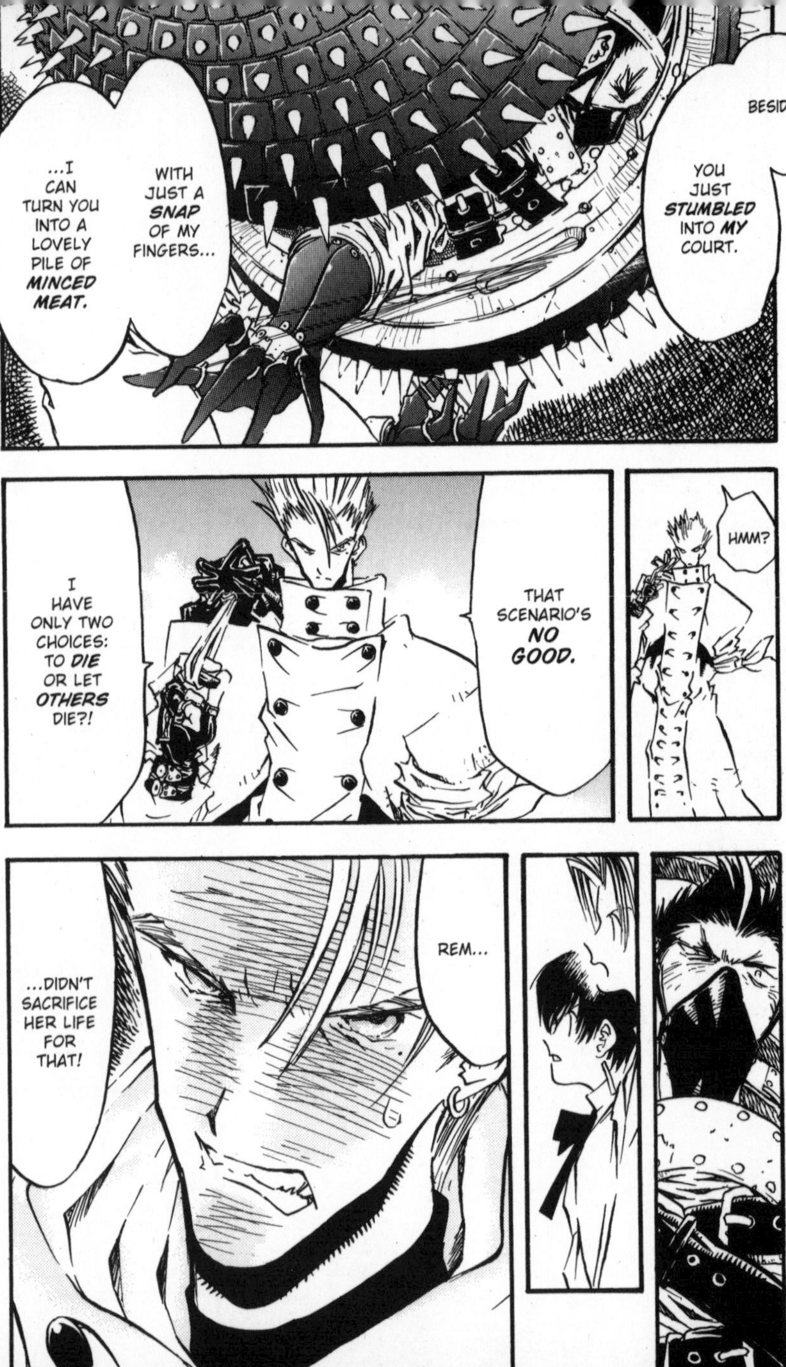
BESIDES...
YOU JUST STUMBLED INTO MY COURT.
WITH JUST A SNAP OF MY FINGERS...
...I CAN TURN YOU INTO A LOVELY PILE OF MINCED MEAT.
HMM?
THAT SCENARIO'S NO GOOD.
I HAVE ONLY TWO CHOICES: TO DIE OR LET OTHERS DIE?!
REM...
...DIDN'T SACRIFICE HER LIFE FOR THAT!

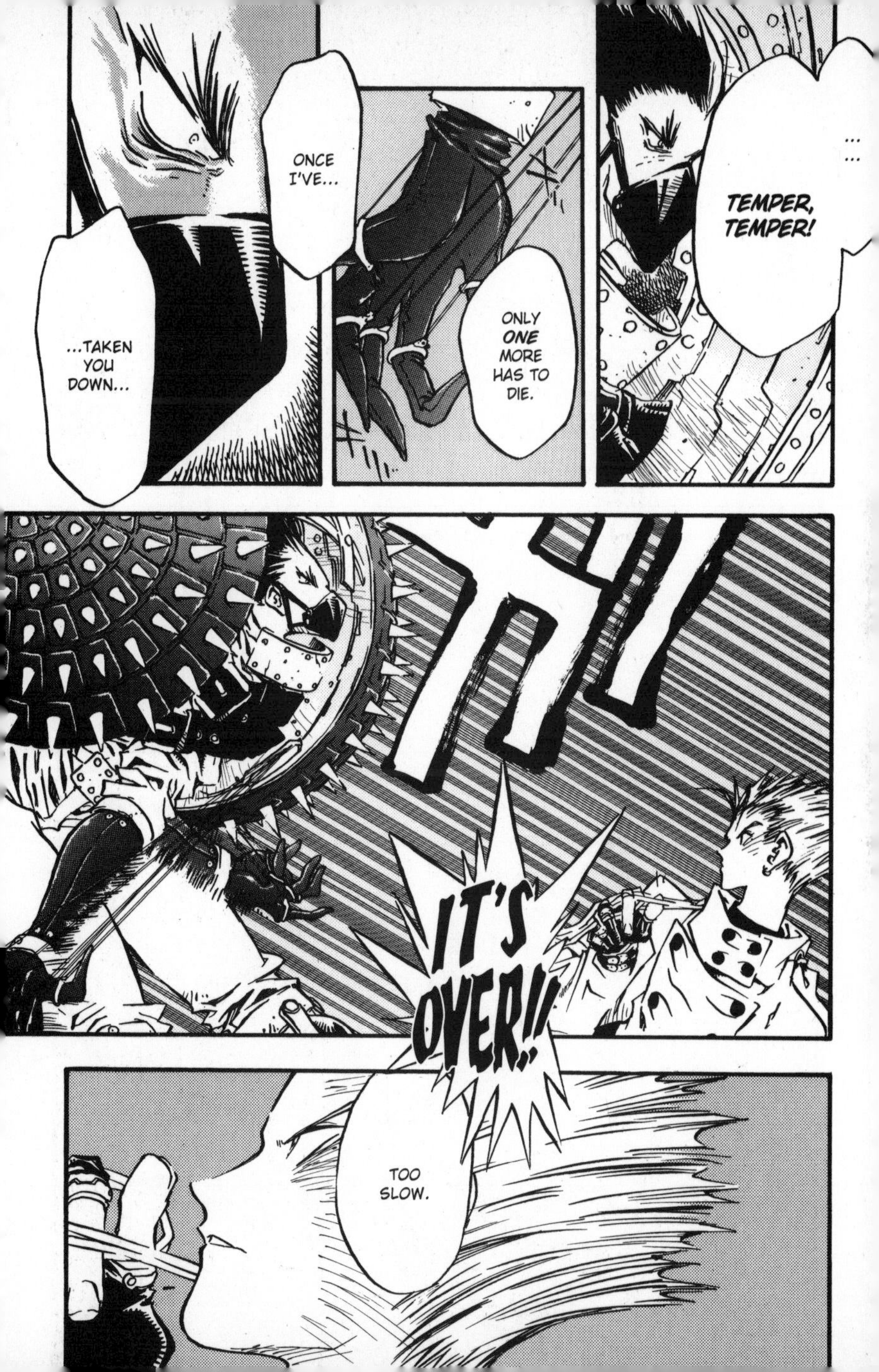
... ...
TEMPER, TEMPER!
ONCE I'VE...
ONLY ONE MORE HAS TO DIE.
...TAKEN YOU DOWN...
IT'S OVER!!
TOO SLOW.

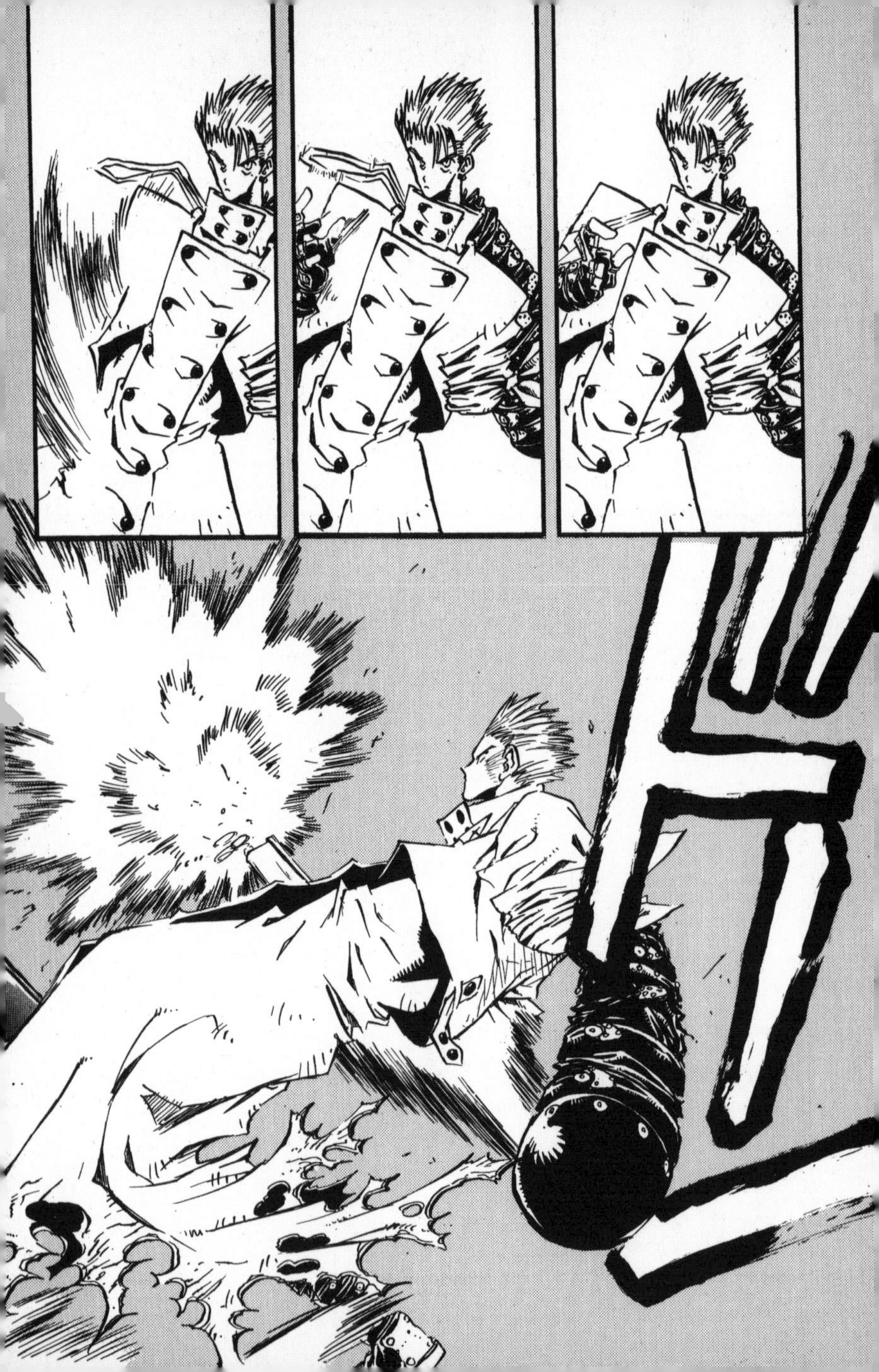

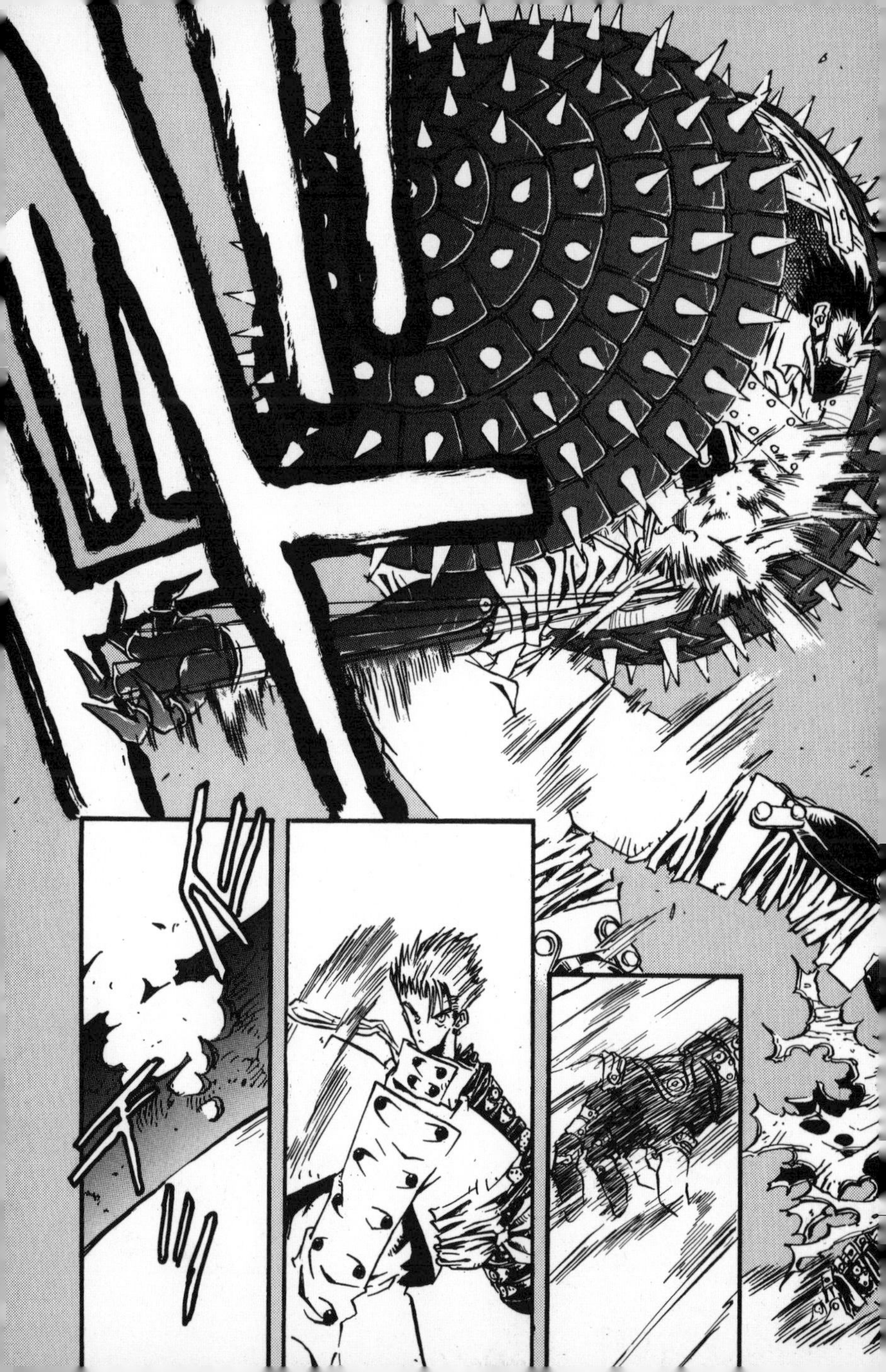

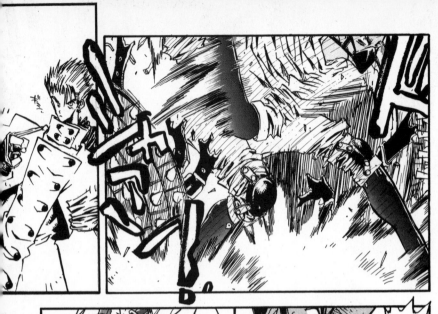

WHA--?!

EH?!

...

OH,
M--

HEY!!

...

126

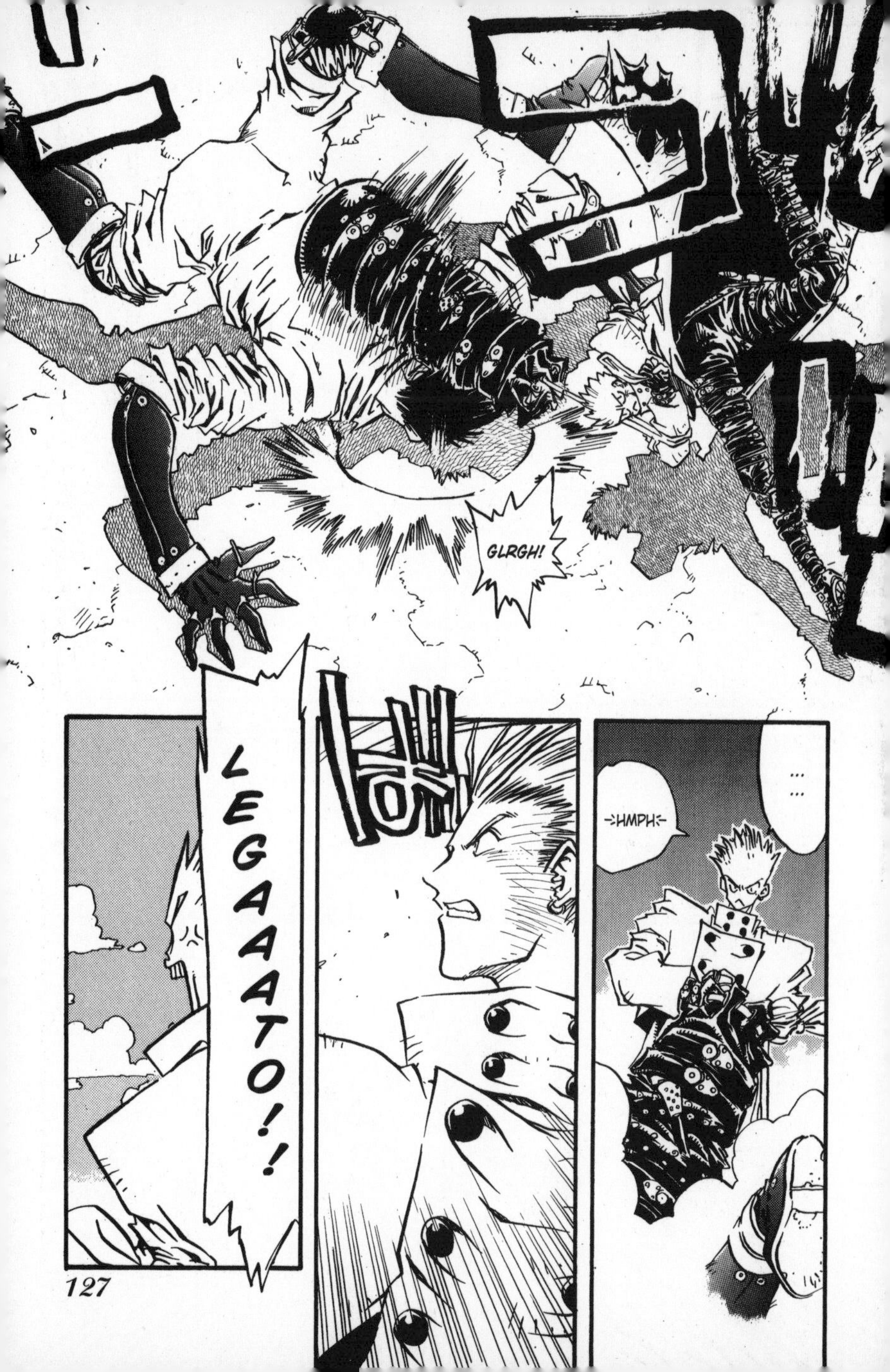
GLRGH!
...
...
-HMPH-
LEGAAAATO!!

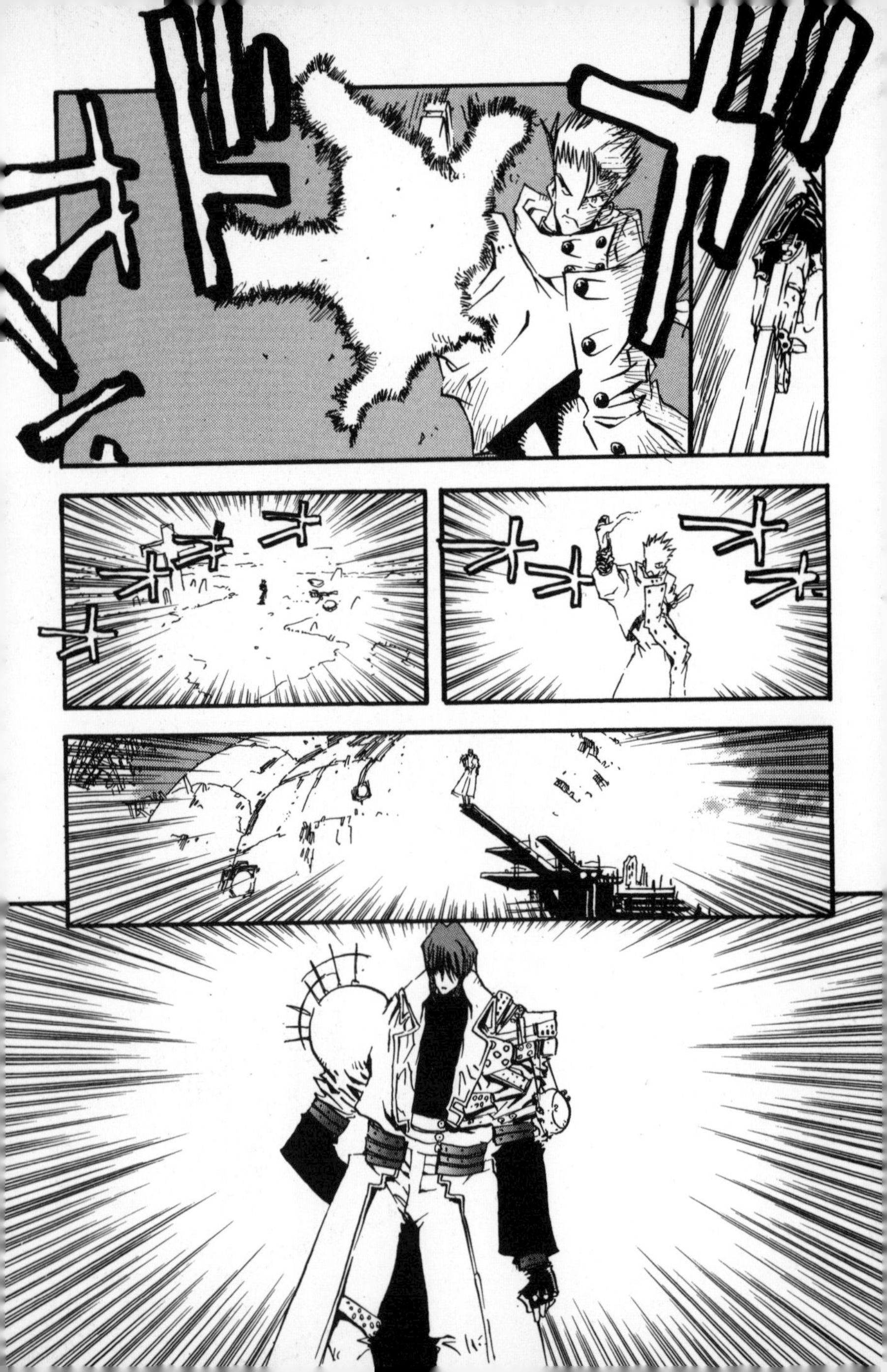
オオオオ
オオオオオ

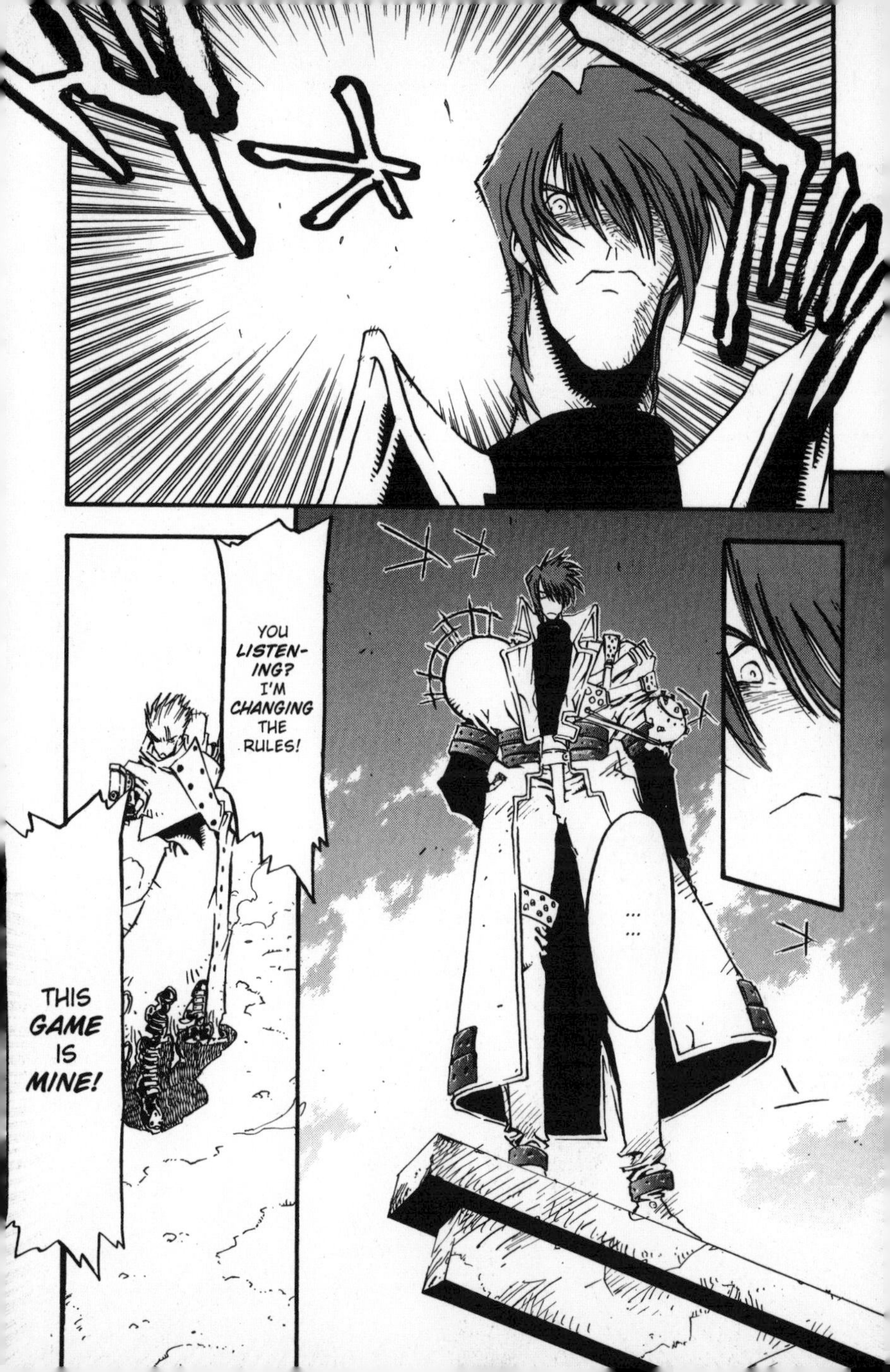
...
...
YOU LISTEN-ING? I'M CHANGING THE RULES!
THIS GAME IS MINE!

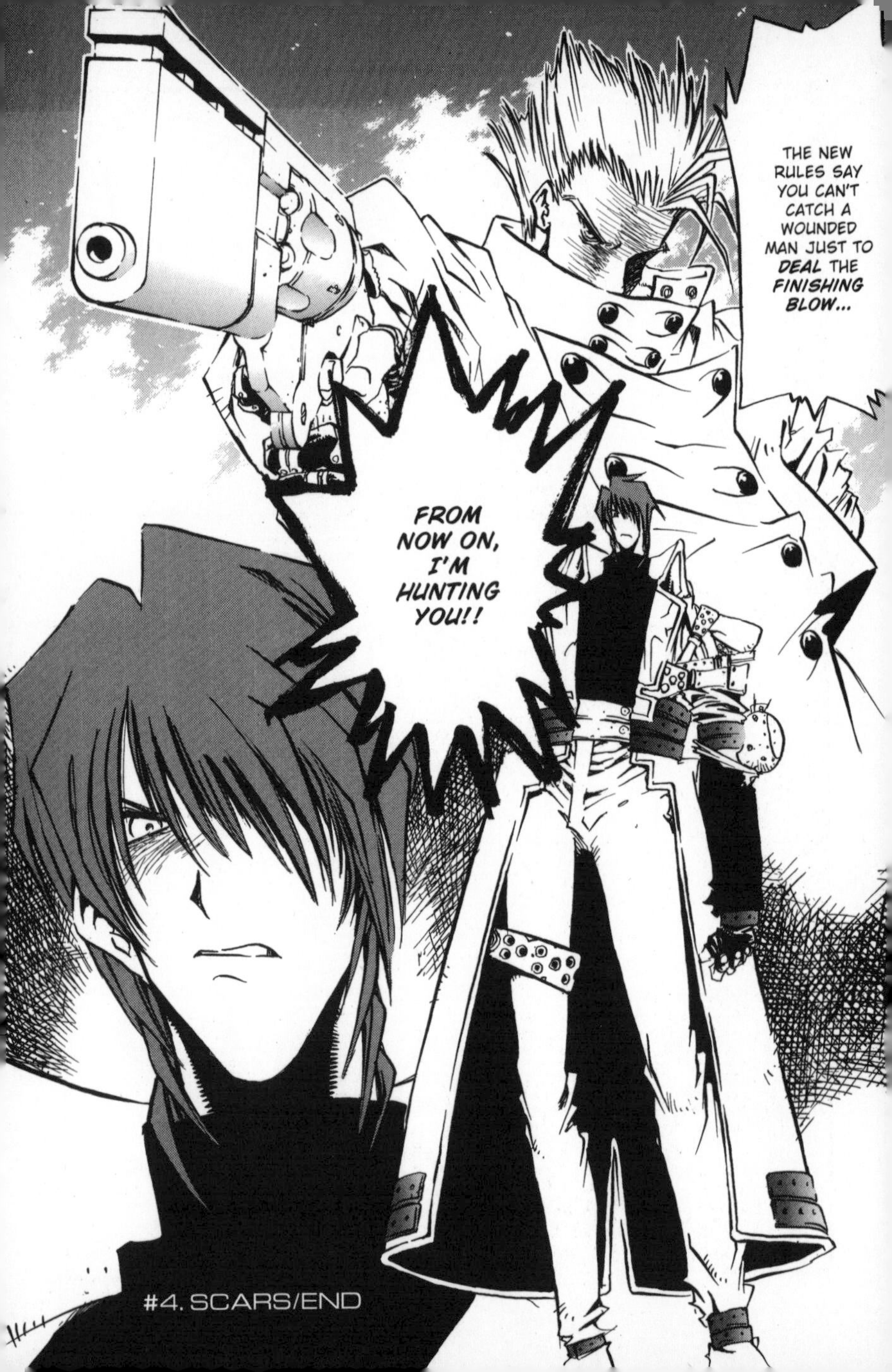
THE NEW RULES SAY YOU CAN'T CATCH A WOUNDED MAN JUST TO DEAL THE FINISHING BLOW...
FROM NOW ON, I'M HUNTING YOU!!
#4. SCARS/END

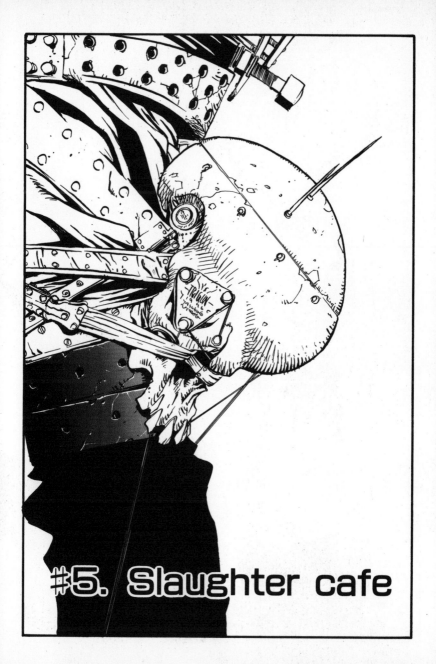

#5. Slaughter cafe

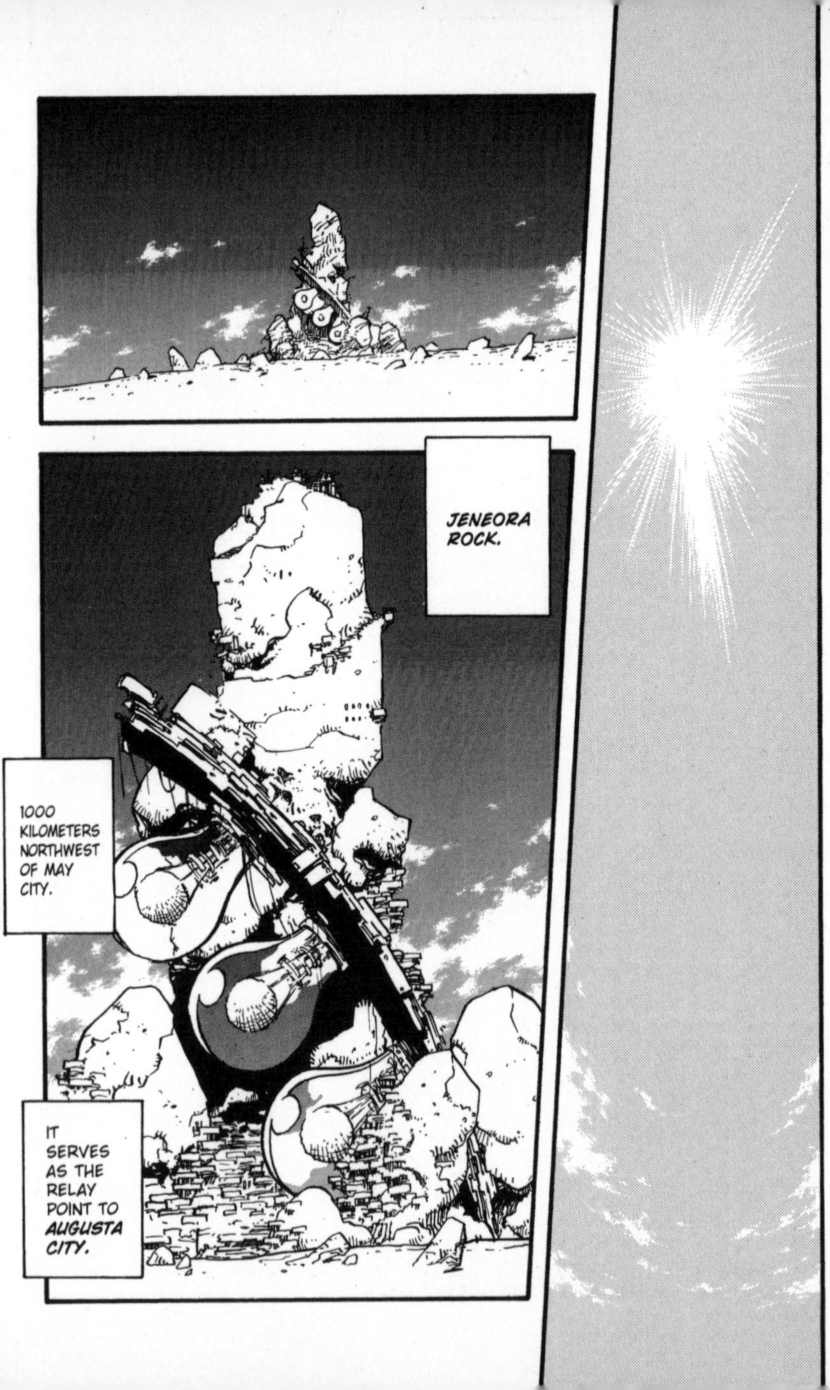
JENEORA ROCK.
1000 KILOMETERS NORTHWEST OF MAY CITY.
IT SERVES AS THE RELAY POINT TO *AUGUSTA CITY*.

...FROM TIME TO TIME, THE HOT WINDS...

...SUMMON VISITORS TO THIS SMALL COUNTRY TOWN.

NATURALLY...

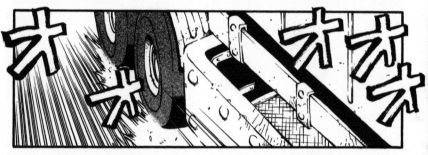

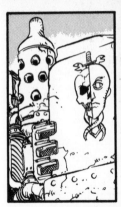

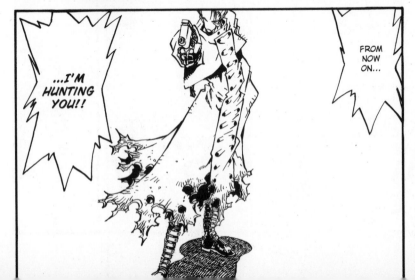

...I'M HUNTING YOU!!

FROM NOW ON...

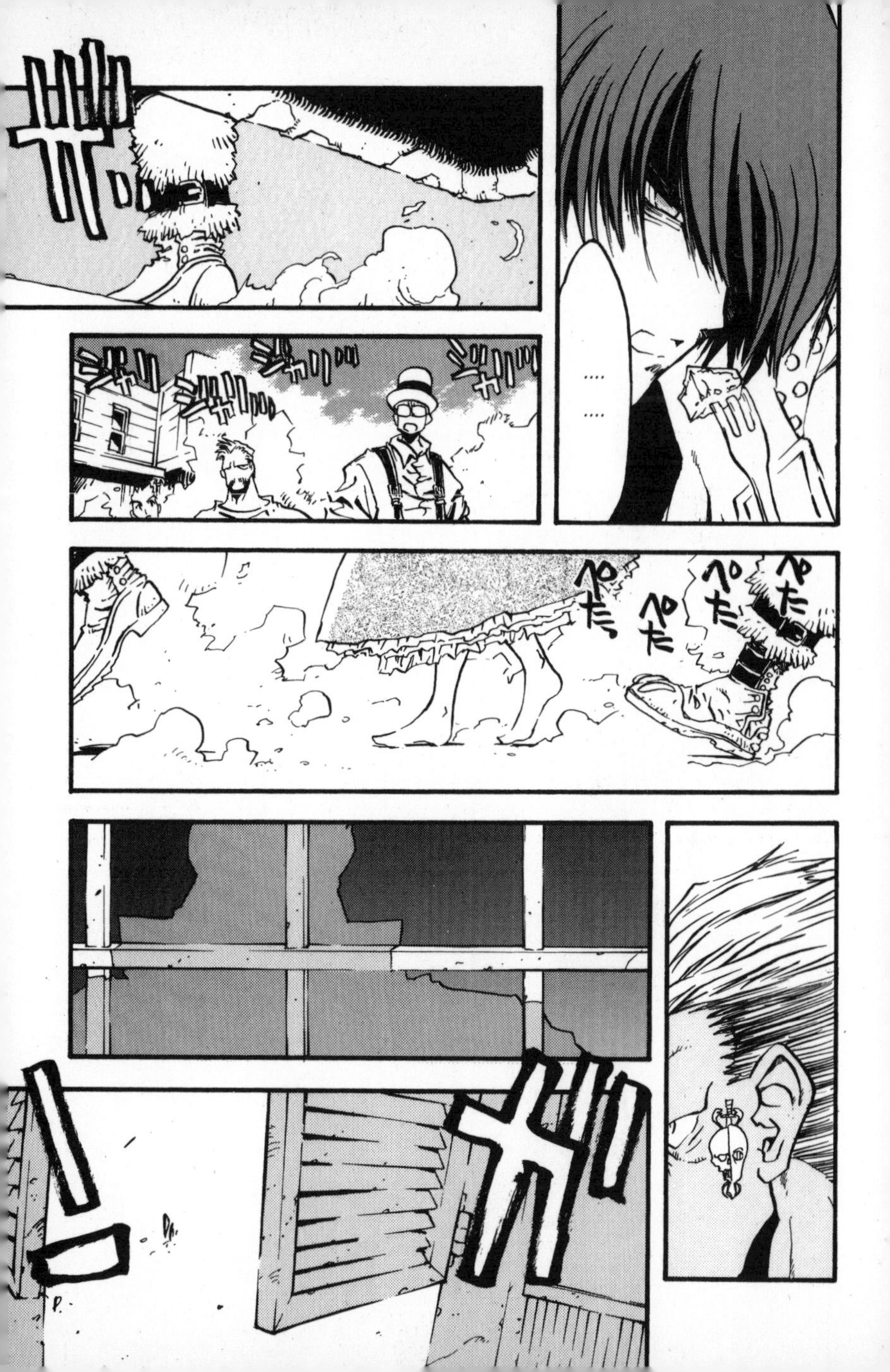
……
……
ザッ
ジャリ
ジャリッ
ジャリッ
ジャリリ
ぺた
ぺた
ぺた
ぺた、
ガッ

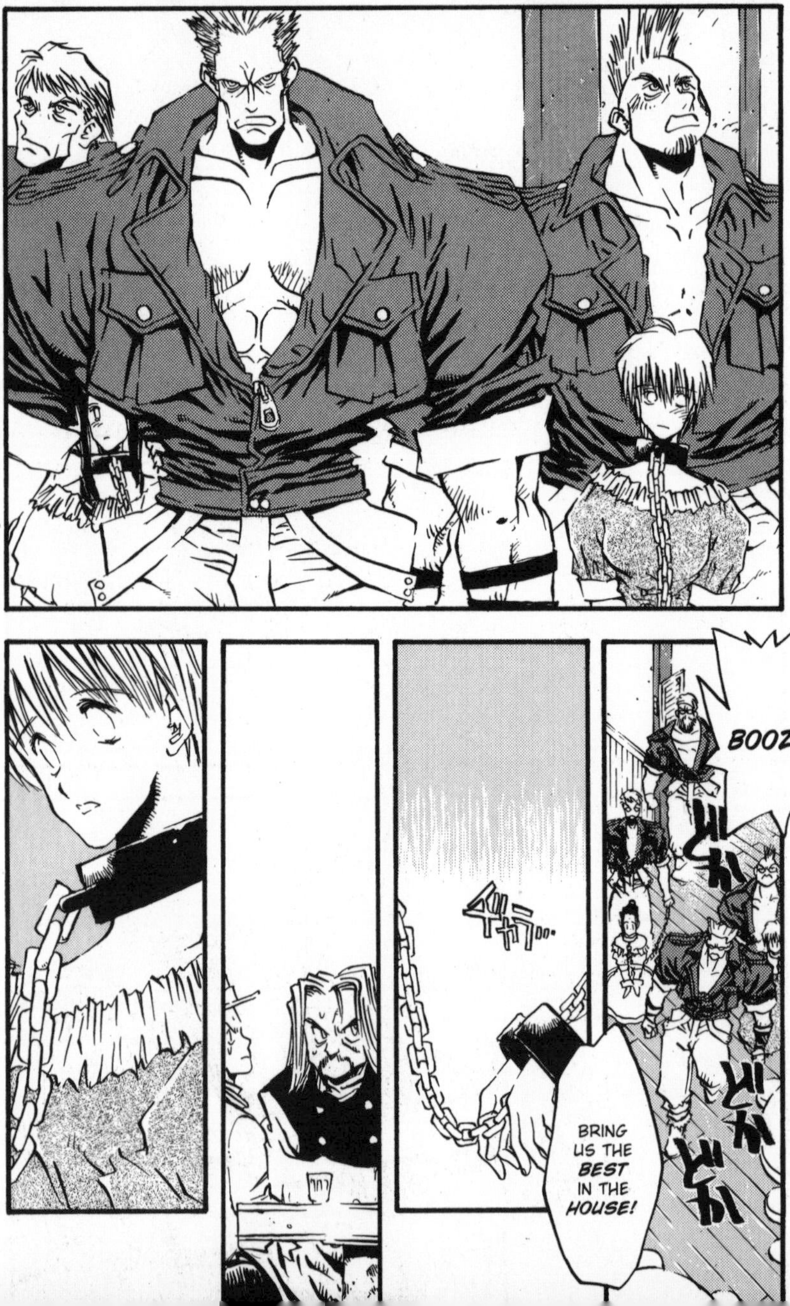
BOOZE!
BRING US THE BEST IN THE HOUSE!

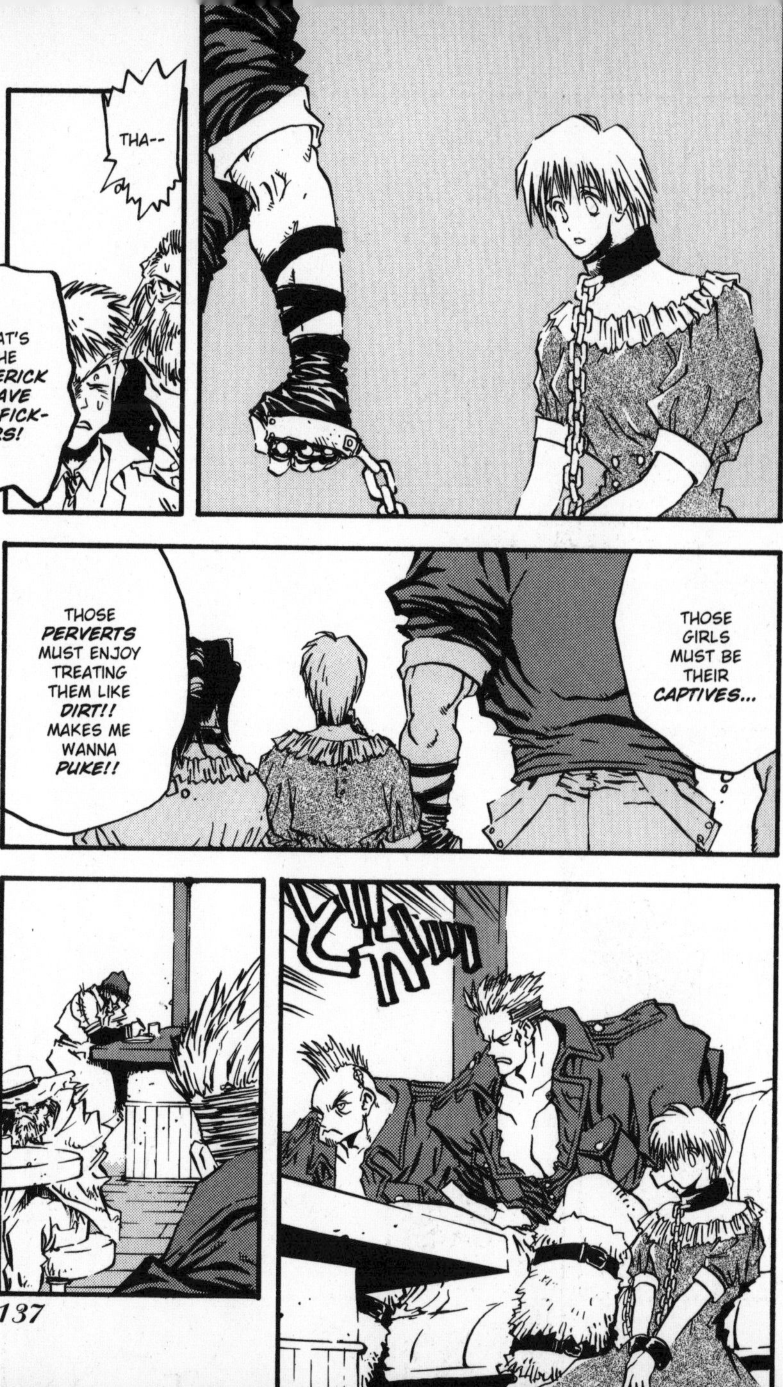
THA--
THAT'S THE RODERICK SLAVE TRAFFICK-ERS!
THOSE GIRLS MUST BE THEIR CAPTIVES...
THOSE PERVERTS MUST ENJOY TREATING THEM LIKE DIRT!! MAKES ME WANNA PUKE!!

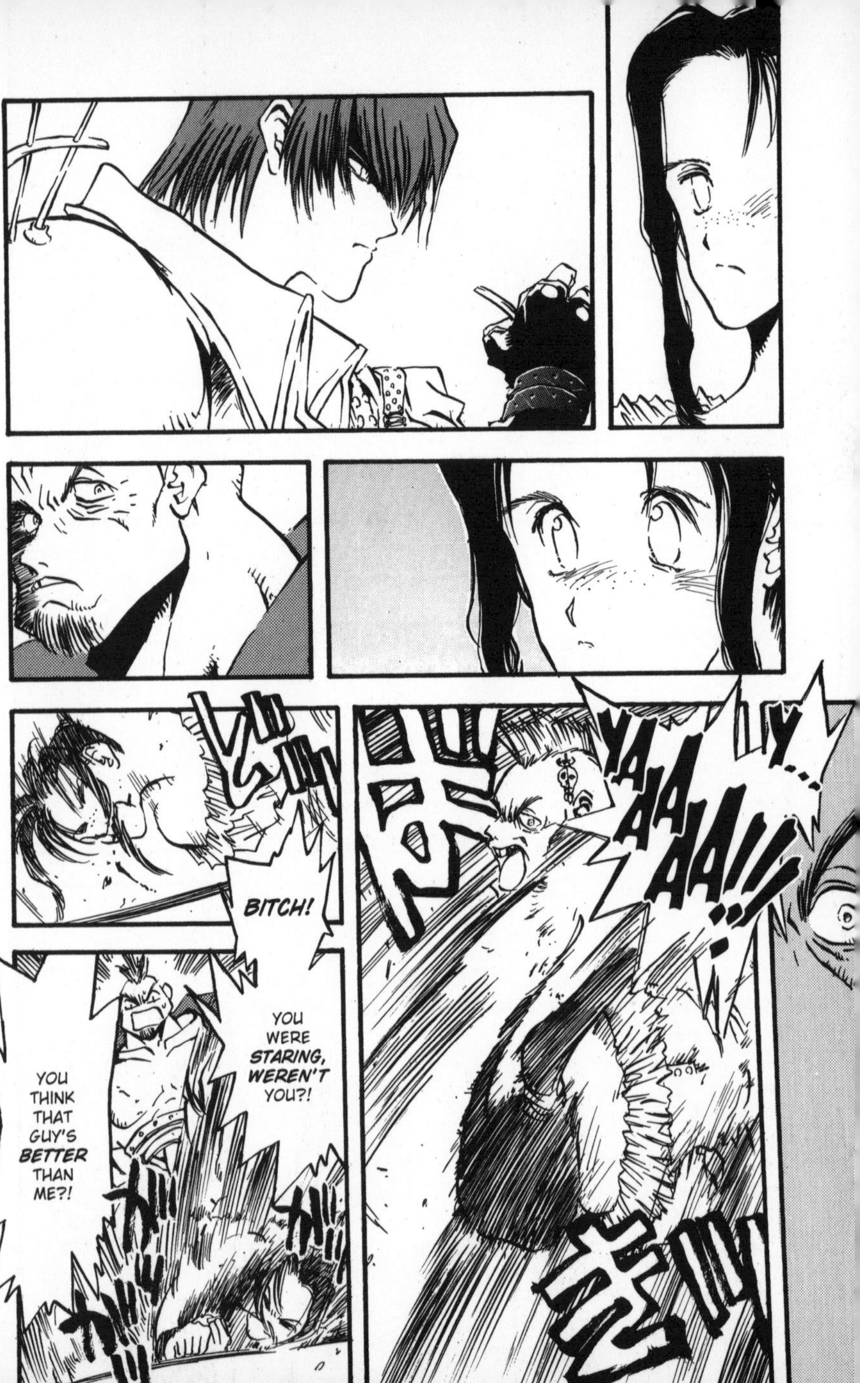
Y...
YAAAAAAA!!
BITCH!
YOU WERE STARING, WEREN'T YOU?!
YOU THINK THAT GUY'S BETTER THAN ME?!

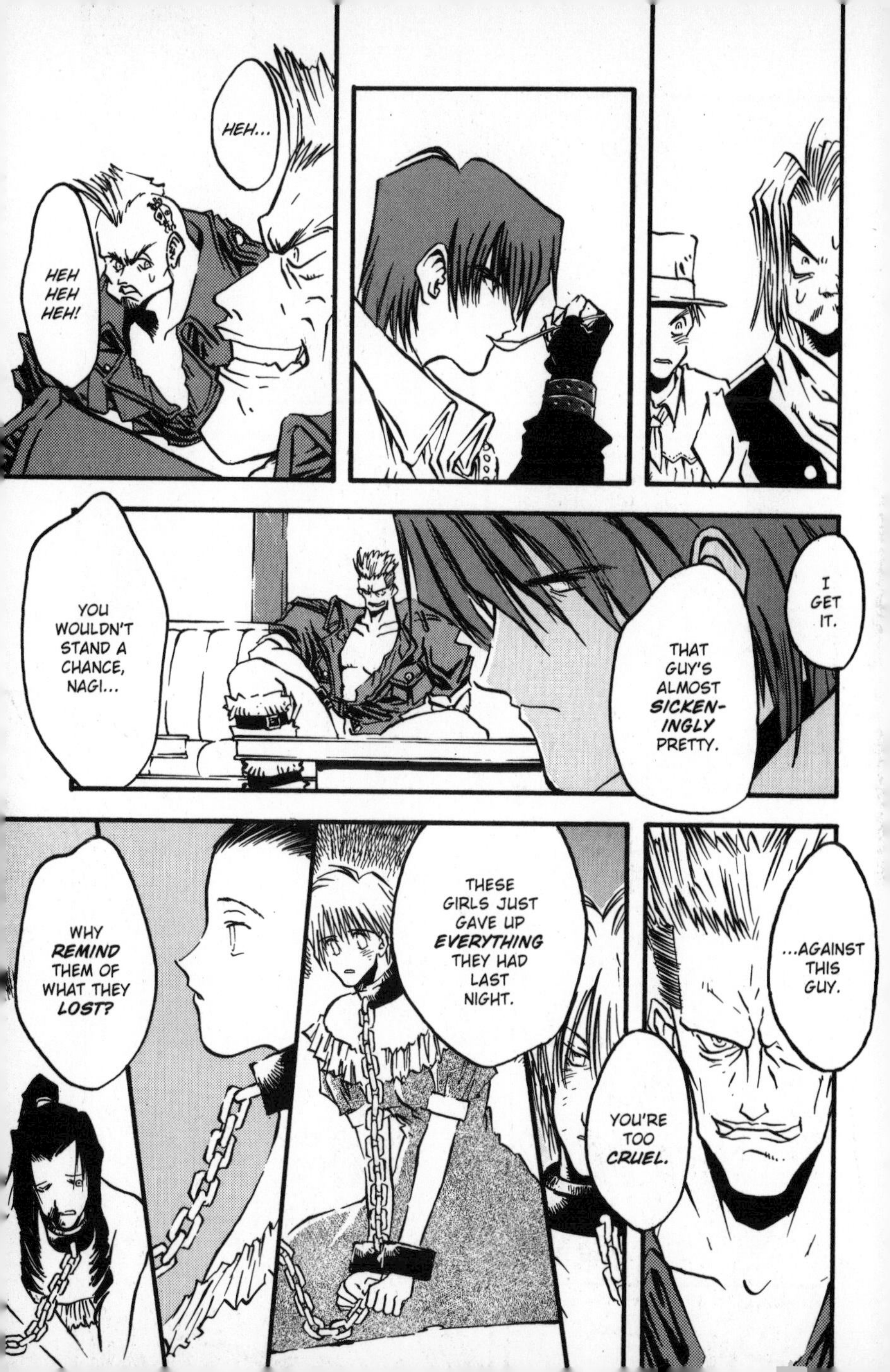
HEH...
HEH HEH HEH!
I GET IT.
THAT GUY'S ALMOST SICKENINGLY PRETTY.
YOU WOULDN'T STAND A CHANCE, NAGI...
...AGAINST THIS GUY.
YOU'RE TOO CRUEL.
THESE GIRLS JUST GAVE UP EVERYTHING THEY HAD LAST NIGHT.
WHY REMIND THEM OF WHAT THEY LOST?

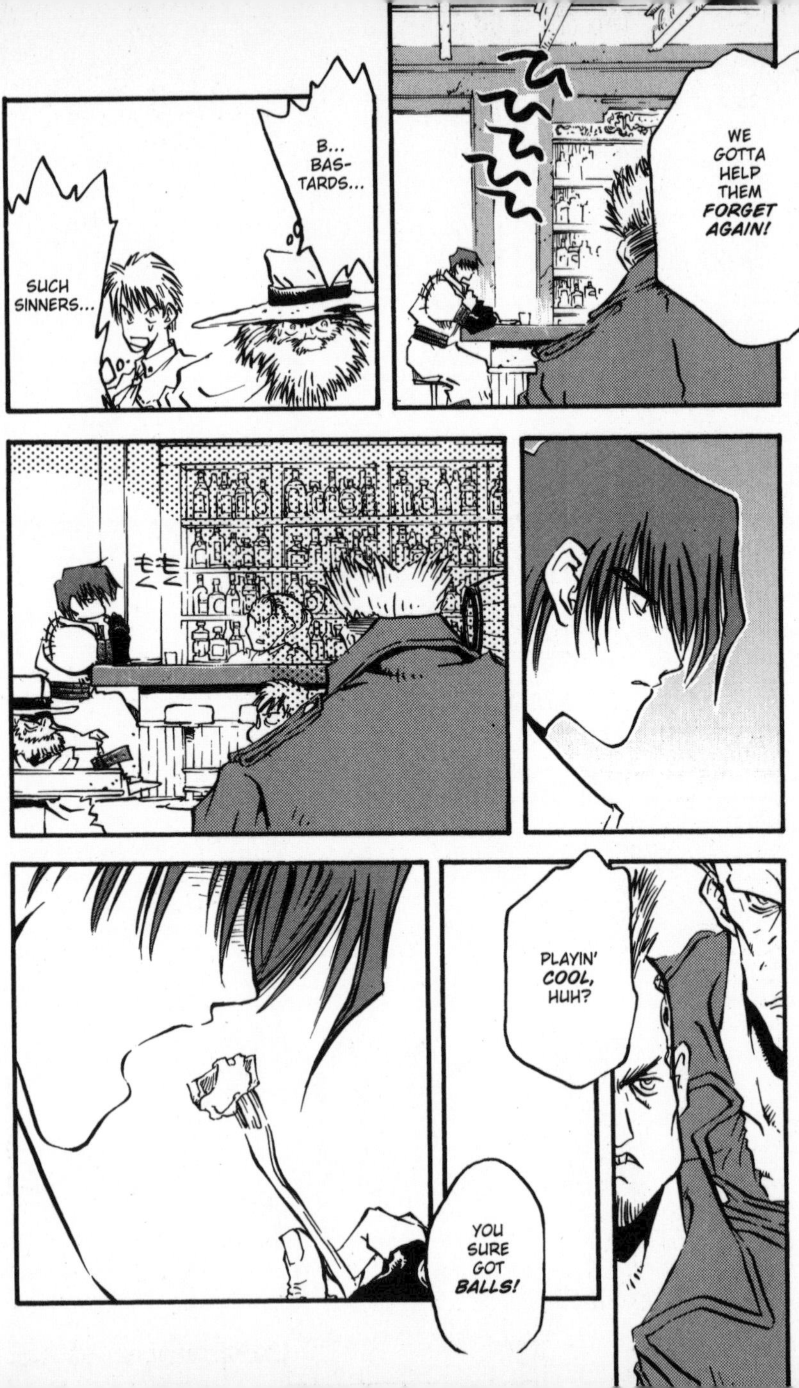
WE GOTTA HELP THEM **FORGET AGAIN!**
B... BAS-TARDS...
SUCH SINNERS...
PLAYIN' **COOL,** HUH?
YOU SURE GOT **BALLS!**

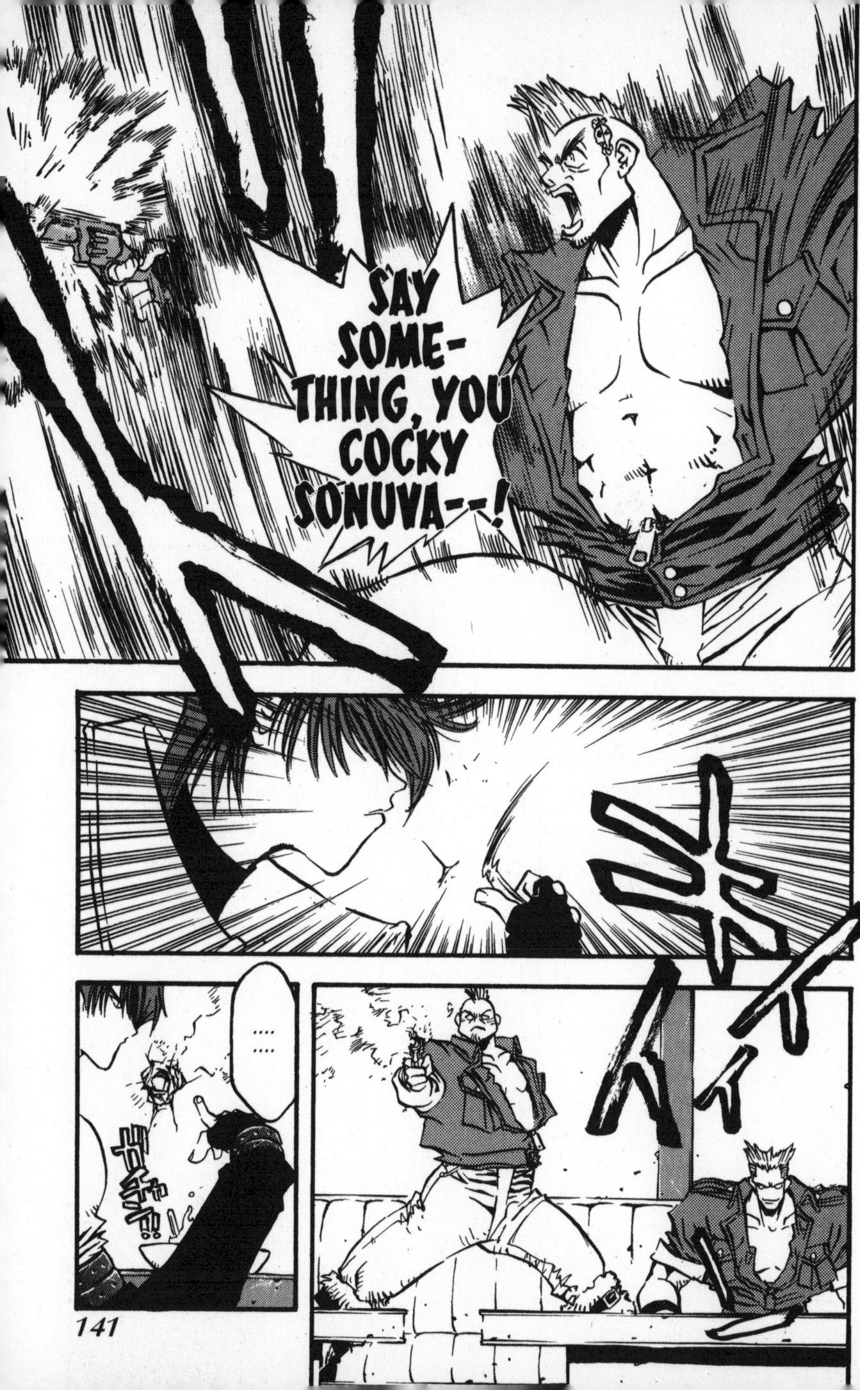
SAY SOME-THING, YOU COCKY SONUVA--!
....
....

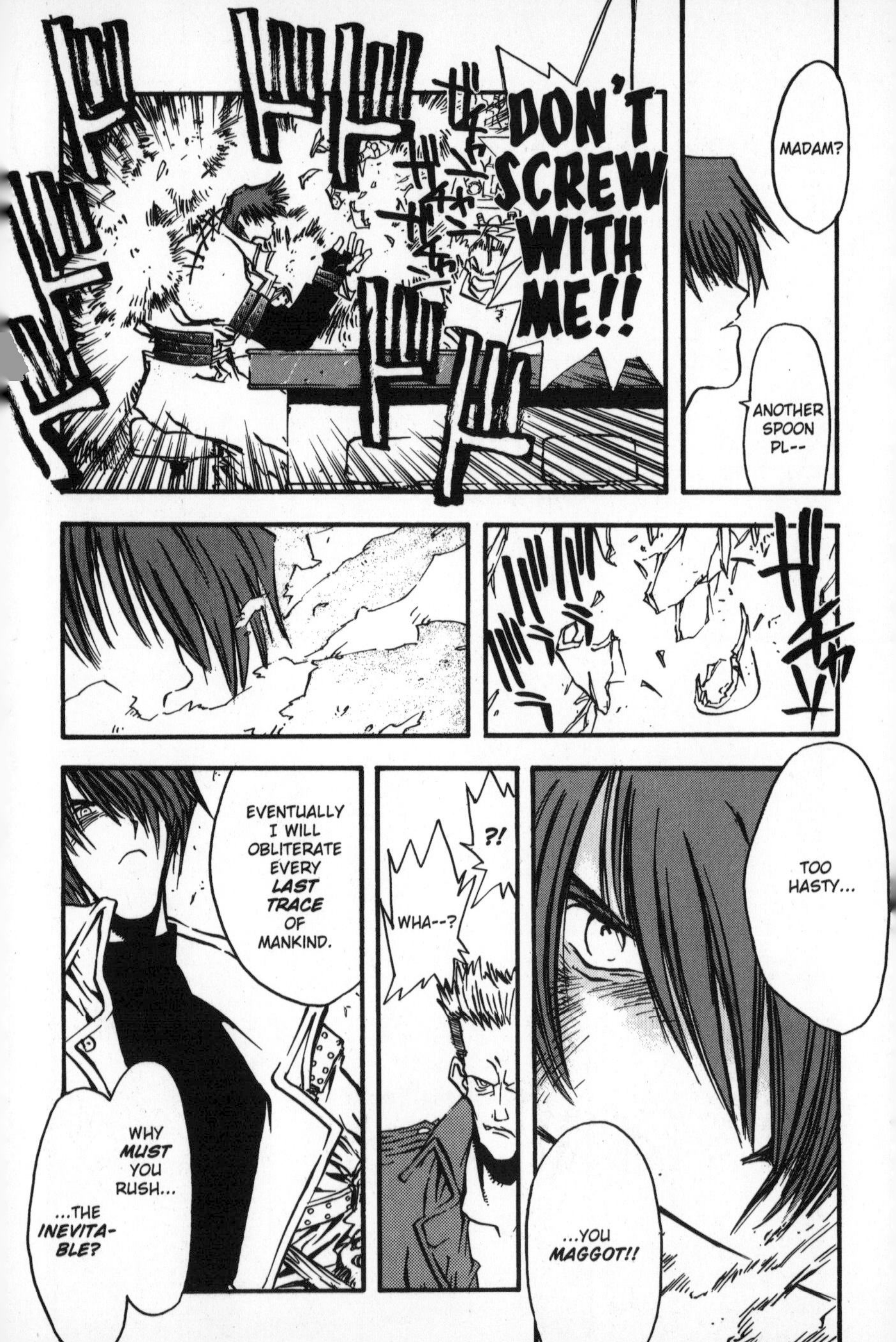
MADAM?
ANOTHER SPOON PL--
DON'T SCREW WITH ME!!
TOO HASTY...
...YOU *MAGGOT!!*
?!
WHA--?
EVENTUALLY I WILL OBLITERATE EVERY *LAST TRACE* OF MANKIND.
WHY *MUST* YOU RUSH...
...THE *INEVITA-BLE?*

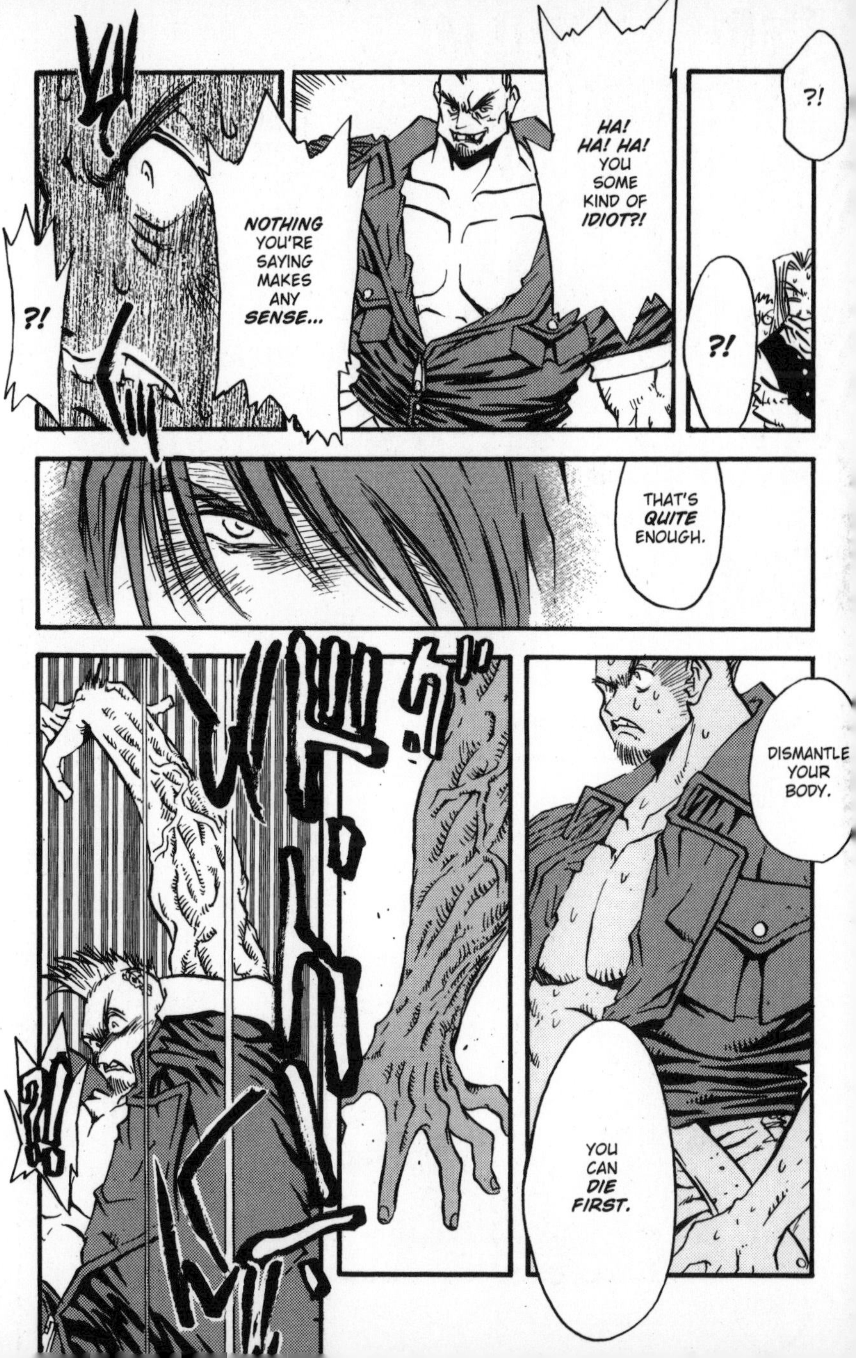
?!
?!
HA! HA! HA! YOU SOME KIND OF IDIOT?!
NOTHING YOU'RE SAYING MAKES ANY SENSE...
?!
THAT'S QUITE ENOUGH.
DISMANTLE YOUR BODY.
YOU CAN DIE FIRST.

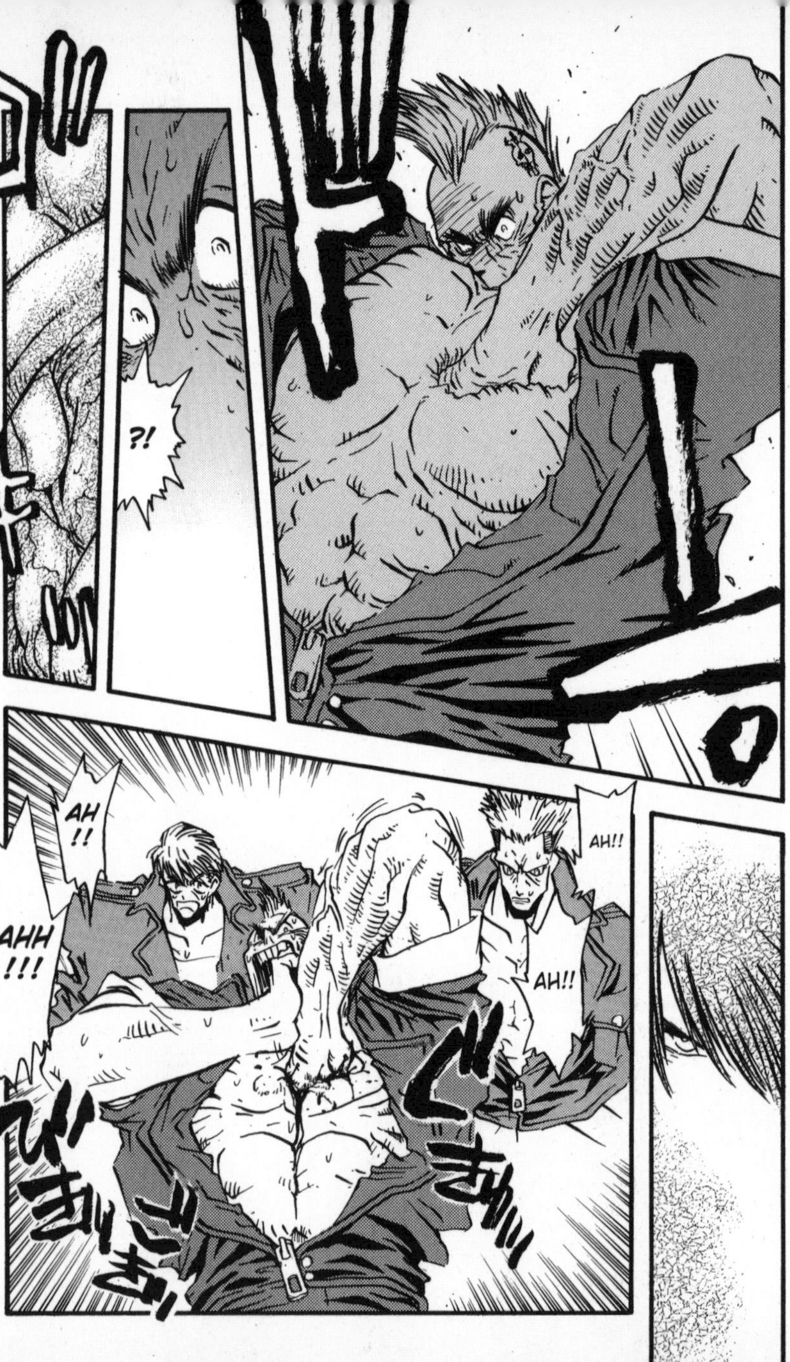

?!
AH!!
AH
!!
AH!!
AHH
!!!

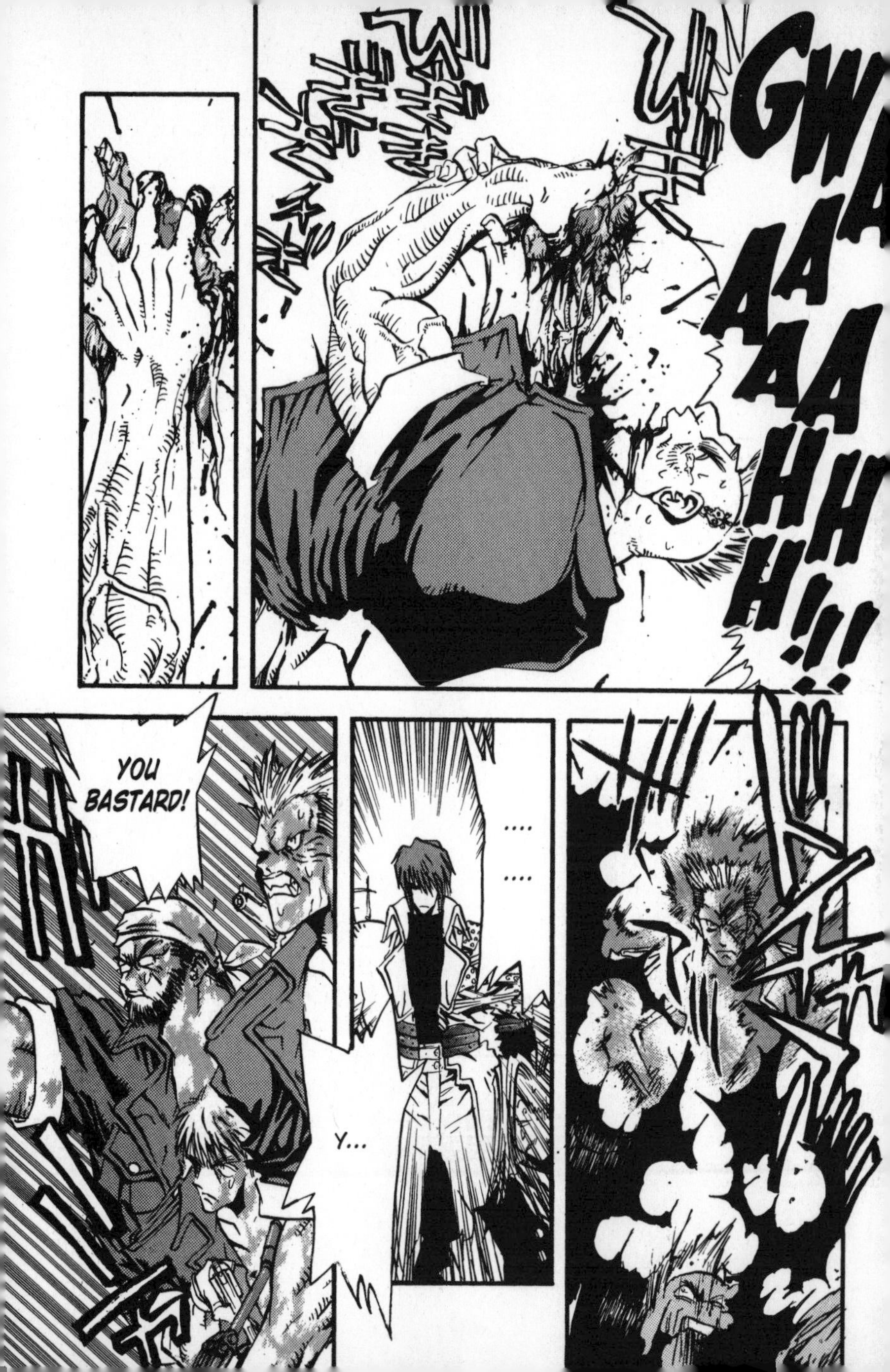
GWAAAAAAHHHHH!!!!
....
....
Y...
YOU BASTARD!

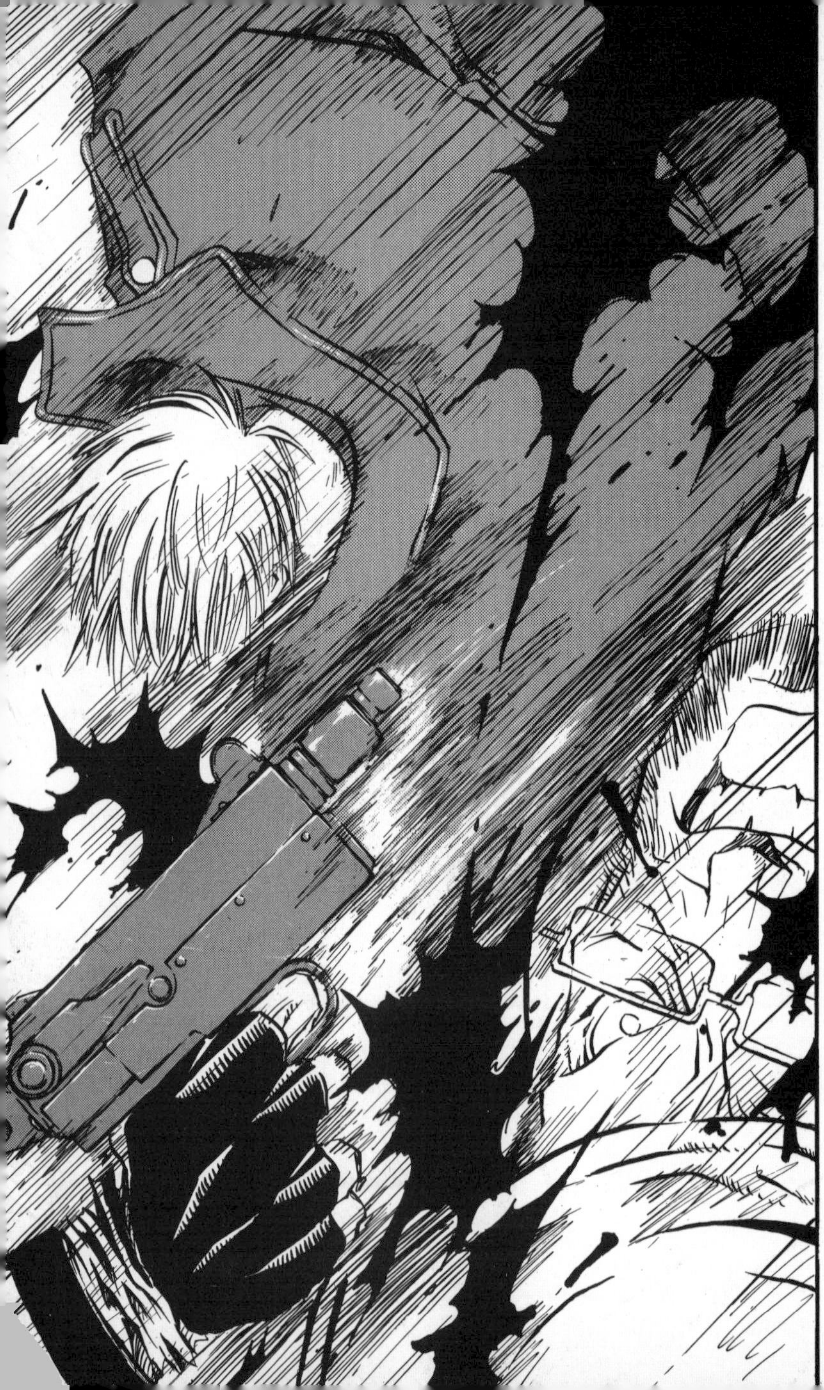

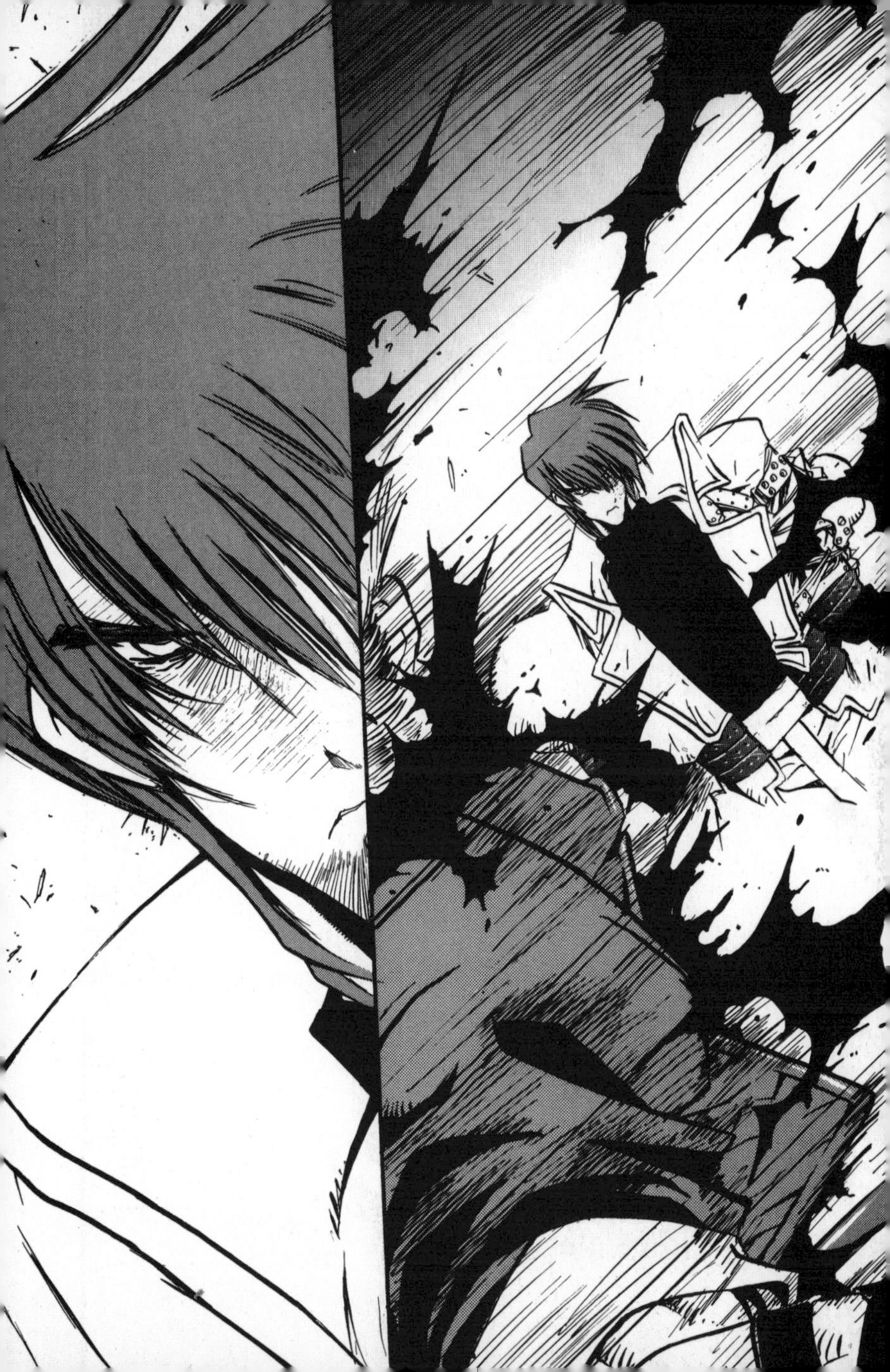

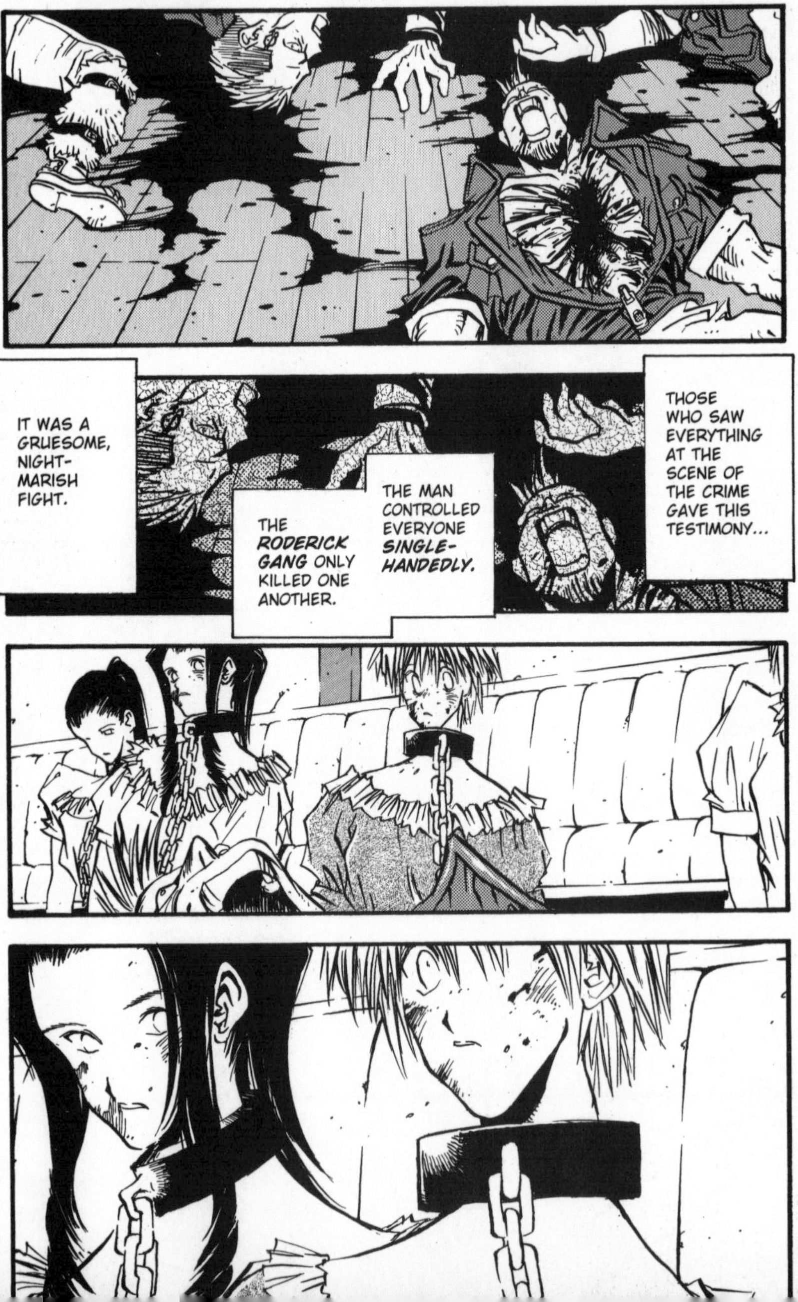
THOSE WHO SAW EVERYTHING AT THE SCENE OF THE CRIME GAVE THIS TESTIMONY...
THE MAN CONTROLLED EVERYONE *SINGLE-HANDEDLY.*
THE *RODERICK GANG* ONLY KILLED ONE ANOTHER.
IT WAS A GRUESOME, NIGHT-MARISH FIGHT.

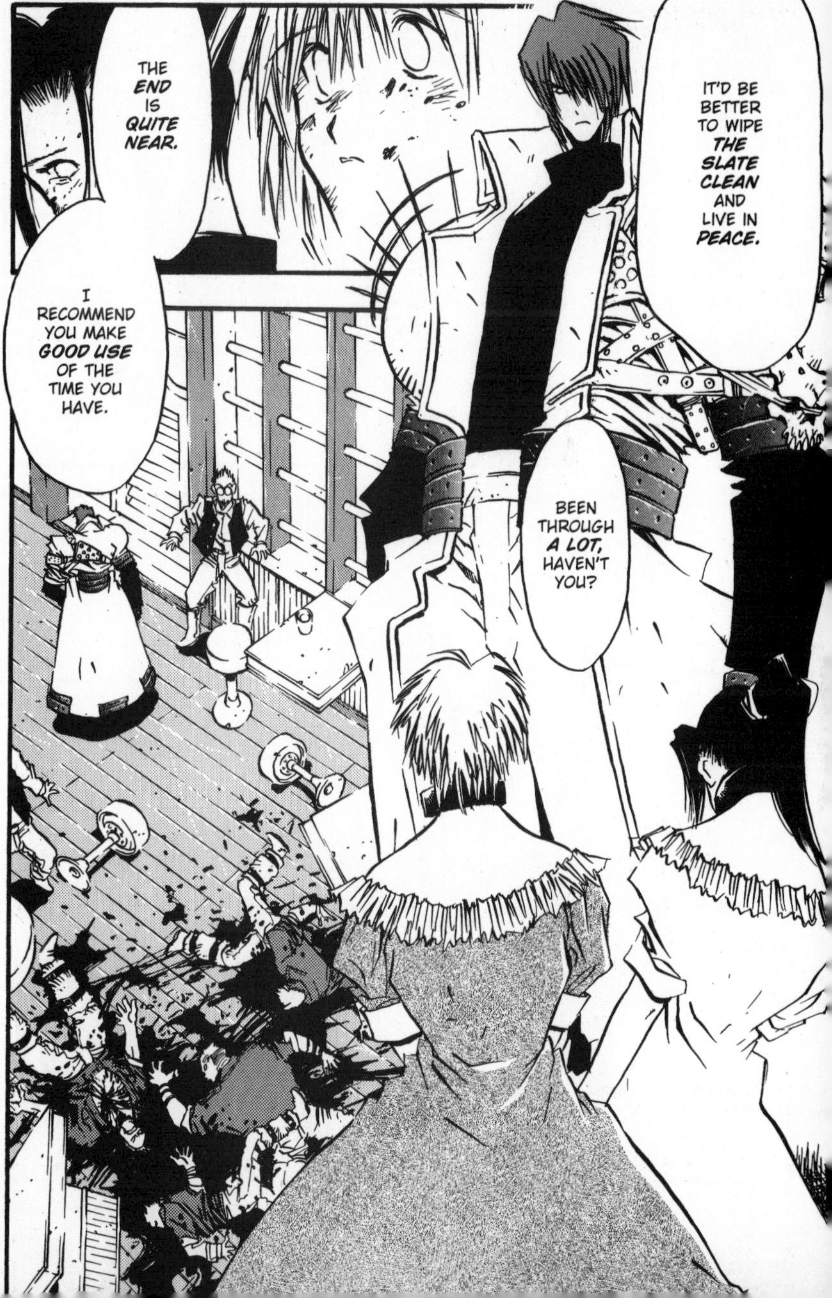
IT'D BE BETTER TO WIPE THE SLATE CLEAN AND LIVE IN PEACE.
BEEN THROUGH A LOT, HAVEN'T YOU?
THE END IS QUITE NEAR.
I RECOMMEND YOU MAKE GOOD USE OF THE TIME YOU HAVE.

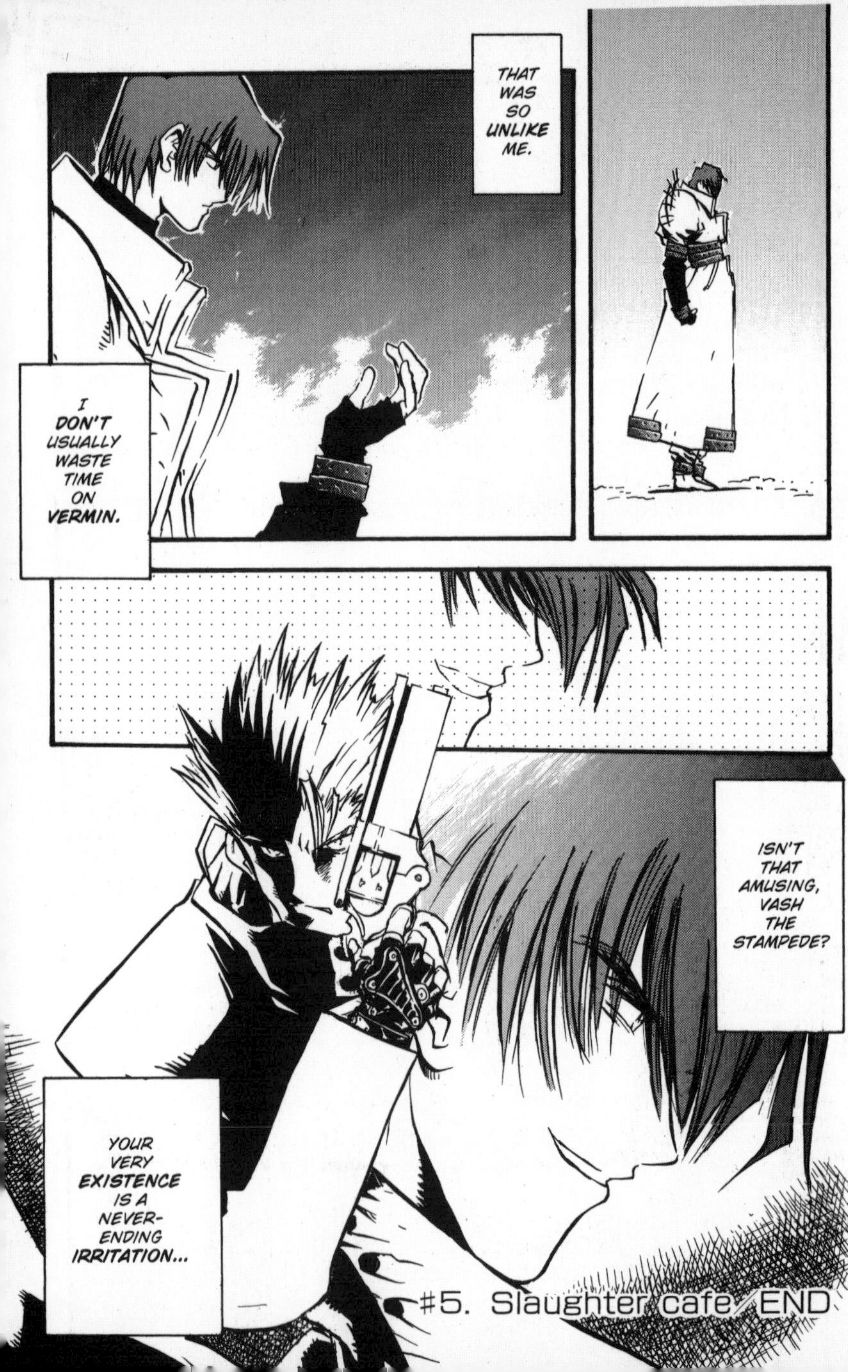
THAT WAS SO UNLIKE ME.
I DON'T USUALLY WASTE TIME ON VERMIN.
ISN'T THAT AMUSING, VASH THE STAMPEDE?
YOUR VERY EXISTENCE IS A NEVER-ENDING IRRITATION...
#5. Slaughter cafe / END

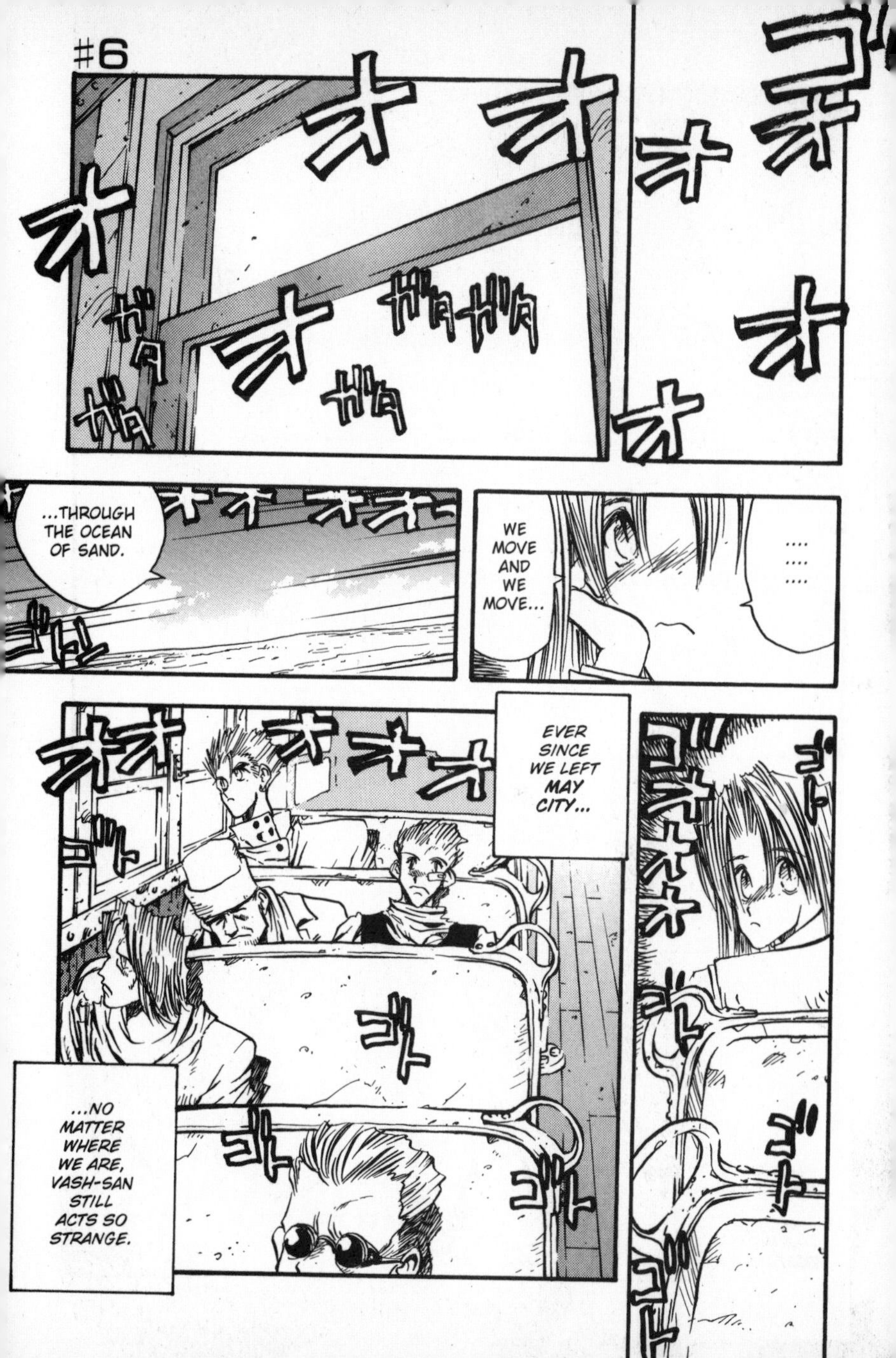
#6
WE MOVE AND WE MOVE...
....
....
....
...THROUGH THE OCEAN OF SAND.
EVER SINCE WE LEFT MAY CITY...
...NO MATTER WHERE WE ARE, VASH-SAN STILL ACTS SO STRANGE.

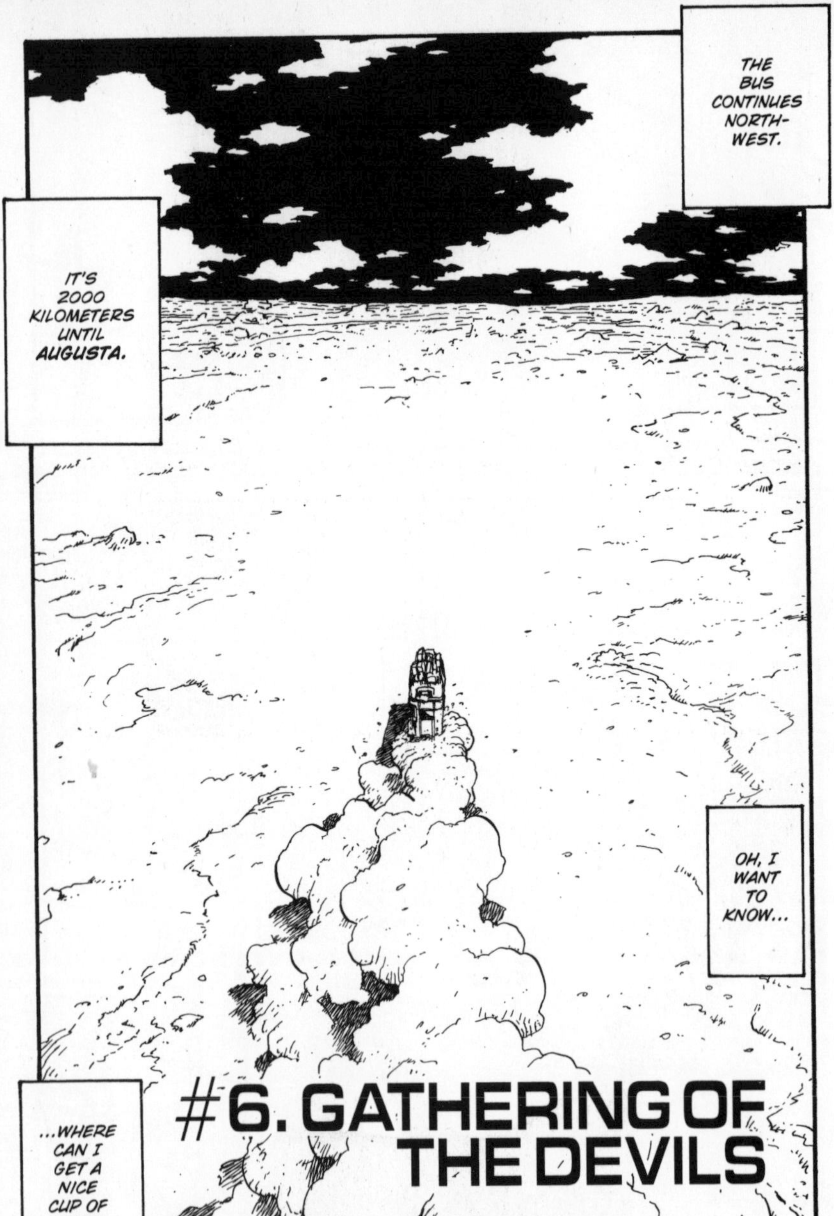
THE BUS CONTINUES NORTH-WEST.
IT'S 2000 KILOMETERS UNTIL AUGUSTA.
OH, I WANT TO KNOW...
...WHERE CAN I GET A NICE CUP OF TEA?
#6. GATHERING OF THE DEVILS

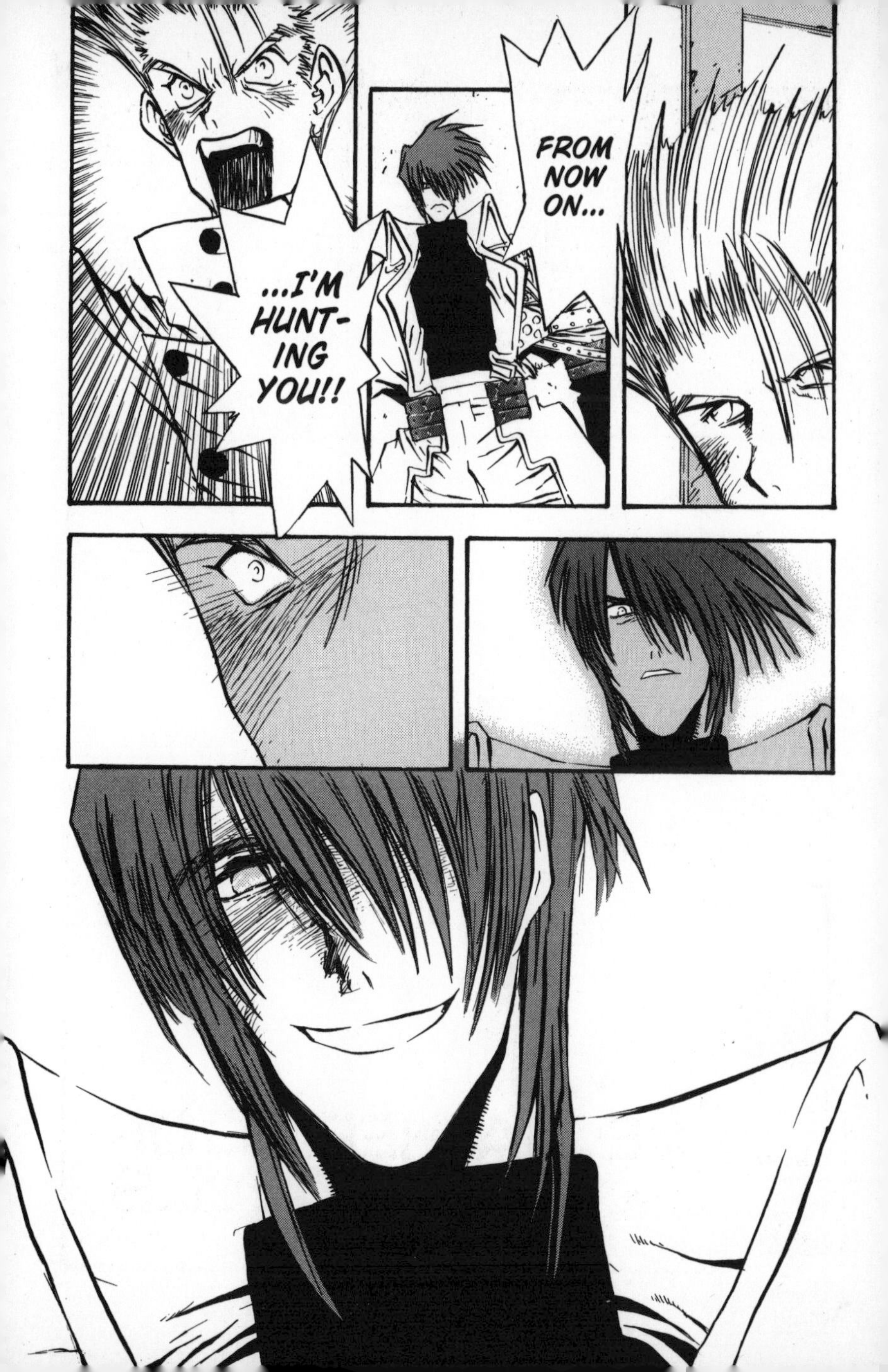
FROM NOW ON...
...I'M HUNT-ING YOU!!

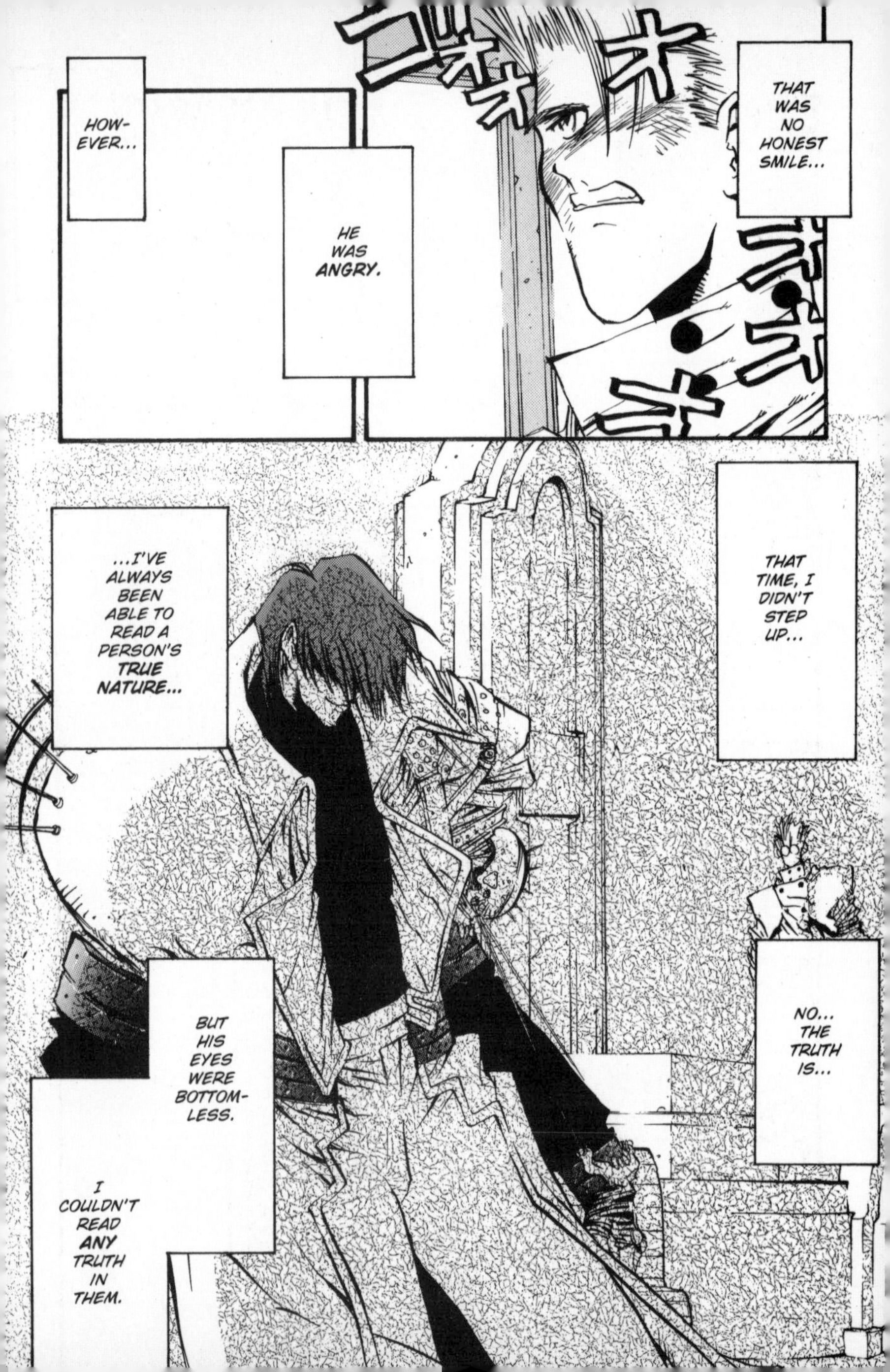
THAT WAS NO HONEST SMILE...
HOW-EVER...
HE WAS ANGRY.
THAT TIME, I DIDN'T STEP UP...
...I'VE ALWAYS BEEN ABLE TO READ A PERSON'S TRUE NATURE...
BUT HIS EYES WERE BOTTOM-LESS.
I COULDN'T READ ANY TRUTH IN THEM.
NO... THE TRUTH IS...

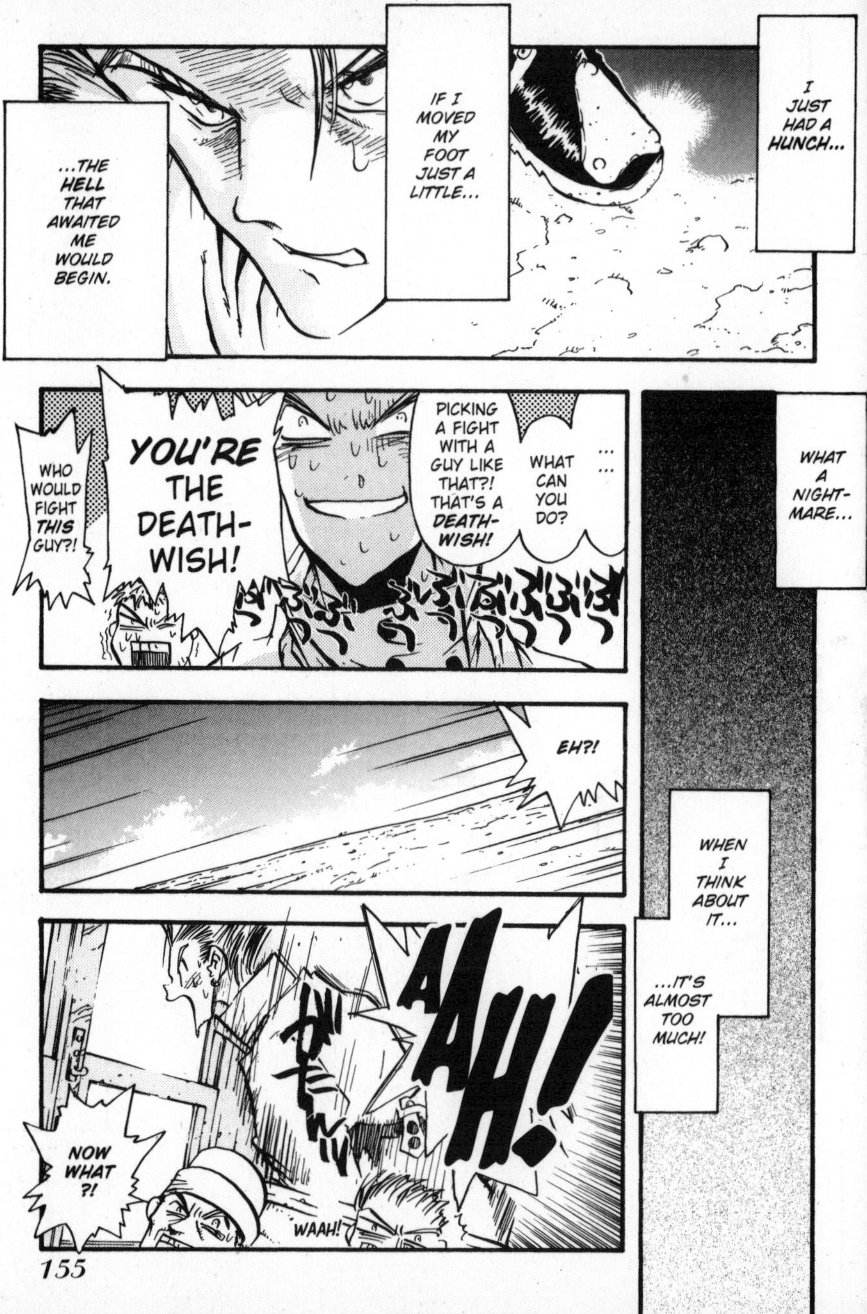
I JUST HAD A HUNCH...
IF I MOVED MY FOOT JUST A LITTLE...
...THE HELL THAT AWAITED ME WOULD BEGIN.
WHAT A NIGHTMARE...
... ...
WHAT CAN YOU DO?
PICKING A FIGHT WITH A GUY LIKE THAT?! THAT'S A DEATH-WISH!
YOU'RE THE DEATH-WISH!
WHO WOULD FIGHT THIS GUY?!
EH?!
WHEN I THINK ABOUT IT...
...IT'S ALMOST TOO MUCH!
AAH!!
WAAH!
NOW WHAT?!

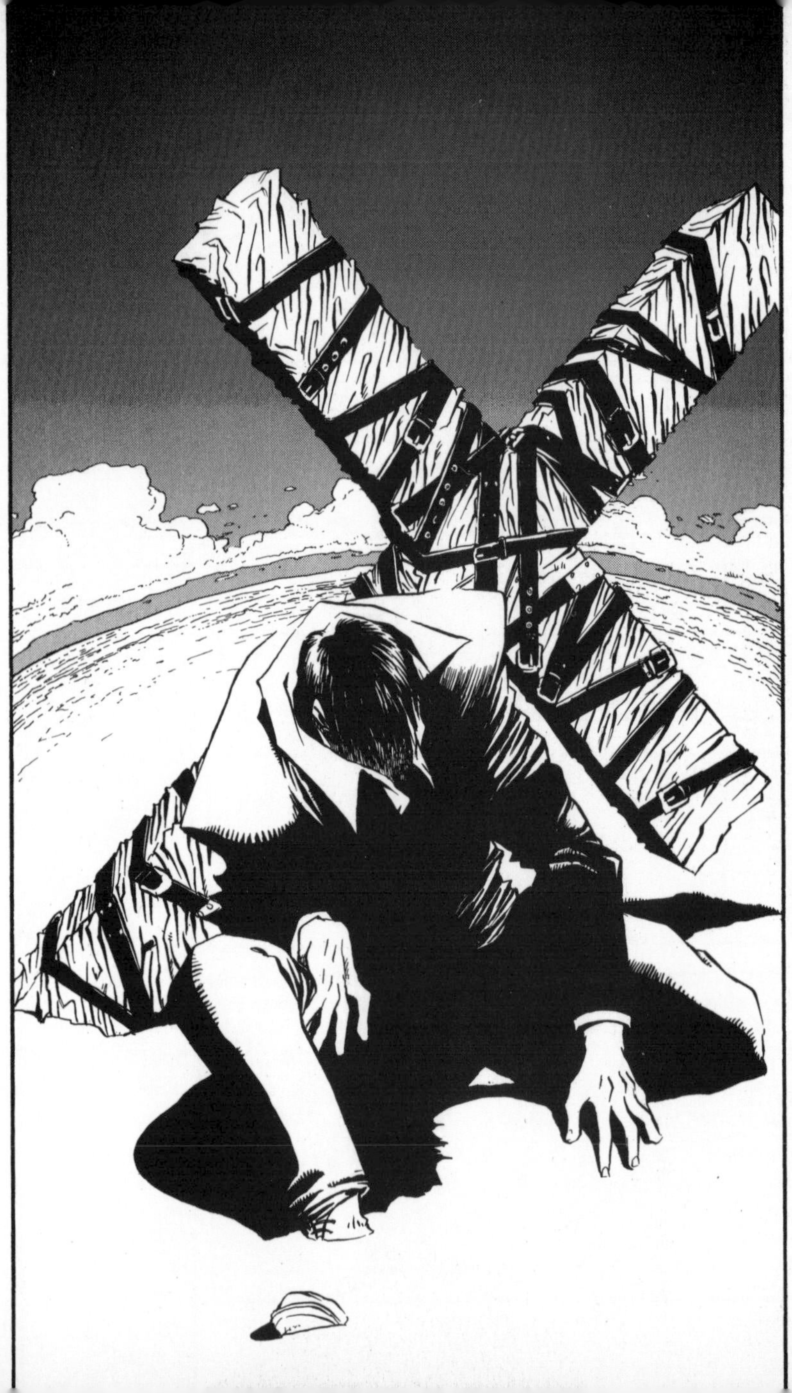

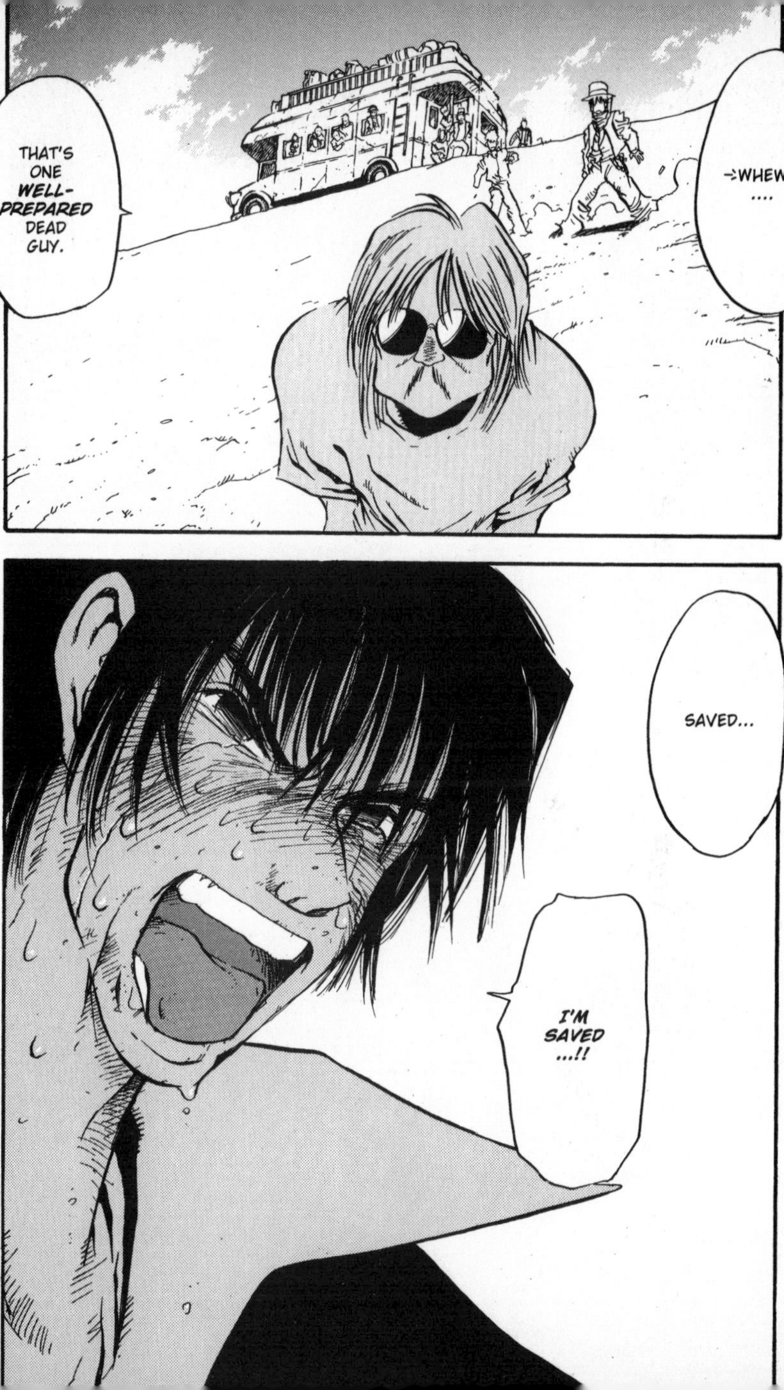
-WHEW- ....
THAT'S ONE WELL-PREPARED DEAD GUY.
SAVED...
I'M SAVED ...!!

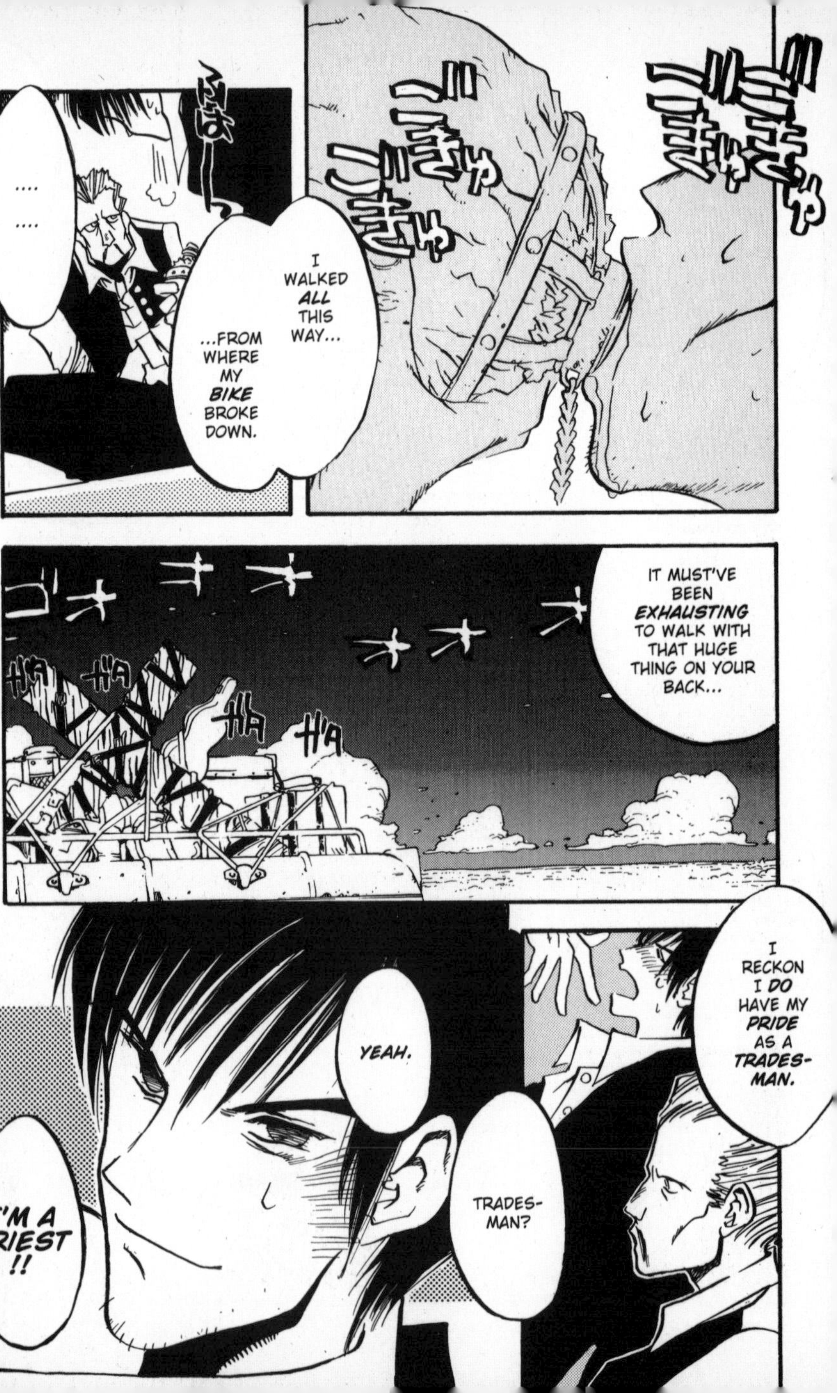
I WALKED ALL THIS WAY...
...FROM WHERE MY BIKE BROKE DOWN.
....
....
IT MUST'VE BEEN EXHAUSTING TO WALK WITH THAT HUGE THING ON YOUR BACK...
I RECKON I DO HAVE MY PRIDE AS A TRADES-MAN.
YEAH.
TRADES-MAN?
I'M A PRIEST!!

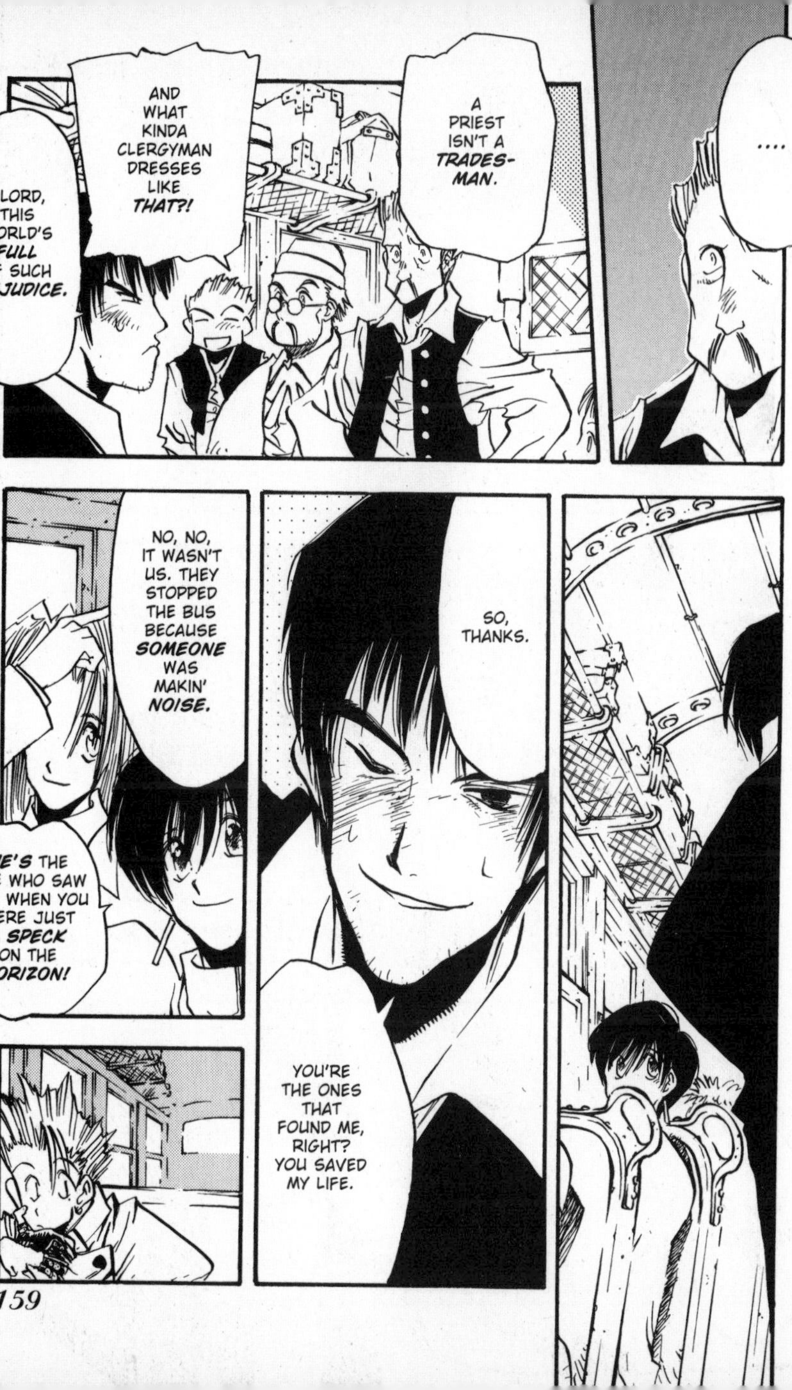
....
A PRIEST ISN'T A *TRADES-MAN*.
AND WHAT KINDA CLERGYMAN DRESSES LIKE *THAT?!*
O LORD, THIS WORLD'S *FULL* OF SUCH *PREJUDICE*.
YOU'RE THE ONES THAT FOUND ME, RIGHT? YOU SAVED MY LIFE.
SO, THANKS.
NO, NO, IT WASN'T US. THEY STOPPED THE BUS BECAUSE *SOMEONE* WAS MAKIN' *NOISE*.
HE'S THE ONE WHO SAW YOU WHEN YOU WERE JUST A *SPECK* ON THE *HORIZON!*

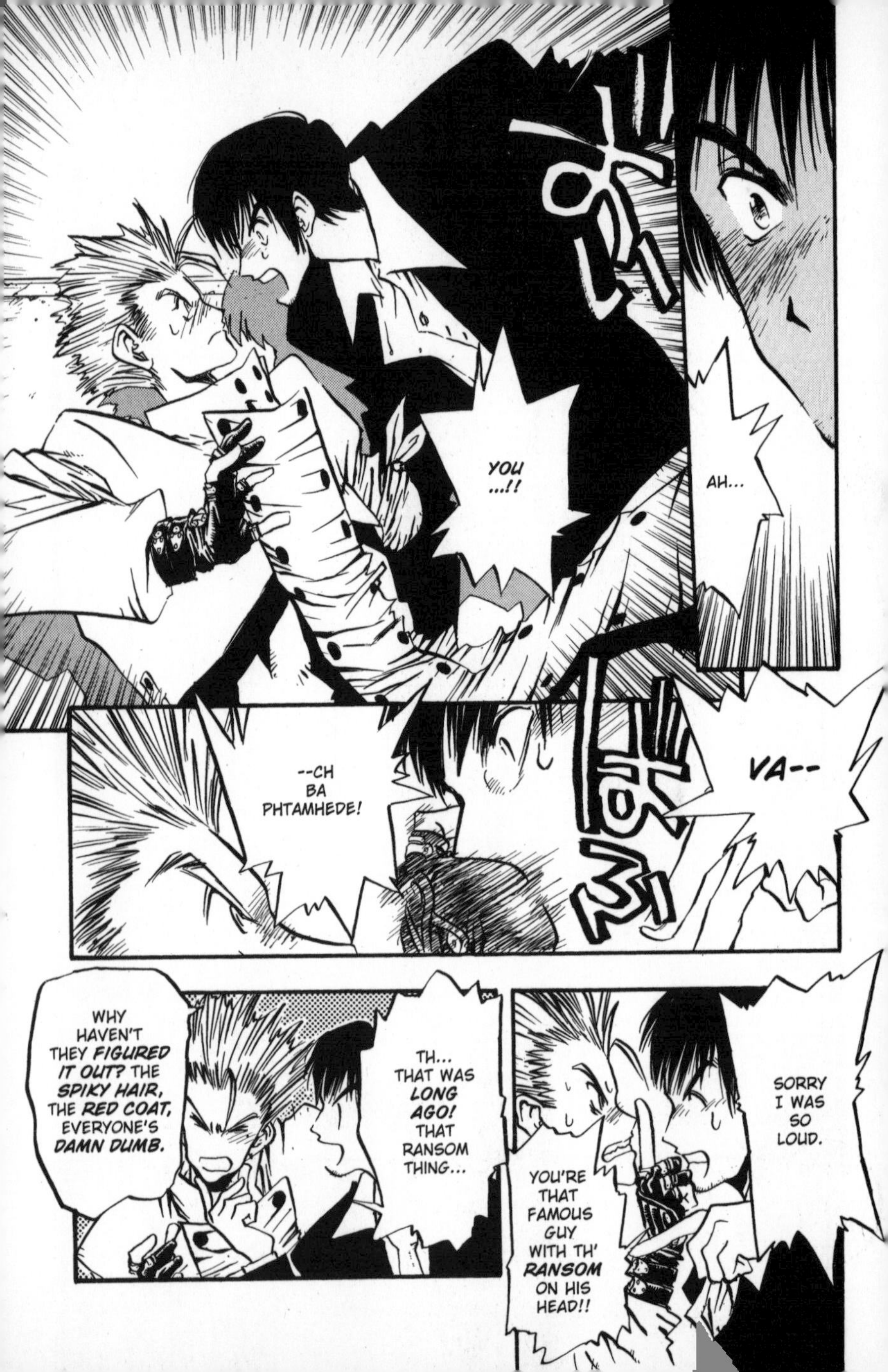
AH...
YOU ...!!
VA--
--CH BA PHTAMHEDE!
SORRY I WAS SO LOUD.
YOU'RE THAT FAMOUS GUY WITH TH' RANSOM ON HIS HEAD!!
TH... THAT WAS LONG AGO! THAT RANSOM THING...
WHY HAVEN'T THEY FIGURED IT OUT? THE SPIKY HAIR, THE RED COAT, EVERYONE'S DAMN DUMB.

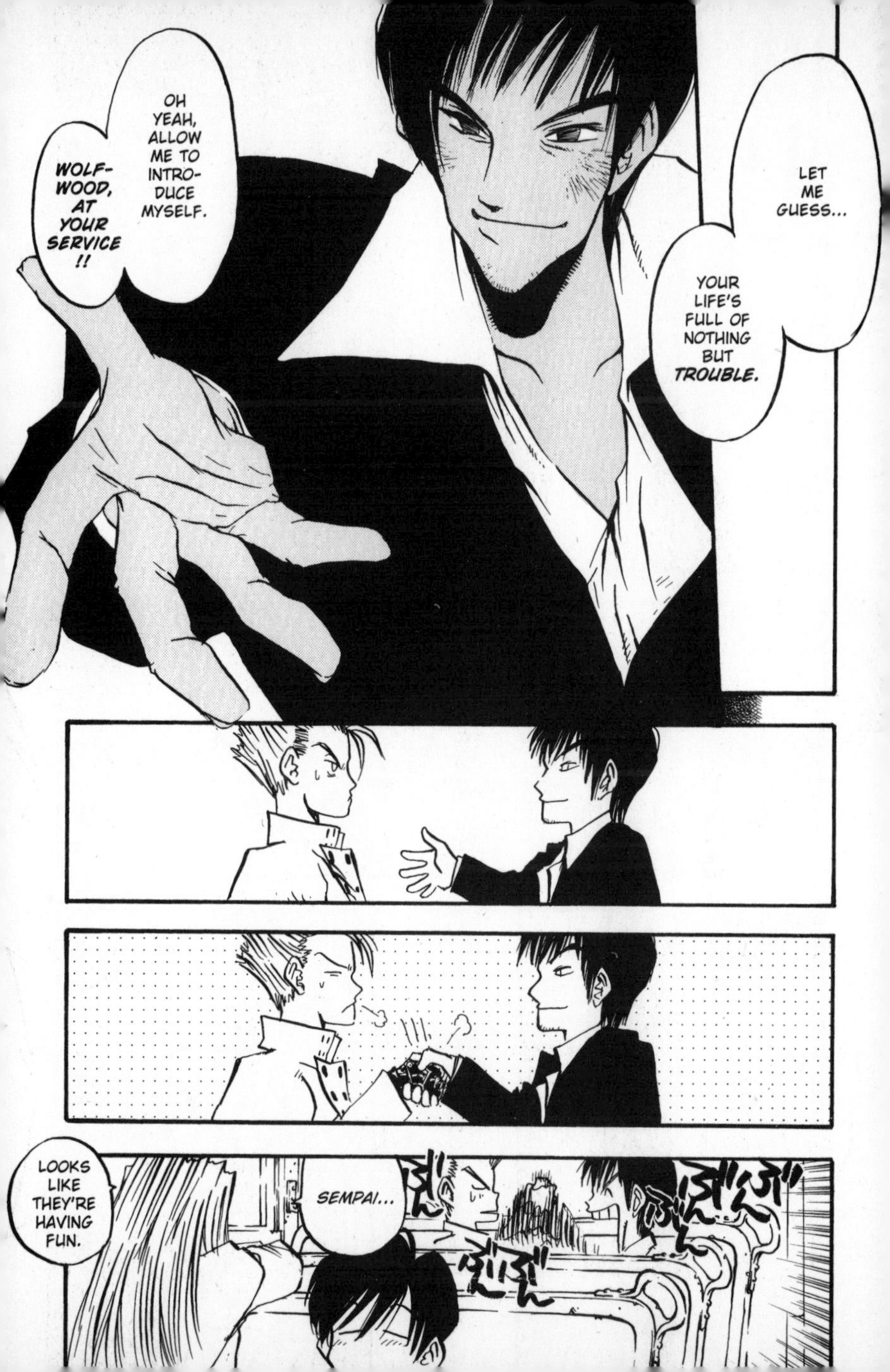
LET ME GUESS...
YOUR LIFE'S FULL OF NOTHING BUT *TROUBLE.*
OH YEAH, ALLOW ME TO INTRO-DUCE MYSELF.
WOLF-WOOD, AT YOUR SERVICE !!
SEMPAI...
LOOKS LIKE THEY'RE HAVING FUN.

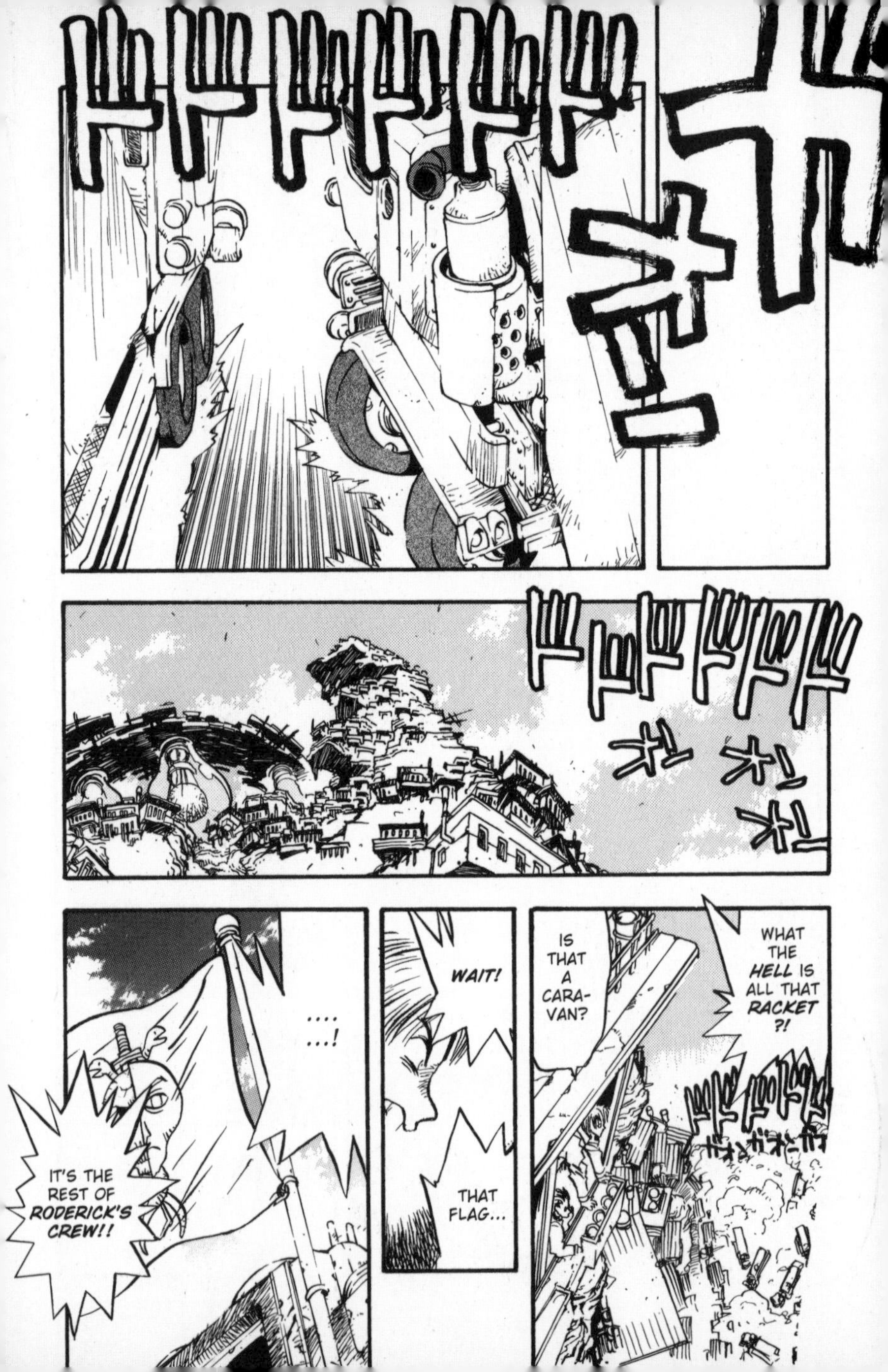
WHAT THE HELL IS ALL THAT RACKET?!
IS THAT A CARA-VAN?
WAIT!
THAT FLAG...
....
...!
IT'S THE REST OF RODERICK'S CREW!!

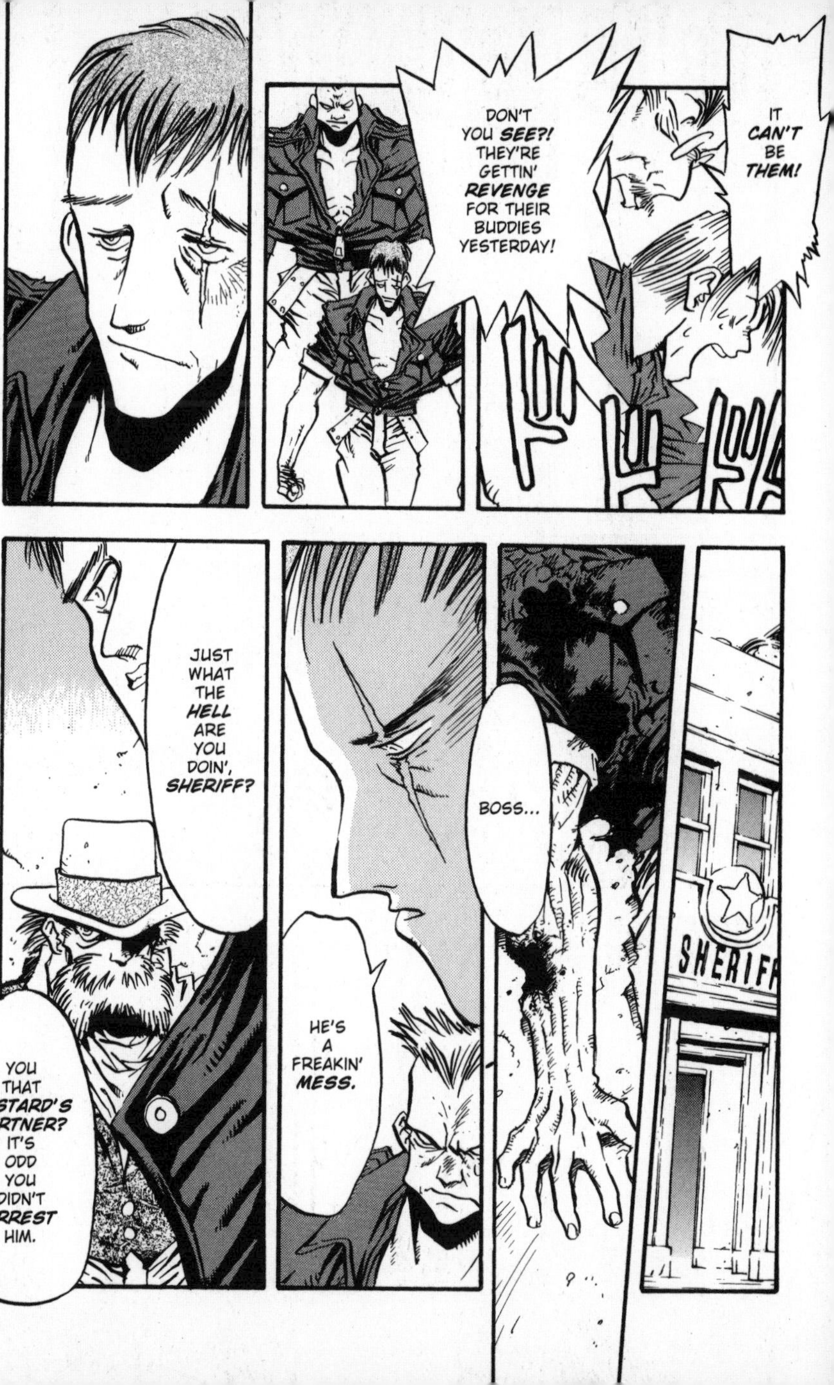
IT CAN'T BE THEM!
DON'T YOU SEE?! THEY'RE GETTIN' REVENGE FOR THEIR BUDDIES YESTERDAY!
SHERIF
BOSS...
HE'S A FREAKIN' MESS.
JUST WHAT THE HELL ARE YOU DOIN', SHERIFF?
YOU THAT BASTARD'S PARTNER? IT'S ODD YOU DIDN'T ARREST HIM.

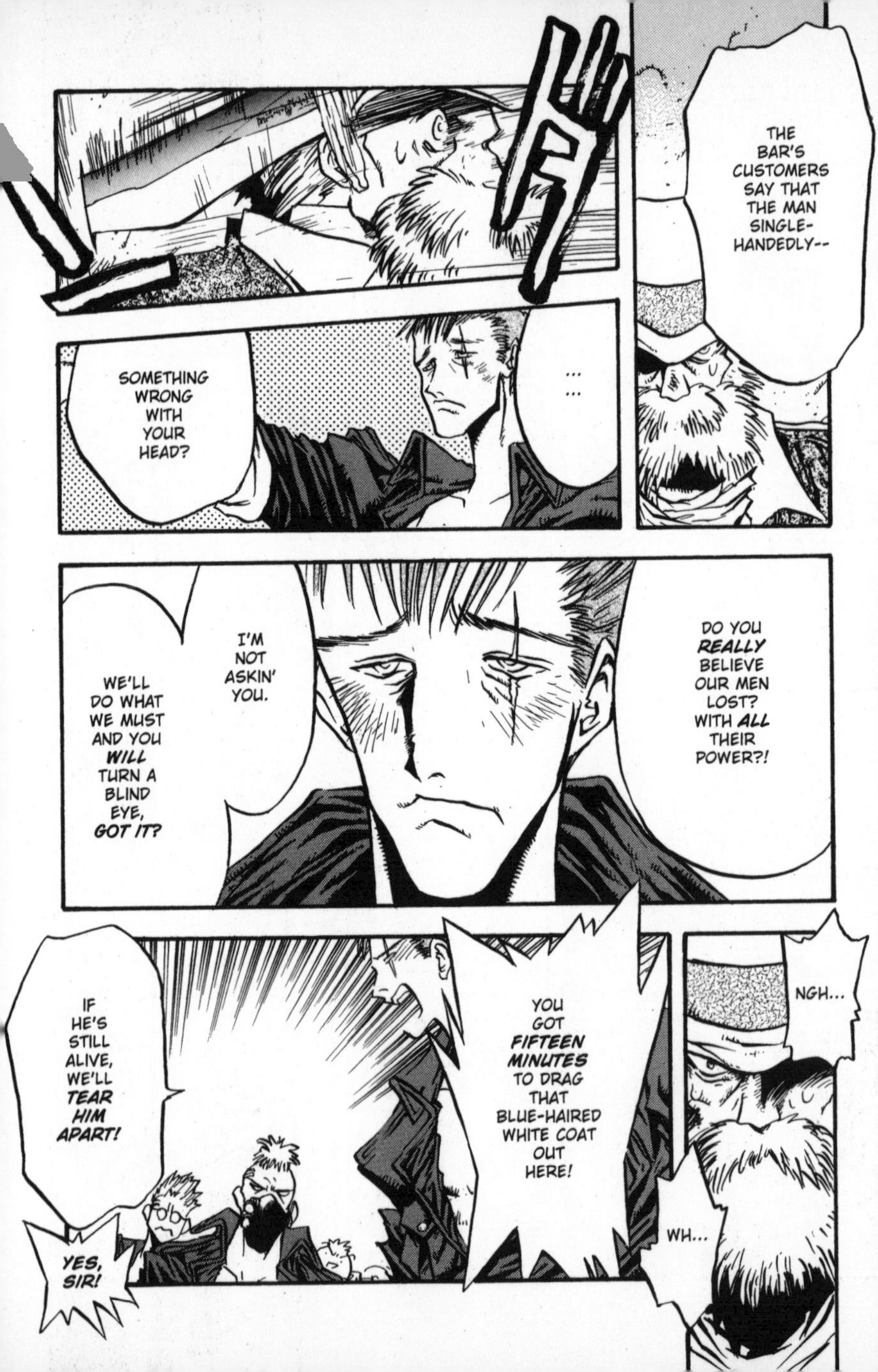
THE BAR'S CUSTOMERS SAY THAT THE MAN SINGLE-HANDEDLY--
... ...
SOMETHING WRONG WITH YOUR HEAD?
DO YOU REALLY BELIEVE OUR MEN LOST? WITH ALL THEIR POWER?!
I'M NOT ASKIN' YOU.
WE'LL DO WHAT WE MUST AND YOU WILL TURN A BLIND EYE, GOT IT?
NGH...
WH...
YOU GOT FIFTEEN MINUTES TO DRAG THAT BLUE-HAIRED WHITE COAT OUT HERE!
IF HE'S STILL ALIVE, WE'LL TEAR HIM APART!
YES, SIR!

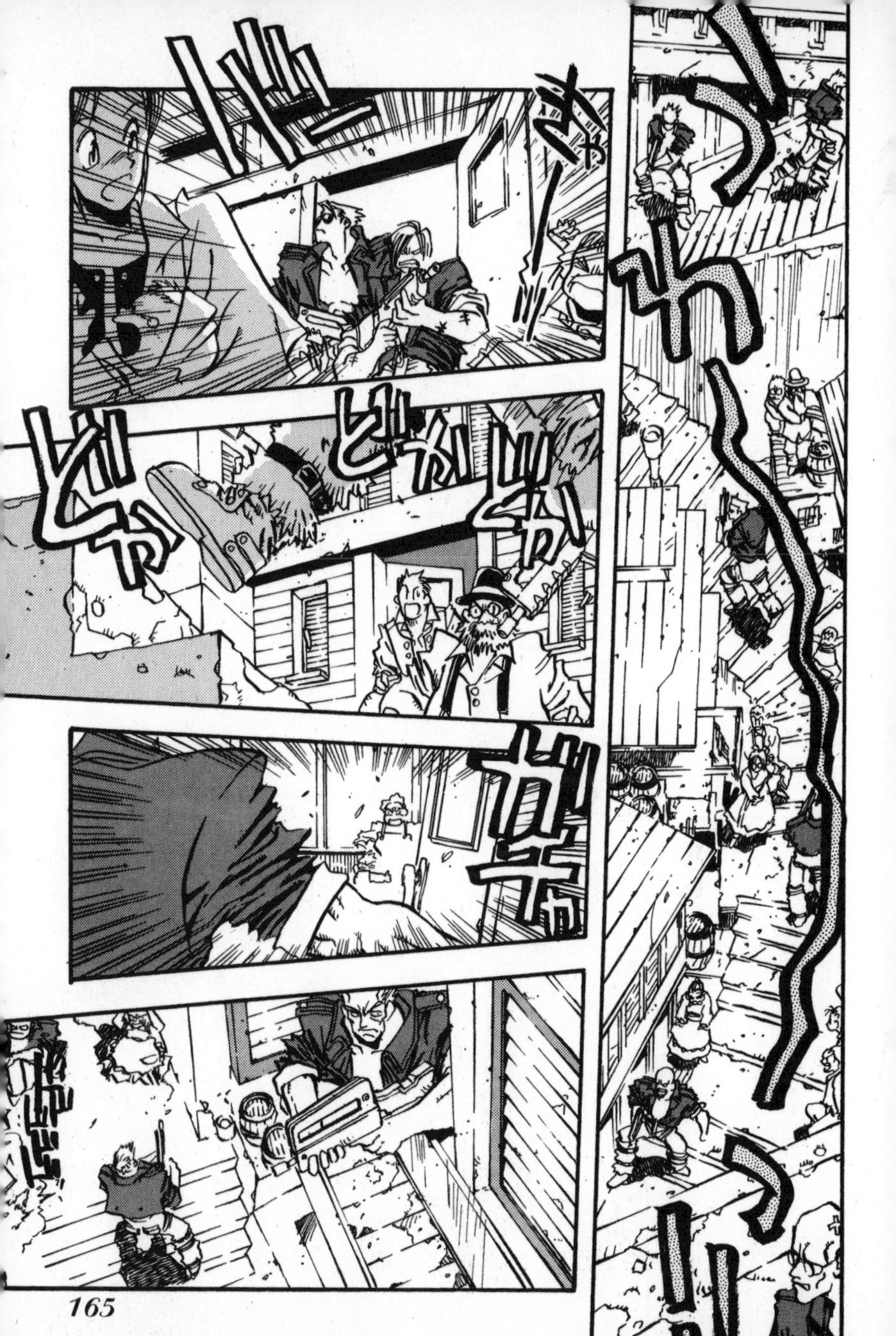
うわ～～っ!!
ぎゃー
どしゃ
ガチャ

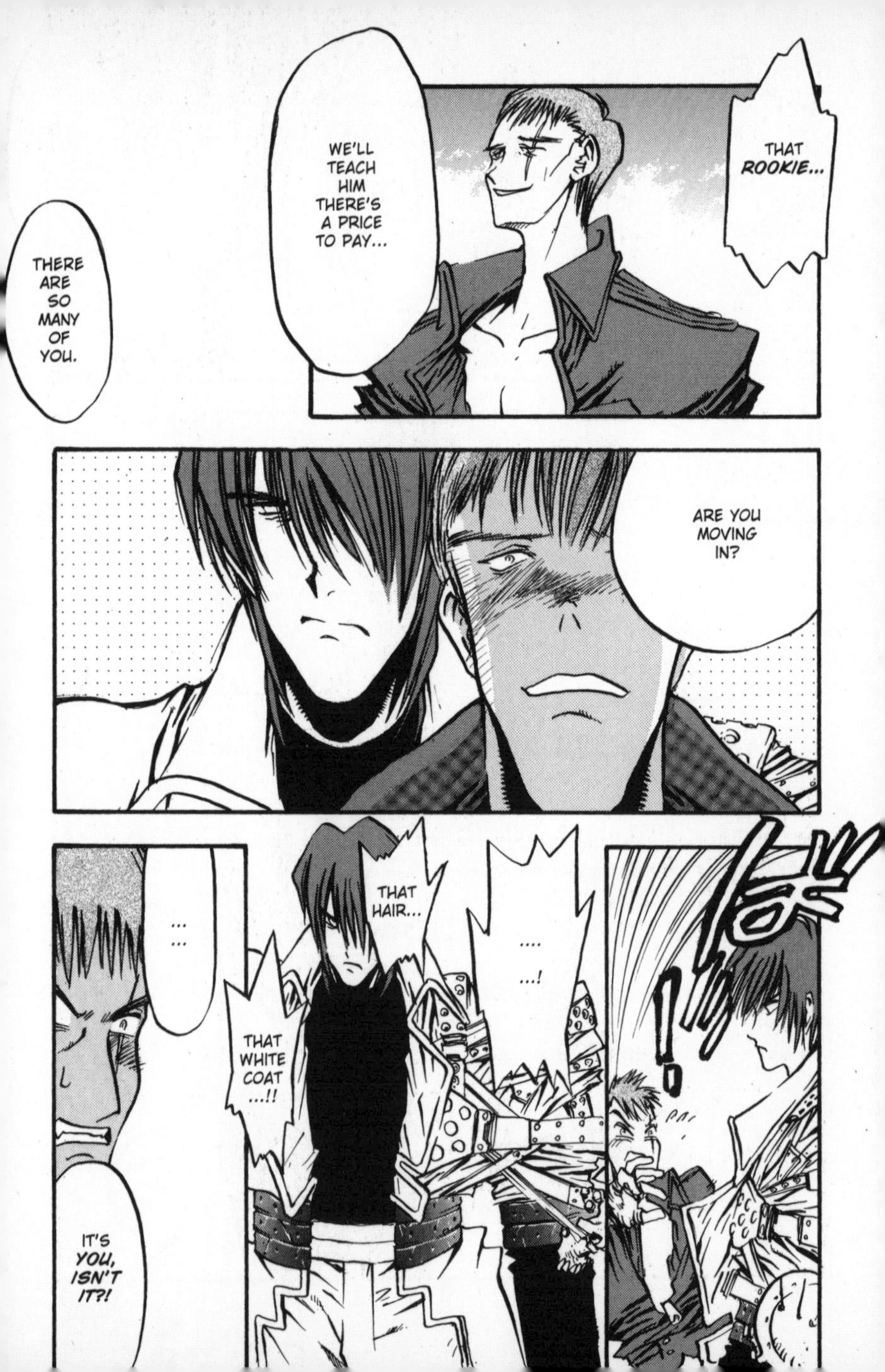
THAT ROOKIE...
WE'LL TEACH HIM THERE'S A PRICE TO PAY...
THERE ARE SO MANY OF YOU.
ARE YOU MOVING IN?
ば
!
THAT HAIR...
....!
THAT WHITE COAT ...!!
... ...
IT'S YOU, ISN'T IT?!

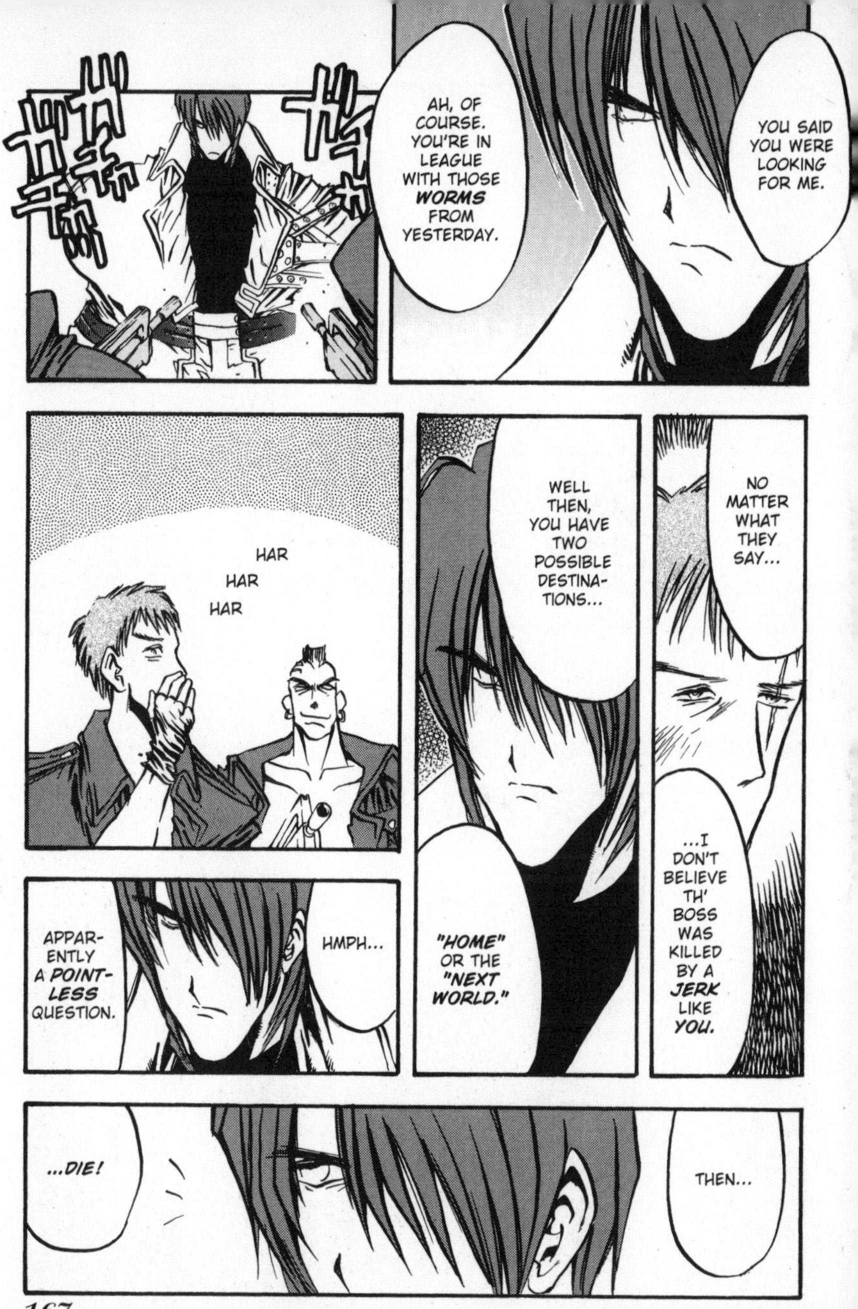
YOU SAID YOU WERE LOOKING FOR ME.
AH, OF COURSE. YOU'RE IN LEAGUE WITH THOSE WORMS FROM YESTERDAY.
NO MATTER WHAT THEY SAY...
...I DON'T BELIEVE TH' BOSS WAS KILLED BY A JERK LIKE YOU.
WELL THEN, YOU HAVE TWO POSSIBLE DESTINATIONS...
"HOME" OR THE "NEXT WORLD."
HAR
HAR
HAR
HMPH...
APPARENTLY A POINTLESS QUESTION.
THEN...
...DIE!

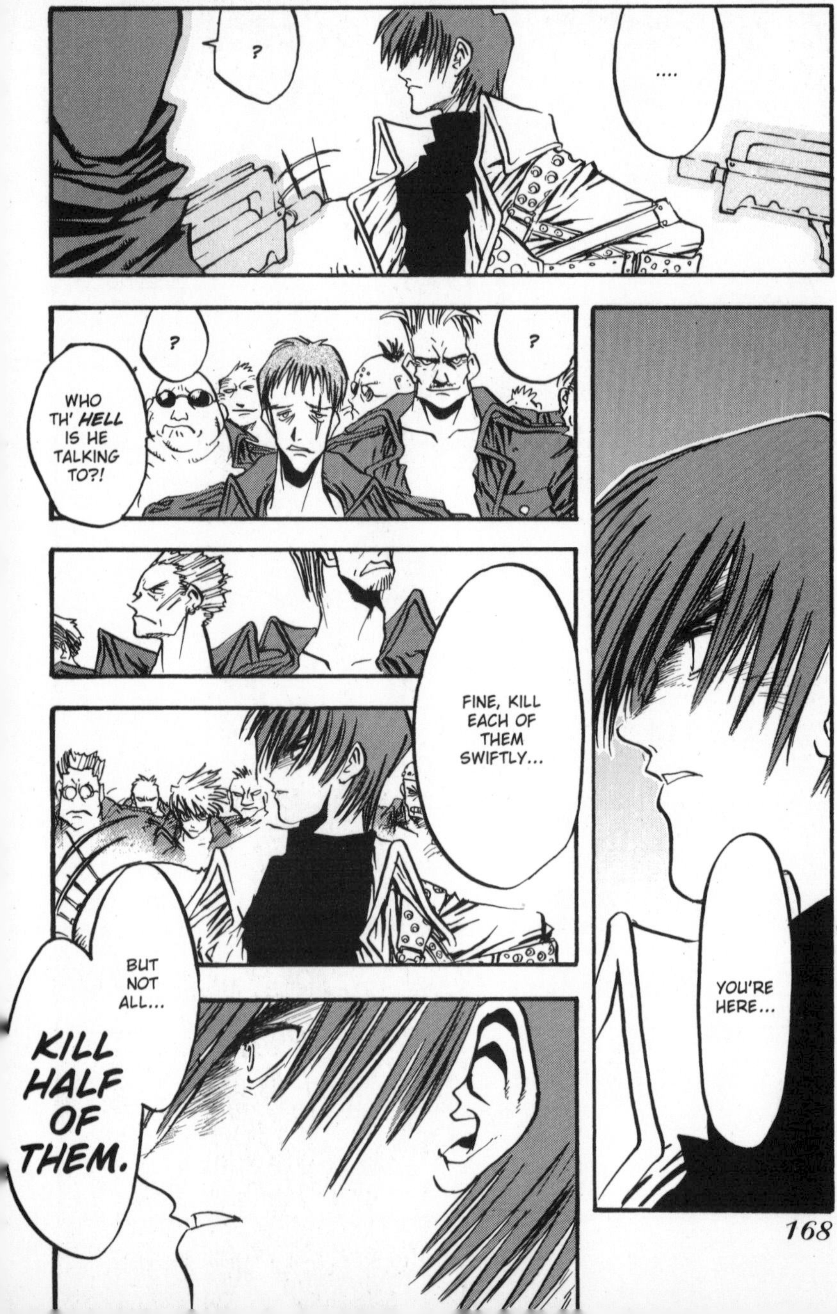
....
?
YOU'RE HERE...
?
?
WHO TH' **HELL** IS HE TALKING TO?!
FINE, KILL EACH OF THEM SWIFTLY...
BUT NOT ALL...
KILL HALF OF THEM.

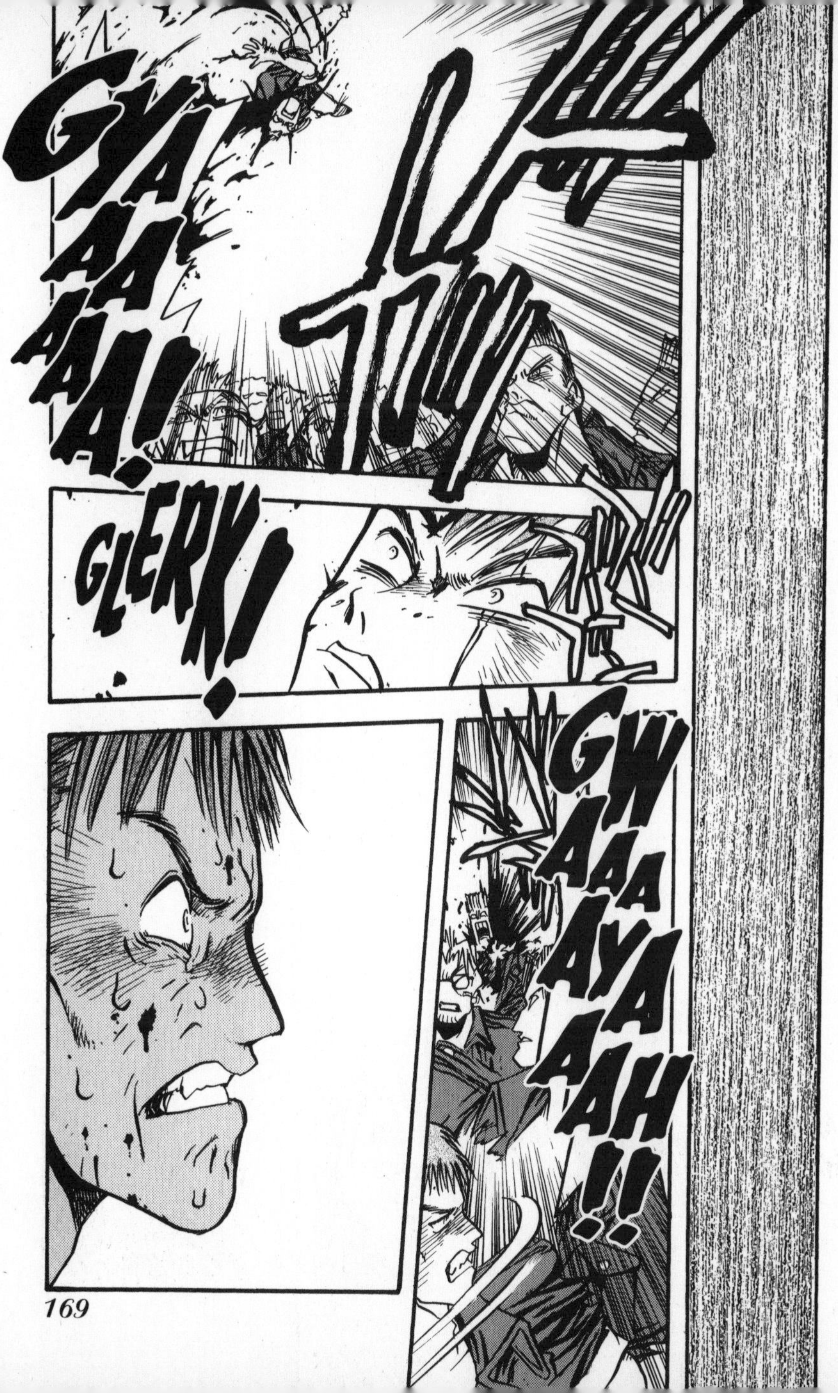
GYAAAAAA!
GLERK!
GWAAAAYAAAAAH!!

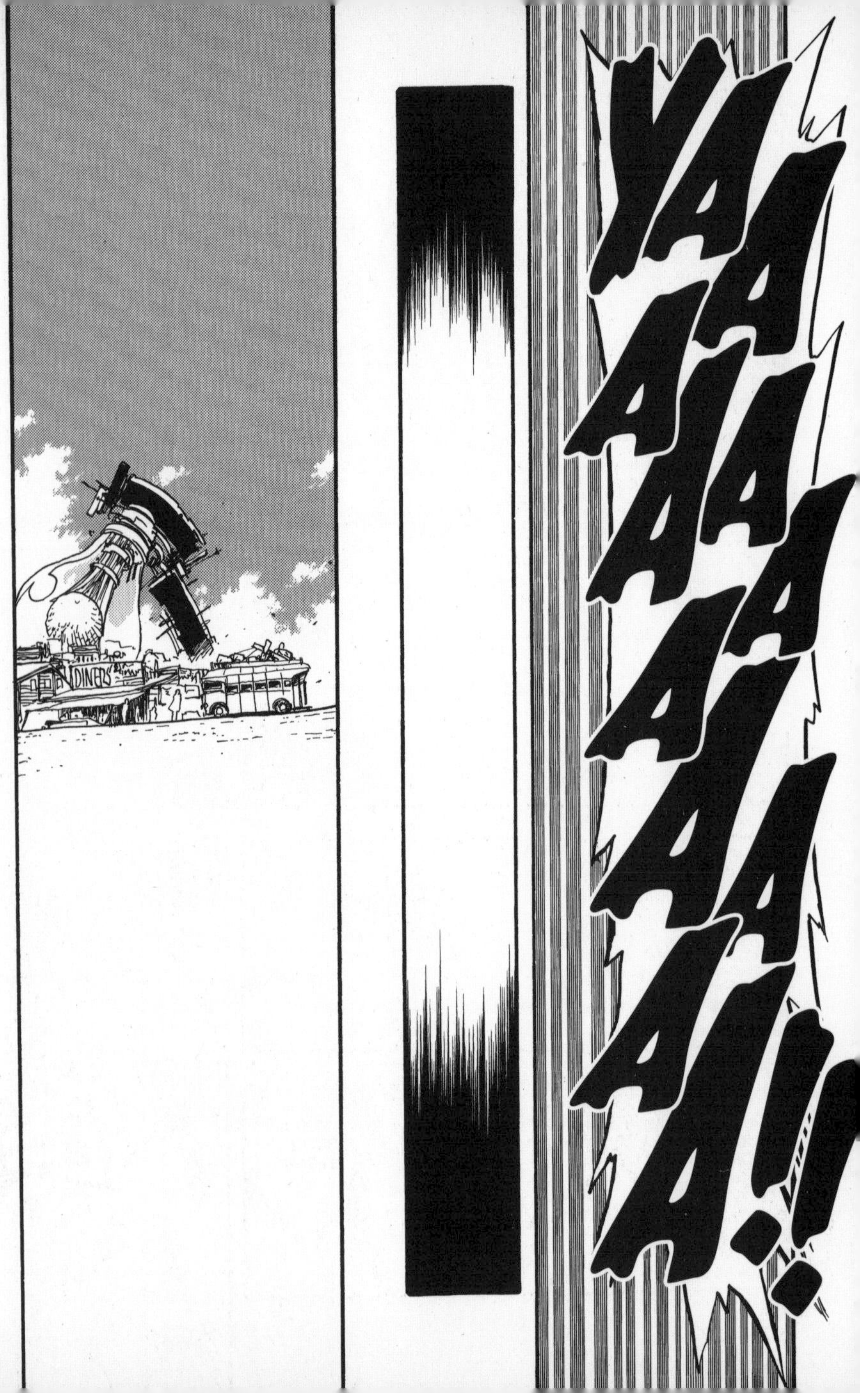
YAAAAAAAAAAAAAA!!

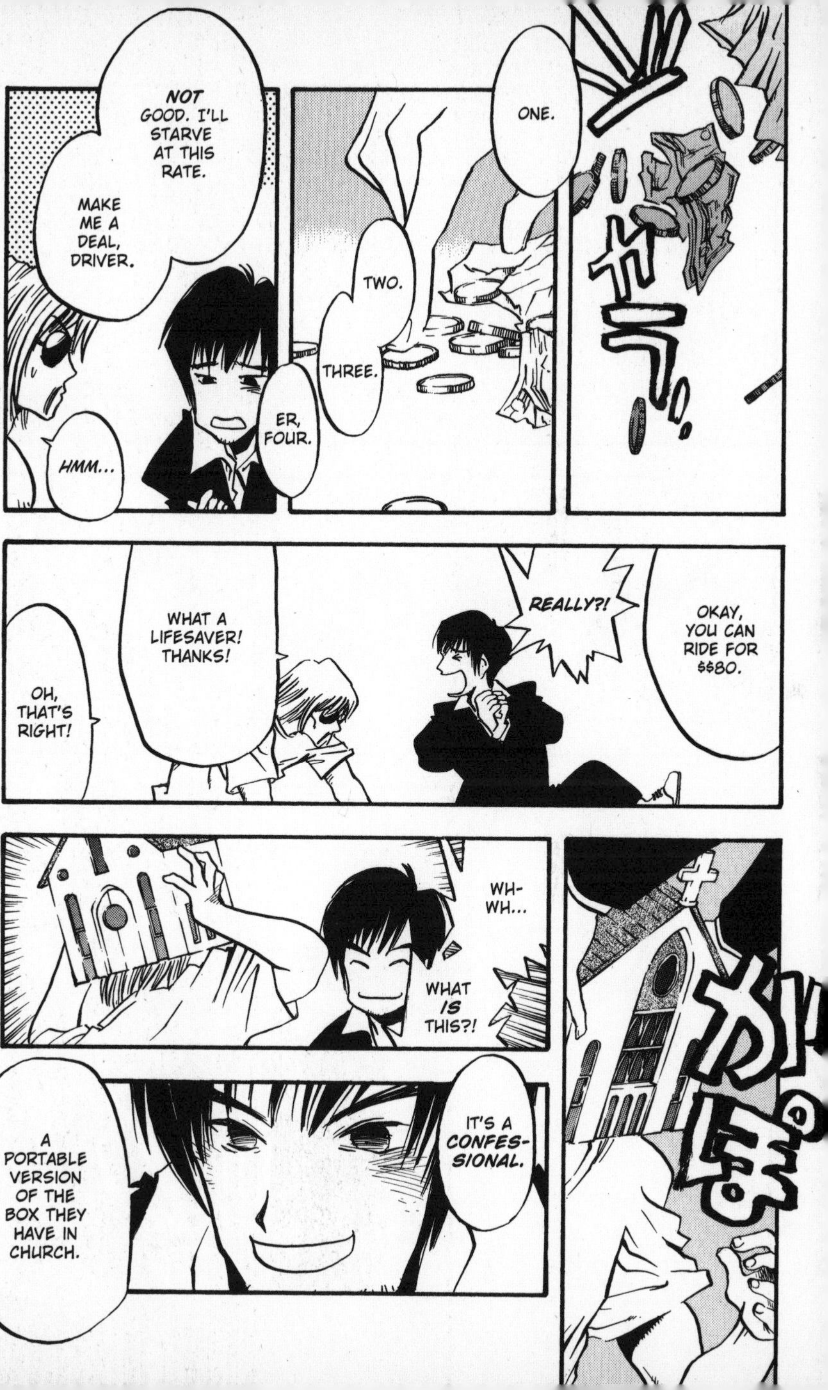
ONE.
TWO.
THREE.
ER, FOUR.
NOT GOOD. I'LL STARVE AT THIS RATE.
MAKE ME A DEAL, DRIVER.
HMM...
OKAY, YOU CAN RIDE FOR $$80.
REALLY?!
WHAT A LIFESAVER! THANKS!
OH, THAT'S RIGHT!
WH- WH...
WHAT IS THIS?!
IT'S A CONFESSIONAL.
A PORTABLE VERSION OF THE BOX THEY HAVE IN CHURCH.

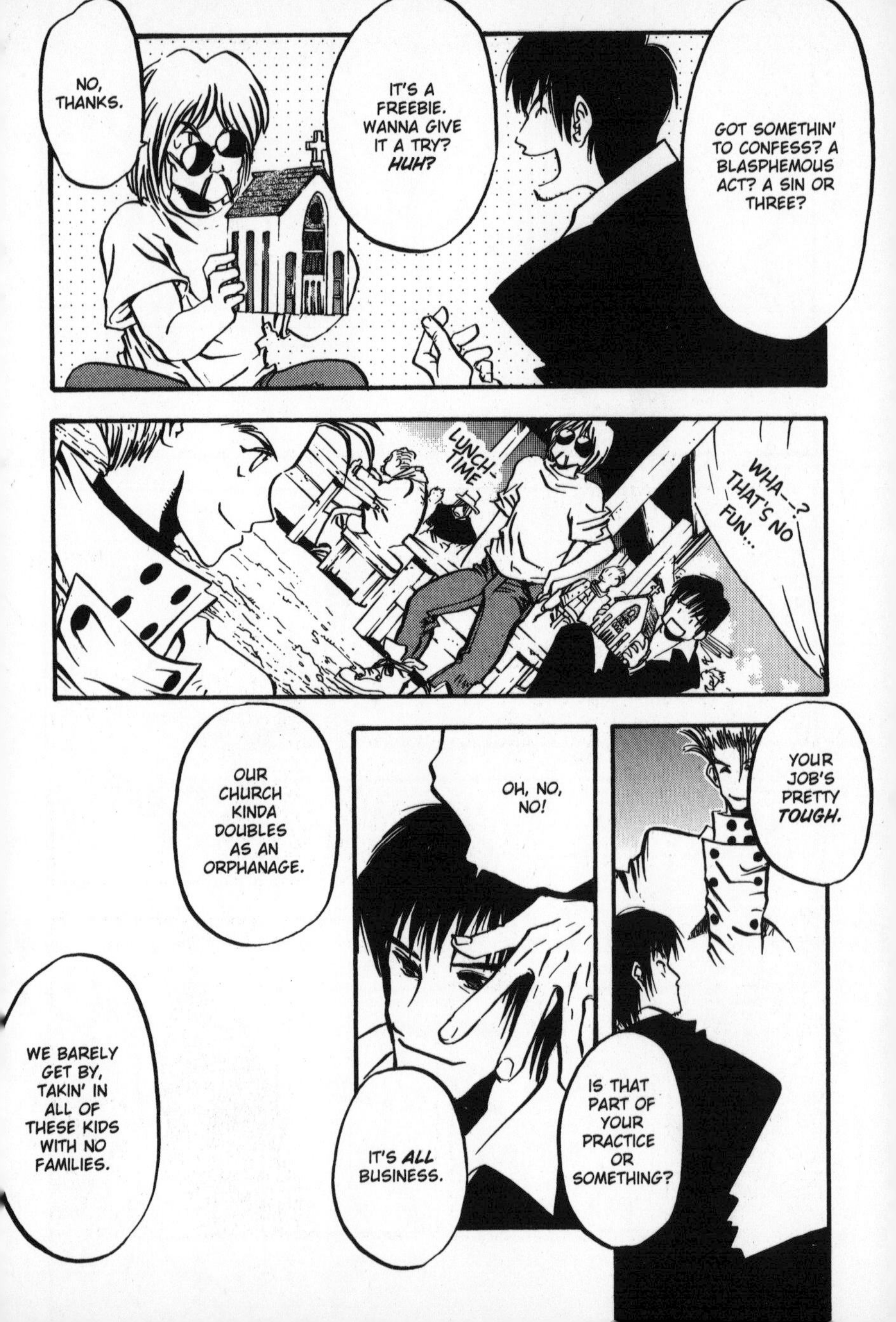
GOT SOMETHIN' TO CONFESS? A BLASPHEMOUS ACT? A SIN OR THREE?
IT'S A FREEBIE. WANNA GIVE IT A TRY? *HUH?*
NO, THANKS.
WHA--? THAT'S NO FUN...
LUNCH-TIME
YOUR JOB'S PRETTY *TOUGH.*
IS THAT PART OF YOUR PRACTICE OR SOMETHING?
OH, NO, NO!
IT'S *ALL* BUSINESS.
OUR CHURCH KINDA DOUBLES AS AN ORPHANAGE.
WE BARELY GET BY, TAKIN' IN ALL OF THESE KIDS WITH NO FAMILIES.

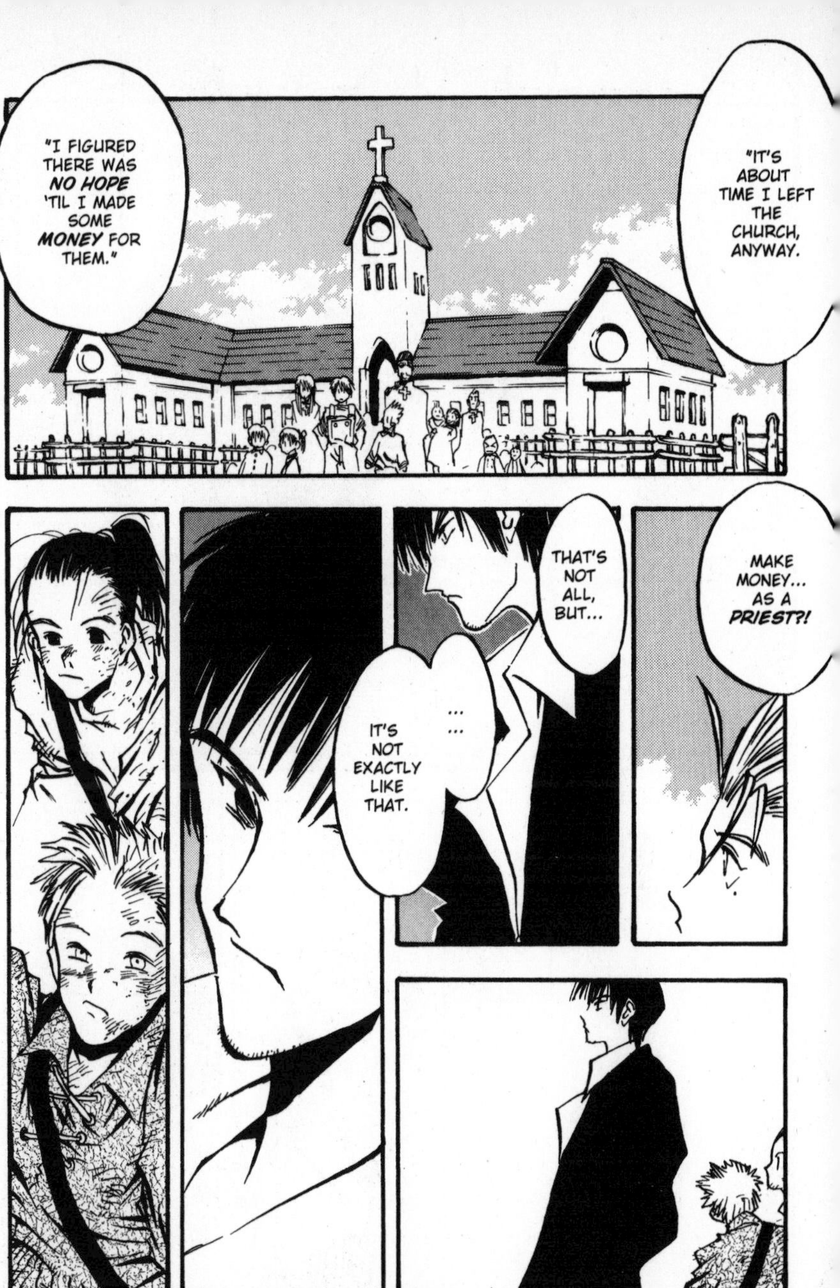
"IT'S ABOUT TIME I LEFT THE CHURCH, ANYWAY.
"I FIGURED THERE WAS NO HOPE 'TIL I MADE SOME MONEY FOR THEM."
MAKE MONEY... AS A PRIEST?!
THAT'S NOT ALL, BUT...
......
IT'S NOT EXACTLY LIKE THAT.

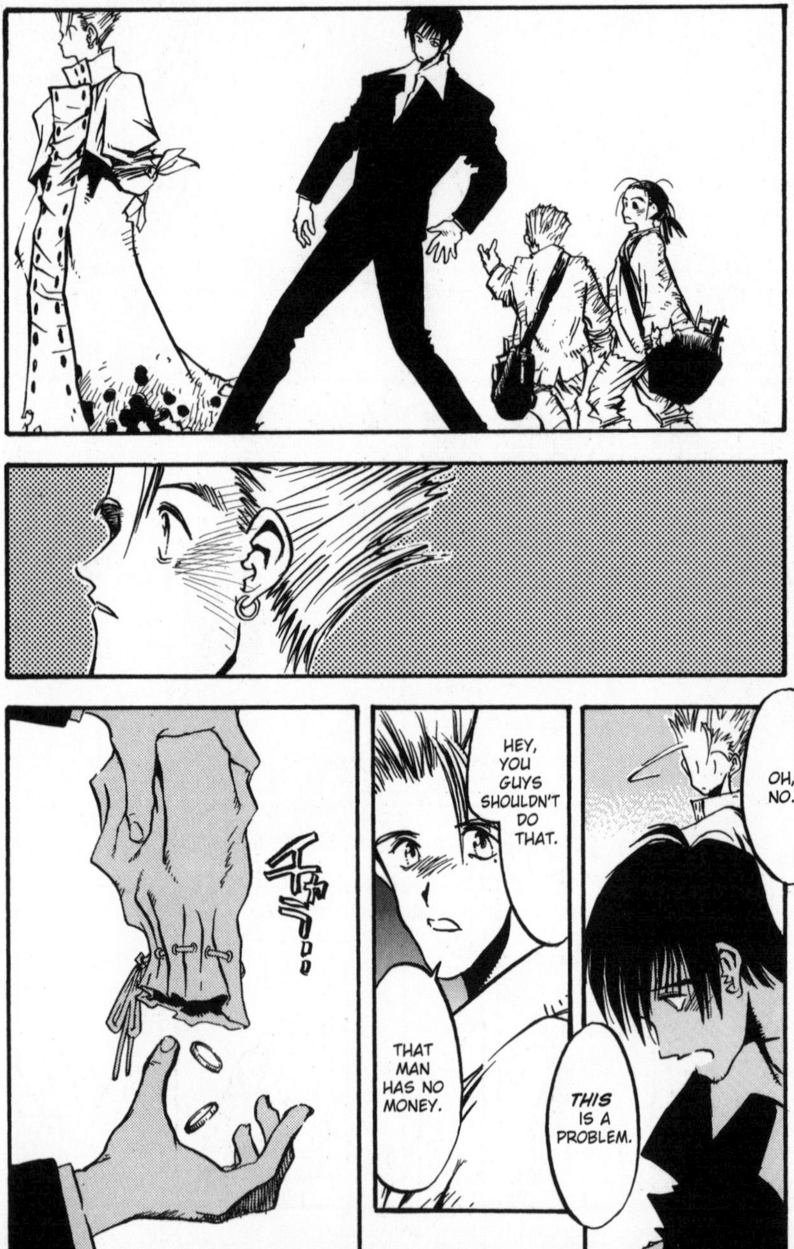
OH, NO.
THIS IS A PROBLEM.
HEY, YOU GUYS SHOULDN'T DO THAT.
THAT MAN HAS NO MONEY.

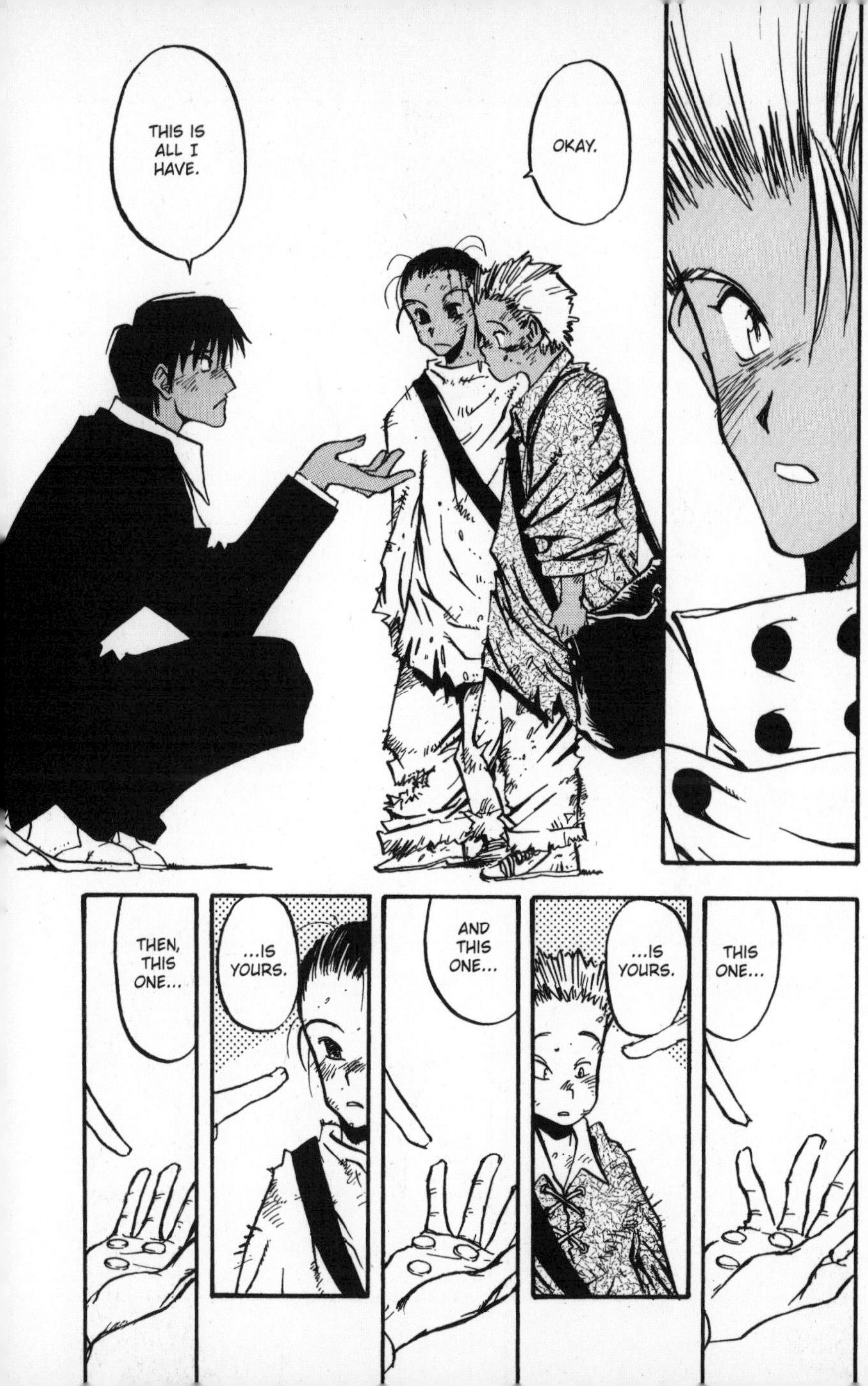
OKAY.
THIS IS ALL I HAVE.
THIS ONE...
...IS YOURS.
AND THIS ONE...
...IS YOURS.
THEN, THIS ONE...

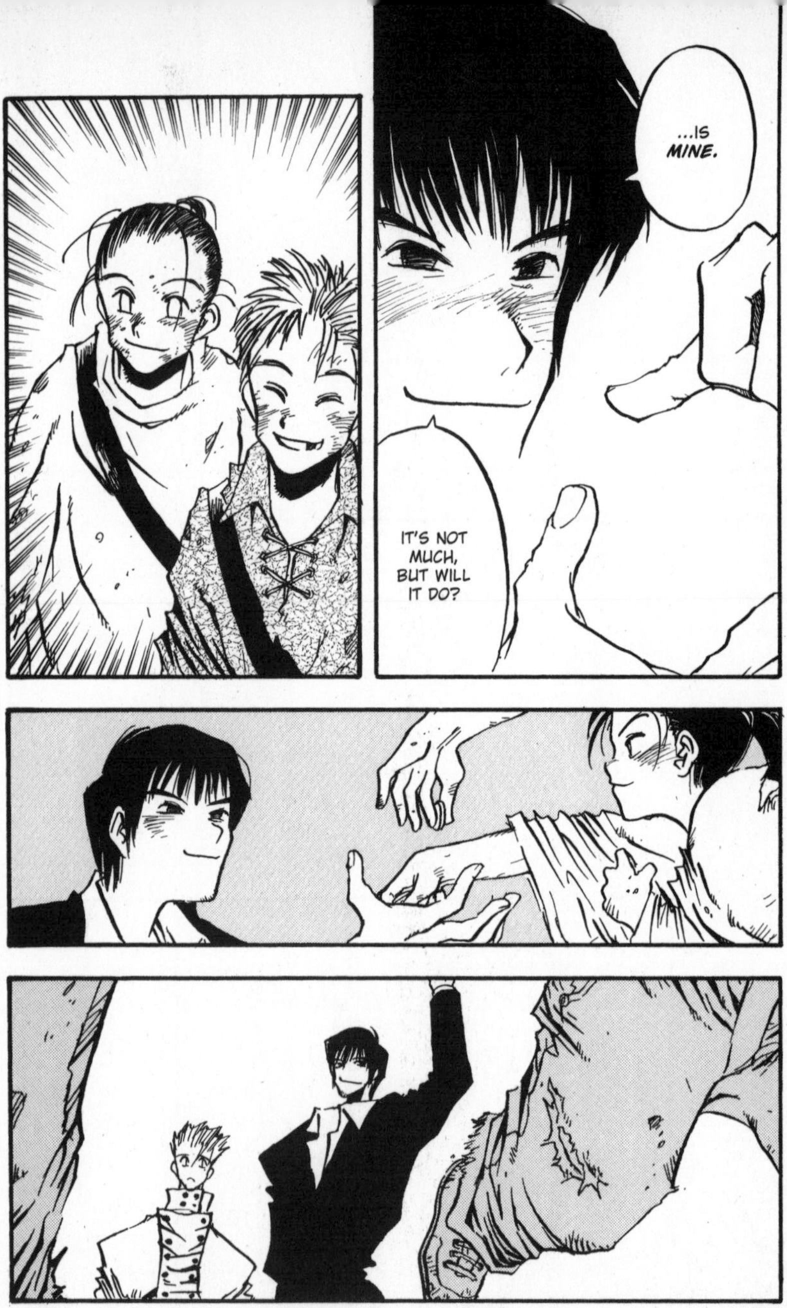
...IS MINE.
IT'S NOT MUCH, BUT WILL IT DO?

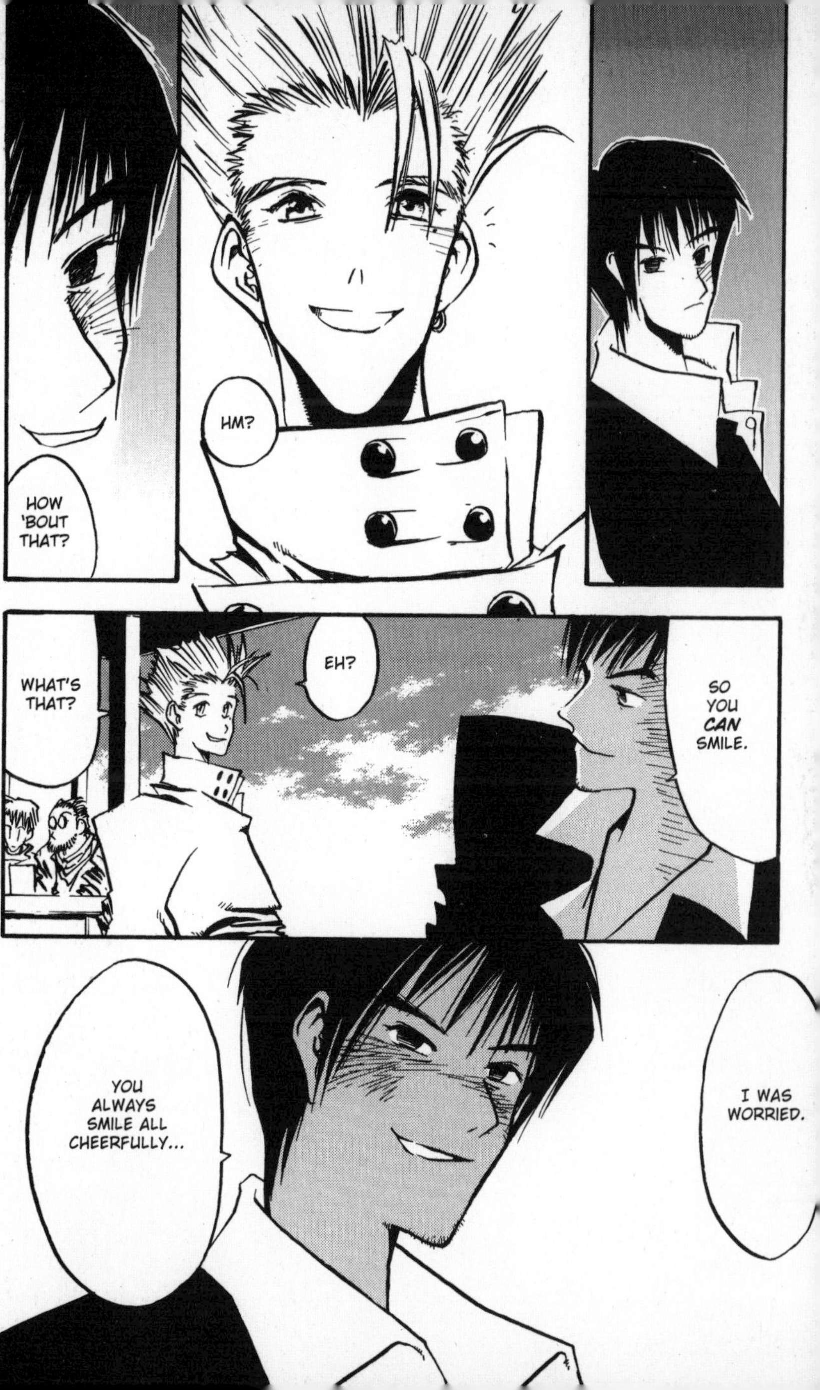
HM?
HOW 'BOUT THAT?
SO YOU ***CAN*** SMILE.
EH?
WHAT'S THAT?
I WAS WORRIED.
YOU ALWAYS SMILE ALL CHEERFULLY...

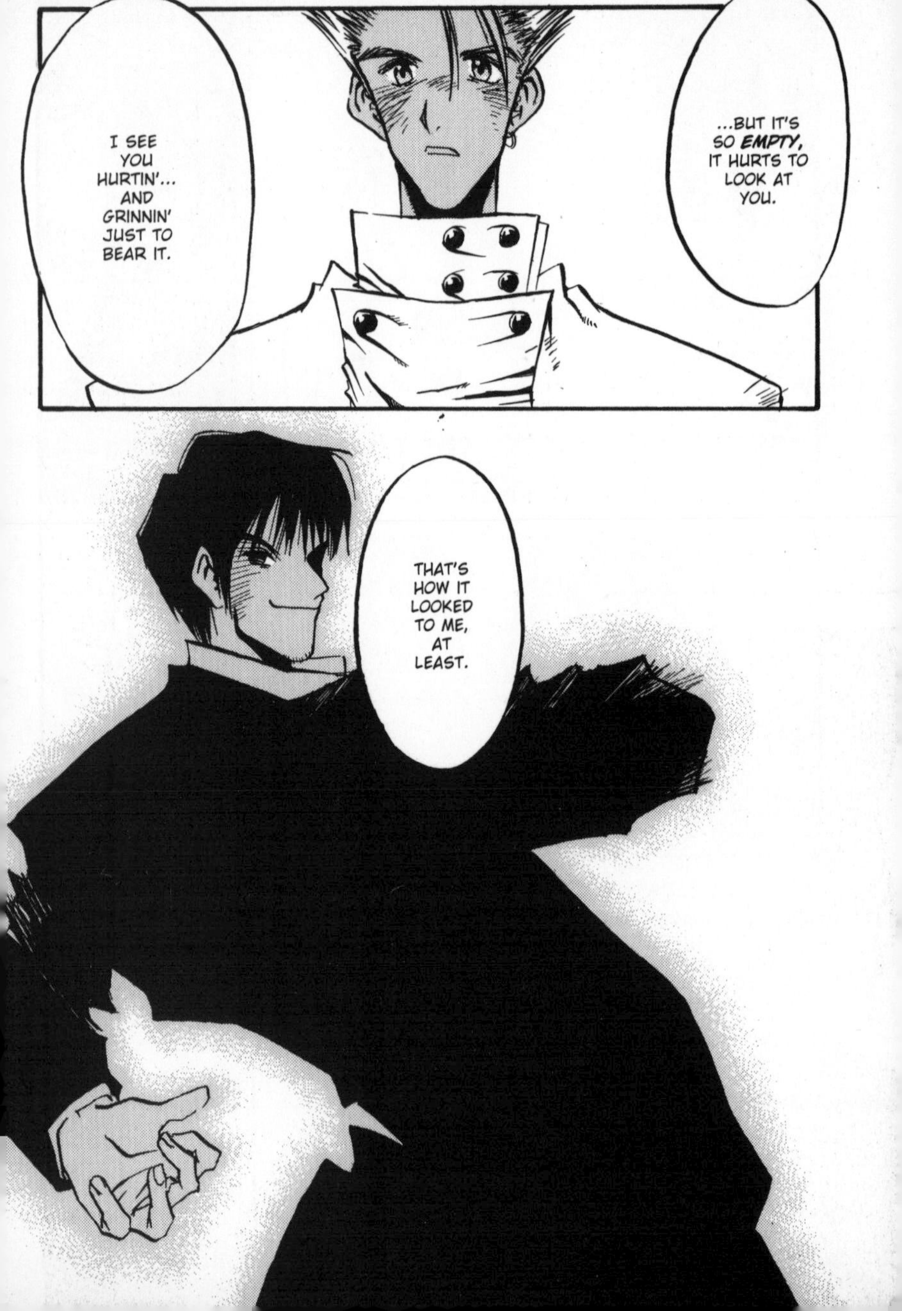
...BUT IT'S SO **EMPTY**, IT HURTS TO LOOK AT YOU.
I SEE YOU HURTIN'... AND GRINNIN' JUST TO BEAR IT.
THAT'S HOW IT LOOKED TO ME, AT LEAST.

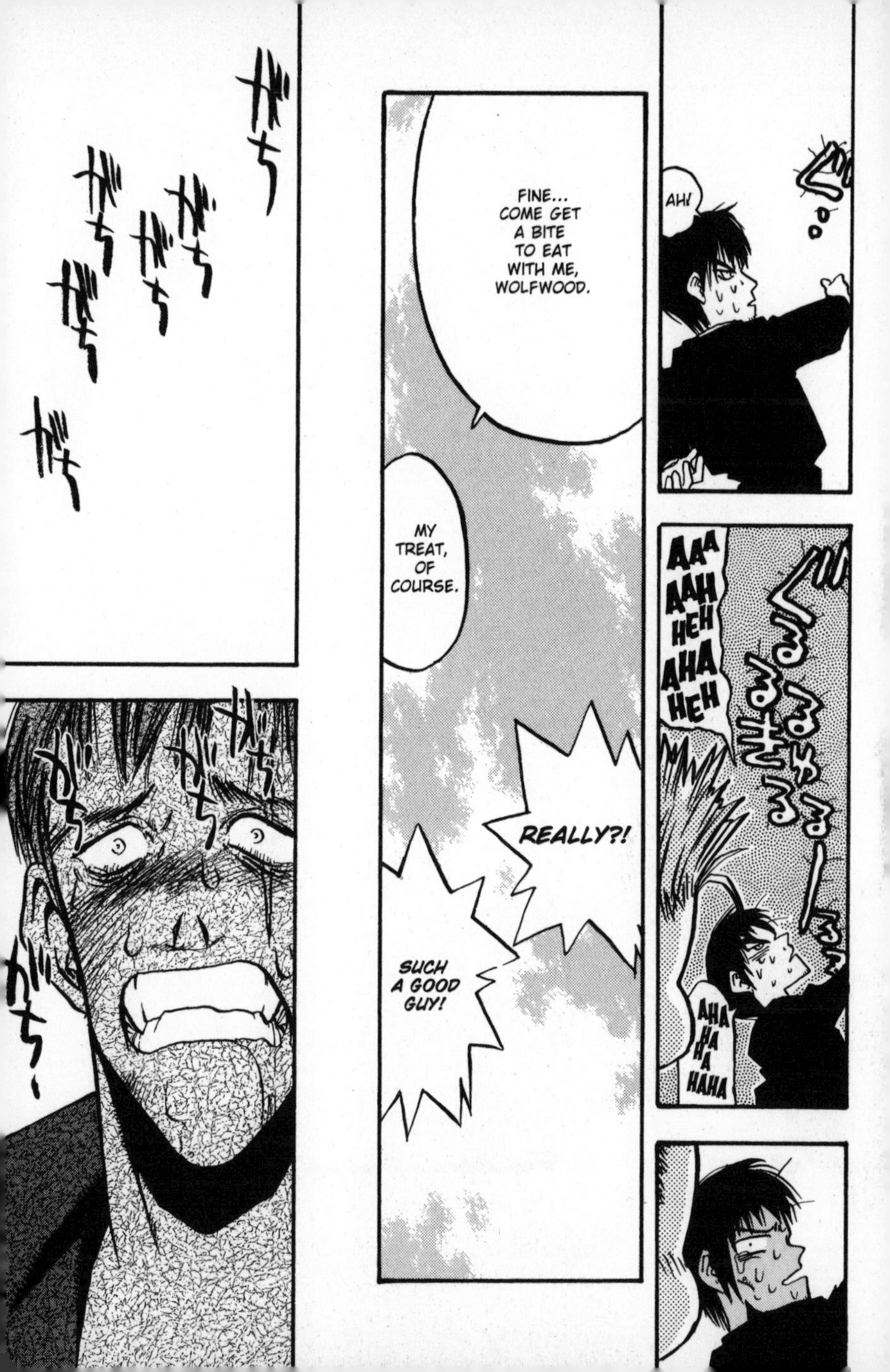
AH!
AAAAAH HEH AHAHA HEH
AHA HA HA HA HAHA
FINE... COME GET A BITE TO EAT WITH ME, WOLFWOOD.
MY TREAT, OF COURSE.
REALLY?!
SUCH A GOOD GUY!

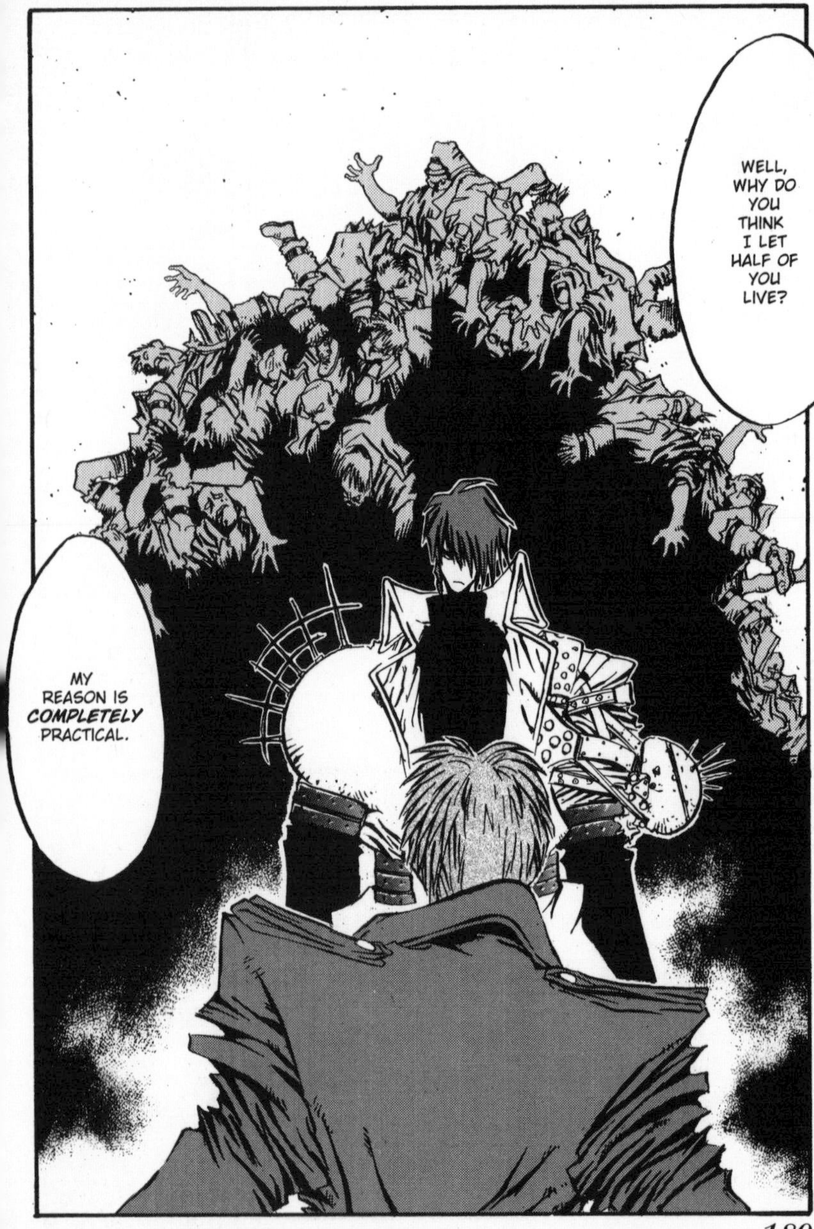
WELL, WHY DO YOU THINK I LET HALF OF YOU LIVE?
MY REASON IS ***COMPLETELY*** PRACTICAL.

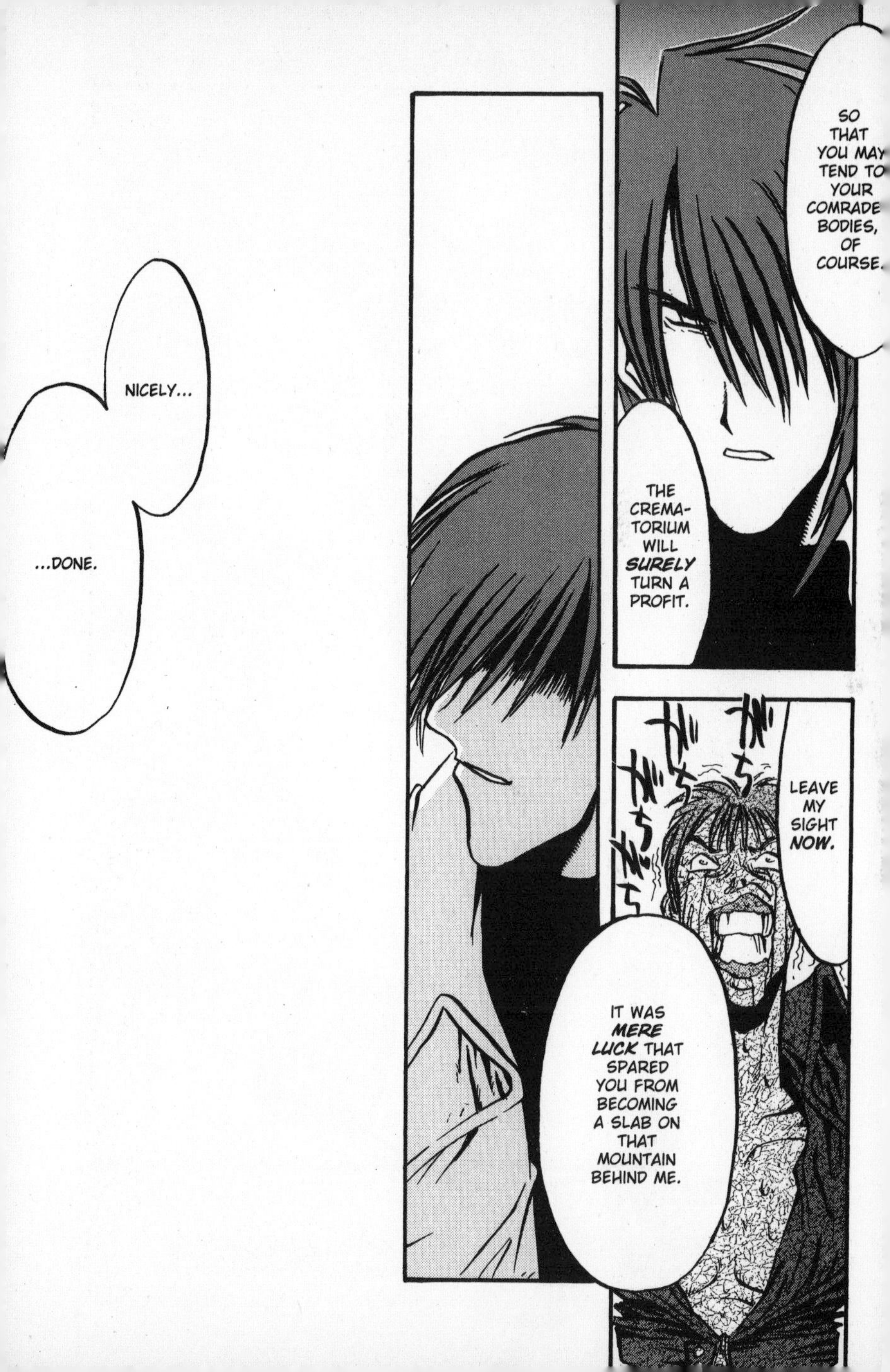
SO THAT YOU MAY TEND TO YOUR COMRADE BODIES, OF COURSE.
THE CREMATORIUM WILL *SURELY* TURN A PROFIT.
LEAVE MY SIGHT *NOW.*
IT WAS *MERE LUCK* THAT SPARED YOU FROM BECOMING A SLAB ON THAT MOUNTAIN BEHIND ME.
NICELY...
...DONE.

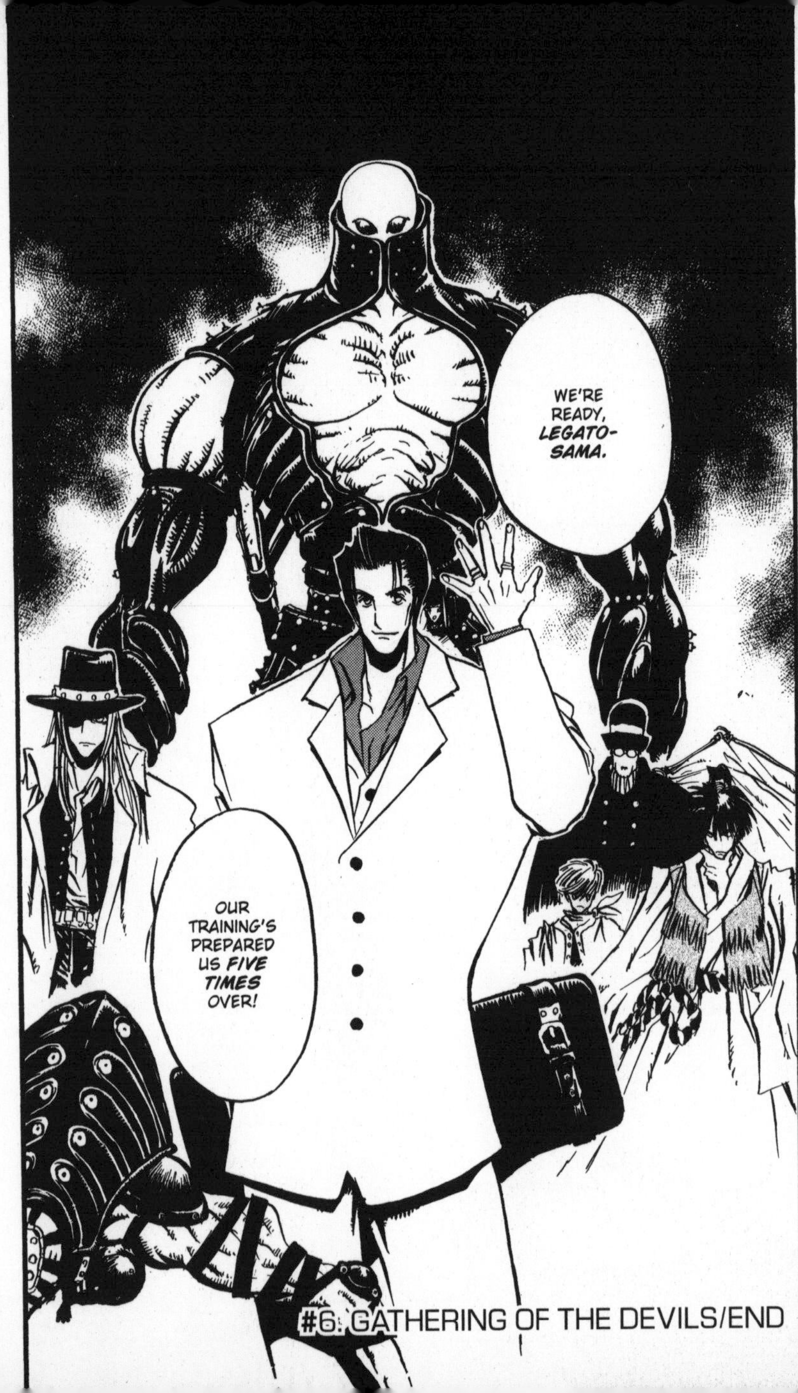
WE'RE READY, *LEGATO-SAMA.*
OUR TRAINING'S PREPARED US *FIVE TIMES* OVER!
#6: GATHERING OF THE DEVILS/END

#7

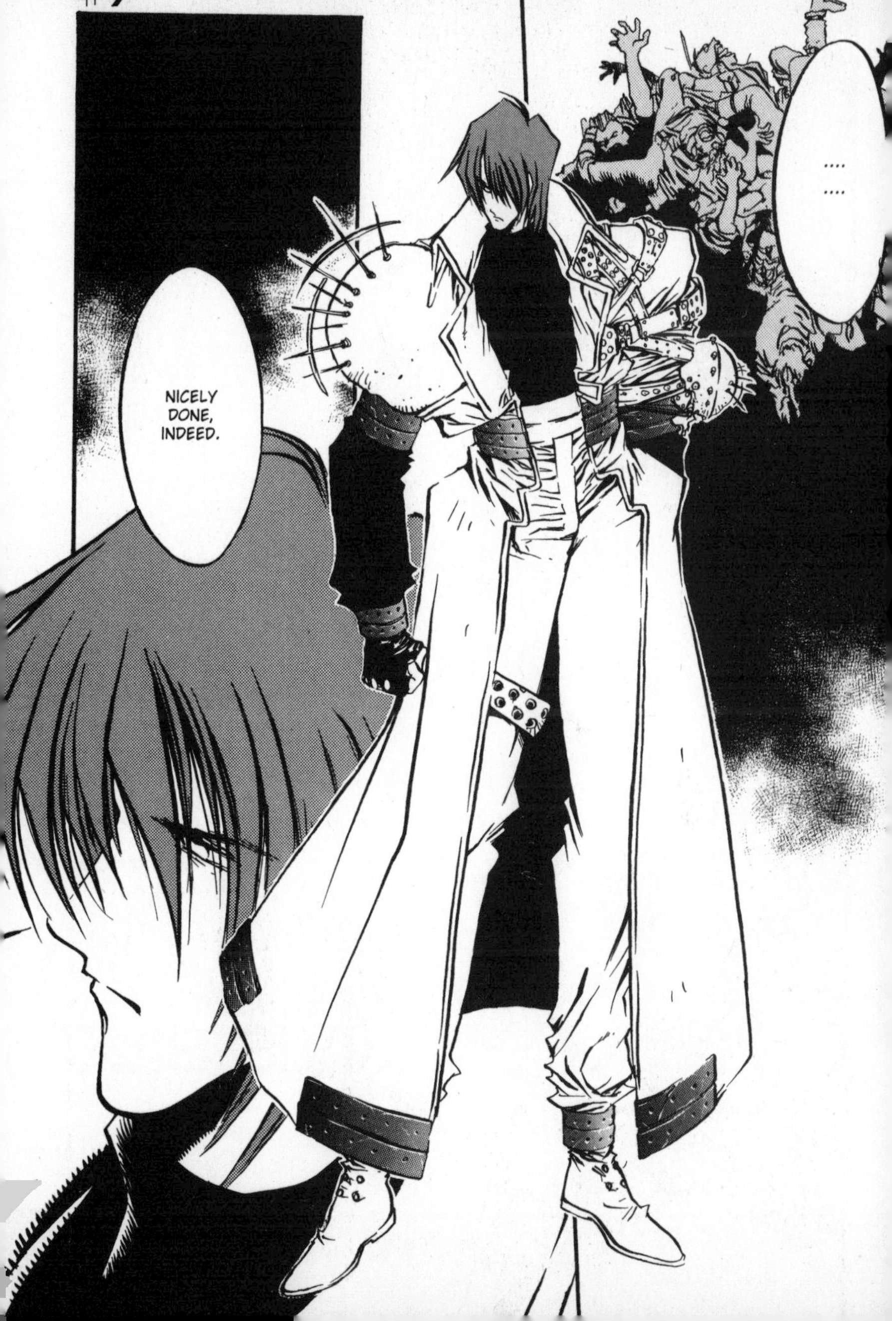
....
....
NICELY DONE, INDEED.

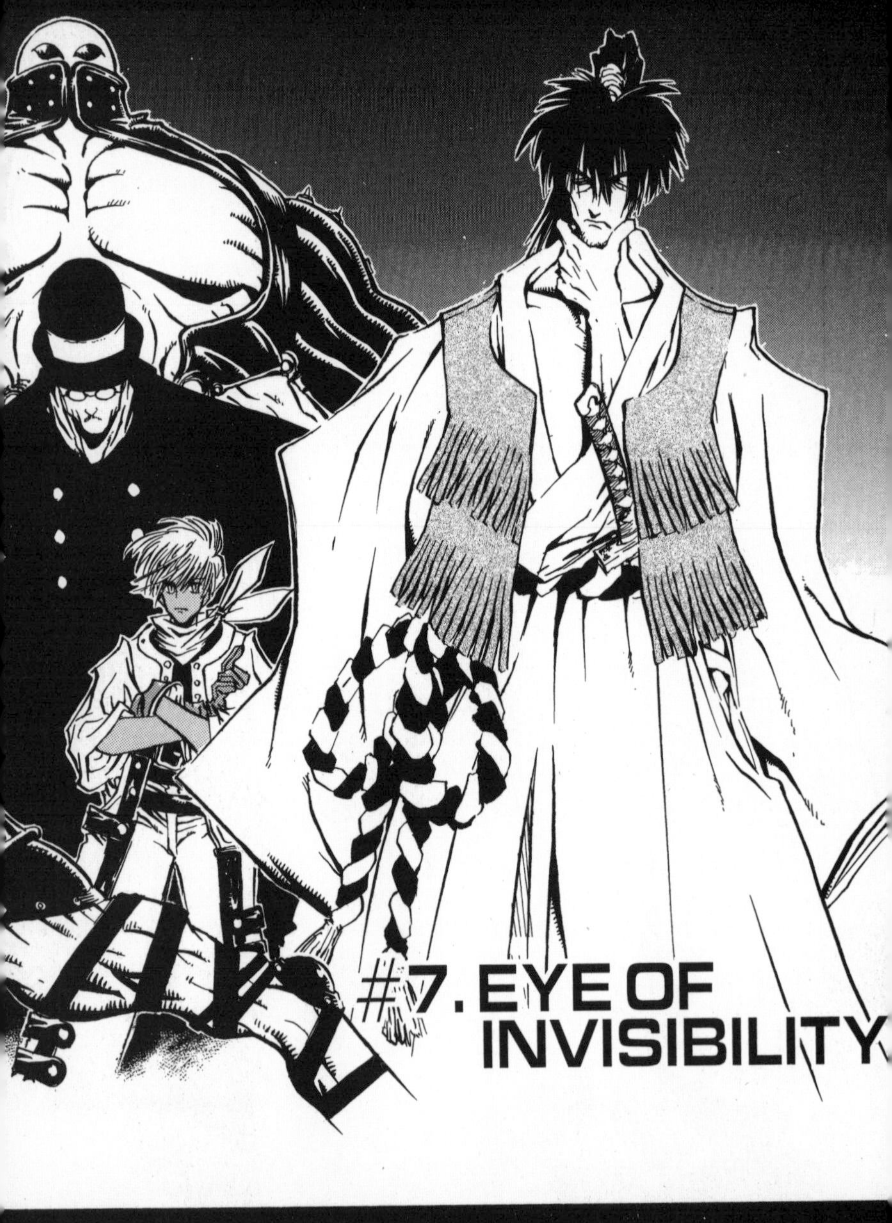
#7. EYE OF INVISIBILITY

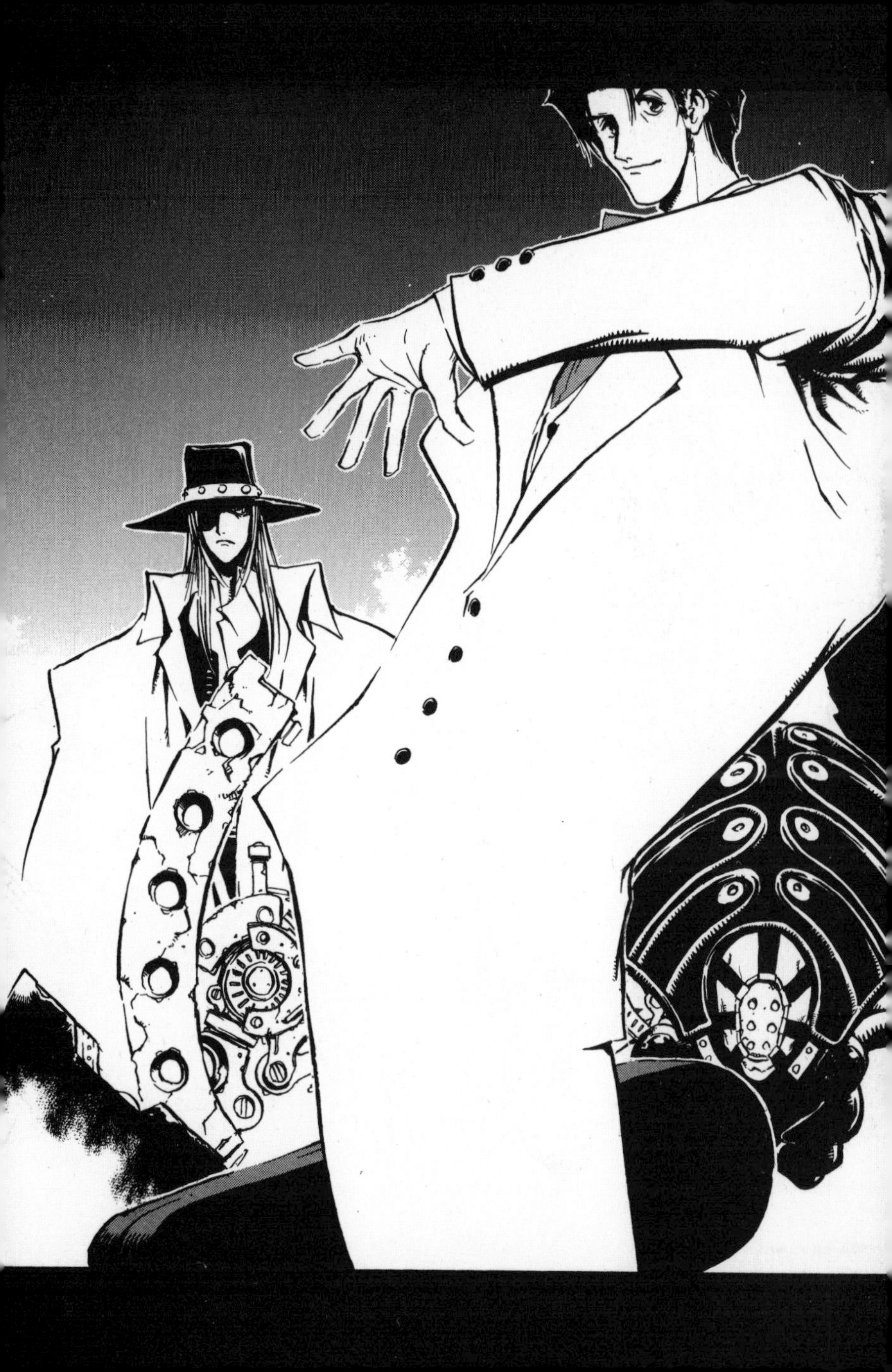

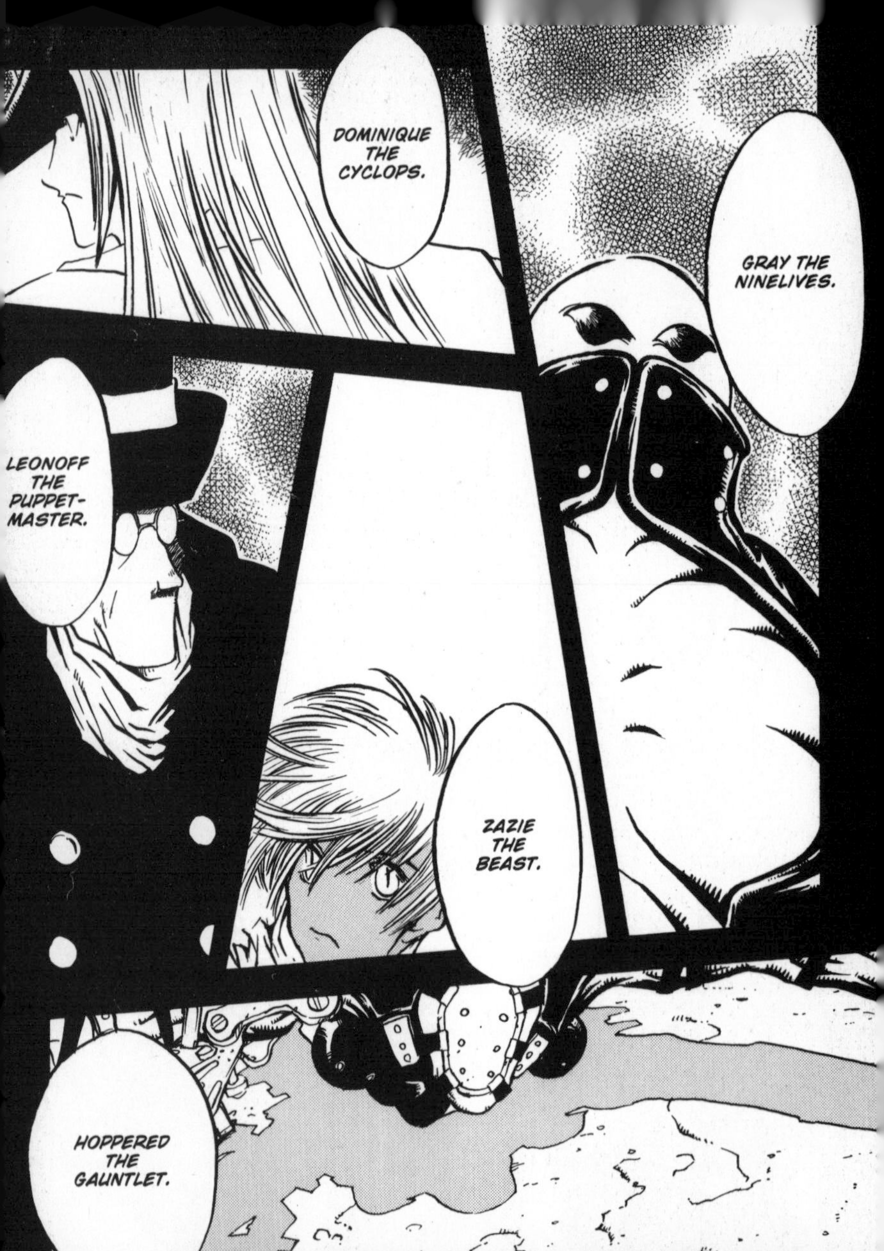
GRAY THE NINELIVES.
DOMINIQUE THE CYCLOPS.
ZAZIE THE BEAST.
LEONOFF THE PUPPET-MASTER.
HOPPERED THE GAUNTLET.

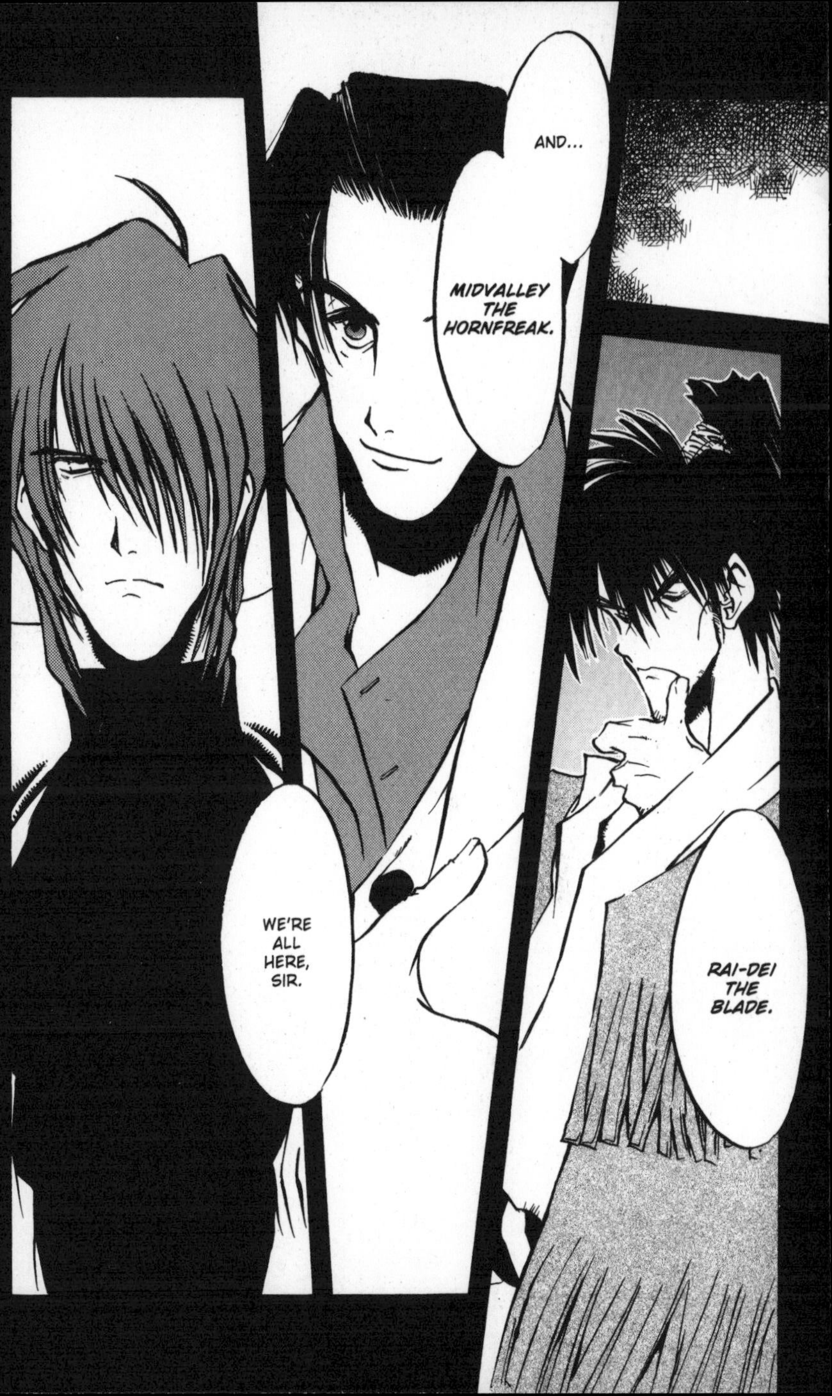
RAI-DEI THE BLADE.
AND...
MIDVALLEY THE HORNFREAK.
WE'RE ALL HERE, SIR.

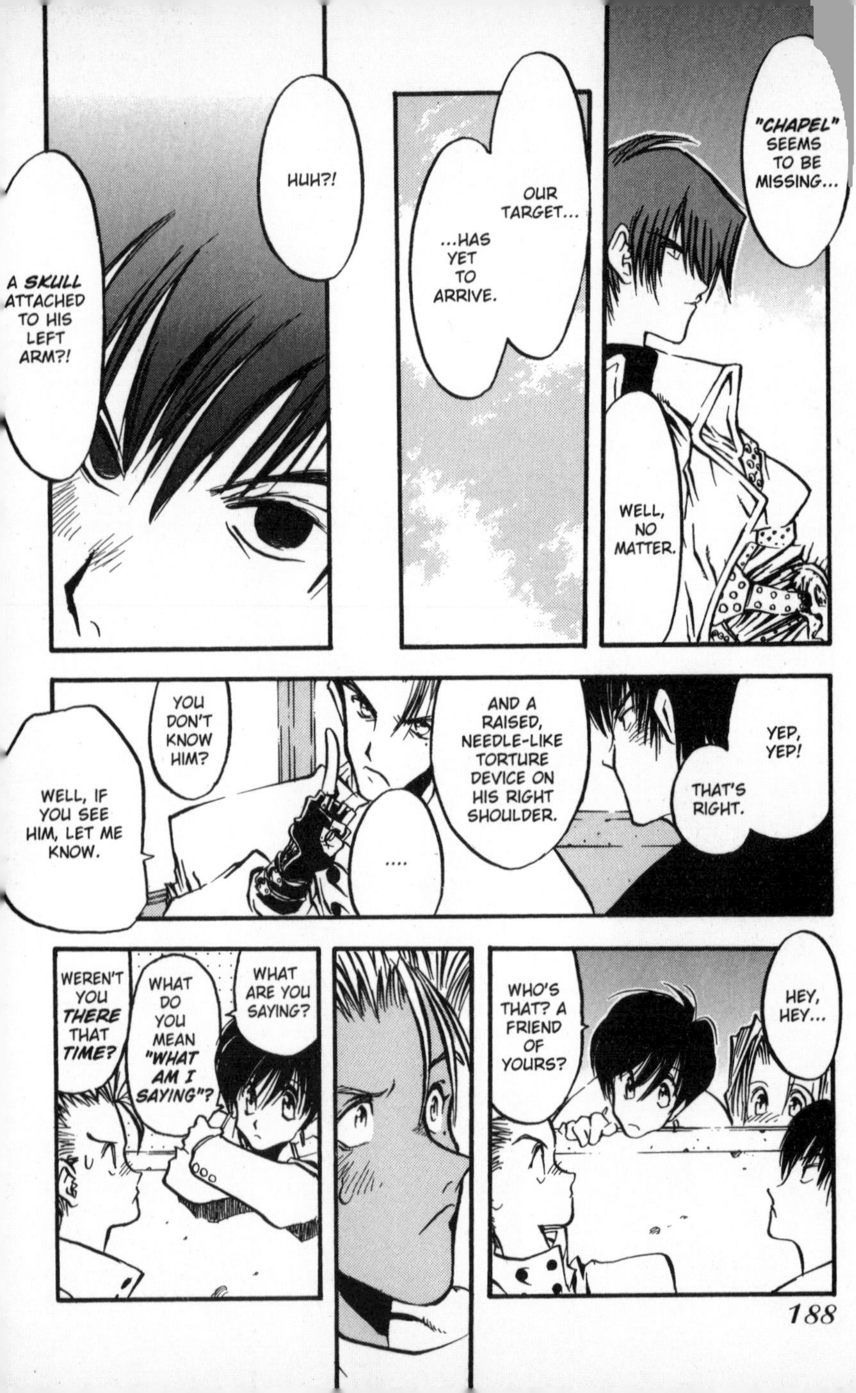
"CHAPEL" SEEMS TO BE MISSING...
WELL, NO MATTER.
OUR TARGET...
...HAS YET TO ARRIVE.
HUH?!
A SKULL ATTACHED TO HIS LEFT ARM?!
YEP, YEP!
THAT'S RIGHT.
AND A RAISED, NEEDLE-LIKE TORTURE DEVICE ON HIS RIGHT SHOULDER.
YOU DON'T KNOW HIM?
....
WELL, IF YOU SEE HIM, LET ME KNOW.
HEY, HEY...
WHO'S THAT? A FRIEND OF YOURS?
WHAT ARE YOU SAYING?
WHAT DO YOU MEAN "WHAT AM I SAYING"?
WEREN'T YOU THERE THAT TIME?

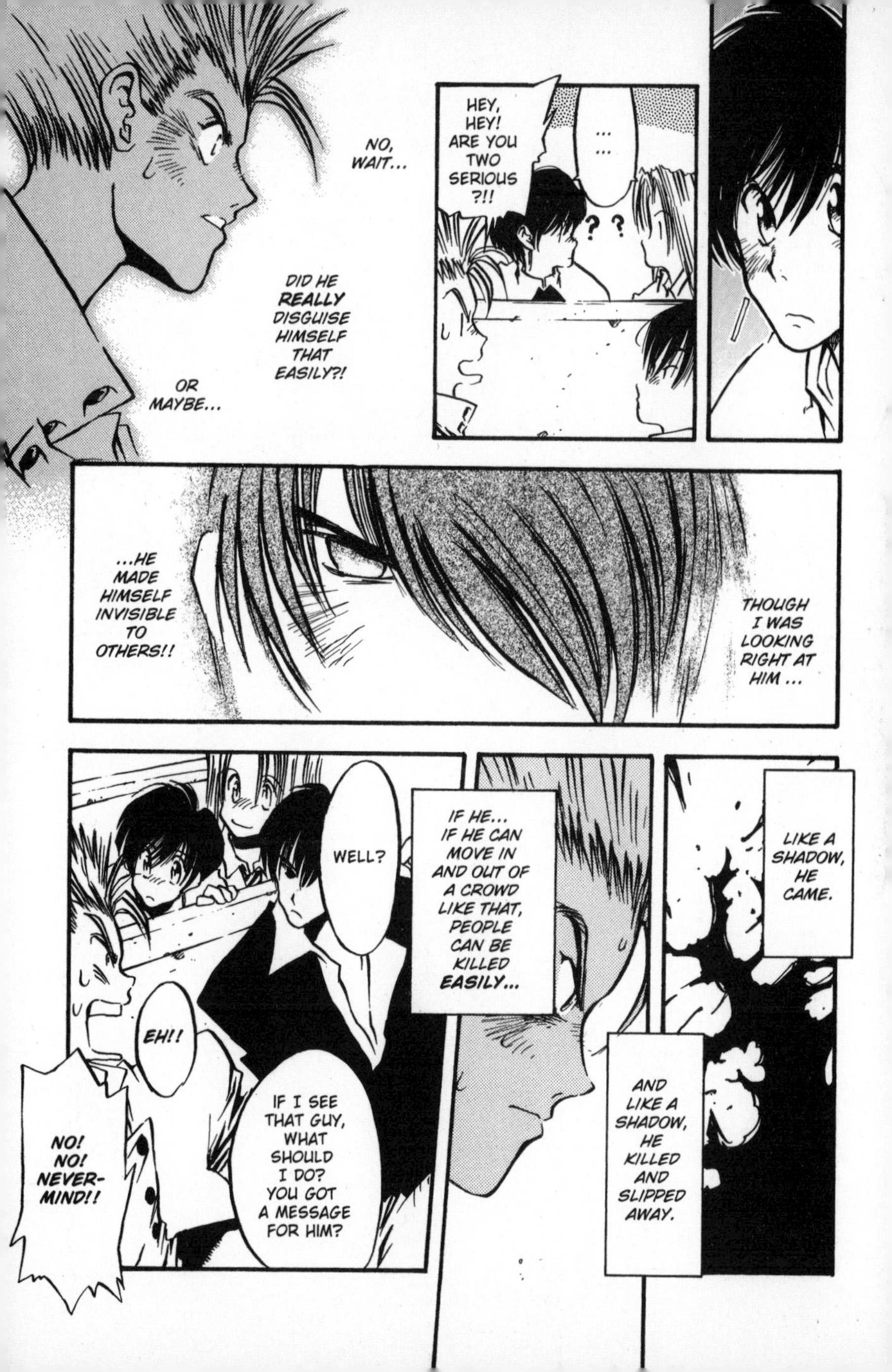
HEY, HEY! ARE YOU TWO SERIOUS ?!!
... ...
? ?
NO, WAIT...
DID HE REALLY DISGUISE HIMSELF THAT EASILY?!
OR MAYBE...
THOUGH I WAS LOOKING RIGHT AT HIM ...
...HE MADE HIMSELF INVISIBLE TO OTHERS!!
LIKE A SHADOW, HE CAME.
AND LIKE A SHADOW, HE KILLED AND SLIPPED AWAY.
IF HE... IF HE CAN MOVE IN AND OUT OF A CROWD LIKE THAT, PEOPLE CAN BE KILLED EASILY...
WELL?
EH!!
IF I SEE THAT GUY, WHAT SHOULD I DO? YOU GOT A MESSAGE FOR HIM?
NO! NO! NEVER-MIND!!

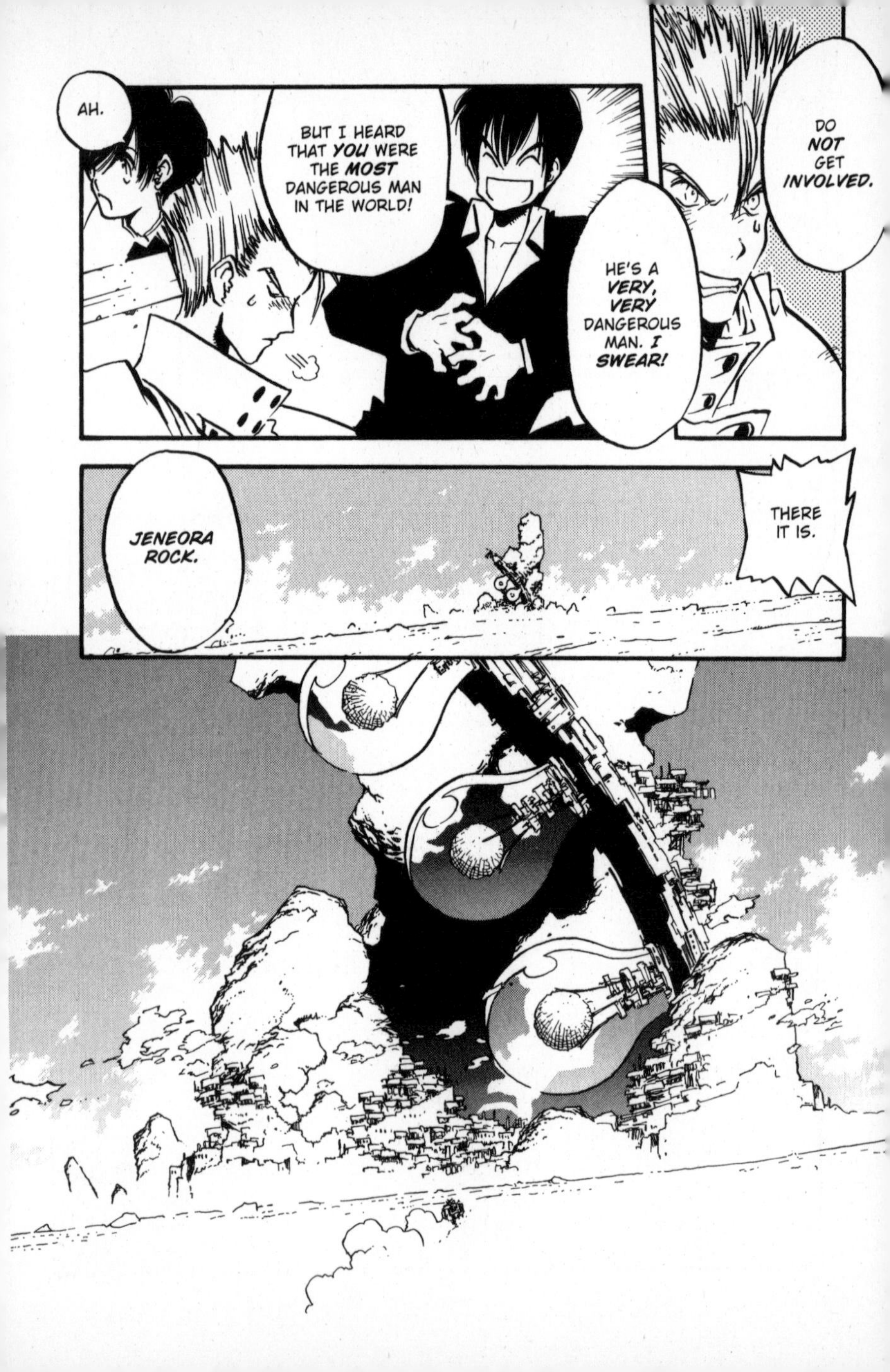
DO NOT GET INVOLVED.
BUT I HEARD THAT YOU WERE THE MOST DANGEROUS MAN IN THE WORLD!
HE'S A VERY, VERY DANGEROUS MAN. I SWEAR!
AH.
THERE IT IS.
JENEORA ROCK.

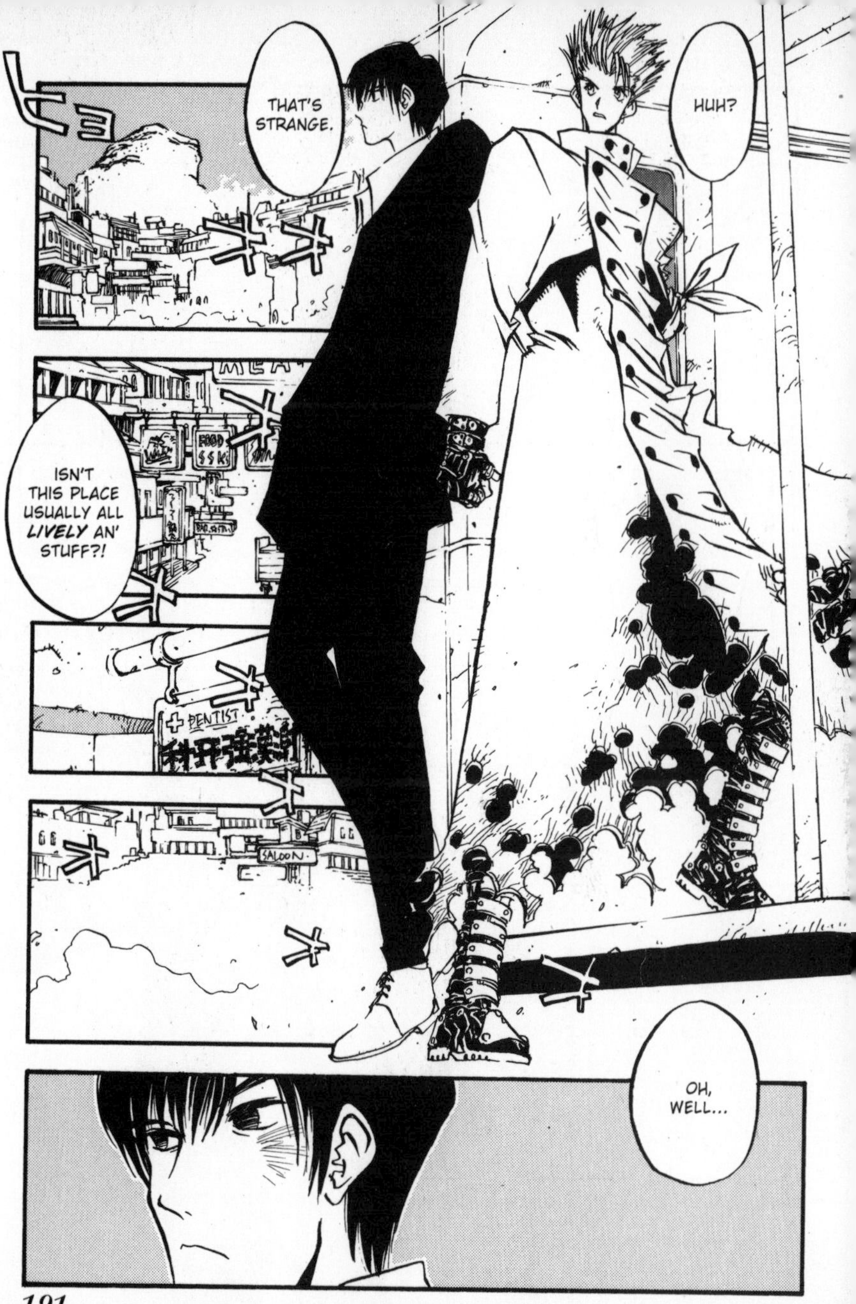
HUH?
THAT'S STRANGE.
ISN'T THIS PLACE USUALLY ALL *LIVELY* AN' STUFF?!
DENTIST
SALOON
OH, WELL...

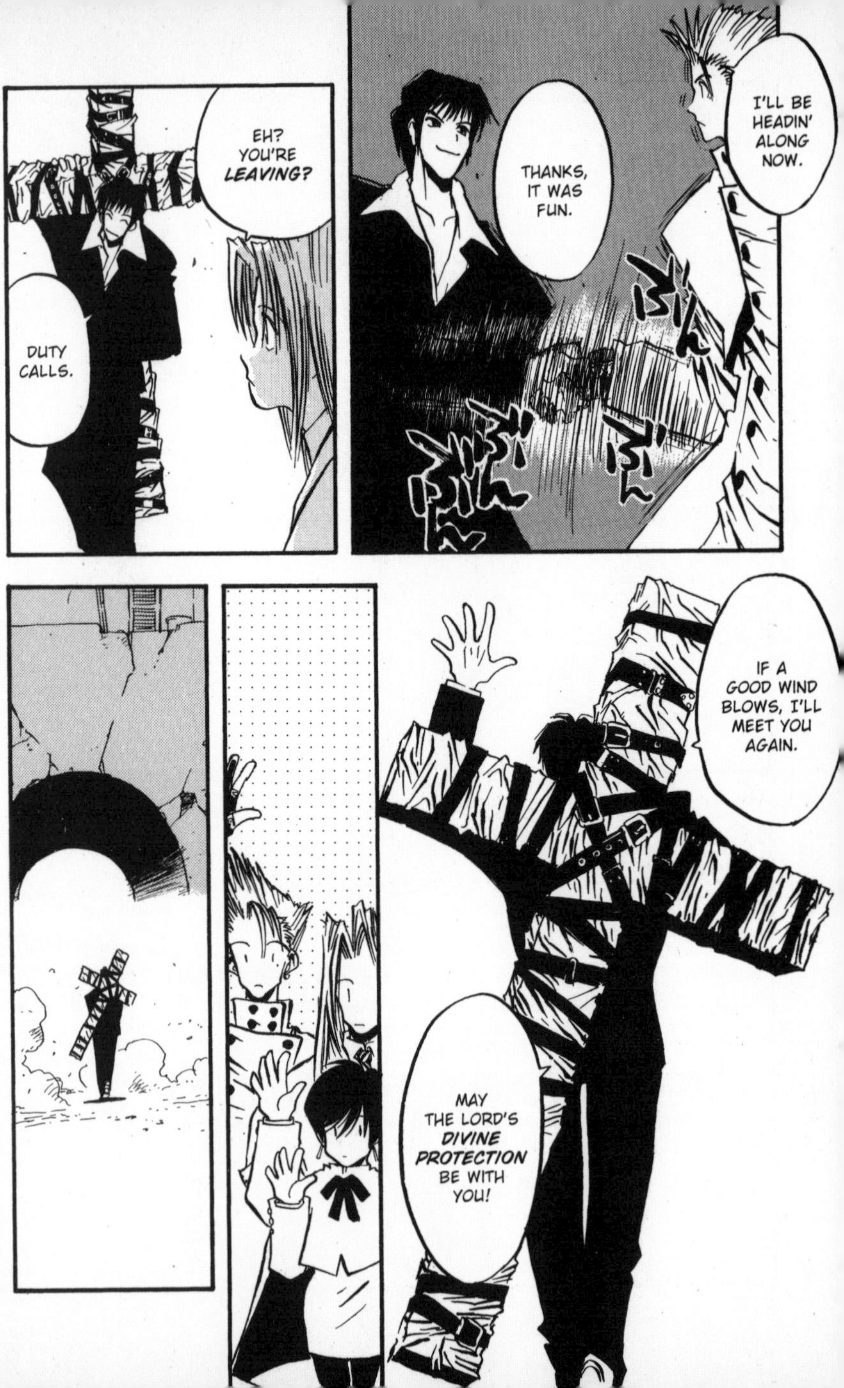
I'LL BE HEADIN' ALONG NOW.
THANKS, IT WAS FUN.
EH? YOU'RE *LEAVING?*
DUTY CALLS.
IF A GOOD WIND BLOWS, I'LL MEET YOU AGAIN.
MAY THE LORD'S ***DIVINE PROTECTION*** BE WITH YOU!

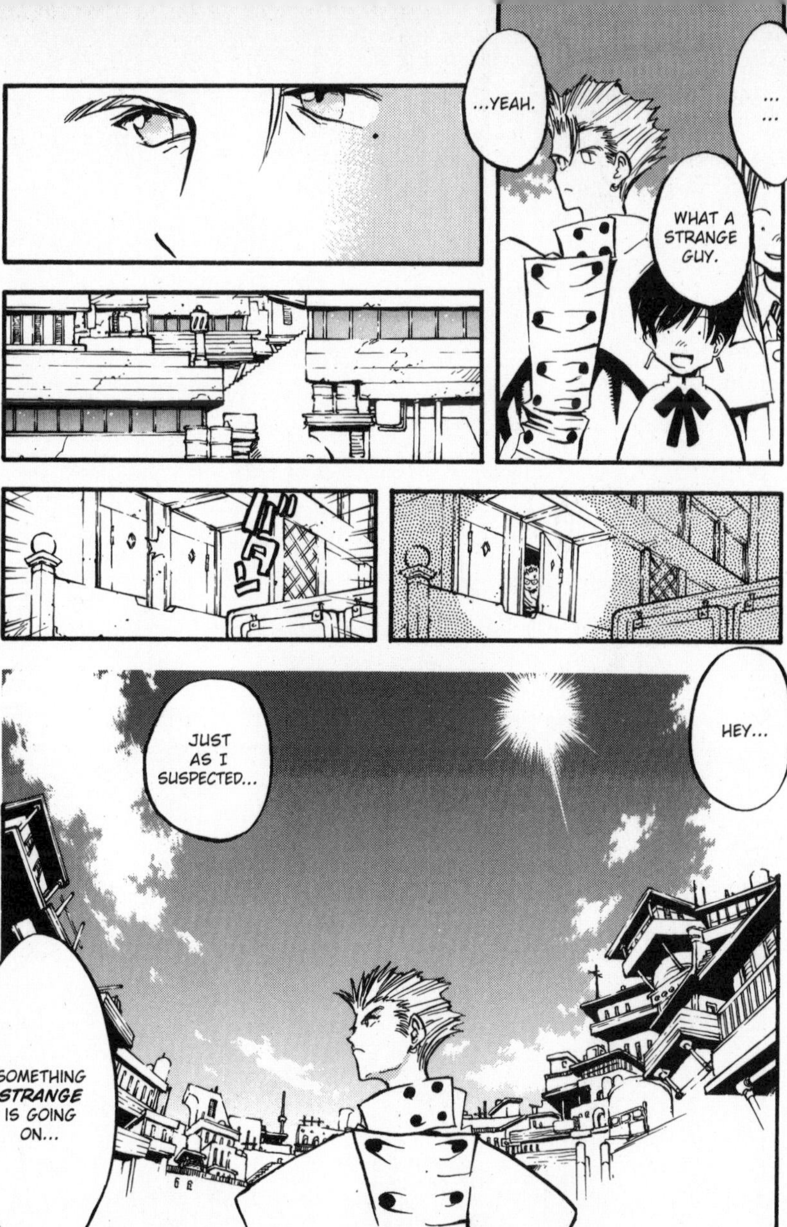
... ...
...YEAH.
WHAT A STRANGE GUY.
HEY...
JUST AS I SUSPECTED...
SOMETHING *STRANGE* IS GOING ON...

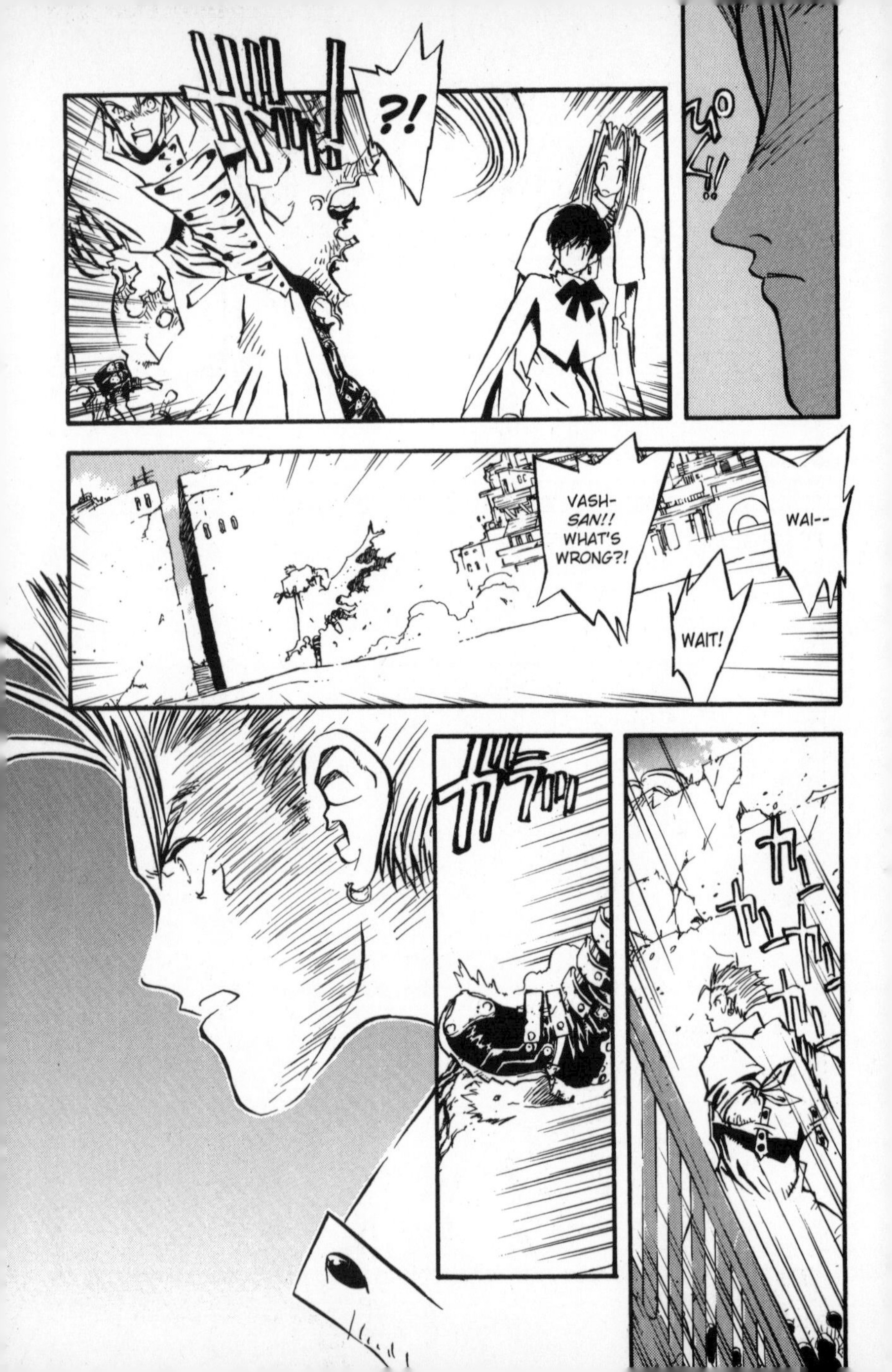
?!
WAI--
VASH-SAN!! WHAT'S WRONG?!
WAIT!

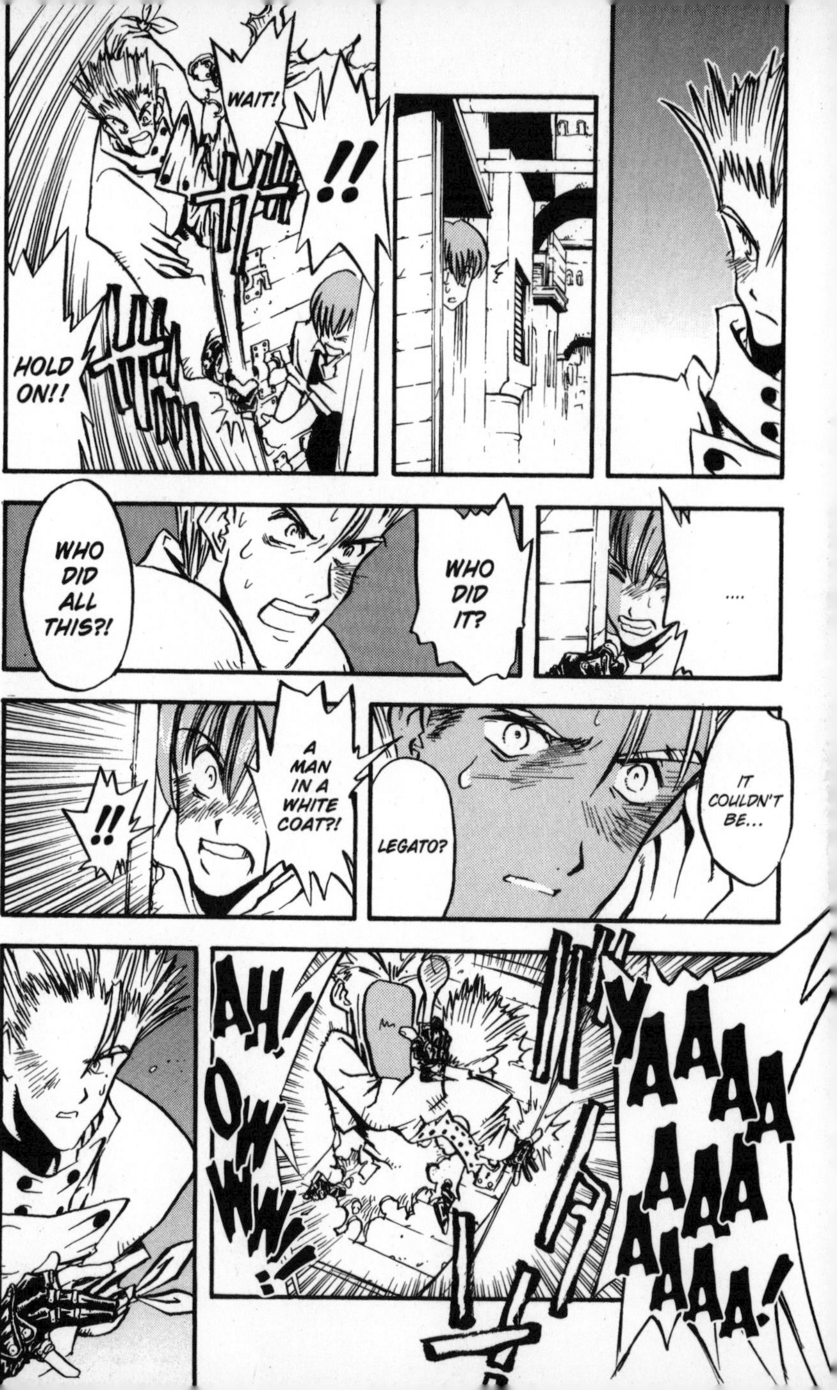
WAIT!
!!
HOLD ON!!
....
WHO DID IT?
WHO DID ALL THIS?!
IT COULDN'T BE...
LEGATO?
A MAN IN A WHITE COAT?!
!!
YAAAAAAAAAAAAA!
AH! OWWWW!!
...

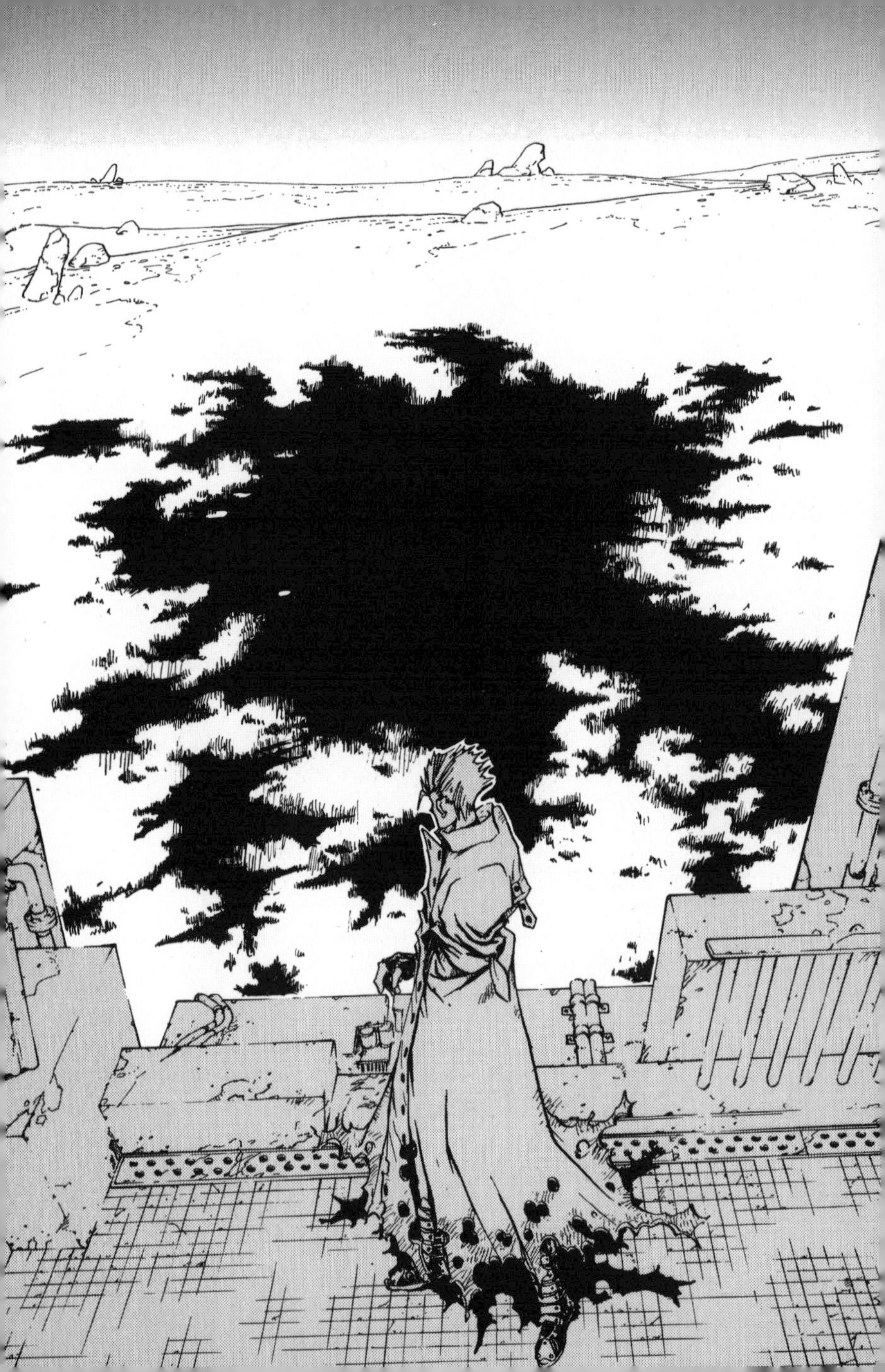

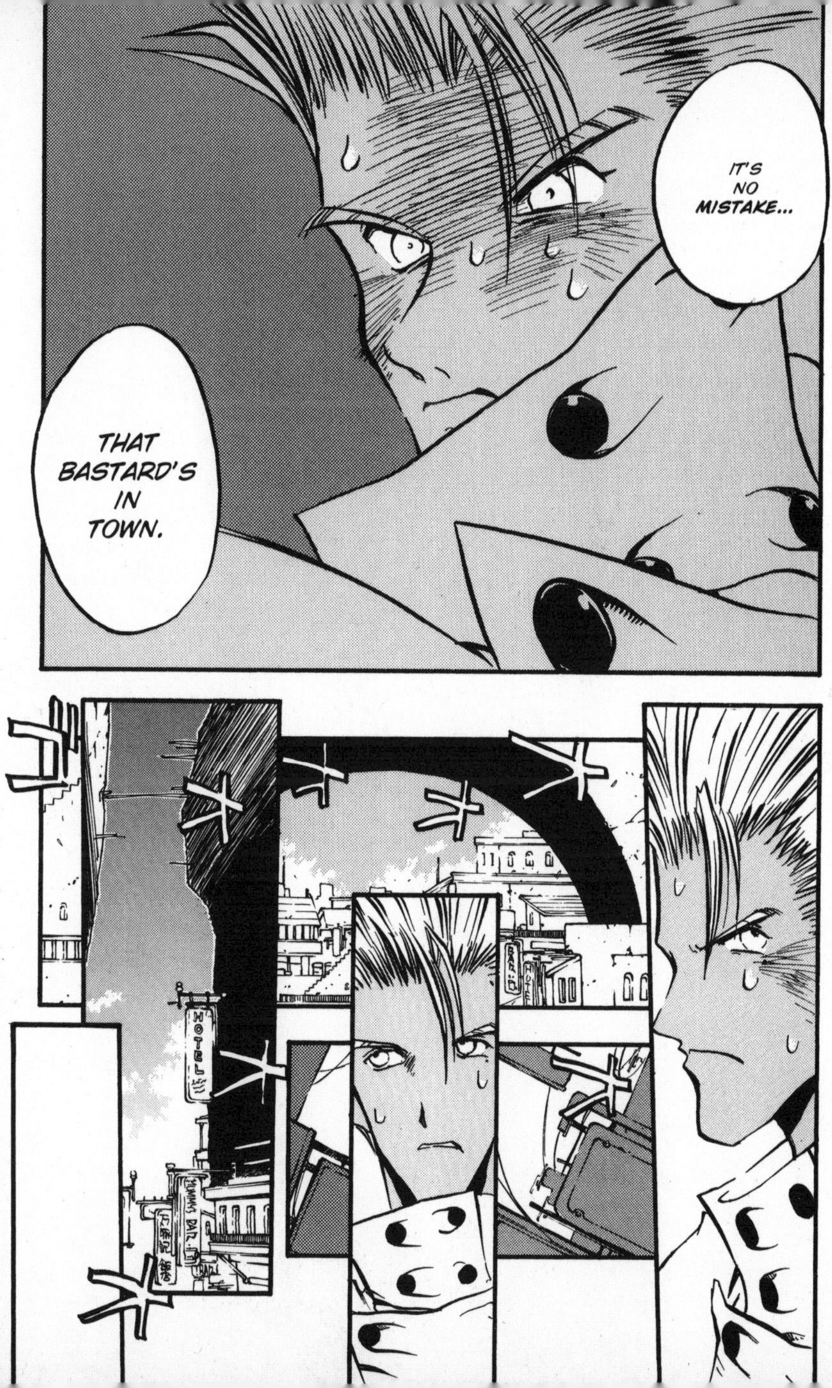
IT'S NO MISTAKE...
THAT BASTARD'S IN TOWN.
HOTEL

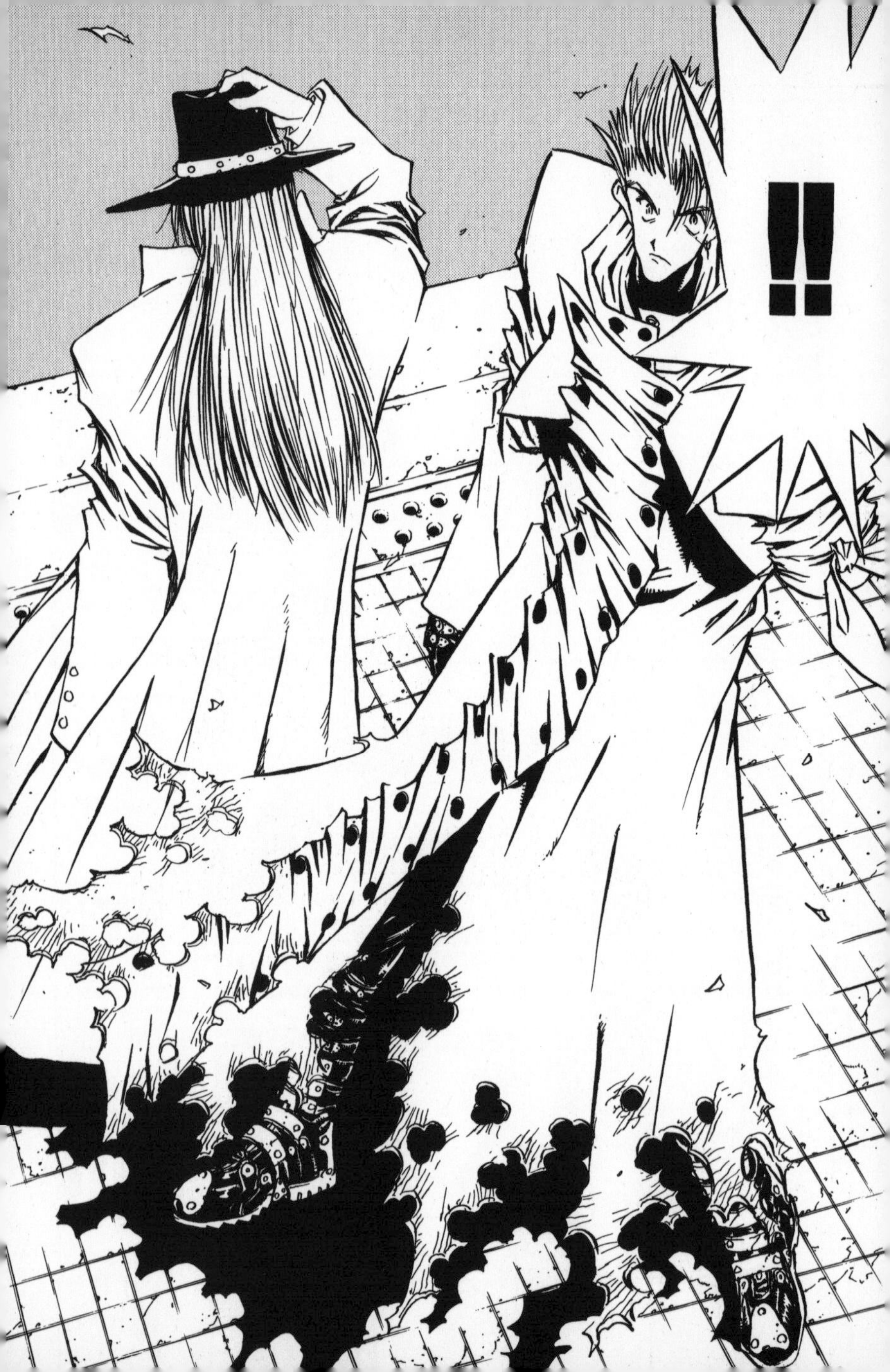
!!

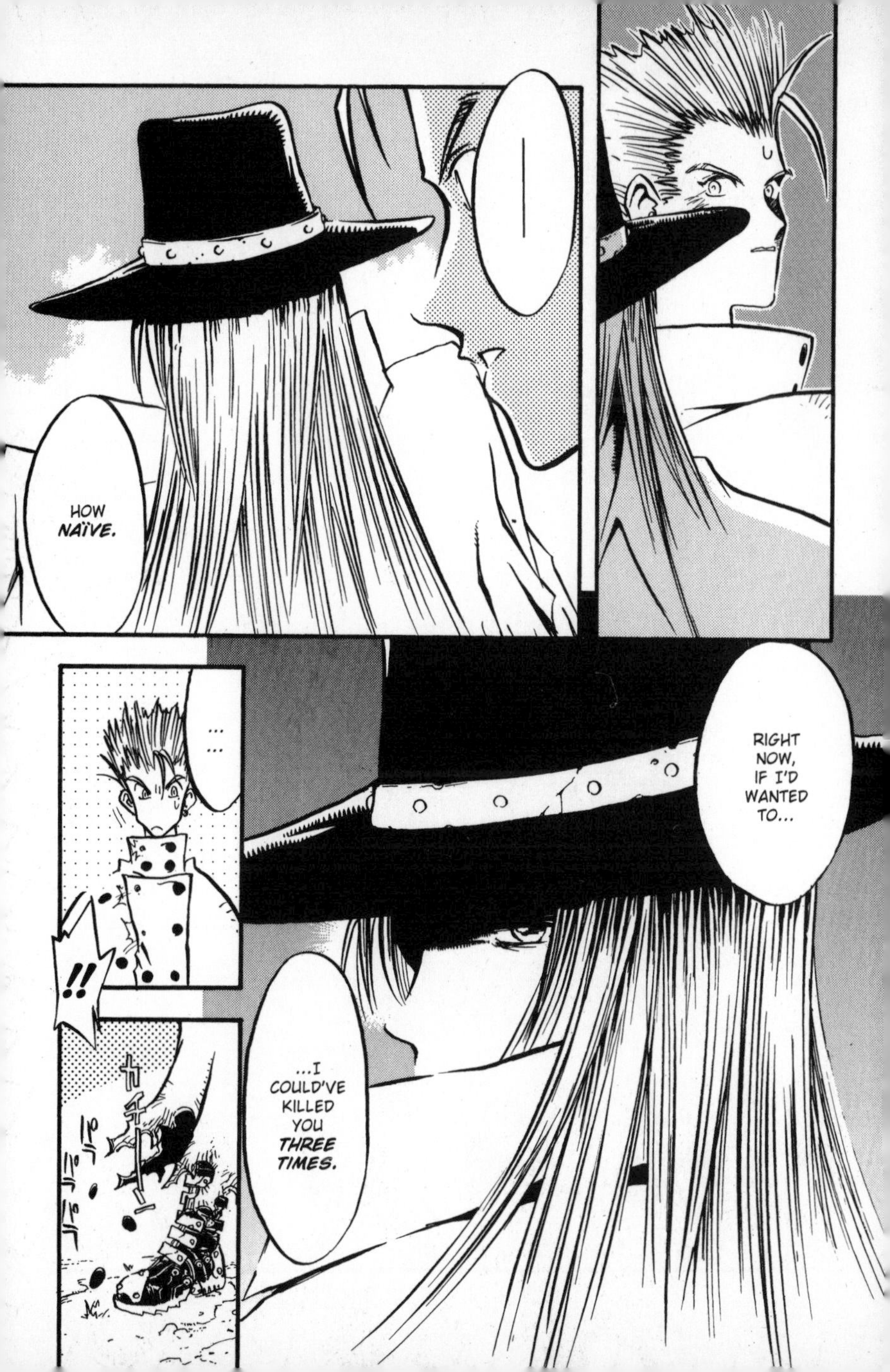
HOW NAÏVE.
RIGHT NOW, IF I'D WANTED TO...
...I COULD'VE KILLED YOU THREE TIMES.
... ...
!!

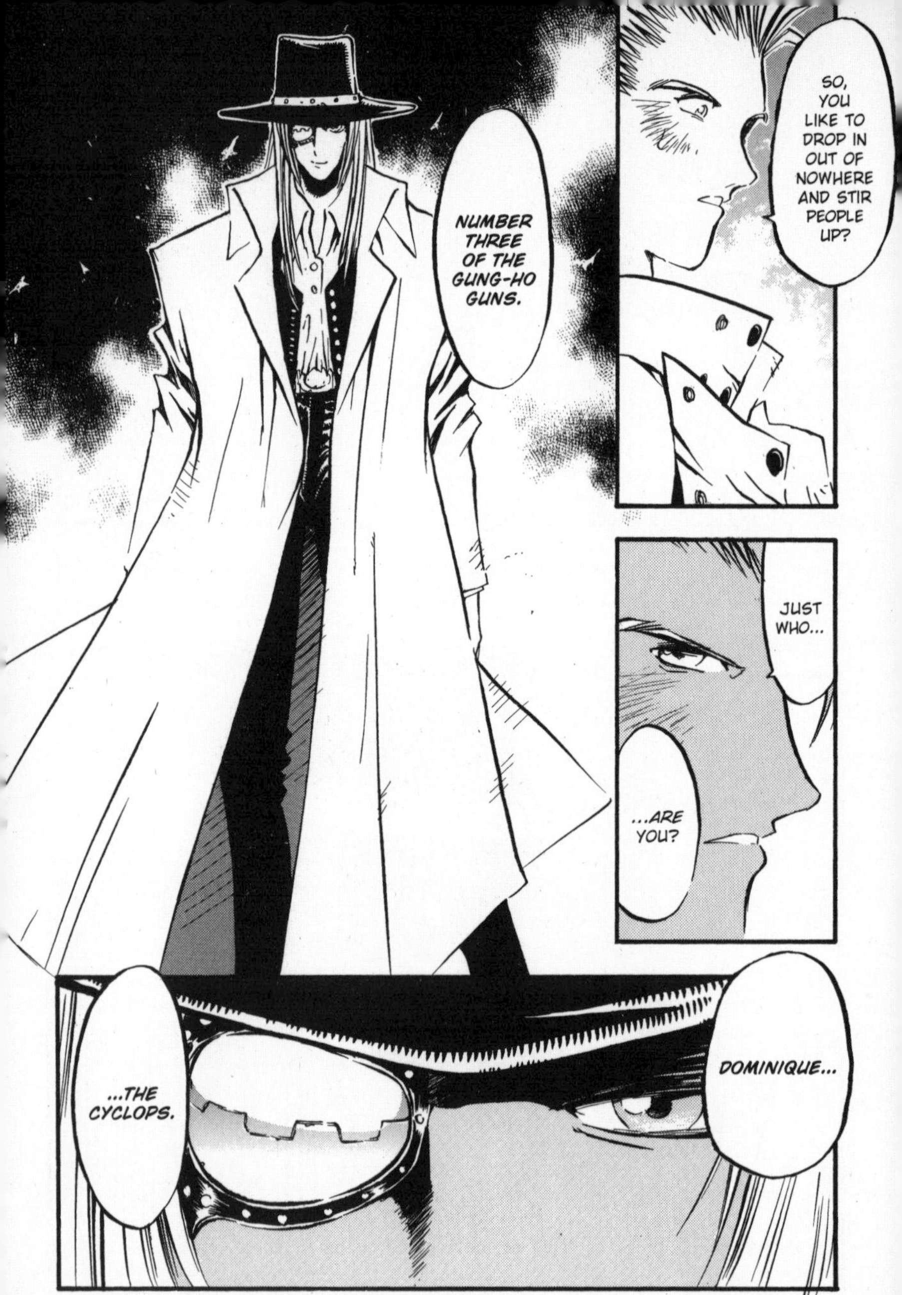
SO, YOU LIKE TO DROP IN OUT OF NOWHERE AND STIR PEOPLE UP?
JUST WHO...
...ARE YOU?
NUMBER THREE OF THE GUNG-HO GUNS.
DOMINIQUE...
...THE CYCLOPS.

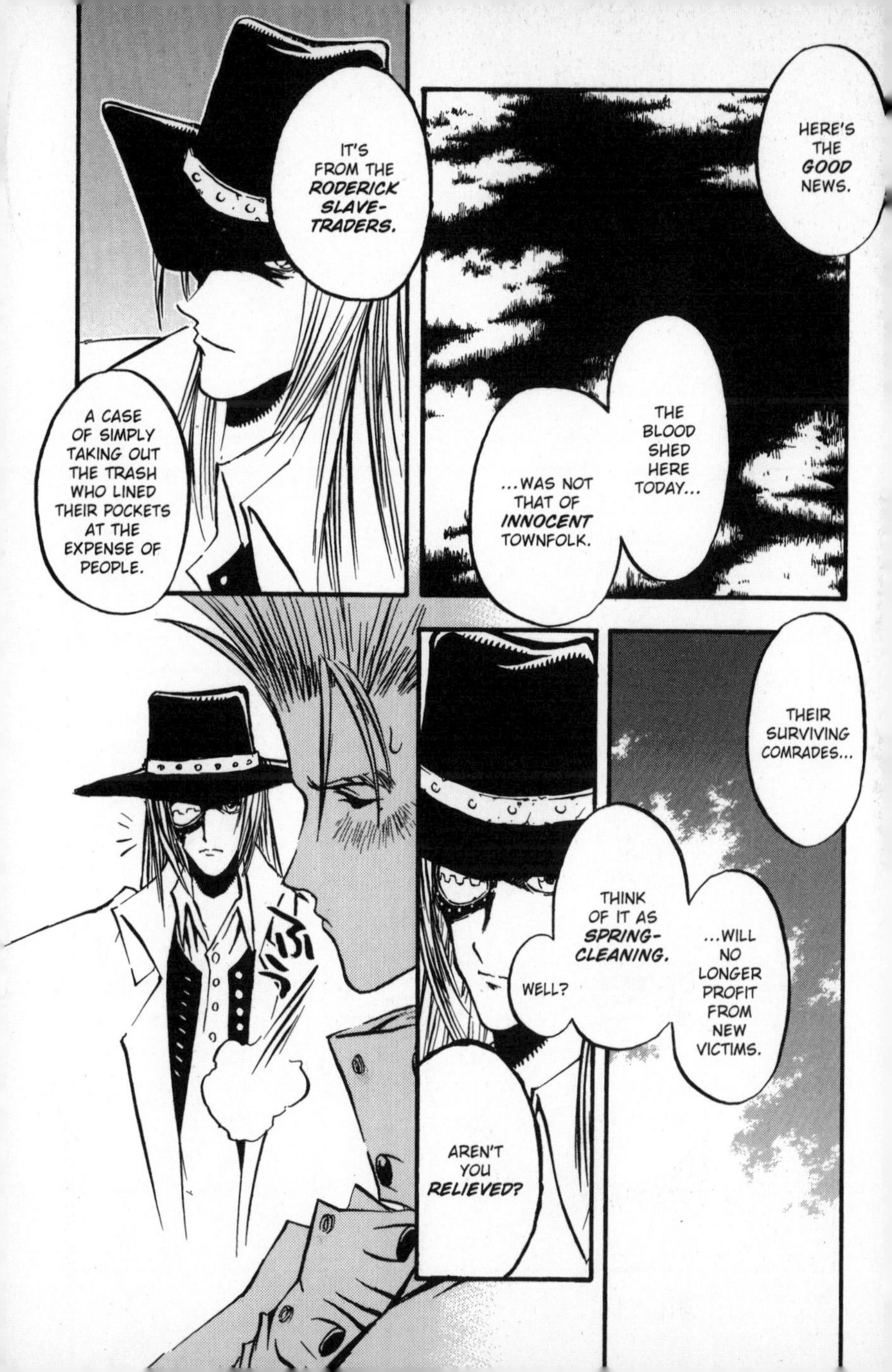
HERE'S THE GOOD NEWS.
THE BLOOD SHED HERE TODAY...
...WAS NOT THAT OF INNOCENT TOWNFOLK.
IT'S FROM THE RODERICK SLAVE-TRADERS.
A CASE OF SIMPLY TAKING OUT THE TRASH WHO LINED THEIR POCKETS AT THE EXPENSE OF PEOPLE.
THEIR SURVIVING COMRADES...
...WILL NO LONGER PROFIT FROM NEW VICTIMS.
THINK OF IT AS SPRING-CLEANING.
WELL?
AREN'T YOU RELIEVED?

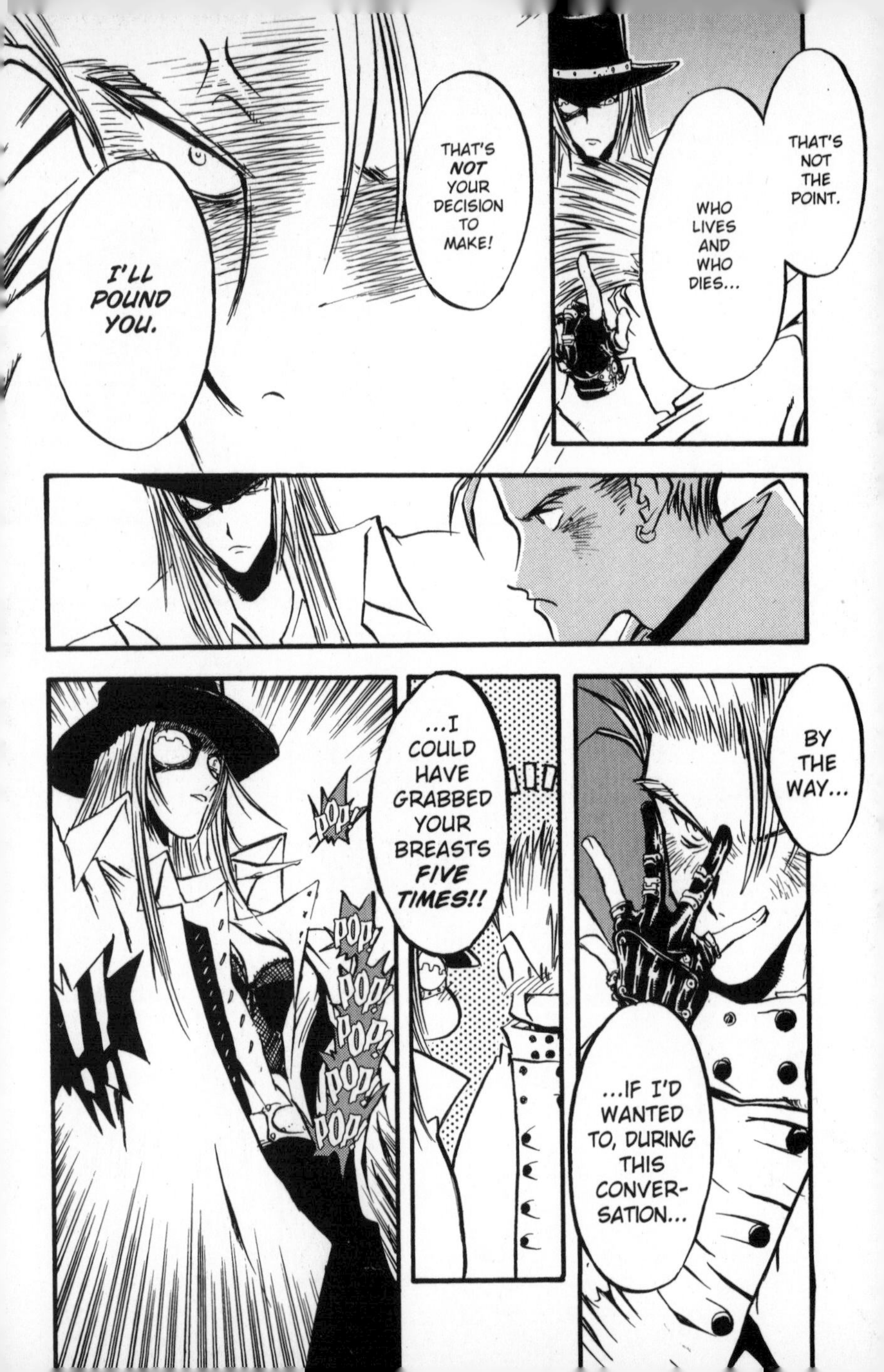
THAT'S NOT THE POINT.
WHO LIVES AND WHO DIES...
THAT'S NOT YOUR DECISION TO MAKE!
I'LL POUND YOU.
BY THE WAY...
...IF I'D WANTED TO, DURING THIS CONVER-SATION...
...I COULD HAVE GRABBED YOUR BREASTS FIVE TIMES!!
POP!
POP!
POP!
POP!
POP!
POP!

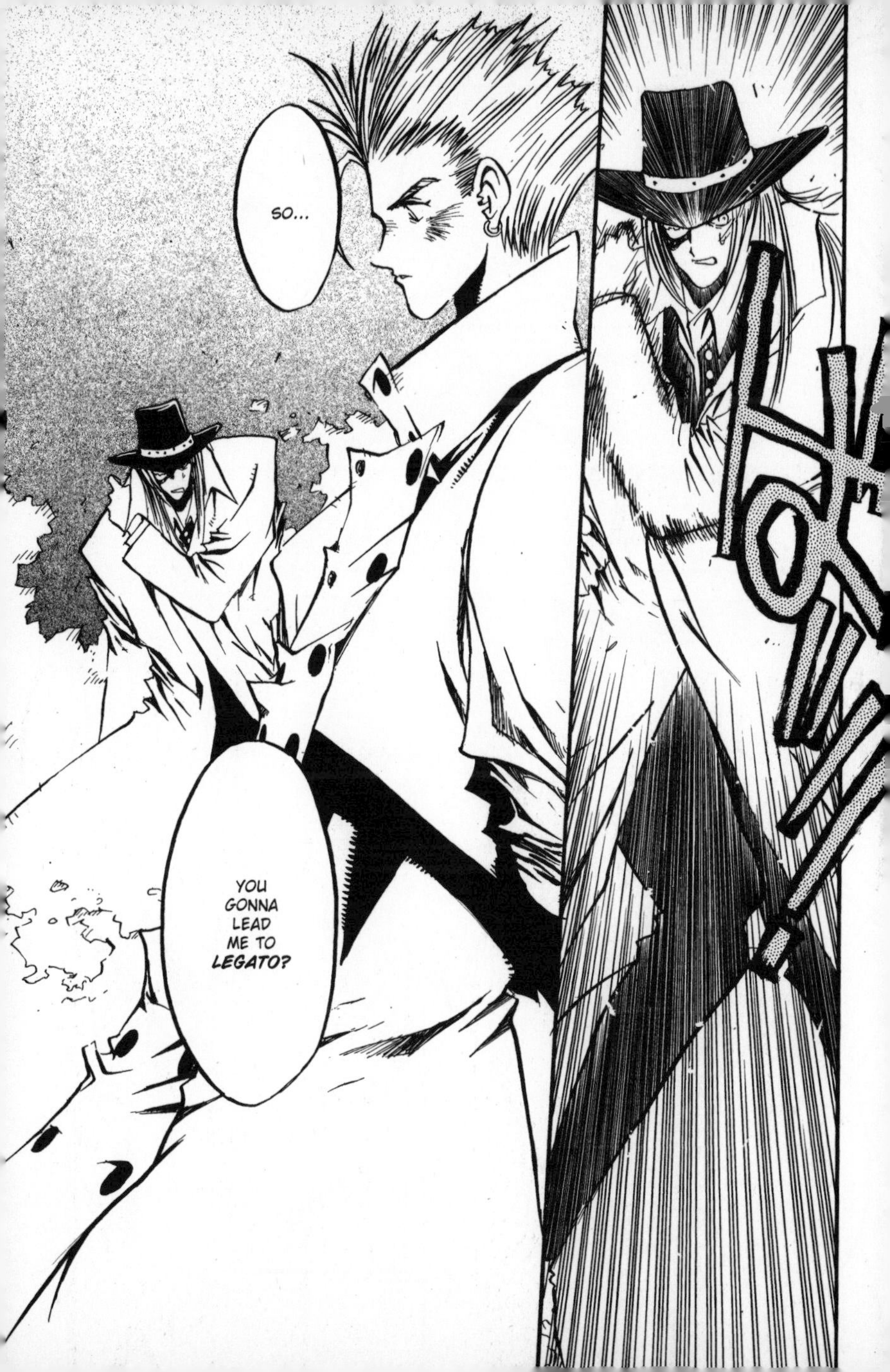
SO...
YOU GONNA LEAD ME TO LEGATO?

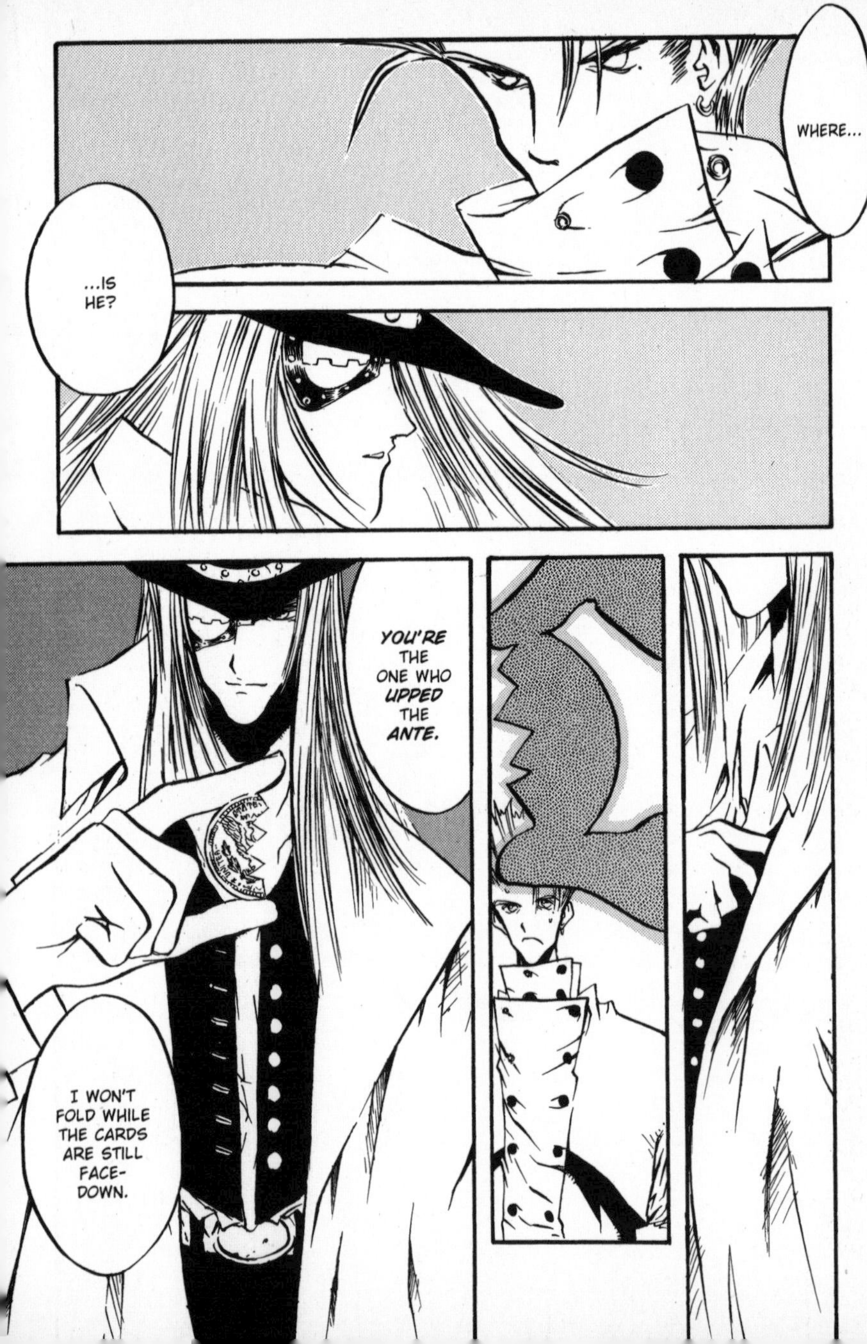
WHERE...
...IS HE?
YOU'RE THE ONE WHO UPPED THE ANTE.
I WON'T FOLD WHILE THE CARDS ARE STILL FACE-DOWN.

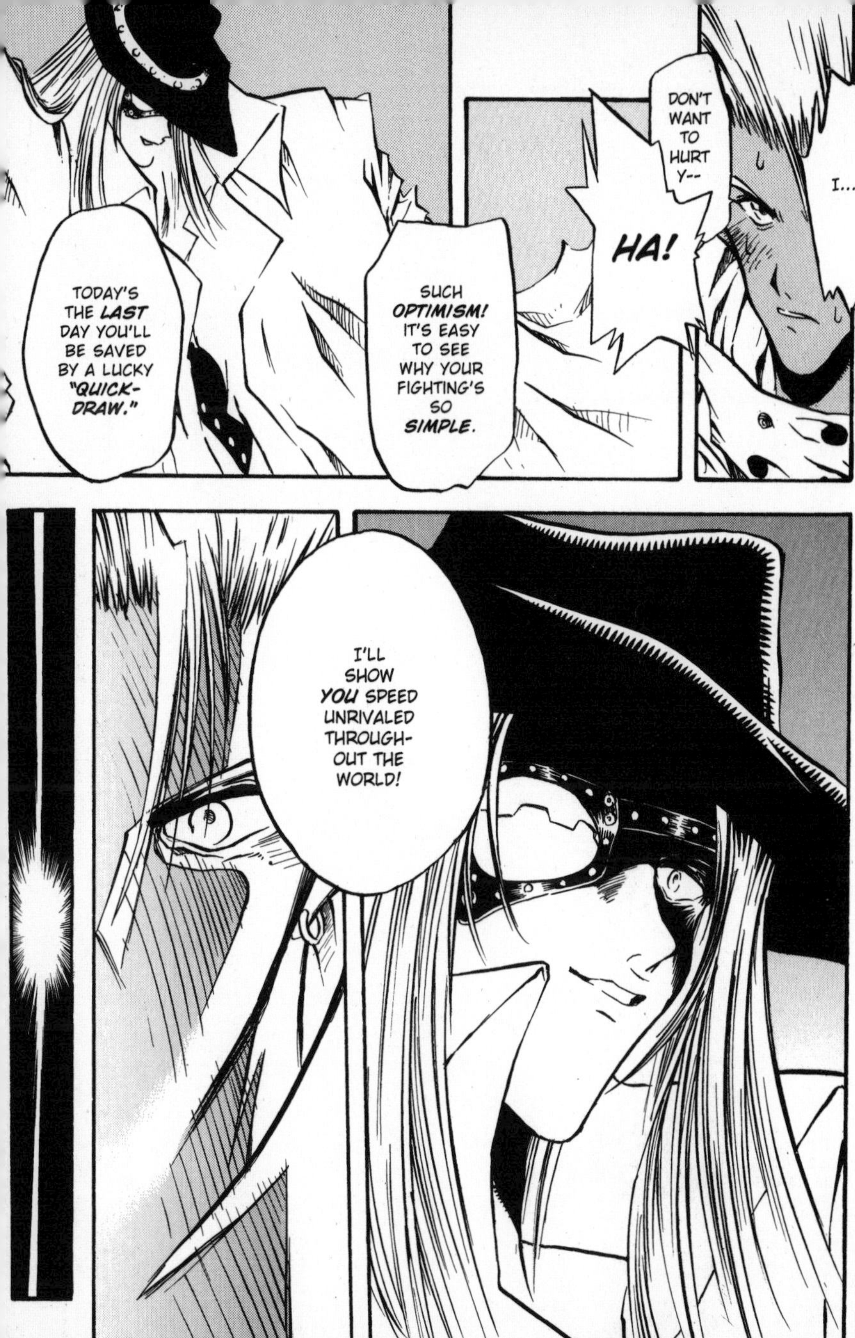
I...
DON'T WANT TO HURT Y--
HA!
SUCH OPTIMISM! IT'S EASY TO SEE WHY YOUR FIGHTING'S SO SIMPLE.
TODAY'S THE LAST DAY YOU'LL BE SAVED BY A LUCKY "QUICK-DRAW."
I'LL SHOW YOU SPEED UNRIVALED THROUGH-OUT THE WORLD!

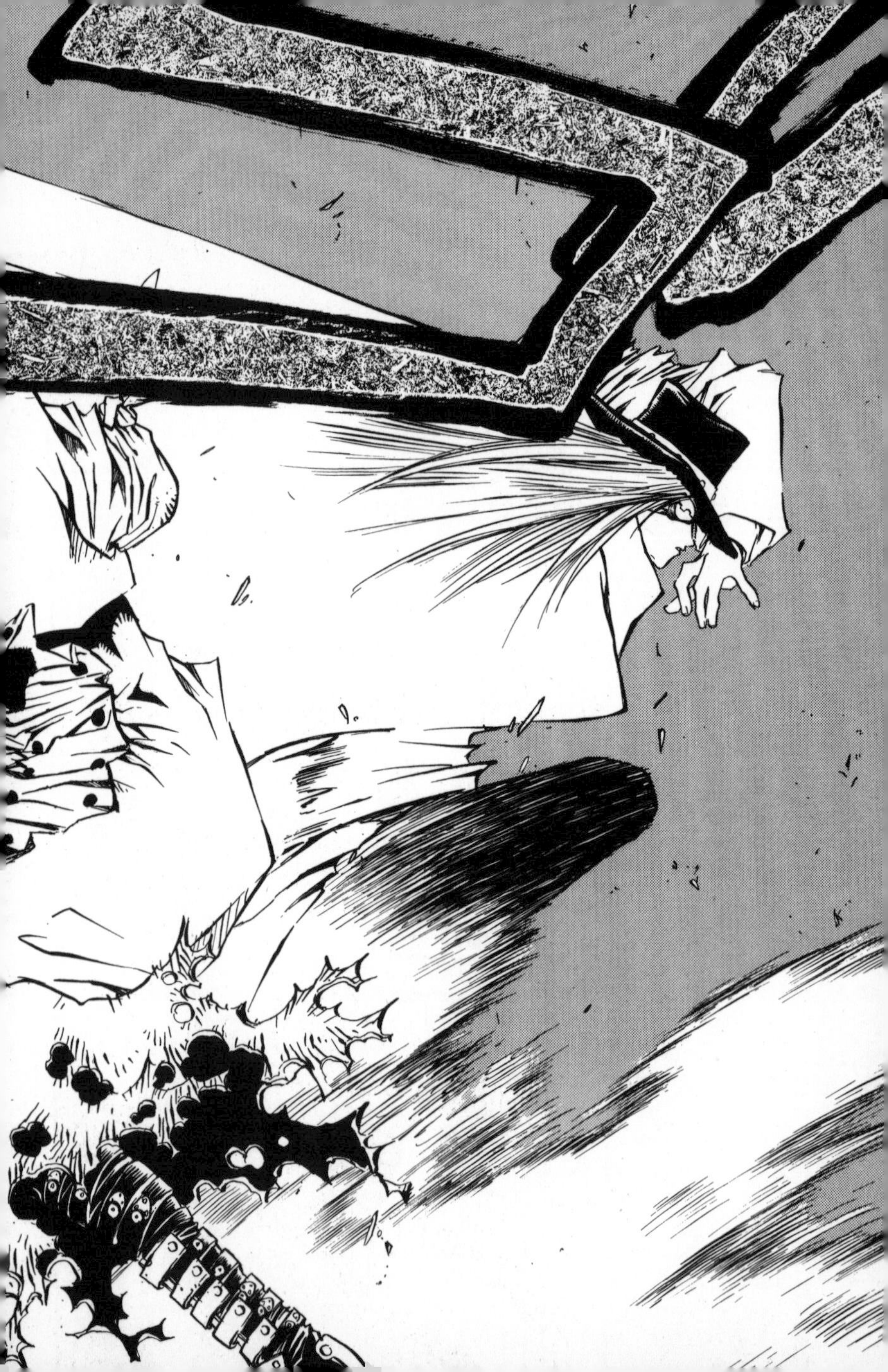

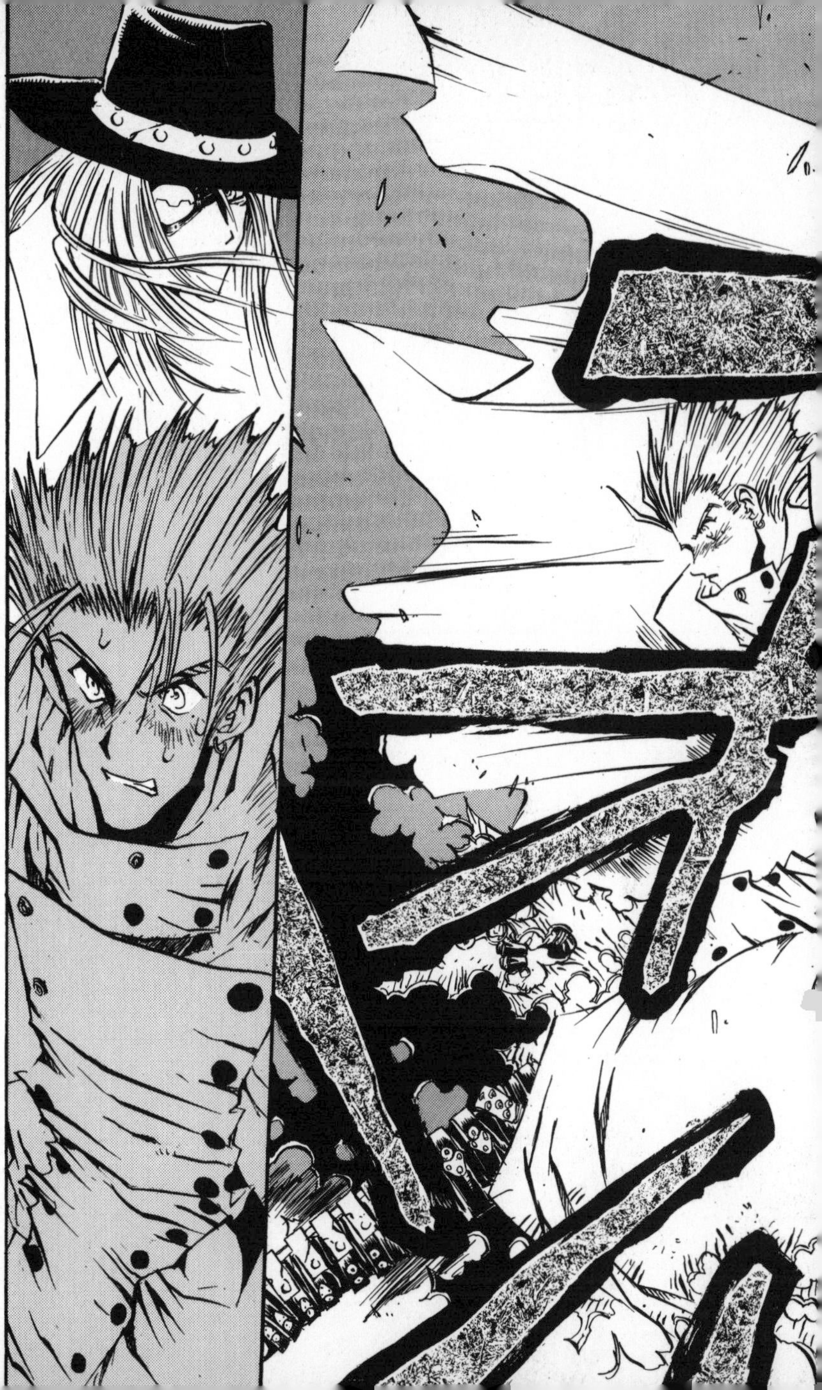

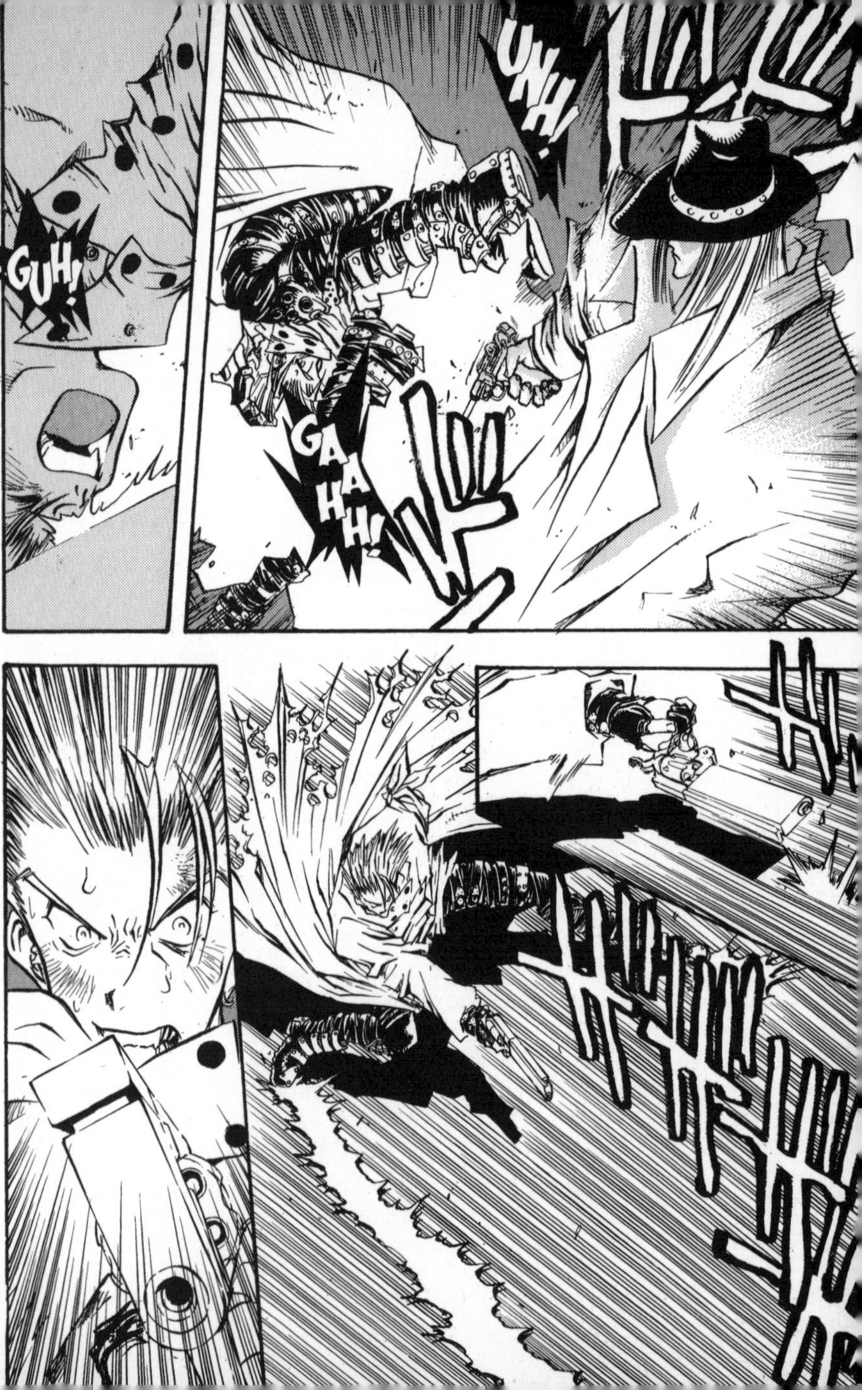
UNH!
GAAHH!
GUH!

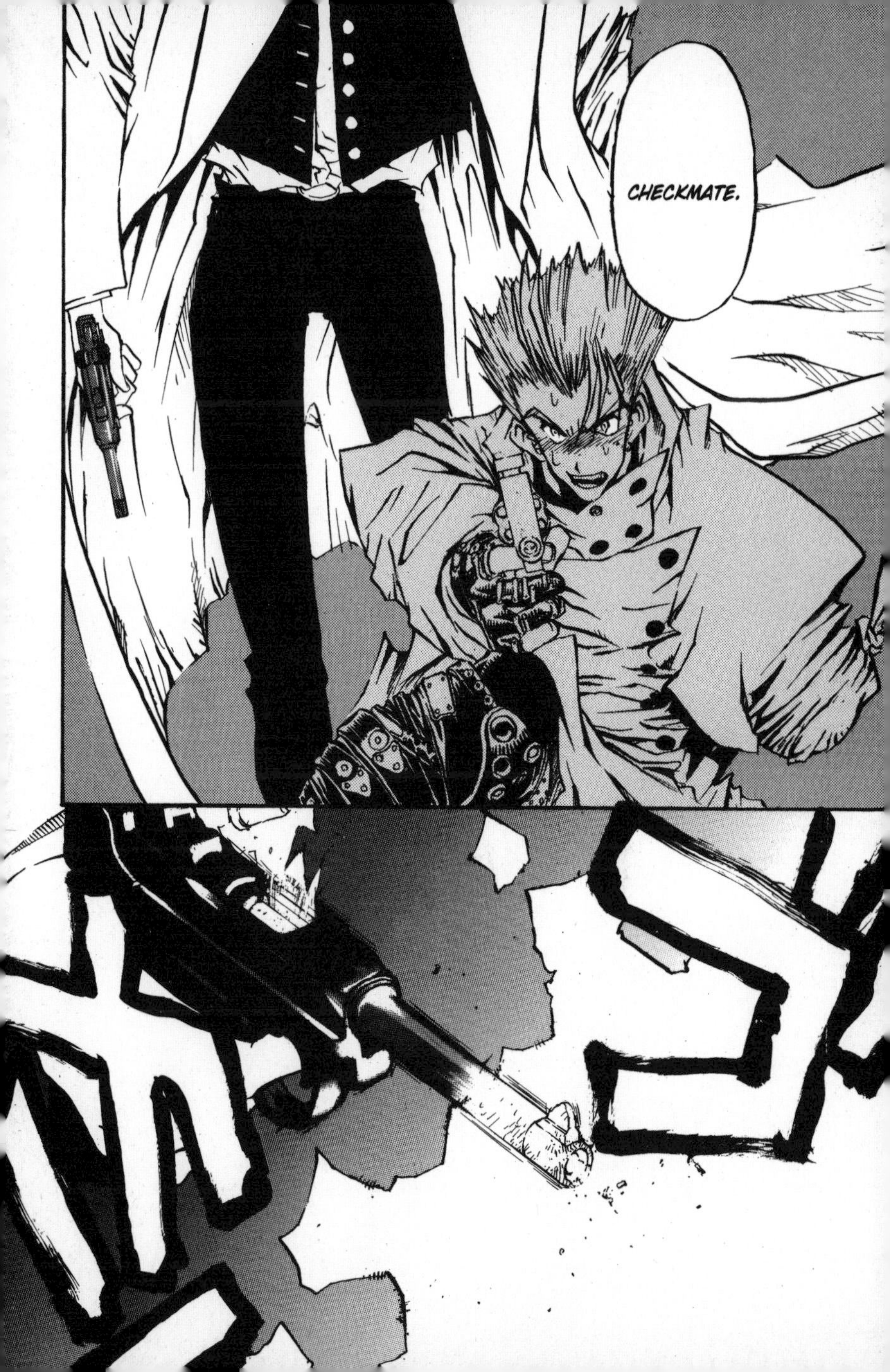
CHECKMATE.

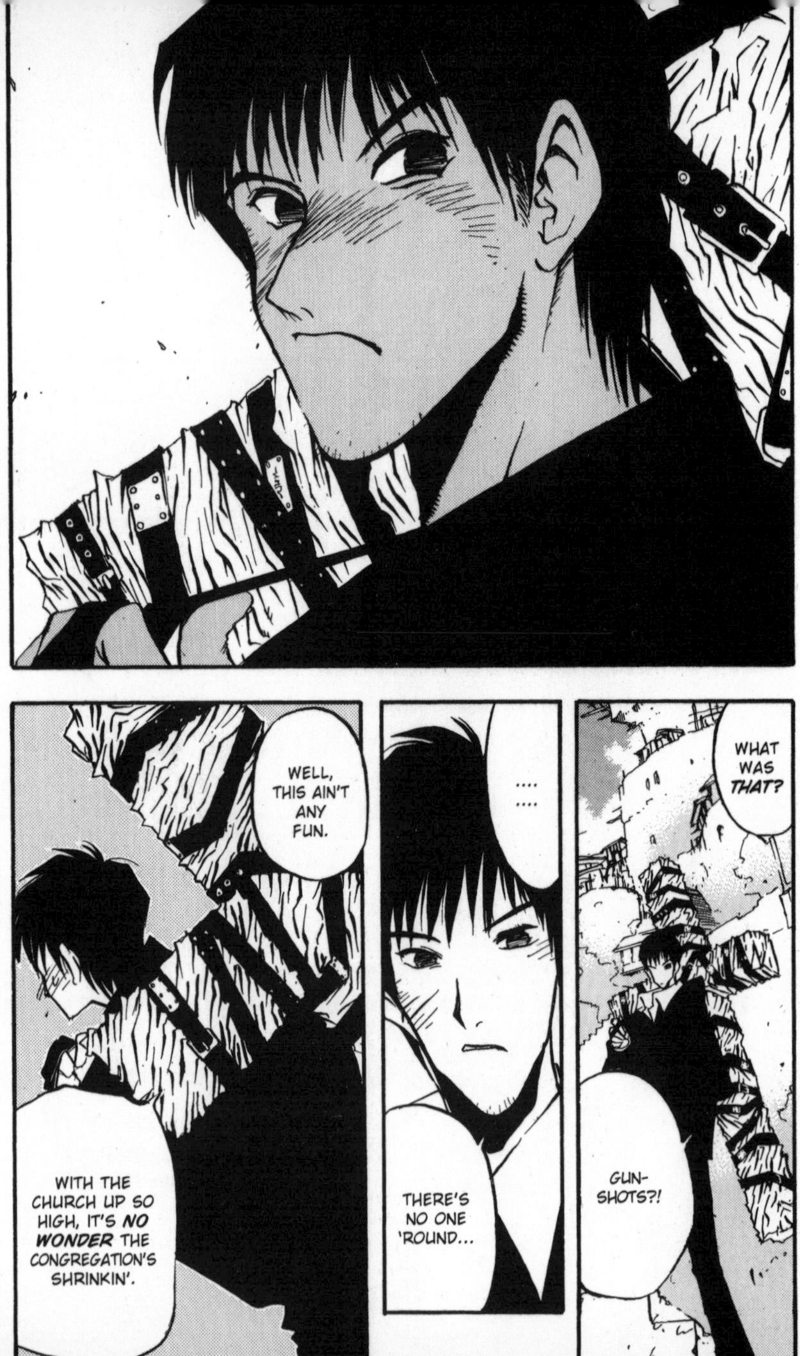
WHAT WAS **THAT?**
GUN-SHOTS?!
....
....
THERE'S NO ONE 'ROUND...
WELL, THIS AIN'T ANY FUN.
WITH THE CHURCH UP SO HIGH, IT'S **NO WONDER** THE CONGREGATION'S SHRINKIN'.

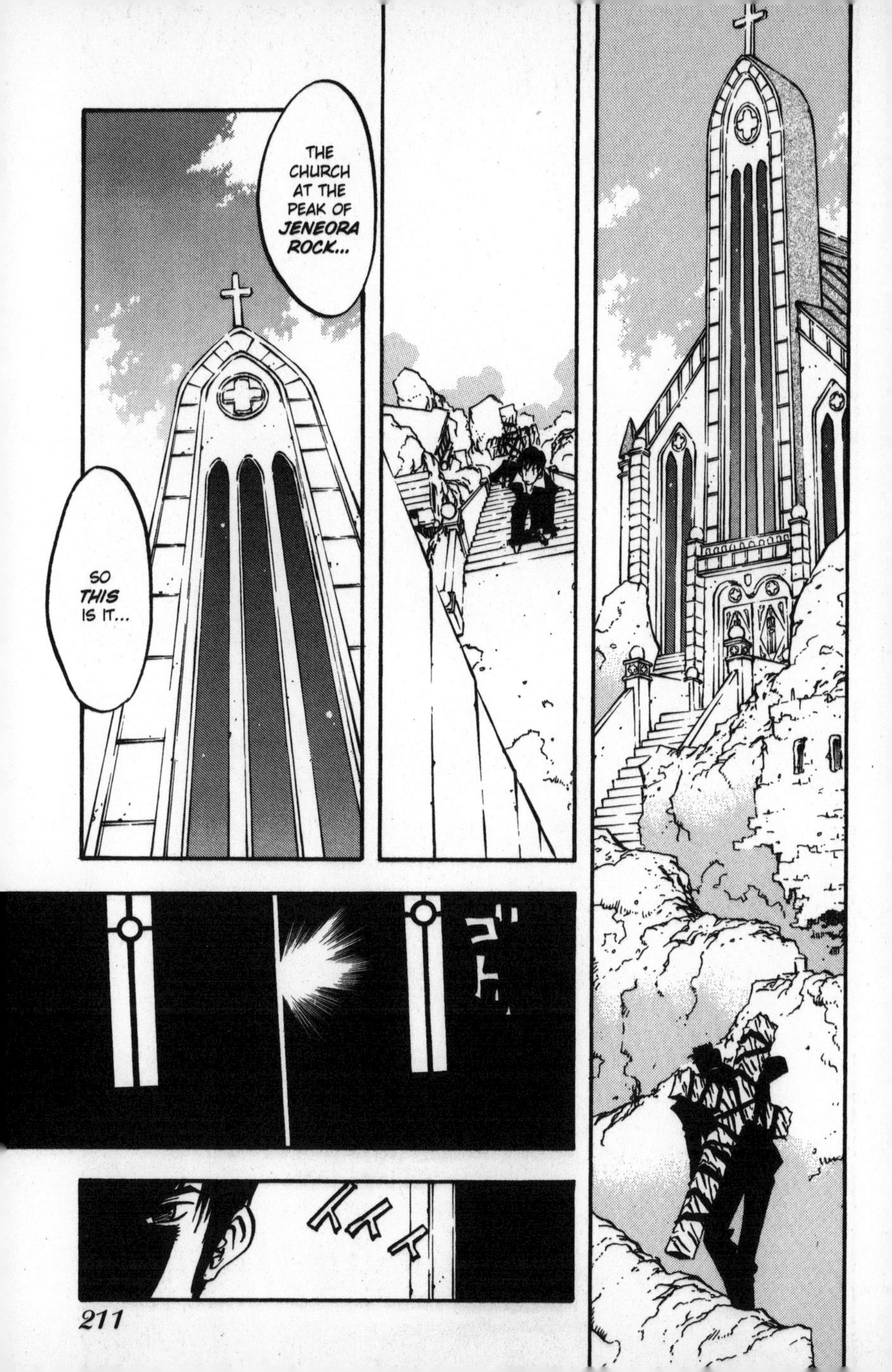
THE CHURCH AT THE PEAK OF *JENEORA ROCK...*
SO *THIS* IS IT...
ゴト

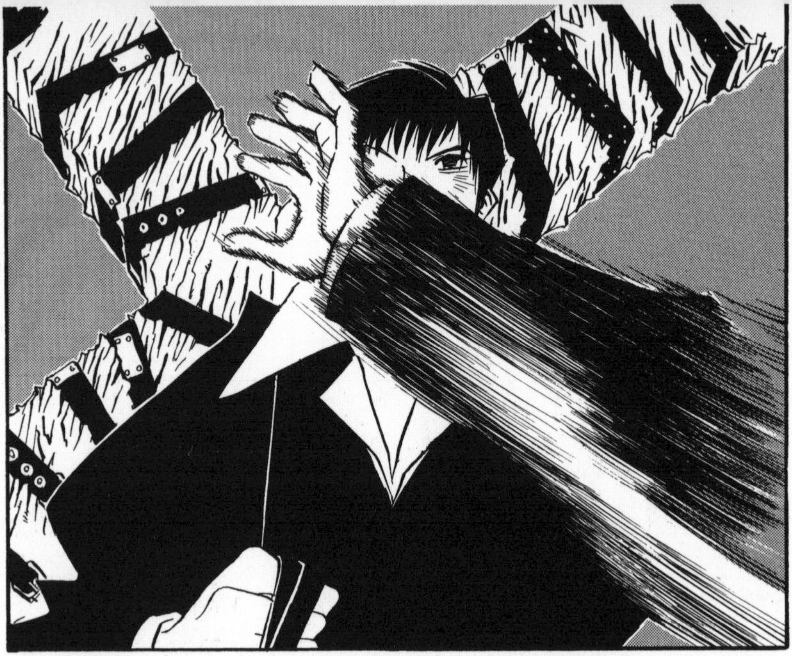
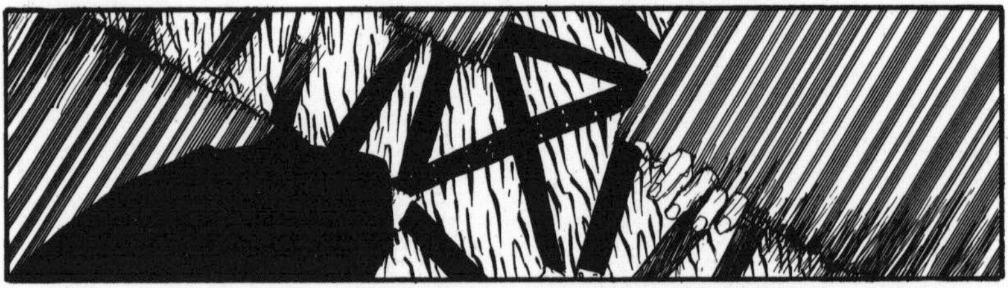
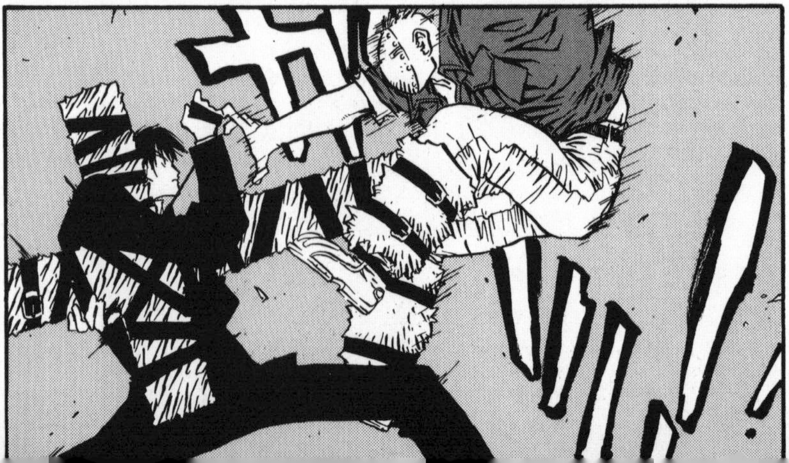

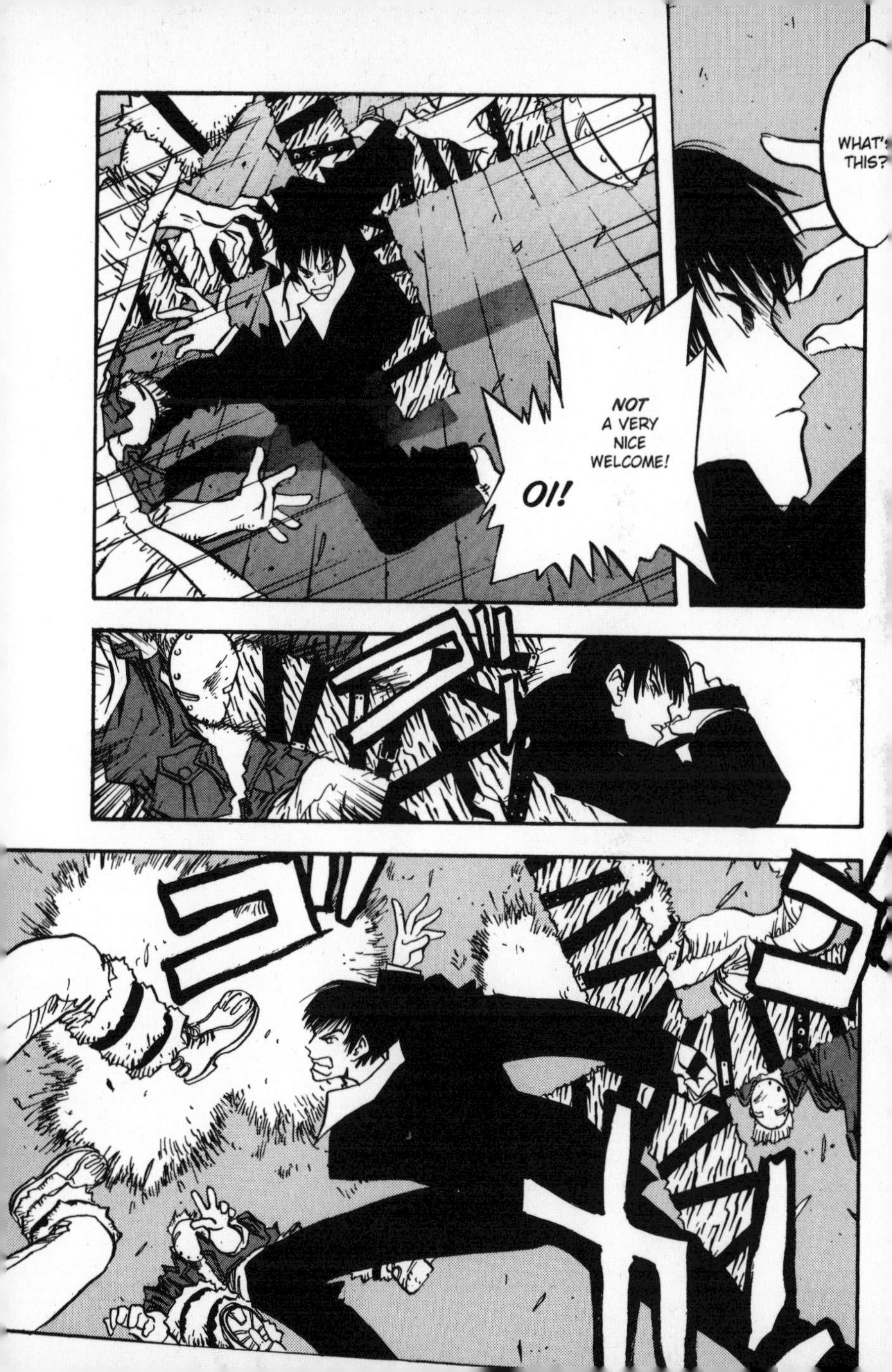
WHAT'S THIS?
NOT A VERY NICE WELCOME!
OI!

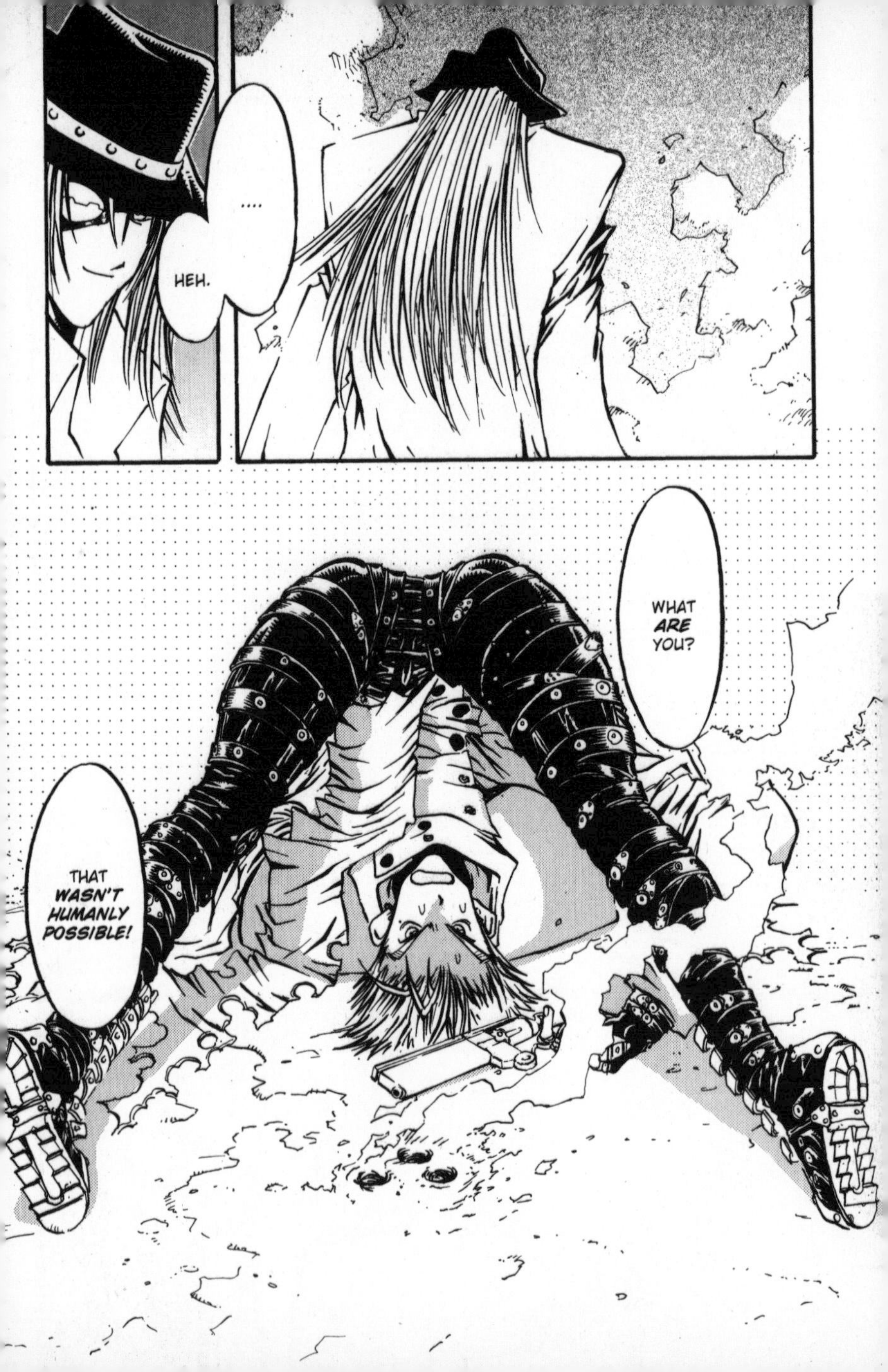
....
HEH.
WHAT *ARE* YOU?
THAT *WASN'T HUMANLY POSSIBLE!*

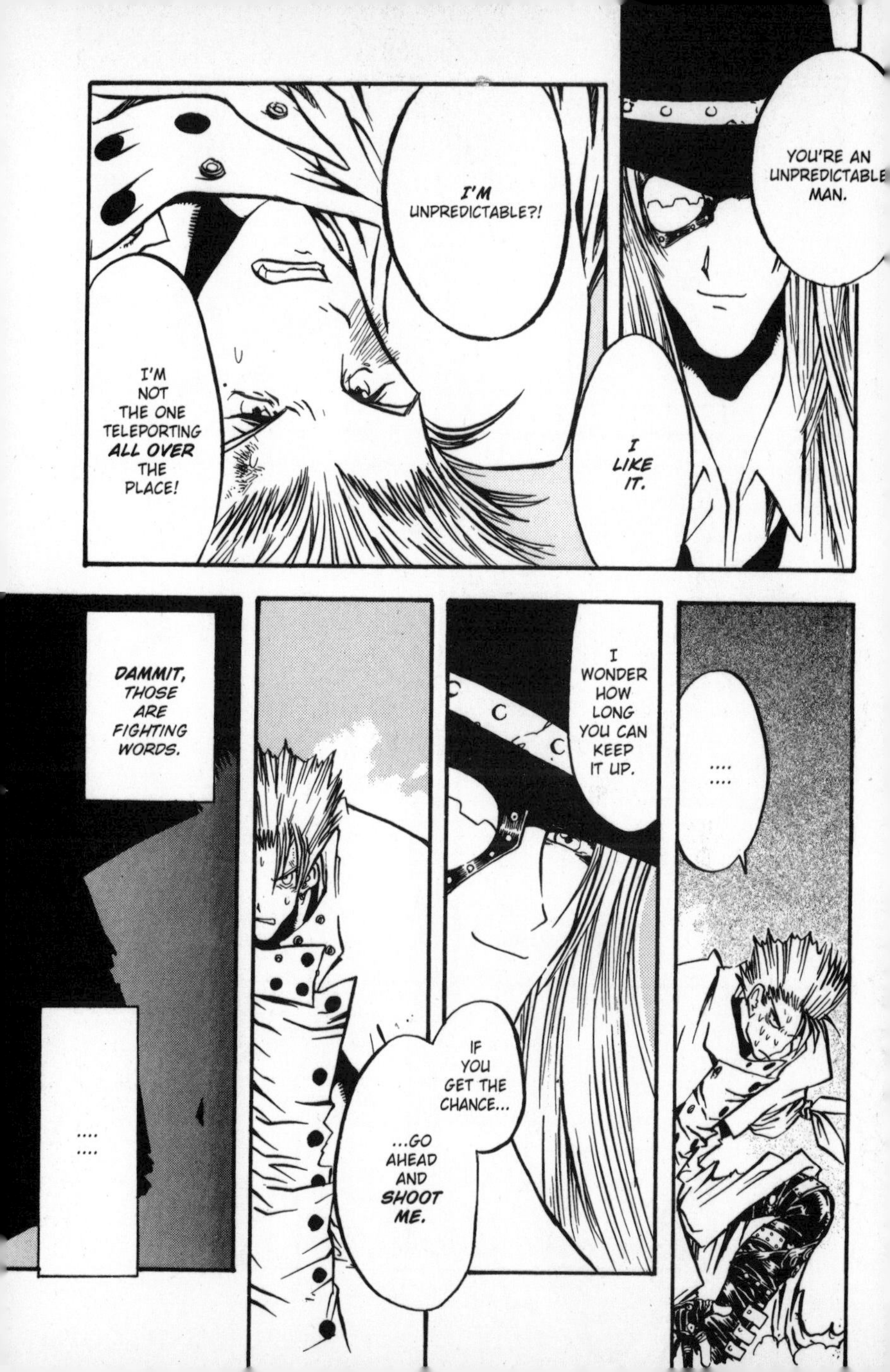
YOU'RE AN UNPREDICTABLE MAN.
I LIKE IT.
I'M UNPREDICTABLE?!
I'M NOT THE ONE TELEPORTING ALL OVER THE PLACE!
....
I WONDER HOW LONG YOU CAN KEEP IT UP.
IF YOU GET THE CHANCE...
...GO AHEAD AND SHOOT ME.
DAMMIT, THOSE ARE FIGHTING WORDS.
....

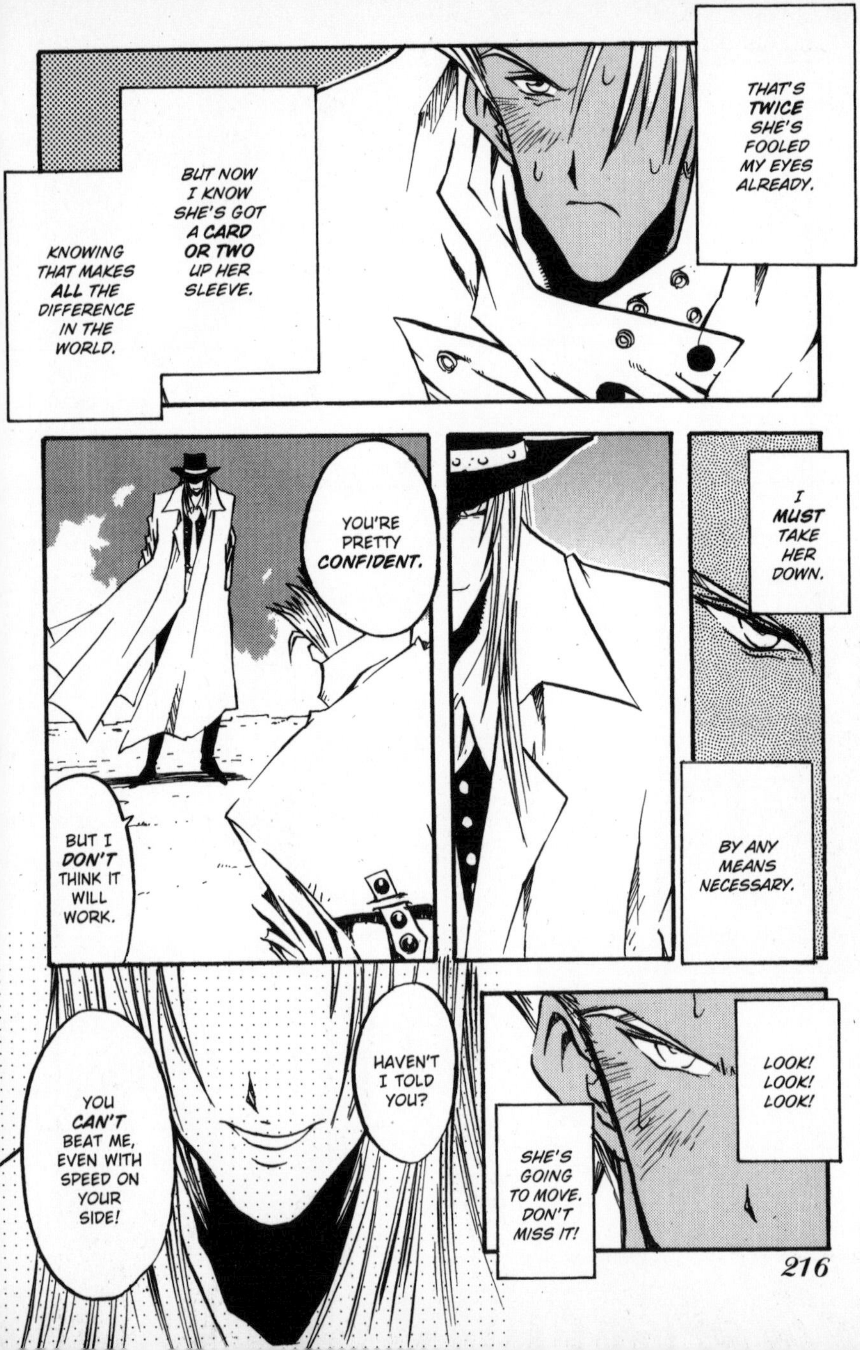
THAT'S TWICE SHE'S FOOLED MY EYES ALREADY.
BUT NOW I KNOW SHE'S GOT A CARD OR TWO UP HER SLEEVE.
KNOWING THAT MAKES ALL THE DIFFERENCE IN THE WORLD.
I MUST TAKE HER DOWN.
BY ANY MEANS NECESSARY.
YOU'RE PRETTY CONFIDENT.
BUT I DON'T THINK IT WILL WORK.
LOOK! LOOK! LOOK!
SHE'S GOING TO MOVE. DON'T MISS IT!
HAVEN'T I TOLD YOU?
YOU CAN'T BEAT ME, EVEN WITH SPEED ON YOUR SIDE!

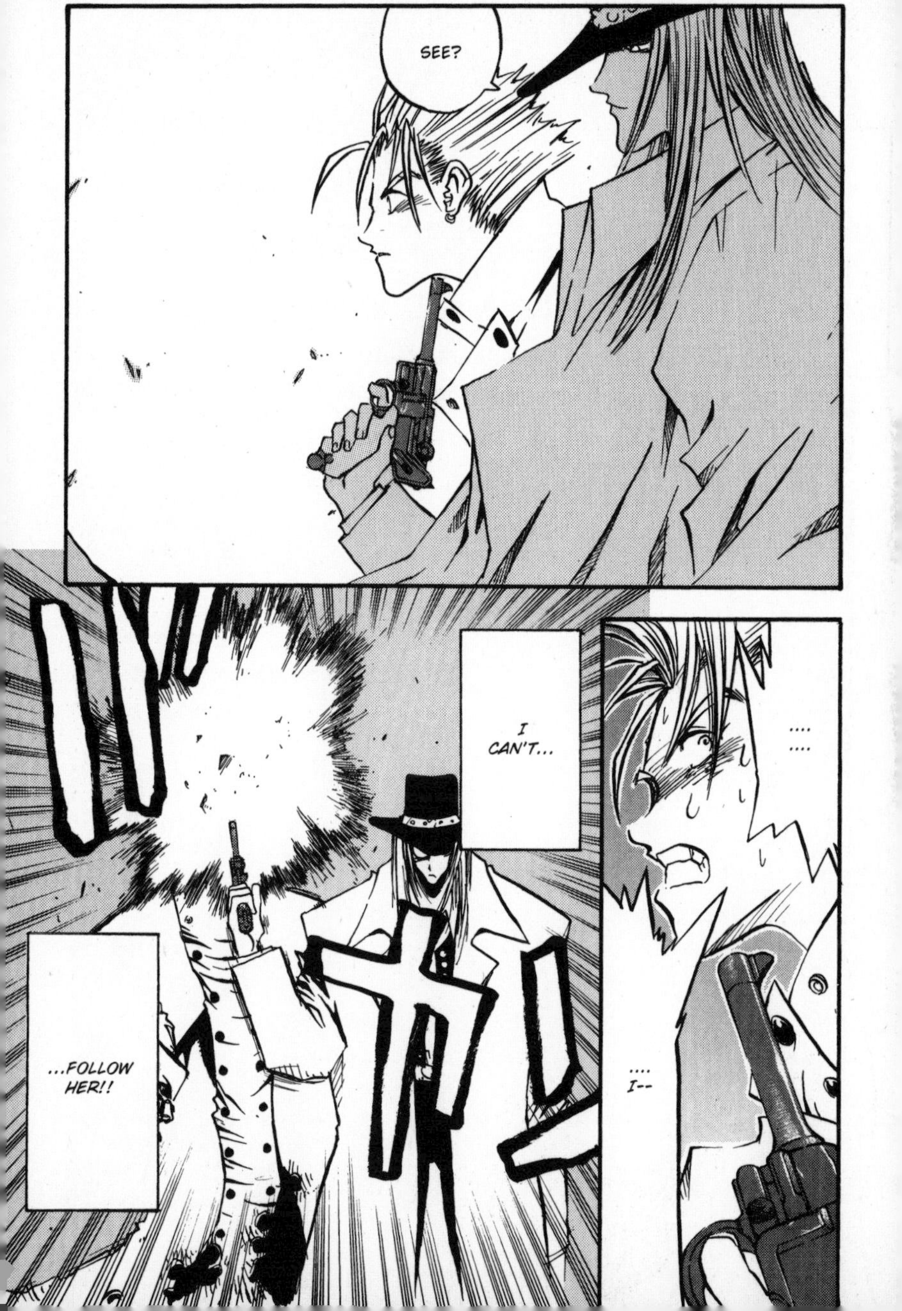
SEE?
....
....
....
I--
I CAN'T...
...FOLLOW HER!!

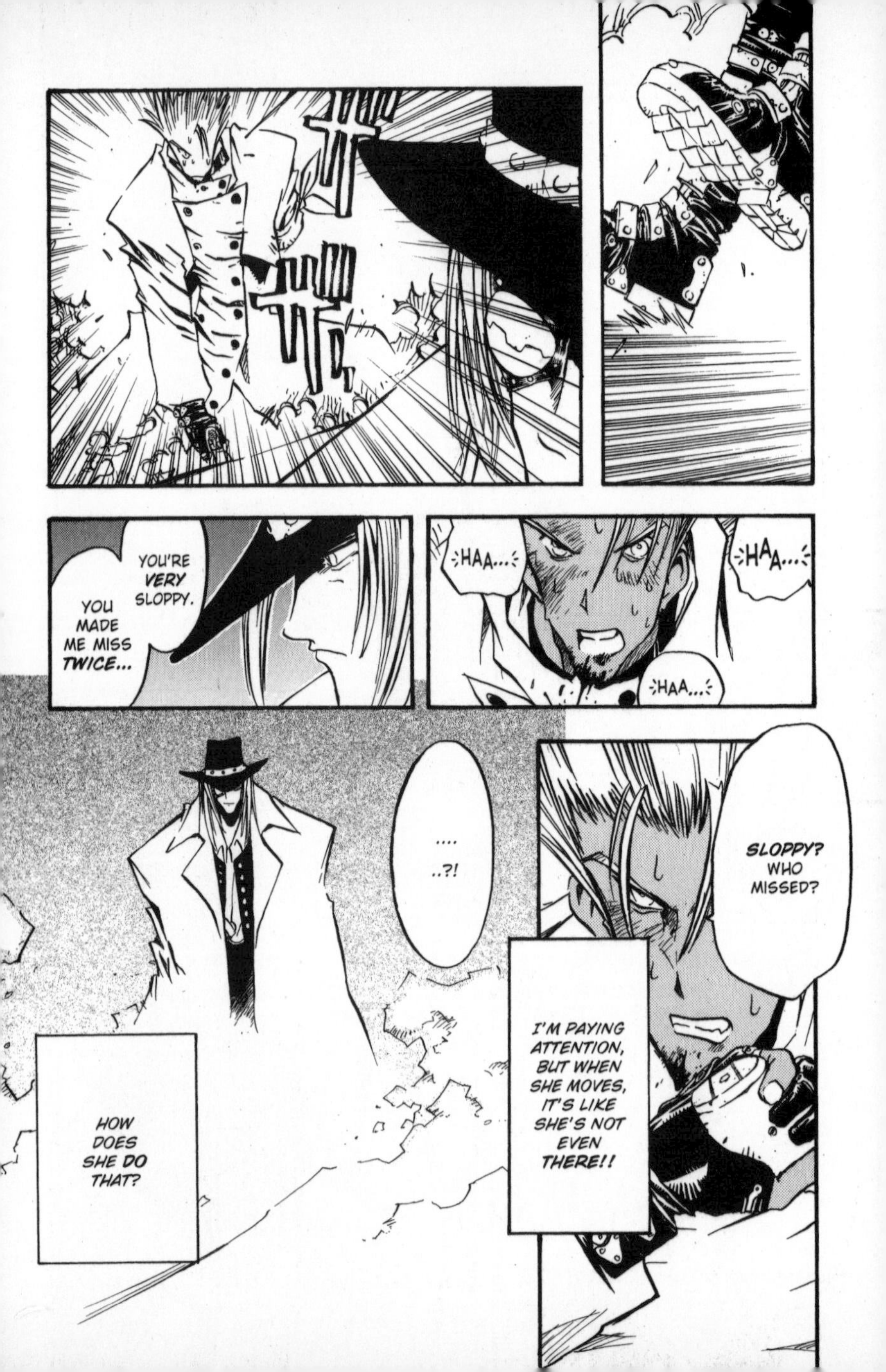
HAA...
HAA...
HAA...
YOU'RE VERY SLOPPY.
YOU MADE ME MISS TWICE...
SLOPPY? WHO MISSED?
I'M PAYING ATTENTION, BUT WHEN SHE MOVES, IT'S LIKE SHE'S NOT EVEN THERE!!
....
..?!
HOW DOES SHE DO THAT?

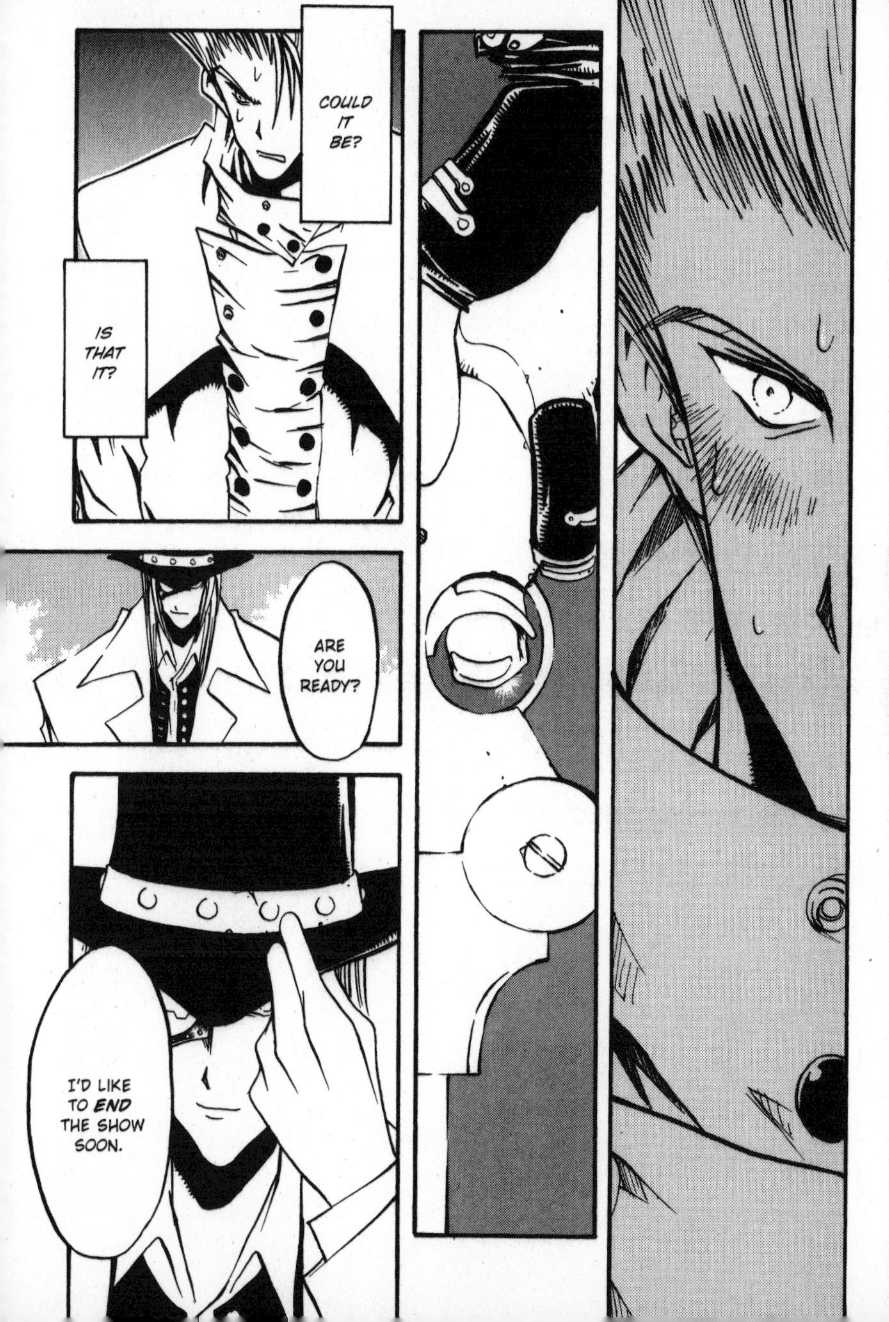
COULD IT BE?
IS THAT IT?
ARE YOU READY?
I'D LIKE TO **END** THE SHOW SOON.

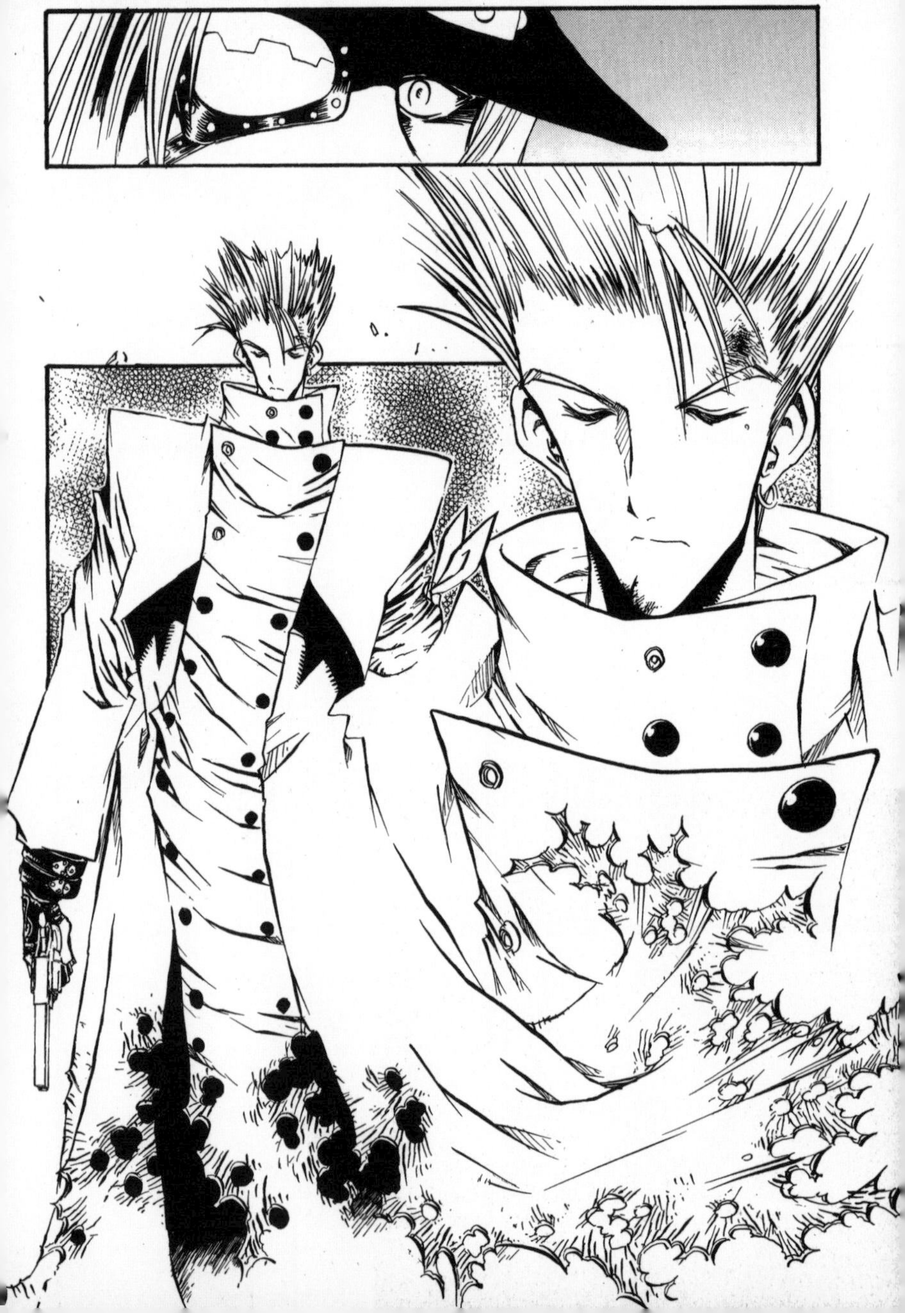

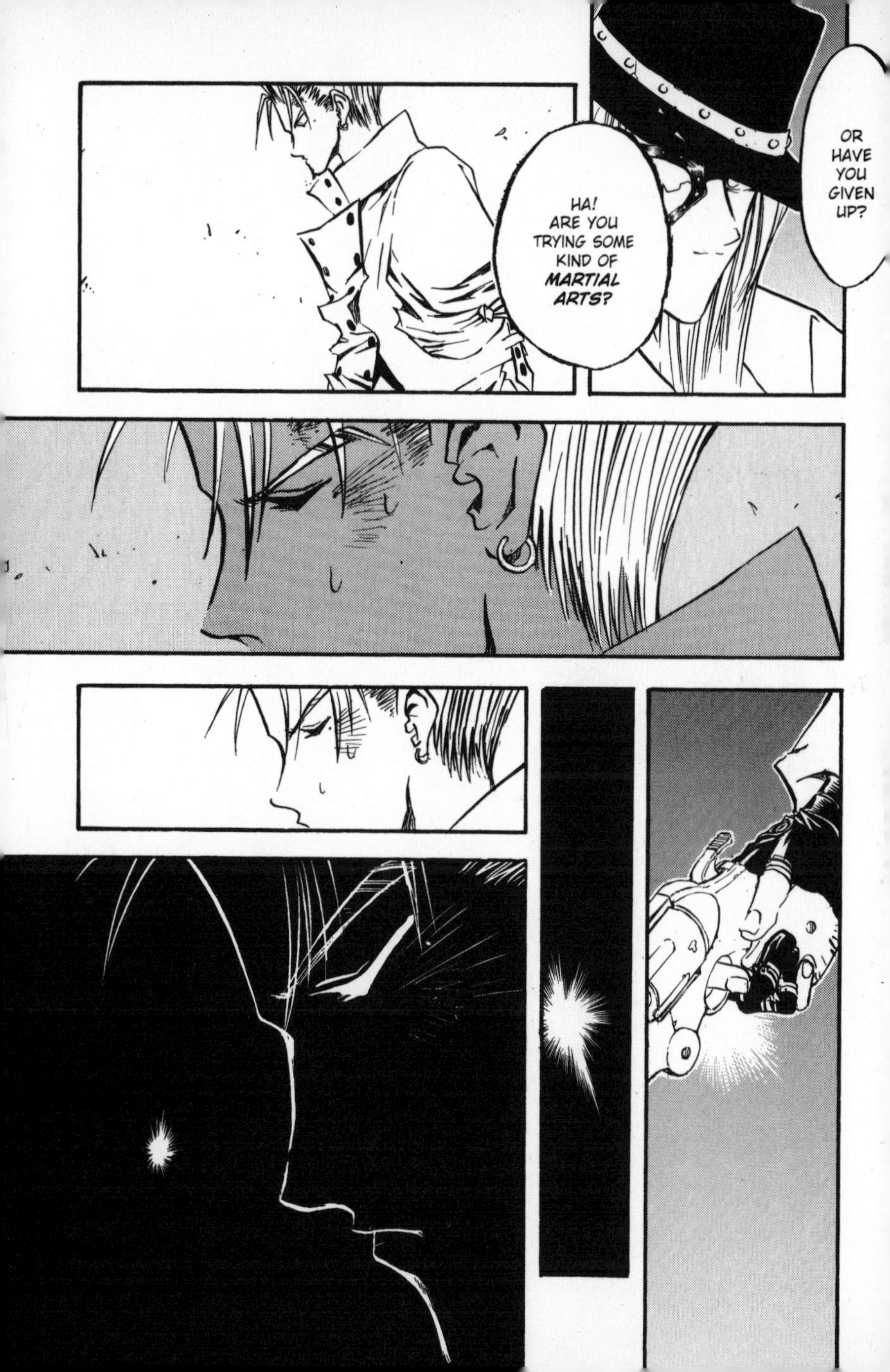
HA! ARE YOU TRYING SOME KIND OF ***MARTIAL ARTS?***
OR HAVE YOU GIVEN UP?

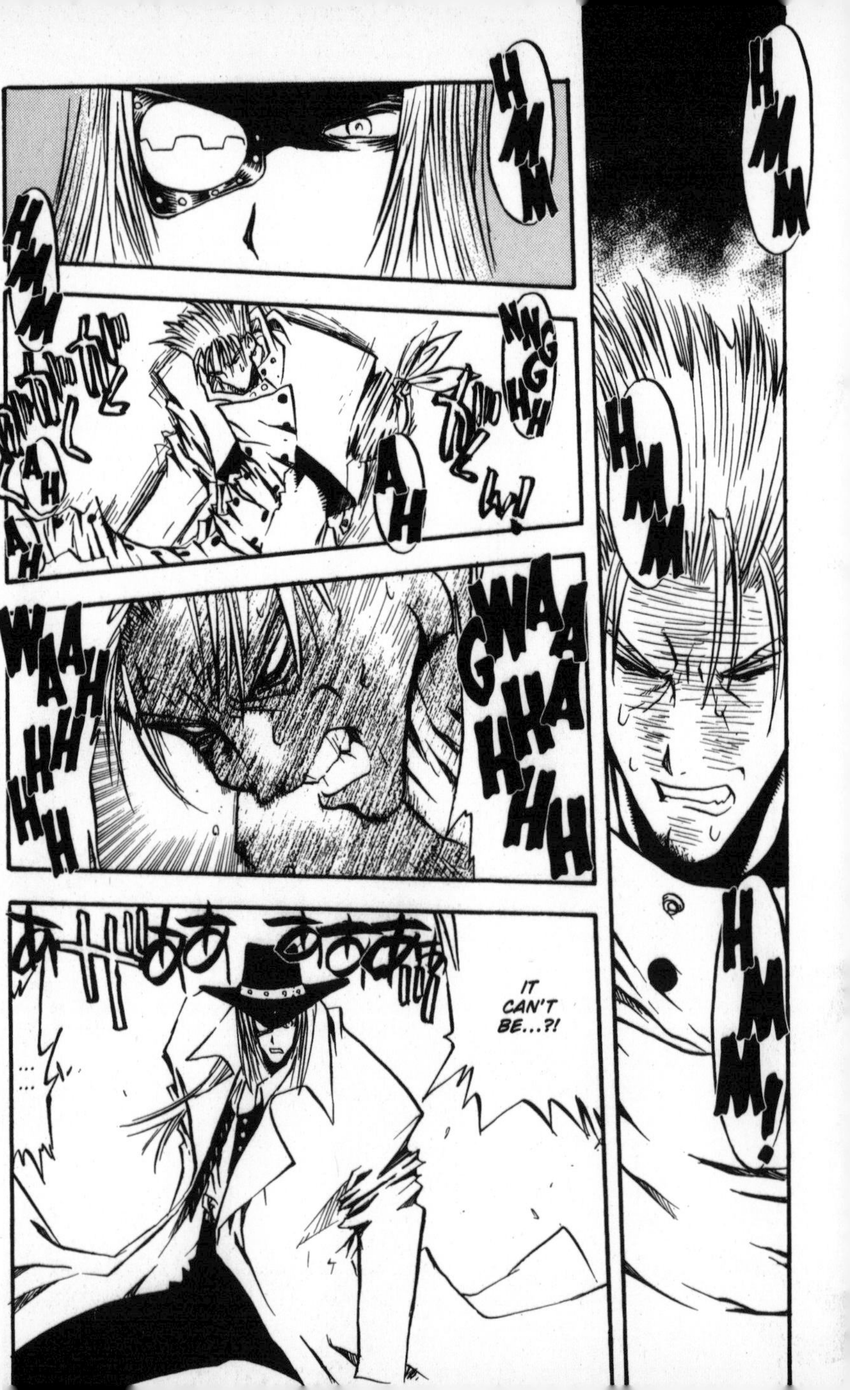

HMMM
HMMM
HMMM!
HMMM
HMMMM
NNGGHH
AH
AH
AH
GWAAAHHAHHHH
WAAHHHHHH
IT CAN'T BE...?!
...
...

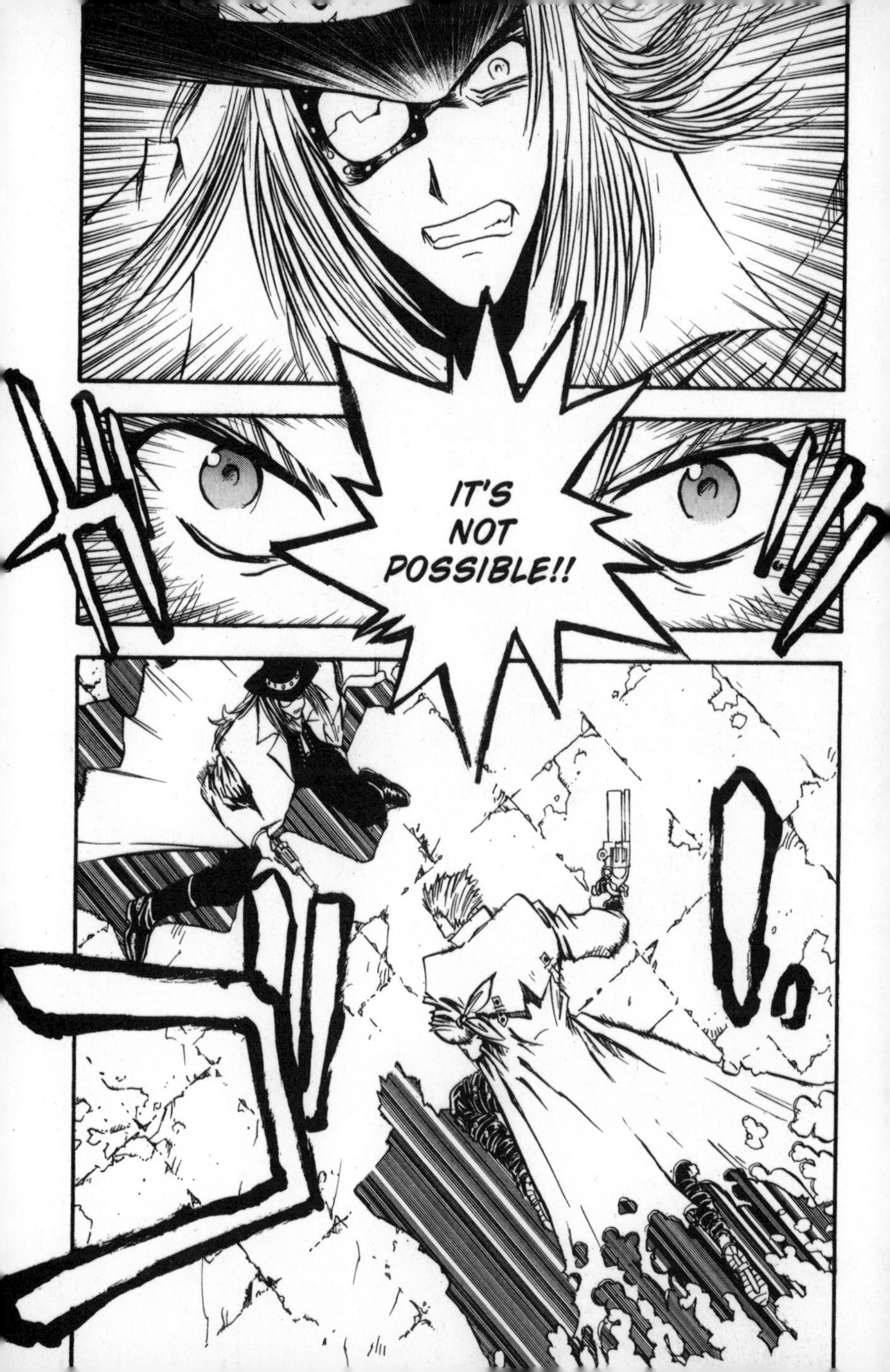
IT'S NOT POSSIBLE!!

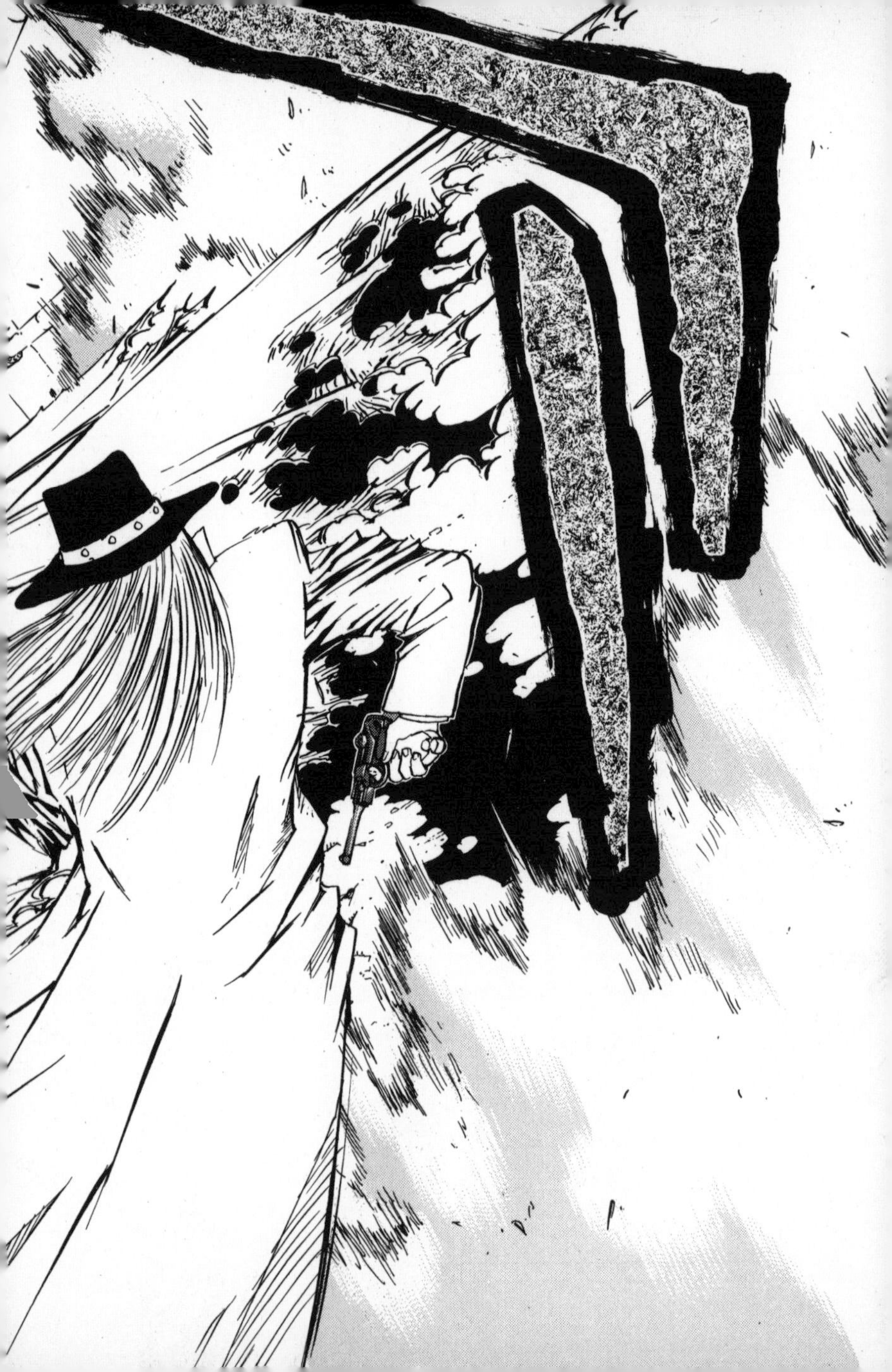

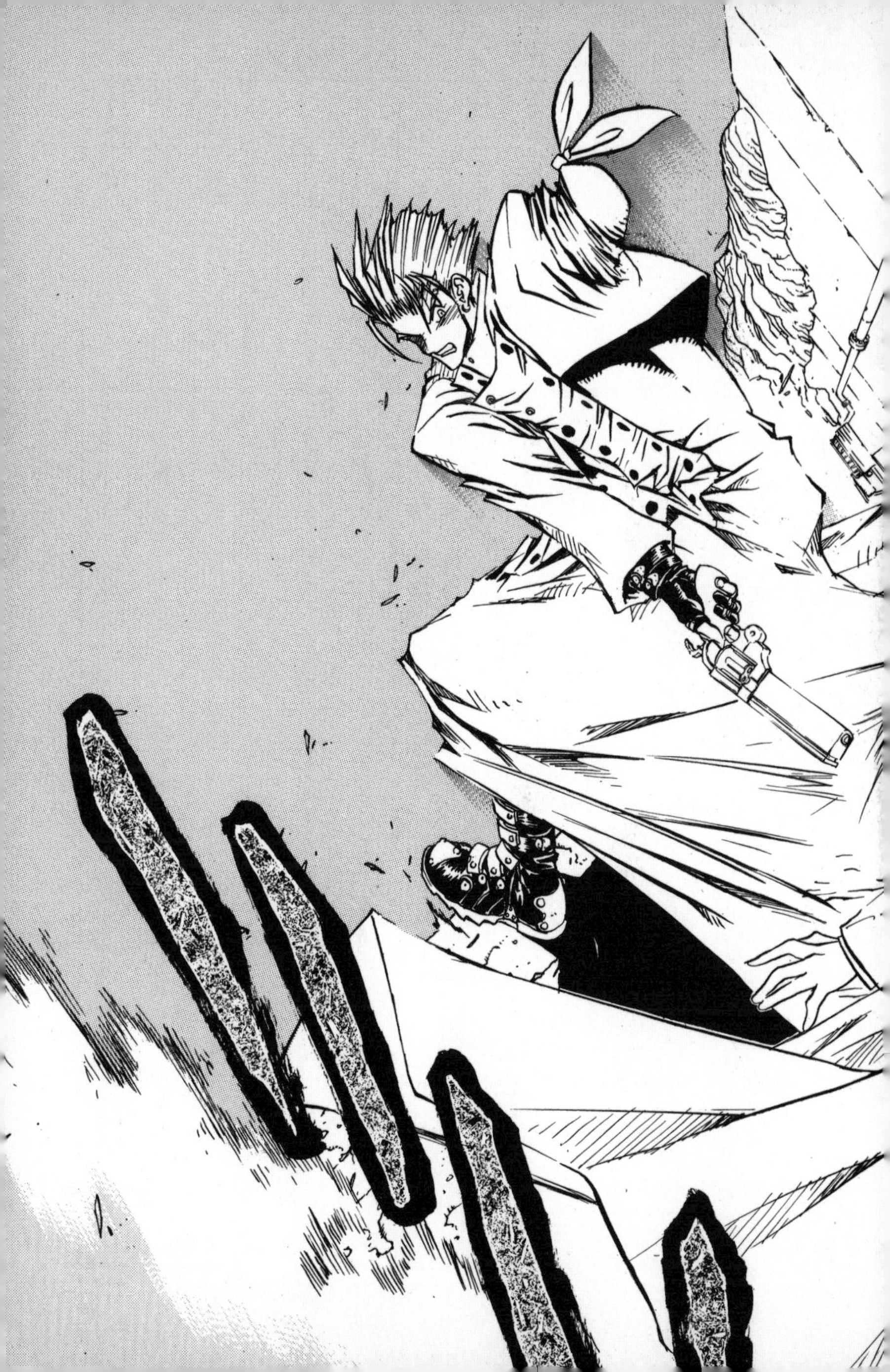

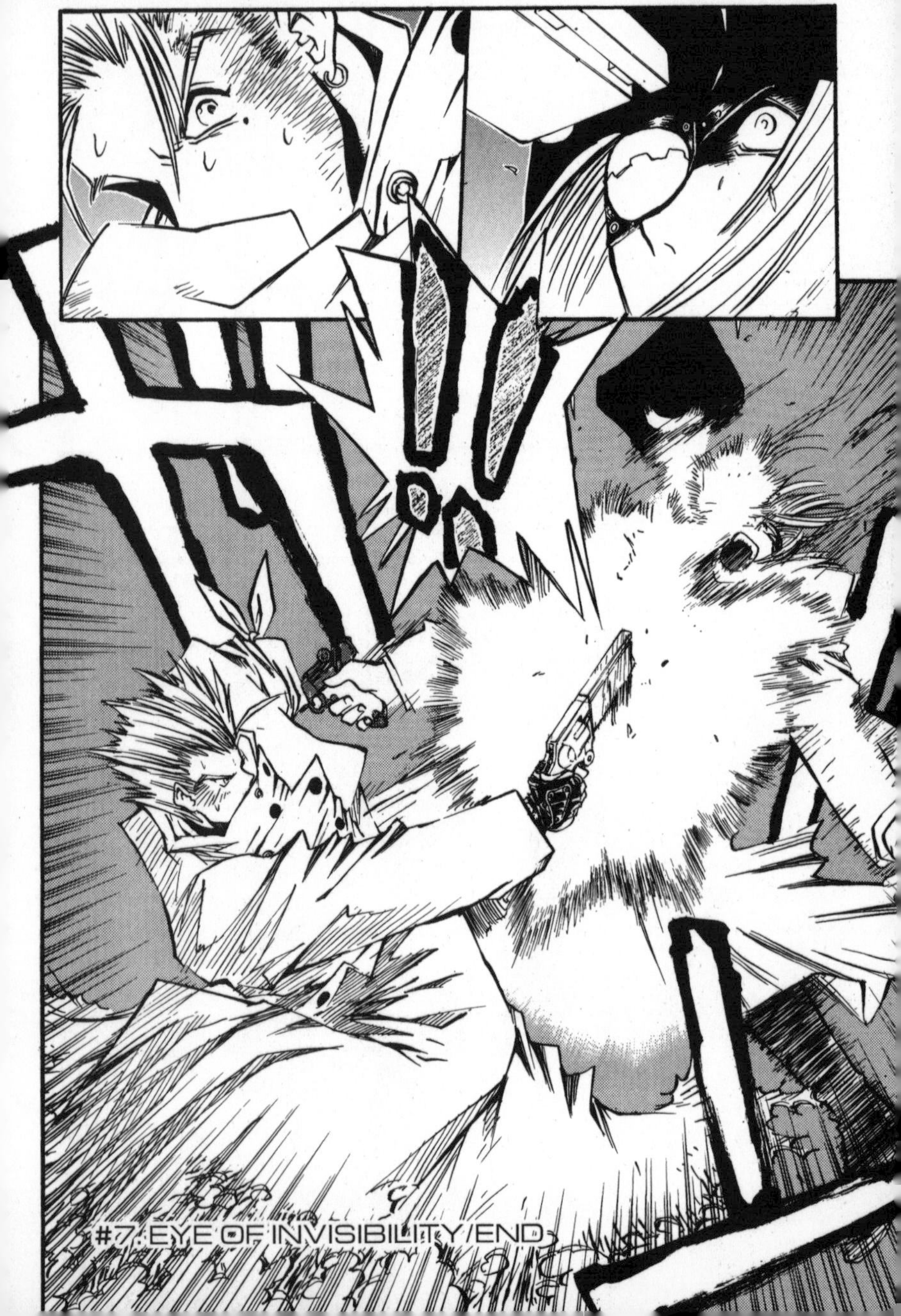
#7: EYE OF INVISIBILITY/END

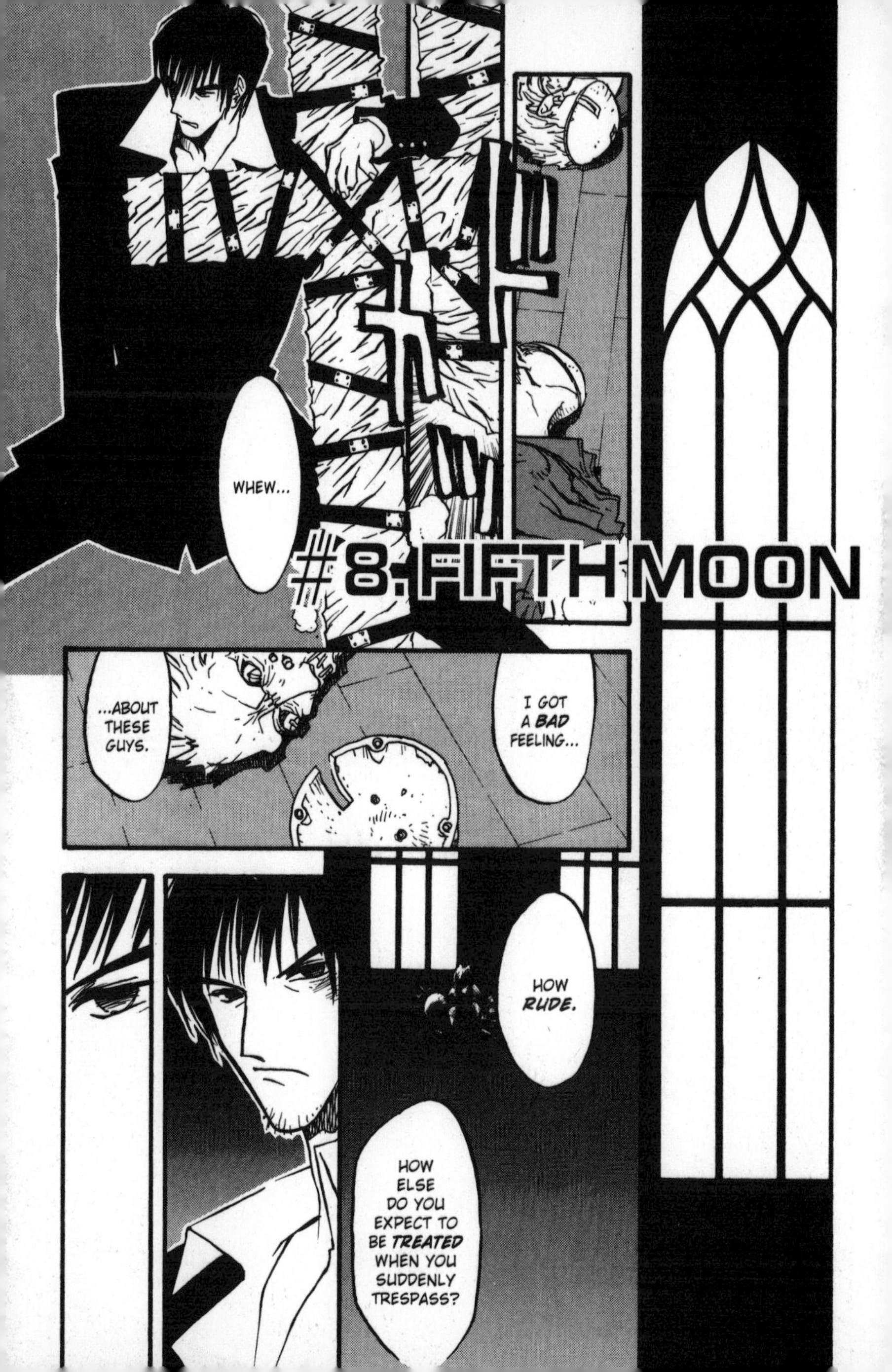
#8. FIFTH MOON
WHEW...
I GOT A *BAD* FEELING...
...ABOUT THESE GUYS.
HOW *RUDE.*
HOW ELSE DO YOU EXPECT TO BE *TREATED* WHEN YOU SUDDENLY TRESPASS?

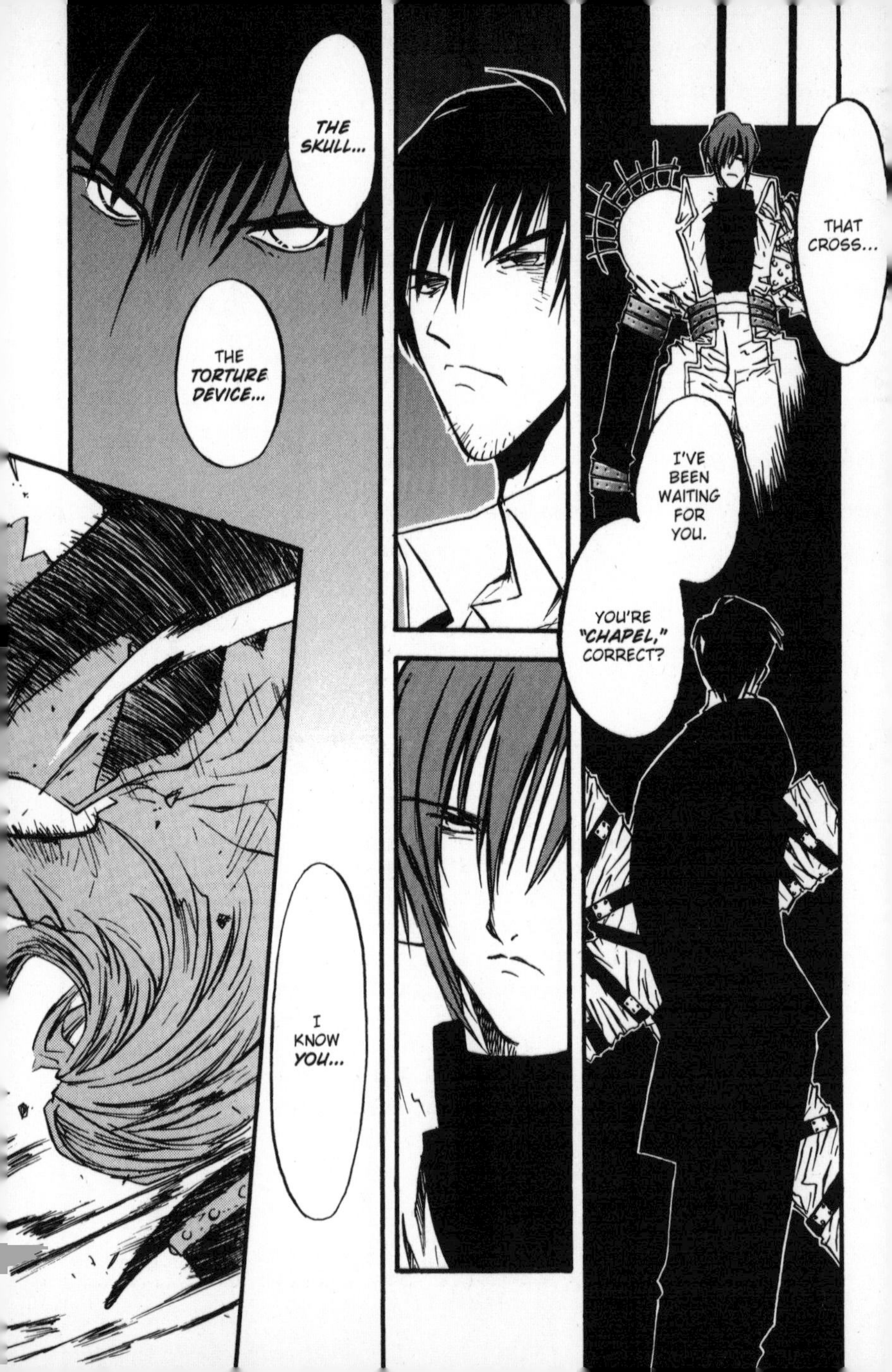
THAT CROSS...
I'VE BEEN WAITING FOR YOU.
YOU'RE "CHAPEL," CORRECT?
THE SKULL...
THE TORTURE DEVICE...
I KNOW YOU...

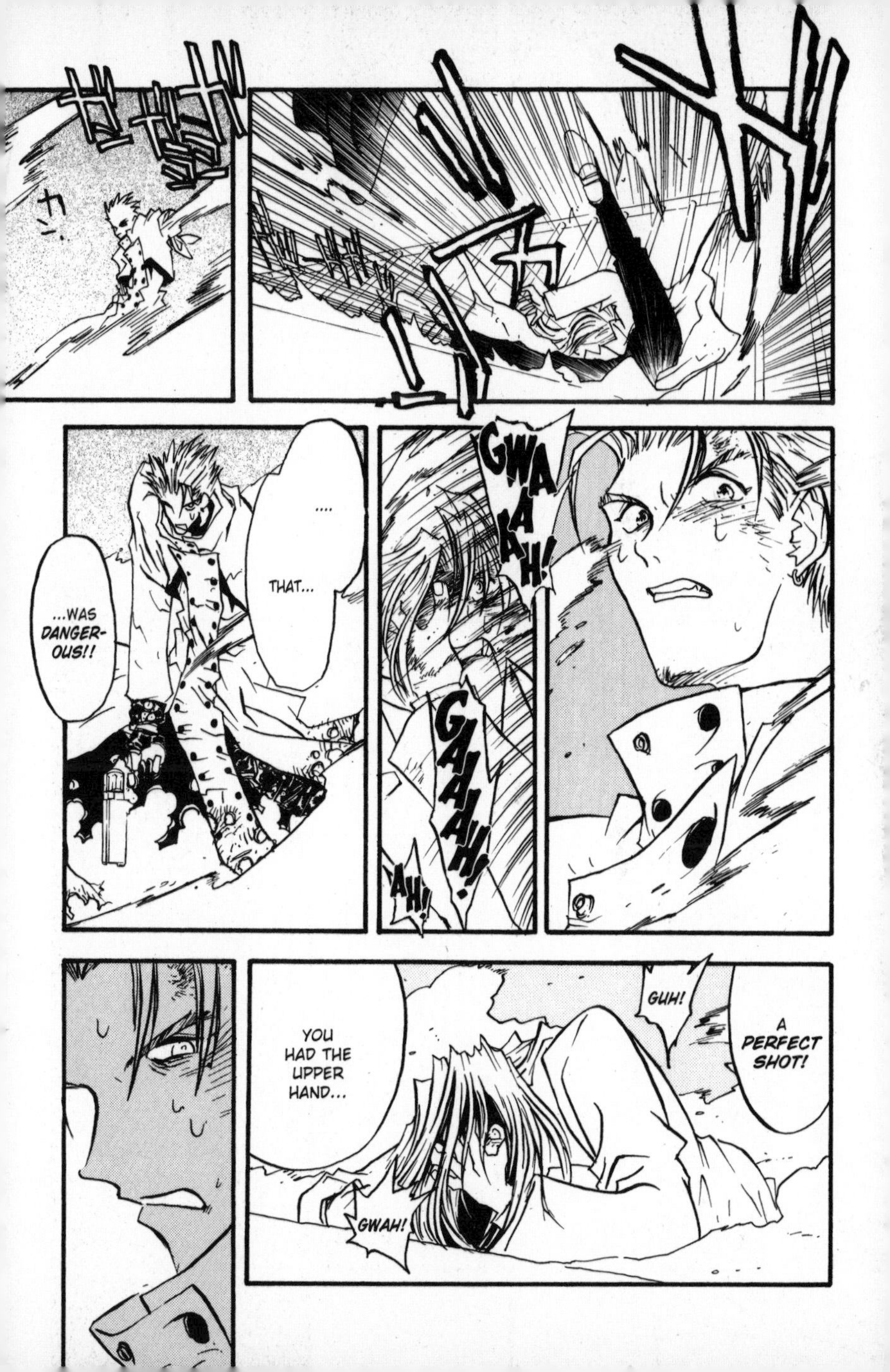
GWAAAH!
GAAAAH!
AH!
....
THAT...
...WAS DANGER-OUS!!
A PERFECT SHOT!
GUH!
YOU HAD THE UPPER HAND...
GWAH!

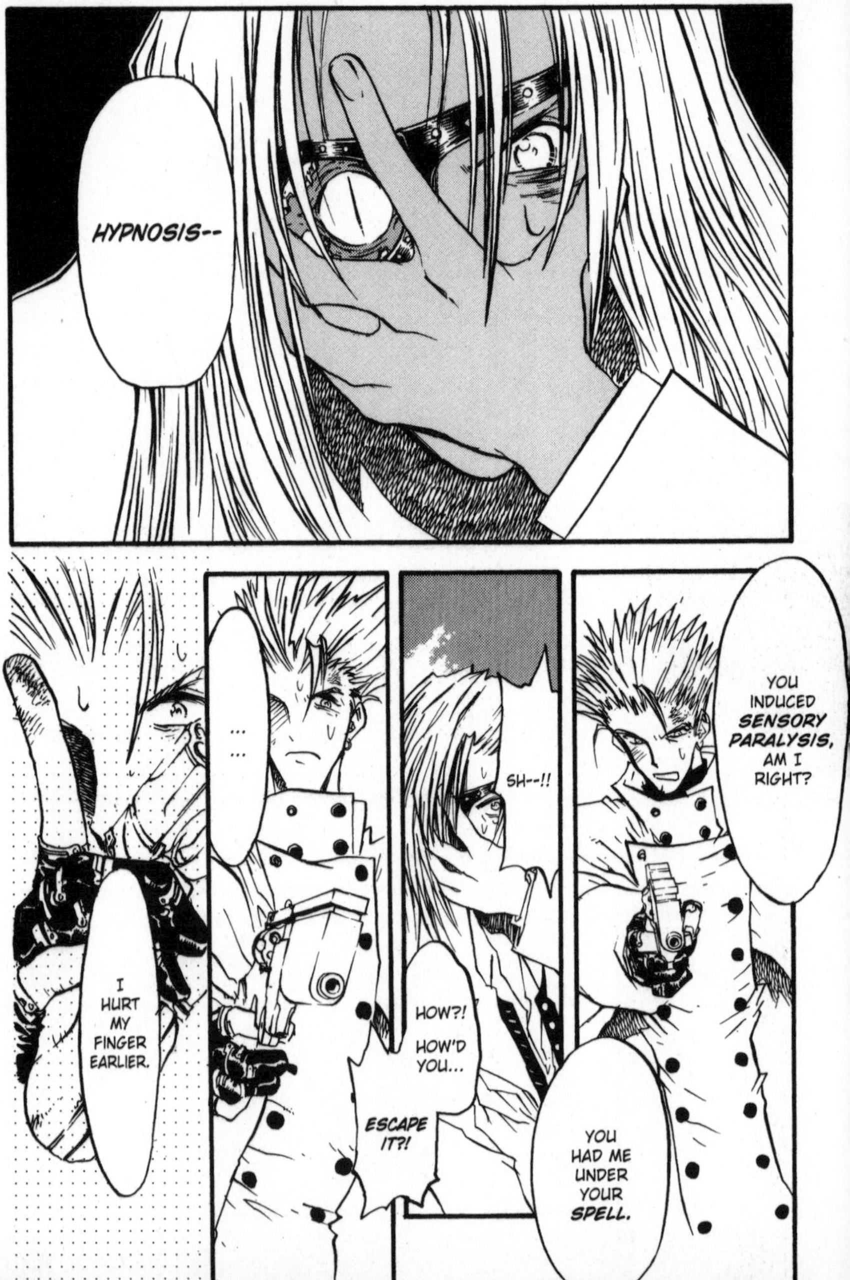
HYPNOSIS--
YOU INDUCED SENSORY PARALYSIS, AM I RIGHT?
YOU HAD ME UNDER YOUR SPELL.
SH--!!
HOW?! HOW'D YOU...
ESCAPE IT?!
... ...
I HURT MY FINGER EARLIER.

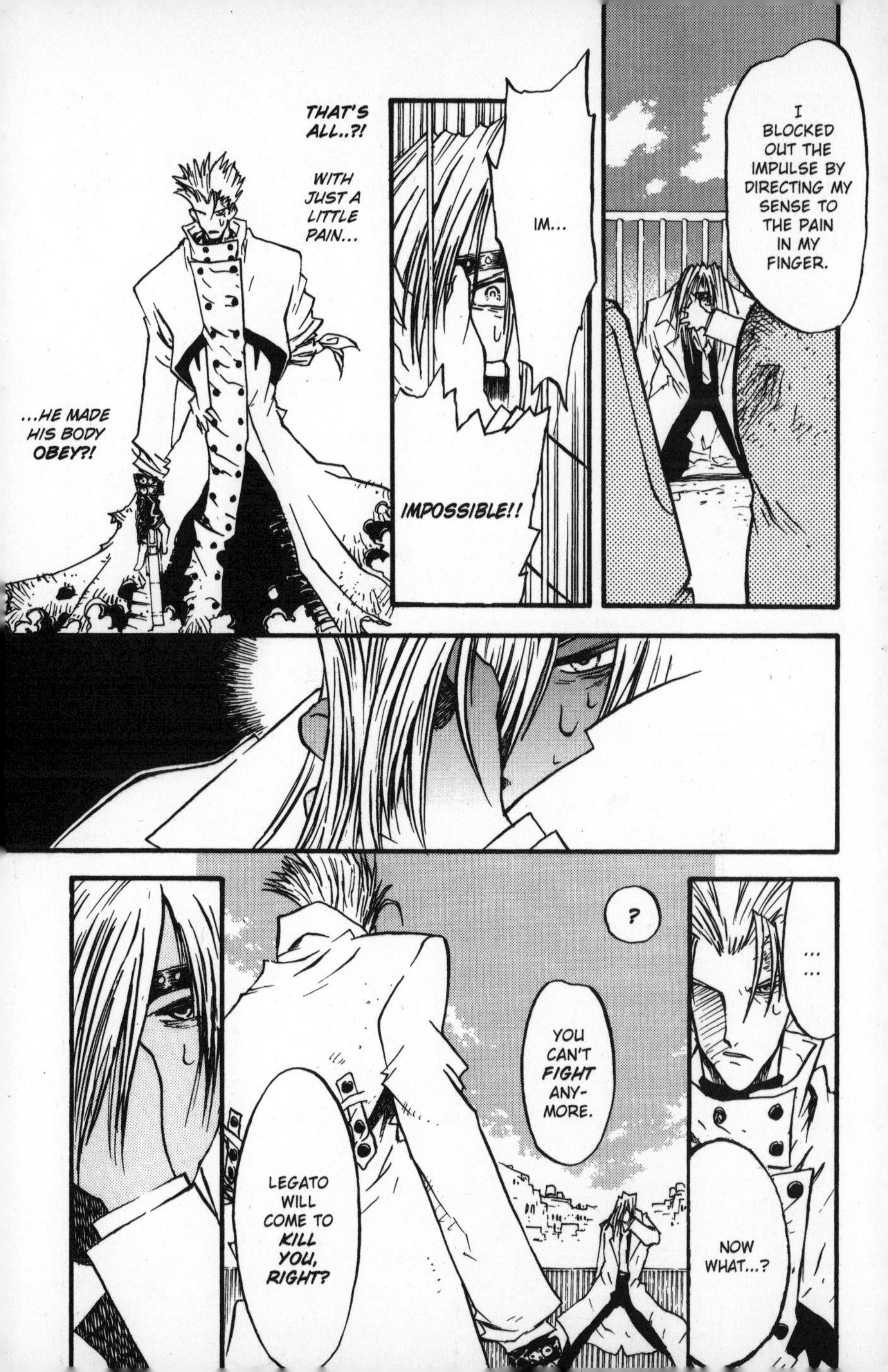

I BLOCKED OUT THE IMPULSE BY DIRECTING MY SENSE TO THE PAIN IN MY FINGER.
IM...
IMPOSSIBLE!!
THAT'S ALL..?!
WITH JUST A LITTLE PAIN...
...HE MADE HIS BODY OBEY?!
......
NOW WHAT...?
?
YOU CAN'T FIGHT ANY-MORE.
LEGATO WILL COME TO KILL YOU, RIGHT?

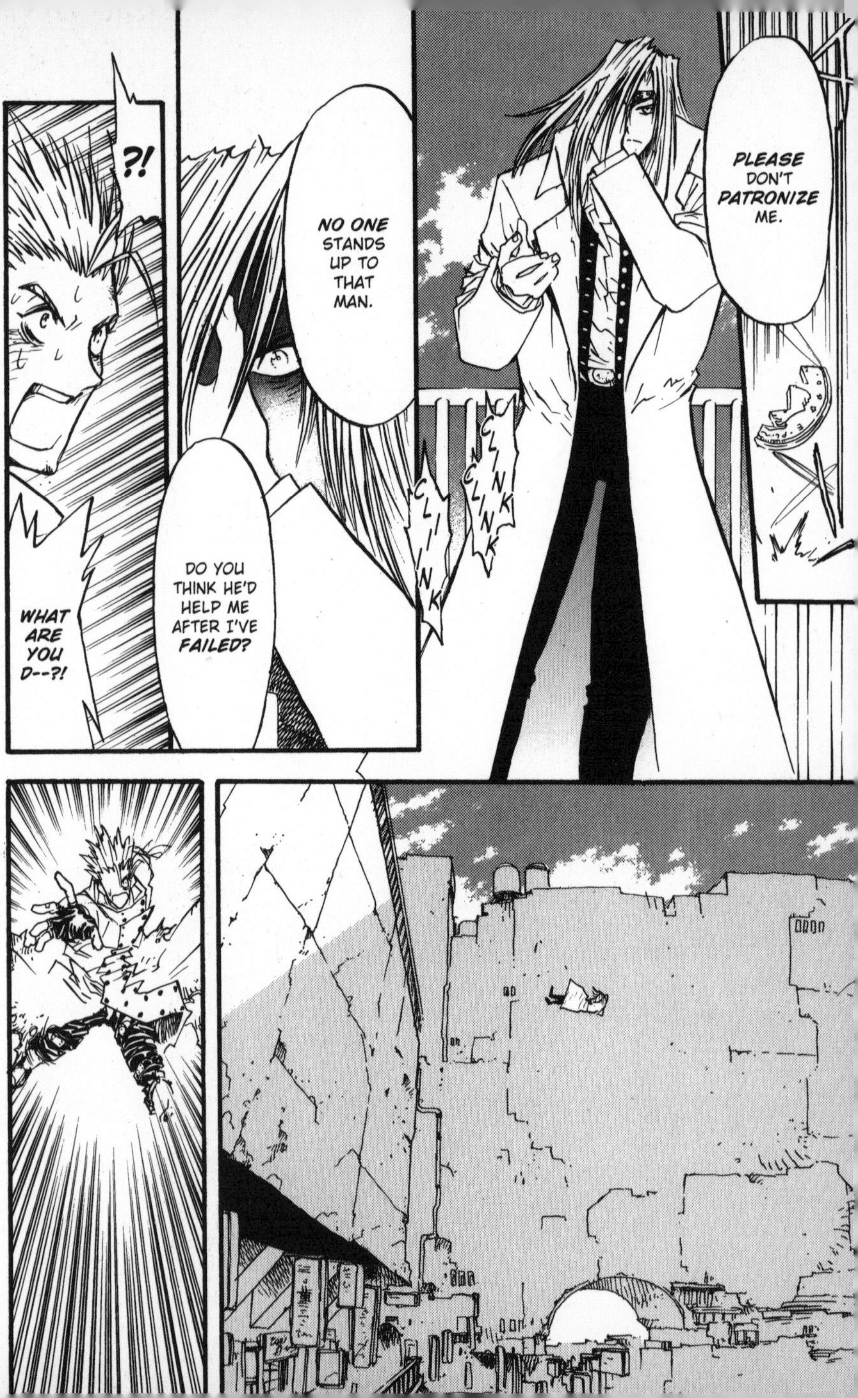
PLEASE DON'T PATRONIZE ME.
CLINK
CLINK
CLINK
NO ONE STANDS UP TO THAT MAN.
DO YOU THINK HE'D HELP ME AFTER I'VE FAILED?
?!
WHAT ARE YOU D--?!

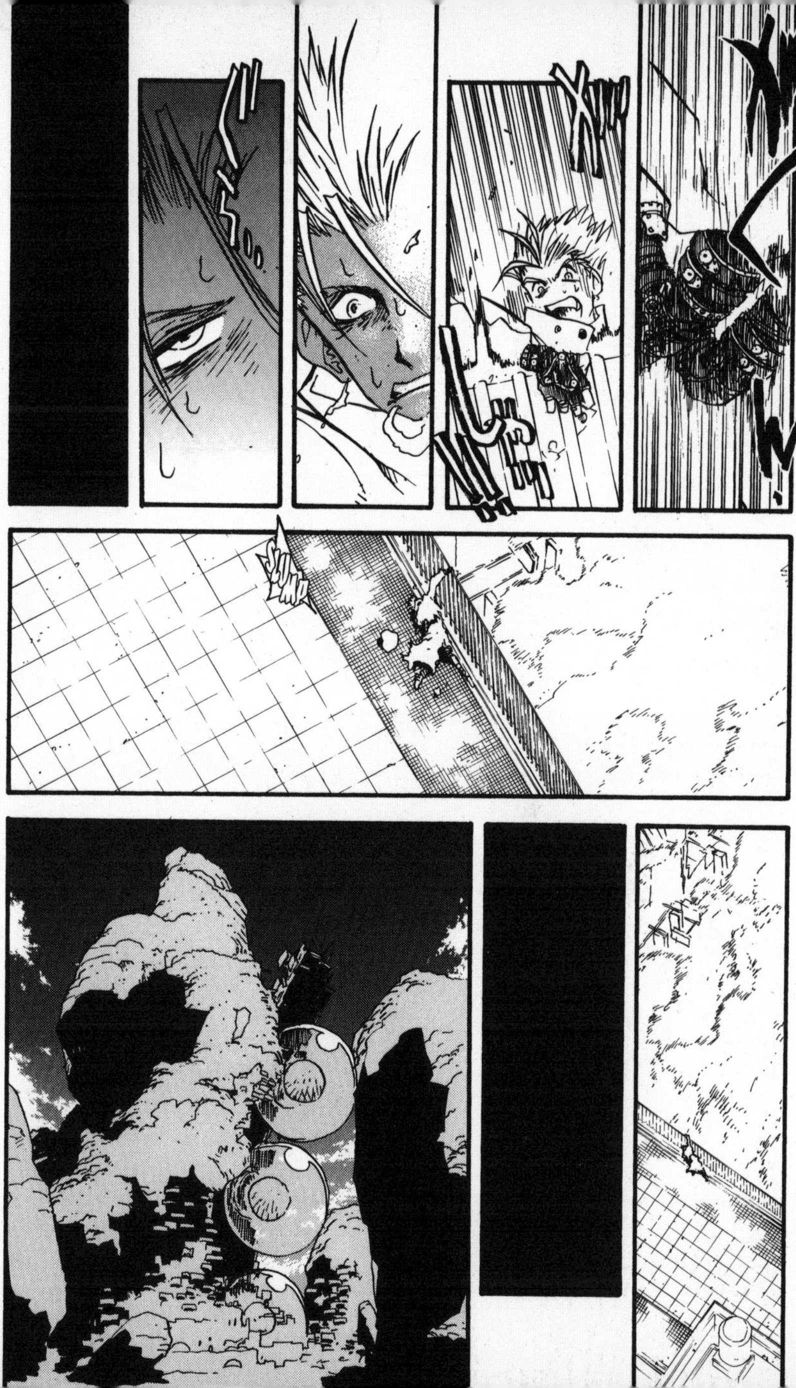
SLUMP

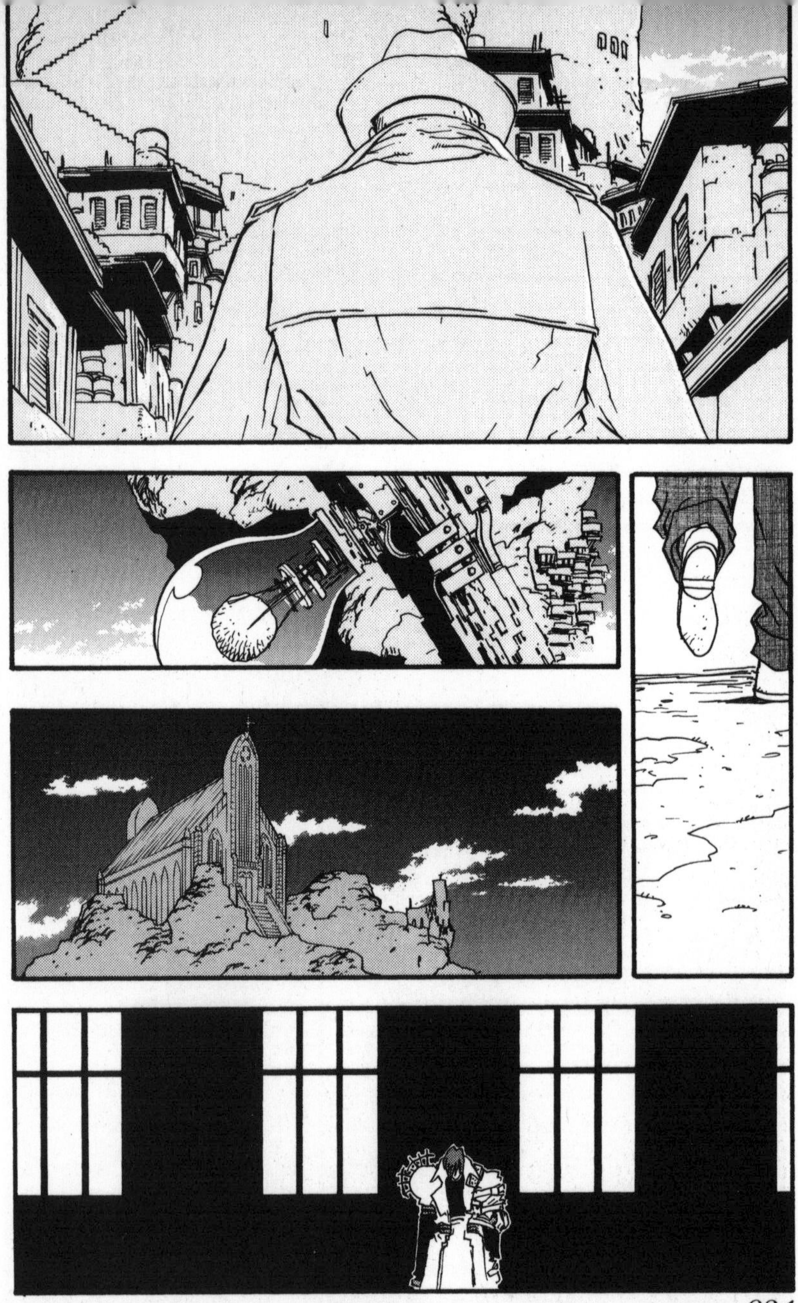

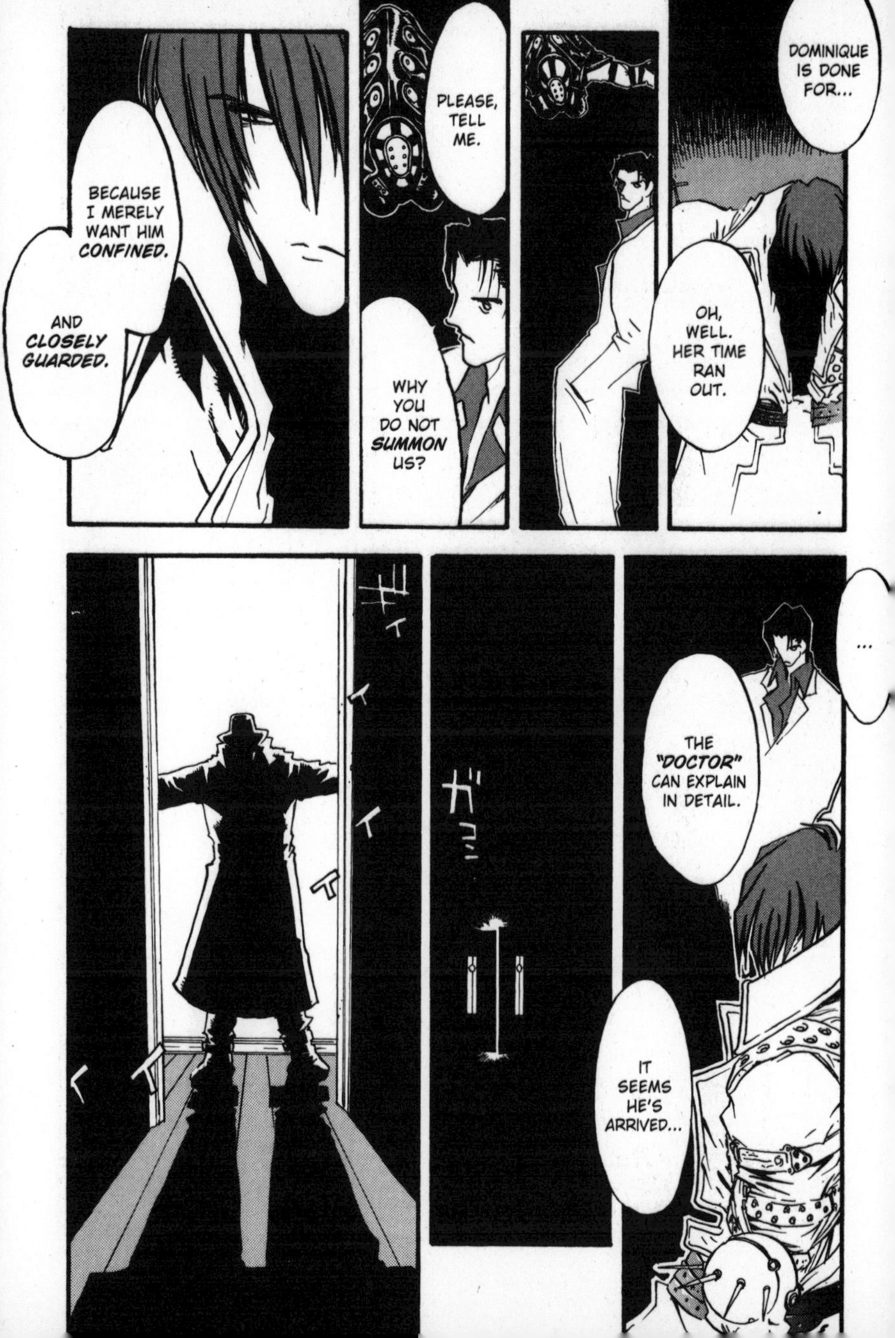
DOMINIQUE IS DONE FOR...
OH, WELL. HER TIME RAN OUT.
PLEASE, TELL ME.
WHY YOU DO NOT SUMMON US?
BECAUSE I MERELY WANT HIM CONFINED.
AND CLOSELY GUARDED.
...
THE "DOCTOR" CAN EXPLAIN IN DETAIL.
IT SEEMS HE'S ARRIVED...

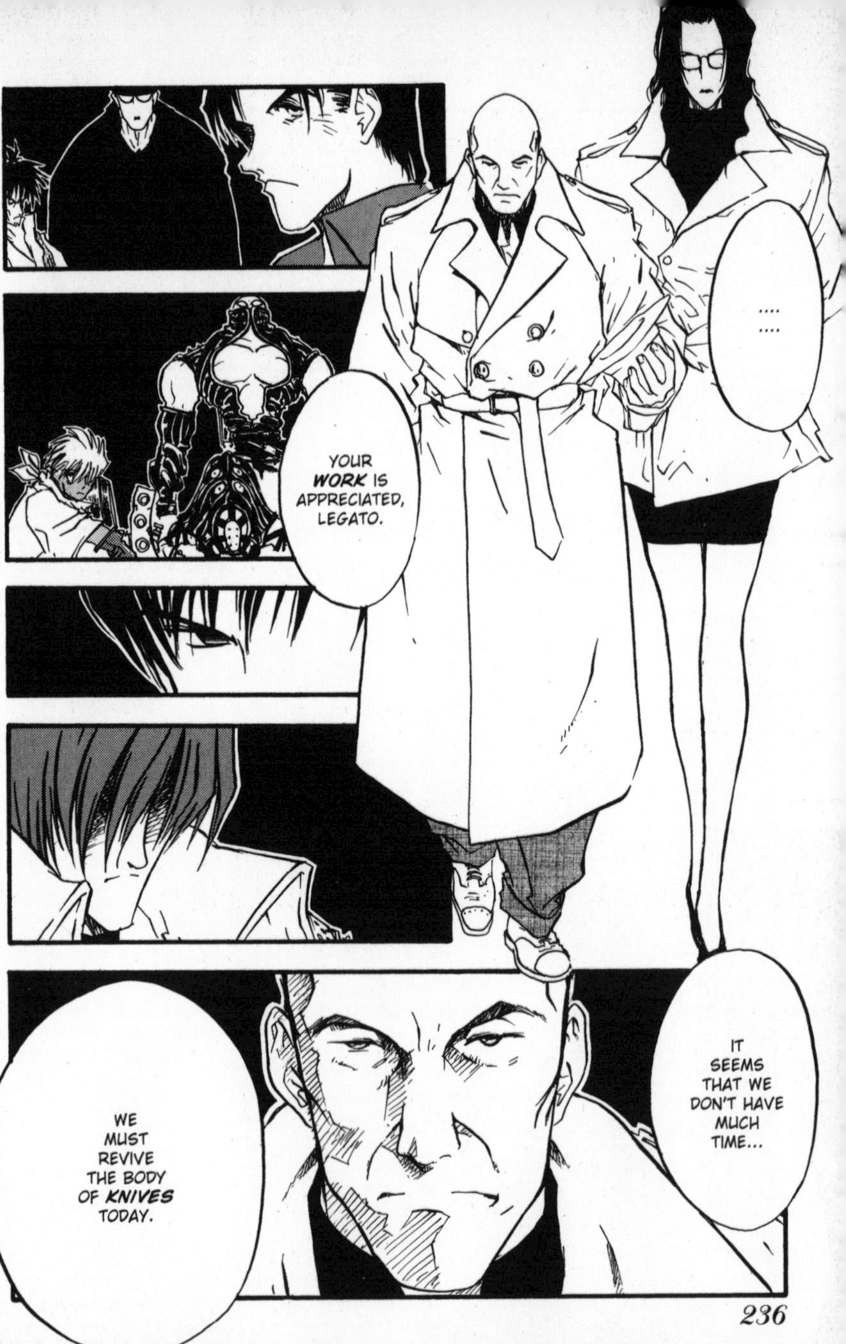
....
....
YOUR WORK IS APPRECIATED, LEGATO.
IT SEEMS THAT WE DON'T HAVE MUCH TIME...
WE MUST REVIVE THE BODY OF KNIVES TODAY.

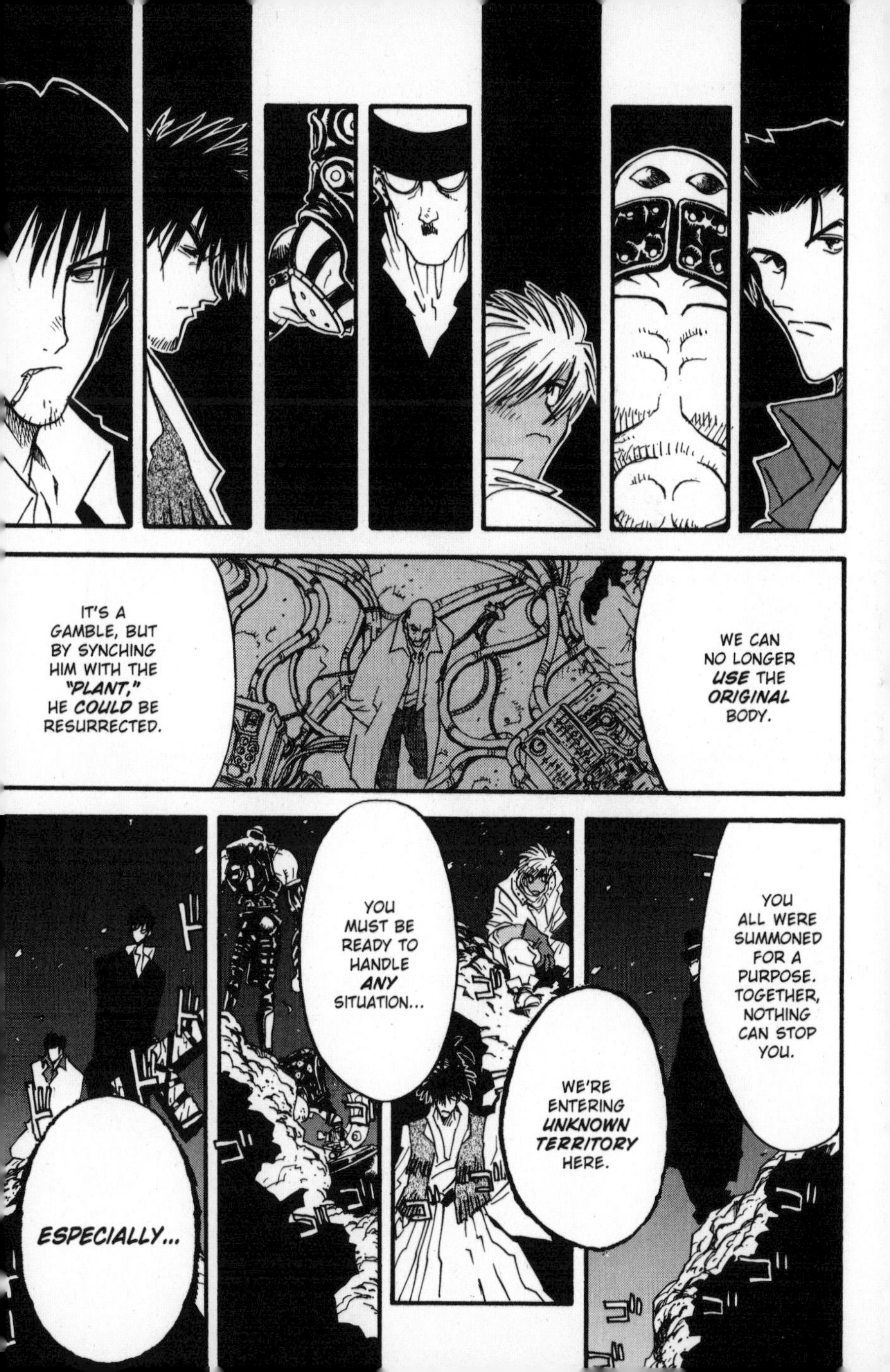
WE CAN NO LONGER USE THE ORIGINAL BODY.
IT'S A GAMBLE, BUT BY SYNCHING HIM WITH THE "PLANT," HE COULD BE RESURRECTED.
YOU ALL WERE SUMMONED FOR A PURPOSE. TOGETHER, NOTHING CAN STOP YOU.
WE'RE ENTERING UNKNOWN TERRITORY HERE.
YOU MUST BE READY TO HANDLE ANY SITUATION...
ESPECIALLY...

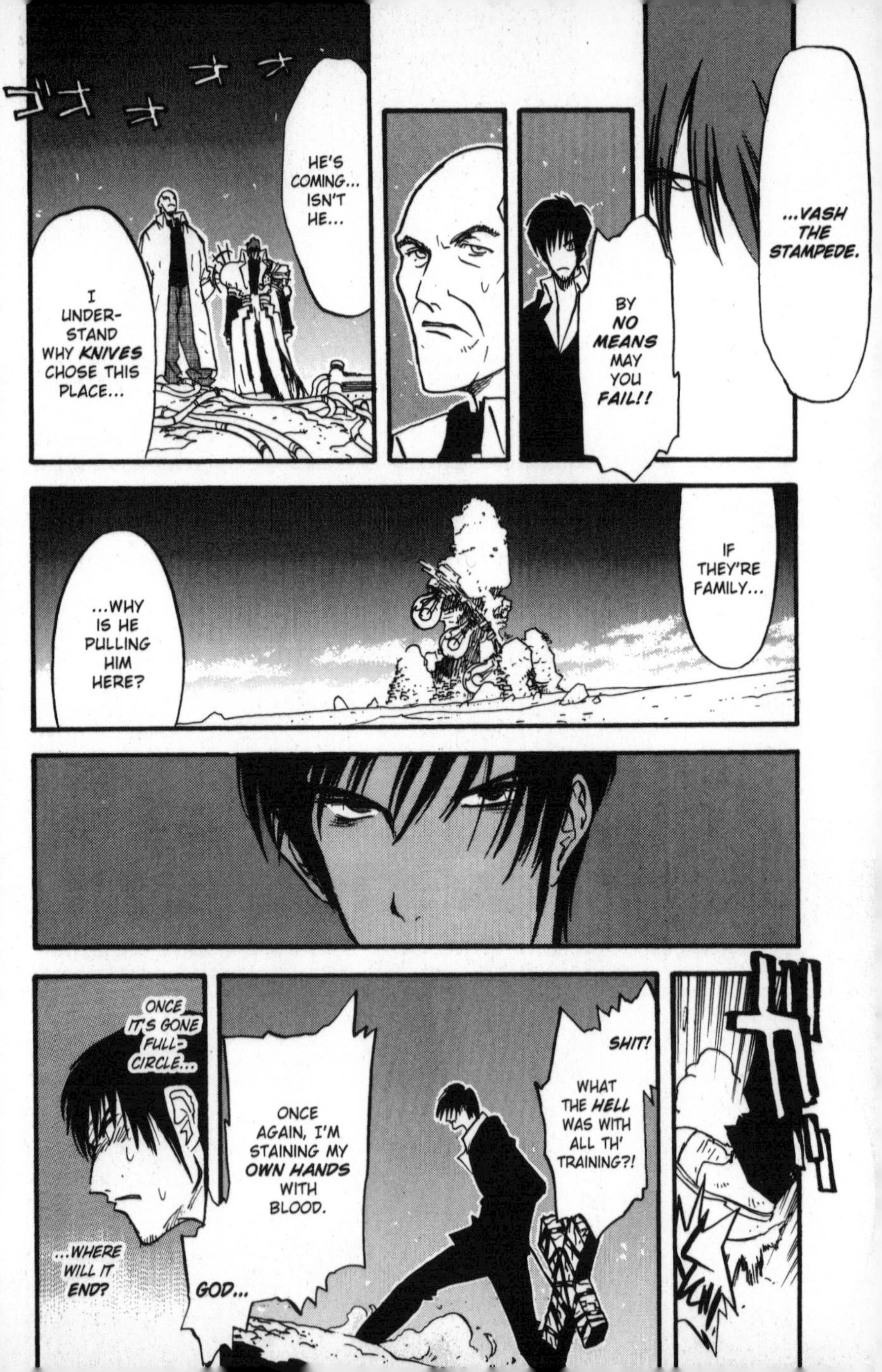

...VASH THE STAMPEDE.
BY NO MEANS MAY YOU FAIL!!
ゴオオオオ
HE'S COMING... ISN'T HE...
I UNDERSTAND WHY KNIVES CHOSE THIS PLACE...
IF THEY'RE FAMILY...
...WHY IS HE PULLING HIM HERE?
SHIT!
WHAT THE HELL WAS WITH ALL TH' TRAINING?!
ONCE AGAIN, I'M STAINING MY OWN HANDS WITH BLOOD.
GOD...
ONCE IT'S GONE FULL-CIRCLE...
...WHERE WILL IT END?

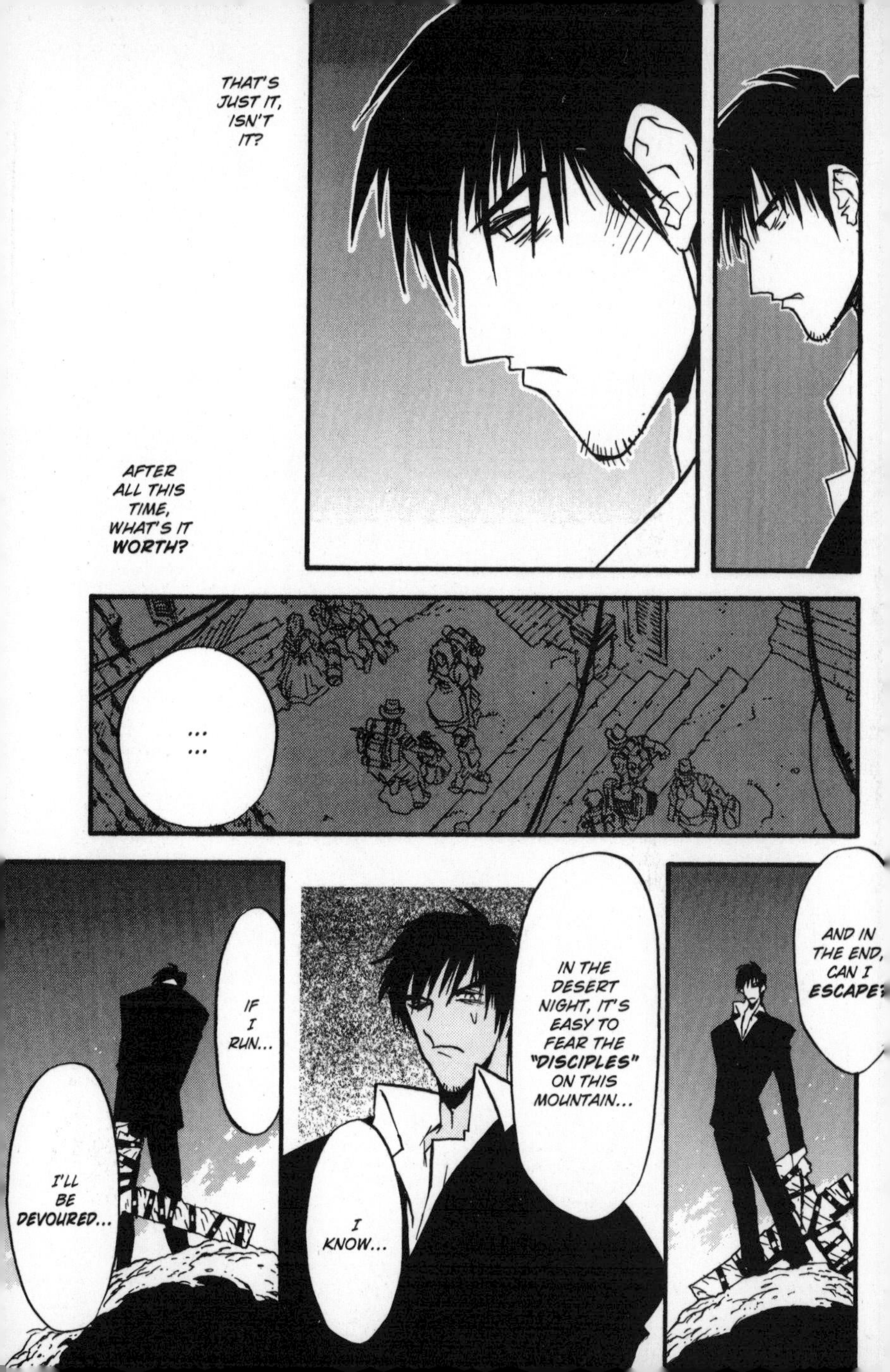
THAT'S JUST IT, ISN'T IT?
AFTER ALL THIS TIME, WHAT'S IT **WORTH?**
... ...
AND IN THE END, CAN I **ESCAPE?**
IN THE DESERT NIGHT, IT'S EASY TO FEAR THE **"DISCIPLES"** ON THIS MOUNTAIN...
I KNOW...
IF I RUN...
I'LL BE DEVOURED...

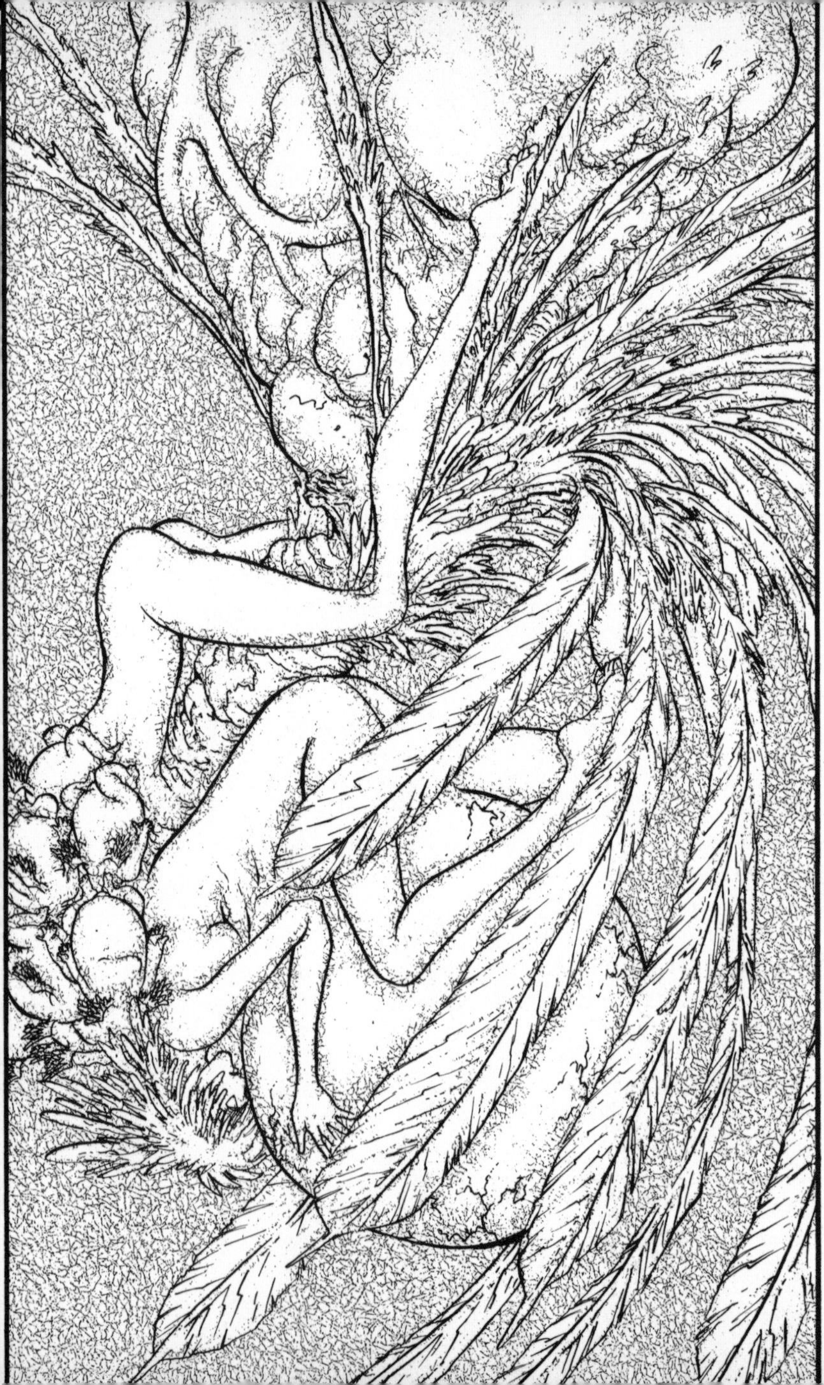

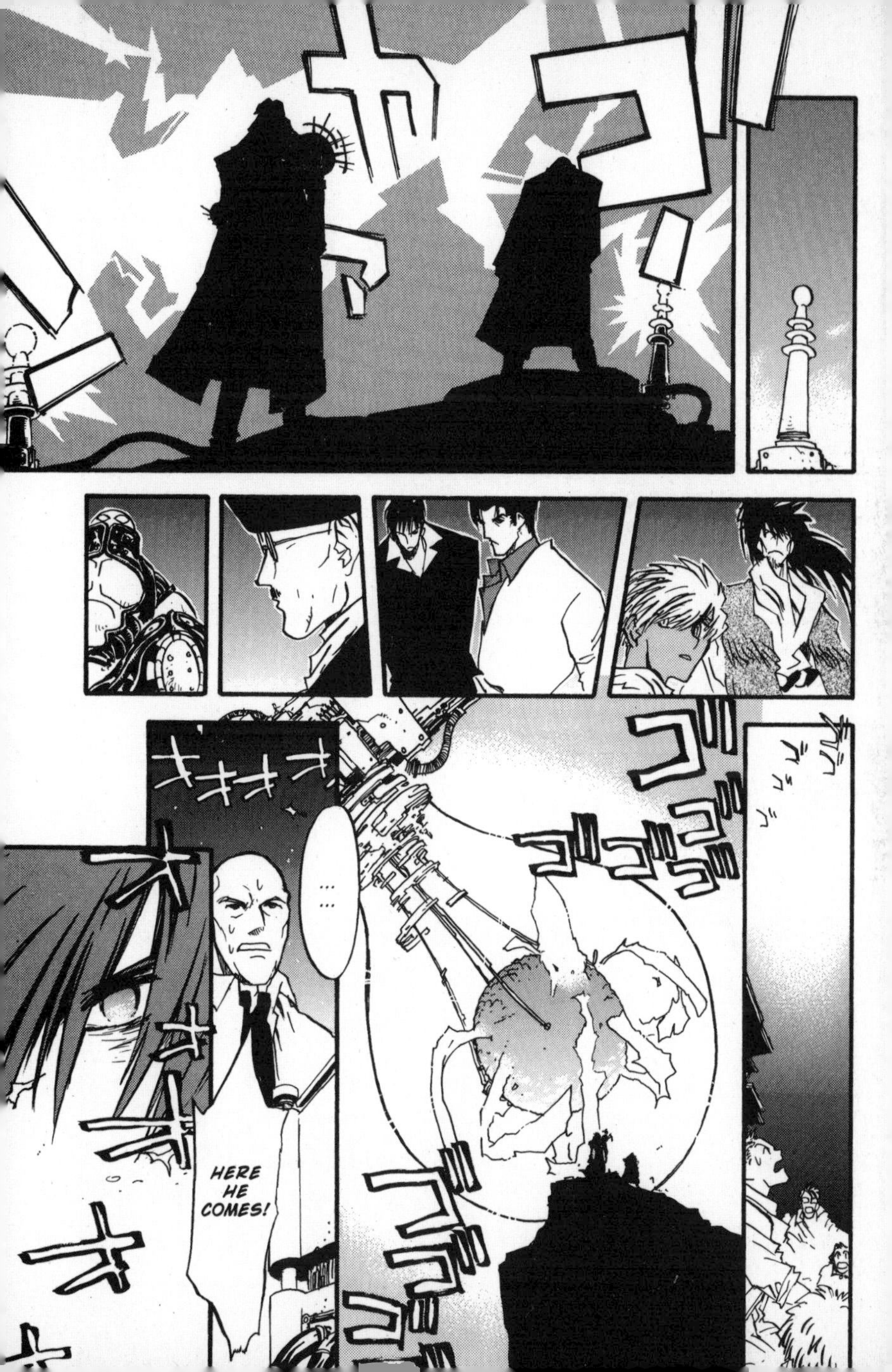

……
HERE HE COMES!

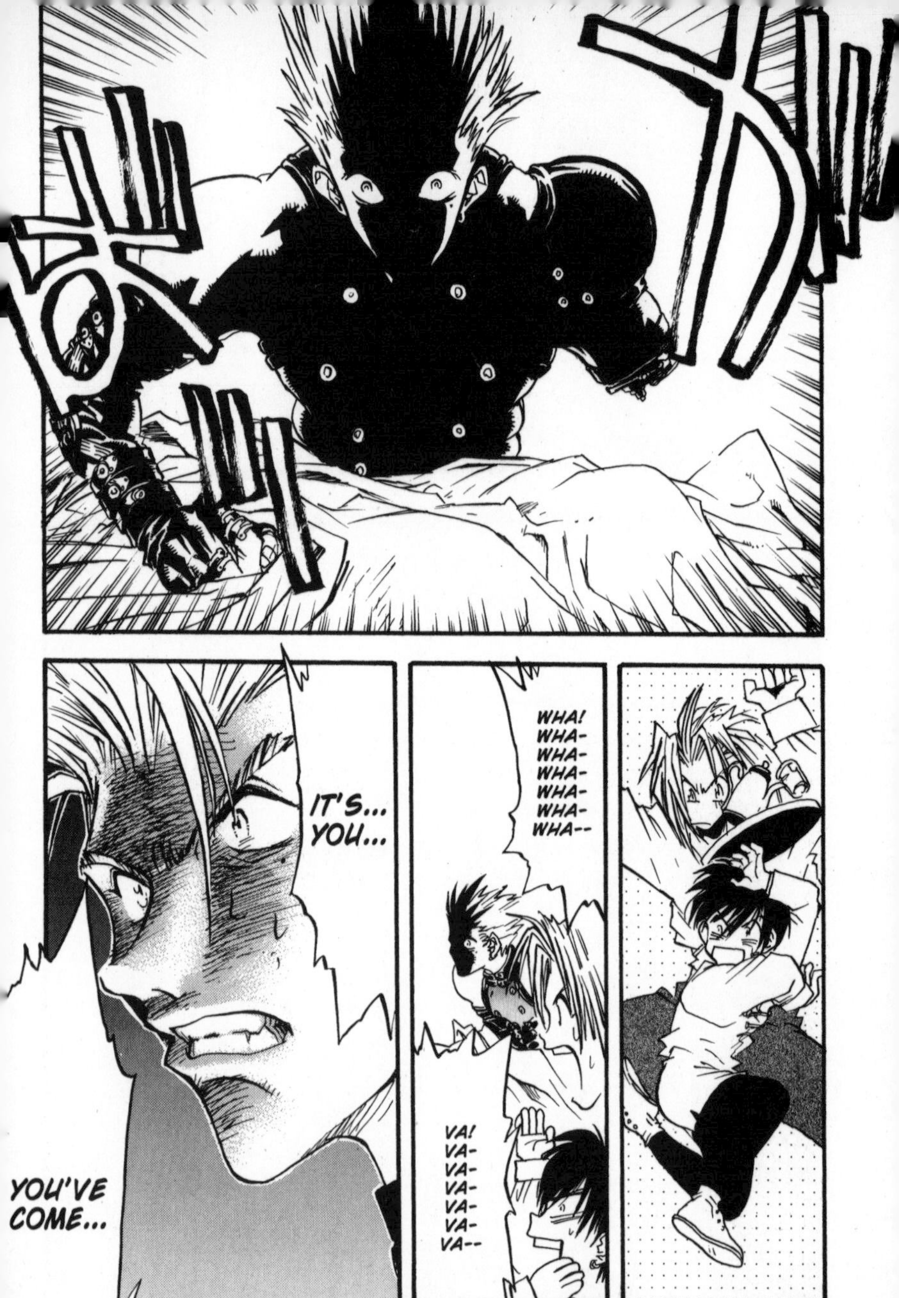
WHA! WHA- WHA- WHA- WHA- WHA- WHA--
VA! VA- VA- VA- VA- VA- VA- VA--
IT'S... YOU...
YOU'VE COME...

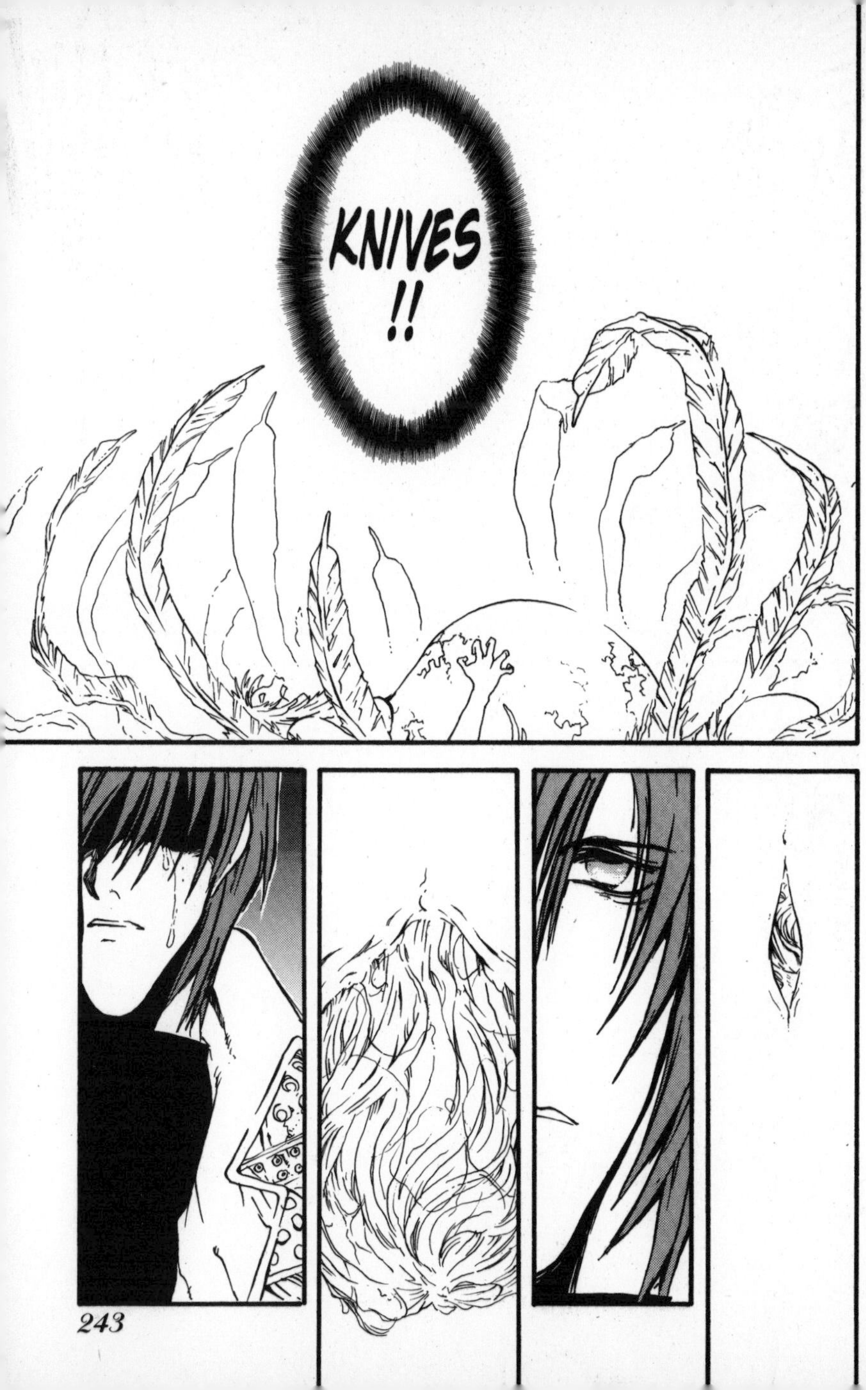
KNIVES !!

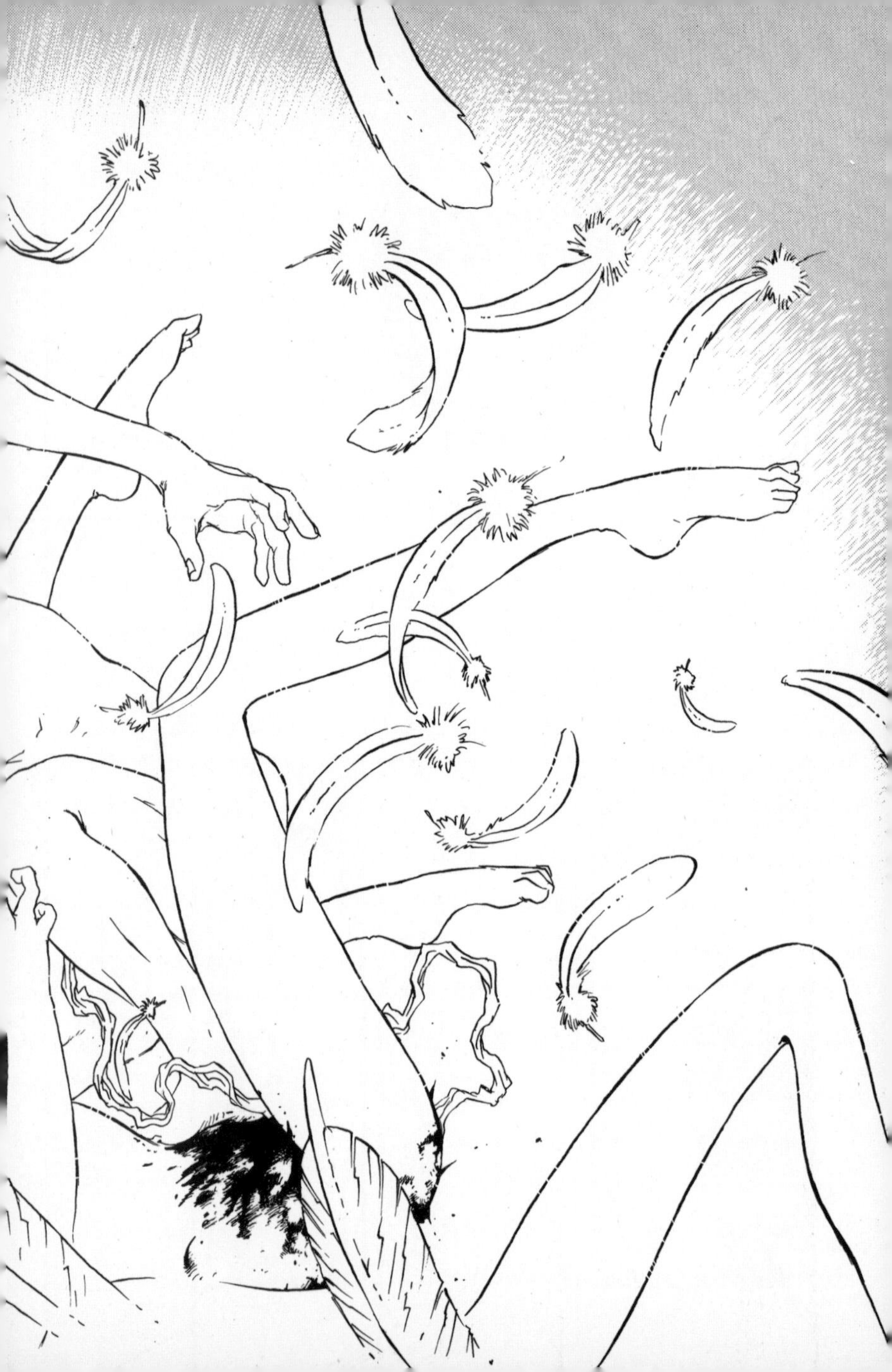

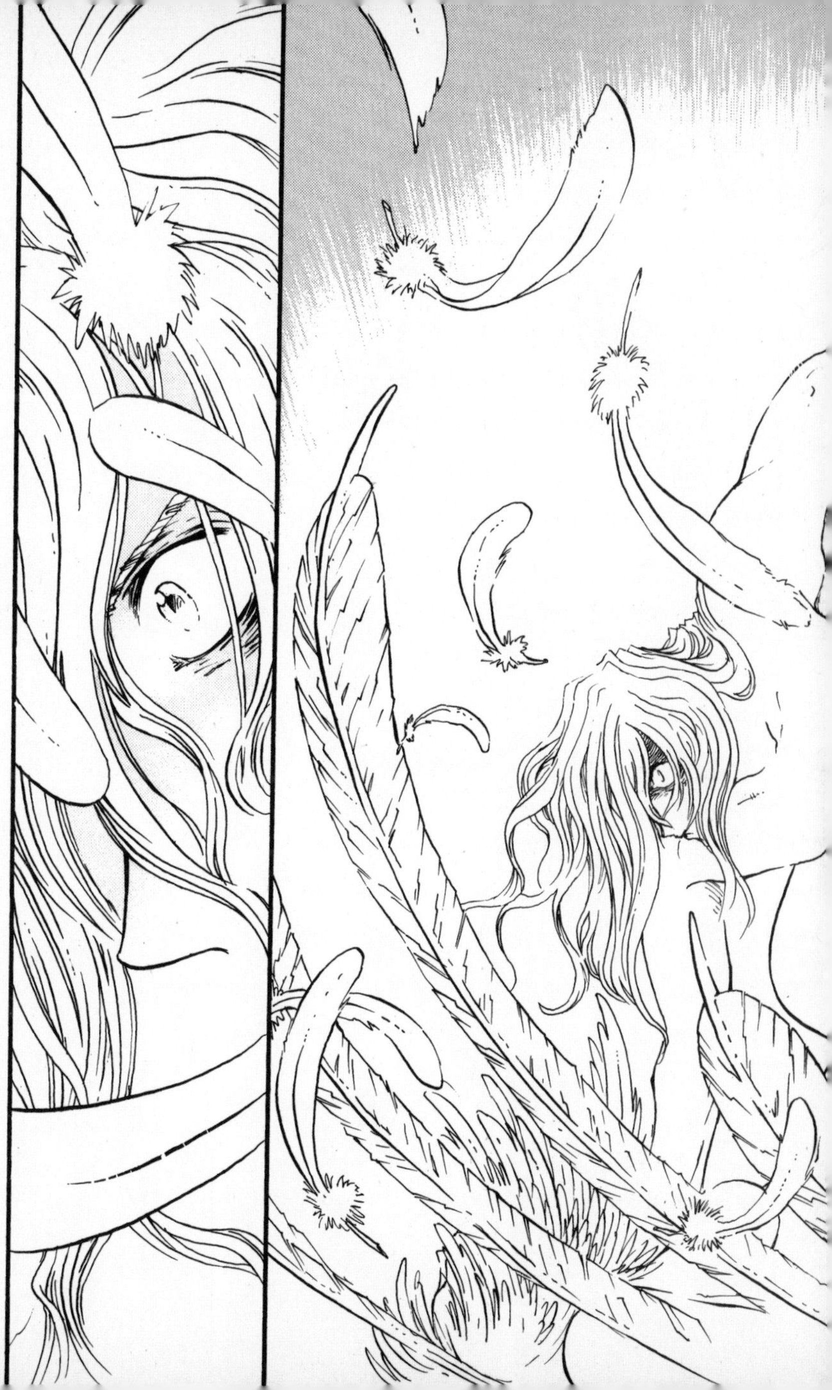

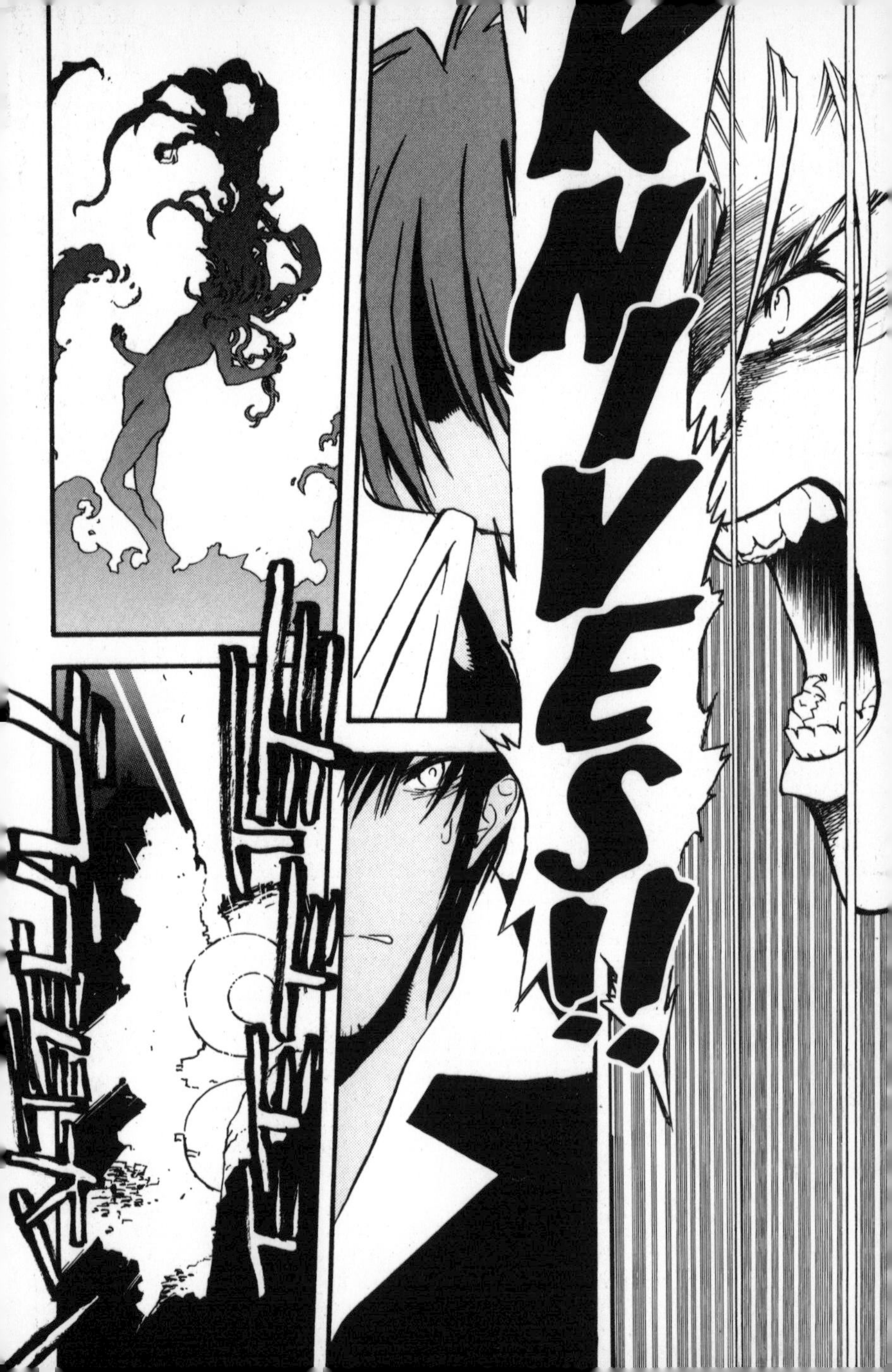
KNIVES!!

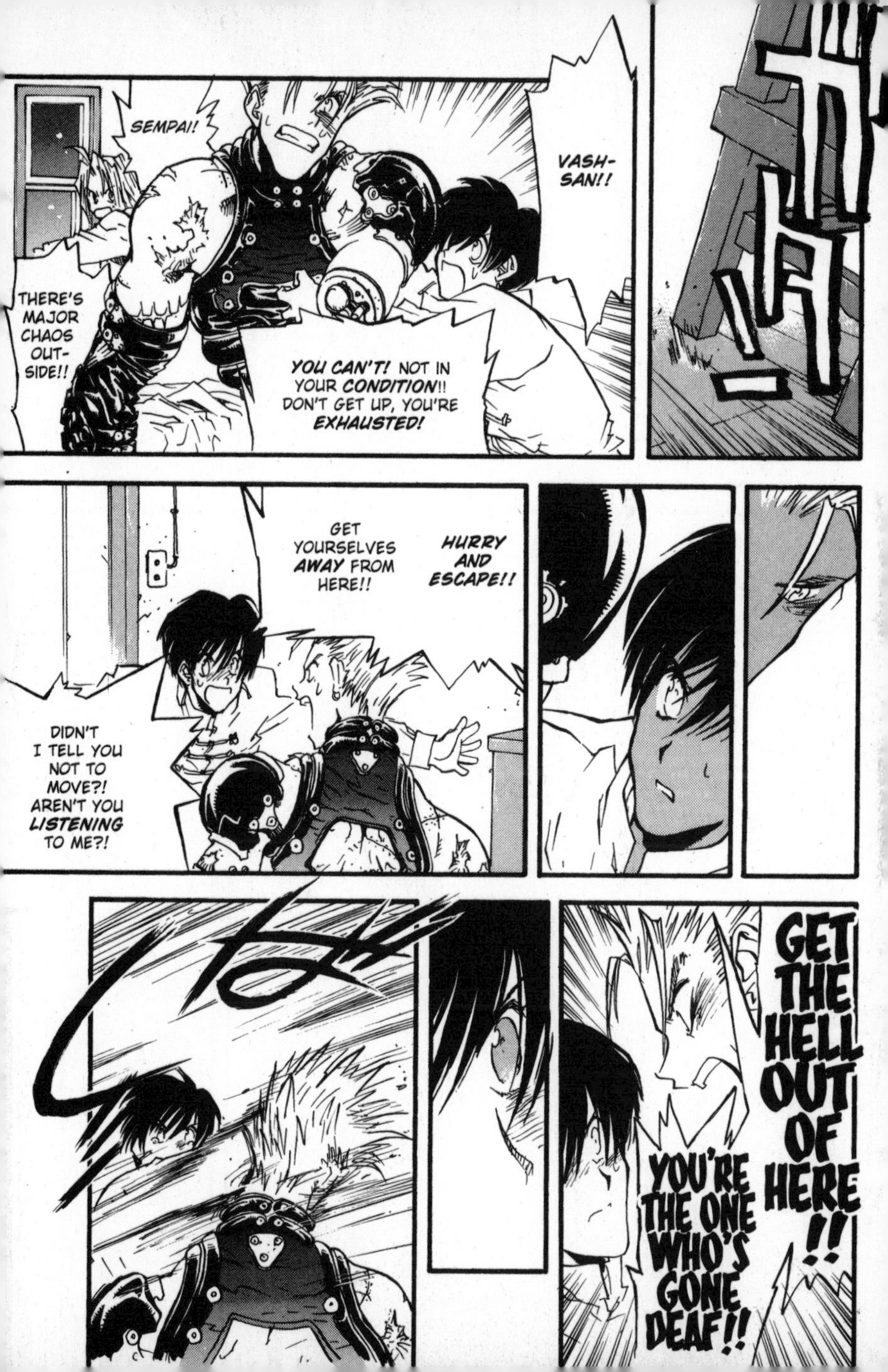
VASH-SAN!!
SEMPAI!
YOU CAN'T! NOT IN YOUR CONDITION!! DON'T GET UP, YOU'RE EXHAUSTED!
THERE'S MAJOR CHAOS OUTSIDE!!
HURRY AND ESCAPE!!
GET YOURSELVES AWAY FROM HERE!!
DIDN'T I TELL YOU NOT TO MOVE?! AREN'T YOU LISTENING TO ME?!
GET THE HELL OUT OF HERE!!
YOU'RE THE ONE WHO'S GONE DEAF!!

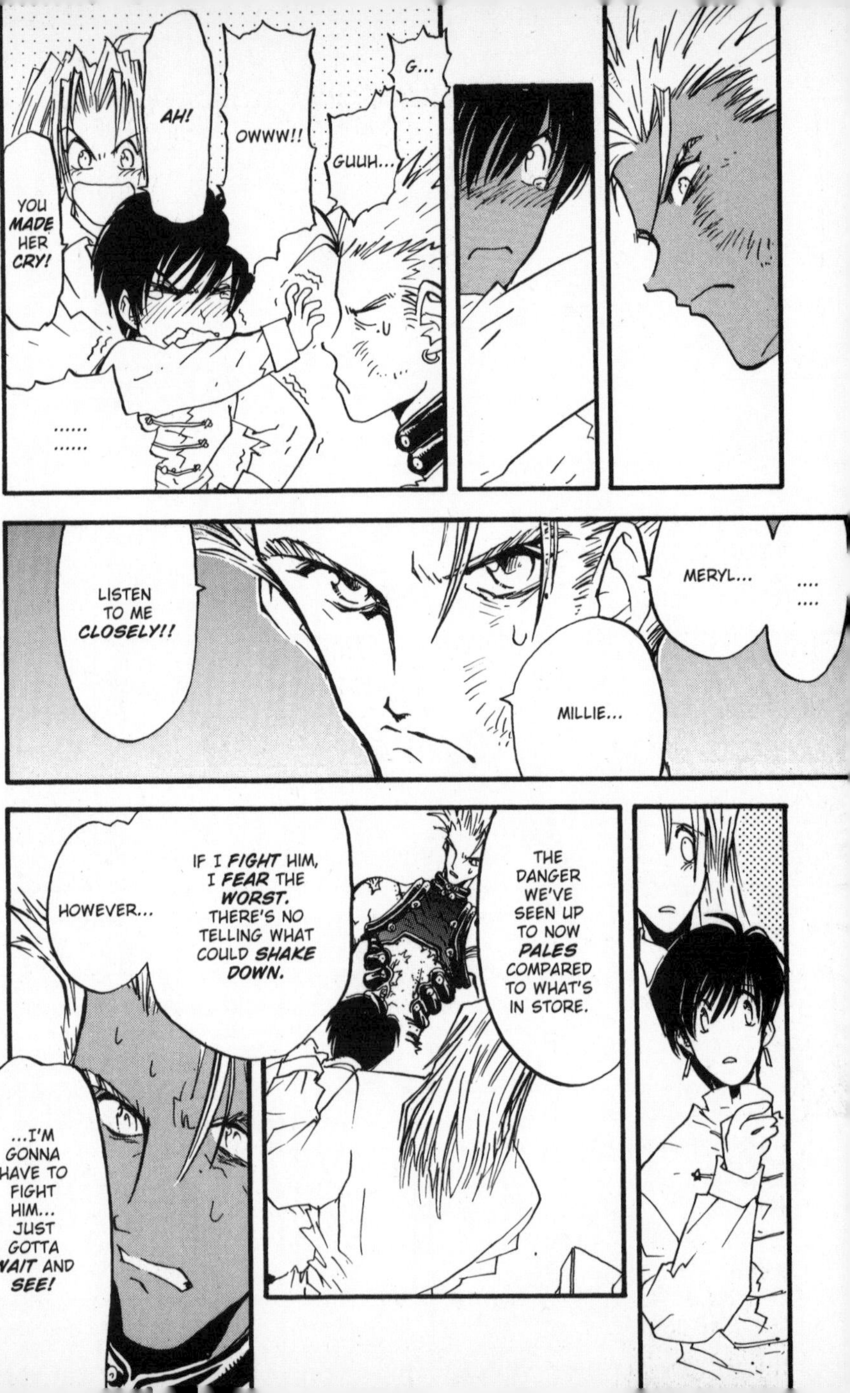
G...
GUUH...
OWWW!!
AH!
YOU MADE HER CRY!
....
MERYL...
....
MILLIE...
LISTEN TO ME CLOSELY!!
THE DANGER WE'VE SEEN UP TO NOW PALES COMPARED TO WHAT'S IN STORE.
IF I FIGHT HIM, I FEAR THE WORST. THERE'S NO TELLING WHAT COULD SHAKE DOWN.
HOWEVER...
...I'M GONNA HAVE TO FIGHT HIM... JUST GOTTA WAIT AND SEE!

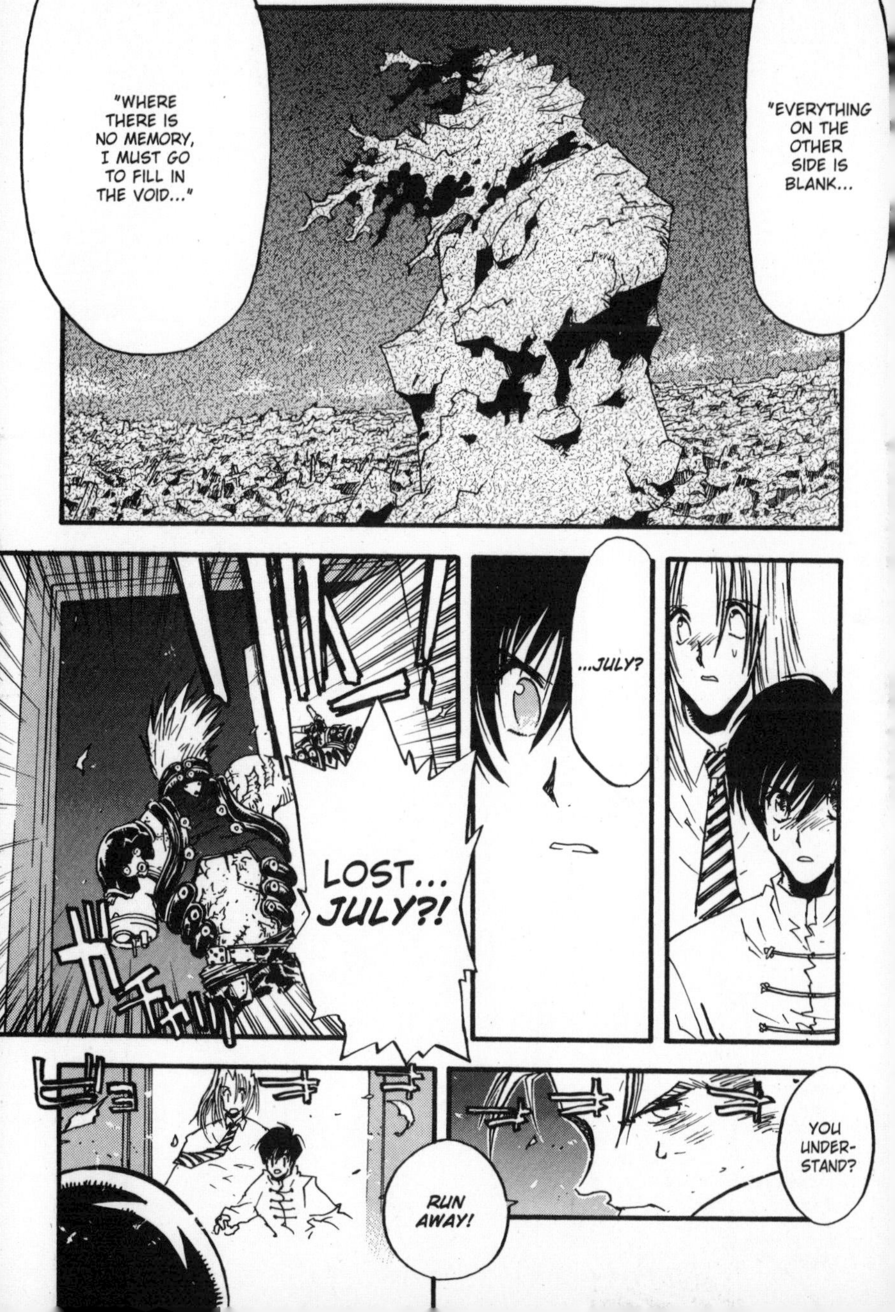
"EVERYTHING ON THE OTHER SIDE IS BLANK...
"WHERE THERE IS NO MEMORY, I MUST GO TO FILL IN THE VOID..."
...JULY?
LOST... JULY?!
YOU UNDER-STAND?
RUN AWAY!

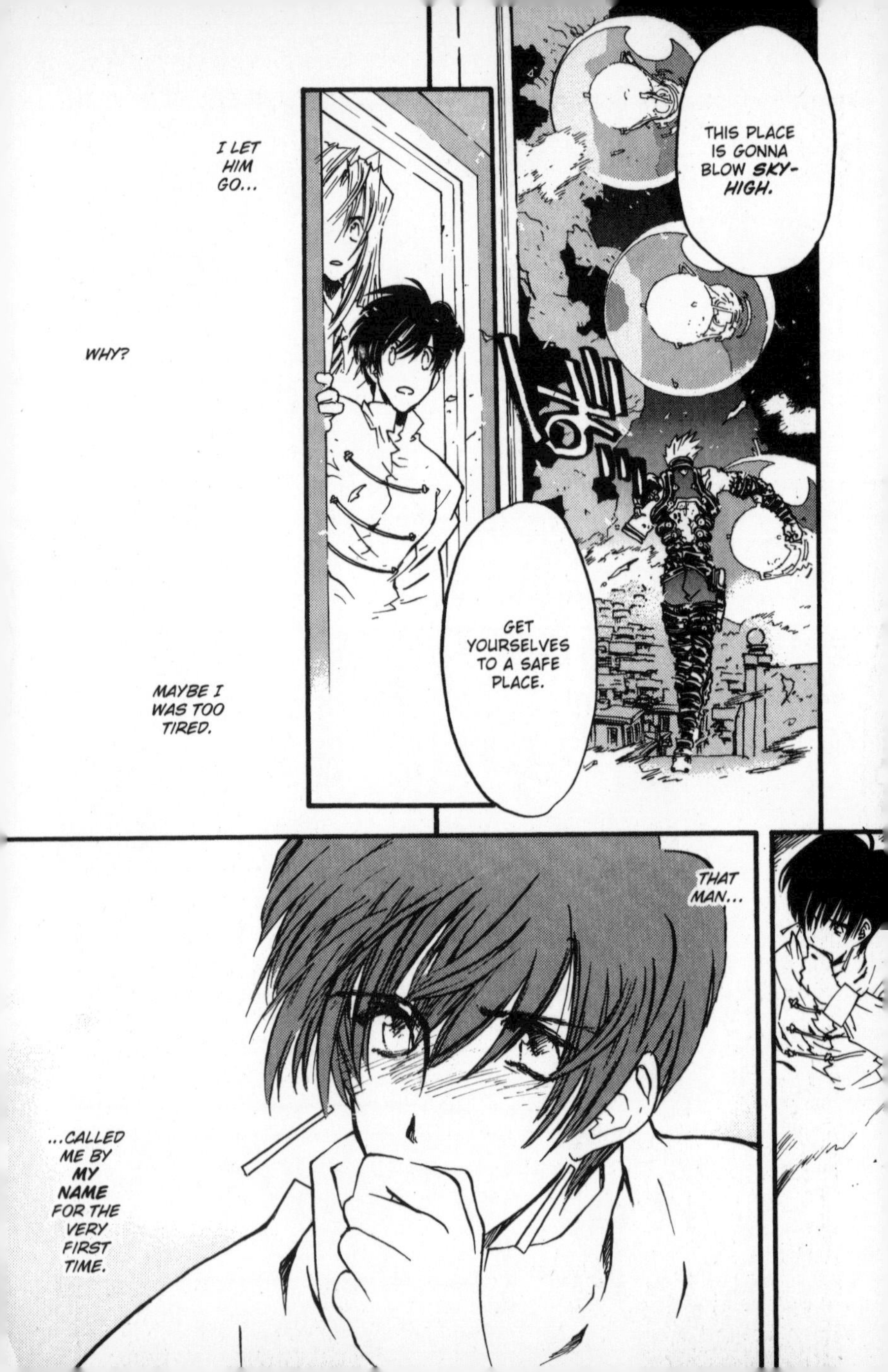
THIS PLACE IS GONNA BLOW SKY-HIGH.
GET YOURSELVES TO A SAFE PLACE.
I LET HIM GO...
WHY?
MAYBE I WAS TOO TIRED.
THAT MAN...
...CALLED ME BY MY NAME FOR THE VERY FIRST TIME.

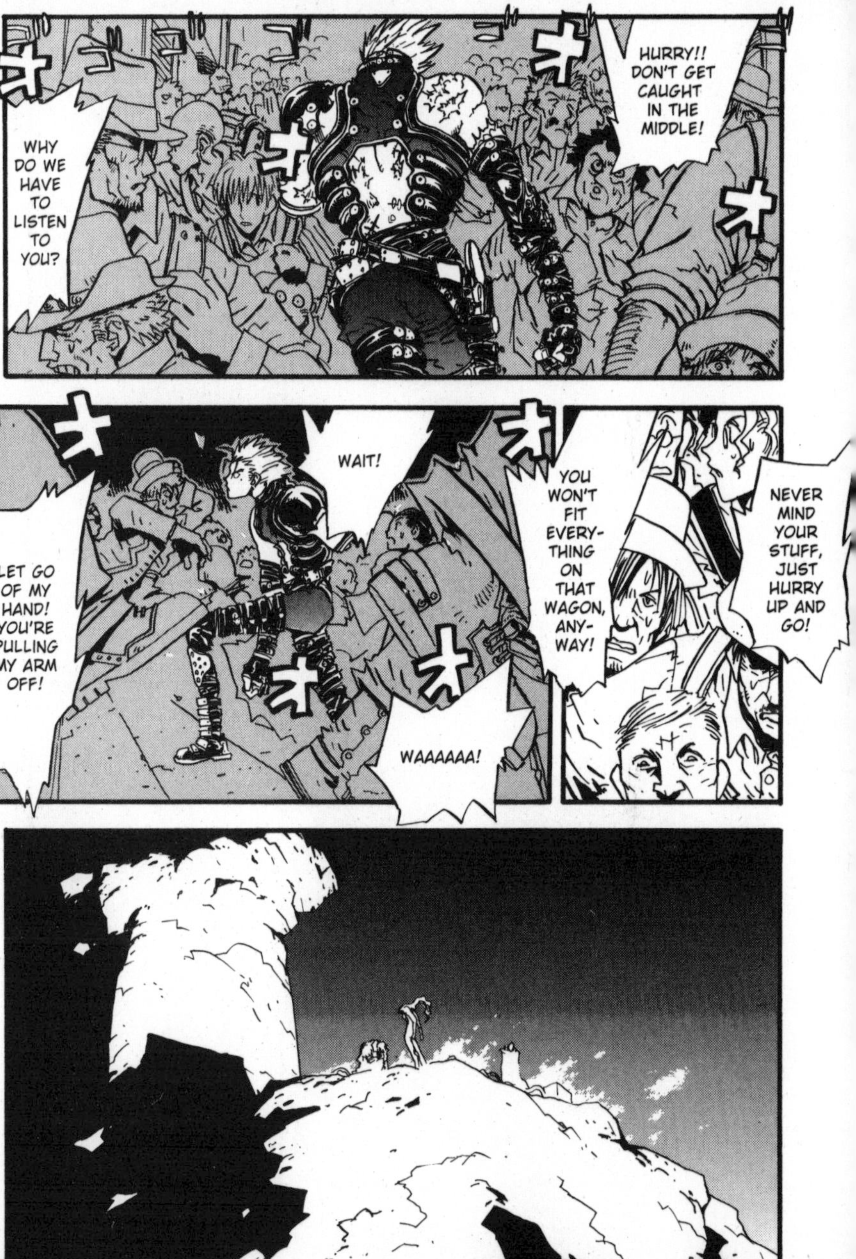
HURRY!! DON'T GET CAUGHT IN THE MIDDLE!
WHY DO WE HAVE TO LISTEN TO YOU?
NEVER MIND YOUR STUFF, JUST HURRY UP AND GO!
YOU WON'T FIT EVERYTHING ON THAT WAGON, ANYWAY!
WAIT!
LET GO OF MY HAND! YOU'RE PULLING MY ARM OFF!
WAAAAAA!

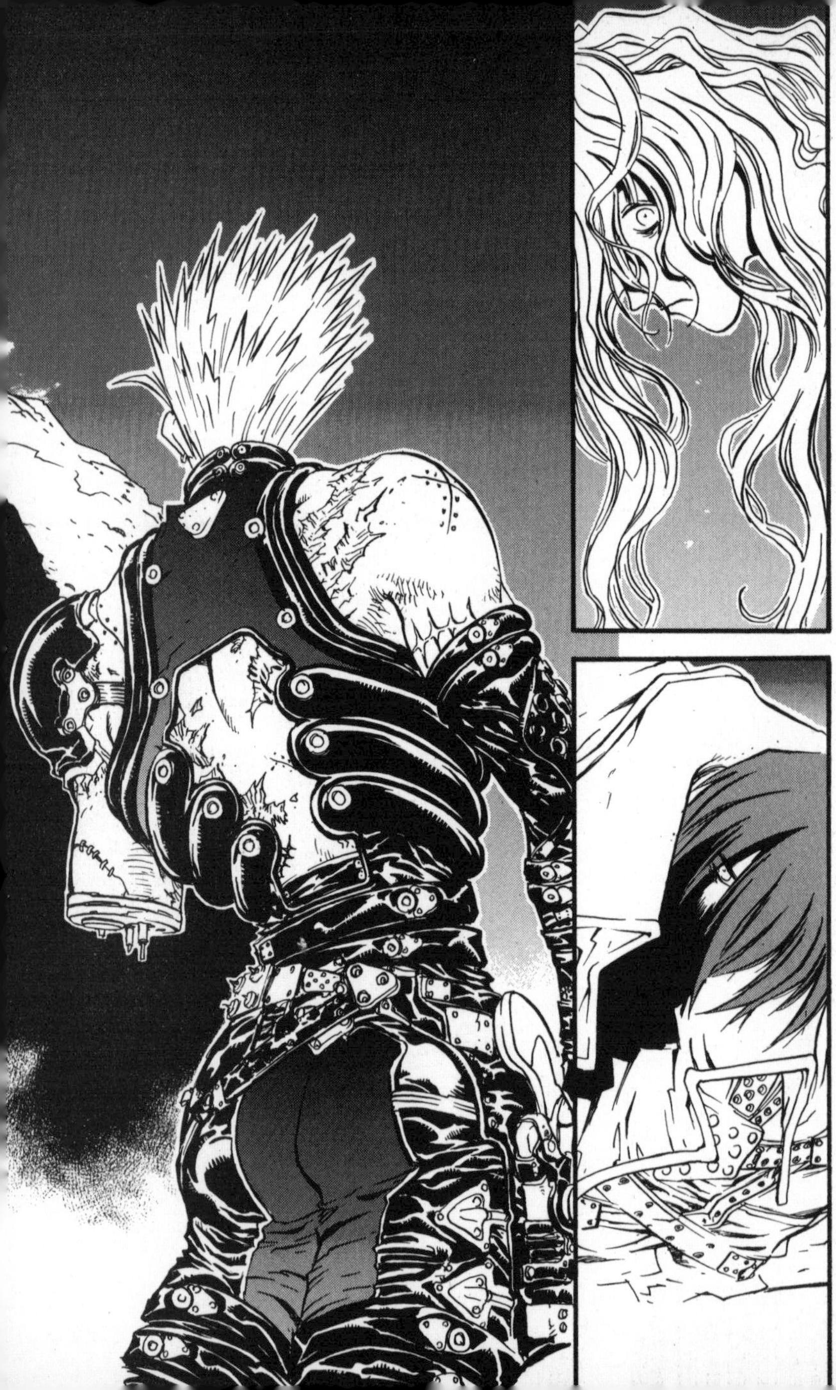

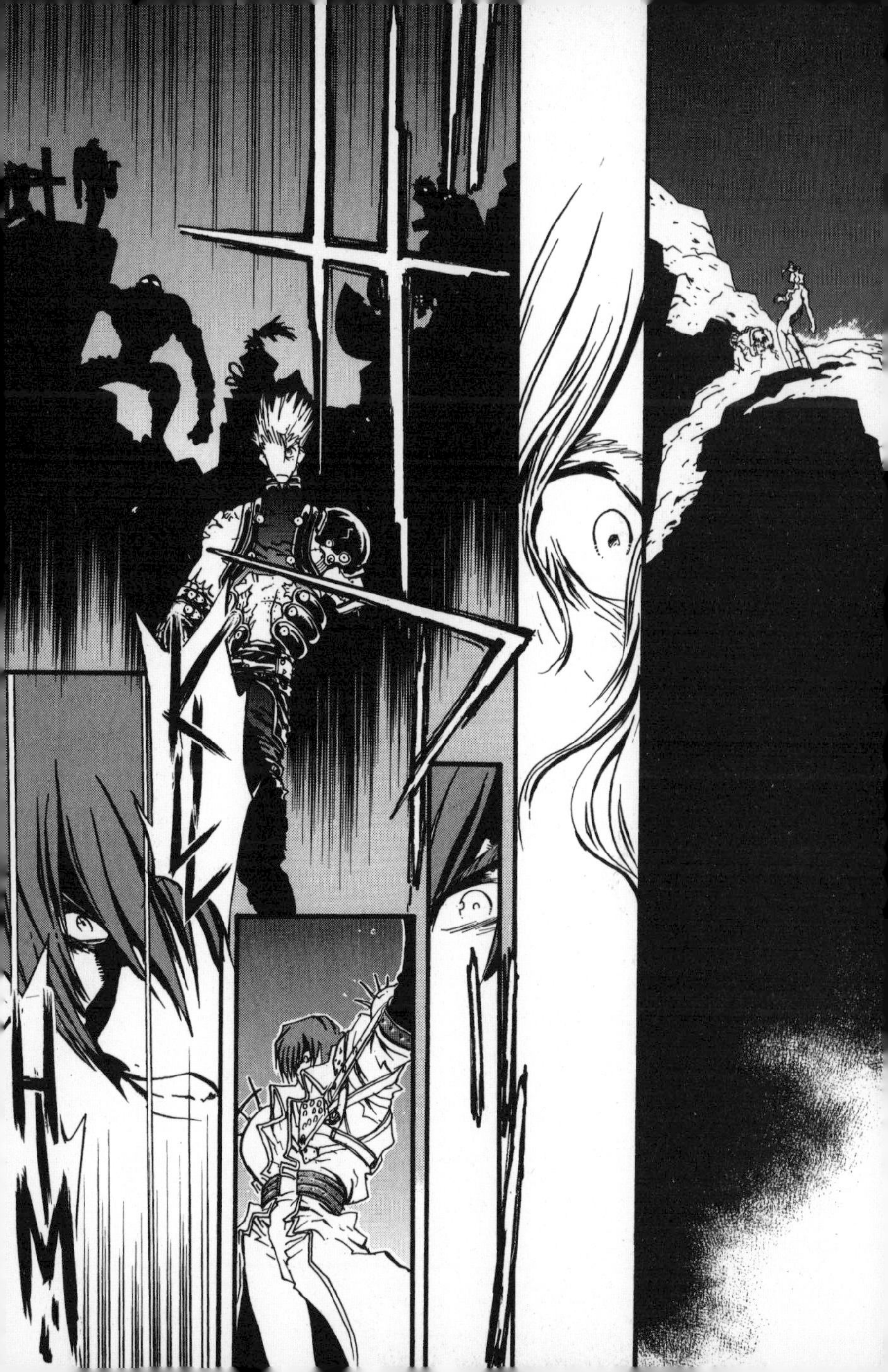
HMM

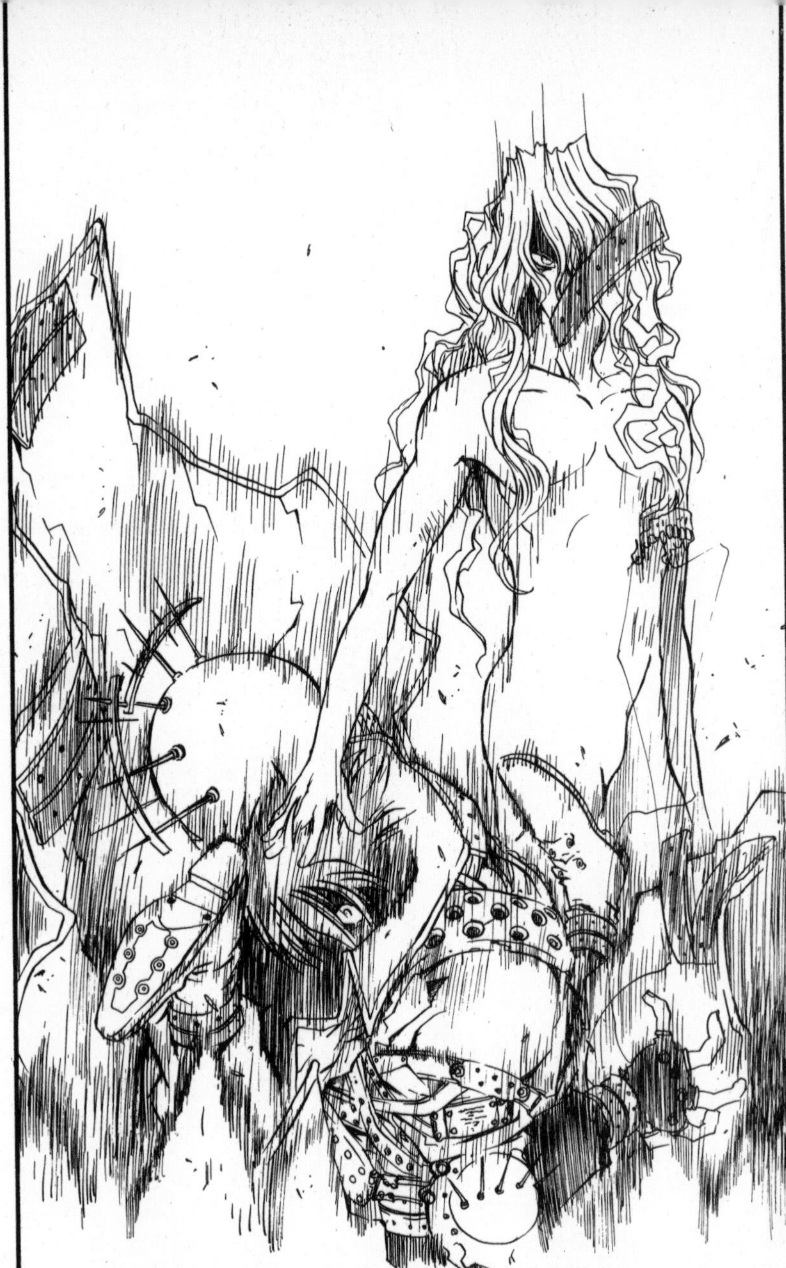

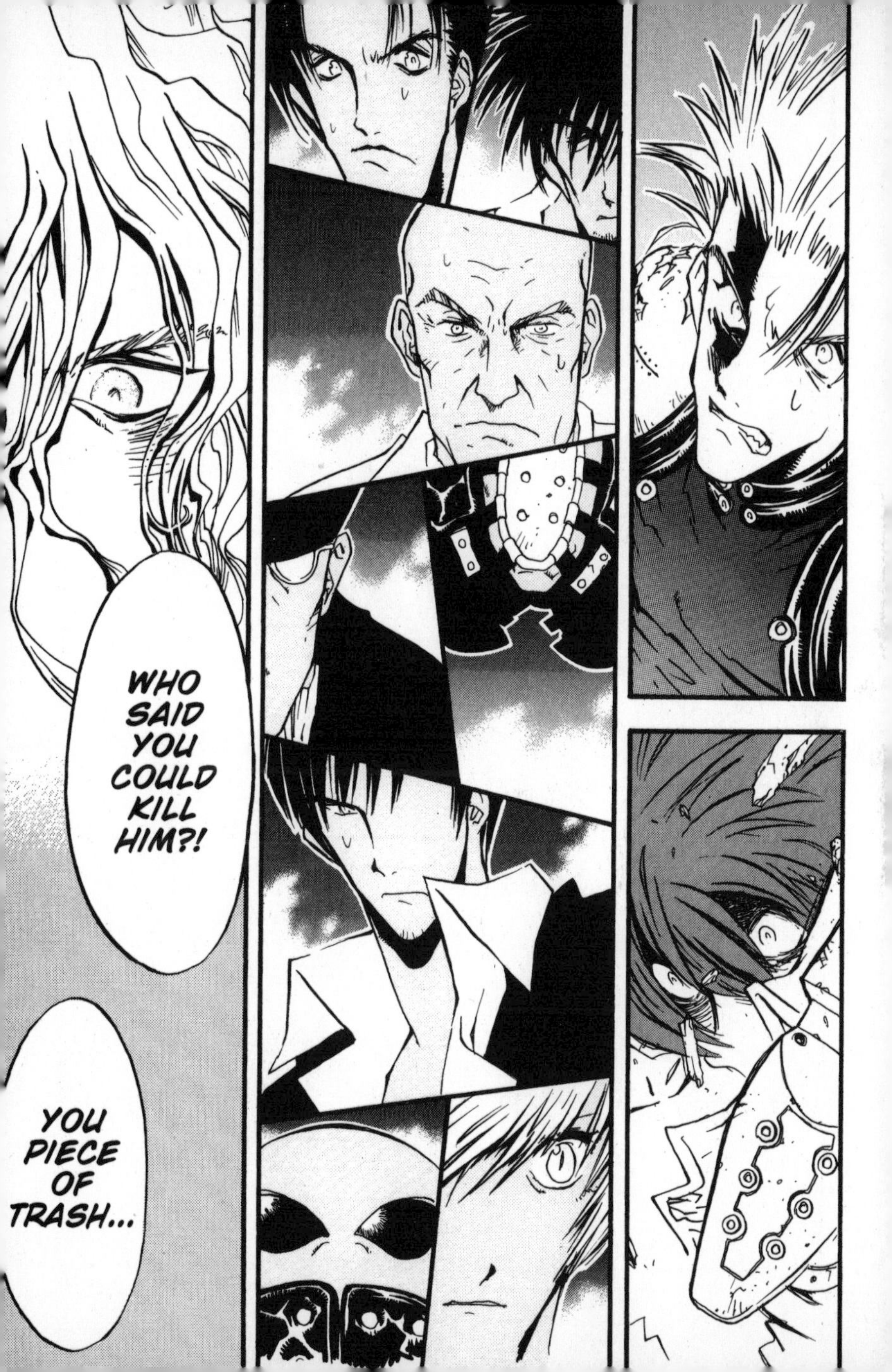
WHO SAID YOU COULD KILL HIM?!
YOU PIECE OF TRASH...

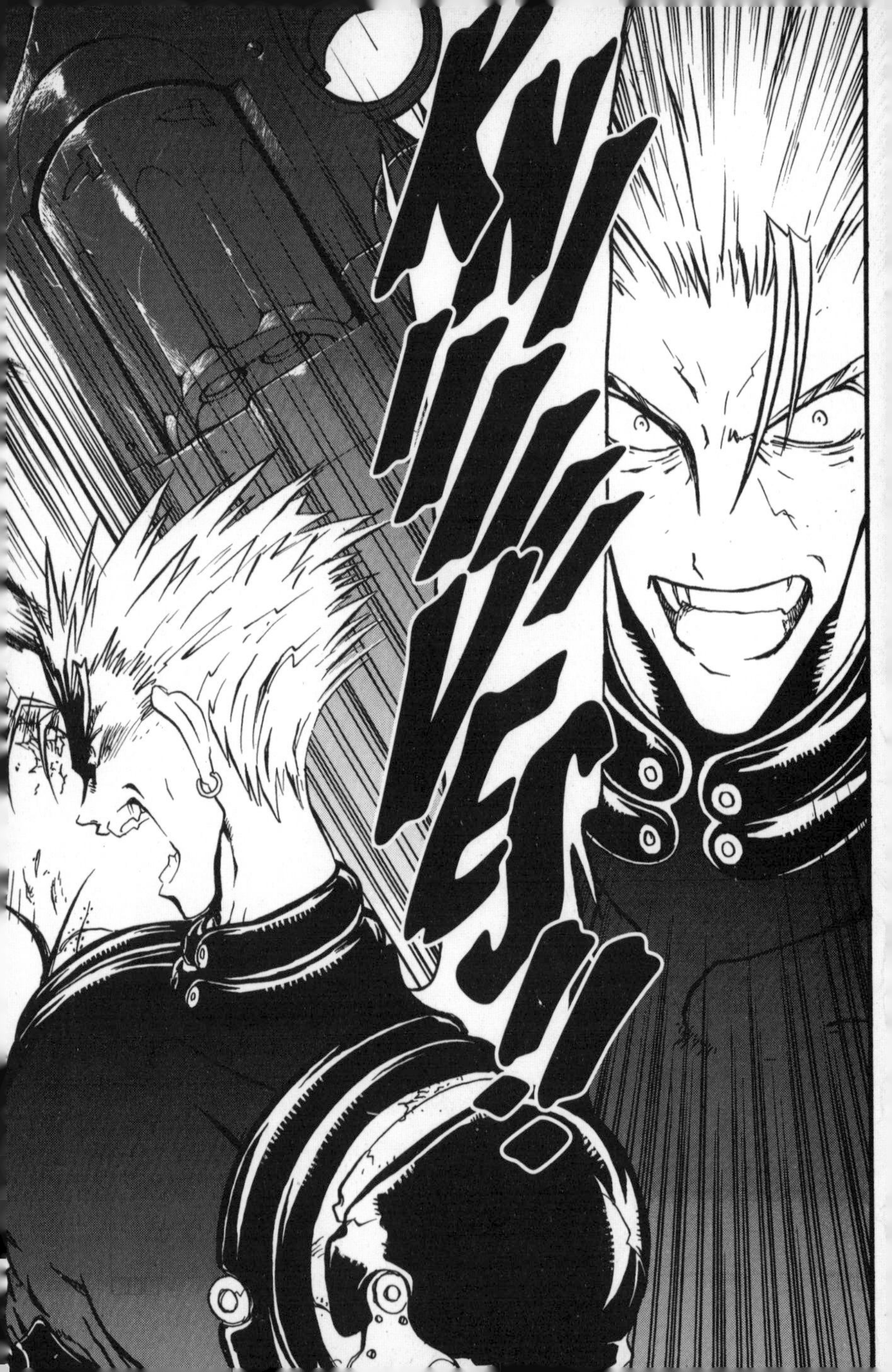

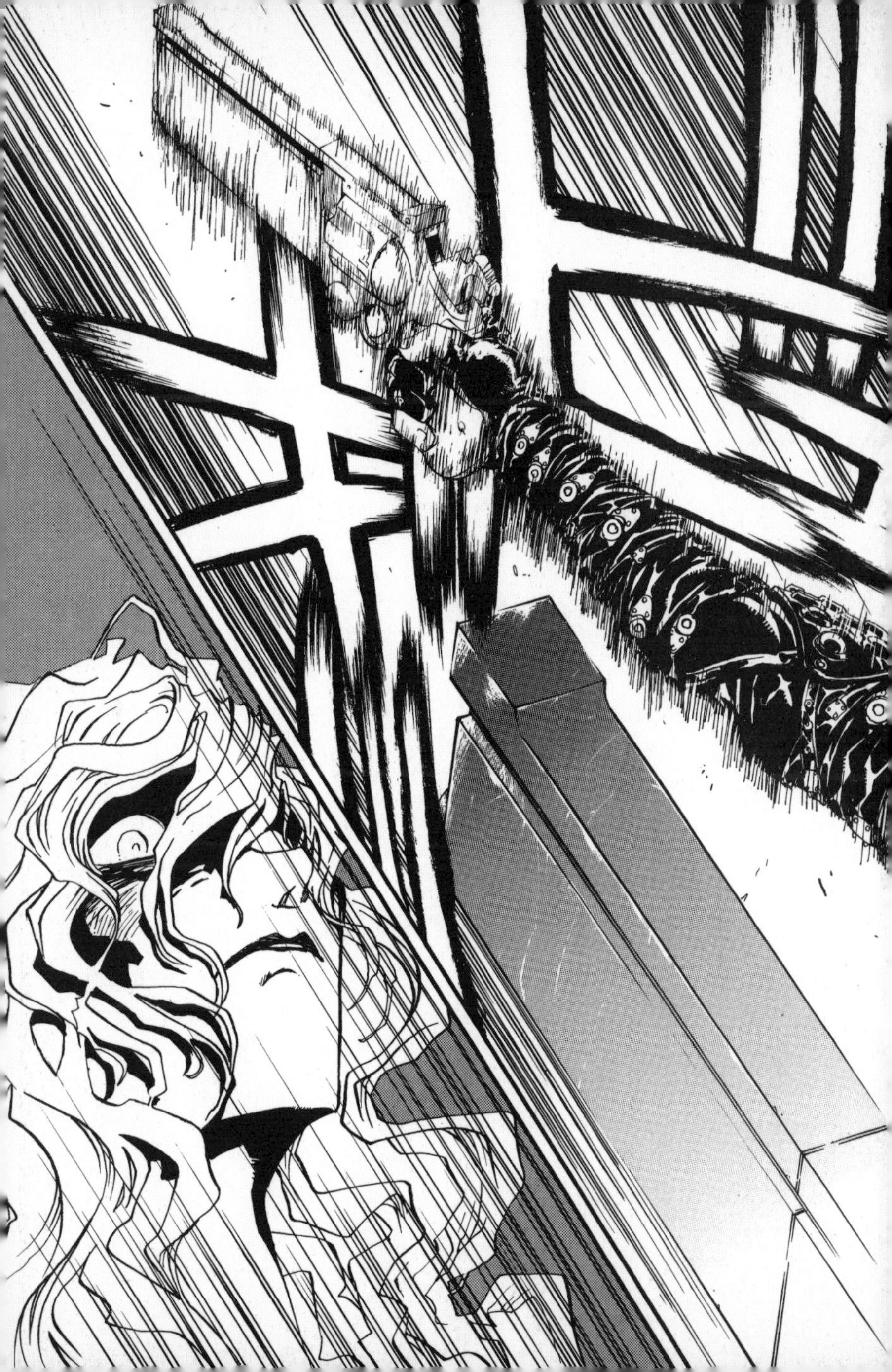

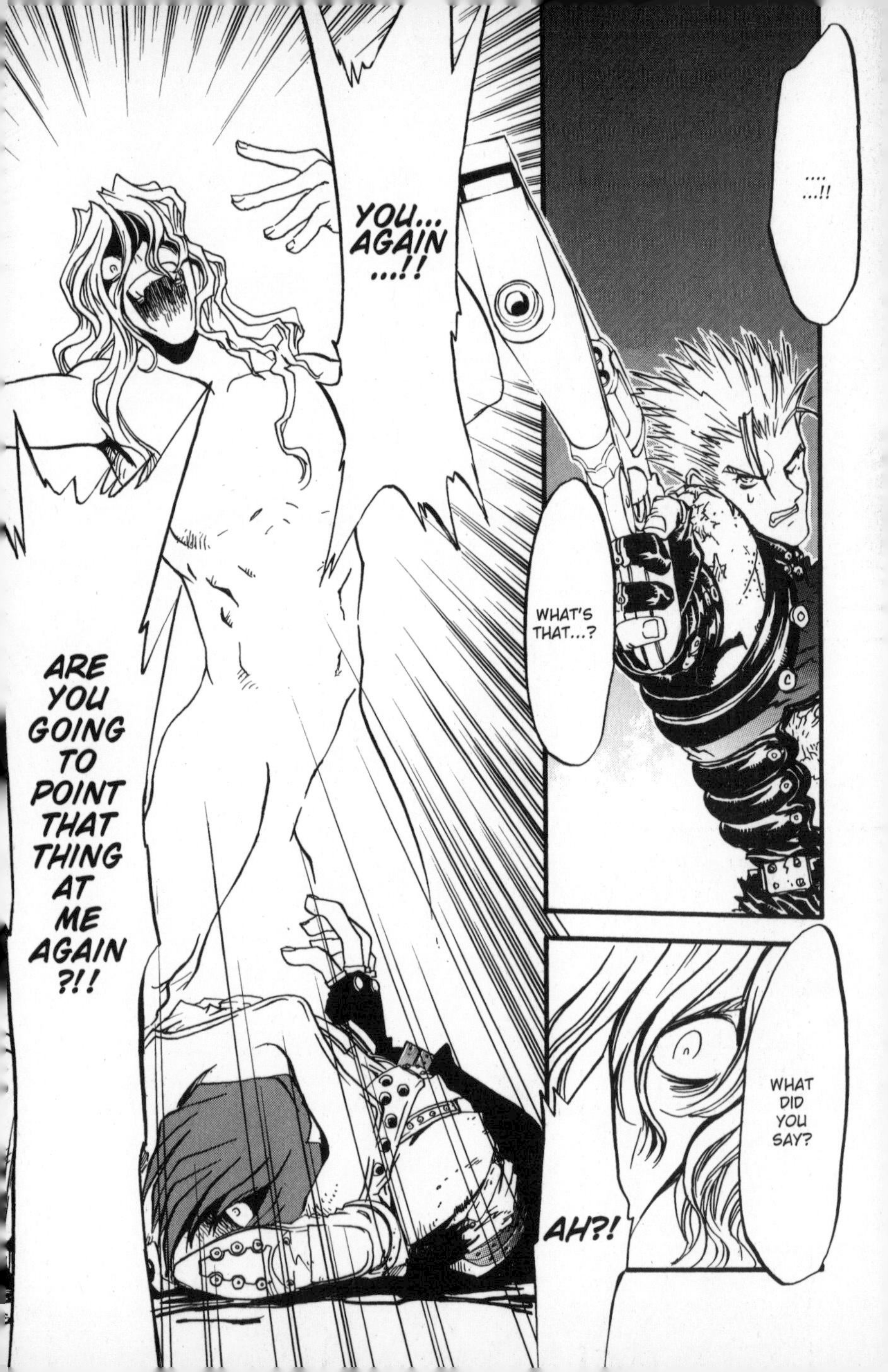
....
...!!
WHAT'S THAT...?
WHAT DID YOU SAY?
AH?!
YOU... AGAIN ...!!
ARE YOU GOING TO POINT THAT THING AT ME AGAIN ?!!

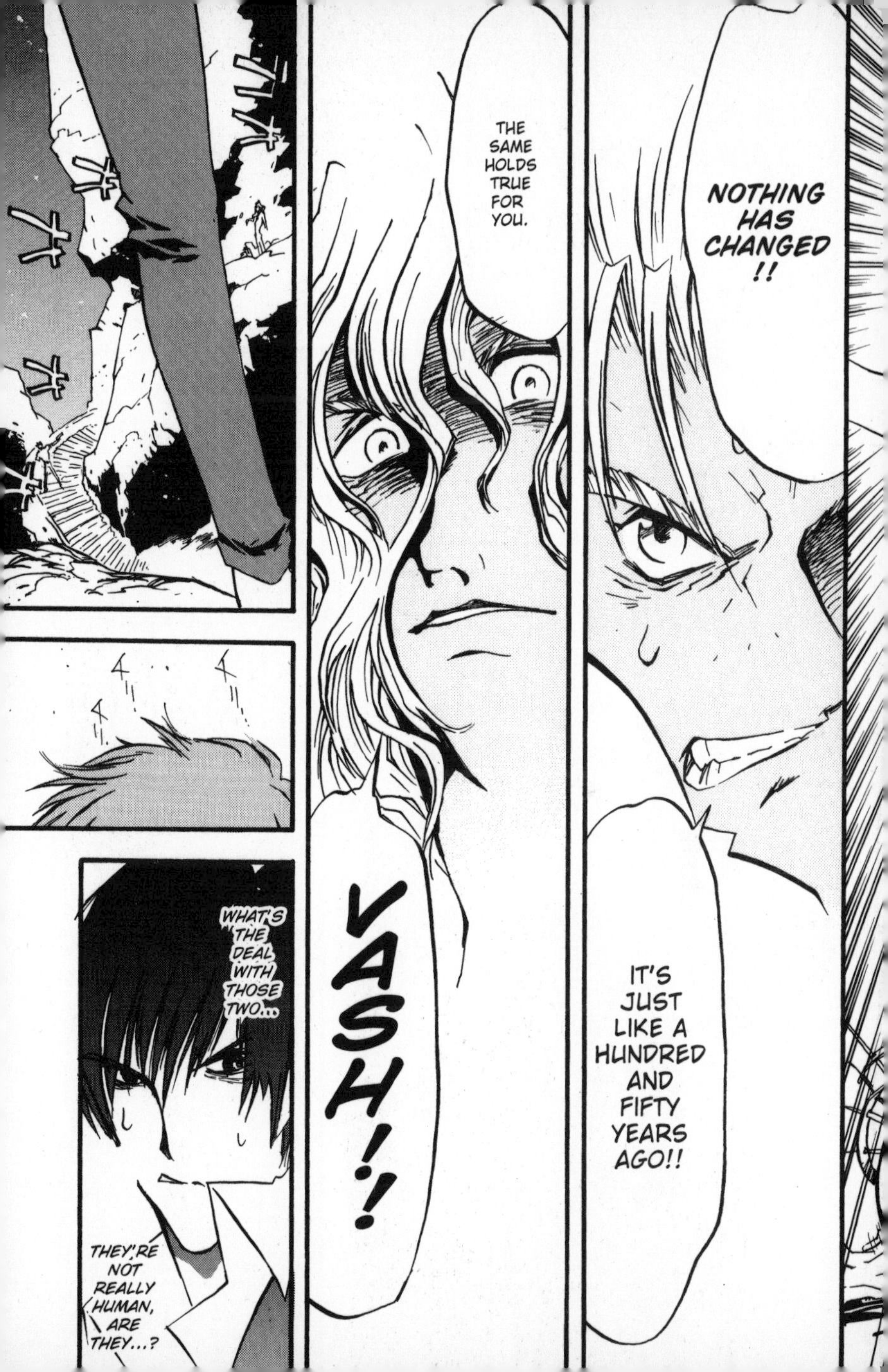
NOTHING HAS CHANGED!!
IT'S JUST LIKE A HUNDRED AND FIFTY YEARS AGO!!
THE SAME HOLDS TRUE FOR YOU.
VASH!!
WHAT'S THE DEAL WITH THOSE TWO...
THEY'RE NOT REALLY HUMAN, ARE THEY...?

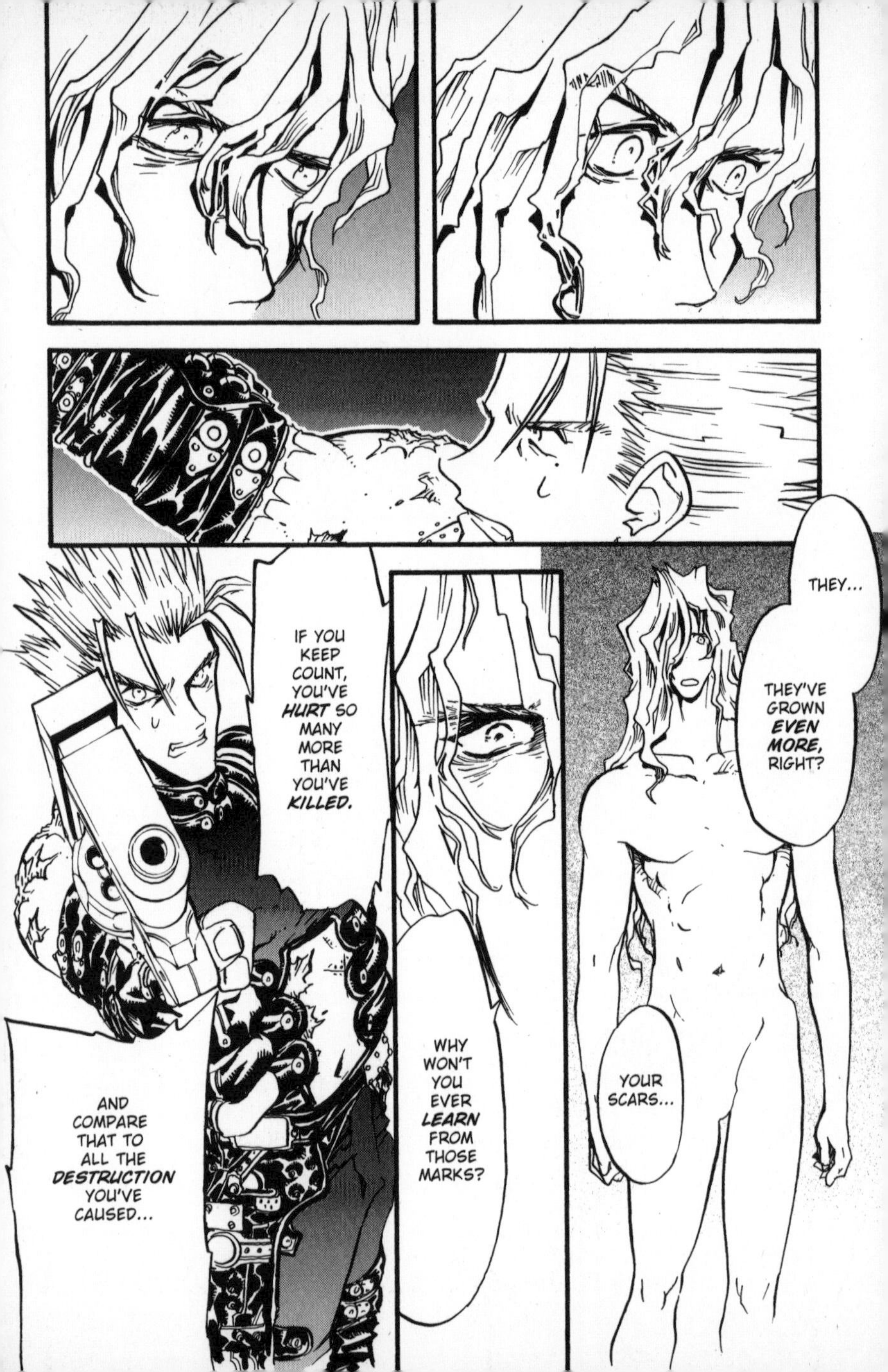
THEY...
THEY'VE GROWN EVEN MORE, RIGHT?
YOUR SCARS...
WHY WON'T YOU EVER LEARN FROM THOSE MARKS?
IF YOU KEEP COUNT, YOU'VE HURT SO MANY MORE THAN YOU'VE KILLED.
AND COMPARE THAT TO ALL THE DESTRUCTION YOU'VE CAUSED...

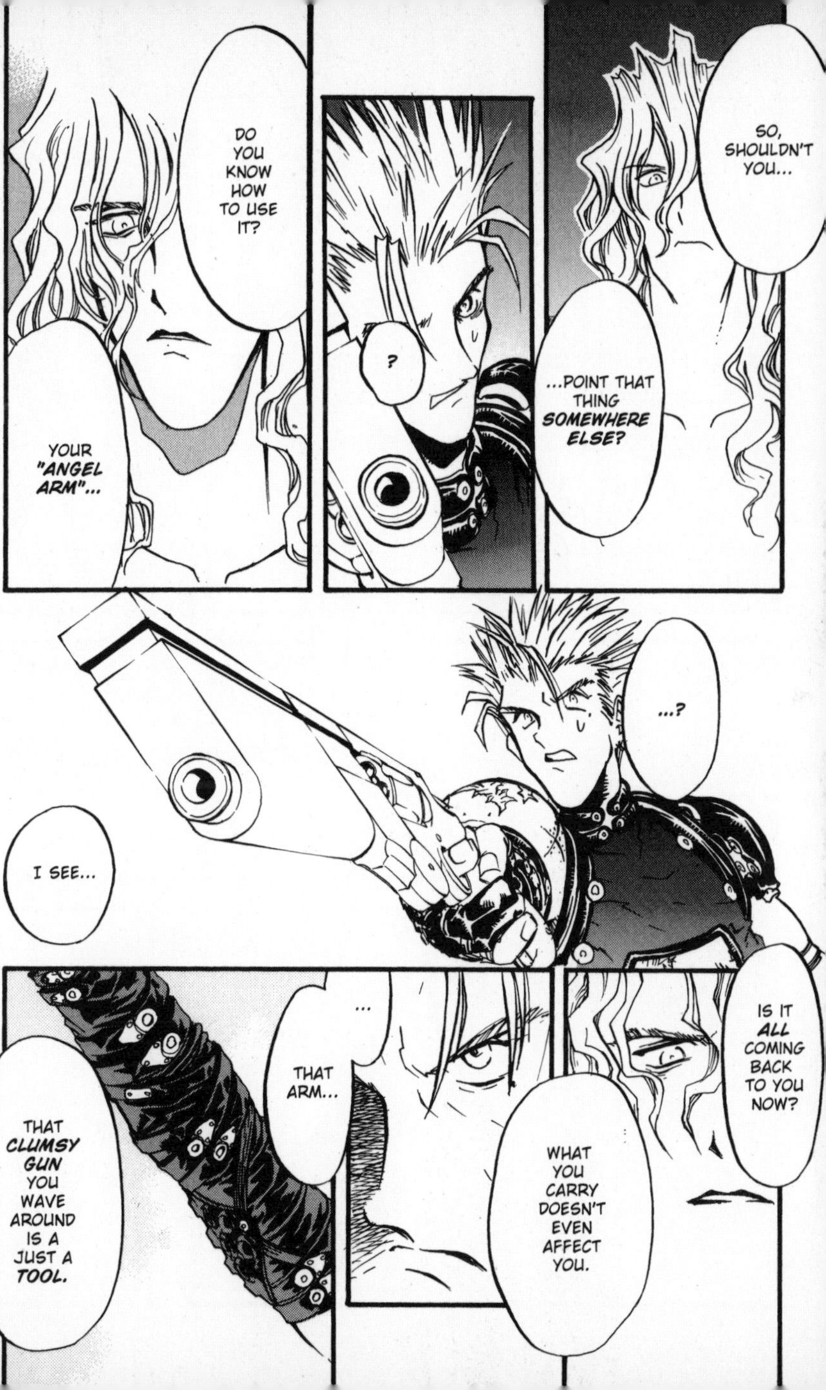
SO, SHOULDN'T YOU...
...POINT THAT THING *SOMEWHERE ELSE?*
?
DO YOU KNOW HOW TO USE IT?
YOUR *"ANGEL ARM"*...
...?
I SEE...
IS IT *ALL* COMING BACK TO YOU NOW?
WHAT YOU CARRY DOESN'T EVEN AFFECT YOU.
...
THAT ARM...
THAT *CLUMSY GUN* YOU WAVE AROUND IS A JUST A *TOOL.*

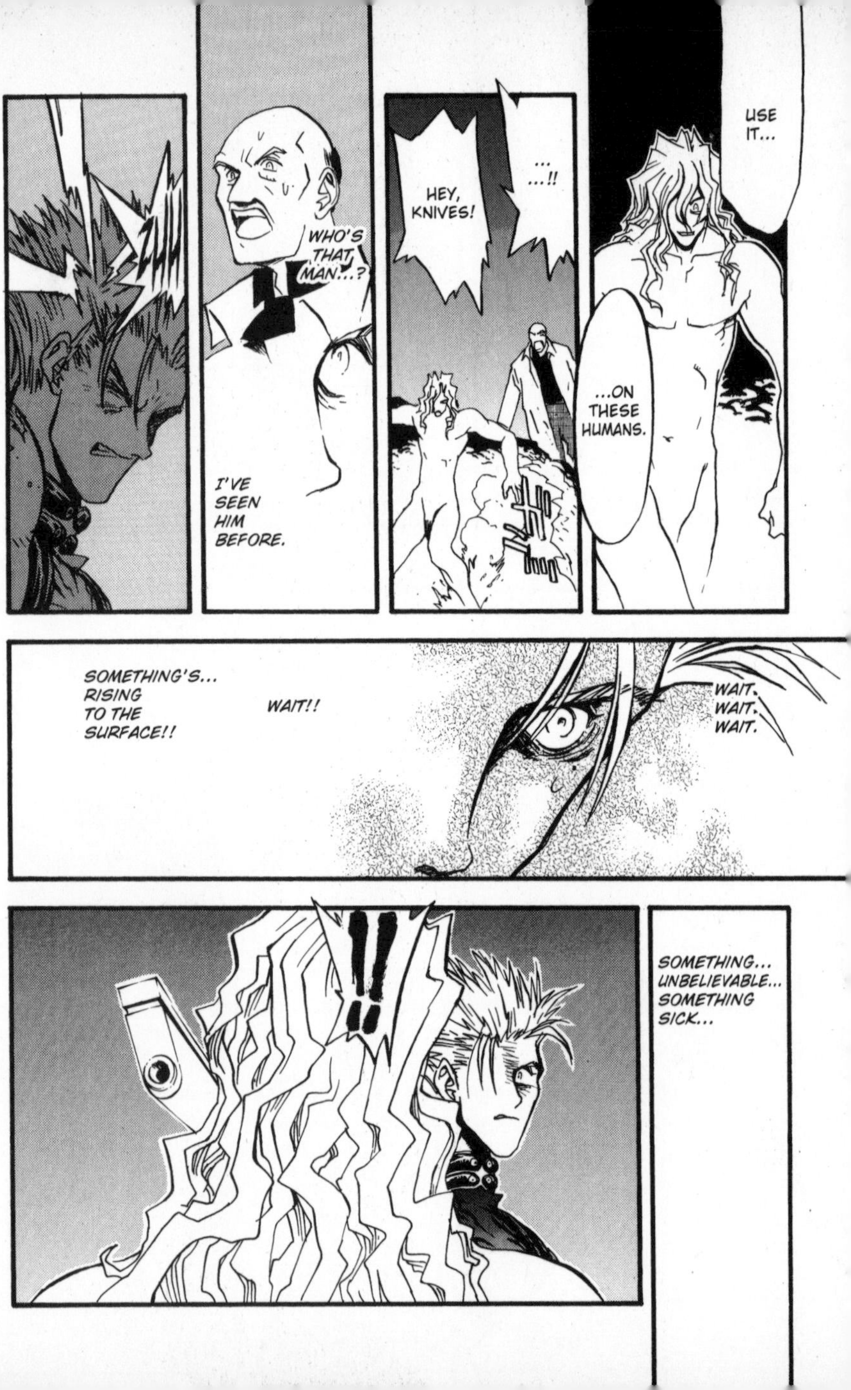
USE IT...
...ON THESE HUMANS.
... ...!!
HEY, KNIVES!
WHO'S THAT, MAN...?
I'VE SEEN HIM BEFORE.
WAIT. WAIT. WAIT.
WAIT!!
SOMETHING'S... RISING TO THE SURFACE!!
SOMETHING... UNBELIEVABLE... SOMETHING SICK...
!!

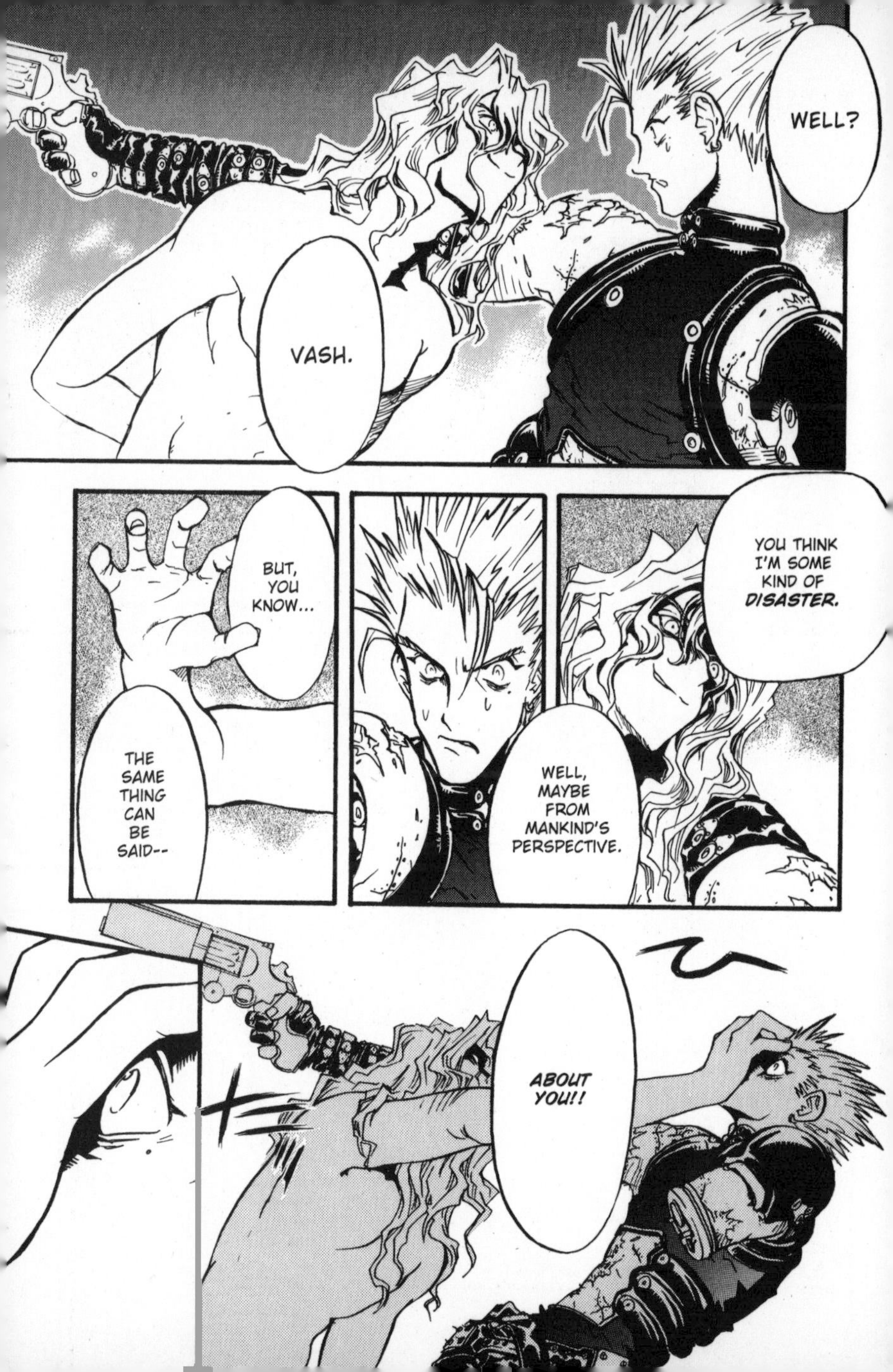
WELL?
VASH.
YOU THINK I'M SOME KIND OF *DISASTER.*
WELL, MAYBE FROM MANKIND'S PERSPECTIVE.
BUT, YOU KNOW...
THE SAME THING CAN BE SAID--
ABOUT YOU!!

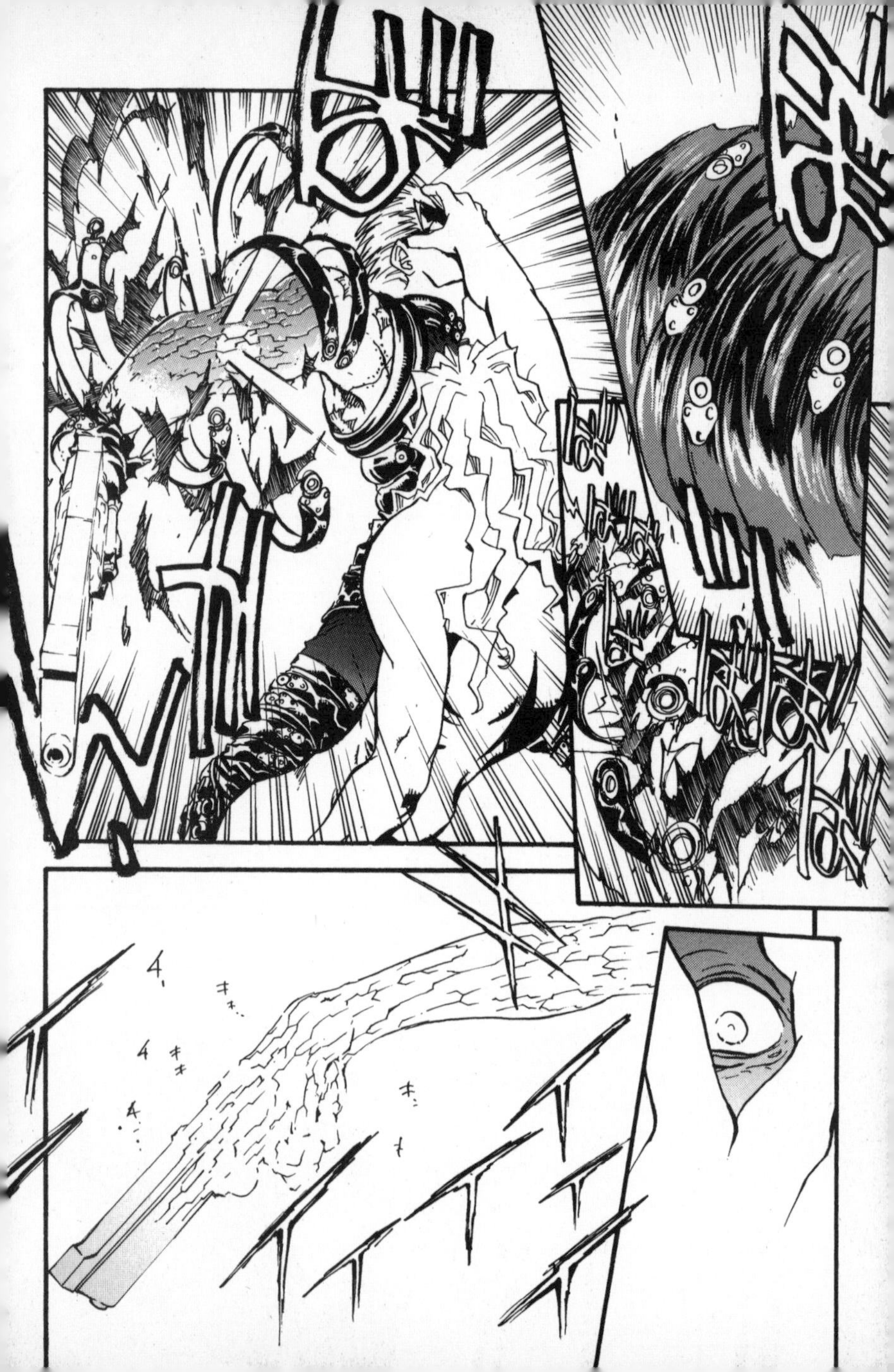

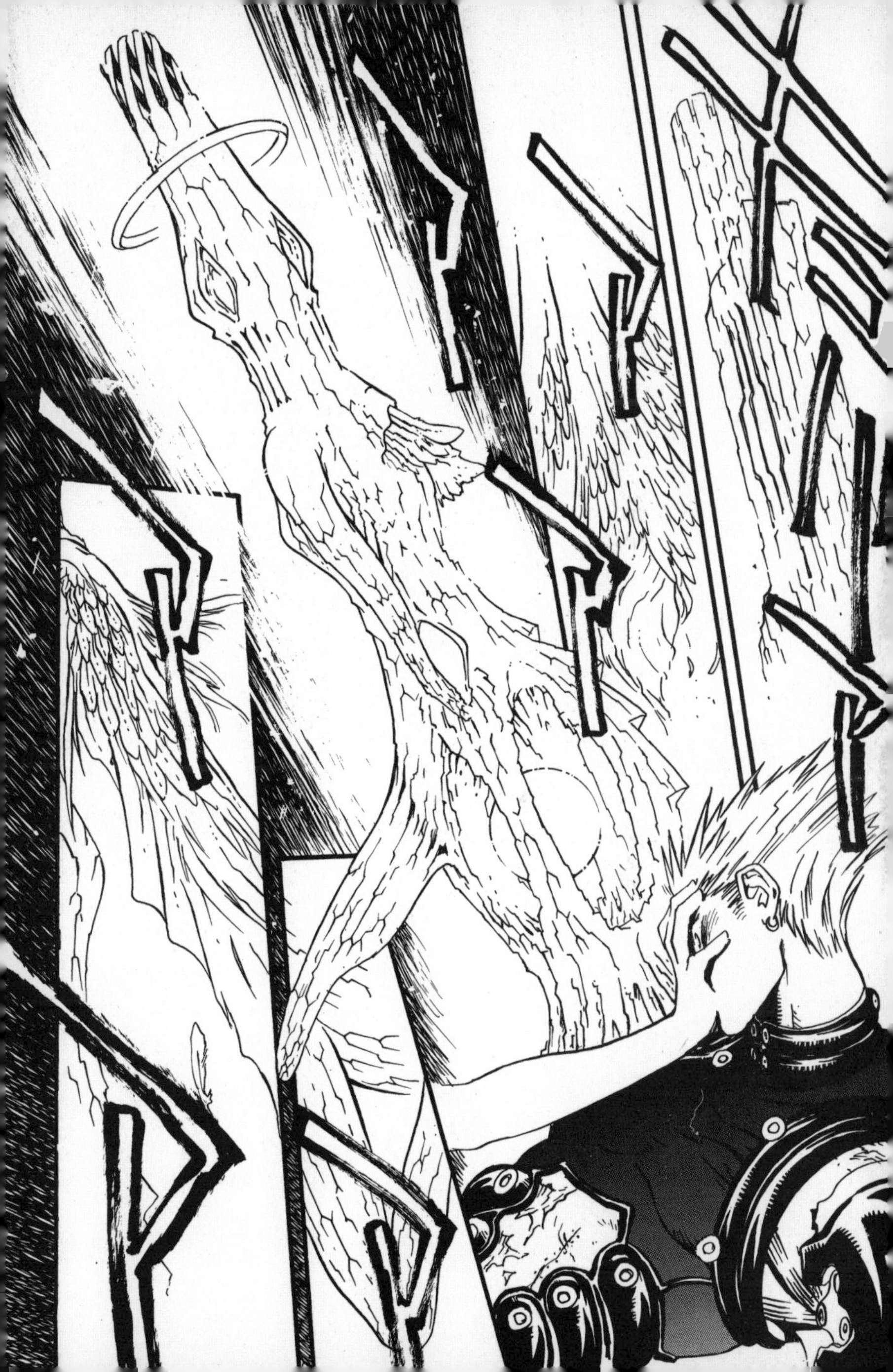

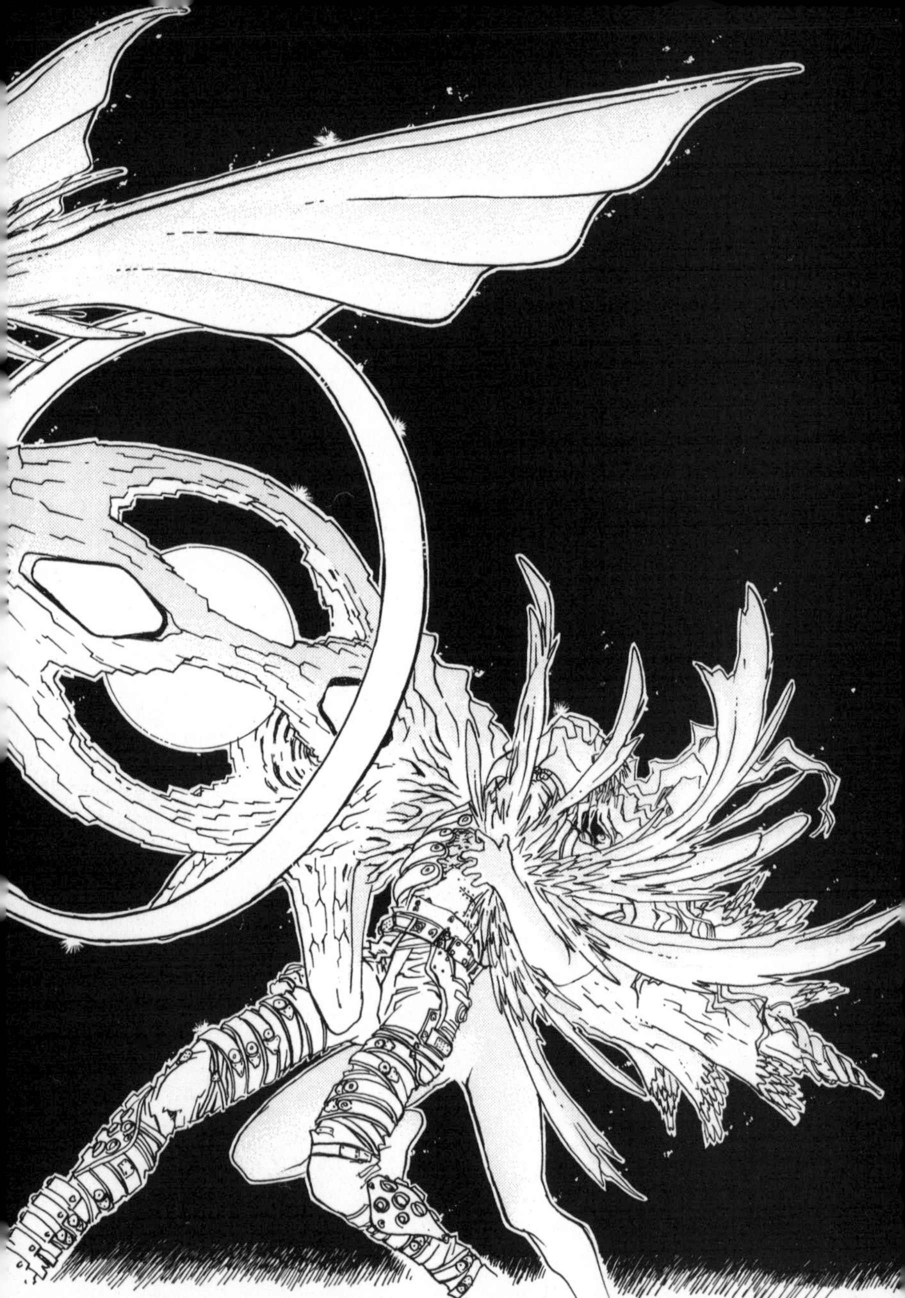

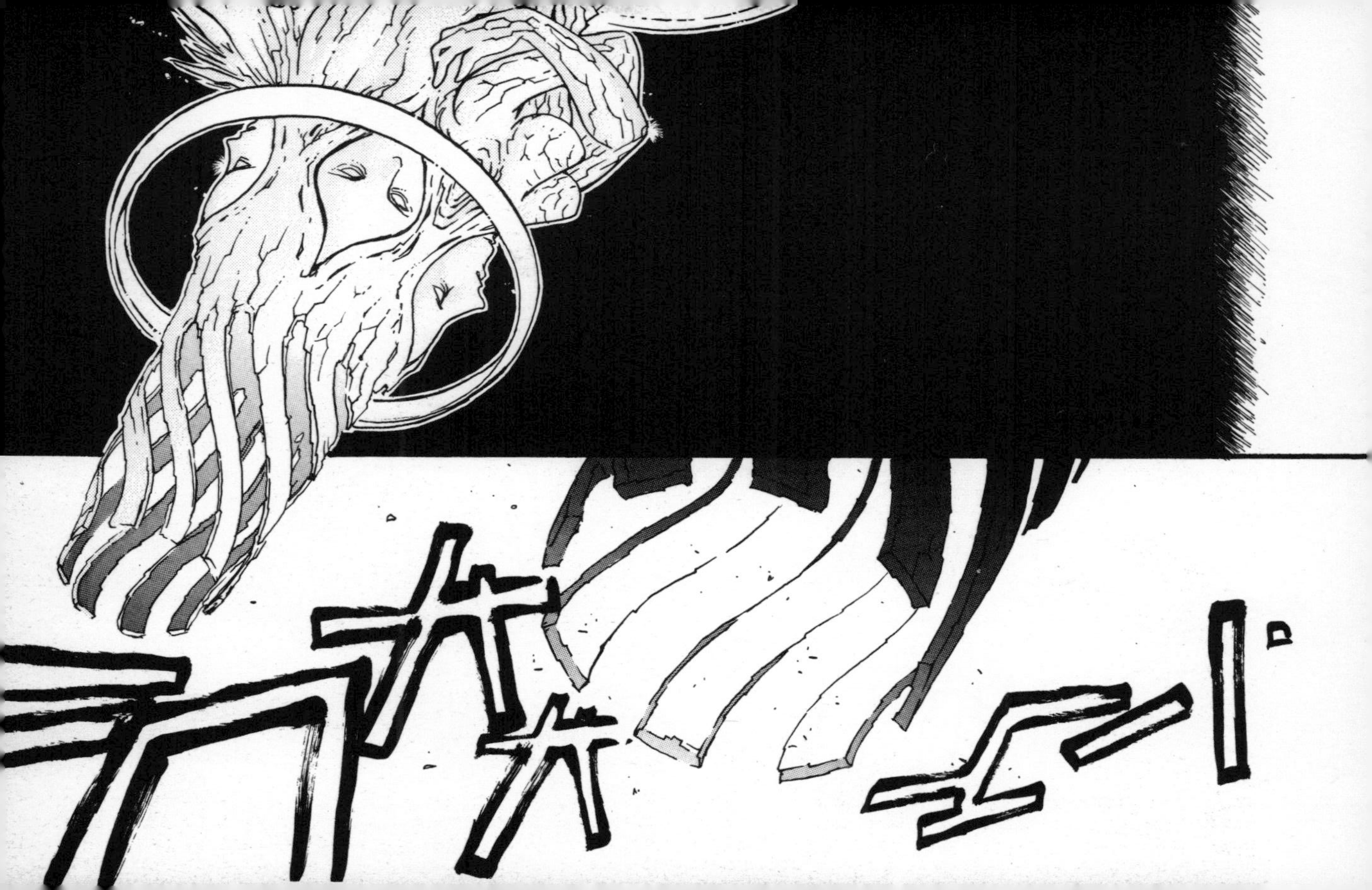

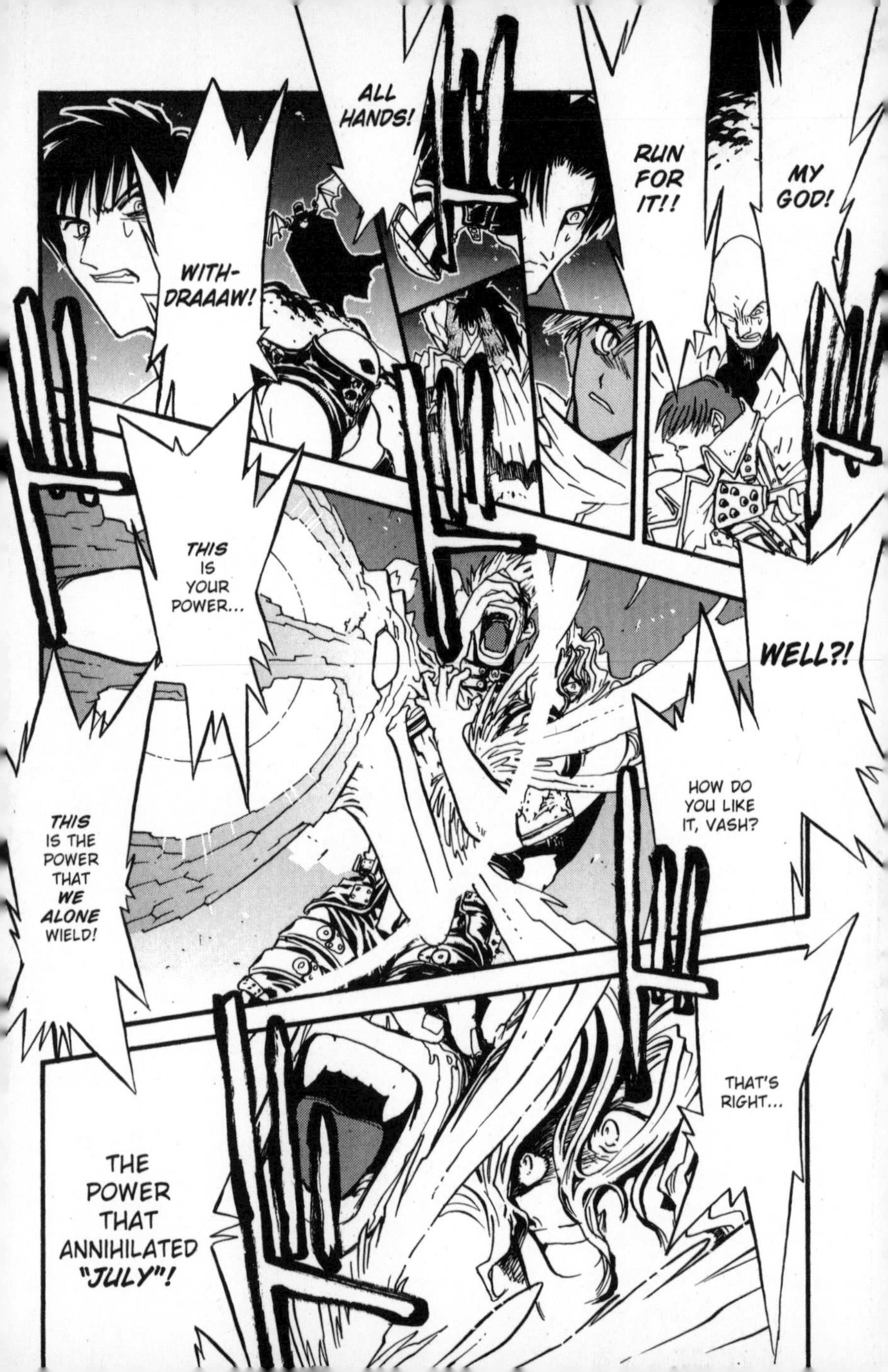
MY GOD!
ALL HANDS!
RUN FOR IT!!
WITH-DRAAAW!
WELL?!
THIS IS YOUR POWER...
HOW DO YOU LIKE IT, VASH?
THIS IS THE POWER THAT WE ALONE WIELD!
THAT'S RIGHT...
THE POWER THAT ANNIHILATED "JULY"!

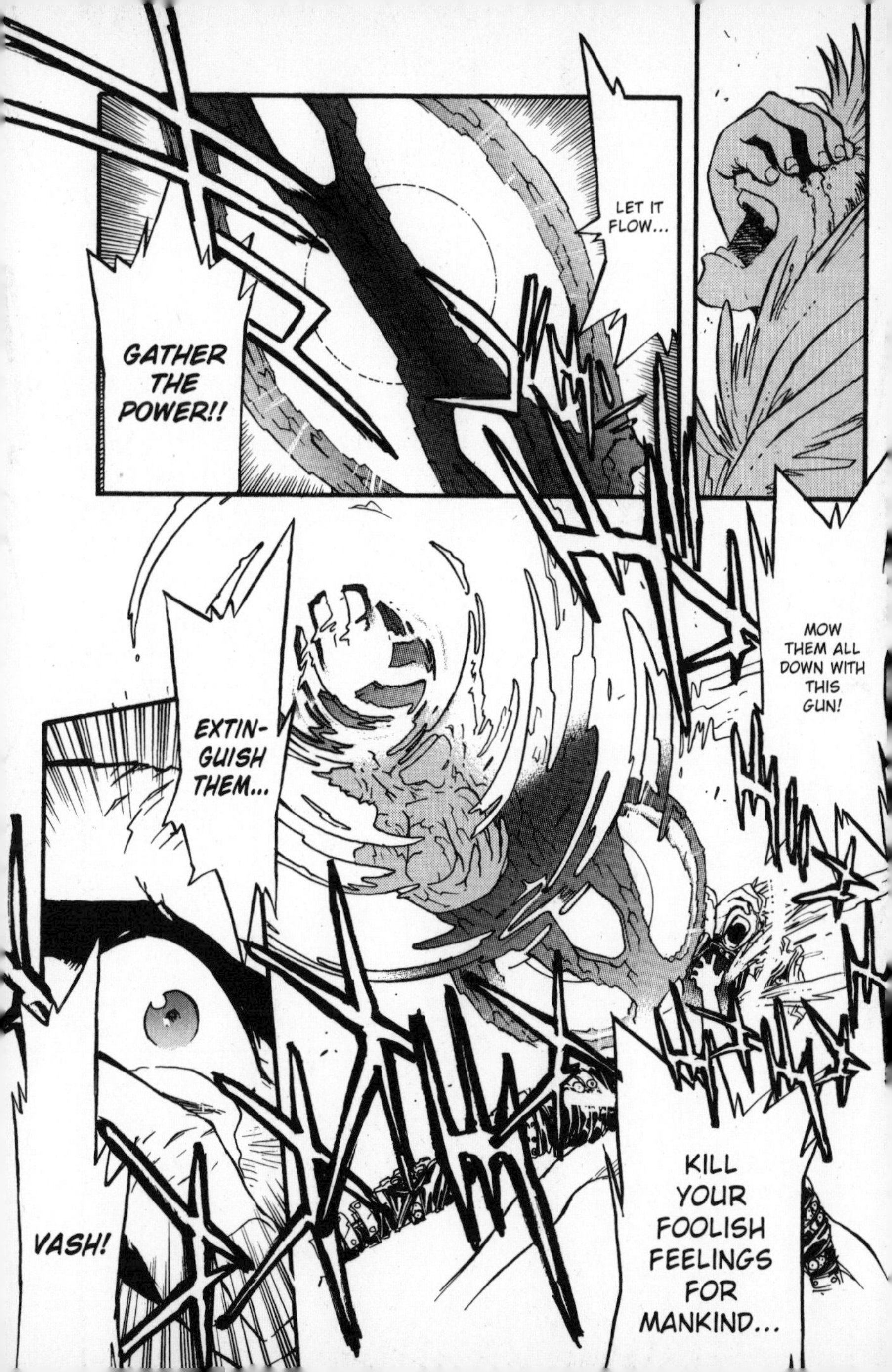
LET IT FLOW...
GATHER THE POWER!!
MOW THEM ALL DOWN WITH THIS GUN!
EXTIN-GUISH THEM...
KILL YOUR FOOLISH FEELINGS FOR MANKIND...
VASH!

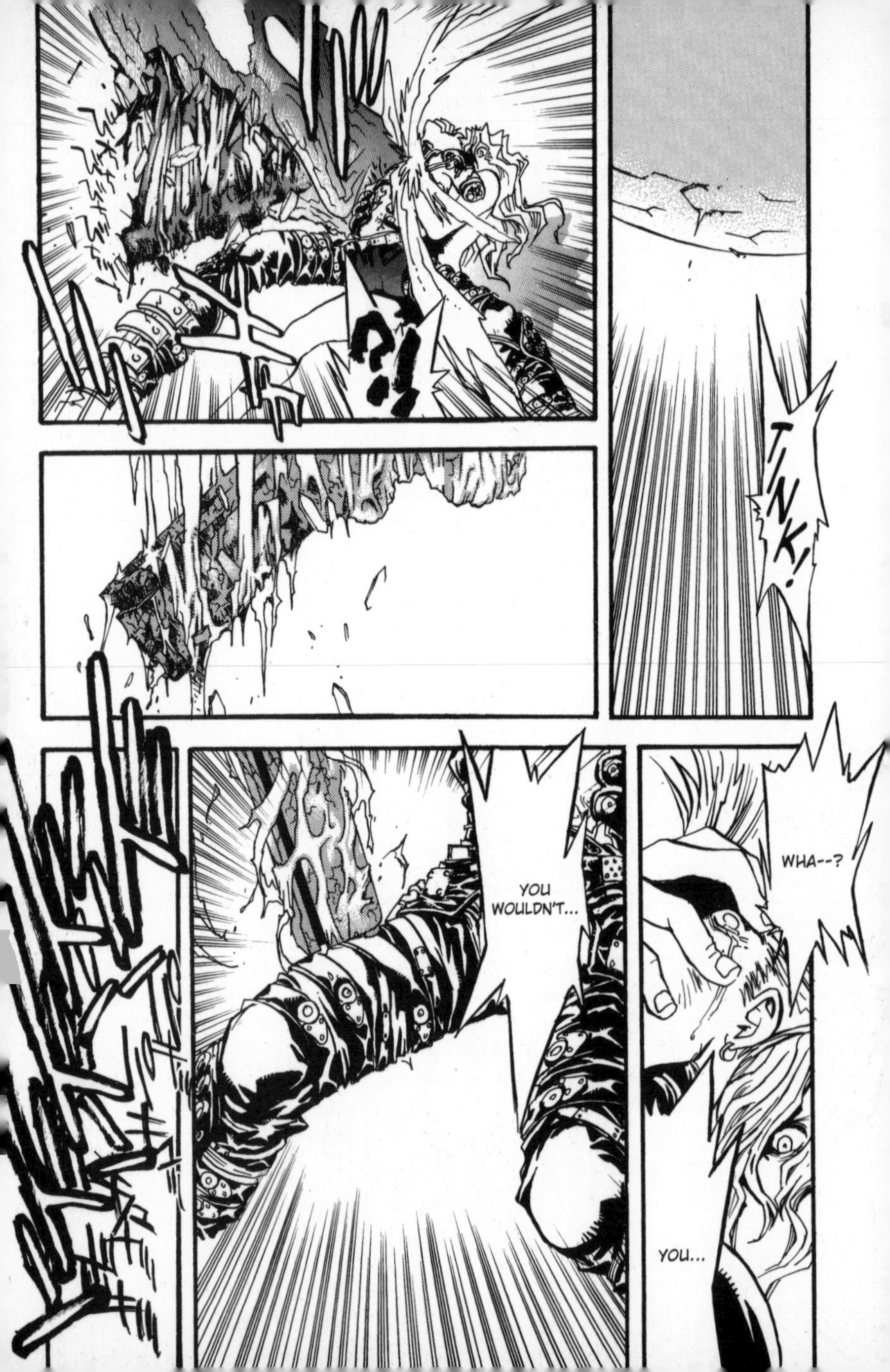
TINK!
?!
WHA--?
YOU...
YOU WOULDN'T...

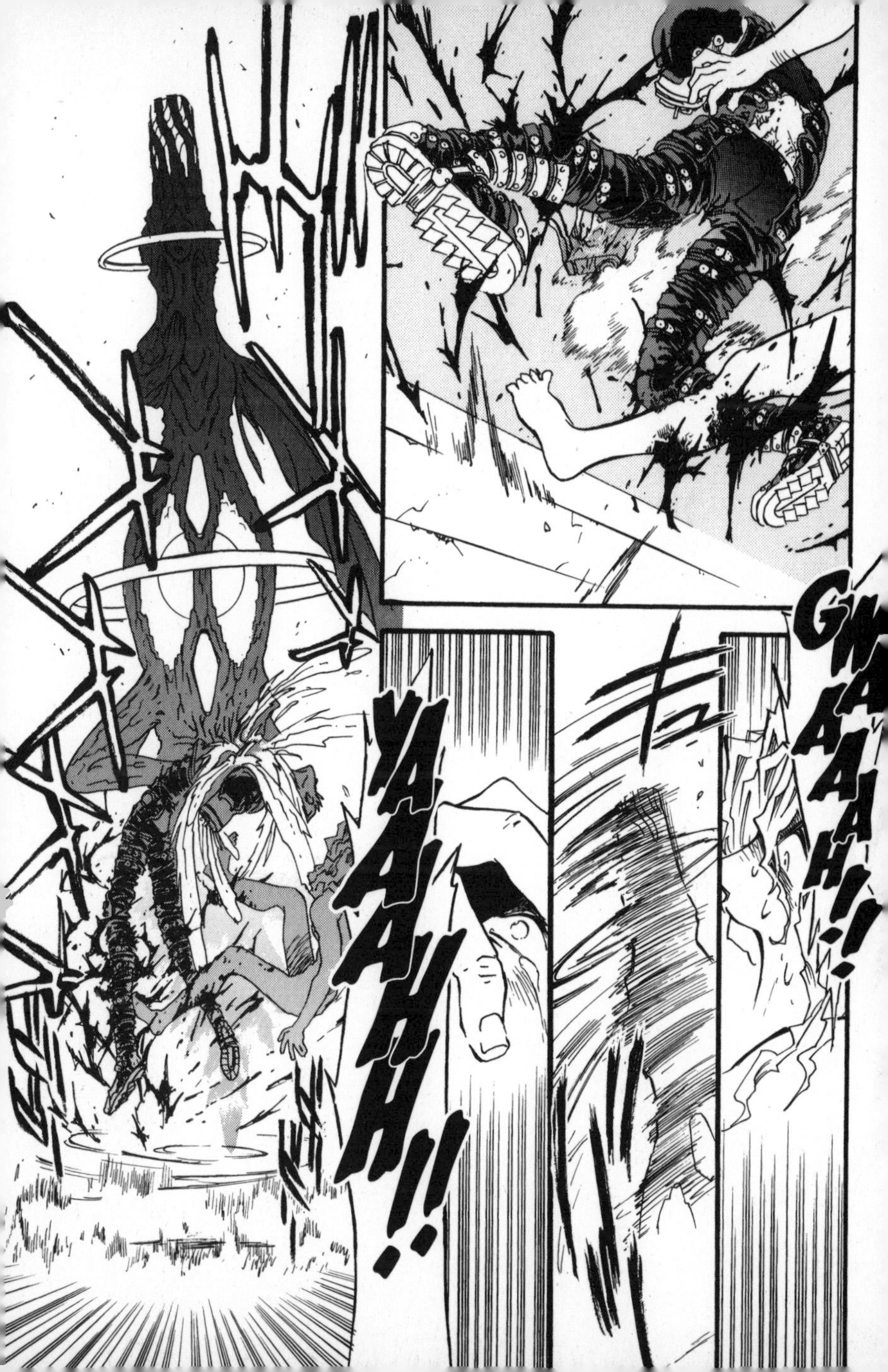
GWAAAAAH!!!
YAAAAH!!

REM...
...

REM...
...

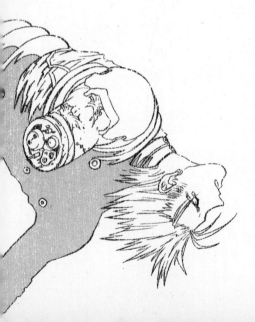

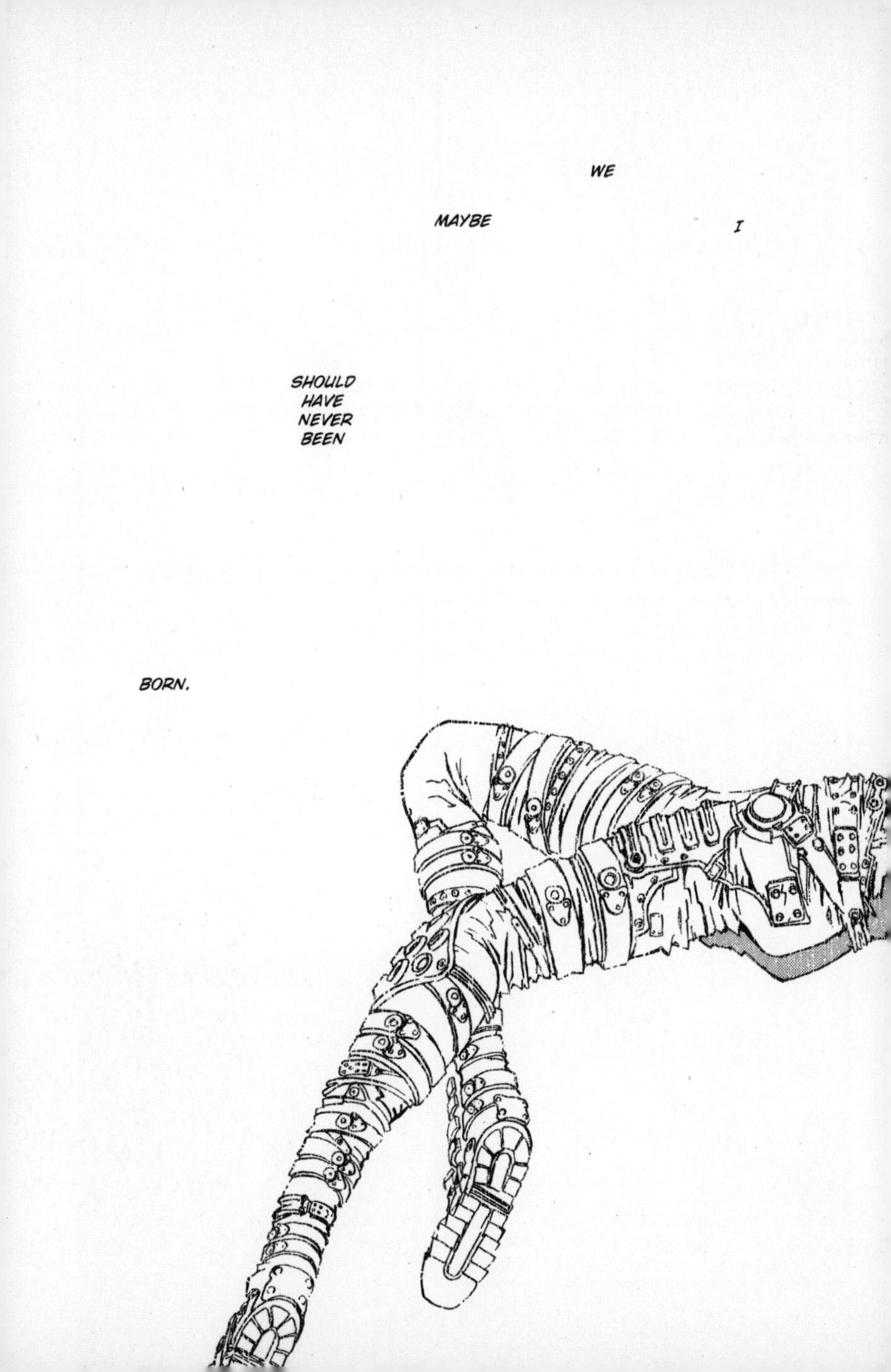

WE

MAYBE   I

SHOULD
HAVE
NEVER
BEEN

BORN.

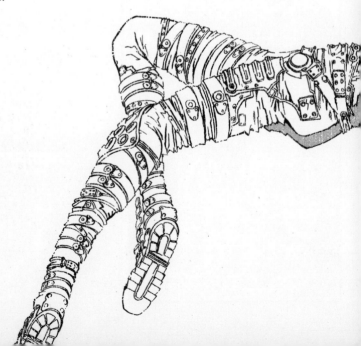

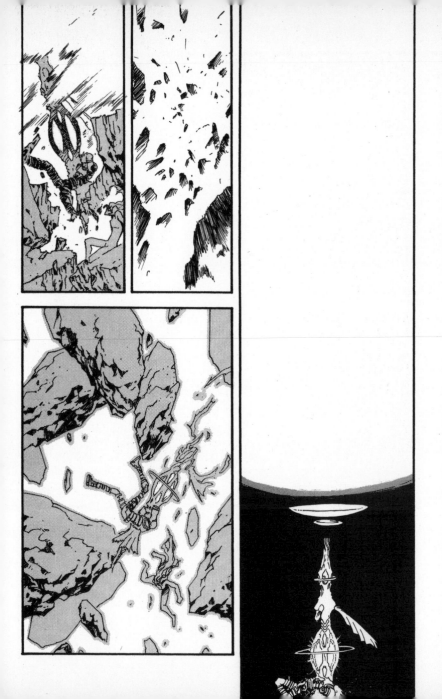

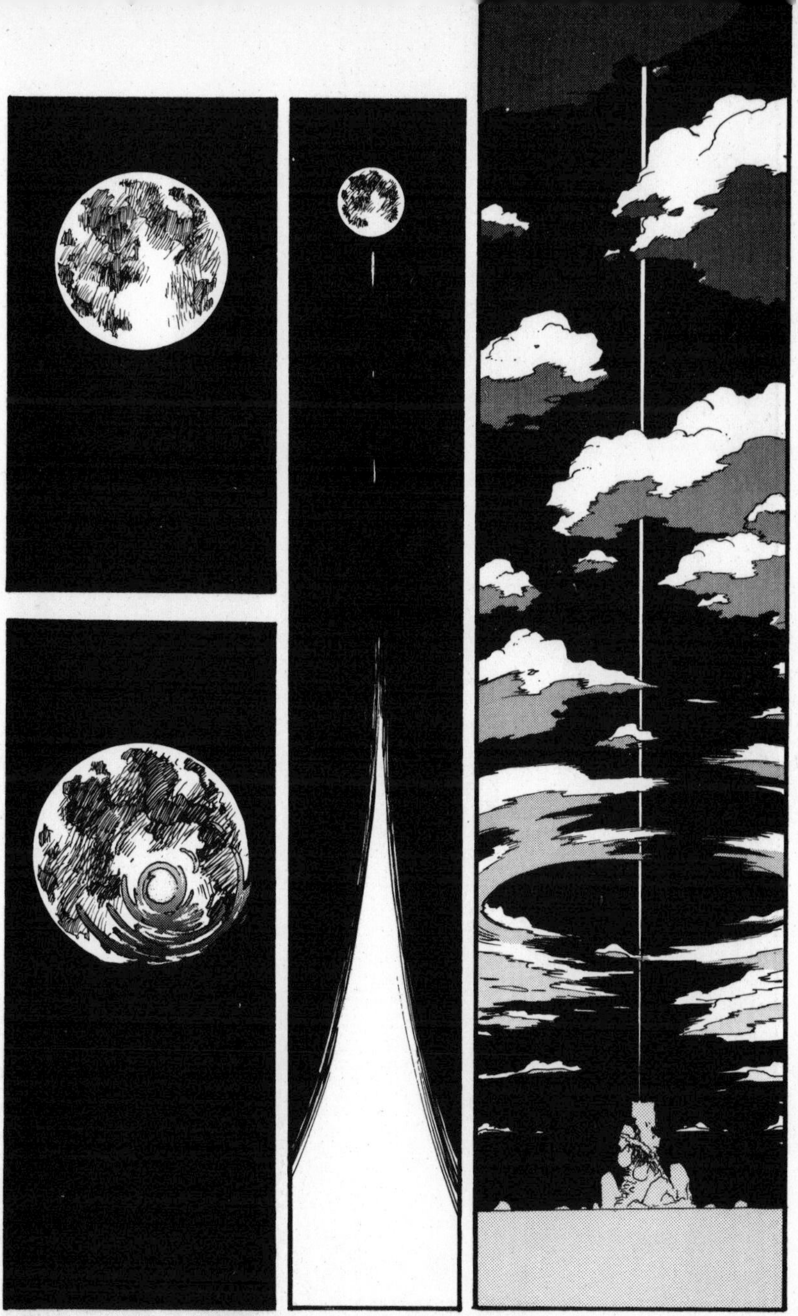

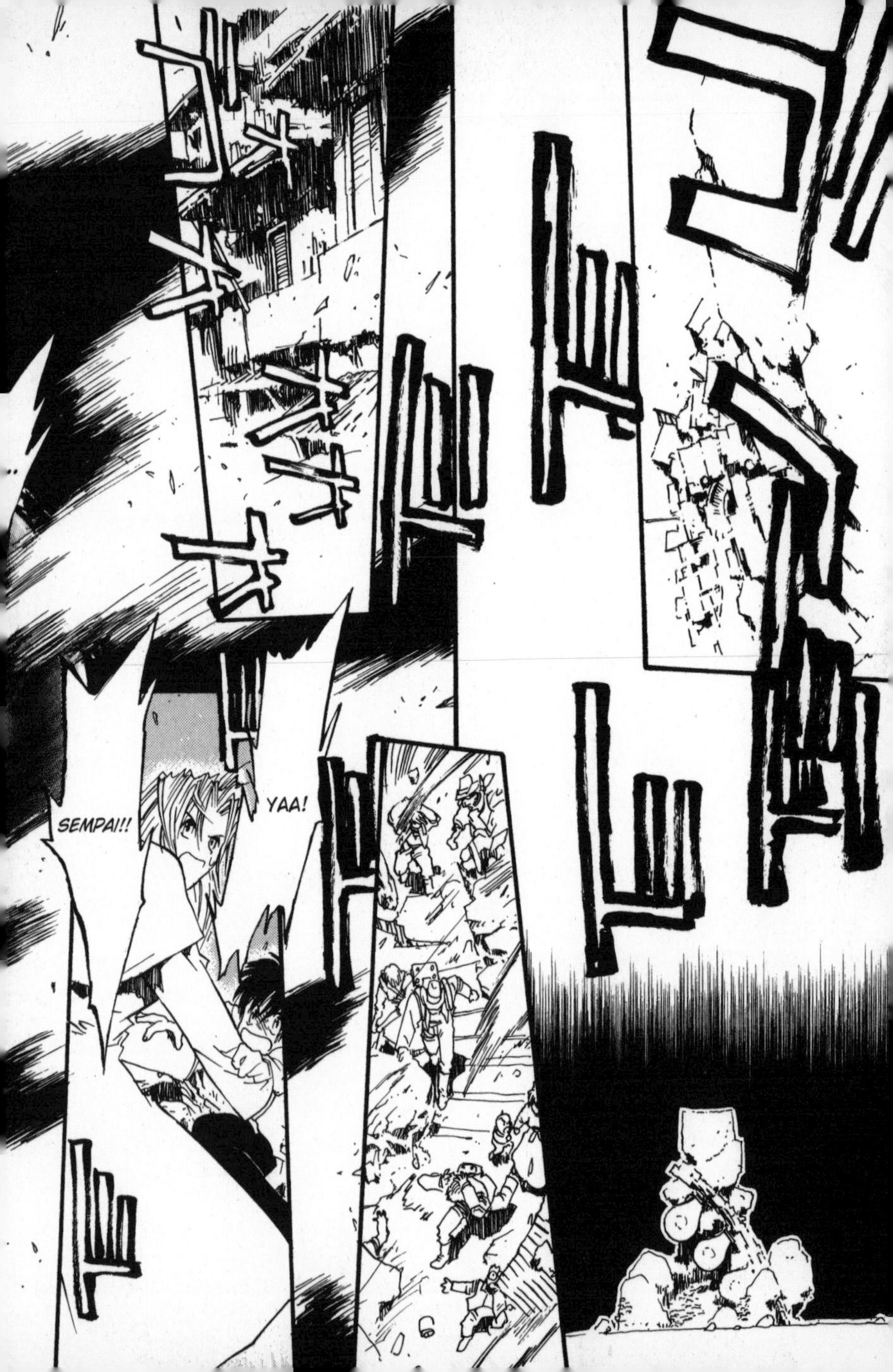
YAA!
SEMPAI!!

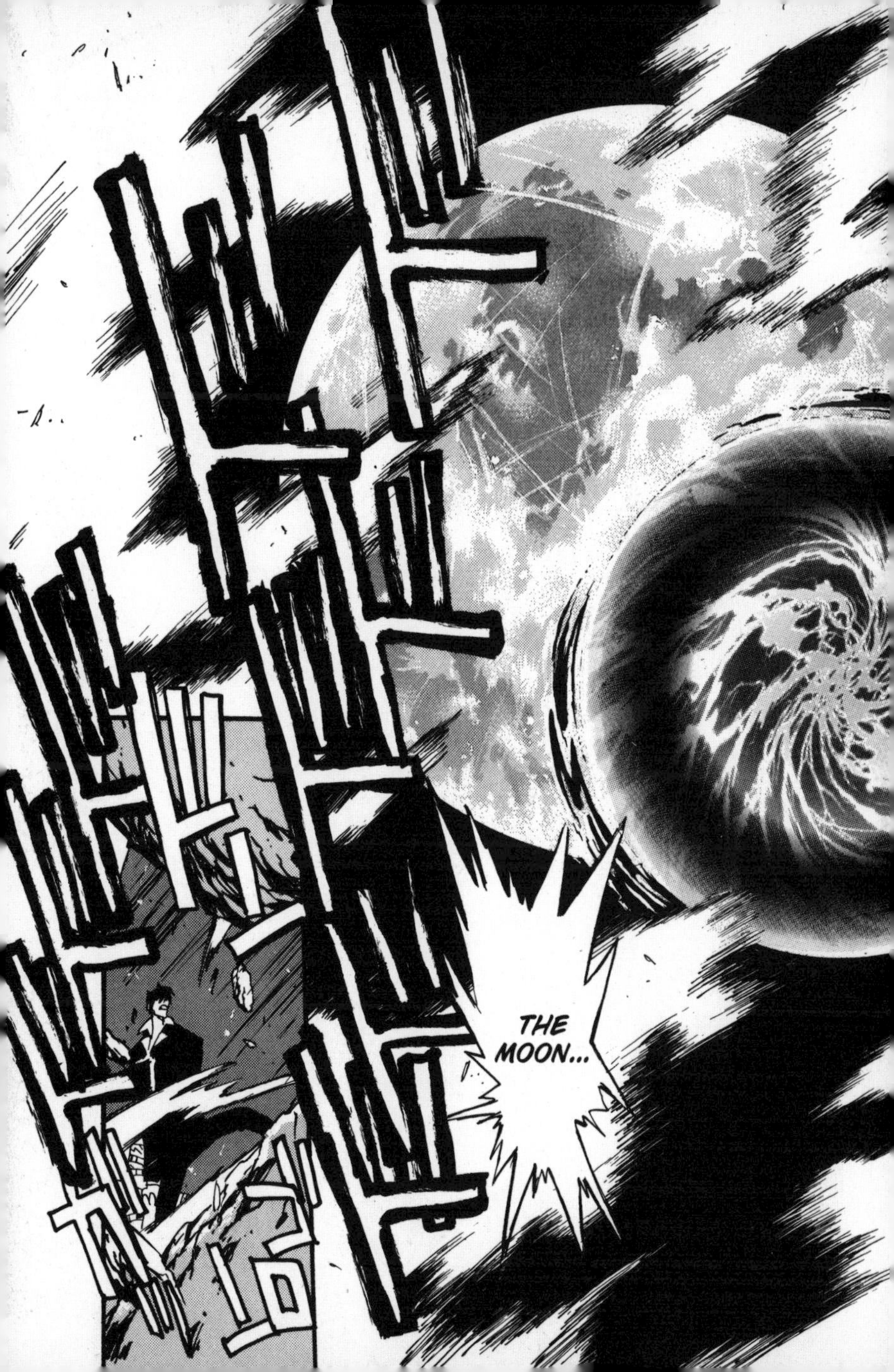
THE MOON...

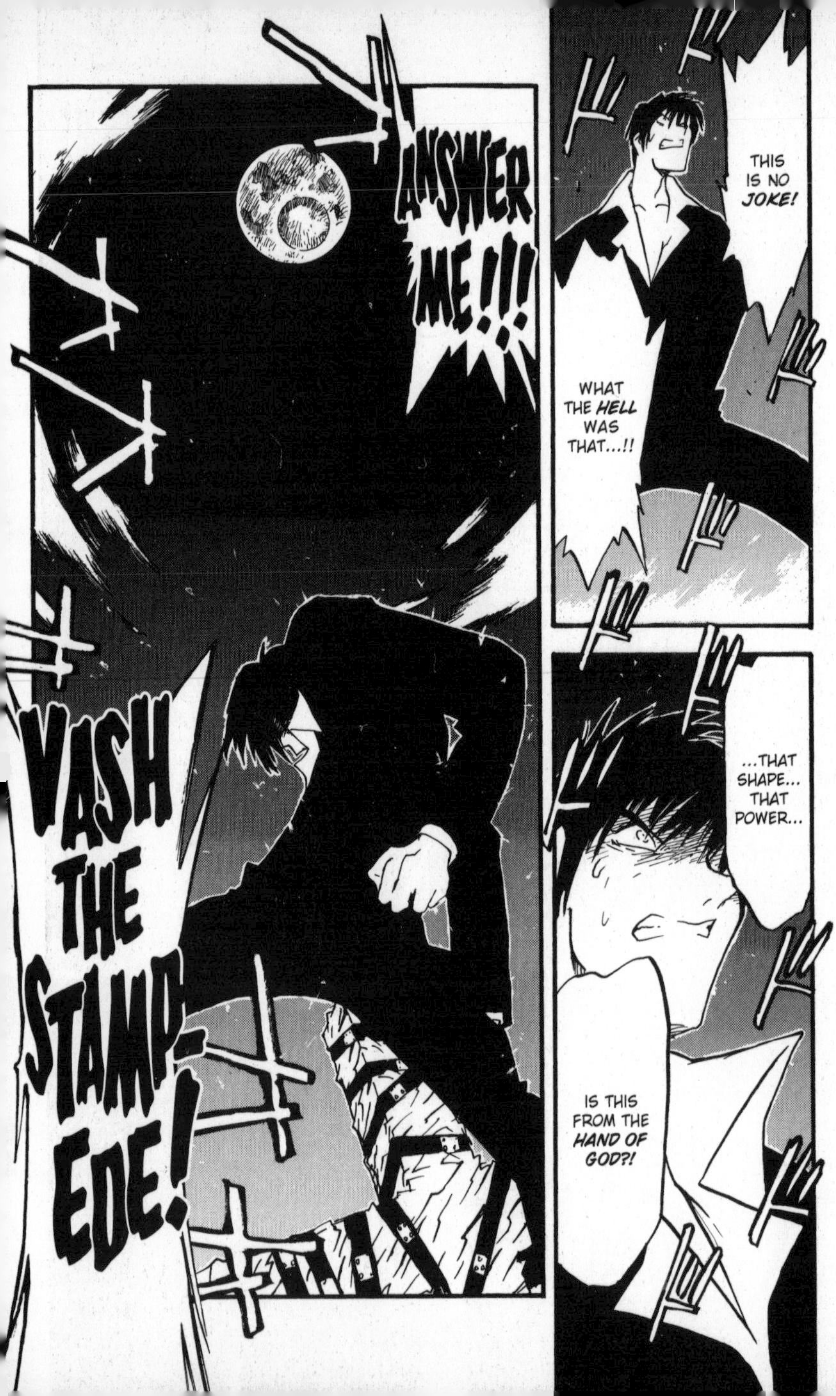
THIS IS NO JOKE!
WHAT THE HELL WAS THAT...!!
...THAT SHAPE... THAT POWER...
IS THIS FROM THE HAND OF GOD?!
ANSWER ME!!!
VASH THE STAMPEDE!

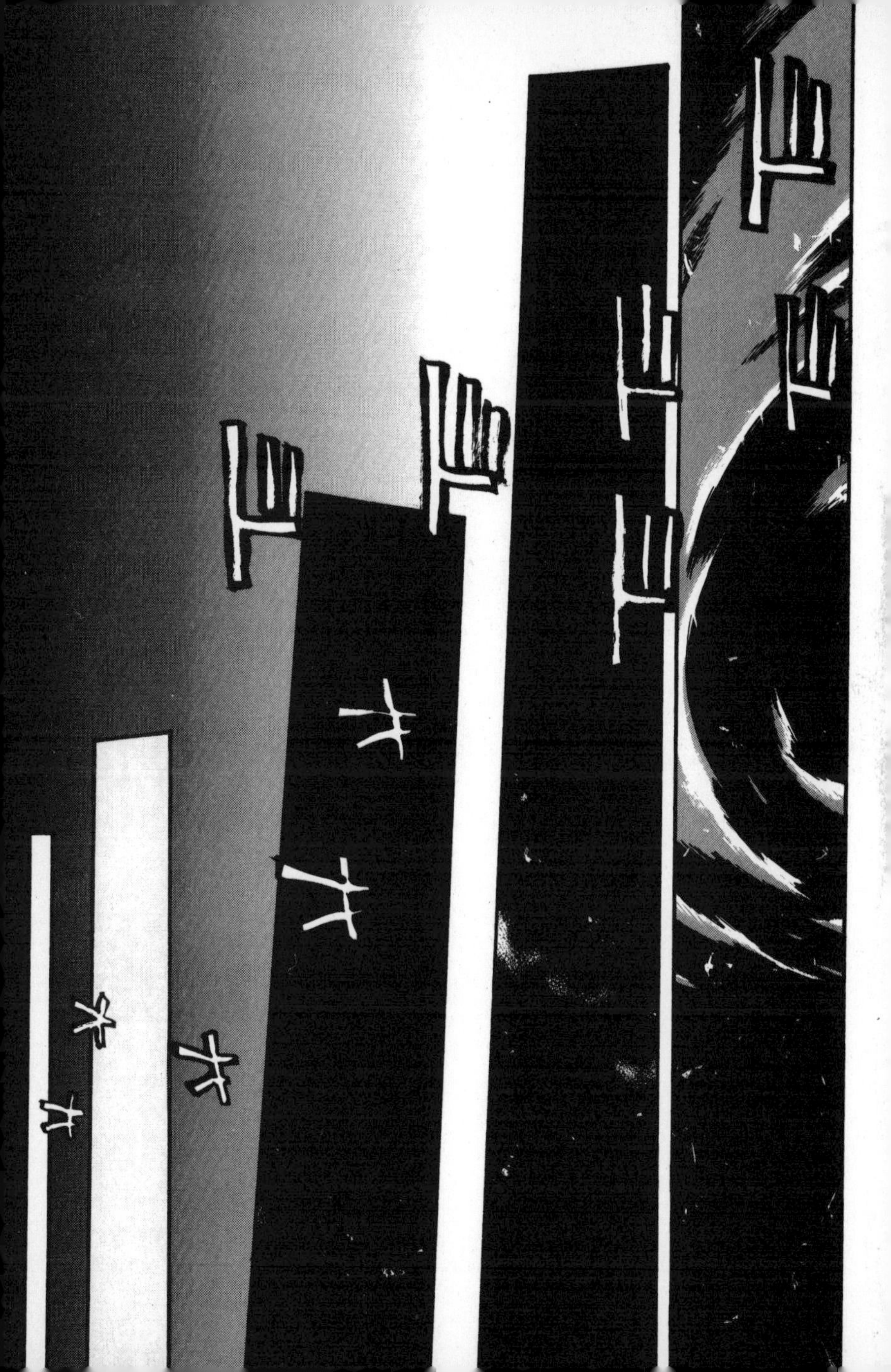

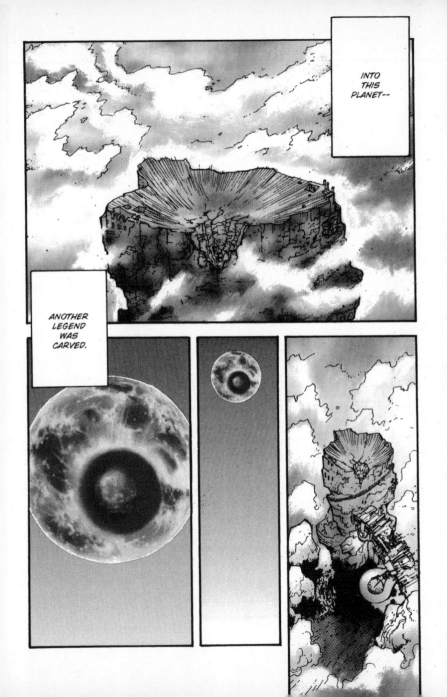

INTO
THIS
PLANET--

ANOTHER
LEGEND
WAS
CARVED.

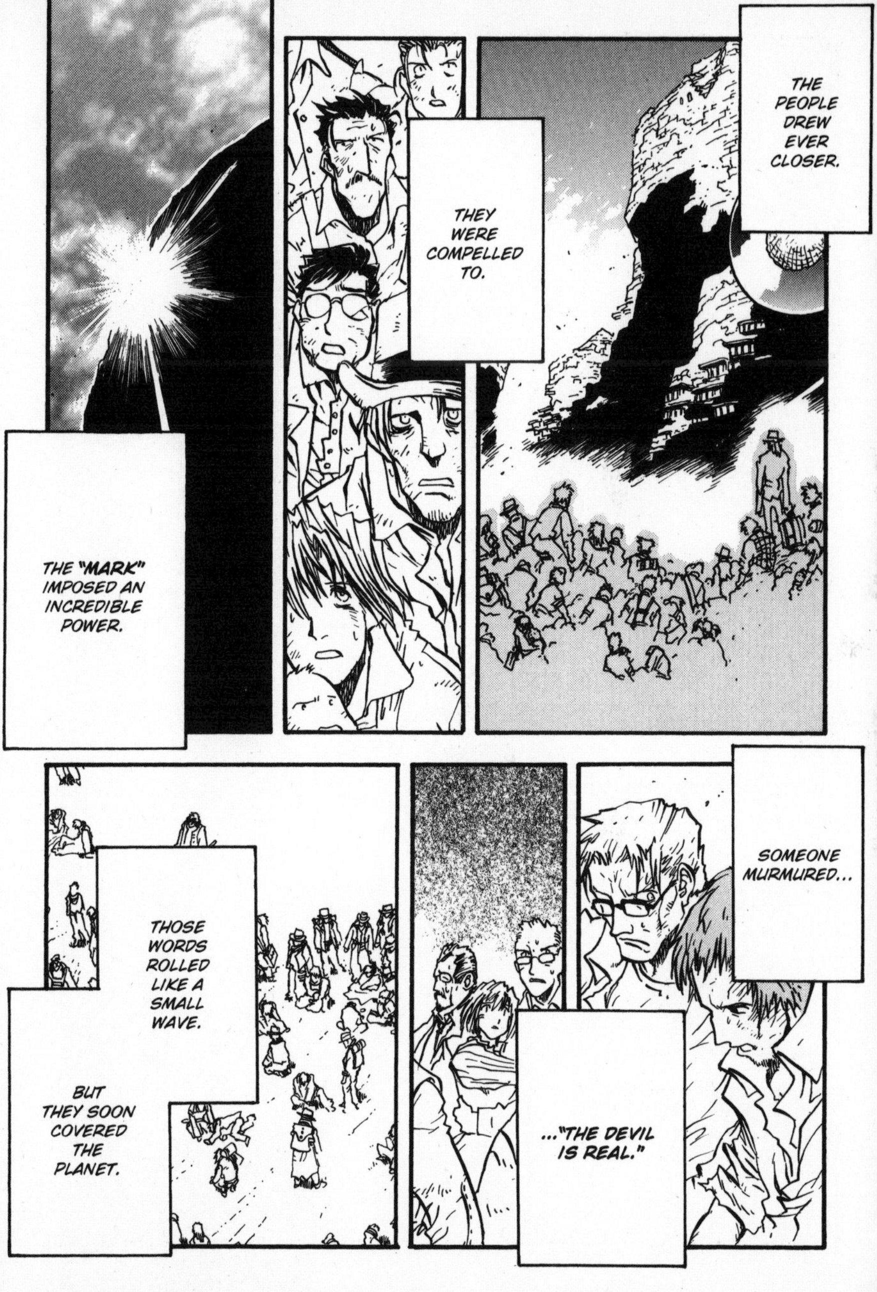
THE PEOPLE DREW EVER CLOSER.
THEY WERE COMPELLED TO.
THE "MARK" IMPOSED AN INCREDIBLE POWER.
SOMEONE MURMURED...
..."THE DEVIL IS REAL."
THOSE WORDS ROLLED LIKE A SMALL WAVE.
BUT THEY SOON COVERED THE PLANET.

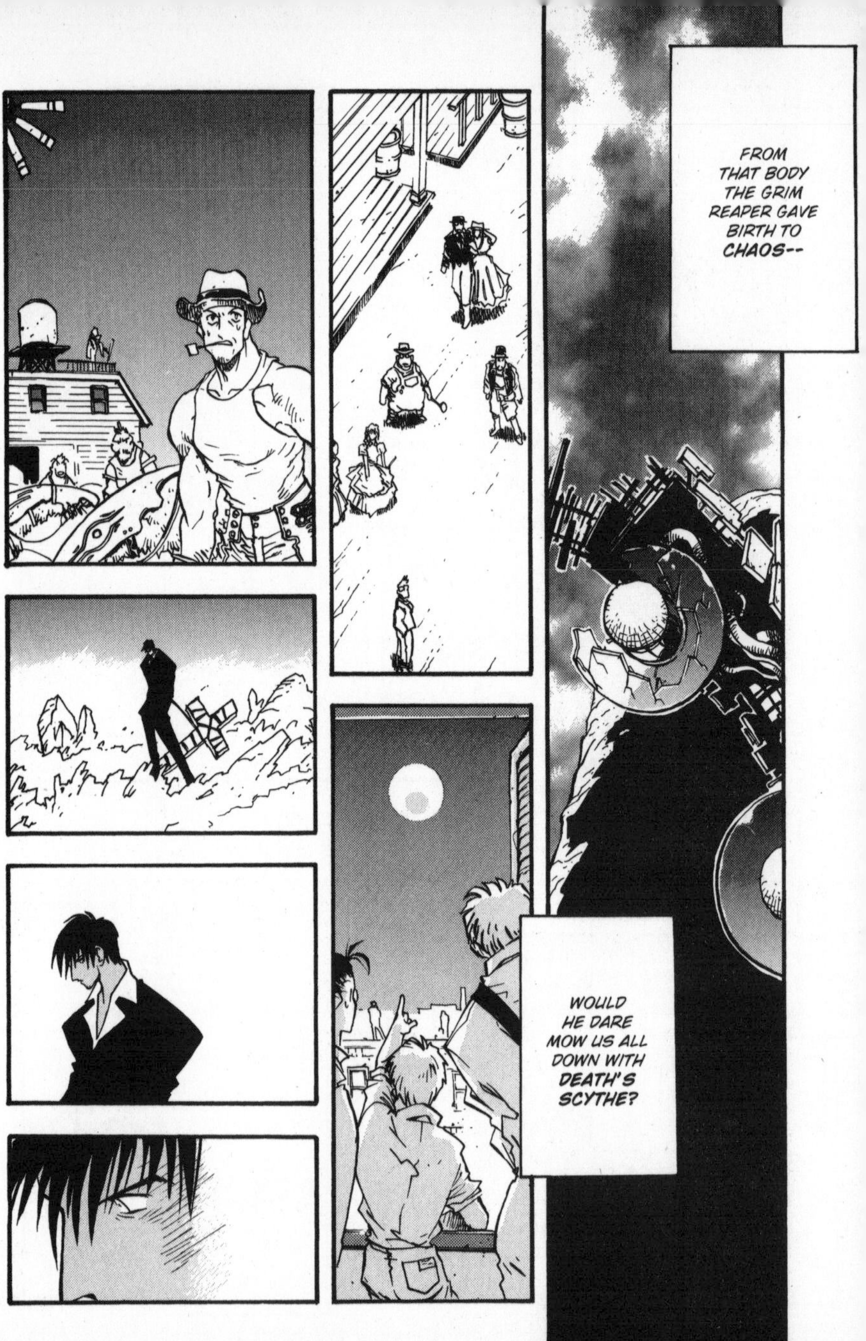
FROM THAT BODY THE GRIM REAPER GAVE BIRTH TO CHAOS--
WOULD HE DARE MOW US ALL DOWN WITH DEATH'S SCYTHE?

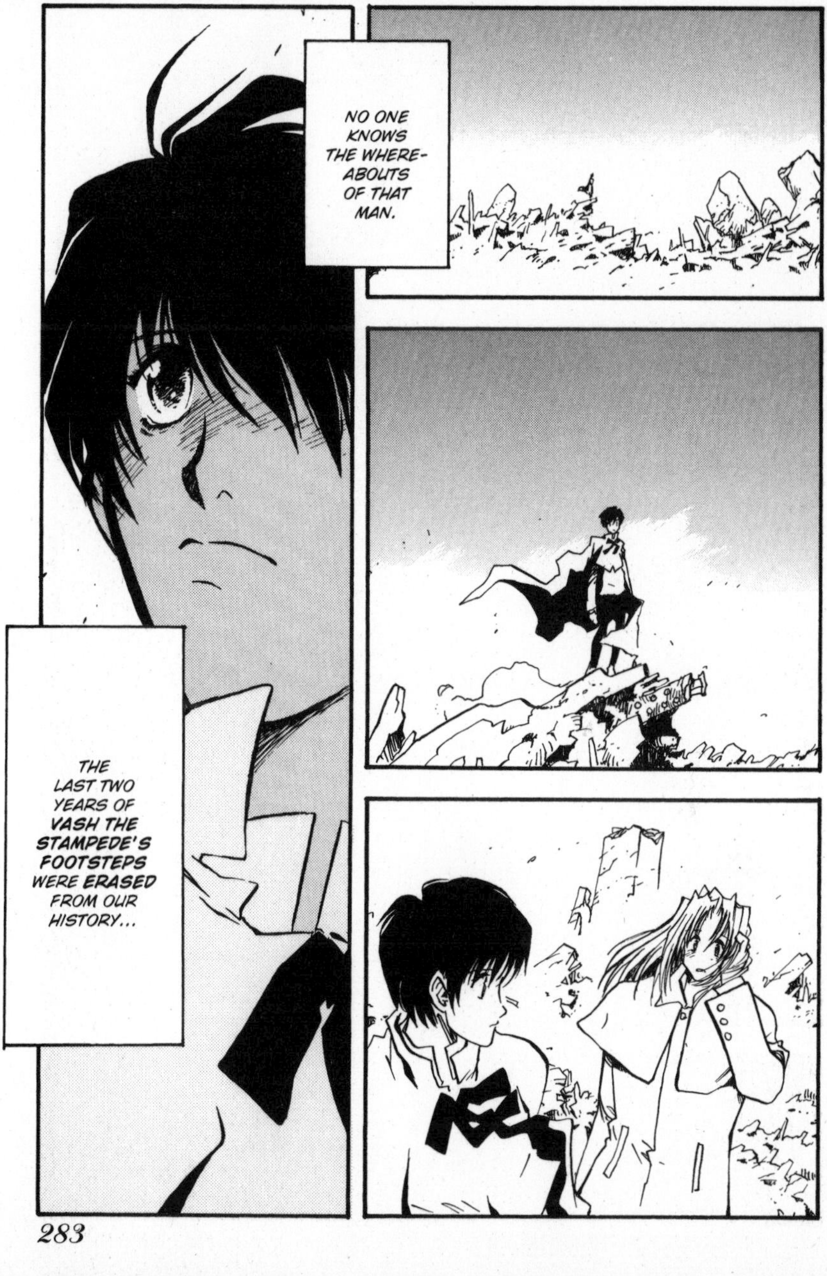
NO ONE KNOWS THE WHERE-ABOUTS OF THAT MAN.
THE LAST TWO YEARS OF VASH THE STAMPEDE'S FOOTSTEPS WERE ERASED FROM OUR HISTORY...

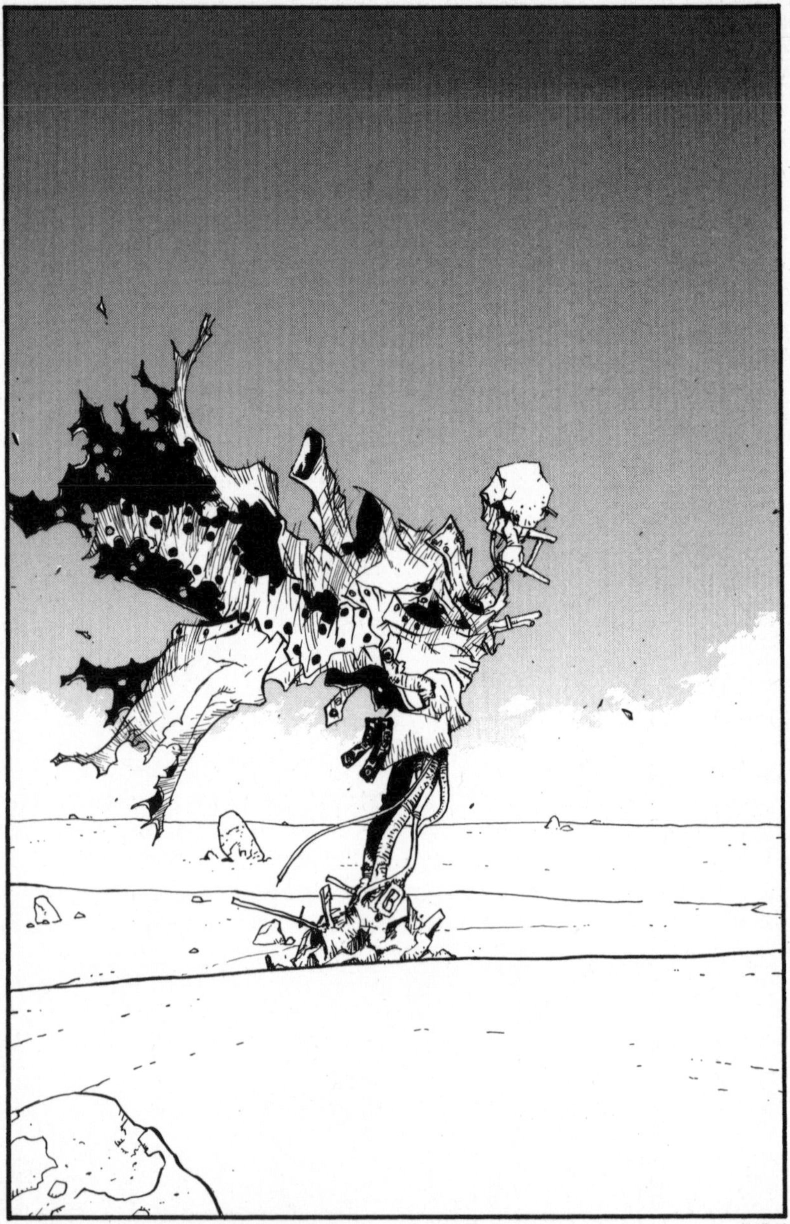

#8. FIFTH MOON/END

TURN TO THE MAXIMUM

TRIGUN YASUHIRO NIGHTOW

TRIGUN
BONUS
TRACKS!!
YASUHIRO NIGHTOW

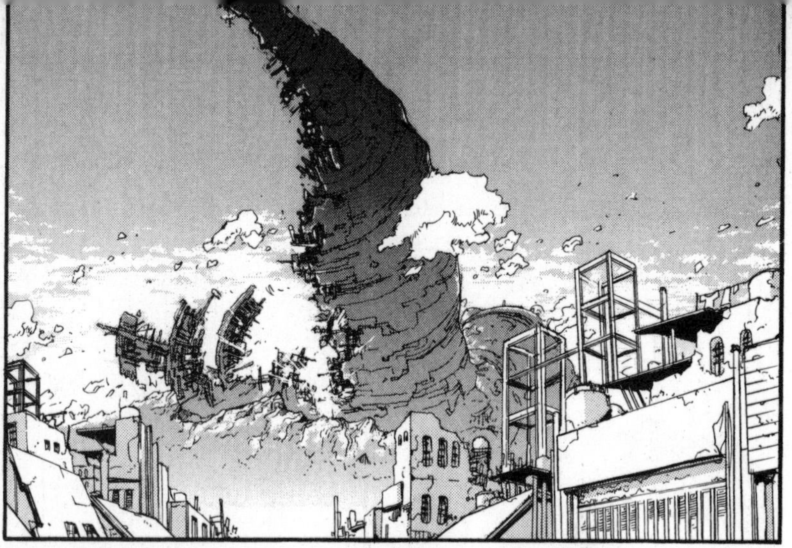

TRIGUN 特別編

DAY IN DAY OUT

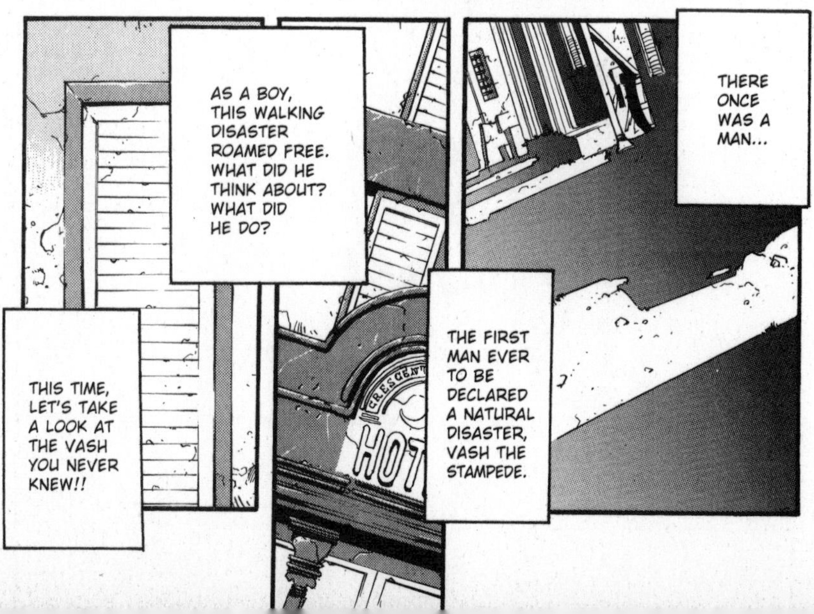
THERE ONCE WAS A MAN...
THE FIRST MAN EVER TO BE DECLARED A NATURAL DISASTER, VASH THE STAMPEDE.
AS A BOY, THIS WALKING DISASTER ROAMED FREE. WHAT DID HE THINK ABOUT? WHAT DID HE DO?
THIS TIME, LET'S TAKE A LOOK AT THE VASH YOU NEVER KNEW!!
HOT
CRESCENT

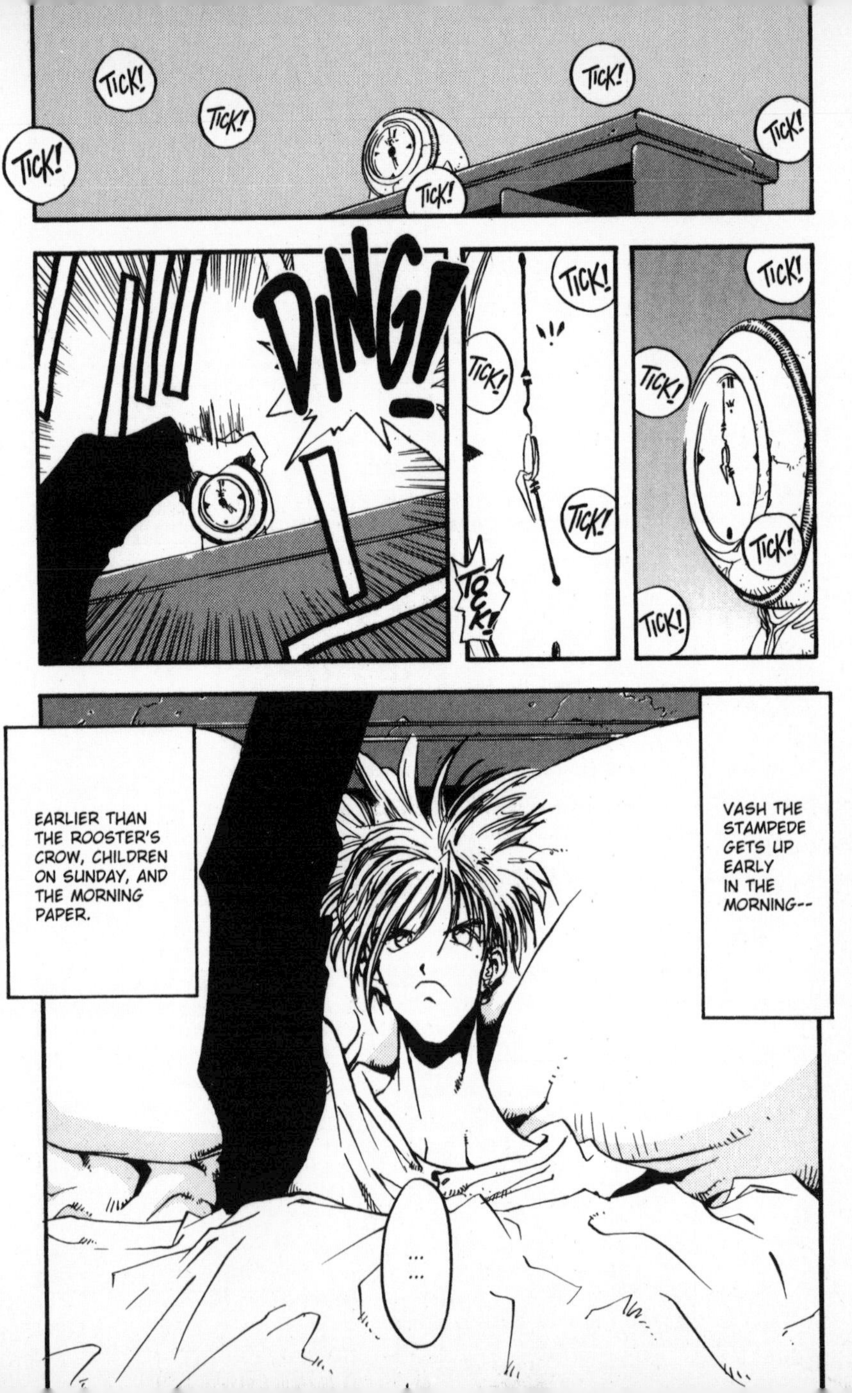
TICK!
TICK!
TICK!
TICK!
TICK!
TICK!
TICK!
TICK!
TICK!
TICK!
TICK!
TICK!
TICK!
TOCK!
DING!
VASH THE STAMPEDE GETS UP EARLY IN THE MORNING--
EARLIER THAN THE ROOSTER'S CROW, CHILDREN ON SUNDAY, AND THE MORNING PAPER.
... ...

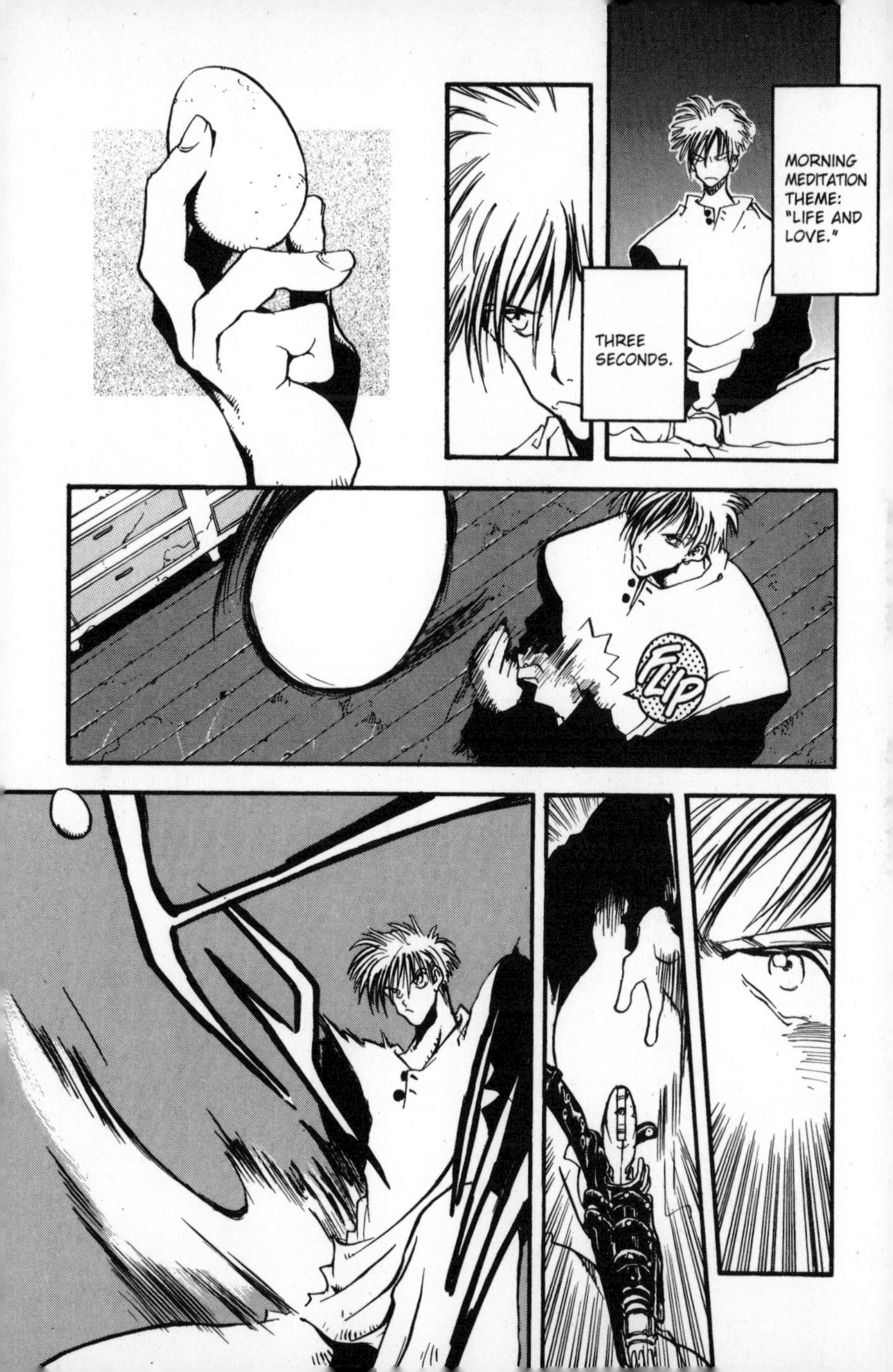
MORNING MEDITATION THEME: "LIFE AND LOVE."
THREE SECONDS.
FLIP

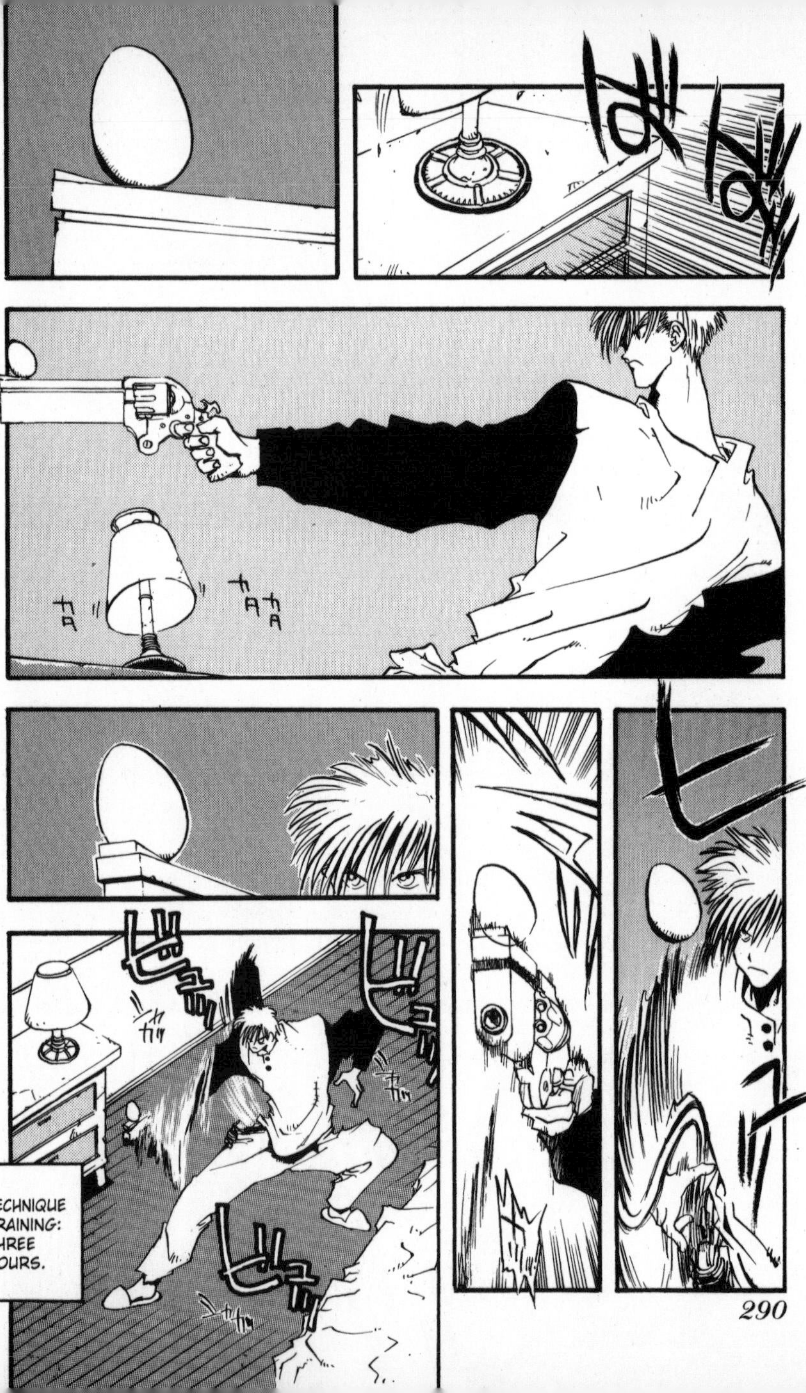
TECHNIQUE TRAINING: THREE HOURS.

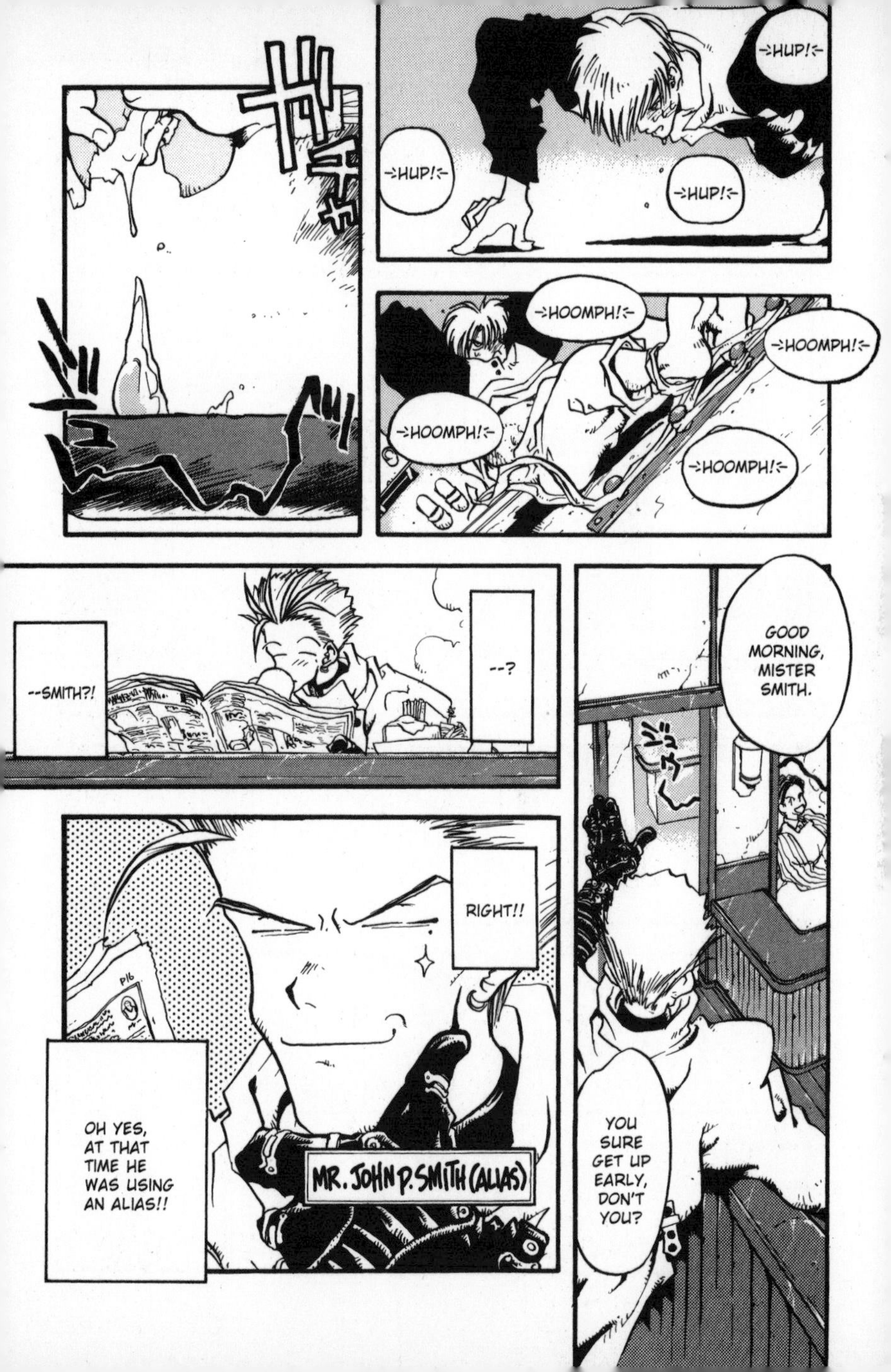
-HUP!-
-HUP!-
-HUP!-
-HOOMPH!-
-HOOMPH!-
-HOOMPH!-
-HOOMPH!-
GOOD MORNING, MISTER SMITH.
YOU SURE GET UP EARLY, DON'T YOU?
--?
--SMITH?!
RIGHT!!
MR. JOHN P. SMITH (ALIAS)
OH YES, AT THAT TIME HE WAS USING AN ALIAS!!

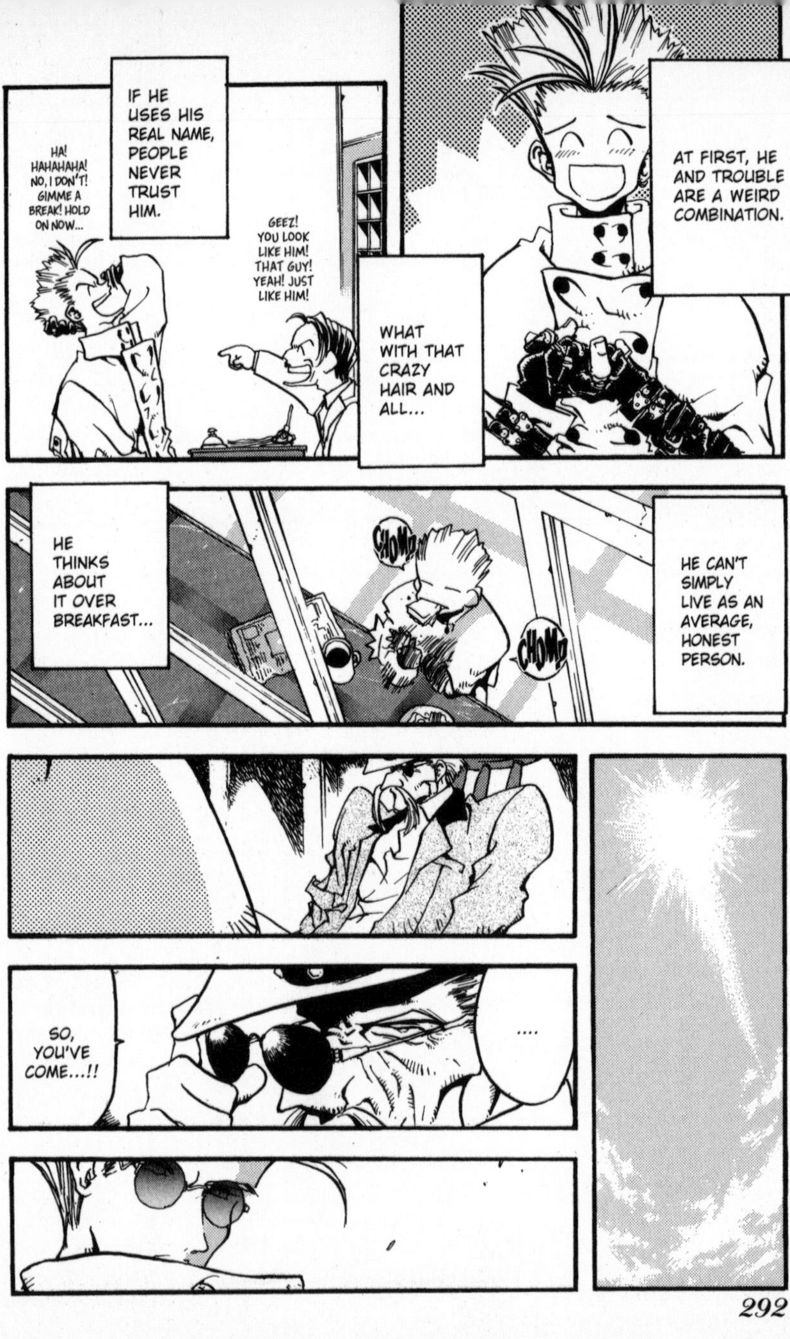
AT FIRST, HE AND TROUBLE ARE A WEIRD COMBINATION.
WHAT WITH THAT CRAZY HAIR AND ALL...
IF HE USES HIS REAL NAME, PEOPLE NEVER TRUST HIM.
GEEZ! YOU LOOK LIKE HIM! THAT GUY! YEAH! JUST LIKE HIM!
HA! HAHAHAHA! NO, I DON'T! GIMME A BREAK! HOLD ON NOW...
HE CAN'T SIMPLY LIVE AS AN AVERAGE, HONEST PERSON.
CHOMP
CHOMP
HE THINKS ABOUT IT OVER BREAKFAST...
....
SO, YOU'VE COME...!!

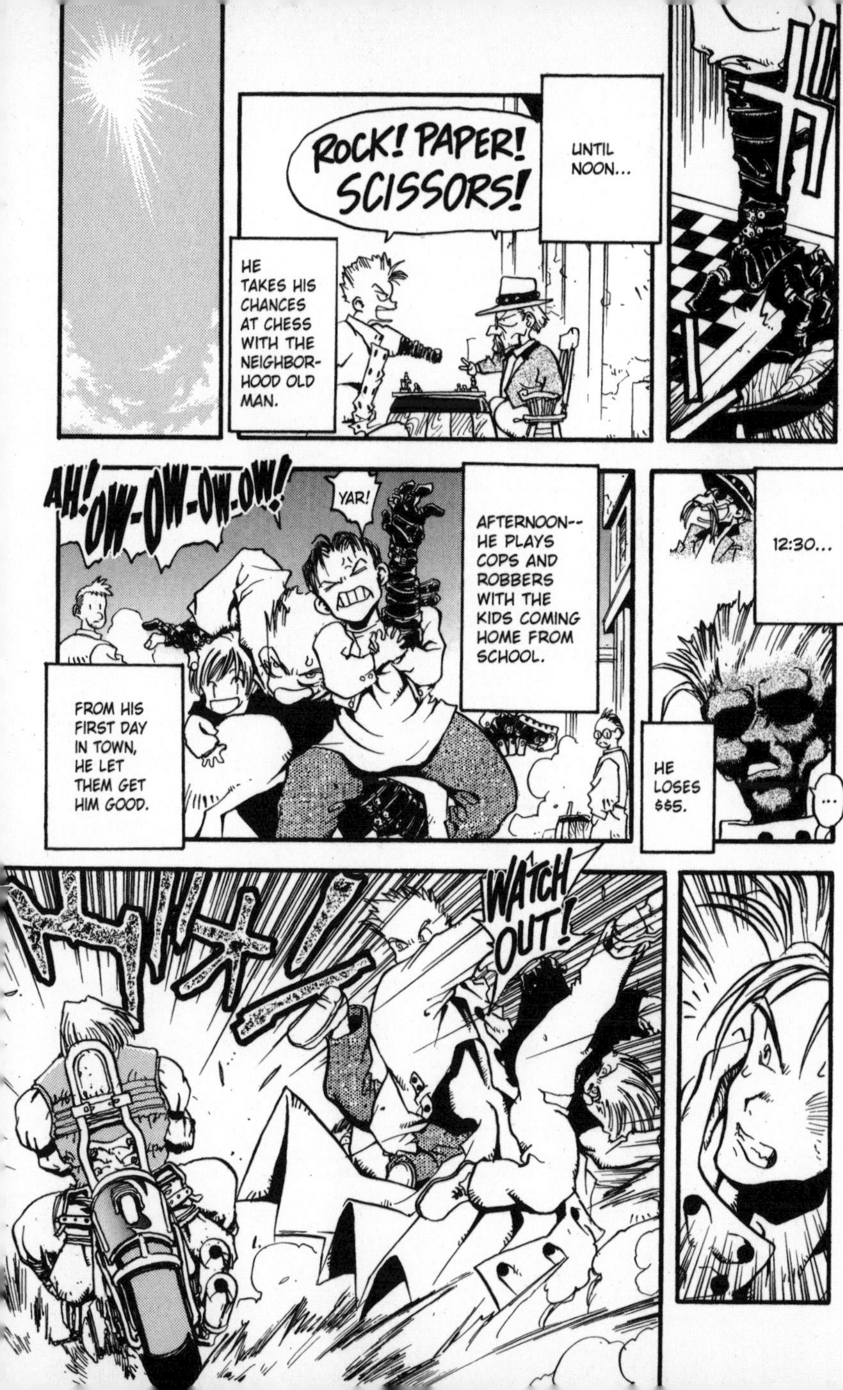
UNTIL NOON...
ROCK! PAPER! SCISSORS!
HE TAKES HIS CHANCES AT CHESS WITH THE NEIGHBORHOOD OLD MAN.
12:30...
HE LOSES $$5.
...
AFTERNOON-- HE PLAYS COPS AND ROBBERS WITH THE KIDS COMING HOME FROM SCHOOL.
YAR!
AH! OW-OW-OW-OW!
FROM HIS FIRST DAY IN TOWN, HE LET THEM GET HIM GOOD.
WATCH OUT!

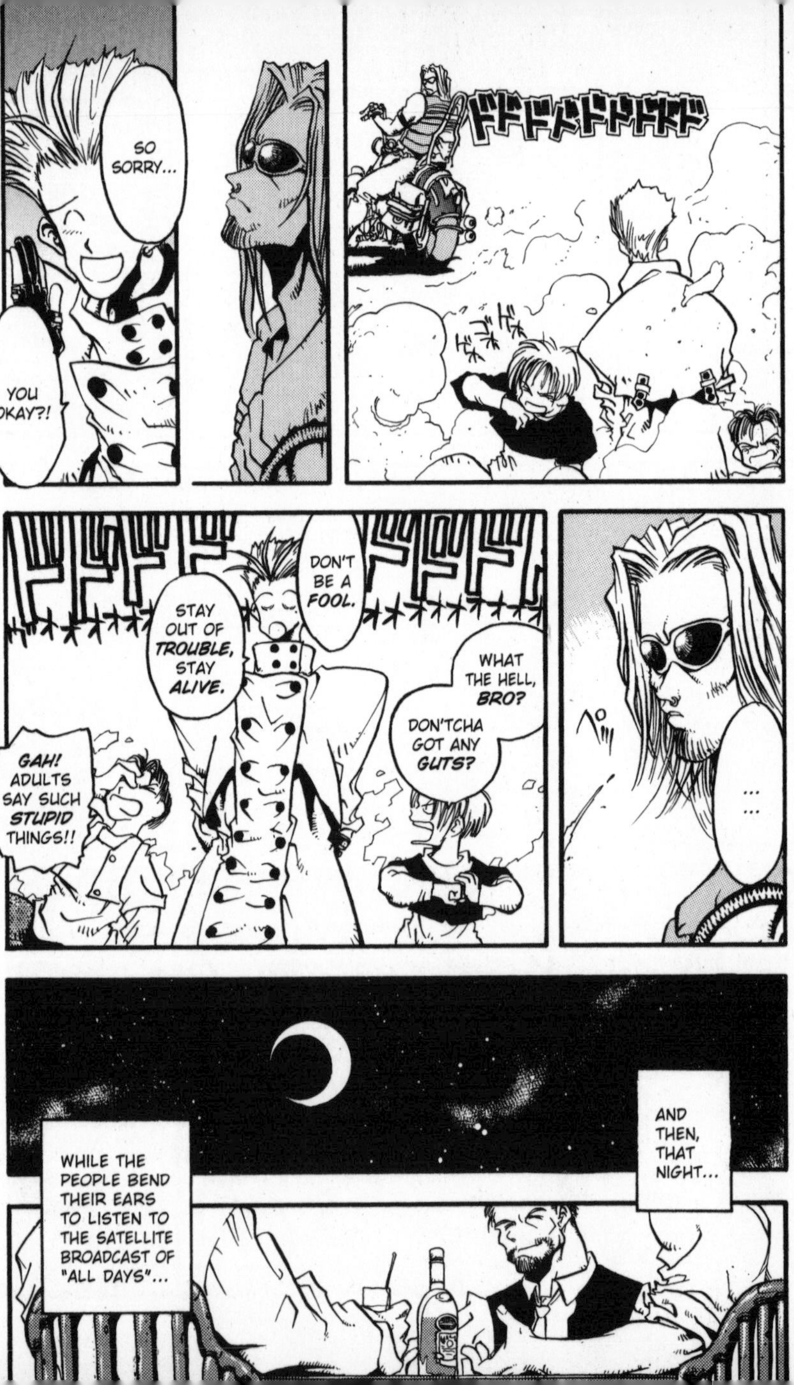
SO SORRY...
YOU OKAY?!
......
WHAT THE HELL, BRO?
DON'TCHA GOT ANY GUTS?
DON'T BE A FOOL.
STAY OUT OF TROUBLE, STAY ALIVE.
GAH! ADULTS SAY SUCH STUPID THINGS!!
AND THEN, THAT NIGHT...
WHILE THE PEOPLE BEND THEIR EARS TO LISTEN TO THE SATELLITE BROADCAST OF "ALL DAYS"...

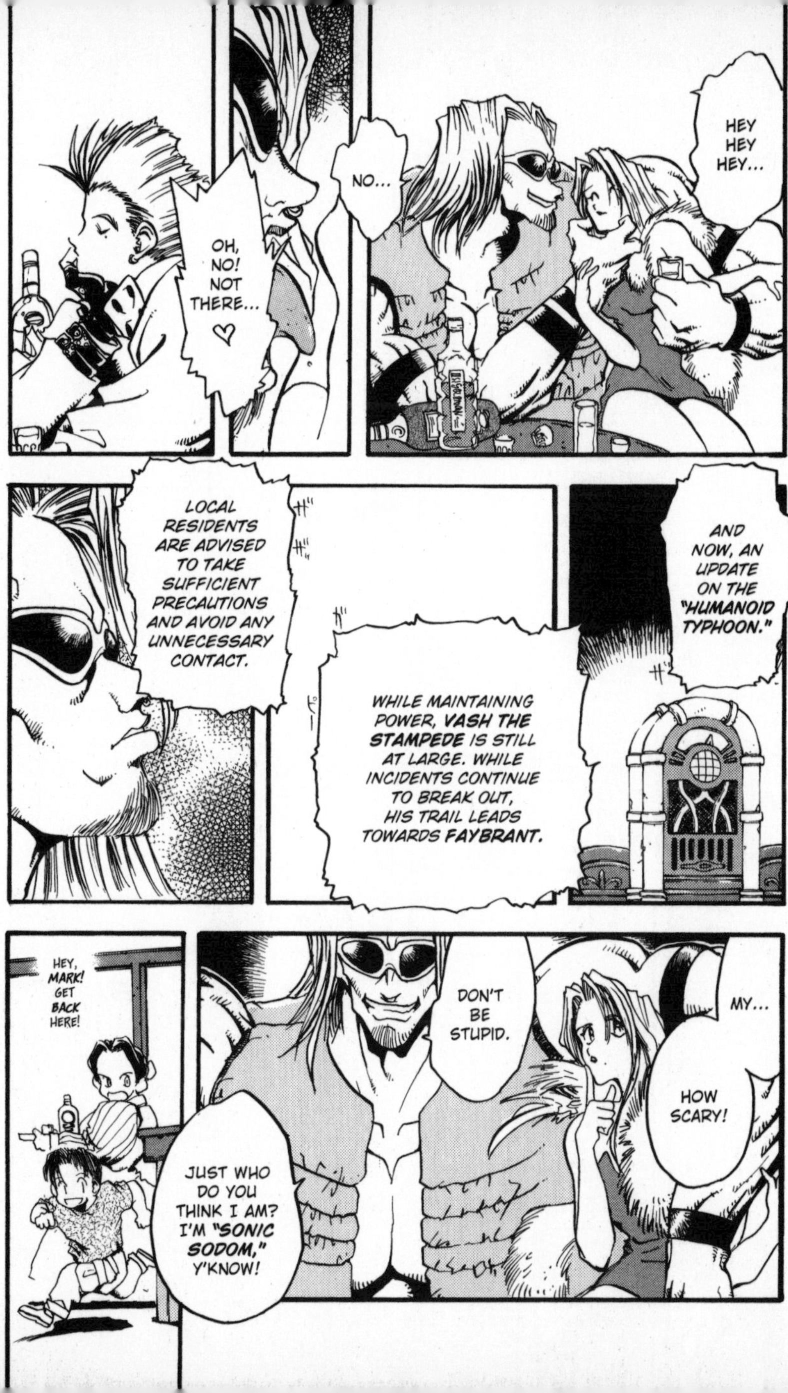
HEY HEY HEY...
NO...
OH, NO! NOT THERE... ♡
AND NOW, AN UPDATE ON THE "HUMANOID TYPHOON."
WHILE MAINTAINING POWER, VASH THE STAMPEDE IS STILL AT LARGE. WHILE INCIDENTS CONTINUE TO BREAK OUT, HIS TRAIL LEADS TOWARDS FAYBRANT.
LOCAL RESIDENTS ARE ADVISED TO TAKE SUFFICIENT PRECAUTIONS AND AVOID ANY UNNECESSARY CONTACT.
MY...
HOW SCARY!
DON'T BE STUPID.
JUST WHO DO YOU THINK I AM? I'M "SONIC SODOM," Y'KNOW!
HEY, MARK! GET BACK HERE!

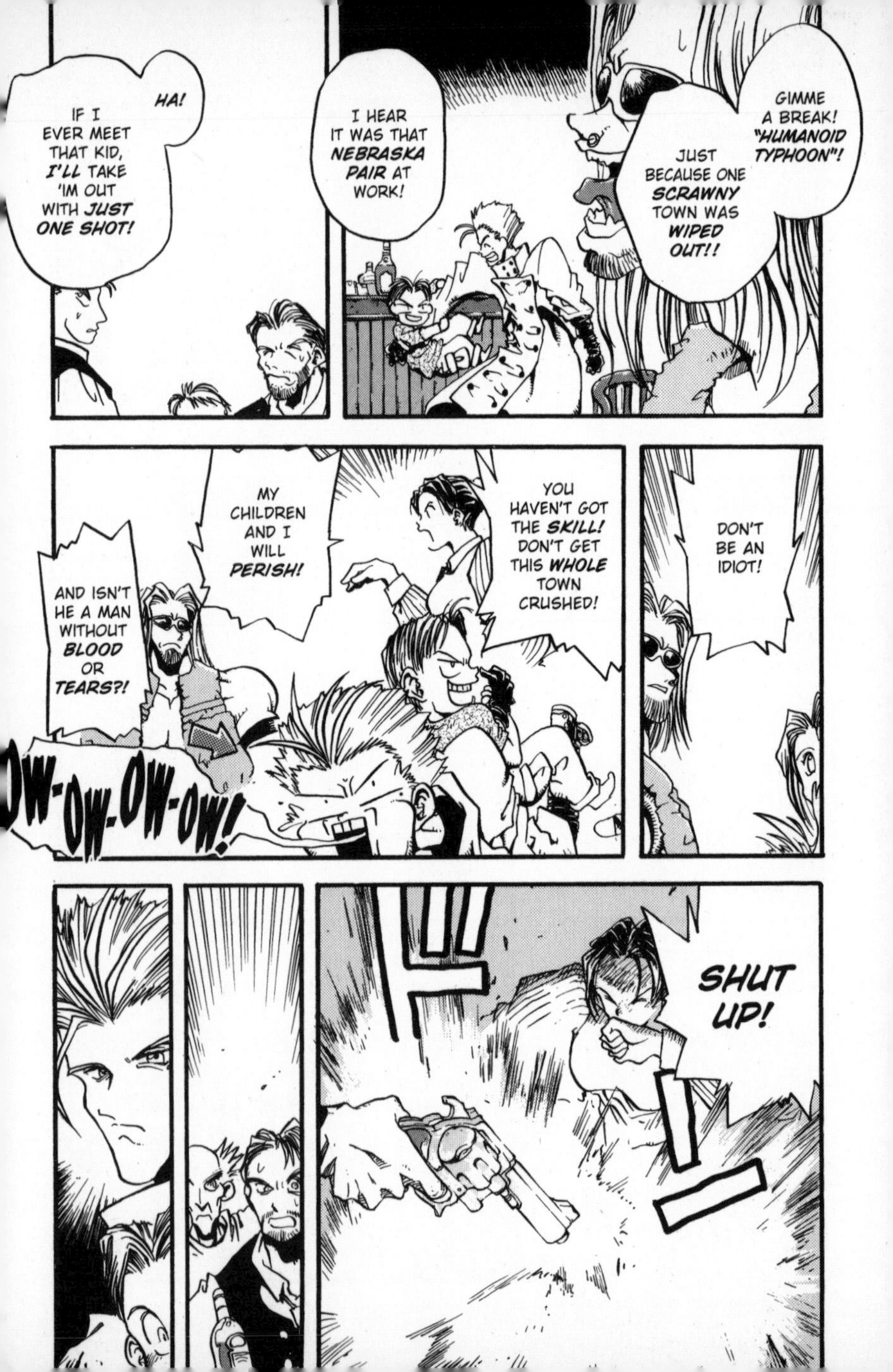
GIMME A BREAK! "HUMANOID TYPHOON"!
JUST BECAUSE ONE SCRAWNY TOWN WAS WIPED OUT!!
I HEAR IT WAS THAT NEBRASKA PAIR AT WORK!
HA! IF I EVER MEET THAT KID, I'LL TAKE 'IM OUT WITH JUST ONE SHOT!
DON'T BE AN IDIOT!
YOU HAVEN'T GOT THE SKILL! DON'T GET THIS WHOLE TOWN CRUSHED!
MY CHILDREN AND I WILL PERISH!
AND ISN'T HE A MAN WITHOUT BLOOD OR TEARS?!
OW-OW-OW-OW!
SHUT UP!

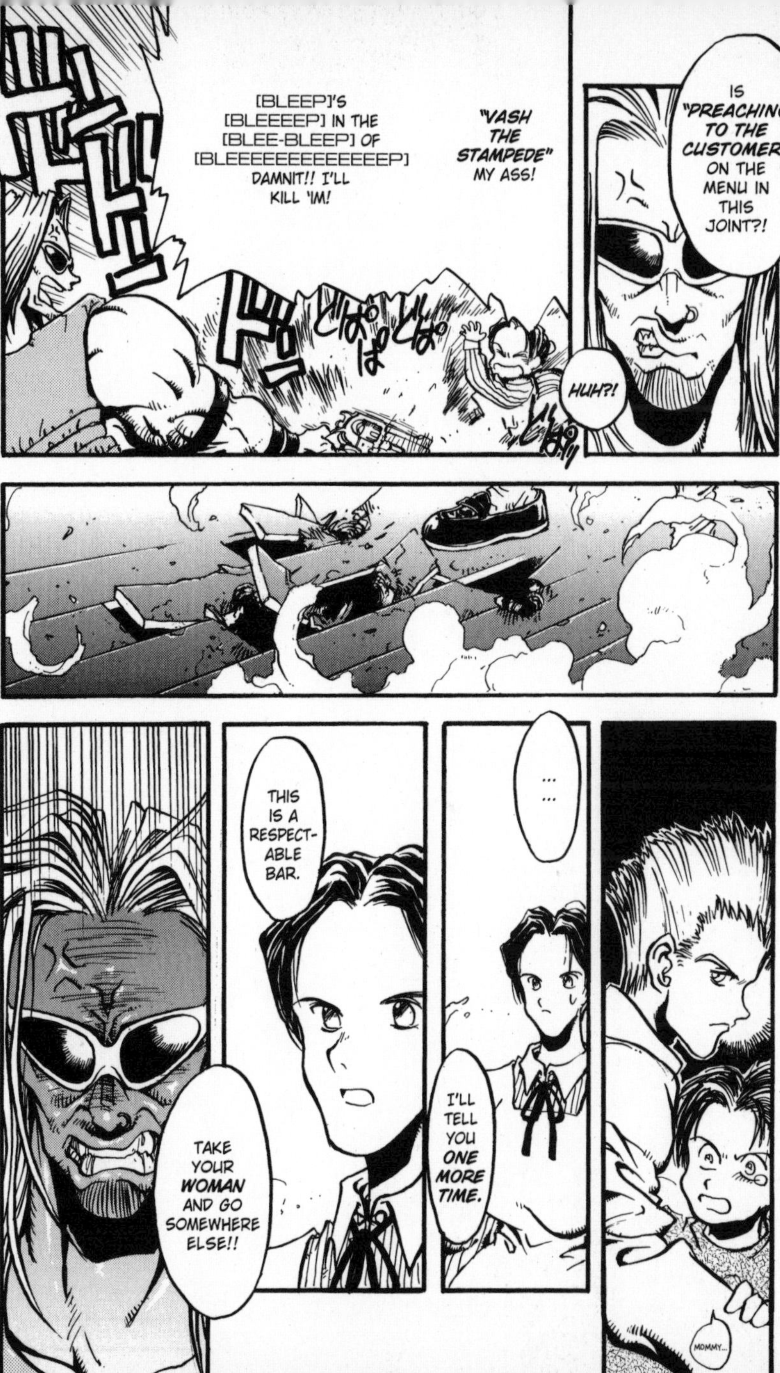

IS "PREACHING TO THE CUSTOMER" ON THE MENU IN THIS JOINT?!
HUH?!
"VASH THE STAMPEDE" MY ASS!
[BLEEP]'s [BLEEEEP] IN THE [BLEE-BLEEP] OF [BLEEEEEEEEEEEEEEP] DAMNIT!! I'LL KILL 'IM!
MOMMY...
... ...
I'LL TELL YOU ONE MORE TIME.
THIS IS A RESPECTABLE BAR.
TAKE YOUR WOMAN AND GO SOMEWHERE ELSE!!

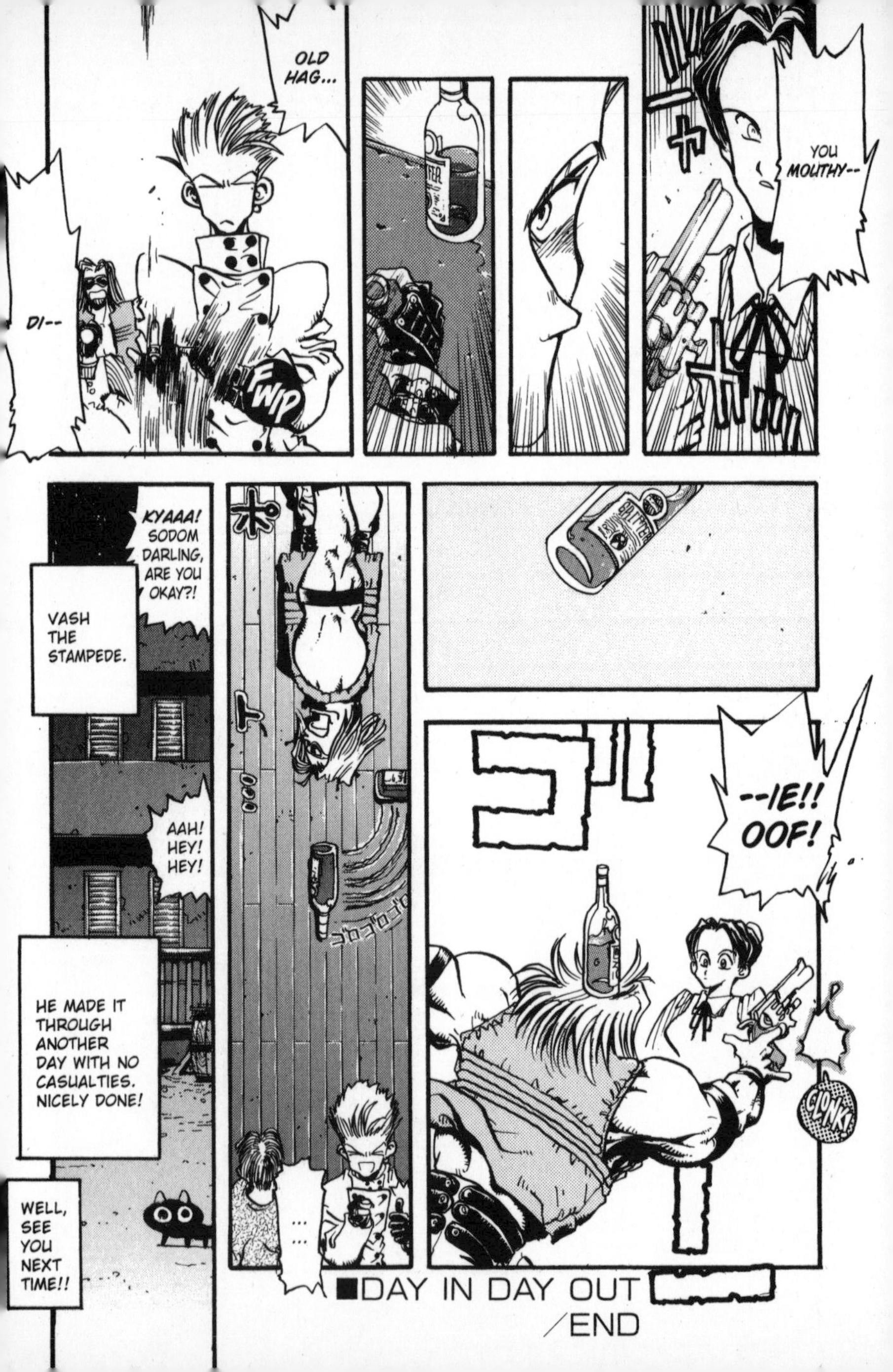
YOU MOUTHY--
OLD HAG...
FWIP
DI--
--IE!! OOF!
CLONK!
...
...
KYAAA! SODOM DARLING, ARE YOU OKAY?!
VASH THE STAMPEDE.
AAH! HEY! HEY!
HE MADE IT THROUGH ANOTHER DAY WITH NO CASUALTIES. NICELY DONE!
WELL, SEE YOU NEXT TIME!!

■DAY IN DAY OUT
/END

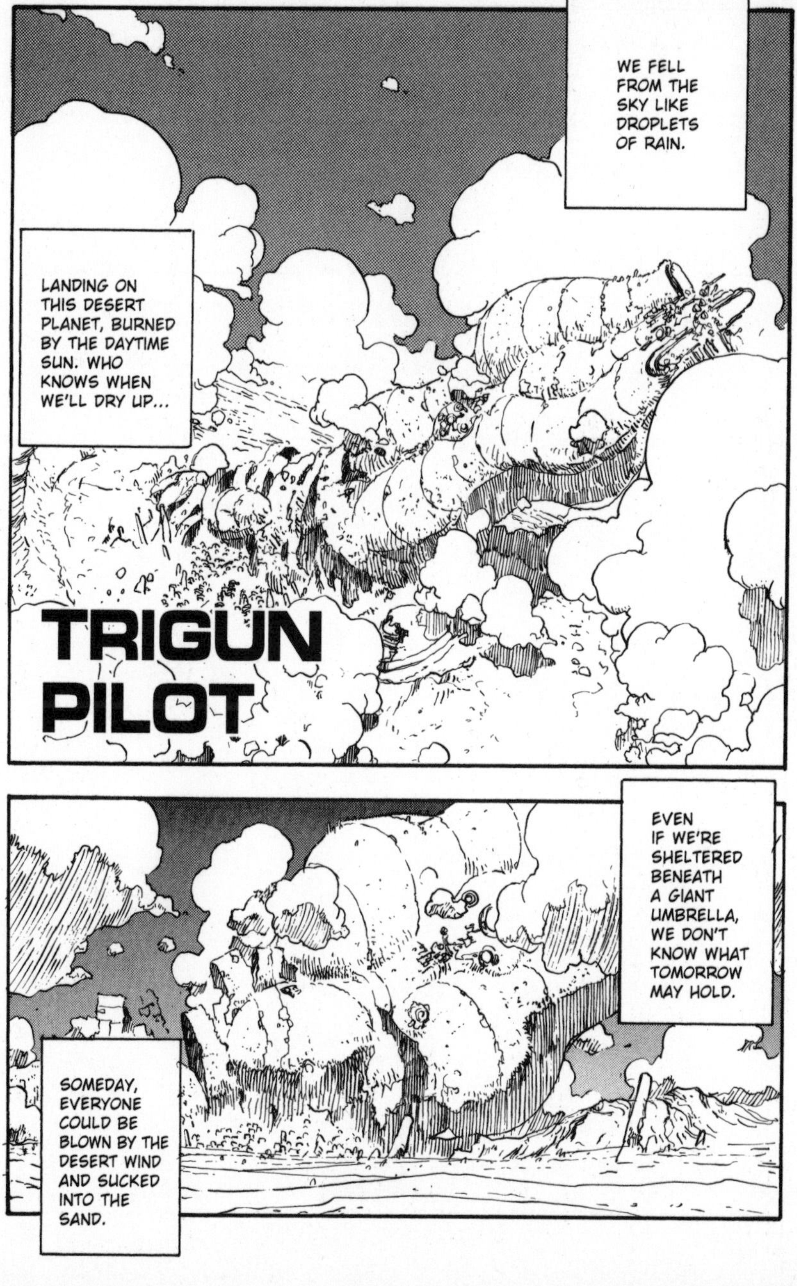
WE FELL FROM THE SKY LIKE DROPLETS OF RAIN.
LANDING ON THIS DESERT PLANET, BURNED BY THE DAYTIME SUN. WHO KNOWS WHEN WE'LL DRY UP...
TRIGUN PILOT
EVEN IF WE'RE SHELTERED BENEATH A GIANT UMBRELLA, WE DON'T KNOW WHAT TOMORROW MAY HOLD.
SOMEDAY, EVERYONE COULD BE BLOWN BY THE DESERT WIND AND SUCKED INTO THE SAND.

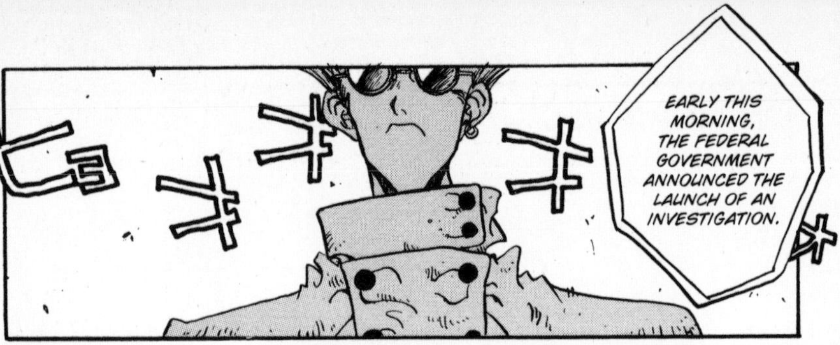
EARLY THIS MORNING, THE FEDERAL GOVERNMENT ANNOUNCED THE LAUNCH OF AN INVESTIGATION.

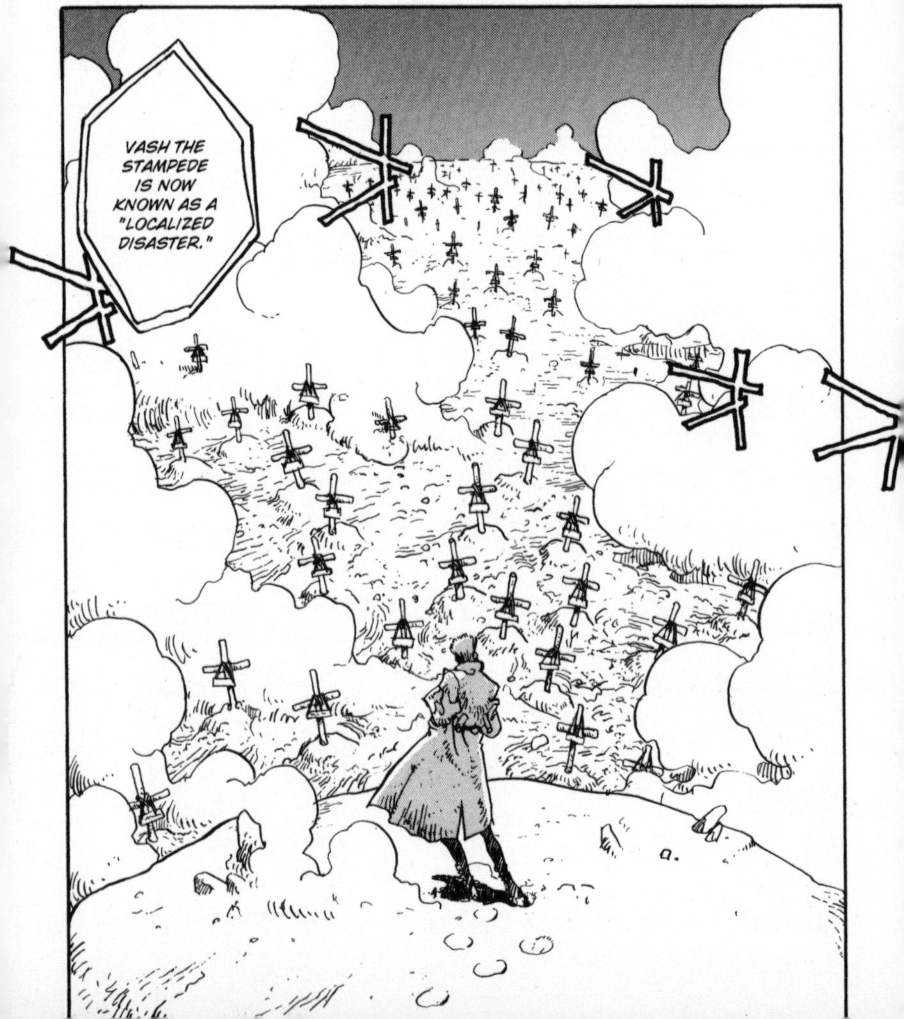
VASH THE STAMPEDE IS NOW KNOWN AS A "LOCALIZED DISASTER."

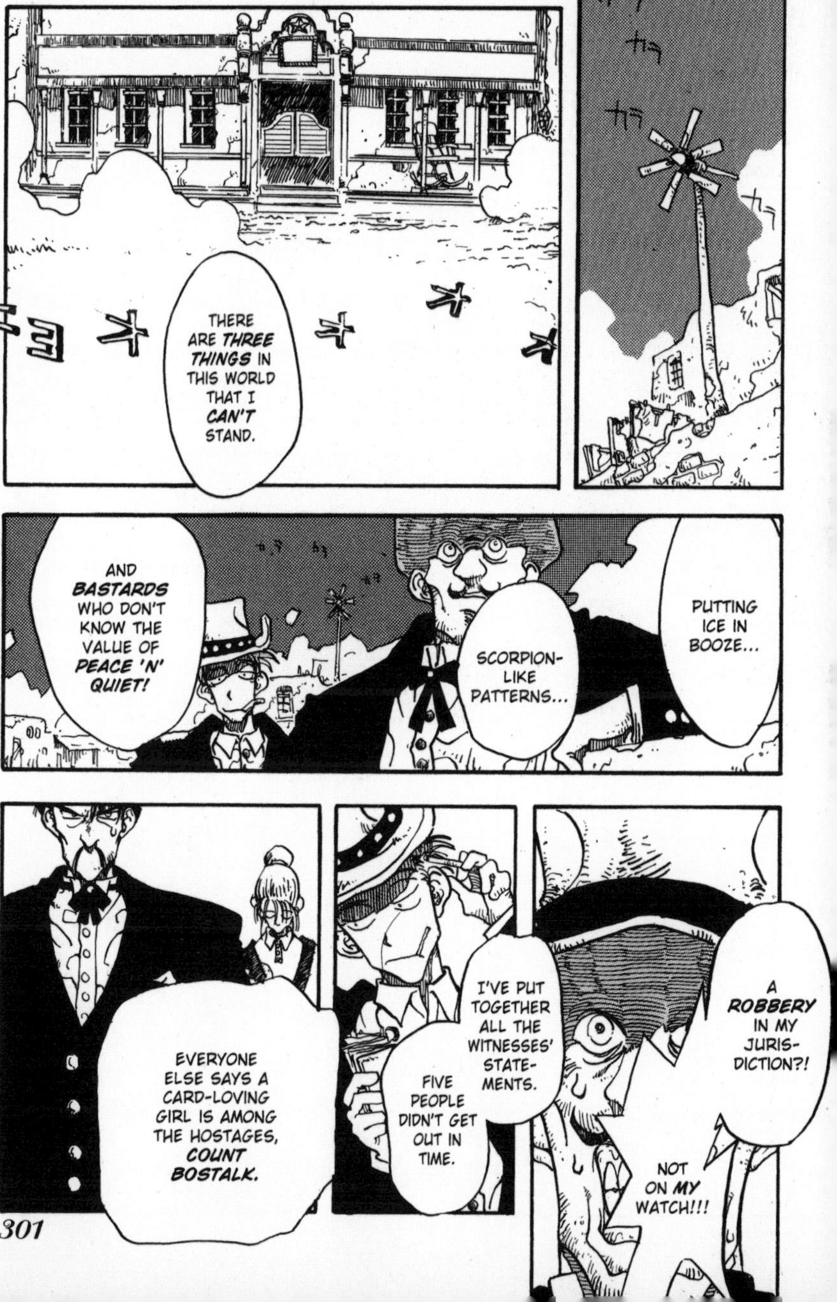
THERE ARE **THREE THINGS** IN THIS WORLD THAT I **CAN'T** STAND.
PUTTING ICE IN BOOZE...
SCORPION-LIKE PATTERNS...
AND **BASTARDS** WHO DON'T KNOW THE VALUE OF **PEACE 'N' QUIET!**
A **ROBBERY** IN MY JURIS-DICTION?!
NOT ON **MY** WATCH!!!
I'VE PUT TOGETHER ALL THE WITNESSES' STATE-MENTS.
FIVE PEOPLE DIDN'T GET OUT IN TIME.
EVERYONE ELSE SAYS A CARD-LOVING GIRL IS AMONG THE HOSTAGES, **COUNT BOSTALK.**

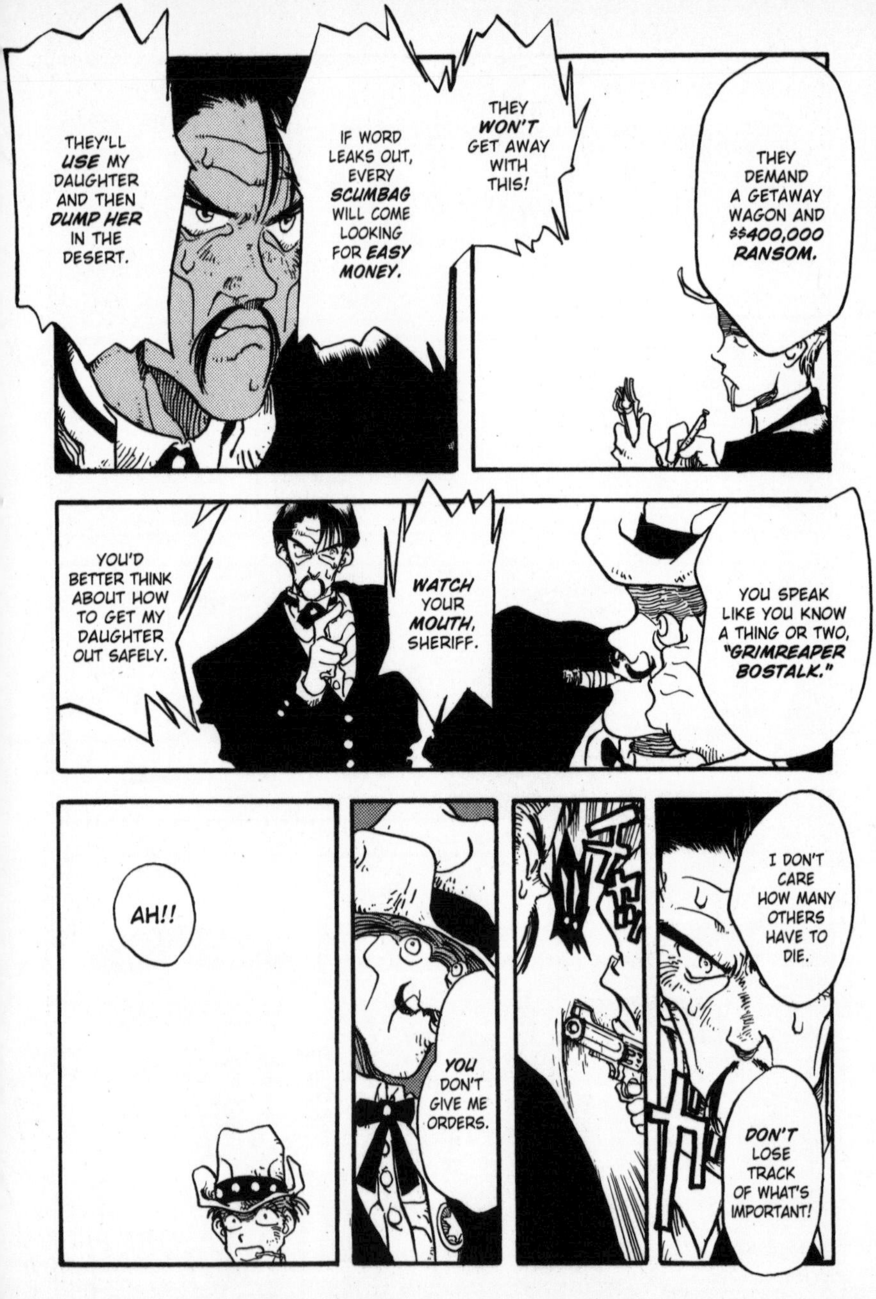
THEY DEMAND A GETAWAY WAGON AND $$400,000 RANSOM.
THEY WON'T GET AWAY WITH THIS!
IF WORD LEAKS OUT, EVERY SCUMBAG WILL COME LOOKING FOR EASY MONEY.
THEY'LL USE MY DAUGHTER AND THEN DUMP HER IN THE DESERT.
YOU SPEAK LIKE YOU KNOW A THING OR TWO, "GRIMREAPER BOSTALK."
WATCH YOUR MOUTH, SHERIFF.
YOU'D BETTER THINK ABOUT HOW TO GET MY DAUGHTER OUT SAFELY.
I DON'T CARE HOW MANY OTHERS HAVE TO DIE.
DON'T LOSE TRACK OF WHAT'S IMPORTANT!
YOU DON'T GIVE ME ORDERS.
AH!!

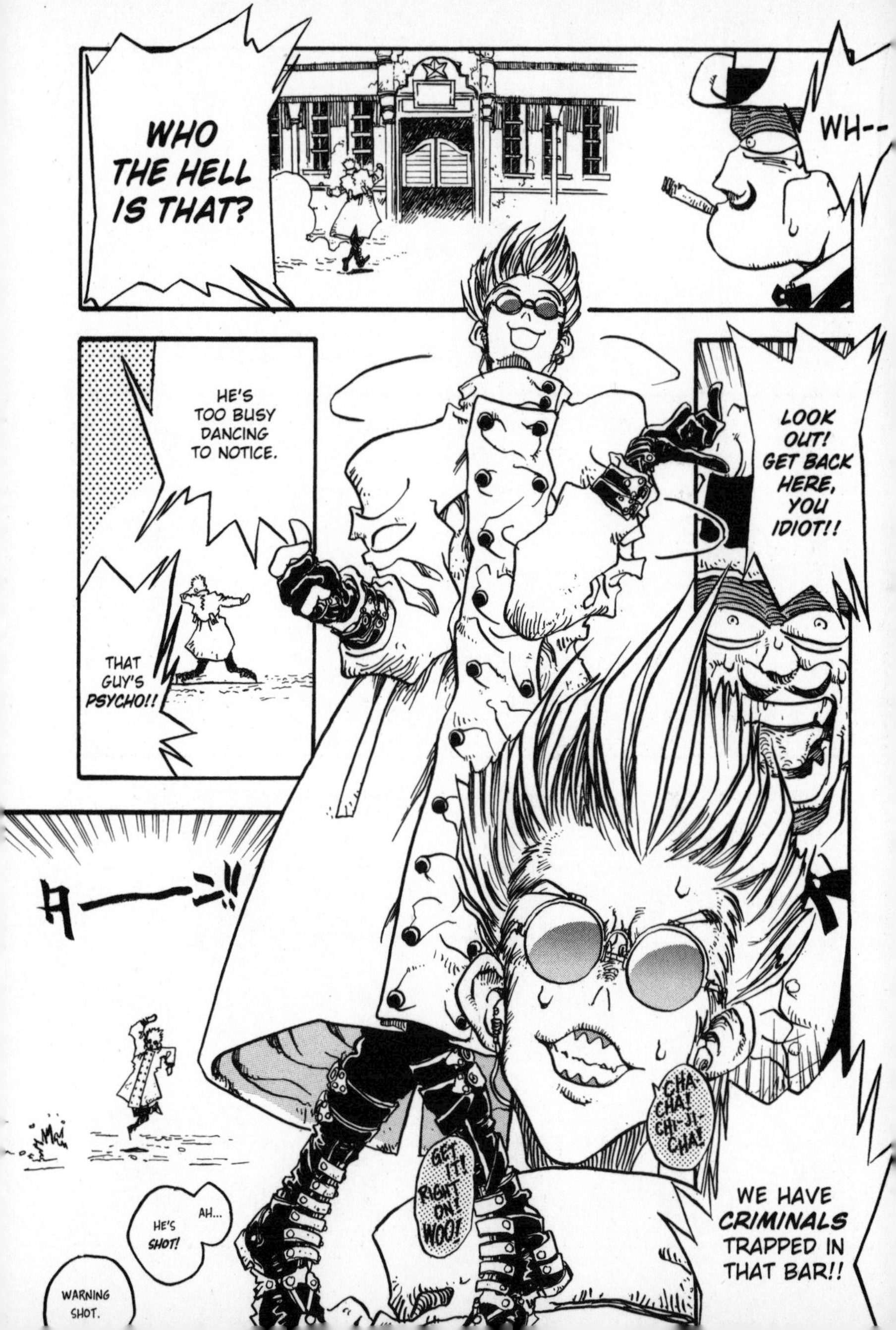
WH--
WHO THE HELL IS THAT?
LOOK OUT! GET BACK HERE, YOU IDIOT!!
HE'S TOO BUSY DANCING TO NOTICE.
THAT GUY'S PSYCHO!!
WE HAVE CRIMINALS TRAPPED IN THAT BAR!!
CHA CHA! CHI-JI-CHA!
GET IT! RIGHT ON! WOO!
ターーーン!!
AH...
HE'S SHOT!
WARNING SHOT.

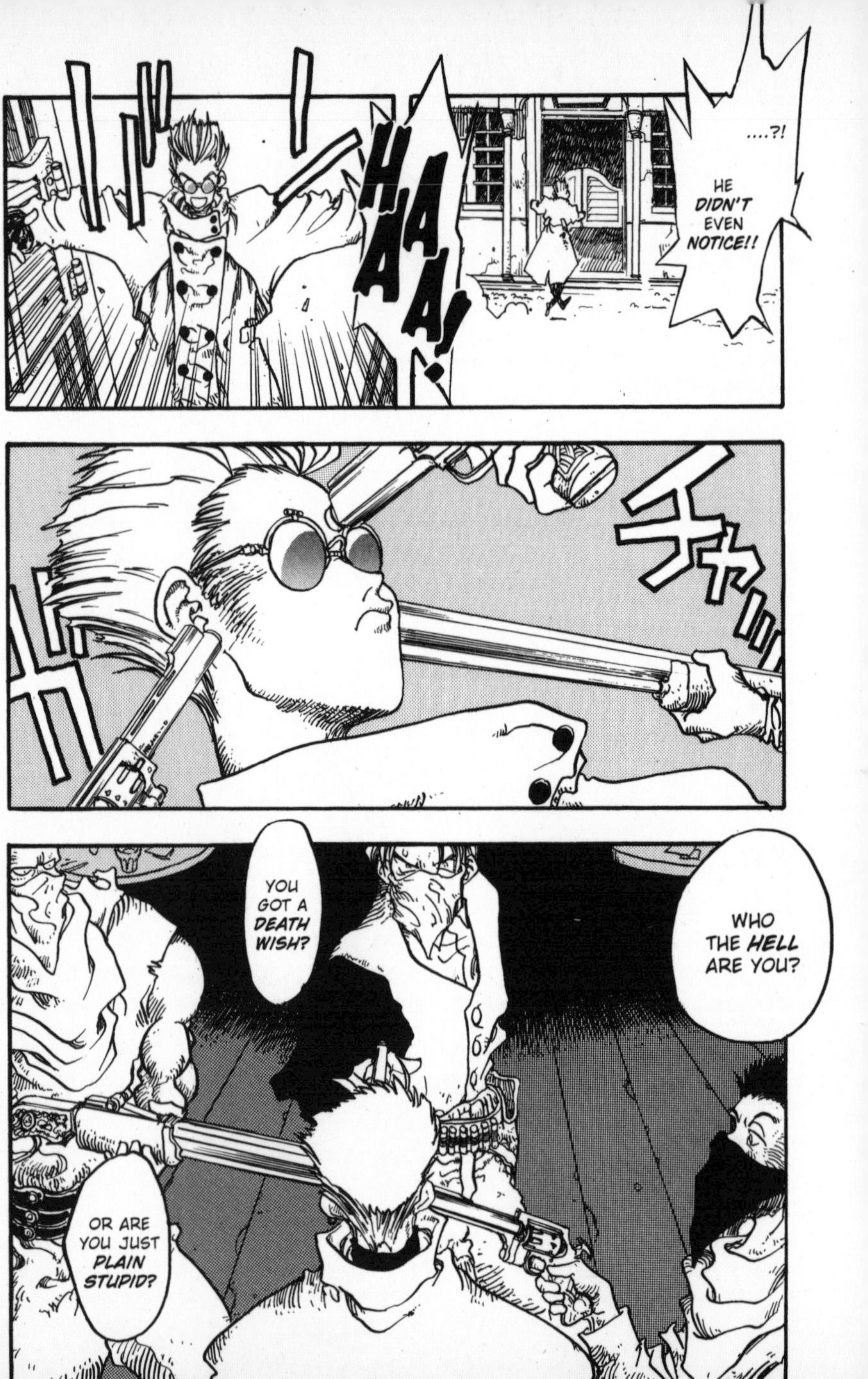
....?!
HE DIDN'T EVEN NOTICE!!
HAAA!
WHO THE HELL ARE YOU?
YOU GOT A DEATH WISH?
OR ARE YOU JUST PLAIN STUPID?

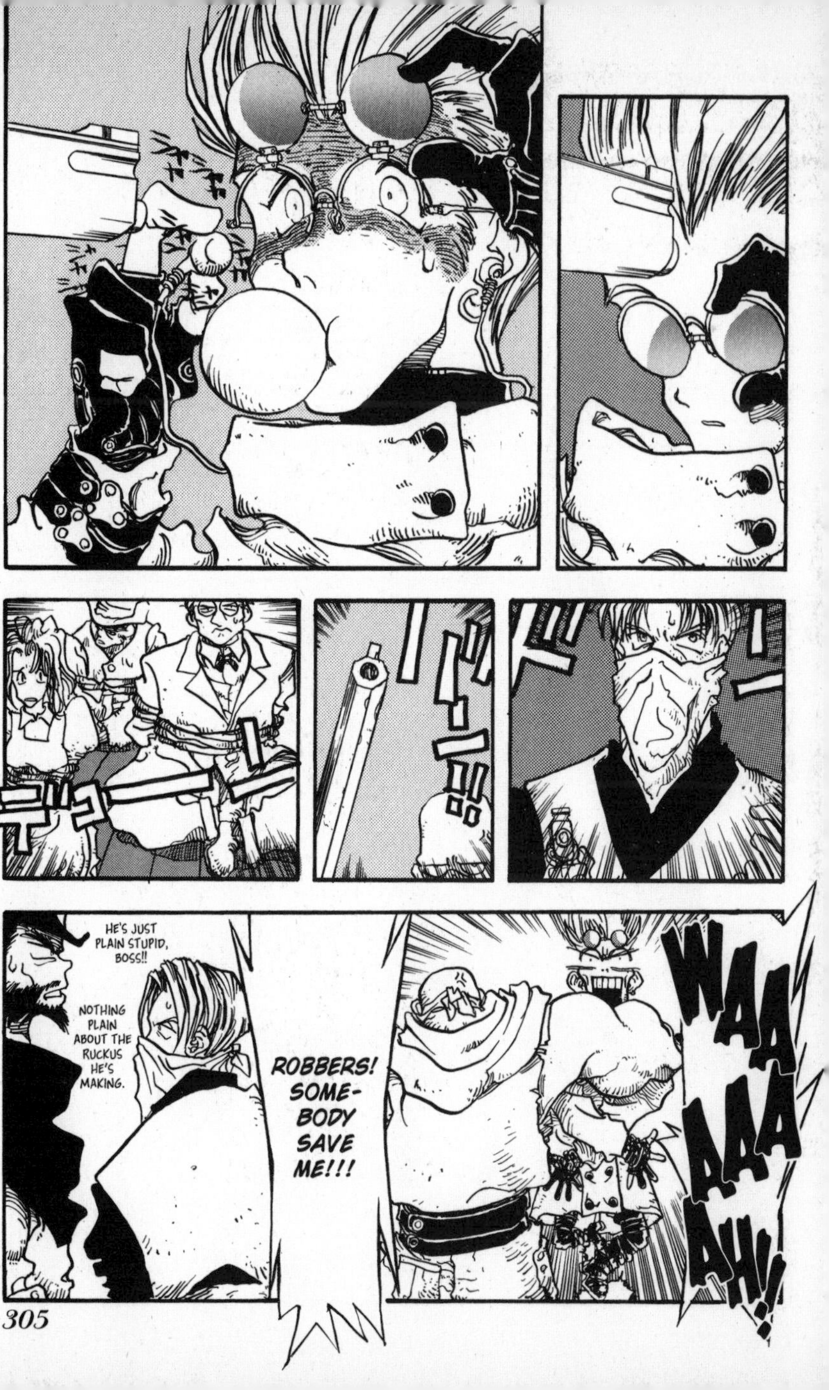
WAAAAAAAH!!
ROBBERS! SOME-BODY SAVE ME!!!
HE'S JUST PLAIN STUPID, BOSS!!
NOTHING PLAIN ABOUT THE RUCKUS HE'S MAKING.

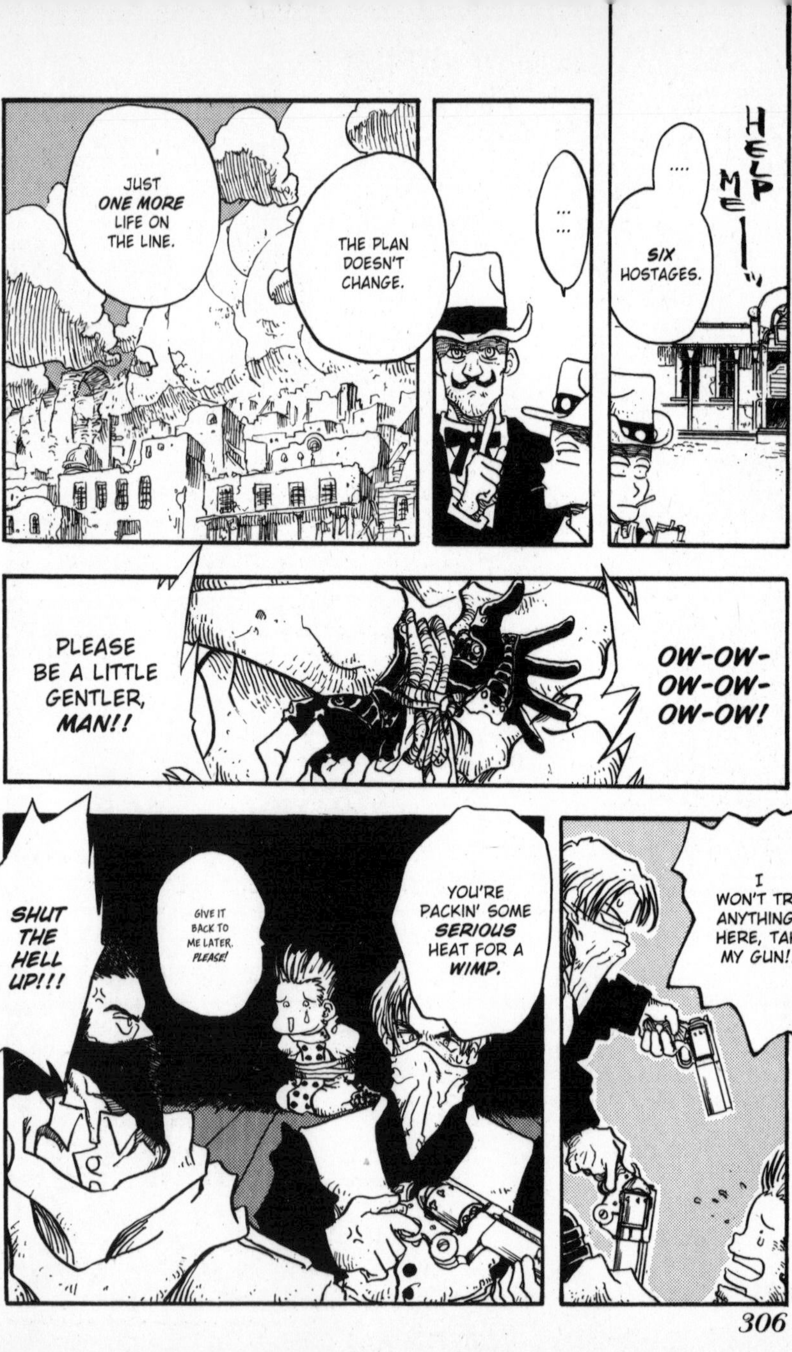

HELP ME—!!
....
SIX HOSTAGES.
... ...
THE PLAN DOESN'T CHANGE.
JUST ONE MORE LIFE ON THE LINE.
OW-OW-OW-OW-OW-OW!
PLEASE BE A LITTLE GENTLER, MAN!!
I WON'T TRY ANYTHING! HERE, TAKE MY GUN!!
YOU'RE PACKIN' SOME SERIOUS HEAT FOR A WIMP.
GIVE IT BACK TO ME LATER. PLEASE!
SHUT THE HELL UP!!!

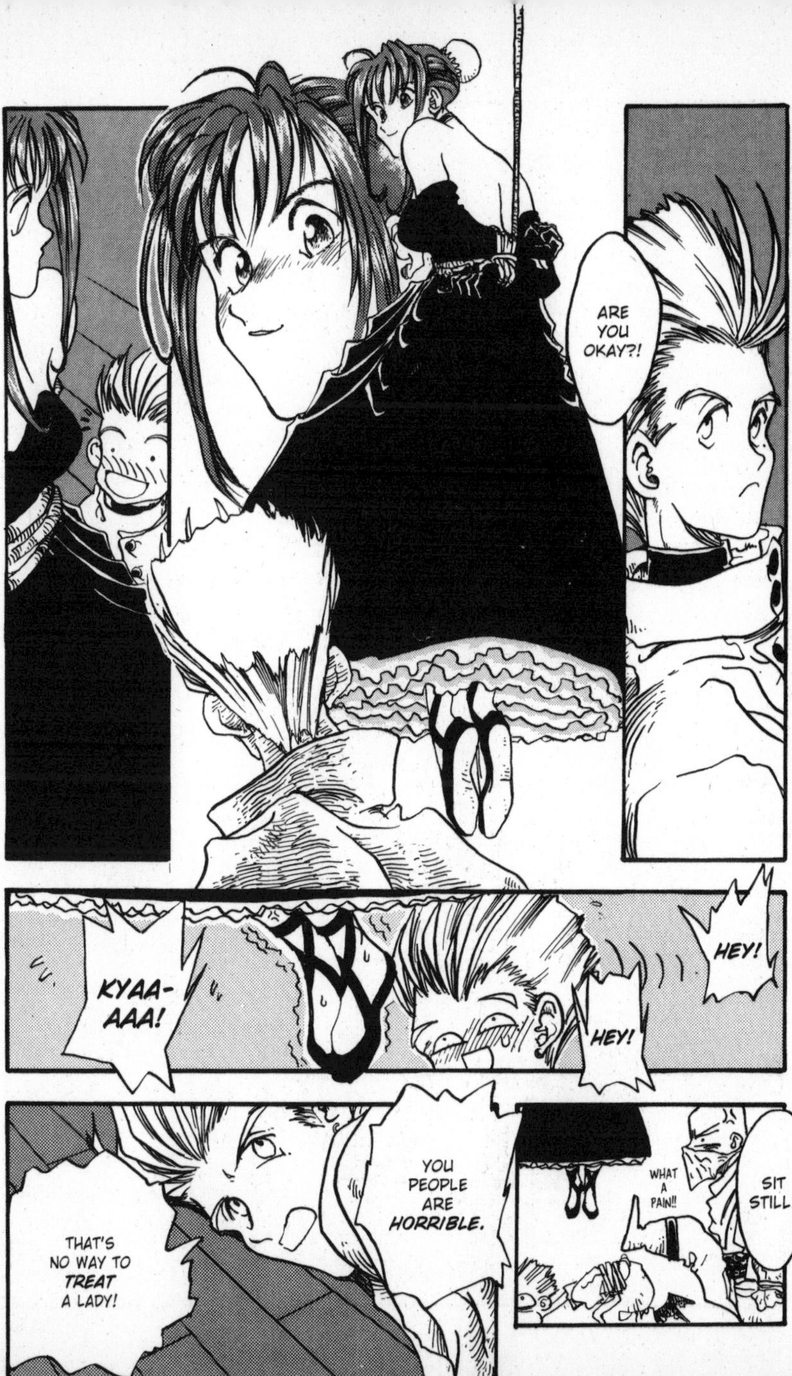
ARE YOU OKAY?!
HEY!
HEY!
KYAA-AAA!
SIT STILL!
WHAT A PAIN!!
YOU PEOPLE ARE HORRIBLE.
THAT'S NO WAY TO TREAT A LADY!

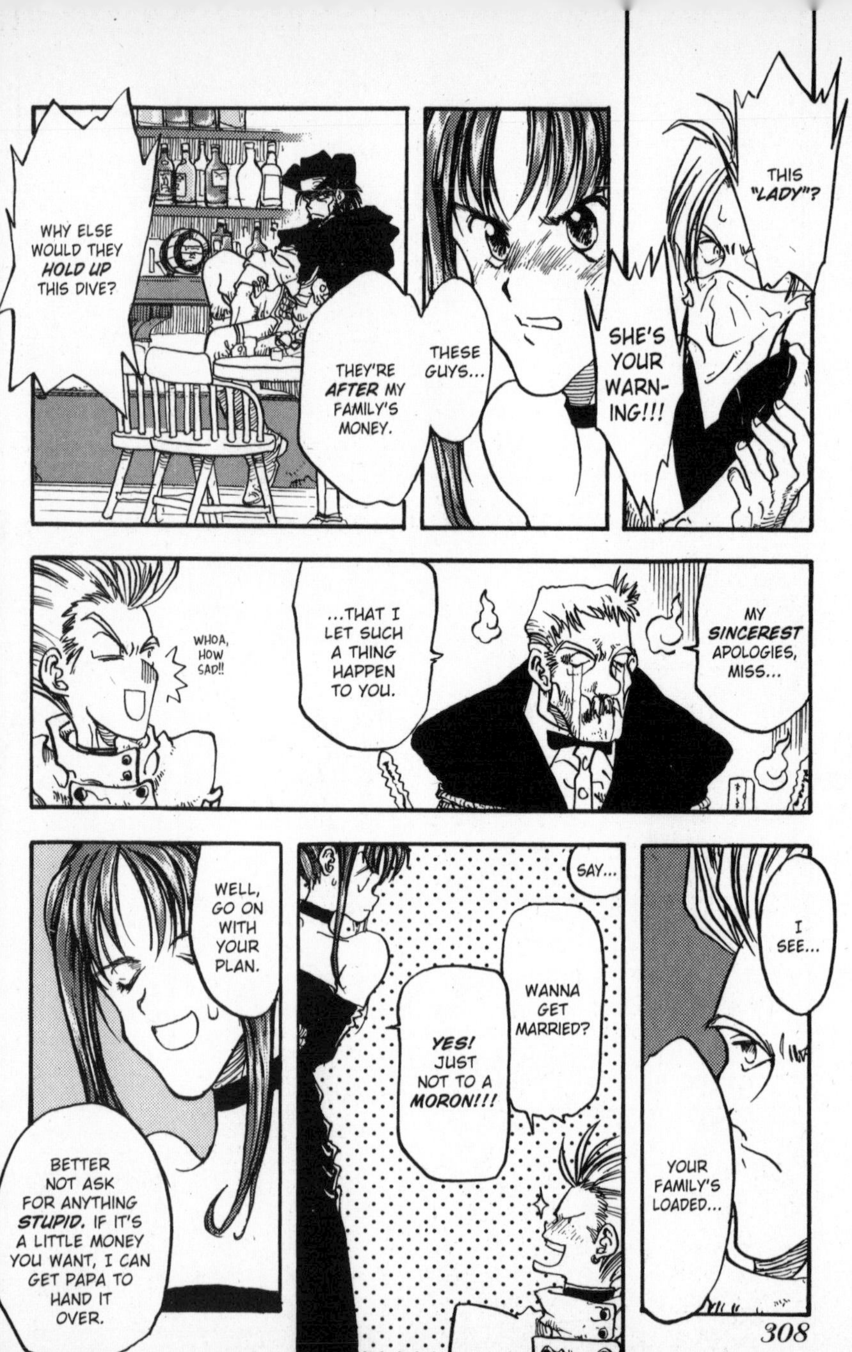

THIS "LADY"?
SHE'S YOUR WARNING!!!
THESE GUYS...
THEY'RE AFTER MY FAMILY'S MONEY.
WHY ELSE WOULD THEY HOLD UP THIS DIVE?
MY SINCEREST APOLOGIES, MISS...
...THAT I LET SUCH A THING HAPPEN TO YOU.
WHOA, HOW SAD!!
I SEE...
YOUR FAMILY'S LOADED...
SAY...
WANNA GET MARRIED?
YES! JUST NOT TO A MORON!!!
WELL, GO ON WITH YOUR PLAN.
BETTER NOT ASK FOR ANYTHING STUPID. IF IT'S A LITTLE MONEY YOU WANT, I CAN GET PAPA TO HAND IT OVER.

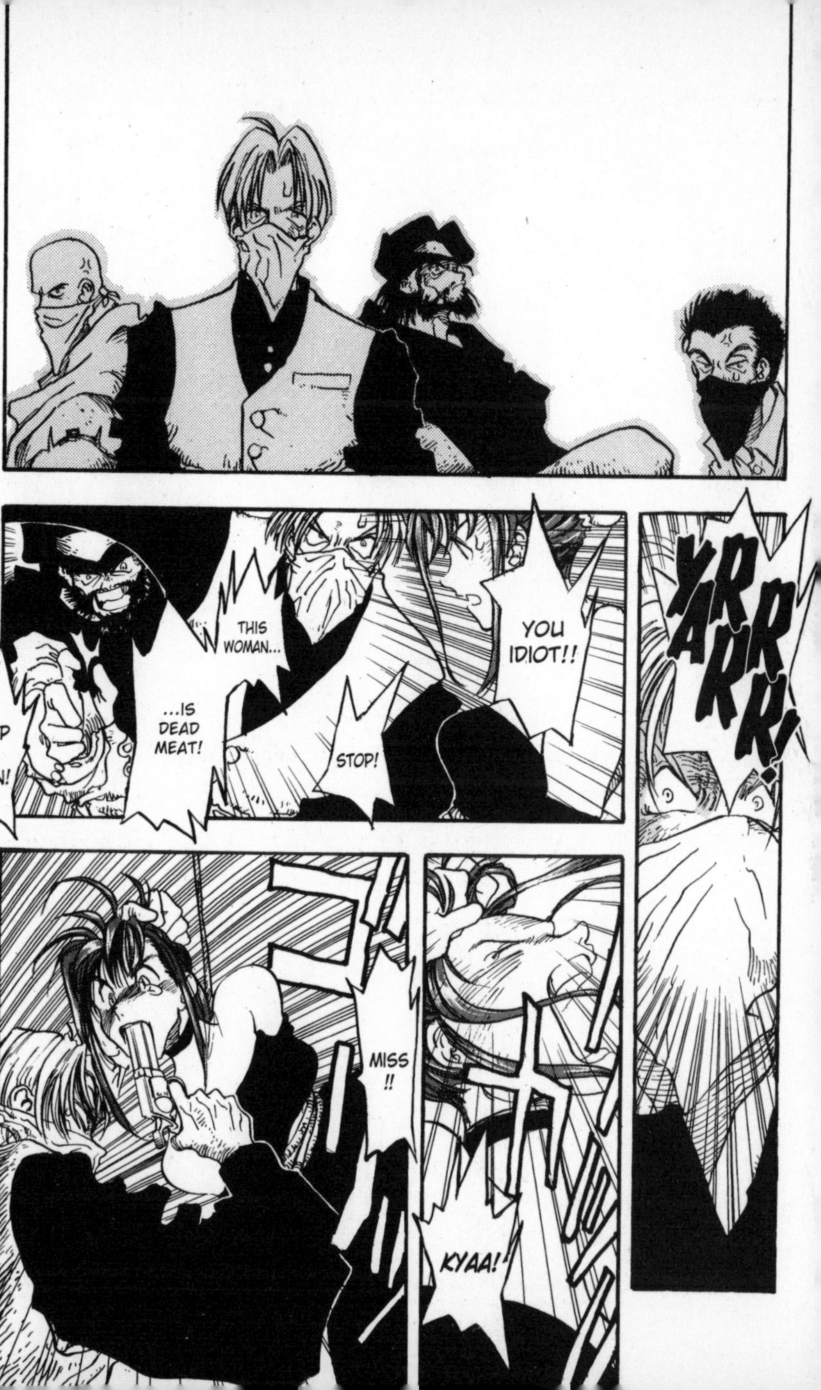
YARRRRR!
YOU IDIOT!!
THIS WOMAN...
STOP!
...IS DEAD MEAT!
STOP IT, JEAN!
KYAA!
MISS!!

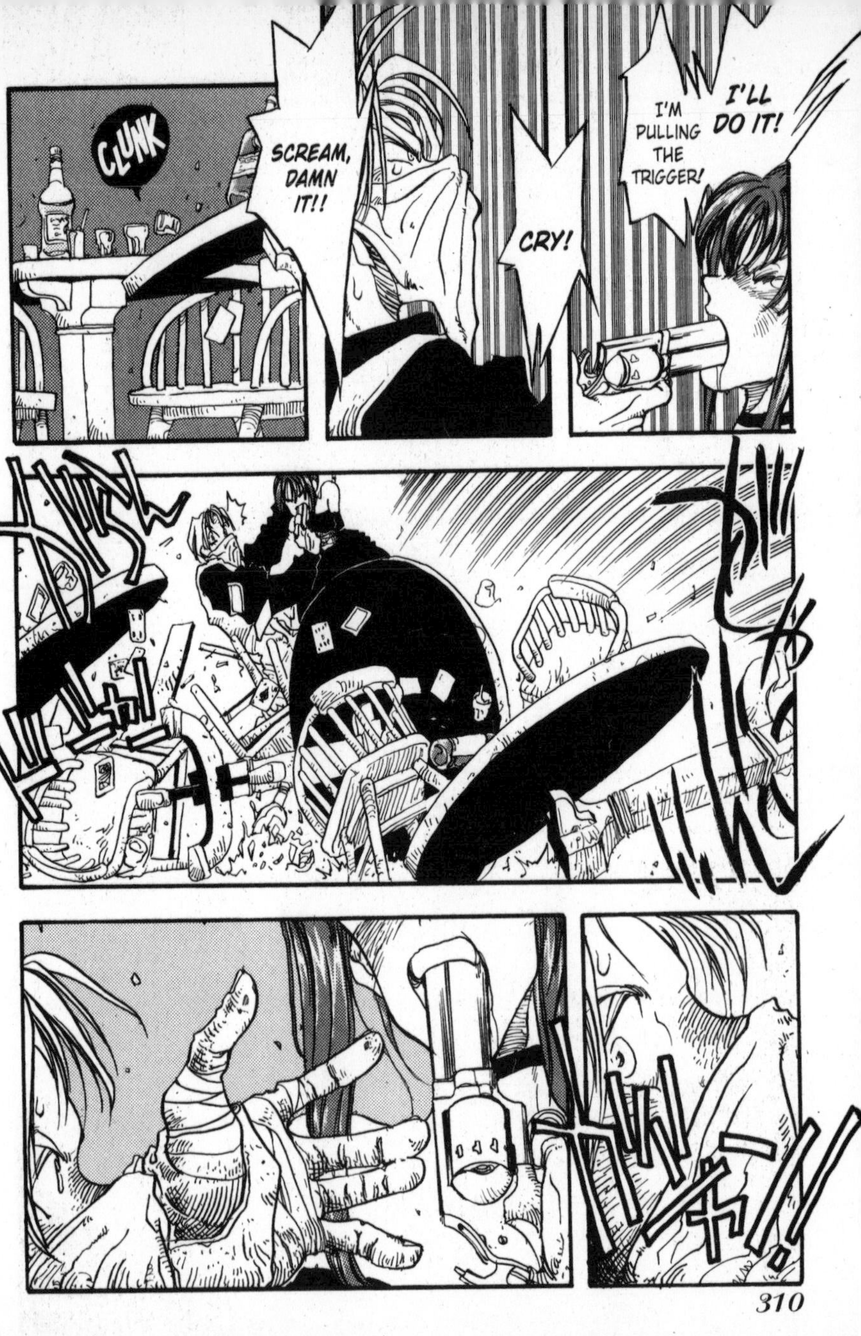
I'LL DO IT!
I'M PULLING THE TRIGGER!
SCREAM, DAMN IT!!
CRY!
CLUNK

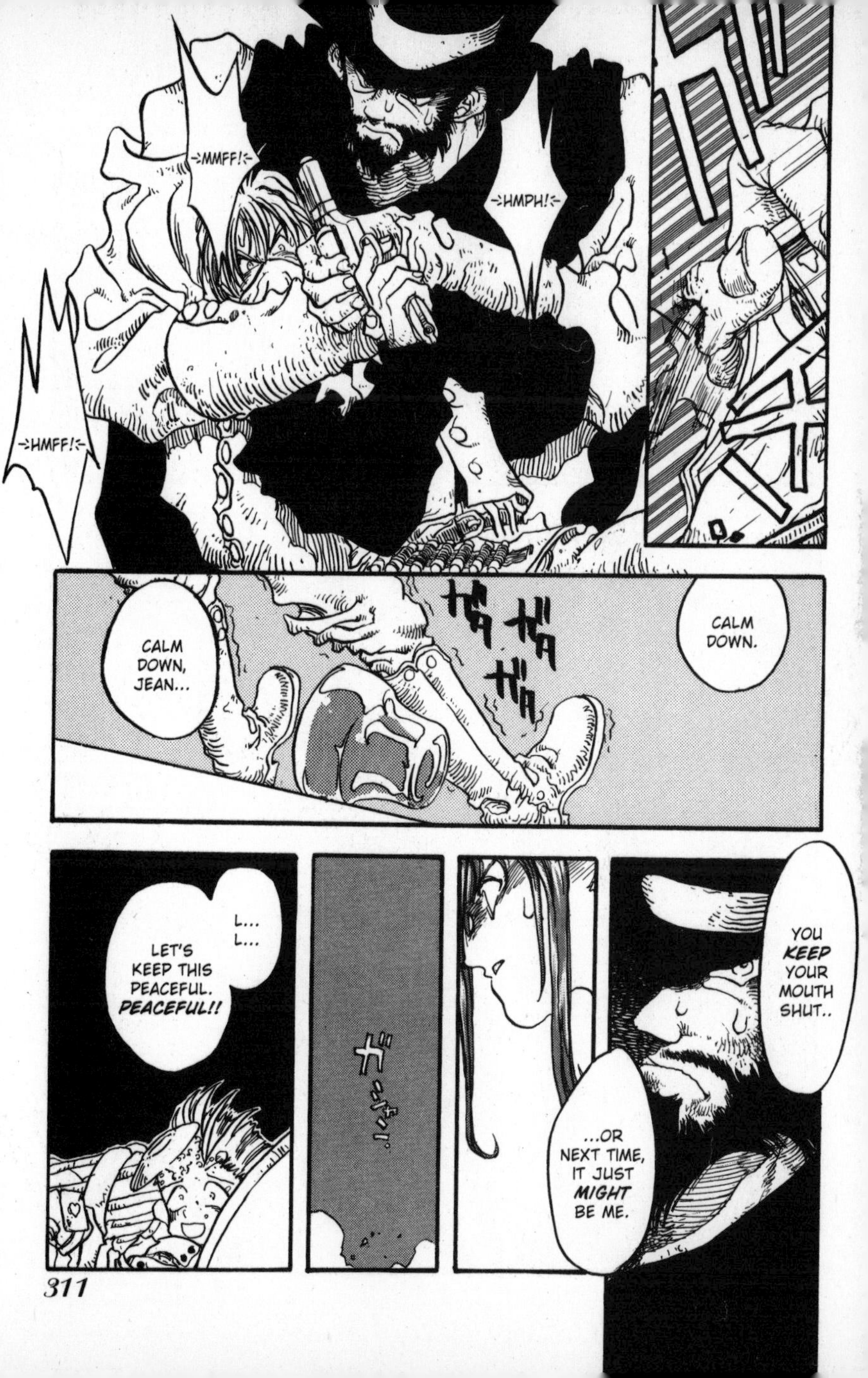

HMPH!
MMFF!
HMFF!
CALM DOWN.
CALM DOWN, JEAN...
ガタ ガタ ガタ
YOU **KEEP** YOUR MOUTH SHUT..
...OR NEXT TIME, IT JUST **MIGHT** BE ME.
L... L...
LET'S KEEP THIS PEACEFUL. ***PEACEFUL!!***

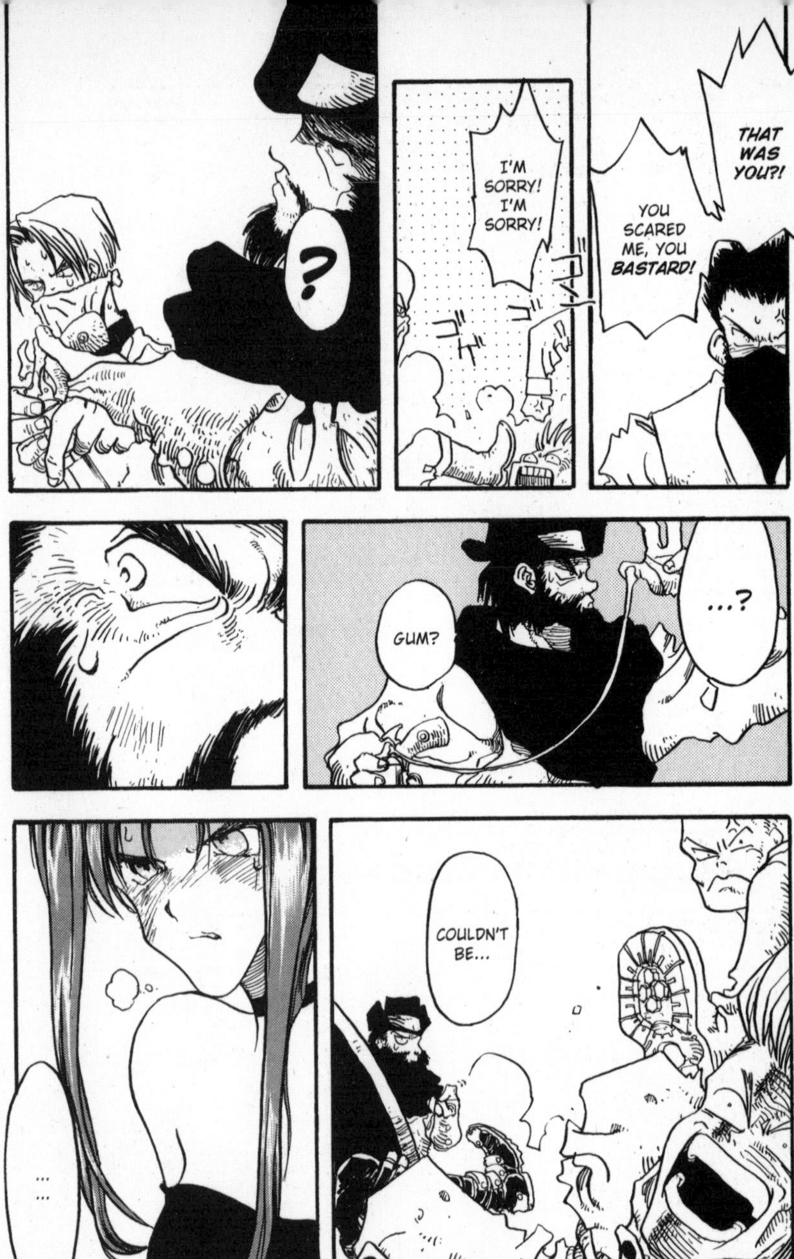
THAT WAS YOU?!
YOU SCARED ME, YOU BASTARD!
I'M SORRY! I'M SORRY!
?
...?
GUM?
COULDN'T BE...
... ...

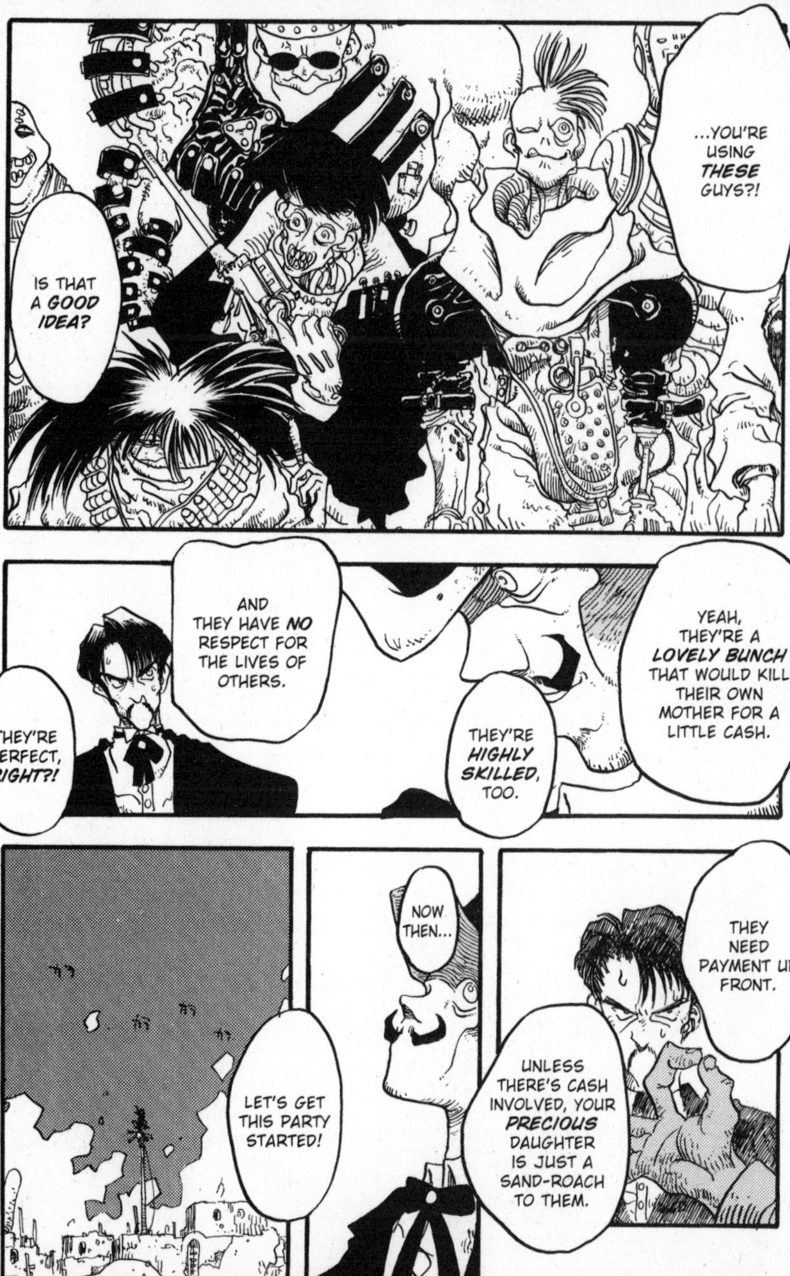
...YOU'RE USING THESE GUYS?!
IS THAT A GOOD IDEA?
YEAH, THEY'RE A LOVELY BUNCH THAT WOULD KILL THEIR OWN MOTHER FOR A LITTLE CASH.
THEY'RE HIGHLY SKILLED, TOO.
AND THEY HAVE NO RESPECT FOR THE LIVES OF OTHERS.
THEY'RE PERFECT, RIGHT?!
THEY NEED PAYMENT UP FRONT.
UNLESS THERE'S CASH INVOLVED, YOUR PRECIOUS DAUGHTER IS JUST A SAND-ROACH TO THEM.
NOW THEN...
LET'S GET THIS PARTY STARTED!

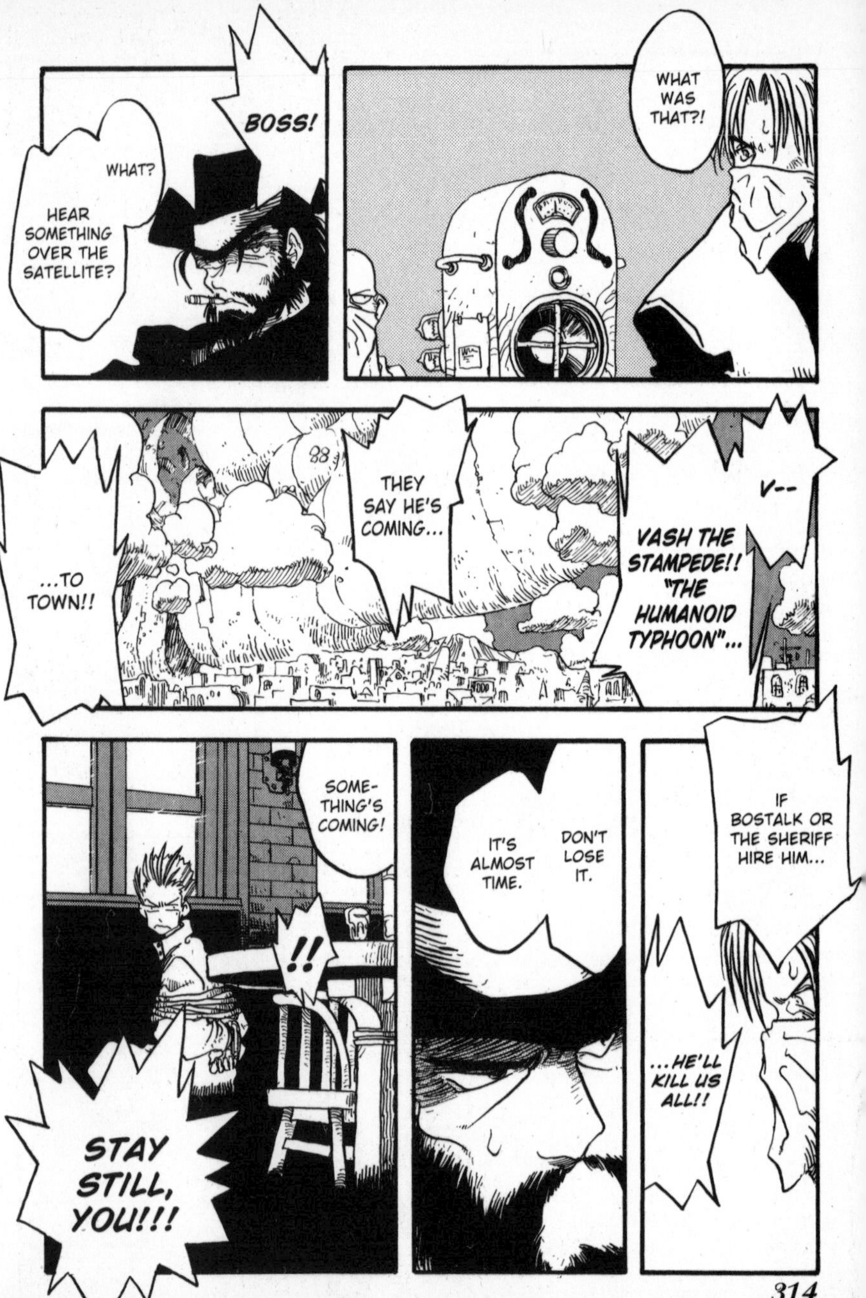
WHAT WAS THAT?!
BOSS!
WHAT? HEAR SOMETHING OVER THE SATELLITE?
V--
VASH THE STAMPEDE!! "THE HUMANOID TYPHOON"...
THEY SAY HE'S COMING...
...TO TOWN!!
IF BOSTALK OR THE SHERIFF HIRE HIM...
...HE'LL KILL US ALL!!
DON'T LOSE IT. IT'S ALMOST TIME.
SOME-THING'S COMING!
!!
STAY STILL, YOU!!!

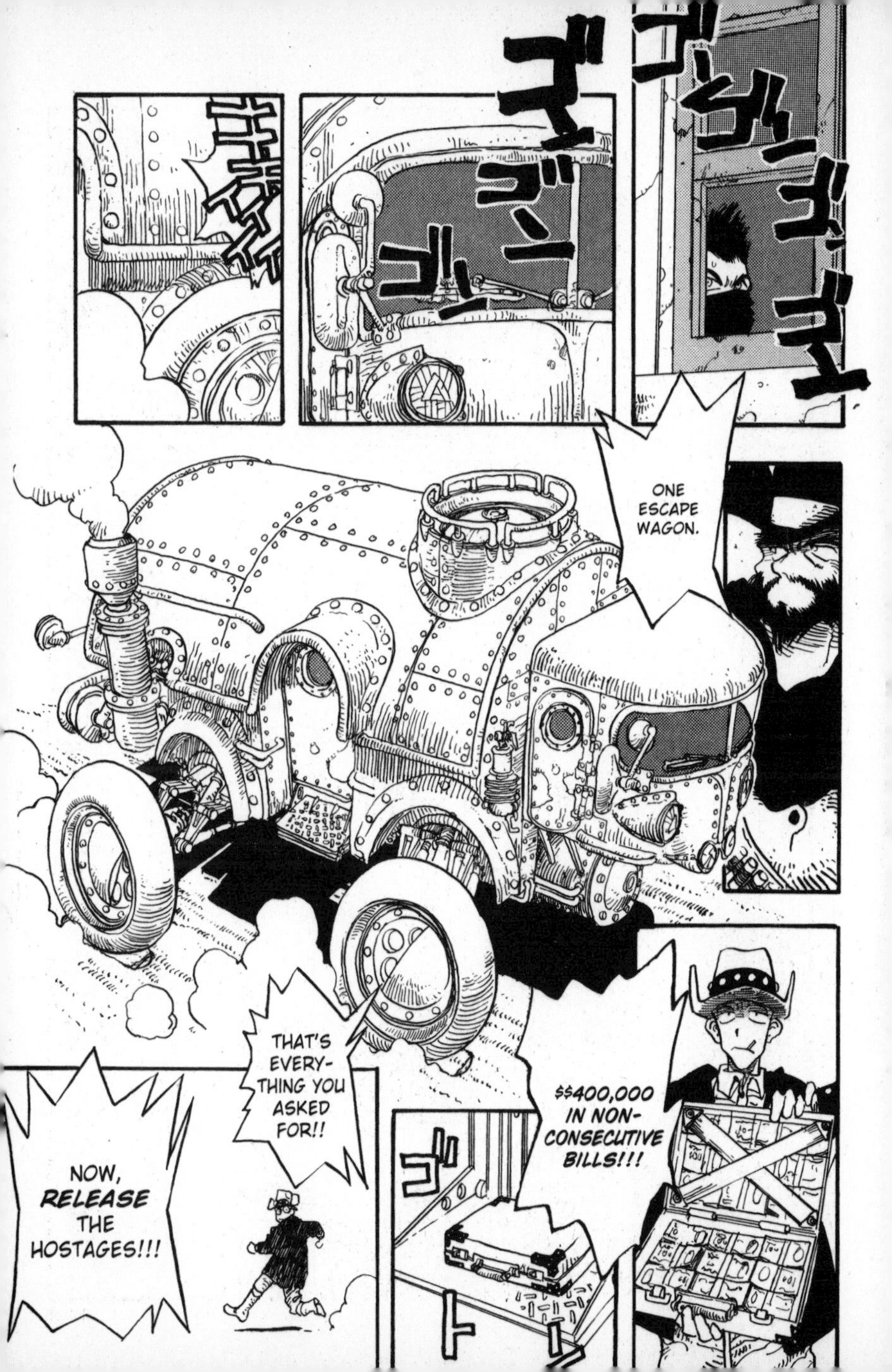
ONE ESCAPE WAGON.
THAT'S EVERYTHING YOU ASKED FOR!!
$$400,000 IN NON-CONSECUTIVE BILLS!!!
ゴト
NOW, RELEASE THE HOSTAGES!!!

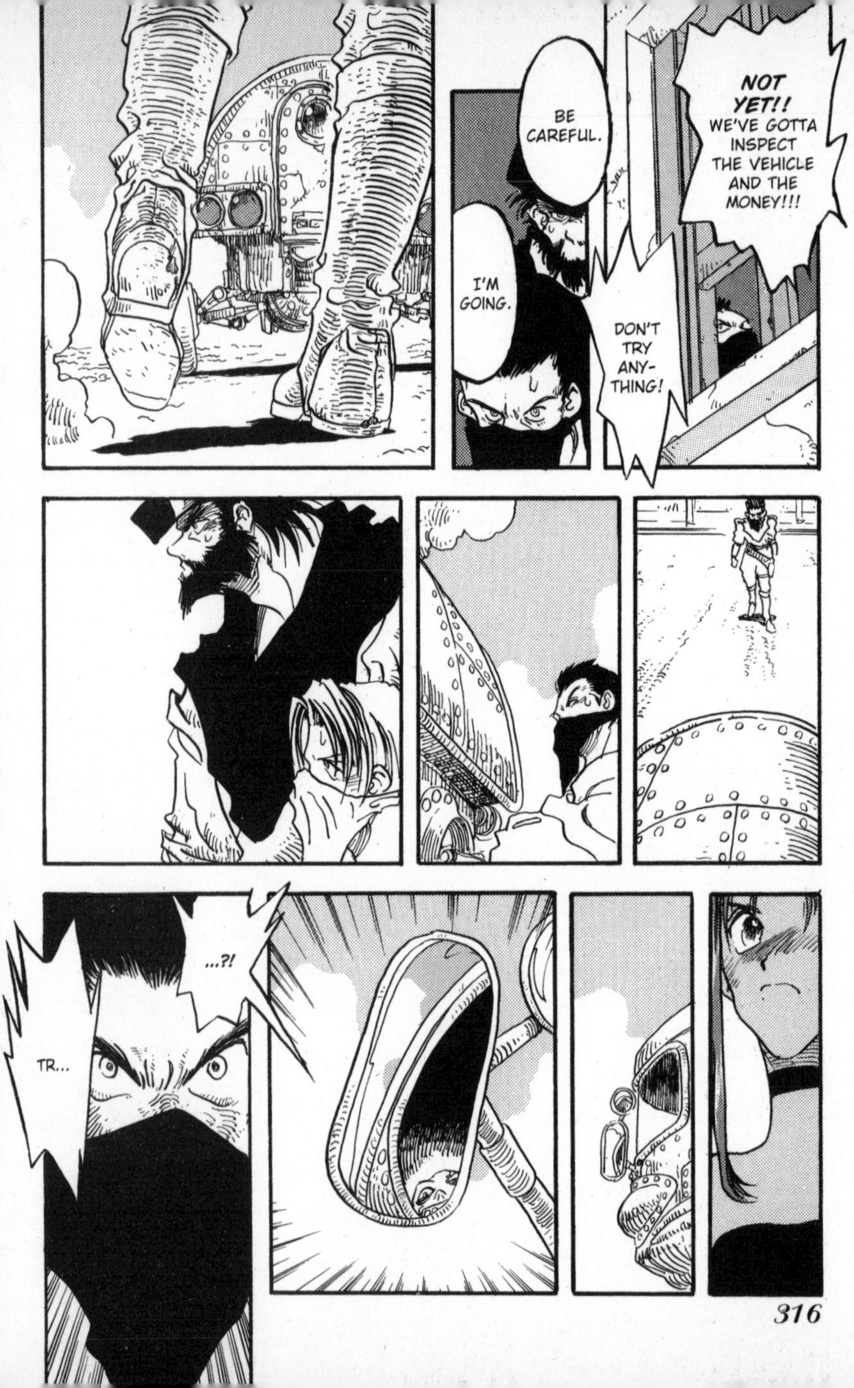
NOT YET!! WE'VE GOTTA INSPECT THE VEHICLE AND THE MONEY!!!
DON'T TRY ANY-THING!
BE CAREFUL.
I'M GOING.
...?!
TR...

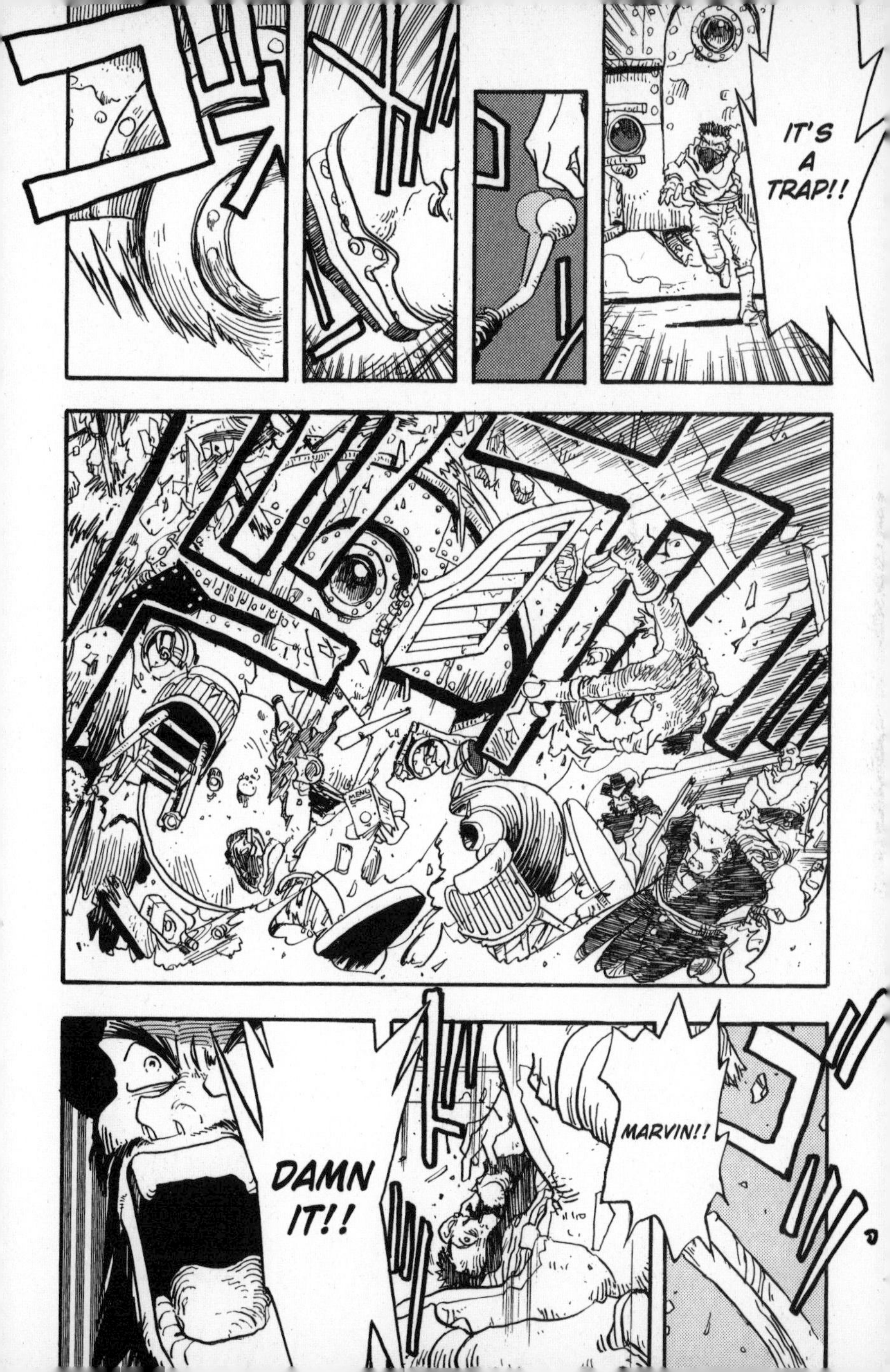
IT'S A TRAP!!
MARVIN!!
DAMN IT!!

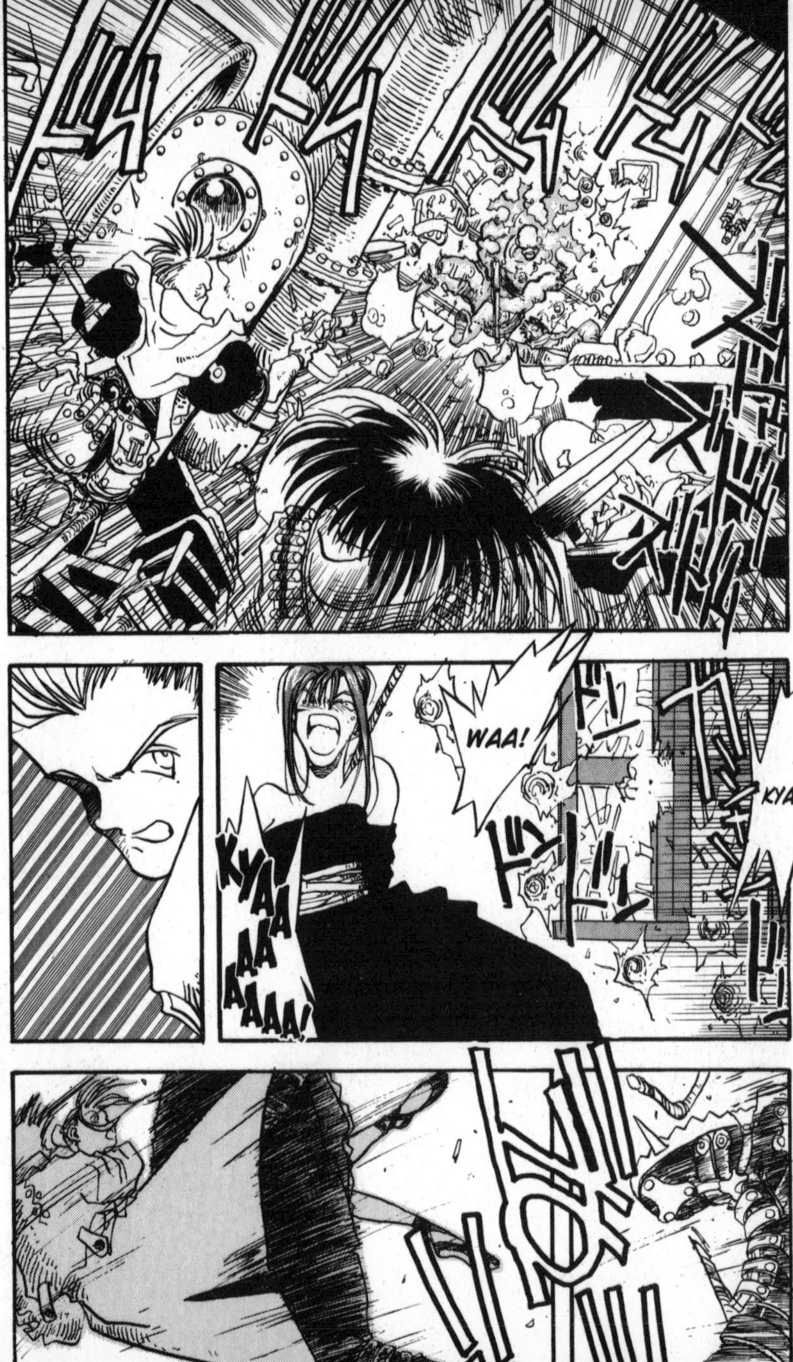
KYAA!
WAA!
KYAAAAAAAAAA!

YOU OKAY?

Y....

YES...

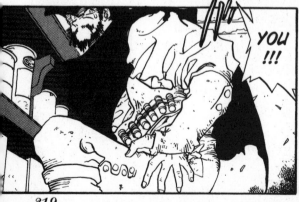

YOU !!!

KYA AAA AAA AA!

319

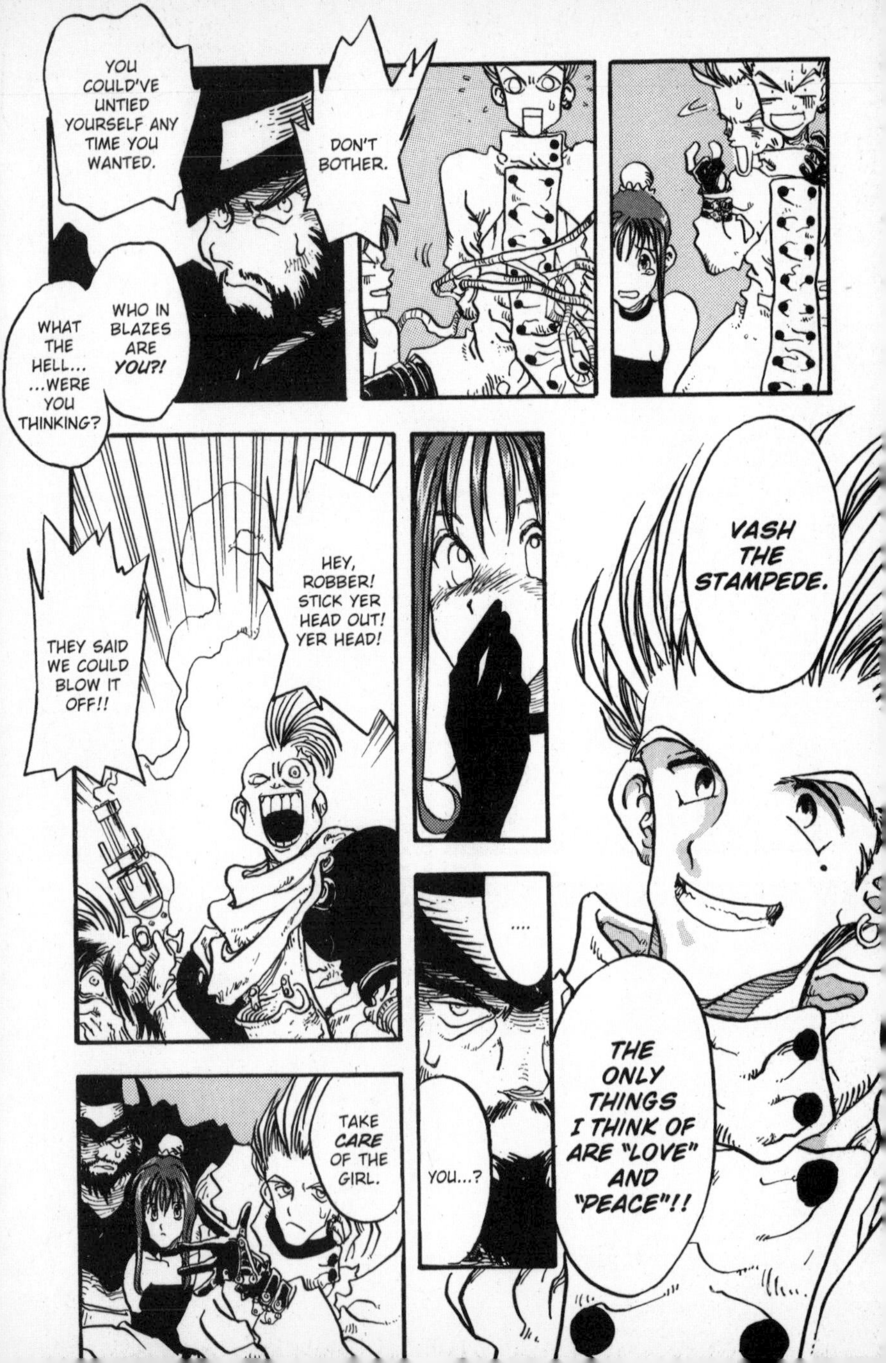
DON'T BOTHER.
YOU COULD'VE UNTIED YOURSELF ANY TIME YOU WANTED.
WHAT THE HELL... ...WERE YOU THINKING?
WHO IN BLAZES ARE *YOU?!*
VASH THE STAMPEDE.
THE ONLY THINGS I THINK OF ARE "LOVE" AND "PEACE"!!
....
YOU...?
HEY, ROBBER! STICK YER HEAD OUT! YER HEAD!
THEY SAID WE COULD BLOW IT OFF!!
TAKE *CARE* OF THE GIRL.

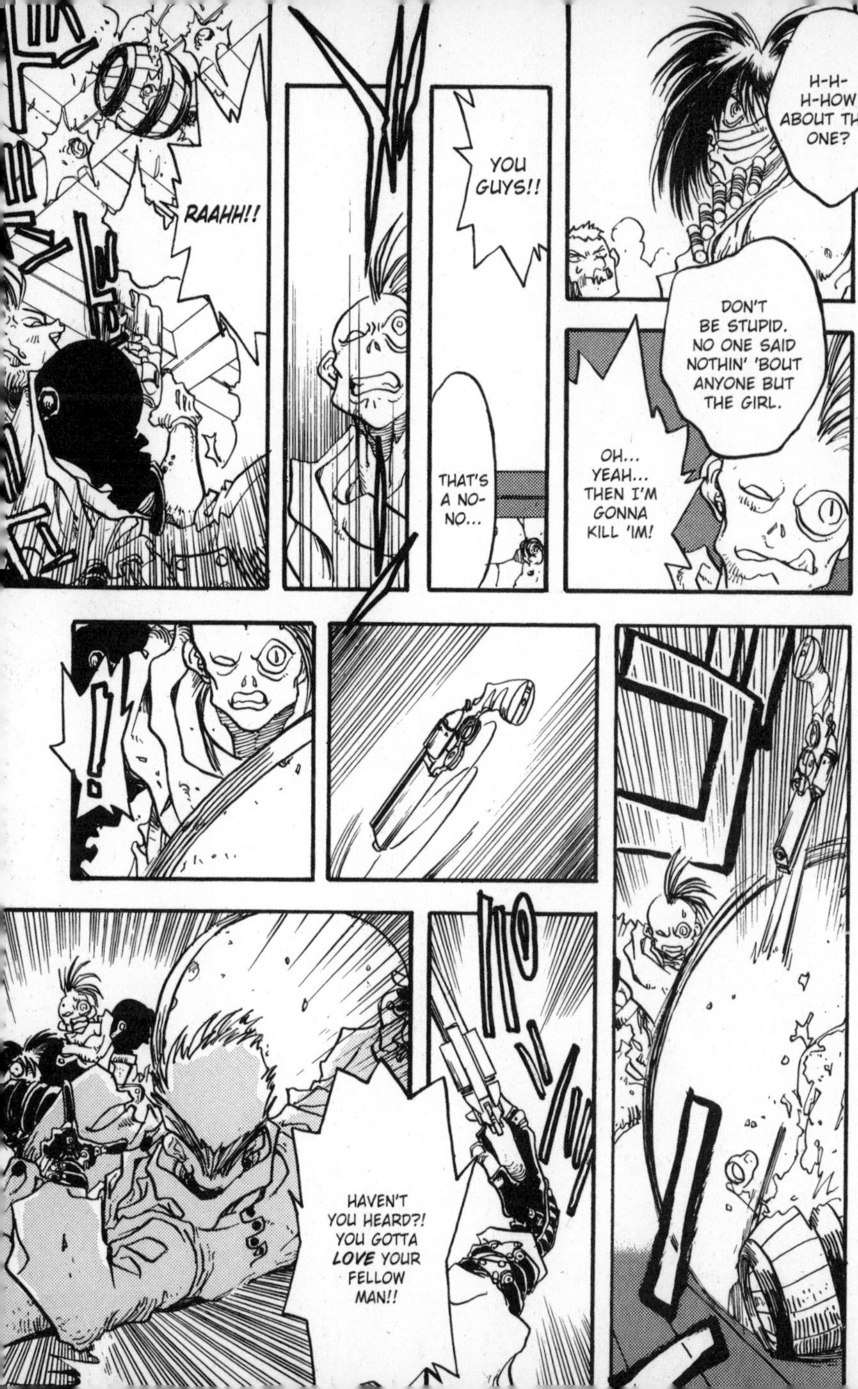
H-H-H-HOW ABOUT THIS ONE?
DON'T BE STUPID. NO ONE SAID NOTHIN' 'BOUT ANYONE BUT THE GIRL.
OH... YEAH... THEN I'M GONNA KILL 'IM!
YOU GUYS!!
THAT'S A NO-NO...
RAAHH!!
HAVEN'T YOU HEARD?! YOU GOTTA *LOVE* YOUR FELLOW MAN!!

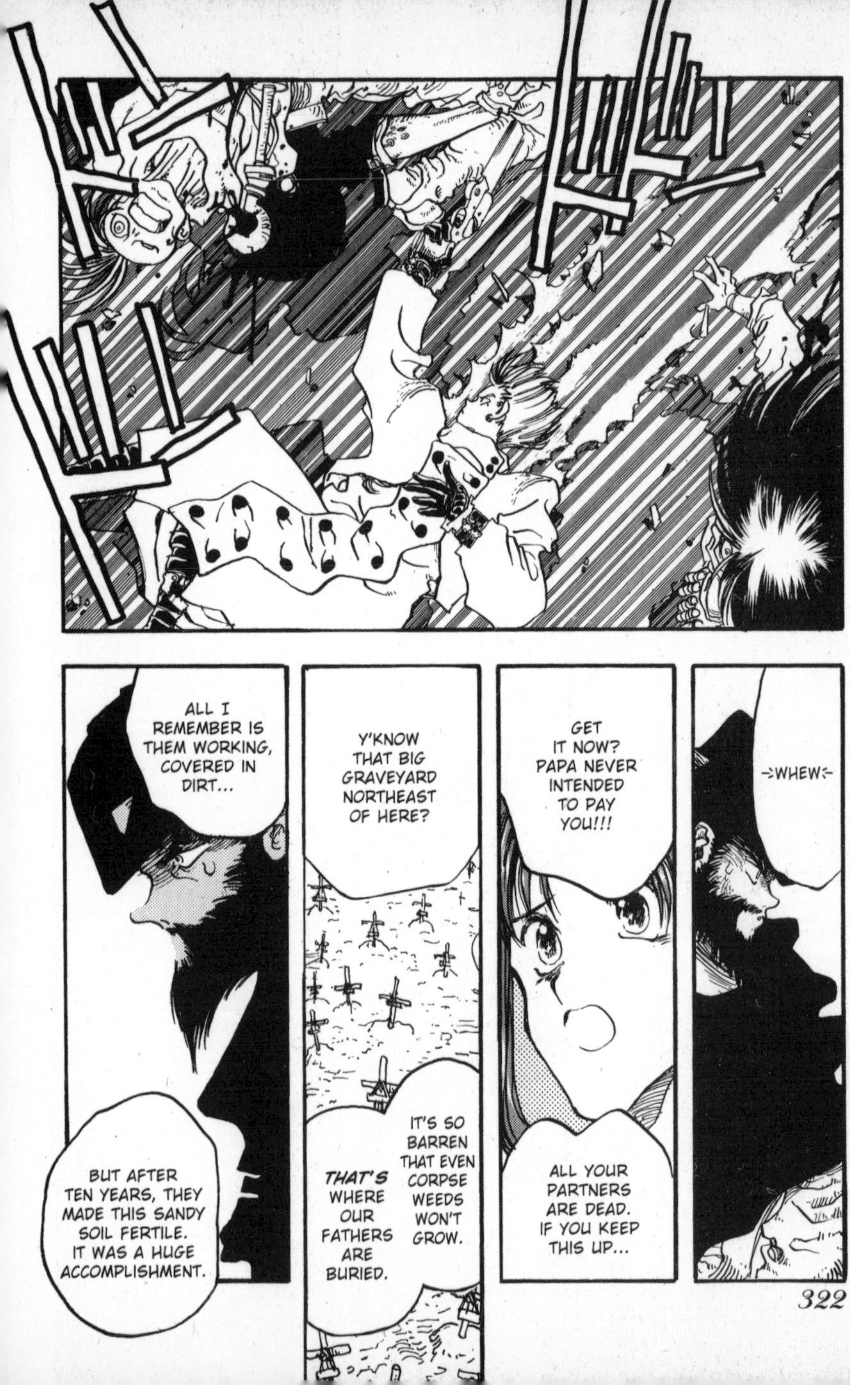
~WHEW~
GET IT NOW? PAPA NEVER INTENDED TO PAY YOU!!!
ALL YOUR PARTNERS ARE DEAD. IF YOU KEEP THIS UP...
Y'KNOW THAT BIG GRAVEYARD NORTHEAST OF HERE?
IT'S SO BARREN THAT EVEN CORPSE WEEDS WON'T GROW.
THAT'S WHERE OUR FATHERS ARE BURIED.
ALL I REMEMBER IS THEM WORKING, COVERED IN DIRT...
BUT AFTER TEN YEARS, THEY MADE THIS SANDY SOIL FERTILE. IT WAS A HUGE ACCOMPLISHMENT.

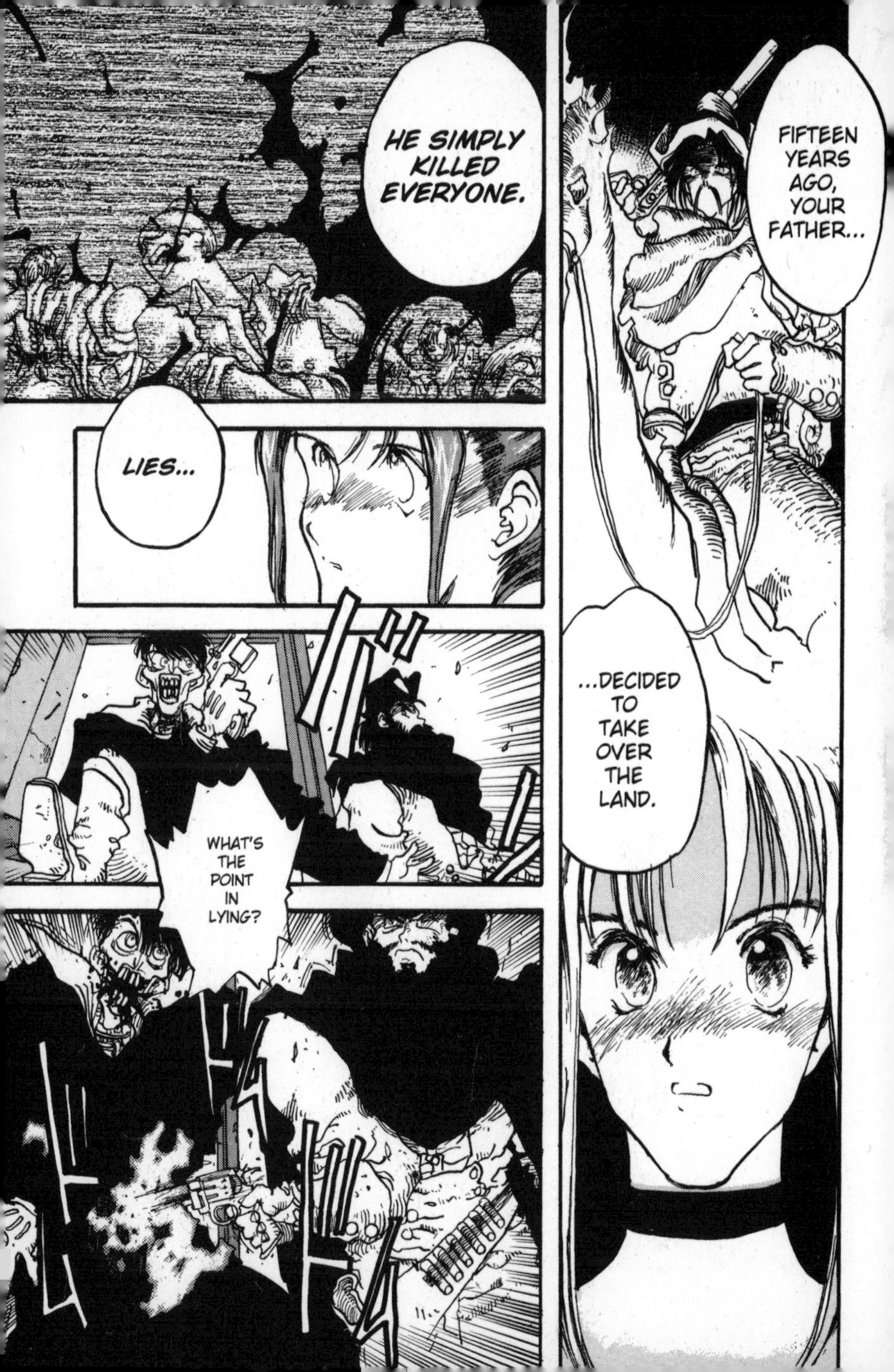
FIFTEEN YEARS AGO, YOUR FATHER...
...DECIDED TO TAKE OVER THE LAND.
HE SIMPLY KILLED EVERYONE.
LIES...
WHAT'S THE POINT IN LYING?

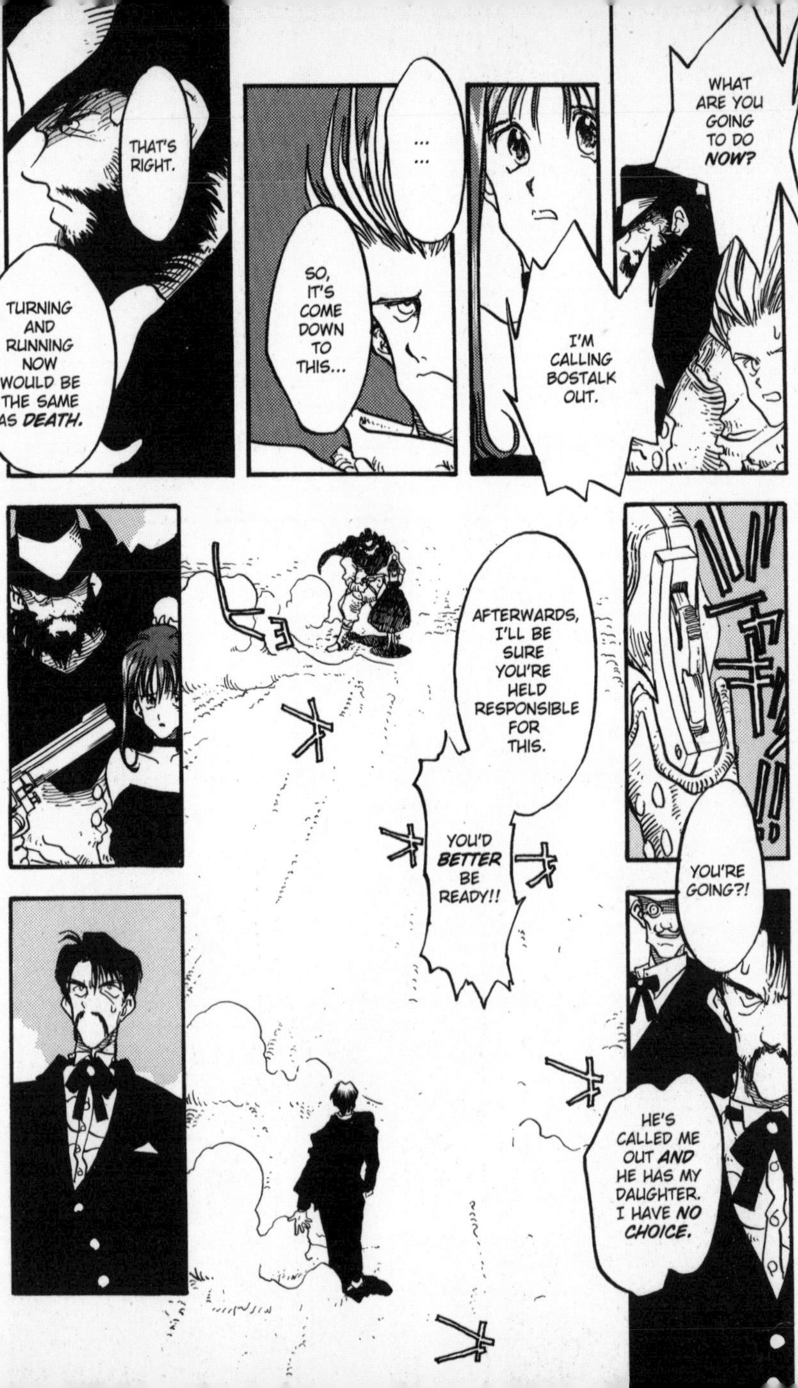

WHAT ARE YOU GOING TO DO NOW?
I'M CALLING BOSTALK OUT.
……
……
SO, IT'S COME DOWN TO THIS...
THAT'S RIGHT.
TURNING AND RUNNING NOW WOULD BE THE SAME AS DEATH.
YOU'RE GOING?!
HE'S CALLED ME OUT AND HE HAS MY DAUGHTER. I HAVE NO CHOICE.
AFTERWARDS, I'LL BE SURE YOU'RE HELD RESPONSIBLE FOR THIS.
YOU'D BETTER BE READY!!

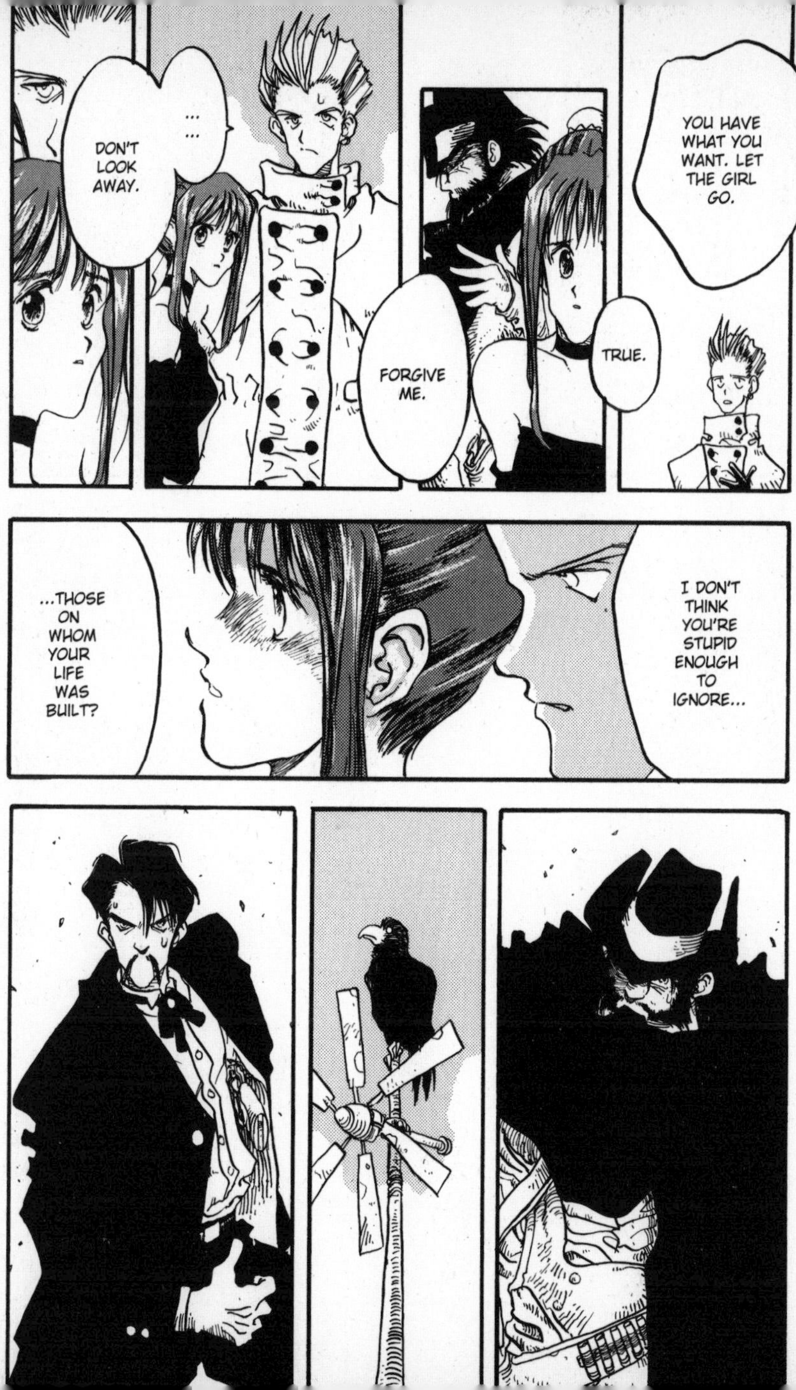
YOU HAVE WHAT YOU WANT. LET THE GIRL GO.
TRUE.
FORGIVE ME.
...
...
DON'T LOOK AWAY.
I DON'T THINK YOU'RE STUPID ENOUGH TO IGNORE...
...THOSE ON WHOM YOUR LIFE WAS BUILT?

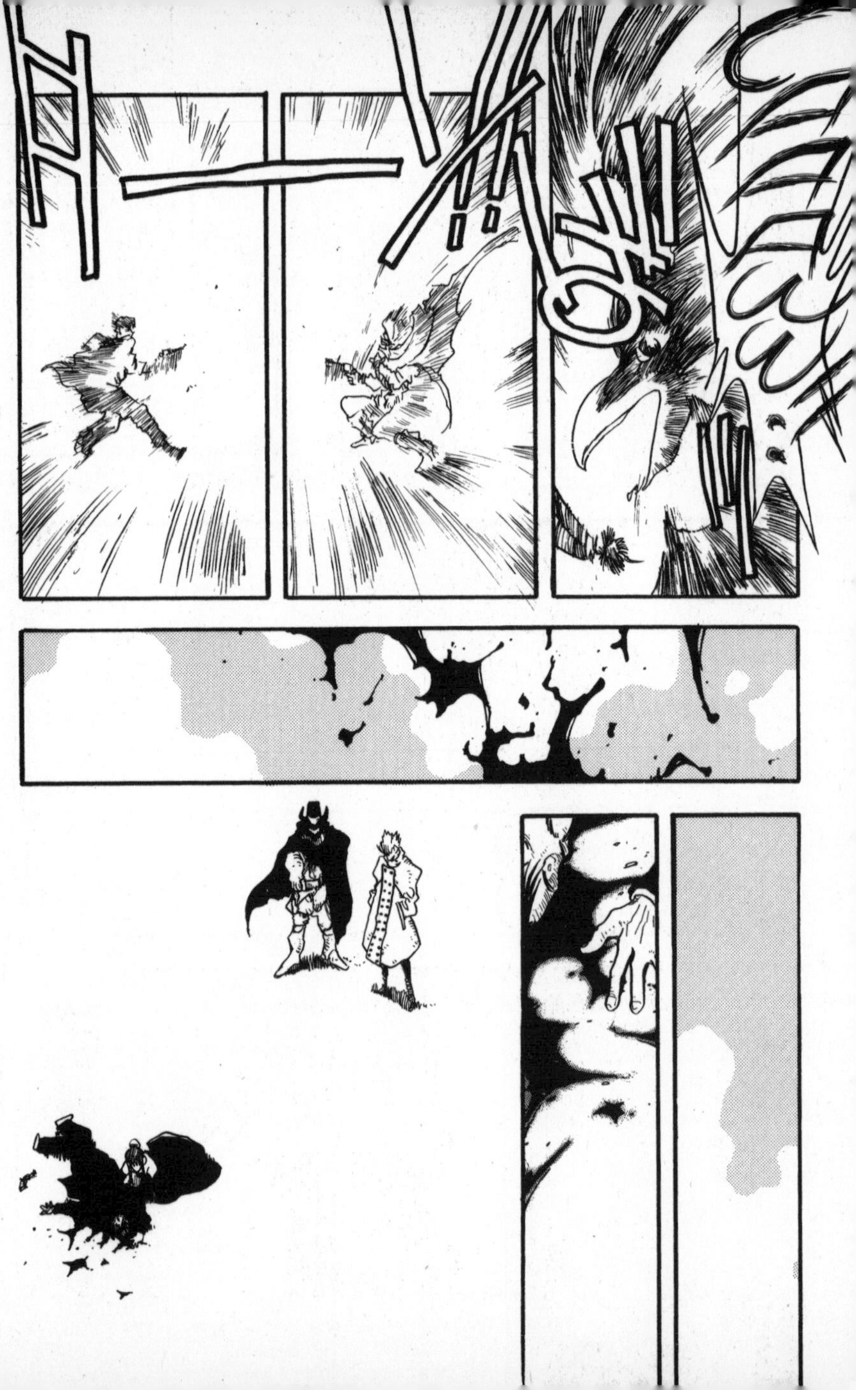

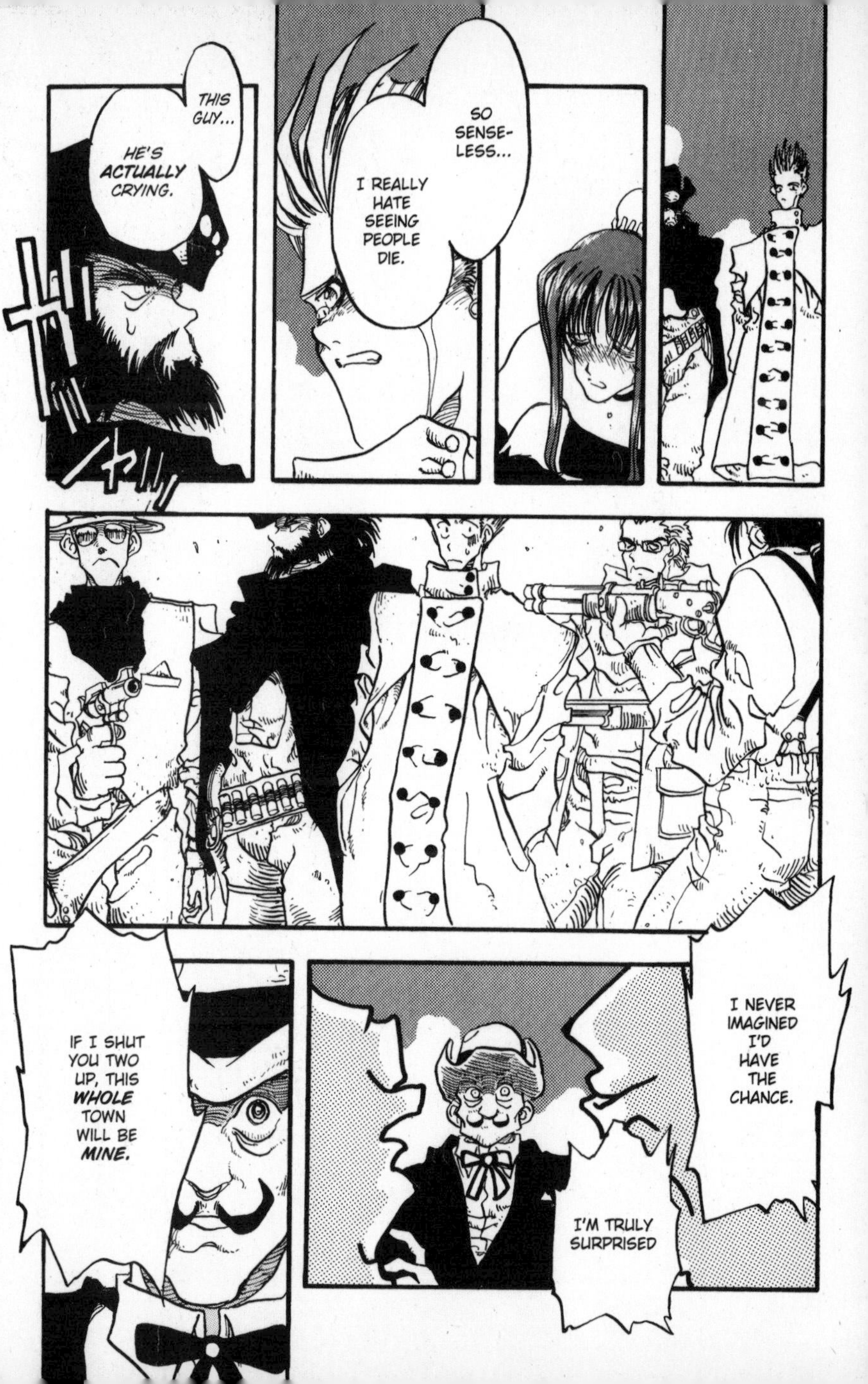
SO SENSELESS...
I REALLY HATE SEEING PEOPLE DIE.
THIS GUY...
HE'S ACTUALLY CRYING.
I NEVER IMAGINED I'D HAVE THE CHANCE.
I'M TRULY SURPRISED
IF I SHUT YOU TWO UP, THIS WHOLE TOWN WILL BE MINE.

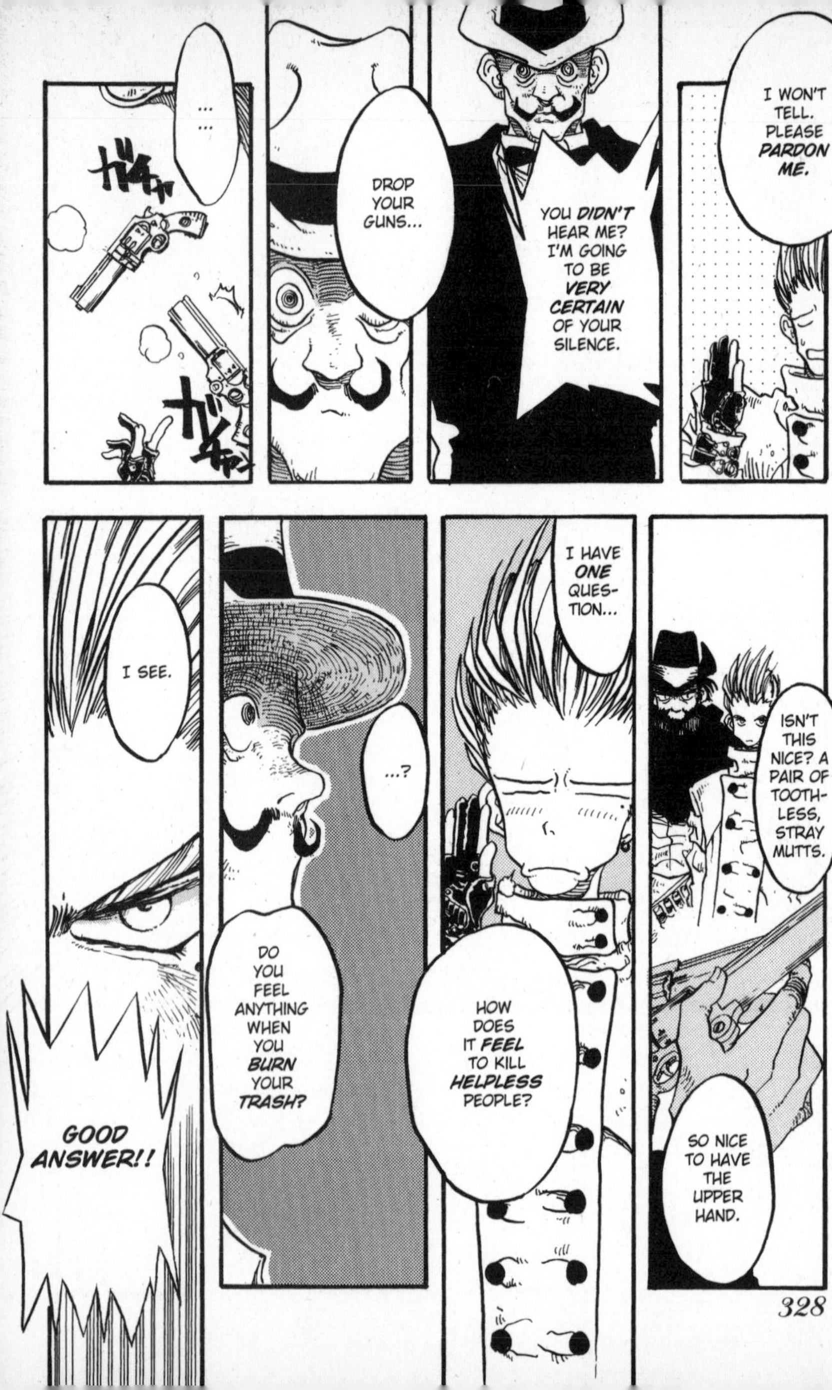
I WON'T TELL. PLEASE PARDON ME.
YOU DIDN'T HEAR ME? I'M GOING TO BE VERY CERTAIN OF YOUR SILENCE.
DROP YOUR GUNS...
... ...
ISN'T THIS NICE? A PAIR OF TOOTH-LESS, STRAY MUTTS.
SO NICE TO HAVE THE UPPER HAND.
I HAVE ONE QUES-TION...
HOW DOES IT FEEL TO KILL HELPLESS PEOPLE?
...?
DO YOU FEEL ANYTHING WHEN YOU BURN YOUR TRASH?
I SEE.
GOOD ANSWER!!

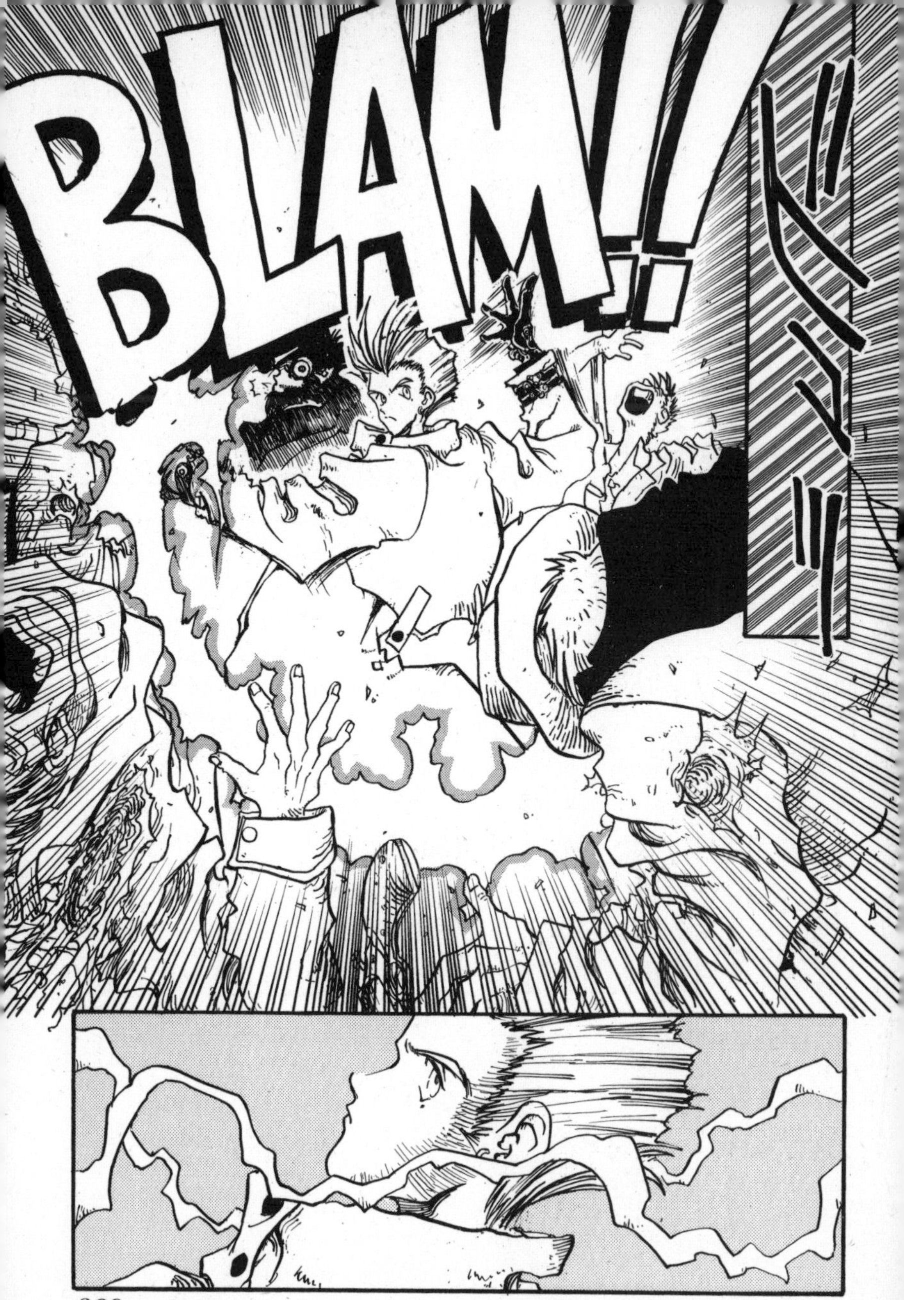
BLAM!!

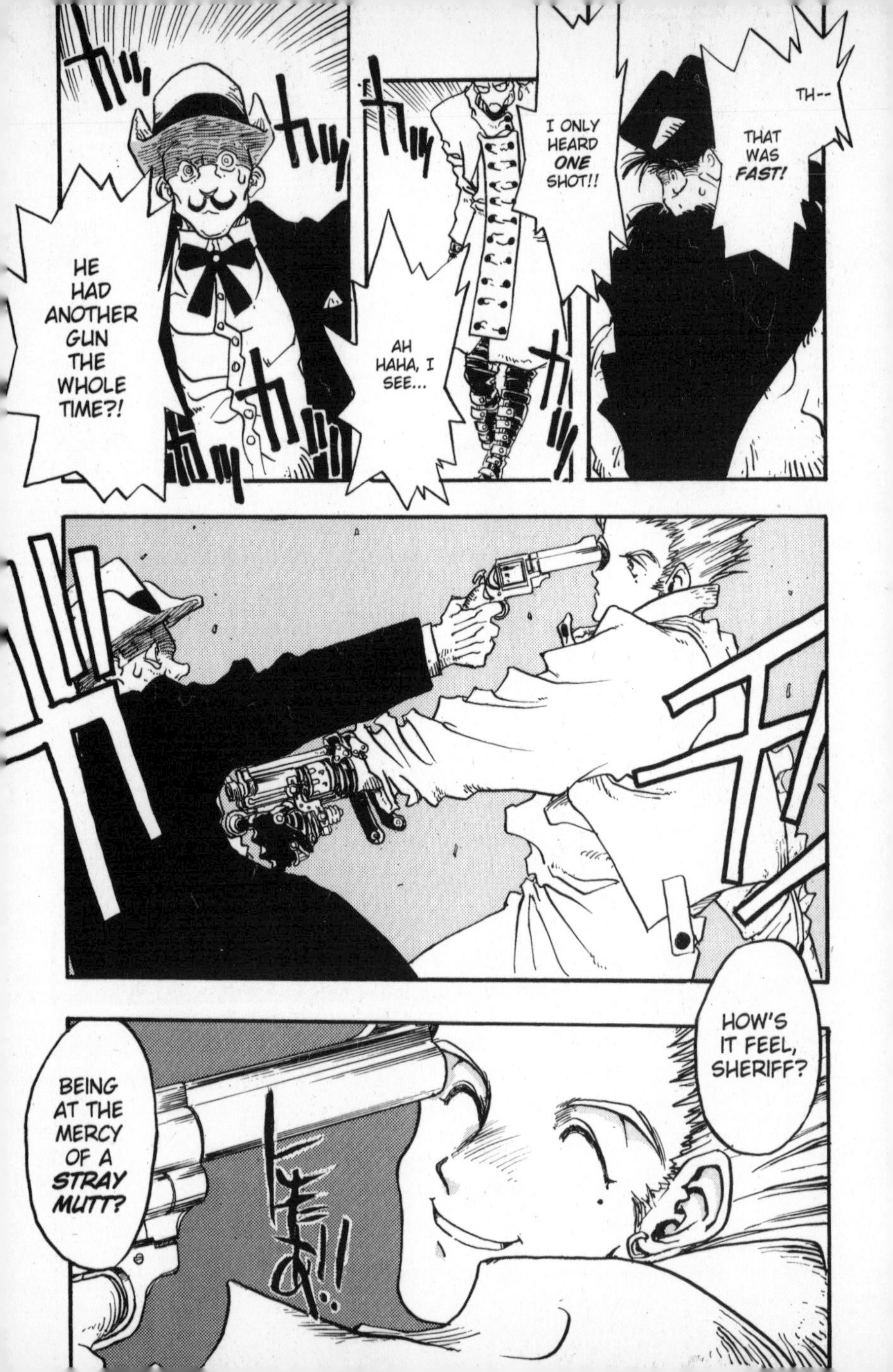
TH--
THAT WAS FAST!
I ONLY HEARD ONE SHOT!!
AH HAHA, I SEE...
HE HAD ANOTHER GUN THE WHOLE TIME?!
HOW'S IT FEEL, SHERIFF?
BEING AT THE MERCY OF A STRAY MUTT?

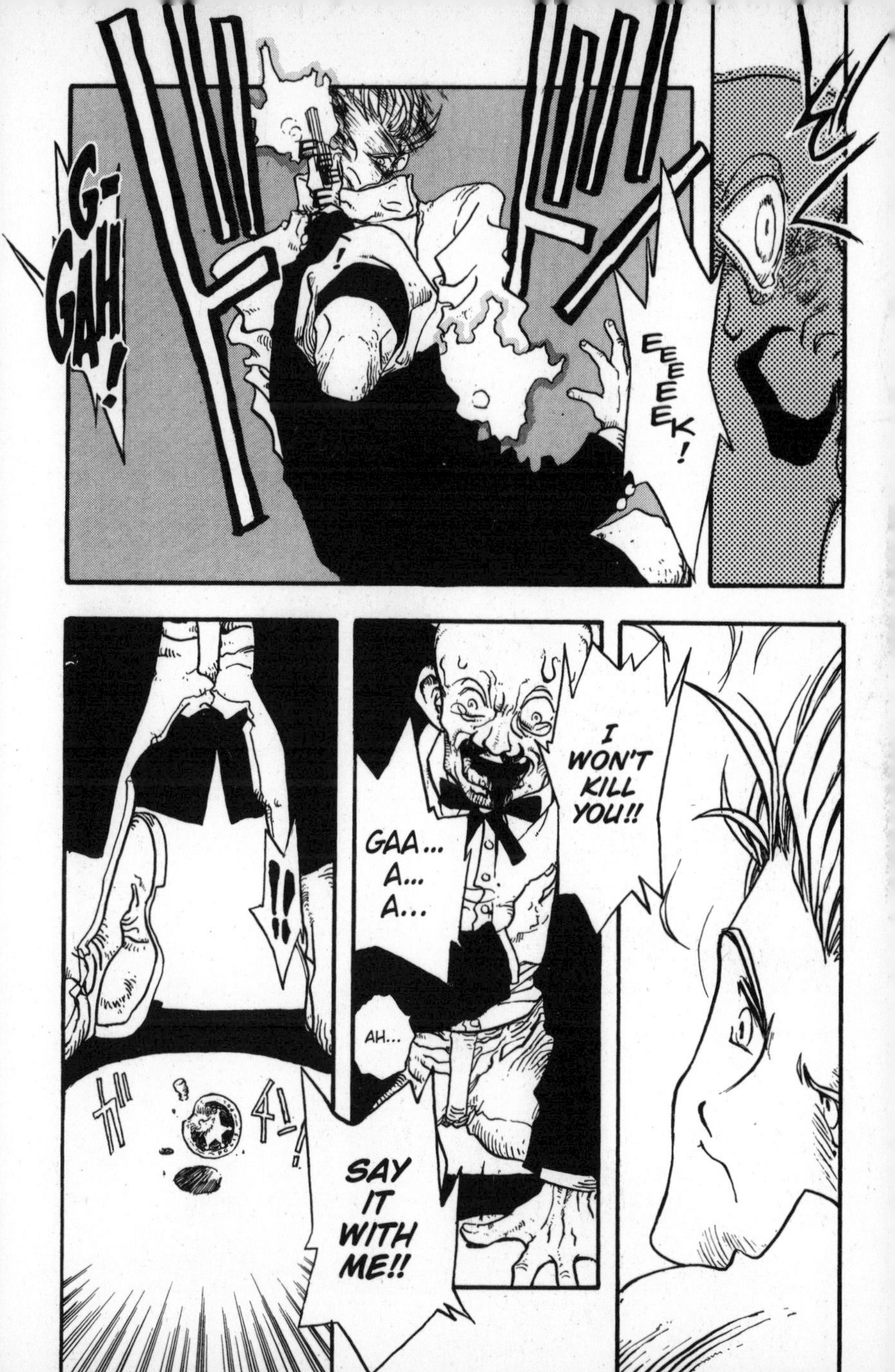
EEEEEK!
G-GAH!
I WON'T KILL YOU!!
GAA... A... A...
AH...
SAY IT WITH ME!!
!!

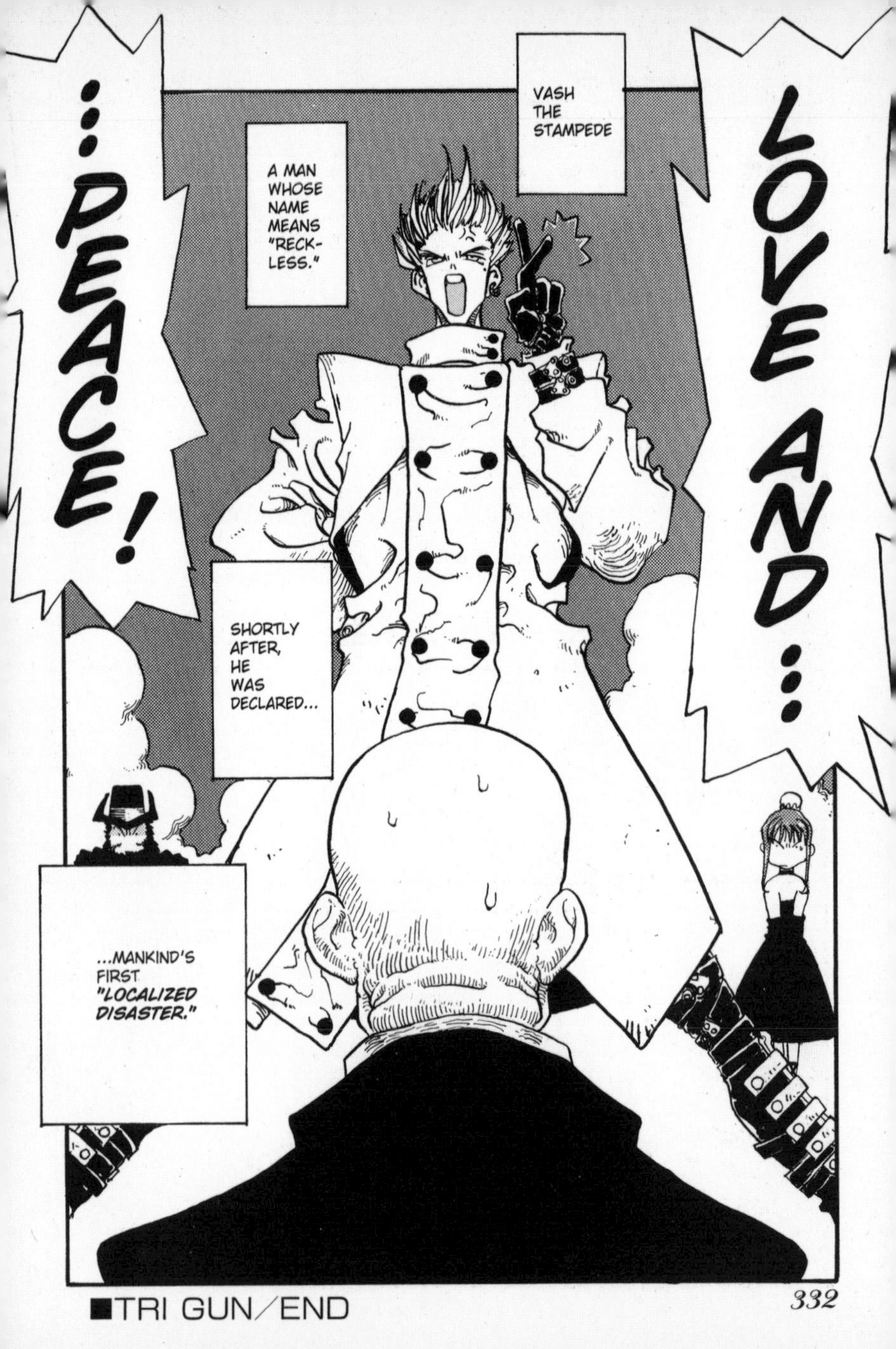
LOVE AND...
...PEACE!
VASH THE STAMPEDE
A MAN WHOSE NAME MEANS "RECKLESS."
SHORTLY AFTER, HE WAS DECLARED...
...MANKIND'S FIRST "LOCALIZED DISASTER."

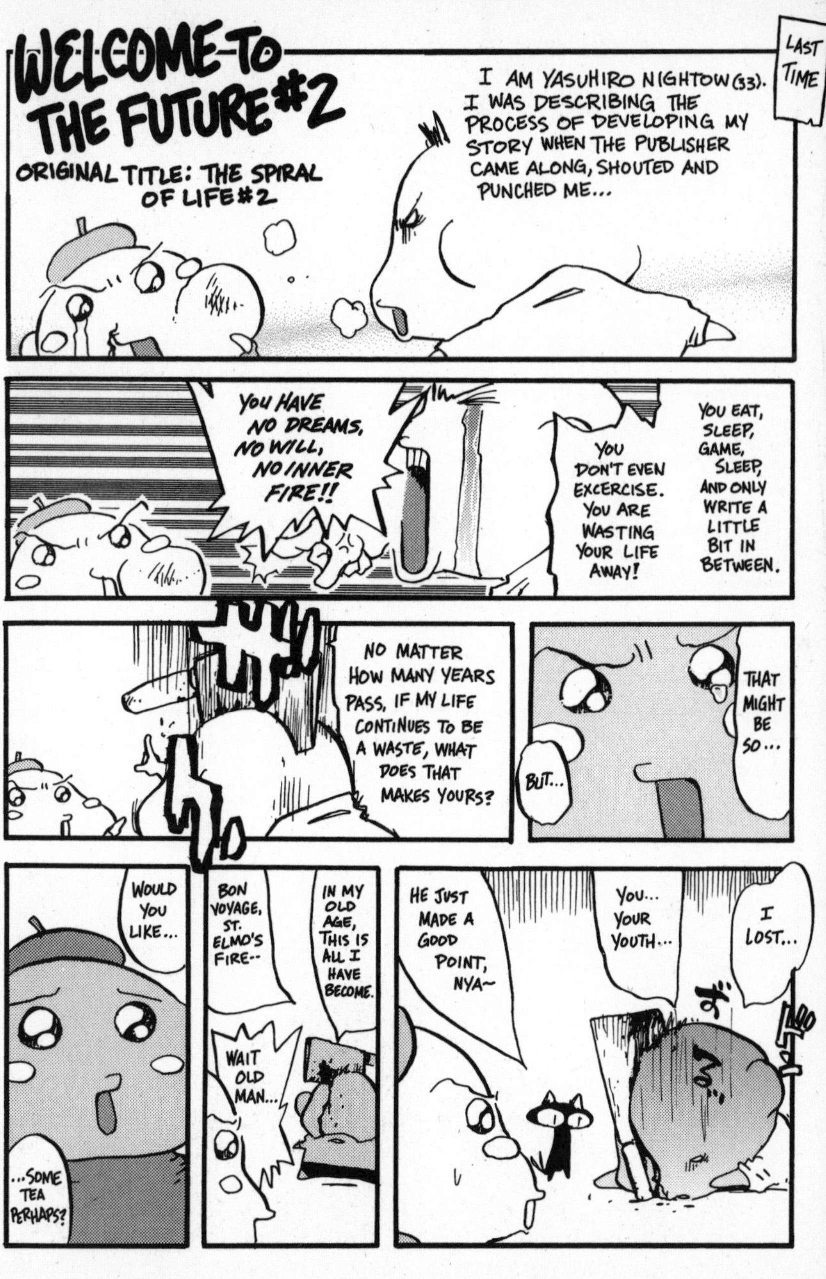
LAST TIME
I AM YASUHIRO NIGHTOW (33). I WAS DESCRIBING THE PROCESS OF DEVELOPING MY STORY WHEN THE PUBLISHER CAME ALONG, SHOUTED AND PUNCHED ME...
WELCOME TO THE FUTURE #2
ORIGINAL TITLE: THE SPIRAL OF LIFE #2
YOU EAT, SLEEP, GAME, SLEEP, AND ONLY WRITE A LITTLE BIT IN BETWEEN.
YOU DON'T EVEN EXCERCISE. YOU ARE WASTING YOUR LIFE AWAY!
YOU HAVE NO DREAMS, NO WILL, NO INNER FIRE!!
THAT MIGHT BE SO...
BUT...
NO MATTER HOW MANY YEARS PASS, IF MY LIFE CONTINUES TO BE A WASTE, WHAT DOES THAT MAKES YOURS?
I LOST...
YOU... YOUR YOUTH...
HE JUST MADE A GOOD POINT, NYA~
IN MY OLD AGE, THIS IS ALL I HAVE BECOME.
BON VOYAGE, ST. ELMO'S FIRE--
WAIT OLD MAN...
WOULD YOU LIKE...
...SOME TEA PERHAPS?

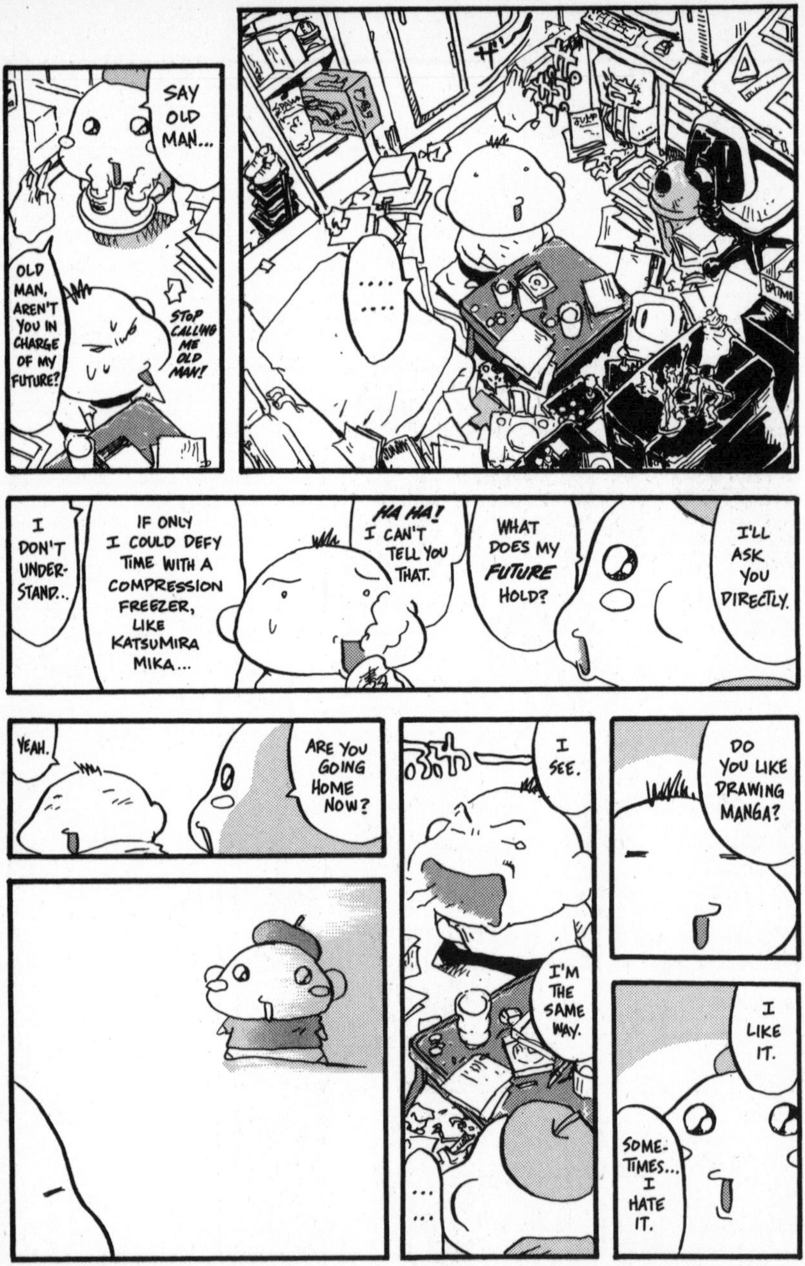
....
....
SAY OLD MAN...
STOP CALLING ME OLD MAN!
OLD MAN, AREN'T YOU IN CHARGE OF MY FUTURE?
I'LL ASK YOU DIRECTLY.
WHAT DOES MY FUTURE HOLD?
HA HA! I CAN'T TELL YOU THAT.
IF ONLY I COULD DEFY TIME WITH A COMPRESSION FREEZER, LIKE KATSUMIRA MIKA...
I DON'T UNDERSTAND...
DO YOU LIKE DRAWING MANGA?
I LIKE IT.
SOMETIMES... I HATE IT.
I SEE.
ふわー
I'M THE SAME WAY.
... ...
ARE YOU GOING HOME NOW?
YEAH.

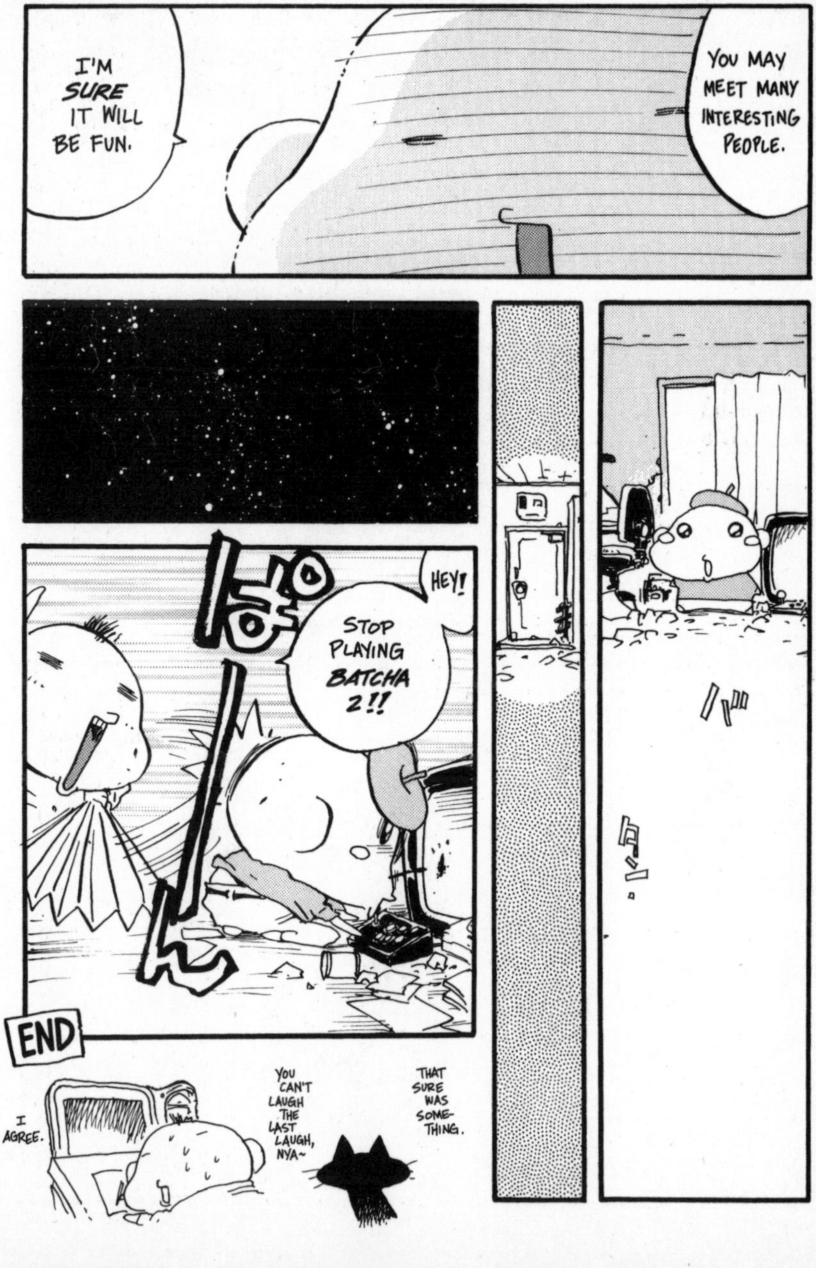

YOU MAY MEET MANY INTERESTING PEOPLE.
I'M SURE IT WILL BE FUN.
HEY!
STOP PLAYING BATCHA 2!!
END
THAT SURE WAS SOME-THING.
YOU CAN'T LAUGH THE LAST LAUGH, NYA~
I AGREE.

STOP

This is the back of the book!

This manga collection is translated into English but oriented in right-to-left reading format at the creator's request, maintaining the artwork's visual orientation as originally published in Japan. If you've never read manga in this way before, take a look at the diagram below to give yourself an idea of how to go about it. Basically, you'll be starting in the upper right corner and will read each balloon and panel moving right to left. It may take some getting used to, but you should get the hang of it very quickly. Have fun!

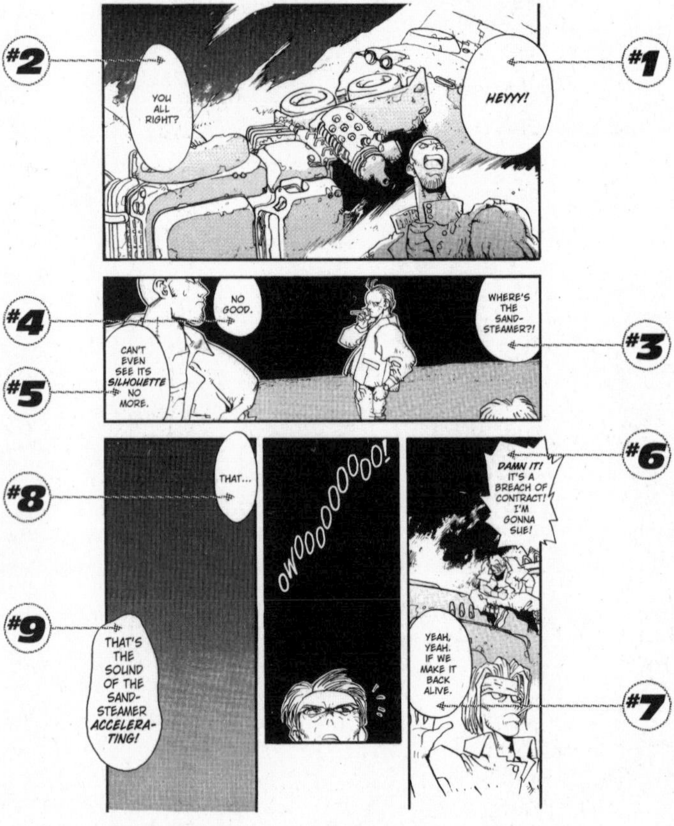

#1
HEYYY!
#2
YOU ALL RIGHT?
#3
WHERE'S THE SAND-STEAMER?!
#4
NO GOOD.
#5
CAN'T EVEN SEE ITS SILHOUETTE NO MORE.
#6
DAMN IT! IT'S A BREACH OF CONTRACT! I'M GONNA SUE!
#7
YEAH, YEAH. IF WE MAKE IT BACK ALIVE.
OWOOOOOOOOOO!
#8
THAT...
#9
THAT'S THE SOUND OF THE SAND-STEAMER ACCELERATING!